PENGUIN BOOKS

COMMAND AND CONTROL

Eric Schlosser is the author of the *New York Times* bestsellers *Fast Food Nation* and *Reefer Madness*. His work has appeared in *The Atlantic Monthly*, *Rolling Stone*, *The New Yorker*, *Vanity Fair*, and *The Nation*.

Praise for *Command and Control* by Eric Schlosser

Finalist for the Pulitzer Prize

A *New York Times* Notable Book of the Year
The Economist Best Books of the Year
Time Best Books of the Year
Politico Best Books of the Year
Gizmodo Best Books of the Year
Chicago Tribune Best Books of the Year
Newsday Best Books of the Year
San Francisco Chronicle Best Books of the Year
Kirkus Reviews Best Books of the Year

"By a miracle of information management, Schlosser has synthesized a huge archive of material, including government reports, scientific papers, and a substantial historical and polemical literature on nukes, and transformed it into a crisp narrative covering more than fifty years of scientific and political change. And he has interwoven that narrative with a hair-raising, minute-by-minute account of an accident at a Titan II missile silo in Arkansas, in 1980, which he renders in the manner of a techno-thriller. . . . *Command and Control* is how nonfiction should be written."
—Louis Menand, *The New Yorker*

"Deeply reported, deeply frightening . . . a techno-thriller of the first order."
—*Los Angeles Times*

"Eric Schlosser detonates a truth bomb in *Command and Control*, a powerful exposé about America's nuclear weapons."
—*Vanity Fair*

"Schlosser's book reads like a thriller, but it's masterfully even-handed, well researched, and well organized. Either he's a natural genius at integrating massive amounts of complex information, or he worked like a dog to write this book. You wouldn't think the prospect of nuclear apocalypse would make for a reading treat, but in Schlosser's hands it does."   —Jonathan Franzen, *The Guardian* (London)

"A devastatingly lucid and detailed new history of nuclear weapons in the U.S."
—Lev Grossman, *Time*

"*Command and Control* ranks among the most nightmarish books written in recent years; and in that crowded company it bids fair to stand at the summit. It is the more horrific for being so incontrovertibly right and so damnably readable. Page after relentless page, it drives the vision of a world trembling on the edge of a fatal precipice deep into your reluctant mind. . . . A work with the multilayered density of an ambitiously conceived novel . . . Schlosser has done what journalism does at its best when at full stretch: he has spent time—years—researching, interviewing, understanding, and reflecting to give us a piece of work of the deepest import."

—*Financial Times*

"Exciting . . . A gripping moment-by-moment account . . . A sophisticated chronicle of U.S. nuclear war strategies, based on exhaustive research . . . If you are dismayed by the violence and chaos in today's world, this book will provide a sense of proportion. The chapter 'Out of Control' is one of several that remind us of brinks more alarming than any we can imagine today, other than global warming."

—Charles Perrow, *The Washington Post*

"Perilous and gripping . . . Schlosser skillfully weaves together an engrossing account of both the science and the politics of nuclear weapons safety. . . . The story of the missile silo accident unfolds with the pacing, thrill, and techno details of an episode of *24*."

—*San Francisco Chronicle*

"Gripping . . . A real-life adventure that's every bit as fascinating as a Tom Clancy thriller . . . Schlosser is clearly on top of his game with *Command and Control*. His stories of nuclear near-misses inspire trepidation, and his description of Cold War political machinations provide hints about the conversations Pentagon officials must be having nowadays when they review the country's war strategies."

—Associated Press

"Eric Schlosser's *Command and Control* is a sobering and frightening yet fascinating account of the unbelievable peril posed by repeatedly mishandled American nuclear weapons. . . . The tale is riveting from start to finish. In the first few chapters, I found myself so repeatedly astounded by Schlosser's recounting of accidents in the early 1950s, I thought: Certainly, it can't get any worse than this. But it kept getting worse—so much so that I started folding the corners of each page that contained what seemed like the most egregious examples of nuclear mishaps and horrors. I now have a 632-page book with roughly a quarter of the pages folded over for reference. *Command and Control* is truly a monumental, Pulitzer-quality work."

—*The Dallas Morning News*

"Disquieting but riveting . . . Schlosser's readers (and he deserves a great many) will be struck by how frequently the people he cites attribute the absence of accidental explosions and nuclear war to divine intervention or sheer luck rather than to human wisdom and skill. Whatever was responsible, we will clearly need many more of it in the years to come." —*The New York Times Book Review*

"Awe-inspiring in its research and organization, *Command and Control: Nuclear Weapons, the Damascus Accident, and the Illusion of Safety* is the most edifying work of nonfiction I have read this year. It is also the most frightening. . . . Schlosser . . . is a masterful guide. His prose is clear, calm, and pinpoint in its precision."
—*Newsday*

"Easily the most unsettling work of nonfiction I've ever read, Schlosser's six-year investigation of America's 'broken arrows' (nuclear weapons mishaps) is by and large historical—this stuff is top secret, after all—but the book is beyond relevant. It's critical reading in a nation with thousands of nukes still on hair-trigger alert. . . . *Command and Control* reads like a character-driven thriller as Schlosser draws on his deep reporting, extensive interviews, and documents obtained via the Freedom of Information Act to demonstrate how human error, computer glitches, dilution of authority, poor communications, occasional incompetence, and the routine hoarding of crucial information have nearly brought about our worst nightmare on numerous occasions."
—*Mother Jones*

"A strange and powerful book . . . Schlosser . . . reminds us that accidents will happen and that current U.S. nuclear policy too often appears to assume otherwise."
—Scott Sagan, *The American Scholar*

"*Command and Control* is really two books in one. The first is a techno-thriller, narrating the Damascus Accident in gripping detail and bringing alive the participants and tough decisions they confronted in dramatic fashion. The second is a more analytic exploration of the challenge at the heart of nuclear command-and-control systems: how to ensure that nuclear weapons are both completely reliable and perfectly safe. Schlosser skillfully fits these two parts together to shine a bright light on the potentially catastrophic combination of human fallibility and complex systems. As in his previous two books, *Fast Food Nation* and *Reefer Madness*, Schlosser has exposed the hidden costs of practices that are widely accepted by the American public."
—*Foreign Affairs*

"Epic pop history."
—*Bloomberg*

"*Command and Control* . . . sometimes reads like a political thriller and sometimes like a science fiction novel. It's easy to forget that the stories within it are true. Mr. Schlosser is a tremendously adept investigative reporter. . . . Once again, [he] has provided readers with another aspect of American life to be simultaneously riveted and repulsed by. The scientific and engineering feats that created nuclear power are admirable, but the question of ultimate purpose has given even the creators pause from the very beginning."
—*Pittsburgh Post-Gazette*

"Schlosser . . . lays out, in unnerving and almost comical detail, the fights between various government agencies over who should be responsible for the bombs, the need for more sophisticated safety systems to prevent accidental detonations (not

to mention apocalyptic freelancing by rogue commanders, à la *Dr. Strangelove*). He also lists the frequent mishaps—bombs set on fire, dropped from planes, lost in crashes, wired improperly, armed by electrical surges and simple human error, or stored in laughably unsecure ways. . . . At just over 600 pages, *Command and Control* approaches cinder-block status, but there is very little in it I would've wanted trimmed. Schlosser brings an uncommonly cool and nonideological eye to a subject that ought to inspire sheer terror."
—*Toronto Star*

"*Command and Control* is the product of six years' labor, through which Schlosser turned himself from a layman to an expert. It is a complex, deliberative, and imaginative work, more of art than of urgent pamphleteering. It is also, like his 2001 book, *Fast Food Nation*, a study in twentieth-century Americana (he notes somewhere that a component of Little Boy—the bomb dropped on Hiroshima—was designed with the aid of a Coke bottle). Having addressed the most familiar American subject, Schlosser has taken up the most opaque one. 'My own ignor-arance,' he writes early on, 'was profound.' Would that knowledge could take us further, faster, toward the better light."
—*The Vancouver Sun*

"Nail-biting . . . thrilling . . . Mixing expert commentary with hair-raising details of a variety of mishaps, [Eric Schlosser] makes the convincing case that our best control systems are no match for human error, bad luck, and ever-increasing tech-nological complexity."
—*Publishers Weekly* (starred review)

"Vivid and unsettling . . . An exhaustive, unnerving examination of the illusory safety of atomic arms."
—*Kirkus Reviews* (starred review)

"The lesson of this powerful and disturbing book is that the world's nuclear arsenals are not as safe as they should be. We should take no comfort in our skill and good fortune in preventing a nuclear catastrophe, but urgently extend our maximum effort to assure that a nuclear weapon does not go off by accident, mistake, or miscalculation."
—Lee H. Hamilton, former U.S. Representative; cochair, Blue Ribbon Commission on America's Nuclear Future; director, the Center on Congress at Indiana University

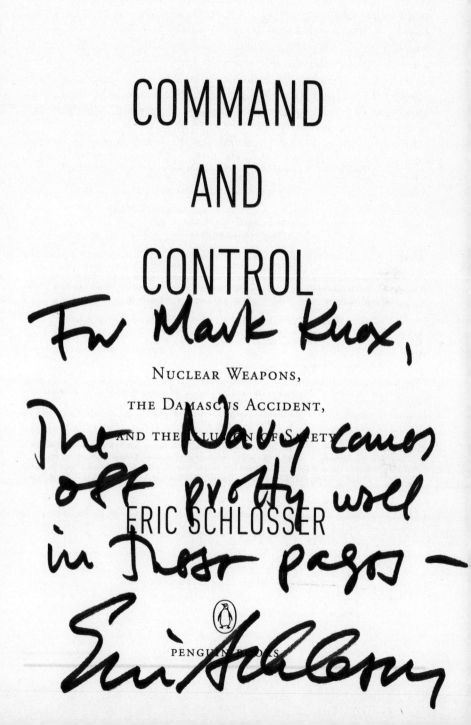

COMMAND
AND
CONTROL

NUCLEAR WEAPONS,

THE DAMASCUS ACCIDENT,

AND THE ILLUSION OF SAFETY

ERIC SCHLOSSER

PENGUIN BOOKS

For Mark Knox,

The Navy comes off pretty well in these pages —

Eric Schlosser

PENGUIN BOOKS
Published by the Penguin Group
Penguin Group (USA) LLC
375 Hudson Street
New York, New York 10014

USA | Canada | UK | Ireland | Australia | New Zealand | India | South Africa | China
penguin.com
A Penguin Random House Company

First published in the United States of America by The Penguin Press,
a member of Penguin Group (USA) LLC, 2013
Published in Penguin Books 2014

THE LIBRARY OF CONGRESS HAS CATALOGED THE HARDCOVER EDITION AS FOLLOWS:

Schlosser, Eric.
Command and control : nuclear weapons, the Damascus Accident, and the illusion of safety / Eric Schlosser.
pages   cm
Includes bibliographical references and index.
ISBN 978-1-59420-227-8 (hc.)
ISBN 978-0-14-312578-5 (pbk.)
1. Nuclear weapons—Accidents—United States—History.   2. Nuclear weapons—Accidents—Arkansas—History.
3. Titan (Missile)—History.   4. United States. Air Force. Strategic Air Command. Strategic Missile Wing, 308th.
5. Nuclear weapons—United States—Safety measures.   6. Nuclear weapons—Government policy—United States.
I. Title.   II. Title: Nuclear weapons, the Damascus Accident, and the illusion of safety.
U264.3.S45 2013
363.17'990976774—dc23
2013017151

Printed in the United States of America
1 3 5 7 9 10 8 6 4 2

BOOK DESIGN BY MEIGHAN CAVANAUGH

ILLUSTRATIONS ON PAGES XXII–XXIII BY GIDEON KENDALL

Ring the bells that still can ring
Forget your perfect offering
There is a crack, a crack in everything
That's how the light gets in.

Leonard Cohen

CONTENTS

AUTHOR'S NOTE

This is a book about the effort to control nuclear weapons—to ensure that one doesn't go off by accident, by mistake, or by any other unauthorized means. The emphasis in these pages isn't on the high-level diplomacy behind arms control treaties. It's on the operating systems and the mind-set that have guided the management of America's nuclear arsenal for almost seventy years. The history of similar efforts in the Soviet Union is largely absent here. Although no less important, such a history requires a knowledge of Russian archives and sources that I lack. *Command and Control* explores the precarious balance between the need for nuclear weapon safety and the need to defend the United States from attack. It looks at the attempts by American scientists, policy makers, and military officers to reconcile those two demands, from the dawn of the nuclear age until the end of the Cold War. And through the story of a long-forgotten accident, it aims to shed light on a larger theme: the mixture of human fallibility and technological complexity that can lead to disaster.

Although most of the events in this book occurred a long time ago, they remain unfortunately relevant. Thousands of nuclear warheads still sit atop missiles belonging to the United States and Russia, ready to be launched at a moment's notice. Hundreds more are possessed by India, China, Pakistan, Israel, North Korea, Great Britain, and France. As of this writing, a nuclear weapon has not destroyed a city since August 1945. But there is no guarantee that such good luck will last.

The fall of the Berlin Wall now feels like ancient history. An entire generation has been raised without experiencing the dread and anxiety of the Cold War, a conflict that lasted almost half a century and threatened to annihilate mankind. This book assumes that most of its readers know little about nuclear weapons, their inner workings, or the strategic thinking that justifies their use. I hope readers who are familiar with these subjects will nevertheless learn a new thing or two here. My own ignorance, I now realize, was profound. No great monument has been built to honor those who served during the Cold War, who risked their lives and sometimes lost them in the name of freedom. It was ordinary men and women, not just diplomats and statesmen, who helped to avert a nuclear holocaust. Their courage and their sacrifices should be remembered.

SELECTED CAST
OF CHARACTERS

The Titan II Missile Combat Crew

Captain Michael T. Mazzaro, the commander, a young officer from Massachusetts with a pregnant wife

Lieutenant Allan D. Childers, the deputy commander, raised in Okinawa, a former DJ in his late twenties

Staff Sergeant Rodney L. Holder, the ballistic missile systems analyst technician, son of a Navy officer, responsible for keeping the Titan II ready to launch

Staff Sergeant Ronald O. Fuller, the missile facilities technician, responsible for the equipment at the launch complex

Lieutenant Miguel Serrano, a trainee studying to become a deputy commander

Propellant Transfer System Team A

Senior Airman Charles T. Heineman, the team chief

Senior Airman David Powell, an experienced Titan II repairman, twenty-one and raised in Kentucky

Airman Jeffrey L. Plumb, nineteen and from Detroit, a novice receiving on-the-job training

Propellant Transfer System Team B

Sergeant Jeff Kennedy, a quality control evaluator for the 308th Strategic Missile Wing, perhaps the best missile mechanic at Little Rock Air Force Base, a former deckhand from Maine in his midtwenties

Colonel James L. Morris, the head of maintenance at the 308th Strategic Missile Wing

Senior Airman James R. Sandaker, a young missile technician from Evansville, Minnesota

Technical Sergeant Michael A. Hanson, the team chief

Senior Airman Greg Devlin, a junior middleweight Golden Gloves boxer

Senior Airman David L. Livingston, a twenty-two-year-old missile repairman from Ohio with a fondness for motorcycles

CIVILIANS IN AND AROUND DAMASCUS

Sid King, the twenty-seven-year-old manager of a local radio station

Gus Anglin, the sheriff of Van Buren County

Sam Hutto, a dairy farmer with land across the road from the missile site

THE DISASTER RESPONSE FORCE

Colonel William A. Jones, the head of the force as well as the base commander

Captain Donald P. Mueller, a flight surgeon manning the force's ambulance

Richard L. English, head of the Disaster Preparedness Unit, a civilian in his late fifties, still fit and athletic, nicknamed "Colonel," who'd served in the Air Force for many years

Technical Sergeant David G. Rossborough, an experienced first responder

SECURITY POLICE OFFICERS

Technical Sergeant Thomas A. Brocksmith, the on-scene police supervisor at the accident site

Technical Sergeant Donald V. Green, a noncommissioned officer in his early thirties who volunteered to escort a flatbed truck to Launch Complex 374-7

Technical Sergeant Jimmy E. Roberts, a friend of Green's who accompanied him on the drive to Damascus

AT THE LITTLE ROCK COMMAND POST

Colonel John T. Moser, commander of the 308th Strategic Missile Wing

AT THE SAC COMMAND POST IN OMAHA

General Lloyd R. Leavitt, Jr., the vice commander in chief of the Strategic Air Command

At Barksdale Air Force Base in Lousiana

Colonel Ben G. Scallorn, a Titan II expert at the Eighth Air Force who'd worked with the missiles since the first silos were built

The Manhattan Project

General Leslie R. Groves, director of the project, who led the effort to build an atomic bomb

J. Robert Oppenheimer, a theoretical physicist, later known as "the father of the atomic bomb," who served as the first director of the Los Alamos Laboratory

Edward Teller, a physicist later known as "the father of the hydrogen bomb," often at odds with the other Los Alamos scientists

George B. Kistiakowsky, a chemist and perhaps the nation's leading explosives expert, later the science adviser to President Dwight D. Eisenhower

Scientists and Engineers at the Weapons Labs

Bob Peurifoy, an engineer from Texas who joined Sandia in 1952 and subsequently became its leading advocate for nuclear weapon safety

Harold Agnew, a physicist from Colorado who helped create the first manmade nuclear chain reaction, filmed the destruction of Hiroshima from an observer plane, and played an important role in nuclear weapon safety efforts at the Los Alamos Laboratory

Carl Carlson, a young physicist at Sandia who in the late 1950s recognized the vulnerability of a nuclear weapon's electrical system during an accident

Bill Stevens, an engineer who became the first head of Sandia's nuclear safety department and worked closely with Bob Peurifoy

Stan Spray, a Sandia engineer who burned, crushed, and routinely tortured nuclear weapon components to discover their flaws

Military Leaders

General Curtis E. LeMay, an engineer who revolutionized American bombing techniques during the Second World War and turned the Strategic Air Command into the most powerful military organization in history

General Thomas S. Power, an Air Force officer who led the firebombing of Tokyo during the Second World War, followed LeMay to the Strategic Air Command, and gained the reputation of being a mean son of a bitch

General Maxwell D. Taylor, an Army officer who championed the nuclear strategy of limited war and served as influential adviser to President John F. Kennedy

Officials in Washington, D.C.

David E. Lilienthal, the first chairman of the Atomic Energy Commission and a strong believer in civilian control of nuclear weapons

Fred Charles Iklé, a RAND analyst who studied the potential consequences of an accidental nuclear detonation and later served as an undersecretary of defense in the Reagan administration

Donald A. Quarles, an engineer whose work at Sandia, the Department of the Air Force, and the Department of Defense helped to promote nuclear weapon safety

Robert S. McNamara, a former automobile executive who, as secretary of defense during the Kennedy and Johnson administrations, struggled to formulate a rational nuclear strategy

ACRONYMS AND ABBREVIATIONS

A-Bomb—an atomic bomb, a weapon deriving its explosive power from the fission of uranium or plutonium atoms

AEC—Atomic Energy Commission, the civilian agency created in 1947 to oversee nuclear weapons and nuclear power

AFSWP—Armed Forces Special Weapons Project, a military agency formed in 1947 to deal with nuclear weapons

B.E. Number—a unique eight-digit number that identifies each of the targets in the Air Force's *Bombing Encyclopedia*

BMEWS—Ballistic Missile Early Warning System, the radar system built after *Sputnik* to detect Soviet missiles heading toward the United States

BOMARC—a ground-launched antiaircraft missile with an atomic warhead, designed by Boeing (BO) and the Michigan Aerospace Research Center (MARC), that was deployed at sites in the United States and Canada

CND—Campaign for Nuclear Disarmament, a British antiwar group whose logo later became known as the "peace symbol"

DEFCON—Defense Readiness Condition, the American military's readiness for hostilities, ranked on a scale from DEFCON 5 (the lowest level of alert) to DEFCON 1 (nuclear war)

DEW Line—the Distant Early Warning Line, a radar system that extended across the Arctic in North America to detect Soviet bombers

DIRECT—Defense Improved Emergency Message Automatic Transmission System Replacement Command and Control Terminal, the Pentagon computer system currently deployed to send and receive a nuclear attack order

DUL—the Deliberate, Unauthorized Launch of a missile

ENIAC—the Electronic Numerical Integrator and Computer, America's first large-scale electronic, digital computer, built for the Army to calculate the trajectory of artillery shells and later used at Los Alamos to help design a thermonuclear weapon

EOD—Explosive Ordnance Disposal, the rendering safe of warheads, bombs, and anything else that might detonate

FCDA—the Federal Civil Defense Administration, which from 1951 until 1979 advised the American public on how to survive a nuclear war

H-Bomb—a hydrogen bomb, the most powerful weapon ever invented, deriving its explosive force not only from nuclear fission but also from nuclear fusion, the elemental power of the sun

ICBM—Intercontinental Ballistic Missile, a missile that can propel a nuclear warhead more than 3,400 miles

JAG—the nickname for a military attorney, a member of the Judge Advocate General's Corps

K crew—a backup crew for the Titan II missile, on call to give advice during an emergency

LOX—liquid oxygen, a propellant that was used as an oxidizer, in combination with rocket fuel, to launch Atlas and Titan I missiles

MAD—Mutually Assured Destruction, a nuclear strategy that seeks to maintain peace by ensuring that adversaries have the capability to destroy one another

MANIAC—the Mathematical Analyzer, Numerical Integrator, and Computer, an early electronic, digital computer used at Los Alamos to help design the first hydrogen bombs

MART—Missile Alarm Response Team, the security police who responded to problems at Titan II missile sites

MFT—Mobile Fire Team, a heavily armed four-man team of Air Force security officers

MIMS—Missile Inspection and Maintenance Squadron, the repair crews who kept Titan II missiles ready to launch

MIRV—Multiple Independently targetable Reentry Vehicle, a ballistic missile carrying two or more warheads that can be aimed at different targets

MIT—Massachusetts Institute of Technology

MSA—a nickname for the vapor-detection equipment built by the Mine Safety Appliance Company and installed in Titan II silos

NATO—North Atlantic Treaty Organization, the military alliance formed in 1949 to defend Western Europe against an attack by the Soviet Union

NORAD—North American Air Defense Command, an organization created in 1958 by the United States and Canada to defend against a Soviet attack, later renamed the North American Aerospace Defense Command

NRC—Nuclear Regulatory Commission, the federal agency that licenses and regulates civilian nuclear power plants

OPLAN—Operations Plan, the term used since 2003 to describe the nuclear war plans of the United States

PAL—Permissive Action Link, a coded device installed within a nuclear warhead or bomb, much like a lock, to prevent unauthorized use of the weapon

PK—Probability of Kill, the likelihood of a target being destroyed

PPM—Parts per Million

PTPMU—Propellant Tank Pressure Monitor Unit, the gauge in a Titan II launch control center that provided digital readouts of the fuel and oxidizer pressures within the missile

PTS—Propellant Transfer System, the facilities and equipment used to handle the fuel and oxidizer for a Titan II missile

RAF—Royal Air Force, the armed service in Great Britain that during the Cold War was responsible for land-based aircraft and missiles

RAND—a think tank in Santa Monica, California, created by the Air Force after the Second World War, whose name was derived from the phrase "Research ANd Development"

RFHCO—Rocket Fuel Handler's Clothing Outfit, a liquidproof, vaporproof outfit with an air pack and a bubble helmet that looked like a space suit, commonly known among Titan II crews as a "ref-co"

RV—Reentry Vehicle, the nose cone of a missile containing its warhead

SAC—Strategic Air Command, the organization that until 1992 was responsible for the long-range bombers, the land-based missiles, and most of the nuclear weapons deployed by the U.S. Air Force

SAGE—Semi-Automatic Ground Environment, an air defense system built in the late 1950s that linked hundreds of radars into a network guided by computers in real time

SIOP—Single Integrated Operational Plan, the name given to the nuclear war plan of the United States from 1960 until 2003

SOCS—Strategic Operational Control System, a communications network employed by the Strategic Air Command during the 1950s, featuring a red telephone at its headquarters in Omaha that could be used to call every SAC air base simultaneously and broadcast a war order through their loudspeakers

SRAM—Short-Range Attack Missile, a missile with a nuclear warhead, launched from the air to hit targets on the ground, that was carried mainly by B-52 bombers, from the early 1970s until 1993

TAC—Tactical Air Command, the organization that from 1946 until 1992 was responsible for the ground support fighter planes of the U.S. Air Force

TACAMO—Take Charge and Move Out, a communications system created by the U.S. Navy that uses aircraft to transmit a nuclear attack order during an emergency

TASS—Telegraphic Agency of the Soviet Union (Telegrafnoe Agentstvo Sovetskogo Soyuza), the official news agency of the Soviet government

TATB—1,3,5-triamino-2,4,6-trinitrobenzene, an "insensitive" high explosive that cannot easily be detonated by fire, shock, or impact

USAAF—United States Army Air Forces, the organization responsible for America's land-based bombers during the Second World War

USAF—United States Air Force, the new and independent armed service that replaced the USAAF in 1947

WSEG—Weapon Systems Evaluation Group, a high-level research unit, employing both military and civilian personnel, that from 1948 until 1976 advised the Joint Chiefs of Staff

WWMCCS—World Wide Military Command and Control System, an organization formed during the Kennedy administration to combine the sensors, computers, command posts, and communications networks of the different armed services into a single centralized system

ZI—Zone of the Interior, a phrase used by the military to describe the continental United States

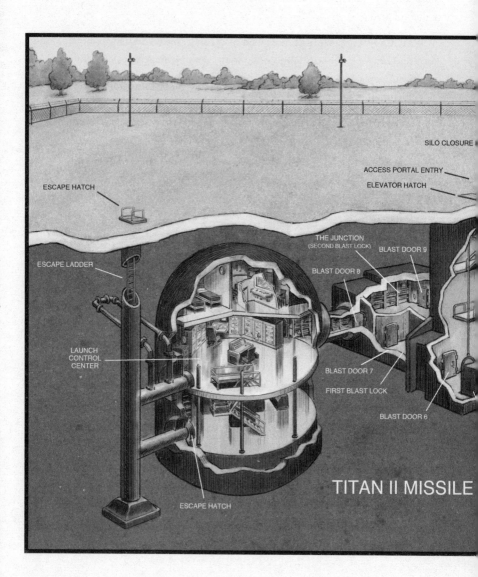

SILO CLOSURE

ACCESS PORTAL ENTRY

ELEVATOR HATCH

ESCAPE HATCH

THE JUNCTION
(SECOND BLAST LOCK)

BLAST DOOR 9

BLAST DOOR 8

ESCAPE LADDER

LAUNCH
CONTROL
CENTER

BLAST DOOR 7

FIRST BLAST LOCK

BLAST DOOR 6

ESCAPE HATCH

TITAN II MISSILE

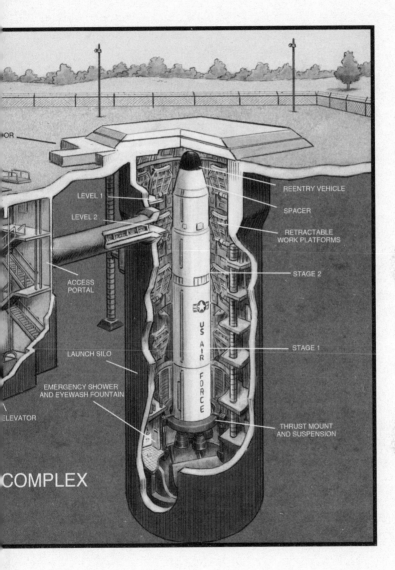

OR

REENTRY VEHICLE

SPACER

RETRACTABLE
WORK PLATFORMS

LEVEL 1

LEVEL 2

STAGE 2

ACCESS
PORTAL

STAGE 1

LAUNCH SILO

EMERGENCY SHOWER
AND EYEWASH FOUNTAIN

ELEVATOR

THRUST MOUNT
AND SUSPENSION

COMPLEX

US AIR FORCE

PART ONE

THE TITAN

Not Good

On September 18, 1980, at about six thirty in the evening, Senior Airman David F. Powell and Airman Jeffrey L. Plumb walked into the silo at Launch Complex 374-7, a few miles north of Damascus, Arkansas. They were planning to do a routine maintenance procedure on a Titan II missile. They'd spent countless hours underground at complexes like this one. But no matter how many times they entered the silo, the Titan II always looked impressive. It was the largest intercontinental ballistic missile ever built by the United States: 10 feet in diameter and 103 feet tall, roughly the height of a nine-story building. It had an aluminum skin with a matte finish and U.S. AIR FORCE painted in big letters down the side. The nose cone on top of the Titan II was deep black, and inside it sat a W-53 thermonuclear warhead, the most powerful weapon ever carried by an American missile. The warhead had a yield of 9 megatons—about three times the explosive force of all the bombs dropped during the Second World War, including both atomic bombs.

Day or night, winter or spring, the silo always felt the same. It was eerily quiet, and mercury vapor lights on the walls bathed the missile in a bright white glow. When you opened the door on a lower level and stepped into the launch duct, the Titan II loomed above you like an immense black-tipped silver bullet, loaded in a concrete gun barrel, primed, cocked, ready to go, and pointed at the sky.

The missile was designed to launch within a minute and hit a target as far as six thousand miles away. In order to do that, the Titan II relied upon a pair of liquid propellants—a rocket fuel and an oxidizer—that were "hypergolic." The moment they came into contact with each other, they'd instantly and forcefully ignite. The missile had two stages, and inside both of them, an oxidizer tank rested on top of a fuel tank, with pipes leading down to an engine. Stage 1, which extended about seventy feet upward from the bottom of the missile, contained about 85,000 pounds of fuel and 163,000 pounds of oxidizer. Stage 2, the upper section where the warhead sat, was smaller and held about one fourth of those amounts. If the missile were launched, fuel and oxidizer would flow through the stage 1 pipes, mix inside the combustion chambers of the engine, catch on fire, emit hot gases, and send almost half a million pounds of thrust through the supersonic convergent-divergent nozzles beneath it. Within a few minutes, the Titan II would be fifty miles off the ground.

The two propellants were extremely efficient—and extremely dangerous. The fuel, Aerozine-50, could spontaneously ignite when it came into contact with everyday things like wool, rags, or rust. As a liquid, Aerozine-50 was clear and colorless. As a vapor, it reacted with the water and the oxygen in the air and became a whitish cloud with a fishy smell. This fuel vapor could be explosive in proportions as low as 2 percent. Inhaling it could cause breathing difficulties, a reduced heart rate, vomiting, convulsions, tremors, and death. The fuel was also highly carcinogenic and easily absorbed through the skin.

The missile's oxidizer, nitrogen tetroxide, was even more hazardous. Under federal law, it was classified as a "Poison A," the most deadly category of man-made chemicals. In its liquid form, the oxidizer was a translucent, yellowy brown. Although not as flammable as the fuel, it could spontaneously ignite if it touched leather, paper, cloth, or wood. And its boiling point was only 70 degrees Fahrenheit. At temperatures any higher, the liquid oxidizer boiled into a reddish brown vapor that smelled like ammonia. Contact with water turned the vapor into a corrosive acid that could react with the moisture in a person's eyes or skin and cause severe burns. When inhaled, the oxidizer could destroy tissue in the upper respiratory system and the lungs. The damage might not be felt immediately. Six to twelve hours after being inhaled, the stuff could suddenly cause headaches, dizziness, difficulty breathing, pneumonia, and pulmonary edema leading to death.

Powell and Plumb were missile repairmen. They belonged to Propellant Transfer System (PTS) Team A of the 308th Strategic Missile Wing, whose headquarters was about an hour or so away at Little Rock Air Force Base. They'd been called to the site that day because a warning light had signaled that pressure was low in the stage 2 oxidizer tank. If the pressure fell too low, the oxidizer wouldn't flow smoothly to the engine. A "low light" could mean a serious problem—a rupture, a leak. But it was far more likely that a slight change in temperature had lowered the pressure inside the tank. Air-conditioning units in the silo were supposed to keep the missile cooled to about 60 degrees. If Powell and Plumb didn't find any leaks, they'd simply unscrew the cap on the oxidizer tank and add more nitrogen gas. The nitrogen maintained a steady pressure on the liquid inside, pushing downward. It was a simple, mundane task, like putting air in your tires before a long drive.

Powell had served on a PTS team for almost three years and knew the hazards of the Titan II. During his first visit to a launch complex, an oxidizer leak created a toxic cloud that shut down operations for three days. He was twenty-one years old, a proud "hillbilly" from rural Kentucky who loved the job and planned to reenlist at the end of the year.

Plumb had been with the 308th for just nine months. He wasn't qualified to do this sort of missile maintenance or to handle these propellants. Accompanying Powell and watching everything that Powell did was considered Plumb's "OJT," his on-the-job training. Plumb was nineteen, raised in suburban Detroit.

Although an oxidizer low light wasn't unusual, Air Force technical orders required that both men wear Category I protective gear when entering the silo to investigate it. "Going Category I" meant getting into a Rocket Fuel Handler's Clothing Outfit (RFHCO)—an airtight, liquidproof, vaporproof, fire-resistant combination of gear designed to protect them from the oxidizer and the fuel. The men called it a "ref-co." A RFHCO looked like a space suit from an early-1960s science fiction movie. It had a white detachable bubble helmet with a voice-actuated radio and a transparent Plexiglas face screen. The suit was off white, with a long zipper extending from the top of the left shoulder, across the torso, to the right knee. You stepped into the RFHCO and wore long johns underneath it. The black vinyl gloves and boots weren't attached, so the RFHCO had roll-down cuffs at the wrists and the ankles to maintain a tight seal. The suit weighed about twenty-two pounds. The RFHCO backpack weighed an additional thirty-five and carried about an hour's worth of air. The outfit was heavy and cumbersome. It could be hot, sticky, and uncomfortable, especially when worn outside the air-conditioned silo. But it could also save your life.

The stage 2 oxidizer pressure cap was about two thirds of the way up the missile. In order to reach it, Powell and Plumb had to walk across a retractable steel platform that extended from the silo wall. The tall, hollow cylinder in which the Titan II stood was enclosed by another concrete cylinder with nine interior levels, housing equipment. Level 1 was near the top of the missile; level 9 about twenty feet beneath the missile. The steel work platforms folded down from the walls hydraulically. Each one had a stiff rubber edge to prevent the Titan II from getting scratched, while keeping the gap between the platform and the missile as narrow as possible.

The airmen entered the launch duct at level 2. Far above their heads was a concrete silo door. It was supposed to protect the missile from the wind and the rain and the effects of a nuclear weapon detonating nearby. The door weighed 740 tons. Far below the men, beneath the Titan II, a concrete flame deflector shaped like a *W* was installed to guide the hot gases downward at launch, then upward through exhaust vents and out of the silo. The missile stood on a thrust mount, a steel ring at level 7 that weighed about 26,000 pounds. The thrust mount was attached to the walls by large springs, so that the Titan II could ride out a nuclear attack, bounce instead of break, and then take off.

In addition to the W-53 warhead and a few hundred thousand pounds of propellants, many other things in the silo could detonate. Electroexplosive devices were used after ignition to free the missile from the thrust mount, separate stage 2 from stage 1, release the nose cone. The missile also housed numerous small rocket engines with flammable solid fuel to adjust the pitch and the roll of the warhead midflight. The Titan II launch complex had been carefully designed to minimize the risk of having so many flammables and explosives within it. Fire detectors, fire suppression systems, toxic vapor detectors, and decontamination showers were scattered throughout the nine levels of the silo. These safety devices were bolstered by strict safety rules.

Whenever a PTS team member put on a RFHCO, he had to be accompanied by someone else in a RFHCO, with two other people waiting as backup, ready to put on their suits. Every Category I task had to be performed according to a standardized checklist, which the team chief usually read aloud over the radio communications network. There was one way to do everything—and only one way. Technical Order 21M-LGM25C-2-12, Figure 2-18, told Powell and Plumb exactly what to do as they stood on the platform near the missile.

"Step four," the PTS team chief said over the radio. "Remove airborne disconnect pressure cap."

"Roger," Powell replied.

"Caution. When complying with step four, do not exceed one hundred sixty foot-pounds of torque. Overtorquing may result in damage to the missile skin."

"Roger."

As Powell used a socket wrench to unscrew the pressure cap, the socket fell off. It struck the platform and bounced. Powell grabbed for it but missed.

Plumb watched the nine-pound socket slip through the narrow gap between the platform and the missile, fall about seventy feet, hit the thrust mount, and then ricochet off the Titan II. It seemed to happen in slow motion. A moment later, fuel sprayed from a hole in the missile like water from a garden hose.

"Oh man," Plumb thought. "This is not good."

New Wave

Earlier that day, Second Lieutenant Allan D. Childers had gotten out of bed around five, showered, put on his uniform, kissed his wife good-bye, grabbed his overnight bag, and headed for the predeparture briefing at Little Rock Air Force Base. Childers was the deputy commander of a Titan II missile combat crew. At seven o'clock every morning, the crews about to pull an alert gathered in a large room at the headquarters of the 308th Strategic Missile Wing. The 308th operated eighteen Titan II launch complexes in Arkansas, each with a single missile and a four-man crew. The wing's motto was *Non sibi sed aliis*—"Not for self but for others." While senior officers and staff stood in the front of the briefing room, each combat crew sat at its own small table.

Childers took a seat with his crew. Captain Michael T. Mazzaro was the commander, a brilliant young officer from Massachusetts, about five foot eight, with thinning brown hair. Staff Sergeant Rodney L. Holder was the missile systems analyst technician, the one who made sure the missile was always ready to go. He looked a lot like Childers, tall and thin with fair hair and glasses. Staff Sergeant Ronald O. Fuller, handsome and baby faced, from Elmira, New York, was the missile facilities technician. His job focused on the workings of the launch site. Once or twice a week, the four of them began their days at one of these briefings and then spent the next twenty-four hours together underground, monitoring their missile; supervising maintenance at the site; constantly practicing, training, and awaiting the order to launch.

Childers hardly fit the stereotype of a warmongering Strategic Air Command (SAC) officer, eager to nuke the Soviets and bring on Armageddon. For about a year before joining the Air Force, he'd been a late-night radio DJ who played mainly acid rock, spent his days surfing, and had hair down to his shoulders. He wasn't a hippie, but he also wasn't harboring any life-long ambition to become a spit-and-polish military officer. He'd spent most of his childhood on the Japanese island of Okinawa, where his father was an aircraft maintenance mechanic for the Air Force. The family home was a Quonset hut, a prefabricated steel building dating back to the Second World War. Although the accommodations were far from luxurious, growing up on that island during the 1960s was idyllic. Childers spent a lot of time lying on the beach and scuba diving. At Kadena Air Force Base the social divide between officers and enlisted men like his father was almost impossible to bridge. The two groups did not mix. But at the local high school nobody seemed to care about military ranks or racial distinctions. White, black, and Asian kids hung out together, and at various times Childers dated not only the daughter of a major but also the daughter of a colonel. Most of the students had a mother or a father in the armed services. The Vietnam War wasn't a distant, abstract conflict debated in the classroom; it touched almost every household directly. Childers had two brothers and a sister, and they were all proud of their father. But none of them wanted anything to do with the military.

After graduating from high school in 1971, Childers went to the University of Arizona, hoping to become an engineer. He dropped out after a few semesters, returned to Okinawa, and found work as a disc jockey at a radio station on the island. He was nineteen, the youngest employee at the station, and they gave him the late-night shift. It was a dream job. From midnight until six in the morning, Childers played his favorite music—Led Zeppelin, Neil Young, Janis Joplin, Jimi Hendrix, Creedence Clearwater Revival. GIs would call the station and make requests. He loved dedicating songs on their behalf and reading messages on the air to their families and girlfriends. After work he'd sleep until noon, and then hit the beach.

The station in Okinawa went off the air in 1973, and Childers moved to Tampa, Florida, hoping to enroll in radio school. But he didn't have enough money for tuition and, after a few months of looking for work, decided to join the Air Force. He expected to wind up in Vietnam, one way or another. Serving at an air base sounded a lot better than carrying a rifle and fighting in the jungle. When Childers enlisted, he filled out a form requesting an assignment with the Armed Forces Radio and Television Service. He thought the Air Force might provide his training to become a radio announcer. But he filled out the form incorrectly and got assigned to the newspaper at Norton Air Force Base in San Bernardino, California. He enjoyed the job and fell for Diane Brandeburg, a budget analyst who worked down the hall. In 1975 his commander persuaded him to become an officer, which would require a college degree. Through the Airman Scholarship and Commissioning Program, he attended Chaminade College of Honolulu, a good place to study and to surf. Diane was stationed at nearby Hickam Air Force Base, and they were married in 1977.

All three of Childers's siblings eventually served in the military. His older brother enlisted in the Army, his sister in the Air Force, his younger brother in the Navy. And all of them wound up with spouses who'd either served in the military or been raised in military families. Childers later realized that they'd been drawn back to a familiar way of life. It offered a good education, a sense of mission, the chance to do something useful, and a strong feeling of comradeship with others who'd chosen to serve.

In the hierarchy of Air Force officers, the fighter pilots and bomber pilots each claimed to be at the top. Despite their intense rivalry, the pilots agreed on at least one thing: missileers occupied a rung far below them. Serving in an underground control center lacked the glamour of flying sorties into enemy territory or gaining command of the skies. Childers's poor eyesight disqualified him from becoming an Air Force pilot, and the missile corps needed officers. Although he knew nothing about intercontinental ballistic missiles (ICBMs) and even less about what a missile officer did, he signed up for the program before graduating from college. He didn't care about the status or traditional Air Force snobbery. The job sounded interesting, and it offered the opportunity to command.

Childers spent six months studying Titan II operations at Sheppard Air Force Base in Texas and Vandenberg Air Force Base in California. Like all Titan II trainees, he carefully read the *Dash-1,* the technical manual that explained every aspect of the missile system. He spent hours in simulators, mock-ups of the control center where launch checklists and hazard checklists were practiced again and again. But he never saw a real Titan II missile until he pulled his first alert in Arkansas and stepped into the silo. It felt cold in there, like walking into a refrigerator, and the missile looked really big.

If an emergency war order arrived from SAC headquarters, every missile crew officer would face a decision with almost unimaginable consequences. Given the order to launch, Childers would comply without hesitation. He had no desire to commit mass murder. And yet the only thing that prevented the Soviet Union from destroying the United States with nuclear weapons, according to the Cold War theory of deterrence, was the threat of being annihilated, as well. Childers had faith in the logic of nuclear deterrence: his willingness to launch the missile ensured that it would never be launched. At Vandenberg he had learned the general categories and locations of Titan II targets. Some were in the Soviet Union, others in China. But a crew was never told where its missile was aimed. That sort of knowledge might inspire doubt. Like four members of a firing squad whose rifles were loaded with three bullets and one blank, a missile crew was expected to obey the order to fire, without bearing personal responsibility for the result.

After six weeks of training at Little Rock, Childers became the deputy commander of a Titan II site in 1979. The following year he was promoted, joining Mazzaro, Holder, and Fuller on an instructor crew. Unlike a typical crew that spent months or years pulling alerts at the same launch complex, an instructor crew brought trainees to different sites. On the morning of September 18, Childers and his crew were planning to bring a student, Second Lieutenant Miguel Serrano, to an overnight alert at Launch Complex 374-5, outside the town of Springhill. The crew always liked going to "4-5." It was closer to the base than some of the other complexes, which meant they could get there faster and get home sooner the next day.

Predeparture briefings always started with a roll call. Once it was clear that every launch complex would be fully staffed, the wing's senior officers talked to the eighty or so combat crew members about maintenance issues, new safety guidelines, changes in the emergency war order, and the latest weather report. The weather was a crucial factor in any maintenance work that involved fuel, oxidizer, or the reentry vehicle. Sometimes the briefings included a slide presentation on intelligence issues and the state of the world.

ON SEPTEMBER 18, 1980, the world was unsettled. The president of Iraq, Saddam Hussein, had announced the previous day that the treaty defining the border between his country and Iran was no longer in effect. Troops from the two nations were already fighting skirmishes in southern Khuzestan, Iran's foreign ministry had condemned "the hostile invasion . . . by the Iraqi regime," and a war over the disputed territory seemed imminent. In Tehran, fifty-two American hostages were still being held captive, almost a year after being seized at the U.S. embassy there. A failed rescue attempt by the U.S. military, during the spring of 1980, had prompted Iran's Revolutionary Guards to remove the hostages from the embassy and scatter them at locations throughout the city. Televised images of Iranian crowds burning American flags and shouting "Death to the Great Satan!" had become a nightly routine, and the American government seemed powerless to do anything about it.

Meanwhile, relations between the United States and the Soviet Union had reached their lowest point since the Cuban Missile Crisis in 1962. The Soviets had invaded Afghanistan nine months earlier, deploying more than 100,000 troops in a campaign that many feared was just the first stage of a wider assault on the oil-producing nations of the Middle East. The United States had responded to the invasion by imposing a grain embargo on the Soviet Union and boycotting the recent Summer Olympics in Moscow.

Neither of those punishments, however, seemed likely to force a Soviet withdrawal from Kabul. The influence of the United States seemed everywhere in decline. On September 17, the International Institute for Strategic Studies, a prominent British think tank, issued a report suggesting that the Soviet Union's new and more accurate ICBMs had made America's ICBMs vulnerable to attack. The United States was falling behind not only in nuclear weaponry, the report claimed, but also in planes, tanks, and ground forces.

Amid this discouraging international news, the mood of the American people seemed equally downbeat. The economy of the United States was in recession, with high inflation and an unemployment rate of about 8 percent. Gasoline shortages raised the prospect of rationing and federal limits on automobile use. Watergate, the Vietnam War, and the energy crisis had shaken faith in the ability of government to accomplish anything. The president of the United States, Jimmy Carter, had offered his own harsh critique of the national state of mind. During a speech broadcast by the three major television networks in prime time, the president warned that the United States faced an invisible threat: "a crisis in confidence." Old-fashioned American optimism had been replaced by a despairing, self-absorbed worship of consumption. "Piling up material goods," Carter said, "cannot fill the emptiness of lives which have no purpose or meaning." The speech ended on a more practical note, outlining half a dozen steps to support renewable energy and eliminate the dependence on foreign oil. The underlying message, however, was that the nation's most important problems could never be solved by Congress or the president, and Carter urged viewers to assume responsibility for their own fate. "All the legislation in the world," he said, "can't fix what's wrong with America."

Many Democrats and Republicans disagreed. They thought that Jimmy Carter was the problem, not some vague, existential crisis of the American soul. It was a presidential election year, and Carter had gained the Democratic nomination after a bitter primary fight with Senator Edward M. Kennedy. Despite the victory, Carter's approval ratings plummeted. The Iranian hostage crisis brought more bad news every day, and an official report on the failed rescue attempt—describing how eight American servicemen died and half a dozen U.S. helicopters full of classified documents were abandoned in the desert—raised doubts about the readiness of the military. Although Carter was a devout Christian, a newly created evangelical group, the Moral Majority, was attacking his support for legalized abortion and a constitutional amendment to guarantee equal rights for women. A midsummer opinion poll found that 77 percent of the American people disapproved of President Carter's performance in the White House—a higher disapproval rate than that of President Richard Nixon at the height of Watergate.

The Republican candidate for president, Ronald Reagan, had a sunnier disposition. "I refuse to accept [Carter's] defeatist and pessimistic view of America," Reagan said. The country could not afford "four more years of weakness, indecision, mediocrity, and incompetence." Reagan called for large tax cuts, smaller government, deregulation, increased defense spending to confront the Soviet threat, and a renewed faith in the American dream. A popular third-party candidate, Congressman John B. Anderson, described himself as a centrist, labeling Reagan a right-wing extremist and Carter "a bumbler." Anderson agreed that things had gone fundamentally wrong in the United States. "People feel that the country is coming apart at the seams," he said.

The nation's underlying anxiety fueled sales of a bestselling nonfiction book in late September: *Crisis Investing: Opportunities and Profits in the Coming Great Depression*. A number of bestselling novels also addressed the widespread fears about America's future. *The Devil's Alternative*, by Frederick Forsyth, described a Soviet plot to invade Western Europe. *The Fifth Horseman*, by Larry Collins and Dominique Lapierre, described a Libyan plot to blackmail the United States with a hydrogen bomb hidden in New York City. *The Spike*, by Arnaud de Borchgrave and Robert Moss, told the story of a left-wing American journalist who uncovers Soviet plans for world domination but cannot persuade his liberal editor to publish them.

Perhaps the most influential bestseller of the year was *The Third World War: August 1985*, a novel written by a retired British officer, General Sir John Hackett. It offered a compelling, realistic account of a full-scale war between NATO and the Soviet bloc. After a long series of European tank

a movie starring the Village People. Punk was dead, too, and taking its place was the lighter, dance-oriented New Wave of Devo, The Police, The B-52's, and Talking Heads. The hard rock of The Rolling Stones had given way to the softer pop sounds of "Emotional Rescue." Led Zeppelin broke up, transforming Van Halen into America's favorite heavy metal band. Turning the radio dial, on almost every FM station, you could hear rough edges becoming smooth. Outlaw country no longer threatened the Nashville establishment. It had fully entered the mainstream, with Willie Nelson's hit "On the Road Again" and Waylon Jennings's "Theme from the *Dukes of Hazzard.*" Bob Dylan now refused to sing any of his old songs. Born again and on the road, he played only gospel. John Lennon was in New York City, recording a new album for the first time in years and looking forward, in a few weeks, to his fortieth birthday. "Life begins at forty," Lennon told an interviewer. "It's like: *Wow!* what's going to happen next?"

In retrospect, it's easy to say that a particular year marked a turning point in history. And yet sometimes the significance of contemporary events is grasped even in the moment. The United States of the 1960s and the 1970s, with its liberalism and countercultural turmoil, was about to become something different. The year 1980, the start of a new decade, was when that change became palpable, in ways both trivial and telling. During the first week of September, the antiwar activist and radical Abbie Hoffman surrendered to federal authorities after more than six years on the run. Before turning himself in, Hoffman sat for a prime-time television interview with Barbara Walters. Another radical leader, Jerry Rubin, had recently chosen a different path. In 1967, Hoffman and Rubin had tossed dollar bills over the balcony at the New York Stock Exchange as a protest against the evils of capitalism. In 1980, Rubin took a job as an investment analyst on Wall Street. "Politics and rebellion distinguished the '60's," he explained in the *New York Times*. "Money and financial interest will capture the passion of the '80's." Rubin had once again spotted a cultural shift and tried to place himself at its cutting edge. At the time, the highest-paid banker in the United States was Roger E. Anderson, the head of Continental Illinois National Bank, who earned about $710,000 a year. The incomes on Wall Street would soon rise. Suits and ties were back in fashion.

Mustaches, beards, and bell-bottoms had become uncool, and an ironic guide to the new zeitgeist, *The Official Preppy Handbook,* was just arriving in stores. During a speech at the Republican convention that summer, Congressman Jack Kemp had noted what others did not yet acknowledge or see: "There is a tidal wave coming, a political tidal wave as powerful as the one that hit in 1932, when an era of Republican dominance gave way to the New Deal."

No Lone Zones

At the predeparture briefing, Childers and his crew learned that "major maintenance" was scheduled at Launch Complex 374-5 that day. The missile was being taken off alert so that the reentry vehicle containing its warhead could be replaced. For an instructor crew, major maintenance was a waste of time. Lieutenant Serrano was training to become a deputy missile combat crew commander, and he needed to practice routine tasks in a control center. Captain Mazzaro found a commander who would switch complexes. Instead of 4-5, the instructor crew would go to 4-7, outside Damascus. The change of plans solved the training issue but delayed the departure of both crews. Entry codes had to be swapped, duty orders rewritten and authenticated. The only important difference between the two launch complexes was their distance from Little Rock Air Force Base. Four-seven was a lot farther away, which meant Childers and his crew probably wouldn't be getting home until noon the next day.

Mazzaro, Childers, Holder, Fuller, and Serrano tossed their bags into the back of an Air Force blue Chevy Suburban, climbed into it, and began the hour-long drive to Damascus. Within a mile, the Suburban's alternator light came on. So they had to turn around, go back to the base, find a new vehicle, move their gear, and fill out paperwork before leaving again. The day was not getting off to a smooth start.

The eighteen Titan II missile complexes in Arkansas were scattered throughout an area extending about sixty miles north of Little Rock Air Force Base and about thirty miles to the east and the west. The missiles were dispersed roughly seven to ten miles from each other, so that in the event of a surprise attack, one Soviet warhead couldn't destroy more than one Titan II silo. In the American West, ICBMs were usually set amid a vast, empty landscape, far from populated areas. In central Arkansas, the Titan II complexes were buried off backcountry roads, near small farms and little towns with names like Velvet Ridge, Mountain Home, Wonderview, and Old Texas. It was an unlikely setting for some of the most powerful nuclear weapons in the American arsenal. The decision to put ICBMs in rural Arkansas had been influenced by political, as well as military, considerations. One of the state's congressmen, Wilbur D. Mills, happened to be chairman of the House Ways and Means Committee when Titan II sites were being chosen.

To reach Launch Complex 374-7, the crew drove west through the towns of Hamlet and Vilonia, then north on Highway 65, a two-lane road that climbed into the foothills of the Ozark Mountains. Slavery had never reached this part of Arkansas, and the people who lived there were overwhelmingly poor, white, hardworking, and self-sufficient. It was the kind of poverty that carried little shame, because everyone seemed to be in the same boat. The local farms were usually thirty to forty acres in size and owned by the same families for generations. Farmers ran cattle, owned a few pigs, grew vegetables in the backyard. They were patriotic and rarely complained about the missiles in the neighborhood. Most of the income generated by the 308th was spent in the area around Little Rock. Aside from the occasional purchase of coffee and doughnuts, the missile crews passing through these rural communities added little to the local economy. For the most part, the airmen were treated warmly or hardly noticed. Despite the poverty, the feel of the place was bucolic. In early fall the fields were deep green, dotted with round bales of hay, and the leaves on the trees—the black gums, sweet gums, maples, and oaks—were beginning to turn.

The population of Damascus was about four hundred. The town consisted of a gas station, a small grocery store, and not much else. A few miles north along Highway 65, right after an old white farmhouse with a rusted tin roof, the combat crew turned left onto a narrow paved road, crossed a cattle guard, and drove half a mile. The launch complex was hidden from view until the road reached the crest of a low hill, and then there it was: a flat, square, three-acre patch of land covered in gravel and ringed in chain link, with the massive silo door in the middle, a couple of paved, rectangular parking areas on either side of it, half a dozen antennae rising from the ground, and a tall wooden pole that had three status lights mounted on top of it, one green, one yellow, one red, and a Klaxon. The green said that all was clear, the yellow warned of a potential hazard, and the red light meant trouble. It rotated like the red lights on an old-fashioned highway patrol car and, accompanied by the loud blare of the Klaxon, warned that there was an emergency on the site—or that the missile was about to take off.

The launch complex didn't look like a high-security, military outpost. The gray concrete silo door could have passed, to the untrained eye, as the cover of a municipal wastewater treatment plant. The sign on the entry gate spelled it out. "WARNING," it said, in red capital letters, followed by these words in capital blue: "U.S. AIR FORCE INSTALLATION, IT IS UN-LAWFUL TO ENTER THIS AREA WITHOUT PERMISSION OF THE INSTALLATION COMMANDER." The barbed wire atop the chain-link fence discouraged a casual stroll onto the property, as did the triangular AN/TPS-39 radar units. Mounted on short metal poles and nicknamed "tipsies," they detected the slightest motion near the silo door or the air intake shaft and set off an alarm.

Captain Mazzaro got out of the truck, picked up the phone at the gate, and notified the control center of their arrival. The gate was unlocked by the crew underground, and Mazzaro walked across the complex to the access portal, a sixteen-foot-square slab of concrete raised about a foot off the ground. Two steel doors lay flat on the slab; beneath one was an elevator, below the other a stairway. Mazzaro opened the door on the left, climbed down a flight of concrete stairs, and waited a moment to be buzzed through another steel door. After he passed through it, the door locked behind him. Mazzaro had entered the entrapment area, a metal stairway enclosed on one side by a wall and on the other by steel mesh that rose to the ceiling. It looked like he'd walked into a cage.

At the bottom of the stairs was another locked door, with a television camera above it. Mazzaro picked up the phone on the wall, called the control center again, pulled a code card from his pocket, and read the six-letter code aloud. After being granted permission to enter, he took out some matches and set the code card on fire. Then he dropped the burning card into a red canister mounted on the steel mesh. The rest of the crew was allowed to enter the complex. They parked the Suburban, checked the site for any signs of weather damage or a propellant leak, headed down the access portal, waited a moment in the entrapment area, then were buzzed through the door at the bottom of the stairs.

The crew descended two more flights and reached an enormous blast door at the bottom of the stairs, about thirty feet underground. The access portal and its metal stairway were not designed to survive a nuclear blast. Everything beyond this blast door was. The steel door was about seven feet tall, five feet wide, and one foot thick. It weighed roughly six thousand pounds. The pair of steel doorjambs that kept it in place weighed an additional thirty-one thousand pounds. The blast door was operated hydraulically, with an electric switch. When the door was locked, four large steel pins extended from it into the frame, creating a formidable, airtight seal. When the door was unlocked, it could easily be swung open or shut by hand. The launch complex had four identical blast doors. For some reason this first one, at the bottom of the access portal, was blast door 6.

Mazzaro picked up a phone near the door and called the control center again. He pushed a button on the wall, someone in the control center pushed a button simultaneously, and the pins in the door retracted from the frame. The crew opened the huge door and stepped into the blast lock, a room about eleven feet long and twelve feet wide. It was a transitional space between the access portal and the rest of the underground complex. Blast door 6 was at one end, blast door 7 at the other. In order to protect the missile and the control center from an explosion, the doors had been wired so that both couldn't be open at the same time. Beyond blast door 7 was another blast lock, "the junction." To the right of it, a long steel-lined tunnel, "the cableway," led to the missile. To the left, a shorter tunnel led to the control center. These two corridors were blocked by opposing blast doors, numbers 8 and 9, that also couldn't be opened at the same time.

Every Titan II launch complex had exactly the same layout: access portal, blast lock, then another blast lock, missile down the corridor to the right, control center down the corridor to the left, blast doors at the most vulnerable entry points. Every complex had the same equipment, the same wiring, lighting, and design. Nevertheless, each had its quirks. Blast door 9 at one site might require frequent maintenance; the control center air-conditioning might be temperamental at another. The typical crew was assigned to a single complex and pulled every alert there. Some crew members had spent two nights a week, for ten years or more, within the same underground facility. But an instructor crew served at different sites, depending on their availability. Al Childers had gotten to know all of the Titan II complexes in Arkansas and, for the most part, couldn't tell the difference between them. Sometimes he had to look at the map on the wall of the control center to remember where he was. One launch complex, however, stood apart from the rest: 373-4 was known as the "ghost site." It was the first complex where Childers was stationed, and odd things seemed to happen there. Pumps that could be operated only by hand suddenly went on by themselves. Lights turned on and off for no reason. Childers didn't believe in the supernatural, and most officers laughed at the idea that the complex might be haunted. But some crew members thought that every now and then it felt pretty odd down there. Rodney Holder was once working in the silo at night with another crew member. The silo had a manually operated elevator that traveled from levels 2 to 8, and the men had left its door open. The bell in the elevator started to ring. It rang whenever the door was open and someone on another level needed the elevator. Holder couldn't think of anyone who might need a ride. He called the control center and learned that nobody else was in the silo. The bell kept ringing. Holder and his partner were spooked, quickly finished their work, and returned to the control center.

———

LAUNCH COMPLEX 373-4 HAD BEEN the site of the worst Titan II accident thus far. On August 9, 1965, the complex outside Searcy, Arkansas, was being modified to make it more likely to survive a nuclear strike. Construction crews were hardening the silo, improving the blast doors, adjusting the hydraulics, installing emergency lights. The reentry vehicle and the warhead had been removed from the missile (serial number 62-0006). But its fuel tanks and oxidizer tanks were full. Four crew members manned the control center, as scores of construction workers labored underground and topside on a hot summer afternoon.

It was Gary Lay's first day on the job. He was seventeen years old and had just graduated from high school in Searcy. His father had found him work at the complex. Lay was glad to have it. The money was good, and the temperature in the silo was a hell of a lot cooler than it was outdoors. Lay had been hired for the summer to do menial tasks and clean up after other workers. He'd never visited a missile complex before. His safety training consisted of watching *You and the Titan II,* a one-hour film. When it was over, Lay was handed a mask with a filter and told, in case of emergency, to use the elevator. He spent the morning at the bottom of the silo, quit for lunch around noon, and came back an hour later.

At approximately one o'clock, Lay was standing in the underground cableway when someone asked him to grab a bucket and a mop from the silo. He walked down the corridor, which entered the silo at level 2. A few minutes later, he was talking to a group of workers in the level 2 equipment area, not far from the emergency escape ladder. Men were busy in all nine levels of the silo, some of them painting, others flushing the hydraulic system that raised and lowered the steel platforms beside the missile. Lay heard a big puff, like the sound of a gas stove being lit, and felt a warm breeze. Then he saw bright yellow flames rising from the floor to the ceiling. He ran to the escape ladder and tried to climb down, but the ladder was jammed with workers. Moments later, the lights went out. Black smoke filled the silo, and it soon felt like the darkest place on earth. Workers were shouting, panicking, desperately trying to find a way out. Lay somehow managed to get back to the level 2 equipment area. He blindly felt his way along the wall, fell down, got back up, and instinctively headed toward the origin of the fire while others ran away from it.

At about the same time that Lay heard the big puff and felt the heat, the FIRE DIESEL AREA light in the control center began to flash red. Klaxons sounded throughout the complex, and the revolving red status light on the outdoor pole lit up. Captain David A. Yount, the crew commander, told everyone to evacuate, giving the order three times over the public address system. And then the power went out.

Pipe fitters who'd been working on the blast doors ran up the access portal stairway. Smoke pouring from a vent in the silo door told workers topside that something was wrong. A number of them tried to get down to the silo but were driven back by thick clouds of smoke. Lay made it to the cableway, then to the control center, suffering from second- and third-degree burns. He was placed in a decontamination shower. While Lay was being rinsed off with cold water, two crew members, Sergeant Ronald O. Wallace and Airman First Class Donald E. Hastings, put on air packs, grabbed fire extinguishers, and prepared to enter the silo. Amid the commotion, they noticed that another worker, Hubert A. Saunders, was calmly sitting in the control center. Saunders had been painting at level 1A of the silo, near the top of the missile, when smoke started drifting toward him. The lights went out just as he reached a ladder, and he climbed twenty feet down in the pitch black. Saunders had worked at Titan II complexes for years and knew the layout. He held his breath while passing through the level 2 equipment area, then crawled on his hands and knees down the cableway. Aside from inhaling some smoke, he was fine. And he'd never let go of his paint can and brush. Wallace and Hastings rushed down the long, dark cableway to battle the fire and rescue survivors. The smoke was so dense that they could not see the floor.

Saunders and Lay were escorted from the complex and taken by ambulance to the hospital in Searcy, where preparations were hastily being made to treat dozens of injured workers. Hours passed, but none arrived. The flash fire in the equipment area on level 2 had filled the silo with smoke, then sucked the oxygen out. The exit to the cableway from level 2 offered the only possibility of escape. Some workers had mistakenly climbed down the ladder toward the bottom of the silo. Others were blocked trying to climb up. One was trapped in the elevator when the power went out. Workers weren't killed by the flames. They were asphyxiated by the smoke. Of the fifty-five men who'd returned to the silo after lunch, only Saunders and Lay left there alive.

Helicopters brought firemen from Little Rock Air Force Base to 373-4, but their work was hampered by the poor visibility. They managed to extinguish a few small fires on level 2, but fire was no longer the real danger. Without power, the site lacked air-conditioning, and as the temperature in the silo rose, so did the pressure in the missile's oxidizer tanks. Nitrogen tetroxide expanded in the heat; its boiling point was only 70 degrees Fahrenheit. By five o'clock that evening, the temperature in the silo was 78 degrees and rising. Opening the silo door would help cool the missile and vent the smoke—but the door couldn't be opened without electrical power. Smoke had seeped into the control center as well, complicating efforts to manage the crisis. All four blast doors had been propped open so workers could freely move within the complex. The pins on blast door 8, at the entrance to the control center, had deliberately been left extended so the door wouldn't shut. And without power, the pins couldn't be retracted. At seven o'clock, SAC headquarters in Omaha warned that if the temperature in the silo wasn't reduced, the missile's stage 2 oxidizer tank was likely to reach an "explosive situation" around midnight.

Firemen and PTS teams worked in the hot, smoke-filled complex to recover bodies, restore power, and prevent an explosion. At ten o'clock, the temperature in the silo reached 80 degrees, then started to fall. Portable lighting units, generators, and industrial air-conditioners were hooked up, and by early morning an even greater disaster had been averted. The fifty-third body was carried from the silo at daybreak.

An Air Force Accident Investigation Board later concluded that a worker who'd been welding on level 2 inadvertently struck a temporary hydraulics line. When the spray of hydraulic fluid hit the arc of the electric welder, it caught fire. The Air Force attributed the accident to human error. But

Gary Lay insisted that nobody had been welding on level 2 and that a mechanical fault had started the fire. He thought that a hydraulics line must have ruptured, spraying flammable oil onto electrical equipment. The missile in the silo wasn't damaged, and the equipment areas were repaired. About one year after the accident, launch crews were back at the complex near Searcy to pull alerts. It looked just like any other complex, except for a few blackened walls in the silo that someone had forgotten to paint.

CHILDERS AND HIS CREW PASSED through blast door 8, walked down the short cableway, and entered the launch control center. The room was round and about thirty-five feet in diameter. It was on the second level of a three-story steel structure, suspended on enormous springs, within a buried concrete cylinder. The walls were two feet thick. The ceiling was covered with a maze of ducts and pipes. The color scheme was a mix of pale turquoise, light gray, the dull silver of unpainted steel. The room had the strong, confident vibe of Eisenhower-era science and technology. It was full of intricately wired machinery and electronics—but did not have a computer. To the right stood a series of steel cabinets that displayed the status and housed the controls of the guidance system, the power and electrical systems, the topside alarm. The cabinets were about seven feet tall and covered with all sorts of switches, gauges, dials, and small round lights. In the center of the room was the commander's console, a small steel desk, turquoise and gray, with rows of square buttons and warning lights. It monitored and controlled the most important functions of the complex. The commander could open the front gate from there, change the warhead's target, enable or abort a launch. In the middle of the console was the launch switch. It was unmarked, blocked by a security seal, and activated by a key. On top of the console was a digital gauge that showed the pressure in the missile's fuel and oxidizer tanks. Two small speakers were bolted to the side of the desk. Throughout the day they broadcast test messages from SAC headquarters and, during wartime, would give the order to launch.

To the left of the commander's console was another small turquoise and gray desk, where the deputy commander sat. It operated the site's communications systems. Directly above the desk was a large, round clock with numbers from 00 through 23 on the face and a thick black casing. The clock was set to Greenwich mean time, so launches at the Titan II sites in Arkansas, Kansas, and Arizona could be synchronized. The deputy commander's launch switch was on the upper left side of the desk. It was round, silver, unmarked, and resembled the ignition switch of an old car. The launch codes and keys were kept in a bright red safe with two brass combination locks, one belonging to the commander, the other to the deputy. It was nicknamed the "go-to-war safe."

If a launch order came over the speakers, the officers were supposed to unlock their locks, open the safe, grab their codes and keys, then return to their consoles. The keys looked unexceptional, like the kind used to unlock millions of American front doors. The codes were hidden inside flat plastic disks called "cookies." The disks were broken open by hand, like fortune cookies, and the codes were read aloud. And if the codes authenticated the emergency war order from SAC headquarters, the launch checklist went something like this:

SURFACE WARNING CONTROL . . . Lighted red.
Remove security seals and insert keys into switches.
Launch keys . . . Inserted.
Circuit breaker 103 on . . . Set.
BVLC – OPERATE Code Word . . . Entered.
Simultaneously (within 2 seconds) turn keys for 5 seconds or until
    sequence starts.
LAUNCH ENABLE . . . Lighted.
BATTERIES ACTIVATED . . . Lighted.
APS POWER . . . Lighted.
SILO SOFT . . . Lighted.
GUIDANCE GO . . . Lighted.
FIRE ENGINE . . . Lighted.
LIFTOFF . . . Lighted.

Assuming that everything worked as planned, the Titan II would be gone within seconds. Its warhead would strike the target in about half an hour. Once the missile left the silo, the crew's job was done. They couldn't destroy a missile midflight or launch another. The complex was designed to be used once.

The Titan II would not launch, however, unless the two keys were turned at the same time; the launch switches were too far apart for one person to activate them both. SAC's "two-man policy" had been adopted to prevent a deranged or fanatic crew member from starting a nuclear war. The butterfly valve lock on the stage 1 rocket engine offered some additional control over who could launch the missile. Oxidizer wouldn't flow into that engine until the correct butterfly valve lock code (BVLC) was used during the launch checklist—and without the oxidizer, the missile would stay in the silo. This code wasn't kept in the safe or anywhere else on the complex. It was transmitted with the emergency war order from SAC. And the valve lock contained a small explosive device. Any attempt to tamper with the lock set off the explosive and sealed the oxidizer line shut.

The SAC two-man rule governed not only how the missile was launched but also how the complex was run. At least two authorized personnel always had to be present and within visual range of each other in the control center. You couldn't allow the other person out of your sight. The same rule applied in the silo, whenever the missile had a warhead. At entrances to the control center and the silo, a warning stenciled in bold red letters said: "NO LONE ZONE, SAC TWO MAN POLICY MANDATORY."

THE COMMANDER AND the deputy commander at every Titan II site were issued .38 caliber revolvers, in case an intruder penetrated the underground complex or a crew member disobeyed orders. Transferring the weapons was part of the turnover checklist, when a new crew arrived for duty. In addition to the handguns and their holsters, Mazzaro and Childers received some bad news from the crew preparing to leave 4-7. Pressure in the stage 2 oxidizer tank was low. A PTS team would have to visit the site, and most of the day would have to be devoted to major maintenance. Before the other crew departed, Mazzaro and Childers opened the safe, made sure the cookies and launch keys were inside, shut it, and installed their own locks.

For the next hour or so Mazzaro, Childers, Holder, and Fuller went through the daily shift verification (DSV) checklist in the control center. They checked every piece of equipment on all three levels of the center, every gauge, switch, and warning light. Level 3 was the basement. It housed the DC power supplies and battery backups, switching equipment for the communications systems, the air-conditioning and ventilation systems. Fresh air was pulled into the control center from outdoors, filtered, cooled, and then sent throughout the rest of the complex. The positive air flow helped to protect the crew from toxic vapors that might drift from the silo. The go-to-war safe, the tall steel cabinets, and the launch consoles were on level 2. The top floor, level 1, had a kitchen, a small round table, four chairs, a toilet, and four beds. The complex had enough food to last for a month, but its emergency diesel generator had enough fuel for only two weeks. During wartime, the crew might find itself eating canned and dehydrated military rations in the dark.

PTS Team A was scheduled to pressurize the stage 2 oxidizer tank at the complex. The eight-man team was led by Senior Airman Charles T. Heineman, who would direct its work from the control center. Airmen David W. Aderhold, Eric Ayala, and Richard D. Willinghurst would remain topside to operate the nitrogen tank. Aderhold and Ayala would be in RFHCO suits. Airmen Roger A. Hamm and Gregory W. Lester would stay in the blast lock as backup to the men working in the silo, ready to put on their RFHCOs in an emergency. And Airmen David Powell and Jeffrey Plumb would enter the silo in RFHCOs, remove the pressure cap, and attach the nitrogen line.

Powell and Plumb hoped to get started on the missile early in the afternoon. But the work platforms wouldn't descend from the silo walls. They were stuck in the upright position. A repair crew was working on them. Something was wrong with the hydraulics system, and troubleshooting with help from the tech manuals couldn't fix it. The hassles continued to mount. The hydropneumatic accumulator was broken, and without it the platforms couldn't be lowered—and the repair crew didn't have the right parts. If pressure in the stage 2 oxidizer tank dropped any further, the missile would have to be taken off alert. SAC headquarters was never pleased when a missile went off alert. And so a helicopter was sent from Little Rock Air Force Base with the parts.

Meanwhile, Rodney Holder and Ron Fuller continued to go through the daily shift verification checklist, walking down the long corridor to the silo. The cableway was essentially a big steel pipe, braced with girders and springs, that stretched almost fifty yards from the blast lock to the silo. The floor was painted gray, the walls and ceilings turquoise. Bundles of pipes and cables snaked overhead and along both sides. It looked like the interior of a submarine that was somehow underground, not underwater. The silo's nine levels were crammed with equipment, and the checklist there took about two hours to complete. It had hundreds of steps. Sometimes crews would cut corners to speed things up. They'd divide the labor—you check this air compressor, I'll check that one—and violate the SAC two-man rule, roaming separately through the silo and comparing notes later. It was faster that way, the violation seemed trivial, and officers in the control center had no way of knowing what the enlisted men were doing in the silo. The television camera in the access portal, aimed at the entrapment area, was the only one in the complex. From the control center you couldn't see what was happening in the cableways, the blast lock, the silo, or topside. There was no periscope. And one officer could not leave the other alone in the control center to check on what crew members were doing elsewhere. That would be a serious violation of the two-man rule.

Holder and Fuller did everything by the book that day. As members of an instructor crew, they took pride in being considered among the best at the job. A standardization-evaluation team was soon going to be judging their work, and Holder wanted a high score. Doing things properly added only fifteen minutes or so to the job. Before joining the Air Force he'd been a construction worker, building highway bridges in rural Arkansas. A career in the military hadn't appealed to him, at first. His father was a former NFL player who joined the Naval Reserve during the Korean War and wound up spending more than two decades as a naval officer. Holder had attended grade schools in three different countries and high schools in four different states. At the age of nineteen, he liked doing construction work but worried about the future. The military promised a more interesting and rewarding life. Joining the Navy wasn't an option; Holder got seasick too easily. So he joined the Air Force, eager to learn about missiles. Working on the Titan II had revealed that, deep down, he was a techno geek. Holder knew his way around the complex better than any of the other crew members. He not only knew what everything was, he could explain how it worked. On September 18, 1980, he was twenty-four years old and had been married for ten months.

The silo door motors on level 1A had to be checked, as did the sump at the bottom of level 9B, and everything in between. The equipment areas of the silo tended to be loud, but the launch duct was lined with sound dampeners, so that the roar of the engines wouldn't cause vibrations and damage the missile. It was so quiet in the launch duct that on hot summer days, when the air-conditioners were struggling, warm oxidizer could be heard bubbling in the tanks. The only problem that Holder and Fuller noted that day was a faulty switch on the hard water tank. The complex had two large water tanks: one inside the silo, extending from levels 3 to 6, and one topside beyond the perimeter fence. The tank within the silo was considered "hard" because it was underground, and therefore shielded from a nuclear blast. It held one hundred thousand gallons of water that would spray into the silo moments before launch. The water helped to suppress the sound of the engines and ensured that flames wouldn't rise up the silo and destroy the missile. The two water tanks were also essential for extinguishing a major fire at the complex. Like a broken float in a toilet that allows only one flush, a faulty switch on the hard water tank could prevent it from refilling automatically. Holder and Fuller noted the problem on the checklist and moved to the next step.

PTS Team A reached the complex around 3:30 in the afternoon, but the platforms still wouldn't lower. Having nothing better to do, the team hung out and played cards around the table in level 1 of the control center. Jeffrey Plumb, who was new to the group, lay on one of the beds. They'd been working since early in the morning and were ready to be finished with the day. PTS teams and launch crews didn't tend to socialize. The PTS guys were a different breed. Outside of work they had a reputation for being rowdy and wild. They had one of the most dangerous jobs in the Air Force—and at the end of the day they liked to blow off steam, drinking and partying harder than just about anyone else at the base. They were more likely to ride motorcycles, ignore speed limits, violate curfews, and toss a commanding officer into a shower, fully clothed, after consuming too much alcohol. They called the missiles "birds," and they were attached to them and proud of them in the same way that good automobile mechanics care about cars. The danger of the oxidizer and the fuel wasn't theoretical. It was part of the job. The daily risks often inspired a defiant, cavalier attitude among the PTS guys. Some of them had been known to fill a Ping-Pong ball with oxidizer and toss it into a bucket of fuel. The destruction of the steel bucket, accompanied by flames, was a good reminder of what they were working with. And if you were afraid of the propellants, as most people would be, you needed to find a different line of work.

Although low pressure in an oxidizer tank could mean a leak, PTS Team A wasn't worried about it. This was the third day in a row that they'd been called out to 4-7. The missile in the silo had recently been recycled. The warhead and the propellants were removed during a recycle, and then the missile was lifted from the silo, hauled back to the base, carefully checked for corrosion and leaks. Later, the same missile might be returned to the complex, or a different one might be shipped there from storage. The fuel and oxidizer pressure often didn't stabilize at the proper levels for weeks after a recycle. PTS teams were accustomed to adding more nitrogen two, three, four times until the tank pressures settled.

At the conclusion of the recycle at 4-7, a Titan II was placed in the silo, filled with propellants, and armed with a warhead. The missile's serial number was 62-0006. The same missile that had been in the silo during the fire at the complex near Searcy now stood on the thrust mount at Launch Complex 374-7 north of Damascus. The odds were slim that the same Titan II airframe, out of dozens, would wind up in those two places.

Bad luck, fate, sheer coincidence—whatever the explanation, neither the launch crew, nor the PTS team, knew that this missile had once been in a silo full of thick smoke and dying men.

By six o'clock in the evening, the platforms had finally been repaired, and the PTS team was ready to do its work. Childers was in the control center, instructing the trainee. Mazzaro and Heineman, the PTS team chief, were there as well, going over the checklist for the procedure. Holder decided to get a few hours of sleep. Although the control center was underground and far removed from the world, it was always noisy. Motors, fans, and pumps were constantly switching on and off. Test messages from SAC were loudly broadcast over the speakers, and telephones rang. The sound had nowhere to go, so it bounced off the walls. Holder never slept well there, even with earplugs. The vibration bothered him more than the noise. The whole place was mounted on springs, and there was so much machinery running that the walls and the floors always seemed to be vibrating. It was the sort of thing you didn't notice, until you became perfectly still, and then it became hard to ignore.

Holder took off his socks and shoes, put on a T-shirt and some pants from an old uniform, and had a bite to eat before bed. He was washing dishes when the Klaxon went off. The sound was excruciatingly loud, like a fire alarm, an electric buzzer inside your head. He didn't think much of it. Whenever a nitrogen line was connected to an oxidizer tank, a little bit of vapor escaped. The vapor detectors in the silo were extremely sensitive, and they'd set off the Klaxon. It happened almost every time a PTS team did this procedure. The launch crew would reset the alarm, and the Klaxon would stop. It was no big deal. Holder kept doing the dishes, the Klaxon stopped—and then ten or fifteen seconds later it started blaring again.

"Dang," Holder thought, "why'd that go off again?" He heard people scurrying on the level below and wondered what was going on. He went halfway down the stairs, looked at the commander's console, and saw all sorts of lights flashing. He thought the PTS team must have spiked the MSA—the vapor detector manufactured by the Mine Safety Appliances Company. If the MSA became saturated with too much vapor, it spiked, going haywire and setting off numerous alarms. That didn't mean any-thing was wrong. But it did mean one more hassle. Now the crew would have to conduct a formal investigation with portable vapor detectors.

Holder went back upstairs and grabbed his boots. When he came down again, Captain Mazzaro was standing and talking on the phone to the command post in Little Rock. Childers was giving orders to the PTS team topside. Something wasn't right. Holder sat at the commander's console and looked down at rows of red warning lights. OXI VAPOR LAUNCH DUCT was lit. FUEL VAPOR LAUNCH DUCT was lit. VAPOR SILO EQUIP AREA, VAPOR OXI PUMP ROOM, and VAPOR FUEL PUMP ROOM were lit. He'd seen those before, when an MSA spiked. But he'd never seen two other lights flashing red: FIRE FUEL PUMP ROOM and FIRE LAUNCH DUCT. Those were serious. There's a problem, Holder thought. And it could be a big one.

Spheres Within Spheres

In the old black-and-white photograph, a young man stands at the bedroom door of a modest home. He wears khakis and a white T-shirt, carries a small metal box, and doesn't smile for the camera. He could be a carpenter arriving for work, with his lunch or his tools in the box. A cowboy hat hangs on the wall, and a message has been scrawled on the door in white chalk: "PLEASE USE OTHER DOOR—KEEP THIS ROOM CLEAN." The photo was taken on the evening of July 12, 1945, at the McDonald Ranch House near Carrizozo, New Mexico. Sergeant Herbert M. Lehr had just arrived with the unassembled plutonium core of the world's first nuclear device. The house belonged to a local rancher, George McDonald, until the Army obtained it in 1942, along with about fifty thousand acres of land, and created the Alamogordo Bombing and Gunnery Range. The plutonium core spent the night at the house, guarded by security officers. A team of physicists from the Manhattan Project was due at nine o'clock the next morning, Friday the thirteenth. After billions of federal dollars spent on this top secret project, after the recruitment of Nobel laureates and many of the world's greatest scientific minds, after revolutionary discoveries in particle physics, chemistry, and metallurgy, after the construction of laboratories and reactors and processing facilities, employing tens of thousands of workers, and all of that accomplished within three years, the most important part of the most expensive weapon ever built was going to be put together in the master bedroom of a little adobe ranch house. The core of the first nuclear device would be not only home made but hand made. The day before, Sergeant Lehr had sealed the windows with plastic sheets and masking tape to keep out the dust.

Although the question of how to control an atomic bomb had inspired a good deal of thought, a different issue now seemed more urgent: Would the thing work? Before leaving Los Alamos, two hundred miles to the north, some of the Manhattan Project's physicists had placed bets on the outcome of the upcoming test, code-named Trinity. Norman F. Ramsey bet the device would be a dud. J. Robert Oppenheimer, the project's scientific director, predicted a yield equal to 300 tons of TNT; Edward Teller thought the yield would be closer to 45,000 tons. In the early days of the project, Teller was concerned that the intense heat of a nuclear explosion would set fire to the atmosphere and kill every living thing on earth. A year's worth of calculations suggested that was unlikely, and the physicist Hans Bethe dismissed the idea, arguing that heat from the explosion would rapidly dissipate in the air, not ignite it. But nobody could be sure. During the drive down from Los Alamos on Friday the thirteenth, Enrico Fermi, who'd already won a Nobel for his discoveries in physics, suggested that the odds of the atmosphere's catching fire were about one in ten. Victor Weisskopf couldn't tell if Fermi was joking. Weisskopf had done some of the calculations with Teller and still worried about the risk.

As Louis Slotin prepared to assemble the plutonium core, the safety precautions were as rudimentary as the work space. Jeeps waited outside the house, with their engines running, in case everyone had to get out of there fast. Slotin was a Canadian physicist in his early thirties. For the past two years at Los Alamos he'd performed some of the most dangerous work, criticality experiments in which radioactive materials were brought to the verge of a chain reaction. The experiments were nicknamed "tickling the dragon's tail," and a small mistake could produce a lethal dose of radioactivity. At the ranch house, Slotin placed a neutron initiator, which was about the size of a gumball, into one of the plutonium hemispheres, attached it with Scotch tape, put the other hemisphere on top, and sealed a hole with a plutonium plug. The assembled core was about the size of a softball but weighed as much as a bowling ball. Before handing it to Brigadier General Thomas F. Farrell, Slotin asked for a receipt. The Manhattan Project was an unusual mix of civilian and military personnel, and this was the nation's first official transfer of nuclear custody. The general decided that if he had to sign for it, he should get a chance to hold it. "So I took this heavy ball in my hand and I felt it growing warm," Farrell recalled. "I got a sense of its hidden power."

The idea of an "atomic bomb," like so many other technological innovations, had first been proposed by the science fiction writer H. G. Wells. In his 1914 novel *The World Set Free*, Wells describes the "ultimate explosive," fueled by radioactivity. It enables a single person to "carry about in a handbag an amount of latent energy sufficient to wreck half a city." These atomic bombs threaten the survival of mankind, as every nation seeks to obtain them—and use them before being attacked. Millions die, the world's great capitals are destroyed, and civilization nears collapse. But the novel ends on an optimistic note, as fear of a nuclear apocalypse leads to the establishment of world government. "The catastrophe of the atomic bombs which shook men out of cities . . . shook them also out of their old established habits of thought," Wells wrote, full of hope, on the eve of the First World War.

The atomic bombs in *The World Set Free* detonated slowly, spewing radioactivity for years. During the 1930s, the Hungarian physicist Leó Szilárd—who'd met with H. G. Wells in 1929 and tried, without success, to obtain the central European literary rights to his novels—conceived of a nuclear weapon that would explode instantly. A Jewish refugee from Nazi Germany, Szilárd feared that Hitler might launch an atomic bomb program and get the weapon first. Szilárd discussed his concerns with Albert Einstein in the summer of 1939 and helped draft a letter to President Franklin D. Roosevelt. The letter warned that "it may become possible to set up a nuclear chain reaction in a large mass of uranium," leading to the creation of "extremely powerful bombs of a new type." Einstein signed the letter, which was hand delivered to the president by a mutual friend. After British researchers concluded that such weapons could indeed be made and intelligence reports suggested that German physicists were trying to make them, the Manhattan Project was formed in 1942. Led by Leslie R. Groves, a brigadier general in the U.S. Army, it secretly gathered eminent scientists from Canada, Great Britain, and the United States, with the aim of creating atomic bombs.

Conventional explosives, like TNT, detonate through a chemical reaction. They are unstable substances that can be quickly converted into gases of a much larger volume. The process by which they detonate is similar to the burning of a log in a fireplace—except that unlike the burning of a log, which is slow and steady, the combustion of an explosive is almost instantaneous. At the point of detonation, temperatures reach as high as 9,000 degrees Fahrenheit. As hot gases expand into the surrounding atmosphere, they create a "shock wave" of compressed air, also known as a "blast wave," that can carry tremendous destructive force. The air pressure at sea level is 14.7 pounds per square inch. A conventional explosion can produce a blast wave with an air pressure of 1.4 million pounds per square inch. Although the thermal effects of that explosion may cause burns and set fires, it's the blast wave, radiating from the point of detonation like a solid wall of compressed air, that can knock down a building.

The appeal of a nuclear explosion, for the Manhattan Project scientists, was the possibility of an even greater destructive force. A plutonium core the size of a tennis ball had the potential to raise the temperature, at the point of detonation, to tens of millions degrees Fahrenheit—and increase the air pressure to many millions of pounds per square inch.

Creating that sort of explosion, however, was no simple task. The difference between a chemical reaction and a nuclear reaction is that in the latter, atoms aren't simply being rearranged; they're being split apart. The nucleus of an atom contains protons and neutrons tightly bound together. The "binding energy" inside the nucleus is much stronger than the energy that links one atom to another. When a nucleus splits, it releases some of that binding energy. This splitting is called "fission," and some elements are more fissionable than others, depending on their weight. The lightest element, hydrogen, has one proton; the heaviest element found in nature, uranium, has ninety-two.

Leó Szilárd realized that bombarding certain heavy elements with neutrons could not only cause them to fission but could also start a chain reaction. Neutrons released from one atom would strike the nucleus of a nearby atom, freeing even more neutrons. The process could become self-sustaining. If the energy was released gradually, it could be used as a source of power to run electrical generators. And if the energy was released all at once, it could cause an explosion with temperatures many times hotter than the surface of the sun.

Two materials were soon determined to be fissile—that is, capable of sustaining a rapid chain reaction: uranium-235 and plutonium-239. Both were difficult to obtain. Plutonium is a man-made element, created by bombarding uranium with neutrons. Uranium-235 exists in nature, but in small amounts. A typical sample of uranium is about 0.07 percent uranium-235, and to get that fissile material the Manhattan Project built a processing facility in Oak Ridge, Tennessee. Completed within two years, it was the largest building in the world. The plutonium for the Manhattan Project came from three reactors in Hanford, Washington.

A series of experiments was conducted to discover the ideal sizes, shapes, and densities for a chain reaction. When the mass was too small, the neutrons produced by fission would escape. When the mass was large enough, it would become critical, a chain reaction would start, and the number of neutrons being produced would exceed the number escaping. And when an even larger mass became supercritical, it would explode. That was the assumption guiding the Manhattan Project scientists. In order to control a nuclear weapon, they had to figure out how to make fissile material become supercritical—without being anywhere near it.

The first weapon design was a gun-type assembly. Two pieces of fissile material would be placed at opposite ends of a large gun barrel, and then one would be fired at the other. When the pieces collided, they'd form a supercritical mass. Some of the most difficult computations involved the time frame of these nuclear interactions. A nanosecond is one billionth of a second, and the fission of a plutonium atom occurs in ten nanoseconds. One problem with the gun-type design was its inefficiency: the two pieces would collide and start a chain reaction, but they'd detonate before most of the material had a chance to fission. Another problem was that plutonium turned out to be unsuitable for use in such a design. Plutonium emits stray neutrons and, as a result, could start a chain reaction in the gun barrel prematurely, destroying the weapon without creating a large explosion.

A second design promised to overcome these problems by increasing the speed at which a piece of plutonium might be made supercritical. The new weapon design was nicknamed, at first, "the Introvert." A sphere of plutonium would be surrounded by conventional explosives. The shock wave from the detonation of these explosives would compress the sphere—and the denser the sphere became, the more efficiently it would trap neutrons. "The more neutrons—the more fission," a secret government manual on nuclear weapons later explained. "We care about neutrons!" Imploding a ball of plutonium to produce an explosion was a brilliant idea. But it was easier said than done. If the conventional explosives failed to produce a shock wave that was perfectly symmetrical, the plutonium wouldn't implode. It would blow to pieces.

Many of the physicists who worked on the Manhattan Project—Oppenheimer, Fermi, Teller, Bethe—later became well known. And yet one of the crucial design characteristics of almost every nuclear weapon built since then was perfected by George B. Kistiakowsky, a tall, elegant chemist. Born in Ukraine and raised in an academic family, Kistiakowsky had fought against the Bolsheviks during the Russian civil war. He later earned a degree at the University of Berlin, emigrated to the United States, and become a professor of chemistry first at Princeton, then at Harvard. By the mid-1940s, he was America's leading expert on explosives. Creating a perfectly symmetrical shock wave required not just the right combination of explosives but also the right sizes and shapes. Kistiakowsky and his team at Los Alamos molded explosive charges into three-dimensional lenses, hoping to focus the shock wave, like the lens of a camera focuses light. Tons of explosives were routinely detonated in the hillsides of Los Alamos, as different lens configurations were tested. Kistiakowsky considered these lenses to be "precision devices," not crude explosives. Each weighed between seventy and one hundred pounds. As the date of the Trinity test approached, he spent long hours at the lab with a dentist's drill, eliminating the air bubbles in lenses and filling the holes with molten explosives. The slightest imperfection could distort the path of a shock wave. The final design was a sphere composed of thirty-two shaped charges—twelve pentagons and twenty hexagons. It looked like a gigantic soccer ball and weighed about five thousand pounds.

The shape and composition of the explosive lenses were irrelevant, however, if the lenses failed to detonate at exactly the same time. The shock wave would travel through the device at a speed of one millimeter per millionth of a second. If a single lens detonated a few ten millionths of a second before the others, it could shatter the plutonium without starting a chain reaction. Blasting caps and Primacord were the detonators usually employed with conventional explosives. But both proved incapable of setting off thirty-two charges simultaneously. The physicist Luis Alvarez and his assistant, Lawrence Johnston, invented a new type of detonator for the job—the exploding-bridgewire detonator. It sent a high-voltage current through a thin silver wire inserted into an explosive. The current vaporized the wire, created a small shock wave, and detonated the explosive. Donald F. Hornig, who was one of the youngest scientists at Los Alamos, devised a contraption, the X-unit, that could store 5,600 volts in a bank of capacitors and then send that electricity instantaneously to all the detonators.

In theory, the X-unit and the exploding bridgewires would set off thirty-two explosive lenses at once, creating the perfect shock wave and imploding the plutonium core. In reality, these new inventions were unpredictable. Cracked insulation frequently caused the detonators to short-circuit. When that happened, they didn't work. And a week before the Trinity test, an X-unit fired prematurely during a lightning storm. It had been triggered by static electricity in the air. The misfire suggested that a nuclear weapon could be set off by a lightning bolt.

At eighteen past three in the afternoon on July 13, 1945, the plutonium core was delivered to a steel tower a couple of miles from the McDonald Ranch House. The tower rose about a hundred feet above the desert and resembled an oil rig with a small shed on top. The rest of the nuclear device sat inside a tent at the base of the tower, awaiting completion. At first, the core wouldn't fit inside it. For a few minutes, nobody could understand why, and then the reason became clear. The plutonium was warm, but the housing that it was supposed to enter had been cooled by the shade of the tent. Once the housing warmed, the core easily slid in. At about four o'clock, a thunderstorm threatened, and the tent started to flap violently in the wind. The small group of scientists left the base of the tower and waited for half an hour at the ranch house until the storm passed. When they returned, Kistiakowsky supervised the placement of the last explosive lenses, and at dusk the device was bolted shut. The next morning, as it was slowly hoisted to the top of the tower, surplus Army mattresses were stacked to a height of fifteen feet directly beneath it, in case the cable broke.

The nuclear device was an assortment of spheres within spheres: first, an outer aluminum casing, then two layers of explosives, then a thin layer of boron and plastic to capture neutrons that might enter from outside the core, then more aluminum, then a tamper of uranium-238 to reflect neutrons that might escape from inside the core, then the ball of plutonium, and finally, at the very center, the gumball-size neutron initiator—a mixture of beryllium and polonium that would flood the device with neutrons, like a nuclear fuse, when the shock wave from the lenses struck. Inside the metal shed atop the tower, the detonators were installed by hand, two for every explosive lens, linked to a pair of X-units. The device now looked like something concocted in a mad scientist's laboratory—a six-foot-tall aluminum globe with a pair of large boxes, the X-units, attached to it and thirty-two thick electrical cables leaving each box, winding around the sphere, and entering evenly spaced holes on its surface.

The Trinity test was scheduled for four in the morning on July 16, but forecasters predicted bad weather. Going ahead with the test could prove disastrous. In addition to the threat of lightning, high winds and rain could carry radioactive fallout as far as Amarillo, Texas, three hundred miles away. Postponing the test had other drawbacks: the device could be damaged by the rain, and President Harry S. Truman was in Potsdam, Germany, preparing to meet with Winston Churchill, the British prime minister, and Joseph Stalin, the general secretary of the Soviet Union's Communist Party. Nazi Germany had recently been defeated, and Truman was about to demand an unconditional surrender from the Japanese. Having an atomic bomb would make it easier to issue that demand. General Groves argued that the test should go forward, as planned, and Oppenheimer agreed. Both men became increasingly nervous, on the evening of the fifteenth, not only about the weather but also about the risk of sabotage. And so Donald Hornig was instructed to "babysit the bomb."

At 9:00 P.M., Hornig climbed to the top of the hundred-foot tower as rain began to fall. He brought a collection of humorous essays, *Desert Island Decameron*. His reading was interrupted by the arrival of a violent electrical storm. Atop the tower in a flimsy metal shed, Hornig sat alone with the book, the fully armed device, a telephone, and a single lightbulb dangling from a wire. He was twenty-five years old and had recently earned a Ph.D. in chemistry at Harvard. Having designed the X-unit, he knew better than anyone how easily it could be triggered by static electricity. Whenever he saw a lightning bolt, he'd count the seconds—one–one thousand, two–one thousand, three–one thousand—until he heard the thunder. Some of the lightning felt awfully close. At midnight, the phone rang, and Hornig was told to come down. Hornig did so, gladly, in the pouring rain. He was the last person to see the device.

The test was pushed back to 5:30 in the morning, right before dawn. The rain ended, and the weather cleared. The radio frequency used to announce the final countdown was similar to that of a local station. Thanks to interference, at the moment of detonation, Tchaikovsky's *Serenade for Strings* cheerfully played in the control bunker. Kistiakowsky stepped out of the bunker to see the fireball and was knocked to the ground by the blast wave. He was about six miles from where the tower had just stood. This is what the end of the world will look like, he thought—this is the last thing the last man will see. Victor Weisskopf saw the flash and felt heat on his face from a distance of ten miles. His heart sank. For a moment, he thought that his calculations were wrong and the atmosphere was on fire. "The hills were bathed in brilliant light," Otto Frisch, a British physicist, observed, "as if somebody had turned the sun on with a switch." General Farrell expressed the mixture of fear, awe, pride, and an underlying attraction that this new power inspired:

The whole country was lighted by a searing light with the intensity many times that of the midday sun. It was golden, purple, violet, gray, and blue. It lighted every peak, crevasse and ridge of the nearby mountain range with a clarity and beauty that cannot be described. . . . It was that beauty the great poets dream about but describe most poorly and inadequately. Thirty seconds after, the explosion came first, the air blast pressing hard against the people and things, to be followed almost immediately by the strong, sustained, awesome roar which warned of doomsday and made us feel that we puny things were blasphemous to dare tamper with the forces heretofore reserved to The Almighty.

Kenneth Bainbridge, the supervisor of the test, turned to Oppenheimer and said, "Now we are all sons of bitches." Within minutes the mushroom cloud reached eight miles into the sky.

THE ATOMIC BOMB was no longer the stuff of science fiction, and the question now was what to do with it. On September 1, 1939, President Franklin D. Roosevelt had issued a statement condemning the "inhuman barbarism" of aerial attacks on civilian populations. Nazi Germany had invaded Poland that day, and the Second World War had begun. Aerial bombardment promised to make the trench warfare of the previous world war—long a symbol of cruel, pointless slaughter—seem almost civilized and quaint. In April 1937 the German air force, the Luftwaffe, had attacked the Spanish city of Guernica, killing a few hundred civilians. Eight months later, the Japanese had bombed and invaded the Chinese city of Nanking, killing many thousands. An era of "total war" had dawned, and traditional rules of warfare seemed irrelevant. President Roosevelt appealed to the European powers for restraint. "The ruthless bombing from the air of civilians in unfortified centers of population," he said, "has profoundly shocked the conscience of humanity."

Roosevelt's appeal for decency and morality had no effect. The city of Warsaw was soon destroyed by German aircraft and artillery, then London was attacked from the air. The British retaliated by bombing Berlin. New theories of airpower were applied on an unprecedented scale. Unlike "tactical" strikes aimed at an enemy's military forces, "strategic" bombing focused on transportation systems and factories, the economic infrastructure necessary for waging war. Strategic assets were usually found in the heart of cities.

At first, the British refrained from deliberate attacks on German civilians. The policy of the Royal Air Force (RAF) changed, however, in the fall of 1941. The Luftwaffe had attacked the English cathedral town of Coventry, and most of the RAF bombs aimed at Germany's industrial facilities were missing by a wide mark. The RAF's new target would be something more intangible than rail yards or munitions plants: the morale of the German people. Bombarding residential neighborhoods, it was hoped, would diminish the will to fight. "The immediate aim is, therefore, twofold," an RAF memo explained, "namely, to produce (i) destruction, and (ii) the fear of death." The RAF Bomber Command, under the direction of Air Marshal Arthur "Bomber" Harris, unleashed a series of devastating nighttime raids on German cities. During Operation Gomorrah in July 1943, RAF bombs started a fire in Hamburg with hurricane-force winds. The first "firestorm" ever ignited by aerial bombardment, it killed about forty thousand civilians.

American bombers participated in Operation Gomorrah and the subsequent RAF attack on Dresden, where perhaps twenty thousand civilians died. But the United States Army Air Forces (USAAF) opposed the British policy of targeting residential areas, known as "de-housing." Instead of the RAF's nighttime "area" bombing, the strategic doctrine of the USAAF called for daytime "precision" bombing. Relying on the Norden bombsight—a device that combined a telescope, a mechanical computer, and an autopilot—the USAAF tried to destroy German factories, ports, military bases, and lines of communication. Precision bombing was rarely precise, and the vast majority of bombs still missed their targets. Nevertheless, American aircrews risked their lives conducting raids in broad daylight to avoid killing German civilians.

In the Pacific War a different set of rules applied. The Japanese were considered racially inferior, often depicted as monkeys or vermin in American propaganda. The Japanese had attacked the United States without warning. They had treated Allied prisoners of war with brutality, employed slave labor, and launched suicide attacks instead of surrendering. They had forced as many as two hundred thousand Korean women to serve as prostitutes in military brothels. They had killed almost one million Chinese civilians with chemical and biological weapons. They had killed millions of other civilians in China, Burma, Korea, Singapore, Malaysia, Cambodia, Vietnam, and the Philippines, war crimes driven by the Japanese belief in their own racial superiority.

At first, the United States conducted only precision bombing raids on Japan. But heavy cloud cover and high-altitude winds made it difficult to hit industrial targets. On the night of March 9, 1945, the Army Air Forces tried a new approach. American planes struck Tokyo with two thousand tons of bombs containing napalm and jellied gasoline. Although a major industrial area was destroyed, the real targets were block after block of Japanese buildings made of wood, paper, and bamboo. Within hours the firestorm consumed one quarter of the city. It killed about one hundred thousand civilians, and left about a million homeless. This was truly, in the words of historian John W. Dower, "war without mercy."

The firebombing of Tokyo wasn't condemned by President Roosevelt. On the contrary, it was soon followed by the firebombing of Nagoya, Osaka, Kobe, Kawasaki, and Yokohama. By the middle of June, the United States had laid waste to Japan's six leading industrial cities. Then American planes launched incendiary attacks on dozens of smaller cities. The level of destruction varied considerably. About one quarter of Osaka was destroyed by fire, one third of Kawasaki, more than half of Kobe. Toyama, a city on the Sea of Japan with chemical plants and a population of about 125,000, was hit the hardest. After a nighttime raid by B-29 bombers, the proportion of Toyama still standing was an estimated 0.5 percent.

As Japanese cities vanished in flames, Leó Szilárd began to have doubts about the atomic bomb. He had been the first to push hard for its development in the United States, but he now opposed its use against Japanese civilians. In June 1945, Szilárd and a group of scientists at the University of Chicago sent a report to the leadership of the Manhattan Project, asking that the power of nuclear weapons be demonstrated to the world at "an appropriately selected uninhabited area." A nuclear attack upon Japan, they contended, would harm the reputation of the United States, make it difficult to secure international control of "this new means of indiscriminate destruction," and start a dangerous arms race. But the die had been cast. A committee of presidential advisers had already decided that a public demonstration of an atomic bomb was too risky, because the weapon might not work; that Japan should not be given any warning of a nuclear attack, for much the same reason; that the bomb should be aimed at a war plant surrounded by workers' housing; and that the goal of the bombing would be "to make a profound psychological impression" on as many workers as possible.

The ideal target of the atomic bomb would be a large city that had not yet been firebombed, so the effects of the new weapon could be reliably assessed. The first four choices of the president's Target Committee were Kyoto, Hiroshima, Yokohama, and Kokura. Secretary of War Henry Stimson insisted that Kyoto be removed from the list, arguing that the city had played too central a role in Japanese art, history, and culture to be wiped out. Nagasaki took its place. The day after the Trinity test, Szilárd and more than sixty-eight other Manhattan Project scientists signed a petition, addressed to the president. It warned that using the atomic bomb against Japan would open the door "to an era of devastation on an unimaginable scale" and place American cities in "continuous danger of sudden annihilation." The petition never reached the president. And even if it had, it probably wouldn't have changed his mind.

Franklin Roosevelt had never told his vice president, Harry Truman, about the Manhattan Project or the unusual weapon that it was developing. When Roosevelt died unexpectedly, on April 12, 1945, Truman had the thankless task of replacing a beloved and charismatic leader during wartime. The new president was unlikely to reverse a nuclear policy set in motion years earlier, at enormous expense, because a group of relatively unknown scientists now considered it a bad idea. Truman's decision to use the atomic bomb was influenced by many factors, and the desire to save American lives ranked near the top. An invasion of Japan was scheduled for

November 1. Former President Herbert Hoover warned Truman that such an invasion would cost between "500,000 and 1,000,000 American lives." At the War Department, it was widely assumed that American casualties would reach half a million. During the recent battle of Okinawa, more than one third of the American landing force had been killed or wounded—and a full-scale invasion of Japan might require 1.8 million American troops. While meeting with the Joint Chiefs of Staff in June 1945, Truman expressed the hope of avoiding "an Okinawa from one end of Japan to the other."

Unlike most presidents, Truman had firsthand experience of battle. During the First World War, half of the men in his infantry division were killed or wounded during the Meuse-Argonne offensive. Standing amid piles of dead American soldiers, the sergeant of his platoon had yelled at the survivors: "Now . . . you'll believe you're in a war." Truman took no pleasure in the deaths of Japanese civilians. But he preferred them to the deaths of young American servicemen. Atomic bombs, he decided, would be dropped on Japan as soon as they were ready.

The Trinity test had been preceded by weeks of careful preparation, and every effort had been made to control the outcome. The device had been slowly and patiently assembled. The wiring and explosives had been repeatedly checked. The tower had been built, the location of the test chosen, and each step of the countdown arranged as part of an elaborate, scientific experiment. Turning an experimental device into an operable weapon presented a new set of challenges. Atomic bombs had to be dropped, somehow, and American aircrews had to survive the detonations. B-29 bombers were secretly retrofitted so that nuclear weapons would fit inside them. And pilots were secretly recruited to fly these "Silverplate" B-29s. They practiced dropping dummy bombs, then banking steeply to escape the blast. Enough fissile material for two nuclear weapons—a gun-type device loaded with uranium-235 and an implosion device with a plutonium core—were readied for use against Japan. The arming and fuzing mechanisms of the bombs would determine when they exploded, whether they exploded, and how much time the bomber crews would have to get as far away as possible.

Both designs relied on the same three-stage fuzing system. When a bomb was released at an altitude of about 30,000 feet, arming wires that linked it to the plane would be pulled out, starting a bank of spring-wound, mechanical clocks inside the weapon. After fifteen seconds, the clocks would close an electrical switch and send power to the firing circuits. At an altitude of 7,000 feet, a set of barometric switches, detecting the change in air pressure, would close another circuit, turning on four radar units, nicknamed "Archies," that pointed at the ground. When the Archies sensed that the bomb was at an altitude of 1,850 feet, another switch would close and the firing signal would be sent. In the gun-type device, that signal would ignite small bags of cordite, a smokeless gunpowder, and shoot one piece of uranium down the barrel at the other. In the implosion device, the firing signal would set off the X-units. Both bomb types were rigged to detonate about 1,800 feet above the ground. That was the altitude, according to J. Robert Oppenheimer, "appropriate for the maximum demolition of light structures." Had the bombs been aimed at industrial buildings, instead of homes, the height of the airburst would have been set lower.

The arming and fuzing mechanisms were repeatedly tested at a bombing range in Wendover, Utah. At the end of a successful test the dummy bomb released a puff of smoke. But no amount of practice could eliminate fears that a real atomic bomb might detonate accidentally. Oppenheimer was especially concerned about the risk. "We should like to know whether the take-off can be arranged," he wrote to a USAAF liaison officer in 1944, "at such a location that the effects of a nuclear explosion would not be disastrous for the base and the squadron." The implosion bomb could be inadvertently set off by a fire, a bullet striking an explosive lens, a small error in assembly.

If a B-29 carrying an implosion bomb was forced to return to its base, the president's Target Committee decided that the crew should jettison the weapon into shallow water from a low altitude. The emergency procedure for a gun-type bomb was more problematic. The gun-type bomb was likely to detonate after a crash into the ocean. Water is a neutron moderator, and its presence inside the bomb would start a chain reaction, regardless of whether the two pieces of uranium slammed together. "No suitable jettisoning ground . . . has been found," the committee concluded in May

1945, "which is sufficiently devoid of moisture, which is sufficiently soft that the projectile is sure not to seat from the impact, and which is sufficiently remote from extremely important American installations whose damage by a nuclear explosion would seriously affect the American war effort." The best advice that the committee could give was hardly reassuring to aircrews, whose bombing runs traversed the Pacific Ocean for thousands of miles: try to remove the cordite charges from the bomb midair and make sure to crash the plane on land.

Captain William S. Parsons was selected to be the "bomb commander and weaponeer" for the first military use of a nuclear weapon. A naval officer who'd spent years researching bomb fuzes, Parsons was chief of the Manhattan Project's ordnance division. At Los Alamos he'd supervised development of the gun-type bomb, which was to be dropped on the city of Hiroshima. Code-named "Little Boy," the bomb was ten feet long and weighed about 10,000 pounds. It contained almost all the processed uranium in existence, about 141 pounds. The relative inefficiency of the design was offset by its simplicity. Although a gun-type bomb had never been tested, Oppenheimer assured Parsons that the odds of "a less than optimal performance . . . are quite small and should be ignored."

The bomb was assembled in an air-conditioned shed on the island of Tinian, where the Silverplate B-29s of the 509th Composite Group were based. Tinian had the largest, busiest airfield in the world, located 1,300 miles southeast of Tokyo and constructed within months of its capture from the Japanese the previous year. The four main runways were a mile and a half long. At the insistence of General Groves, the Manhattan Project's dedication to secrecy was so rigorous that even the Army Air Forces officer who commanded Tinian was not told about the atomic bomb or the mission of the unusual B-29s stationed there. Worried that a nuclear accident might kill thousands of American servicemen and destroy an airfield crucial to the war effort, Captain Parsons decided, without informing Groves, that the final steps of assembling Little Boy would not be completed until the plane carrying it had flown a safe distance from the island.

At three in the morning on August 6, 1945, Parsons and another weaponeer, Morris Jeppson, left the cockpit and climbed into the bomb bay of a

B-29 named *Enola Gay*, after the pilot's mother. The plane was flying at an altitude of five thousand feet, about sixty miles off the coast of Tinian. After making sure that three green safing plugs were inserted into the bomb, Parsons unscrewed the back of it while Jeppson held a flashlight and air turbulence bounced the plane. Nobody had ever done this procedure to a weapon containing fissile material, let alone to one dangling from a single hook in a darkened bomb bay. The men kneeled on a narrow aluminum platform that had been installed the previous day. It took Parsons about twenty minutes to put four small silk bags of cordite into the breech of the gun barrel, reattach the primer wires, and close the back of the bomb. Four and a half hours later, Jeppson returned to the bomb bay alone. The plane was now at about nine thousand feet, nearing the coast of Japan, and the bomb bay felt a lot colder. The green safing plugs blocked the electrical circuit between the fuzing system and the cordite. Jeppson replaced them with red arming plugs. Little Boy was now fully armed, drawing power from its own batteries and not from the plane.

The city of Hiroshima spread across half a dozen islands in the delta of the Ota River. Much of the population had fled to the countryside, leaving about three hundred thousand people in town. The aiming point for Little Boy was the Aioi Bridge, far from the industrial plants on the other islands. The bridge lay in the heart of the city, near the headquarters of the Second Army, amid a residential and commercial district. The bomb was dropped from the *Enola Gay* at about 8:16 A.M., fell for about forty-four seconds, and detonated at an altitude of roughly 1,900 feet.

At ground zero, directly beneath the airburst, the temperature reached perhaps 10,000 degrees Fahrenheit. Everyone on the bridge was incinerated, and hundreds of fires were ignited. The blast wave flattened buildings, a firestorm engulfed the city, and a mushroom cloud rose almost ten miles into the sky. From the plane, Hiroshima looked like a roiling, bubbling sea of black smoke and fire. A small amount of fissile material was responsible for the devastation; 98.62 percent of the uranium in Little Boy was blown apart before it could become supercritical. Only 1.38 percent actually fissioned, and most of that uranium was transformed into dozens of lighter elements. About eighty thousand people were killed in Hiroshima and more than two thirds of the buildings were destroyed because 0.7 gram of uranium-235 was turned into pure energy. A dollar bill weighs more than that.

The Trinity test had been kept secret, the bright flash in the desert dismissed by the War Department as an explosion at an ammunition dump. But the need for secrecy had passed, and publicity about the new weapon would send a clear message about America's military strength not only to Japan but also to the Soviet Union. On August 6, President Truman announced that an atomic bomb, harnessing "the basic power of the universe," had just destroyed Hiroshima. "We are now prepared to obliterate more rapidly and completely every productive enterprise the Japanese have above ground in any city," Truman warned. "If they do not now accept our terms they may expect a rain of ruin from the air, the like of which has never been seen on this earth." But the Japanese government still would not agree to an unconditional surrender, insisting that the emperor be allowed to remain on his throne. The day after Hiroshima's destruction, the governor of the local prefecture encouraged survivors to find "an aroused fighting spirit to exterminate the devilish Americans."

Meanwhile, another atomic bomb, nicknamed "Fat Man," was being assembled at a special building on Tinian. The floor of the building had been coated with rubber and lined with copper wire to minimize the chance that static electricity would cause a spark. The bomb was a Mark 3 implosion device, and putting it together presented more of a challenge than the assembly of Little Boy. Captain Parsons compared the effort to "rebuilding an airplane in the field." Fat Man was scheduled for delivery on August 11, with the city of Kokura as its target. The prospect of bad weather moved the date forward to the ninth.

At around midnight, the night before the bomb was to be loaded onto a Silverplate B-29, a technician named Bernard J. O'Keefe noticed something wrong with the master firing cable that was supposed to connect the Archies to the X-unit. The cable and the X-unit both had female plugs. Somehow the cable had been installed backward. It would take a couple of days to disassemble the layers of spheres and explosives, remove the cable, and reinstall it properly. "I felt a chill and started to sweat in the air-conditioned room," O'Keefe recalled. He decided to improvise. With help from another technician, he broke one major safety rule after another, propping the door open to bring in extension cords and using a soldering iron to attach the right plugs. It was risky to melt solder in a room with five thousand pounds of explosives. The two men fixed the cable, connected the plugs, and didn't tell anyone what they'd done.

The attempt to drop Fat Man on Kokura, the site of Japan's largest arsenal, did not go smoothly. After the bomb was loaded onto a B-29 called *Bockscar*, one of the plane's fuel pumps malfunctioned before takeoff. Major Charles W. Sweeney, the twenty-five-year-old pilot commanding his first combat mission, decided to proceed with six hundred gallons of fuel inaccessible in a reserve tank. Four hours after leaving Tinian, flashing red lights on the flight test box suddenly indicated that the bomb's fuzes had been activated. The red lights could mean the weapon was fully armed and ready to explode. Sweeney considered jettisoning the bomb over the ocean, but let Philip Barnes, the assistant weaponeer, tinker with the flight test box. Barnes quickly checked the blueprints, looked inside the box, and found that a couple of rotary switches had been set in the wrong position. The bomb wasn't armed, and the crew was relieved to hear it.

Poor weather dogged the flight, with dark clouds and heavy turbulence. *Bockscar* circled for forty minutes at a rendezvous point over Japan, wasting fuel, waiting for another American plane that never arrived. Sweeney opened the bomb bay doors over Kokura, but the city was shrouded in smoke and haze. He had strict orders to drop the bomb visually, not by radar. *Bockscar* spent almost an hour over Kokura, made three unsuccessful bombing runs, and drew antiaircraft fire. The city was spared by the poor visibility. Sweeney had enough fuel for one run at the secondary target, Nagasaki. He dropped the bomb there, worried that the plane might have to be ditched in the ocean, and barely made it to the American air base at Okinawa.

Fat Man missed its aiming point by more than a mile. Instead of detonating above the central commercial district, the bomb went off above an industrial area on the western outskirts of Nagasaki. About one fifth of the plutonium fissioned, and the force of the explosion was equal to about

21,000 tons of TNT (21 kilotons). The bomb proved more powerful and efficient than the gun-type device used at Hiroshima, which had an explosive force of between 12 and 18 kilotons. But the damage was less severe in Nagasaki. A series of hills protected much of the city from the blast wave, and a firestorm never erupted, despite winds that reached more than six hundred miles an hour. About forty thousand people were killed in Nagasaki, at least twice that number were injured, and more than one third of the homes were destroyed. Ground zero was approximately five hundred feet south of the Mitsubishi Steel Works. According to one report, the plant was left "bent and twisted like jelly." The bomb also leveled the nearby Mitsubishi Arms Factory, where the torpedoes fired at Pearl Harbor were made.

Most of the casualties in Hiroshima and Nagasaki resembled those caused by incendiaries and conventional bombs. About half of the victims burned to death, and about one third were killed by debris. But two new types of casualty appeared. Flash burns were caused by the extraordinarily hot, though brief, detonation of the atomic bombs. Traveling in straight lines at the speed of light, the thermal radiation was strong enough to kill everyone within a mile of ground zero who was unprotected by walls or other objects that could block ultraviolet and infrared rays. Serious burns were possible at a distance of two miles. Thick clothing offered some protection, because the flash lasted less than a second. White clothes tended to reflect thermal radiation, while darker colors absorbed it. A number of victims suffered flash burns that mimicked the dark and light patterns of their kimonos.

The effects of ionizing radiation—primarily gamma rays emitted during the first minute after detonation—were even more disturbing. Perhaps one fifth of the deaths at Hiroshima and Nagasaki were due to "radiation sickness." People who'd survived the blast and the fires soon felt nauseated and tired. Some became ill within hours, while others seemed perfectly healthy for days before feeling unwell. Gamma rays had damaged the ability of their cells to replicate. The symptoms preceding their deaths were horrific: fever, vomiting, delirium, bloody diarrhea, internal bleeding, bleeding from the eyes and the mouth.

For decades some historians have questioned whether the use of atomic bombs was necessary. They have argued that Japan was already militarily defeated, that the blockade of Japanese ports had strangled the country's economy, that an American invasion would never have been required, that a conventional bombing campaign alone could have forced a surrender, that the Soviet Union's declaration of war on Japan had a greater impact than the atomic bombs, that a demonstration of one atomic bomb would have provided a sufficient shock to the Japanese psyche, that a promise the emperor could retain his throne would have saved hundreds of thousands of lives.

These counterfactual arguments, though compelling, can never be proved. But the historical facts remain. Hiroshima was destroyed on August 6. Two days later the Soviet Union declared war on Japan. Nagasaki was struck on the ninth, and the following day, General Korechika Anami, the minister of war, still urged the Japanese people to fight, "even though we have to eat grass and chew dirt and lay in the field." On August 14, Emperor Hirohito overruled his generals and agreed to an unconditional surrender. "The enemy has for the first time used cruel bombs," he explained, "and the heavy casualties are beyond measure."

Potential Hazards

For a moment Powell and Plumb just stood there, stunned, looking down at the fuel pouring out of the missile and the white mist floating upward, reaching level 6, level 5, level 4.

Oh, my God, Plumb thought, we've got to get the hell out of here.

Powell radioed the control center. There's some kind of white, milky substance in the air at level 7, he said. And that's all he said.

Captain Mazzaro told the PTS team chief, Charles Heineman, that his men should leave the silo immediately. Heineman ordered them to evacuate and return to the blast lock.

Powell motioned to Plumb: let's go. The missile was now shrouded in fuel vapor, and the cloud was approaching the platform where they stood.

Mazzaro was puzzled. He wondered what this white substance could be. He thought about the maintenance that had been performed in the silo earlier in the day. What could the stuff be? He didn't want to notify the command post at Little Rock Air Force Base until he had a better idea of what was happening. Mazzaro asked Heineman, who was sitting nearby, if he could think of anything.

The Klaxon went off, and the FUEL VAPOR LAUNCH DUCT light on the commander's console began flashing red.

Powell and Plumb left the silo and closed the door. Powell wanted to take the elevator down to a lower level, look at the base of the missile, and assess the damage. But the team chief ordered him and Plumb to get out of the cableway and enter the blast lock, where the backup team was stationed. Roger Hamm and Gregory Lester opened blast door 9 for them, let them in, and then Lester quickly pulled it shut. They popped the helmets off their RFHCOs, as Hamm locked the door. Powell threw the wrench handle onto the floor and cursed.

Mazzaro turned off the Klaxon. The FUEL VAPOR LAUNCH DUCT light made no sense. Why would that come on, when the PTS crew was pressurizing the stage 2 oxidizer tank? He asked for vapor readings from the mine safety appliance, which were displayed on a panel in the blast lock. Three old-fashioned gauges there showed the vapor levels in the silo. Needles on the gauges moved to the right as the amount of vapor increased. The PTS team reported that the oxidizer level was ten parts per million—and the fuel vapor level was forty parts per million, almost the maximum reading. One of those gauges had to be wrong. There couldn't be fuel vapors and oxidizer vapors in the silo at the same time; the two would have mixed and caused an explosion. Mazzaro wondered which gauge was correct. Then the needle on the fuel vapor gauge surged all the way to the right, and the MSA spiked.

The Klaxon went off again, and Al Childers looked up. He'd ignored it the first time, but now realized that something was wrong. He was sitting at a table behind the commander's console, filling out paperwork that recommended his student, Miguel Serrano, for another alert. Suddenly the console was lit up like a Christmas tree. Rows of warning lights were flashing red. Then Childers heard somebody say there was a fire in the hole, got up from the table, grabbed a copy of the *Dash-1*, searched the manual for the fire checklist, found it, and started going through each step. Now the SPRAY lights were lit, which meant that the fire suppression system had been automatically triggered. Thousands of gallons of water were pouring into the launch duct. Childers pushed the SURFACE WARNING CONTROL button, turning on the red beacon topside, and contacted the PTS team up there.

Eric Ayala was in his RFHCO suit, standing near the nitrogen tank on the hardstand, when he heard over the radio that Powell and Plumb were backing out of the silo. Then he heard "fire in the hole" and Childers ordering everyone topside to evacuate the site. Ayala and his partner, Richard Willinghurst, quickly took off their RFHCOs. The third member of the team, David Aderhold, was sitting in a truck parked near the access portal, monitoring the radio. The truck held four extra RFHCOs, air packs, dewar units to refill them with air, and a portable shower. After hearing the order to evacuate, he helped Ayala and Willinghurst pack up their suits. Everyone jumped into the truck, leaving an empty pickup behind, and then Willinghurst drove toward the gate. A white cloud floated from the silo exhaust shaft, like smoke rising from a chimney.

Childers called the command post and said there was a fire in the silo. Mazzaro was already on the phone with Little Rock. Holder came down the stairs, noticed the commotion, and sat at the commander's console. The warning lights didn't make sense—FUEL VAPOR LAUNCH DUCT, OXI VAPOR LAUNCH DUCT, FIRE LAUNCH DUCT. One of those might be correct, but not all three at the same time. Holder decided to go through the checklists for a fuel leak, an oxidizer leak, a fire. One of the first steps for any propellant leak was to check the propellant tank pressure monitor unit (PTPMU), the digital readout on top of the console. It displayed the pressure levels in each of the missile's four tanks. Holder pushed the buttons on the PTPMU and recorded the numbers in his log book. For some reason, the pressure in the stage 1 fuel tank seemed low.

It was 6:40 in the evening, about ten minutes after the first Klaxon had sounded. Ronald Fuller was going through all three checklists, too. He closed the blast valve—sealing the ventilation system, cutting off the control center from the air outdoors—and began to set up a portable vapor detector near blast door 8. It would warn if toxic fumes were seeping into the room.

The gate phone rang, and Childers answered it. The PTS crew topside wanted to leave the complex. Childers opened the gate for them and then returned to the fuel vapor checklist. He couldn't understand why the purge fan in the silo wouldn't go on. The purge fan was supposed to clear out any fuel vapors. He kept pushing the PURGE button but nothing happened. Then he remembered that if there was a fire, they didn't want the fan to go on. It would pull fresh air into the silo and feed the fire.

"Can my people come back into the control center?" Heineman asked. Childers said yes. He'd thought it was useful to keep Powell, Plumb, and the others in the blast lock, monitoring the vapor levels on the panel. But then he remembered that the MSA automatically shut off whenever the sprays went on, so that water wouldn't be sucked into the vapor sensors. Too many things seemed to be happening at once; it felt hard to stay on top of them all. Powell and Plumb entered the control center in their RFHCOs, Hamm and Lester in thermal underwear. In the rush to get out of the blast lock, the two had left their RFHCOs in boxes on the floor there. Blast door 8 was swiftly closed and locked. Heineman joined his men, and the group huddled near the door.

"There's got to be a malfunction," Childers said, three or four times. Too many warning lights were flashing at once. But even if it was a malfunction, the crew had to act as though the hazards were real. Childers asked Serrano if he'd ever plotted a toxic corridor on a map.

Serrano replied that he'd once taken a class on it.

"Well, get over here," Childers said. "You're going to watch me do it."

With a map, a compass, a grease pencil, and a protractor, Childers started to plot on a map where a cloud of fuel, smoke, or oxidizer would travel outdoors. The wind speed was almost zero, good news for the nearby houses and farms but not for the crew. A toxic cloud would hover and swirl directly above the missile complex.

Captain Mazzaro was still on the phone to the command post, where a Missile Potential Hazard Team was being formed. At the direction of the wing commander, the officers and airmen on the base who knew the most about the Titan II were being recalled to duty: maintenance and operations supervisors, the chief of safety, the chief of missile engineers, an electrical engineer, a bioenvironmental engineer, a backup missile combat crew, among others. Security police were calling homes and searching classrooms to gather the team. And a Missile Potential Hazard Net was being established—a conference call linking the command post at Little Rock with experts at SAC headquarters in Omaha, the Ogden Air Logistics Center at Hill Air Force Base in Utah, and the headquarters of the Eighth Air Force at Barksdale Air Force Base in Louisiana. One of the command post's first decisions was to send a Missile Alarm Response Team (MART) to the launch complex. A pair of security officers stationed at a nearby missile site grabbed their gas masks and hurried to Damascus.

While Fuller was setting up the portable vapor detector near the blast door, he overheard one of the PTS crew say something about a dropped socket. Fuller asked what had happened in the silo. After hearing the story, Fuller said they needed to tell the commander. Powell stepped forward, admitted to dropping the socket, and began to cry. He described how it fell and hit the thrust mount, how fuel sprayed from the missile like water from a hose. When he was done, the room fell silent.

"Holy shit," thought Holder.

Captain Mazzaro told Powell to come over to the phone and tell the command post exactly what had happened. Powell got on the line and repeated the story. The details were incredible—but plausible.

Things fell all the time in the silo: nuts, bolts, screwdrivers, flashlights, all sorts of tools. They always fell harmlessly into the *W* at the bottom of the silo, and then someone had to climb down and get them. You could drop a socket a thousand times from a platform at level 2 without its ever bouncing off the thrust mount and hitting the missile. And even if it did hit the missile, it would probably cause a dent, and nothing more, and nobody would ever know.

Half an hour after the accident, everyone realized what they were dealing with—a major fuel leak, maybe a fire. The *Dash-1* didn't have a checklist for this scenario. Now it was time to improvise, to figure out what could be done to save the missile and the warhead and the ten men in the underground control center.

SID KING WAS HAVING DINNER at a friend's house when he got a call from the board operator at KGFL, the AM radio station in Clinton, Arkansas. It sounds like there's something going on at the Titan II silo in Damascus, the operator said, a leak or something. King was the manager and part-owner of KGFL, as well as its roving reporter. His friend Tom Phillips was the station's sales rep. Clinton was about seventeen miles north of Damascus, along Highway 65—and Choctaw, where Phillips lived, was even closer to the missile site.

Let's run down there and check it out, King suggested. Phillips thought that sounded like a good idea. They said good-bye to their wives and got into KGFL's mobile unit, a Dodge Omni that King had fitted with a VHF transmitter and a big antenna. The nickname of the subcompact, the "Live Ear," was painted on both sides, along with the station's call letters.

King was twenty-seven years old. He'd been raised in Providence, a town with a population of approximately one hundred, about an hour east of Damascus. His father was a jack-of-all-trades—a math teacher who also sold real estate, cut hair, and managed a movie theater to support the family and their small farm. King had an idyllic, small-town childhood but also dreamed of some day leaving rural Arkansas for Hollywood. At Arkansas State University, he studied radio and television, encouraged by a great uncle who'd been one of the first TV weathermen in Arkansas. During the summers, King was the drummer of the house band at Dogpatch USA, an amusement park in the Ozarks featuring Li'l Abner and other characters created by the cartoonist Al Capp. The house band played for hours every night, mainly Dixieland jazz, soft rock like "Joy to the World," and show tunes like "Sunrise, Sunset," from *Fiddler on the Roof.*

Working at Dogpatch was a lot of fun, and King got a full-time job there after college. He fell for Judi Clark, a tap dancer at the park, and the two soon got married. Backed by a brother-in-law, King started looking for a good place in Arkansas to open a new radio station. Clinton, they decided, was the place. It was the county seat of Van Buren County, in the foothills of the Ozarks, with a population of about 1,600 and a downtown that attracted shoppers from throughout the area. In 1977, KGFL went on the air as a 250-watt "sunset" station, licensed to broadcast only during daylight hours. King wanted the station to assume the role that a small-town newspaper would have played a generation earlier. KGFL started each day with the national anthem. It played gospel music for about half an hour, then switched to country and western. During the morning, it broadcast phone-in shows like "Trading Post," a radio flea market that allowed local callers to buy and sell things. In the afternoon, when kids got out of school, the station began to play rock-and-roll, and that's what it played until going off the air at dusk. King's wife opened a dance studio near the station, teaching jazz, tap, and ballet to children. Her studio was on the second floor of the only two-story building in downtown Clinton.

Sid King and Tom Phillips were about the same age. They'd met at Dogpatch, where Phillips had played Li'l Abner. And they were already familiar with the Titan II site in Damascus. KGFL had covered an accident there a couple of years earlier. At about three in the morning on January 27, 1978, an oxidizer trailer parked on the hardstand had started to leak. The trailer was heated to ensure that the oxidizer remained above 42 degrees during the winter. But the thermostat was broken. Instead of keeping the oxidizer at about 60 degrees, the heater pushed it to more than 100 degrees, far beyond its boiling point. A brown plume of oxidizer floated from the trailer, eventually becoming a cloud half a mile long and a hundred yards wide.

The crew in the underground control center had no idea that the trailer topside was leaking oxidizer. The leak was discovered about five hours later by the missile crew arriving at the site to pull an alert that morning. The crew spotted the cloud of oxidizer from the road, turned around, drove back to Damascus, and called the command post from a pay phone. A PTS team with RFHCO suits was flown by helicopter to Launch Complex 374-7. They fixed the leak and lowered the temperature of the oxidizer by spraying the trailer with cold water for hours. The missile site's neighbors were not pleased by the incident. A cloud of oxidizer had drifted across nearby farms, killing more than a dozen cattle, sickening a farmer who'd gotten up early to milk his cows, and forcing the evacuation of a local elementary school. The farmer later filed a multimillion-dollar lawsuit against the Air Force and the companies that made the trailer.

Gus Anglin, the sheriff of Van Buren County, was standing with a state trooper on the shoulder of Highway 65, near the access road to the silo, when King and Phillips rolled up in the Live Ear. Anglin was in his early forties, thin and wiry, the sort of rural sheriff who knew the names of all the teenagers in town, knew their parents, and knew the right threat to make kids slow down, go home, or stop doing what they were just doing. Van Buren County didn't have much crime, aside from petty theft, some pot growing, and the occasional domestic dispute—and yet Anglin still found himself constantly answering the phone in the middle of the night and leaving his house to deal with all kinds of unexpected things. He wore a badge and drove a squad car but didn't carry a gun, unless the situation seemed to demand one. He and a couple of deputies had to cover thousands of square miles in the county, which took him away from his wife and two children for long stretches of time. Anglin felt obligated to answer every call personally, from the minor ones to the most urgent. That was what the Van Buren County sheriff was supposed to do, a lesson learned from his father-in-law, who'd previously held the job and hired him to serve as a deputy.

During the early-morning leak in 1978, Anglin had evacuated Damascus residents who lived in the path of the oxidizer. The experience had left him frustrated with the Air Force. At first the Air Force didn't know what was happening—and then it didn't want to tell him. Again and again, he was assured that the reddish brown cloud posed no serious threat. He and one of his deputies inhaled a fair amount of oxidizer while escorting people out of their homes. It made both of them sick. After Anglin got the dry heaves and vomited in the road, the two were airlifted by helicopter to the hospital at Little Rock Air Force Base. They were given a clean bill of health and released within a few hours. But Anglin got headaches and didn't feel right for weeks. Now a column of what looked like white smoke rose into the sky from the same missile complex. Once again, nobody from the Air Force had bothered to give him a call.

King said hello to the sheriff and the state trooper. Let's go down there and see what's going on, Anglin suggested. The four men walked down the access road, wondering what was wrong this time, as the evening light grew dim. They reached the perimeter fence and stopped for a second. All of a sudden, out of nowhere, a couple of Air Force security officers appeared with M-16 rifles and asked what they were doing there.

"I'm the sheriff of the county," Anglin said. "And it looks like you've got another problem. We're just trying to figure out what we need to do. Do we need to evacuate people?"

"No, no, we've got everything under control," one of the security officers replied. The command post at Little Rock was on top of the situation.

Anglin and the state trooper turned around and started walking back toward the highway. The sheriff did not look pleased. King started firing questions at the security officers: What exactly is the problem? Is that smoke? Is there a fire? One of the officers was about to answer, then asked King and Phillips if they worked for the sheriff's department. When King said no, we're with KGFL, the officer's response was blunt: "Sir, get your ass out of here."

The two young men laughed as they returned to their car. "Boy, he wasn't in too good a mood," Phillips said. They decided to stick around for a while, alongside the highway, and see what happened next. But first they had to get a message to the station. The transmitter on the Omni wasn't strong enough to send a signal over the nearby hill on Highway 65, so they drove to the top of it. King asked the technician at the station to contact the Associated Press and KATV, the ABC affiliate in Little Rock. Tell them something's wrong at the Titan II complex in Damascus, King said. Then they drove down the hill, parked near the access road, and waited.

CHILDERS AND HOLDER TOOK TURNS at the console where the commander normally sat. Mazzaro stood at the other console or paced back and forth in the room. He was one of the finest missile combat crew commanders that either of them had met, but now he seemed distracted. Every few minutes, one of them would push the HAZARD ALERT LOGIC RESET button. It was supposed to turn off any warning lights that were malfunctioning, that were signaling a nonexistent problem. Not long after Powell admitted to having dropped the socket, the RESET button was pushed, and the OXI VAPOR LAUNCH DUCT light went out. That confirmed what Childers and Holder already suspected: there was no oxidizer leak. At least one potential hazard could be ruled out. They knew that the stage 1 fuel tank was leaking and that fuel vapors were filling the silo. But was there really a fire?

Holder thought that once the tank was pierced, fuel vapors began to interact with the oxidized aluminum panels in the silo. He didn't think there was a roaring fire. It was more likely a smoldering one, hot enough to set off the fire detectors. The PTS crew topside had given conflicting accounts of the cloud leaving the exhaust vent, at first describing it as white, later as "green smoke." Childers thought there was a fuel leak, pure and simple, that had somehow registered as a fire. Fuel vapors were easily mistaken for smoke. He couldn't explain, however, why the fire detectors had been triggered. They were mechanical devices containing a sliver of metal that melted at 140 degrees. They should be reliable. Perhaps the hazard warning circuitry had malfunctioned, signaling that the detectors had been triggered when they hadn't. In any event, the sprays in the silo would help. Water would dilute the fuel, making it less flammable and explosive. And if there was a smoldering fire, the water would extinguish it.

A new set of problems soon emerged. Every five minutes Holder had been recording the stage 1 tank pressures from the PTPMU. The ideal pressure for both the fuel and the oxidizer tanks was 11.5 pounds per square inch (psi). About half an hour after the accident, the fuel pressure had dropped to 5.5, while the oxidizer pressure had risen to 18.6. The combination of water and fuel in the silo created heat, increasing the pressure in the oxidizer tank. If the pressure became too great, the tank would rupture and the oxidizer would pour out. It would mix with the fuel in the silo, causing an explosion.

Meanwhile, the leak was lowering the pressure in the stage 1 fuel tank. The small hole allowed fuel to leave the tank but didn't let air enter it. The stage 1 fuel tank sat at the bottom of the missile and supported much of its weight. The Titan II's aluminum skin was about the width of a nickel. In much the same way that a car is supported by the air in its tires, not the rubber, the huge missile was bolstered by the 85,000 pounds of rocket fuel in its stage 1 tank. That tank wasn't supposed to be empty when the others were full—unless the missile was flying hundreds of miles off the ground. If the fuel tank on the bottom collapsed, the oxidizer tank directly above it would tumble and burst. The two propellants would mix, and the missile would explode.

The pressure levels in both of the stage 1 tanks were now moving in opposite directions: one was rising, due to the heat; the other was falling, due to the leak. The oxidizer tank was likely to rupture when its pressure rose to about 25 or 30 psi. And the fuel tank was likely to collapse when its pressure fell to somewhere between −2 and −3 psi.

At half past seven, about an hour after the accident, the pressure in the fuel tank was 2.6, and the pressure in the oxidizer tank was 18.8.

Holder suggested shutting down the power to the missile. The socket might have struck an electrical panel and started a fire. But even if it hadn't, having power in the silo might somehow give off a spark that would ignite the fuel vapor. Although the suggestion felt like grasping at straws, Holder thought it was something they could actually do, instead of just sitting there. A checklist was composed with help from the Missile Potential Hazard Team. Everyone agreed that circuit breaker 13, which supplied power to the PTPMU, should be left on so that tank pressure readings could still be obtained.

As Holder read the first sentence of the checklist and prepared to turn off circuit breakers, a light on the commander's console indicated that the sprays had stopped. The hard water tank in the silo had run out of water. It was supposed to be refilled automatically by the soft water tank topside. But the faulty switch on the hard water tank that Holder and Fuller noticed during the morning inspection had prompted someone, months or even years earlier, to close the pipe linking the two tanks. About a hundred thousand gallons of water had sprayed into the silo, and an additional hundred thousand were still available topside. The crew, however, had no way of getting that extra water. The indicator said the pump in the silo was still pumping, and yet nothing was coming out of it. Childers tried to turn off the pump, concerned that its electric motor might produce a spark. He kept pushing the button but the pump wouldn't stop.

At about five past eight, the LAUNCH DUCT TEMP HIGH HIGH warning light flashed red. The temperature in the silo had reached 80 degrees, and without the sprays of cold water, it would keep climbing. The pressure in the fuel tank was down to 0.4 psi. The pressure in the oxidizer tank was 19.5 and rising fast.

Captain Mazzaro asked for permission to evacuate the control center. Permission was denied.

The Missile Potential Hazard Team in Little Rock had a plan. The RFHCOs that Powell and Plumb had worn still held about forty minutes of air. The suits in the blast lock hadn't been used. They were good for at least an hour. According to Little Rock's plan, the PTS crew would retrieve the RFHCOs from the blast lock, put them on, check the MSA, and report the vapor levels in the equipment area of the silo. If the levels were low enough, the men would proceed to the equipment area and turn on the purge fan. That might clear some of the fuel vapors out of the silo.

It was worth a try. Fuller, Lester, and Powell stood beside blast door 8. Powell kept his hand on the button. He unlocked the door, and Lester slowly cracked it open. The blast lock was filled with a white, hazy mist that smelled like fuel and smoke. Lester slammed the door, and Powell locked it.

The RFHCOs in the blast lock were now useless, contaminated, and the control center didn't have enough suits for the job. The safety rules required at least two people with RFHCOs as backup, whenever a team went Category I. The PTS crew topside had four RFHCOs on their truck, but nobody could reach them on the radio.

It was twenty minutes past eight. The pressure in the fuel tank was −0.4 psi. At least that's what the gauge said. The PTPMU hadn't been calibrated for negative readings, and the actual pressure could have been even lower. The pressure in the oxidizer tank had risen to 23.4.

The PTS team chief, Heineman, asked if they could be evacuated.

Childers and Holder finished shutting off the power to the missile and, at the direction of the command post, turned off the air-conditioning in the silo, too. Although the air conditioner cooled the silo, it could also produce a spark and ignite the fuel. Childers didn't want to evacuate, and neither did Holder. They wanted to stay put. They were good friends, discussed the issue quietly, and agreed about what should be done. Mazzaro's wife and Fuller's wife were pregnant; Mazzaro's was due to have the baby any day. We ought to let the other guys leave, Childers and Holder decided. We'll stay here and ride this thing out. They volunteered to remain in the control center. It was important for someone to stay there. The two could monitor the PTPMU, keep an eye on the hazard lights, or even open the silo door. They felt confident that the blast doors would hold. "If the missile blows," Holder said, "I think we'll be OK."

The strength of a blast wave is measured by the overpressure it produces—the amount of air pressure greater than that found at sea level, measured in pounds per square inch. An overpressure of 0.5 psi shatters windows. An overpressure of 2 psi destroys wooden homes, and an overpressure of 8 psi knocks down brick walls. The Titan II silo door was designed to withstand a nuclear detonation with an overpressure of 300 psi. The underground blast doors were even stronger. They were supposed to protect the crew not only from a nuclear detonation outside but also from a missile explosion within the silo. The enormous doors on both sides of the blast lock, theoretically, would survive an overpressure of 1,130 psi.

At half past eight, about two hours after the accident, the wing commander ordered everyone to evacuate the complex. The pressure in the stage 1 fuel tank had fallen to –0.7 psi. The safety of the crew could not be guaranteed. The missile could explode at any moment.

While Mazzaro and Childers stuffed top secret documents into the floor safe, Holder and Fuller put on gas masks and went downstairs to level 3 of the control center to open the emergency escape hatch. It wasn't easy. The hatch was a metal dome attached to the wall by thick screws. The men took turns unscrewing them with a large ratchet. The hatch opened a little more with each twist of the ratchet. Holder took off his gas mask. He was out of breath and didn't think the mask was necessary—yet. He'd opened the escape hatch a few times during inspections. But he'd never been inside the narrow, ten-foot tunnel beyond it. The tunnel led to a steel ladder, embedded in the concrete wall of an air shaft, that traveled about fifty feet upward to the surface.

Childers couldn't close the door to the safe. There were too many documents crammed inside it. The command post told him not to worry about them, to leave the door open. But he felt uncomfortable leaving it that way. Although the launch keys and the cookies were securely locked in a different safe, the emergency war order checklists were among these documents. Someone who got hold of them would learn a great deal about how to issue a launch order and how to countermand one. The issue soon became moot. The safe wouldn't close, the crew had to evacuate, and nobody else was likely to be entering the control center soon.

Once the escape hatch was open, the PTS team went down to level 3, wearing gas masks. The missile combat crew members grabbed their hand-guns and put on their holsters. Before departing from the control center, they took the phone off the hook, so that officers on the line at Little Rock could hear if any Klaxons, alarms, or portable vapor detectors went off. And the crew switched the diesel generator to manual. That way the gen-erator wouldn't automatically turn on if power to the entire complex was later shut off, an option being considered. Motors and pumps in the equip-ment areas of the silo were still running—because the circuit breakers to shut them off were inside the silo. Ideally, the crew wouldn't have left any-thing running that might cause a spark. But they'd done the best they could. They put on their gas masks and hurried downstairs.

Fuller entered the hatch first, carrying a flashlight. It was pitch black in the narrow tunnel as he crawled toward the air shaft on his hands and knees. The PTS team and Serrano went next. Childers told them to look after the trainee.

"Put him in the middle of you guys," Childers said, "because I'm not going to have him hurt."

Holder followed them into the tunnel. He'd fought hard against evacu-ating the place, but now that it was time to go, he couldn't wait to get the hell out. Upstairs in the control center, the intruder alarm went off. Fuller must have reached the surface and pushed open the grate, interrupting the radar beams aimed at the air shaft. The tipsie unit had detected the move-ment and activated the alarm, as though someone was trying to get into the control center, not out of it.

Childers went through the hatch, leaving Captain Mazzaro to go last. The tunnel was dank and dark, like a drainage pipe, and he had to crawl through a pool of rusty water to the air shaft. Childers was terrified. The rungs of the ladder were on the far side of the shaft, you had to reach across to grab them, and it was incredibly dark. Childers was breathing hard in the gas mask as he climbed and couldn't see the ladder. He raised a hand and felt above his head for each rung, anxious to move as fast as possible, afraid of slipping and falling to the bottom of the shaft. The control center had felt safe—now they really were vulnerable and unprotected. At the top of the ladder, Holder and Fuller pulled him from the air shaft onto the gravel. The three waited for Mazzaro, lifted him out, and started to run.

The wind seemed to be blowing to the east, carrying the white cloud from the exhaust vents toward the entry gate. So the men headed west. The PTS crew had already found the breakaway section of the fence, removed the quick-release pins, and pushed it down. Mazzaro, Childers, Fuller, and Holder followed them through the gap in the fence, trying to circle the site and reach the front gate without passing through the cloud. The masks would protect their lungs, but fuel vapor could be readily absorbed through their skin. The crew made it about three quarters of the way around the fence before the wind changed direction, blowing the white mist right toward them. "You've got to be kidding me," Holder thought, ready to be miles away from this place.

When Sergeant Thomas A. Brocksmith arrived at the access road to the complex, he noticed that some law enforcement officers and reporters were already there. He introduced himself to the Van Buren County sheriff. Brocksmith was the on-scene supervisor, responsible for Air Force security at the site. The sheriff asked what was going on. The only information we have, Brocksmith replied, is that there's a possible hazard on the complex, but there's no need for an evacuation at this point. About twenty minutes later, Brocksmith was ordered by the command post to drive toward the complex. He put on a gas mask, guided his pickup truck down the access road, and could see that something was seriously wrong. Gray smoke was billowing about fifty feet into the air and drifting over the entry gate. He parked the truck in the clear zone surrounding the fence. The complex was empty, quiet, and still. He looked around for anything out of the ordinary. Aside from the smoke, nothing about the complex seemed unusual. And then someone pounded hard on the passenger door of his truck, yelling, "Get out of here, get out of here." The noise scared Brocksmith, who looked at the door and saw ten men in the dark wearing gas masks and Air Force uniforms. Somehow, they all crowded into the pickup, and he drove it out of there fast.

In the abandoned control center, the hazard lights flashed, the intruder alarm rang, the escape hatch hung wide open, and water slowly dripped from the tunnel onto the concrete floor.

Part Two

MACHINERY OF CONTROL

The Best, the Biggest,
and the Most

Hamilton Holt's dream of world peace finally seemed within reach. For decades he'd campaigned with one civic group after another, trying to end the perpetual conflict between nations, races, and religions. A graduate of Yale from a wealthy family, he'd worked closely with Andrew Carnegie at the New York Peace Society before the First World War. Holt championed the American Peace Society, the World Peace Foundation, the League to Enforce Peace, the League of Nations, the Conciliation Internationale, and the American Society of International Law. He was also a founder of the National Association for the Advancement of Colored People. He edited a reform newspaper, ran for the U.S. Senate in 1924, lost by a wide margin, became the president of Rollins College the following year, and created a unique educational system there. Lectures were eliminated, and faculty members were hired by the students. College life didn't end his work on behalf of disarmament. During the 1930s, Holt erected a Peace Monument on the Rollins campus in Winter Park, Florida. The monument was a German artillery shell from the First World War set atop a stone plinth. The inscription began: "PAUSE, PASSER-BY, AND HANG YOUR HEAD IN SHAME . . ."

In the spring of 1946, Holt hosted a conference on world government at Rollins. An idea that had long been dismissed as impractical and naive was now widely considered essential. Much of Europe, Russia, China, and

Japan lay in ruins. About fifty million people had been killed during the recent war. The United States had been spared the destruction of its cities—and at first, the stunning news of the atomic bomb inspired relief at the swift defeat of Japan, as well as pride in American know-how. And then the implications began to sink in. General Henry H. "Hap" Arnold, commander of the United States Army Air Forces, warned the public that nuclear weapons "destructive beyond the wildest nightmares of the imagination" might someday be mounted on missiles, guided by radar, and aimed at American cities. Such an attack, once launched, would be impossible to stop. Despite having emerged from the conflict with unprecedented economic and military power, the United States suddenly felt more vulnerable than at any other time in its history. "Seldom if ever has a war ended leaving the victors with such a sense of uncertainty and fear," CBS correspondent Edward R. Murrow noted, "with such a realization that the future is obscure and that survival is not assured."

Hamilton Holt had attended the San Francisco Conference that created the United Nations, only weeks before the bombing of Hiroshima and Nagasaki. But the United Nations, Holt thought, wasn't really a world government. It was just another league of sovereign states, doomed to failure. The men who attended the conference at Rollins College felt the same way, and they were hardly a bunch of wild-eyed radicals. Among those who signed Holt's "Appeal to the Peoples of the World" were the president of the Standard Oil Company of Ohio, the chairman of the National Association of Manufacturers, three U.S. senators, one U.S. Supreme Court justice, a congressman, and Albert Einstein. The appeal called for the United Nations' General Assembly to be transformed into the legislative branch of a world government. The General Assembly would be authorized to ban weapons of mass destruction, conduct inspections for such weapons, and use military force to enforce international law. "We believe these to be the minimum requirements," the appeal concluded, "of a world government capable of averting another war in the atomic era."

Within weeks of the conference at Rollins, a collection of essays demanding international control of the atomic bomb became a *New York Times* bestseller. Its title was *One World or None*. And a few months later, an opinion poll found that 54 percent of the American people wanted the United Nations to become "a world government with power to control the armed forces of all nations, including the United States."

To a remarkable degree, even the U.S. military thought that the atomic bomb should be outlawed or placed under some form of international mandate. General Arnold was a contributor to *One World or None*. He'd been a leading proponent of strategic airpower and supervised the American bombing of both Germany and Japan. The stress had taken its toll. Arnold suffered four heart attacks during the war, and his essay in *One World or None* was a final public statement before retirement. The appeal of nuclear weapons, he wrote, was simply a matter of economics. They had lowered "the cost of destruction." They had made it "too cheap and easy." An air raid that used to require five hundred bombers now needed only one. Atomic bombs were terribly inexpensive, compared to the price of rebuilding cities. The only conceivable defense against such weapons was a strategy of deterrence—a threat to use them promptly against an enemy in retaliation. "A far better protection," Arnold concluded, "lies in developing controls and safeguards that are strong enough to prevent their use on all sides."

General Carl A. Spaatz, who replaced Arnold as the Army Air Forces commander, was an outspoken supporter of world government. General George C. Kenney, the head of the recently created Strategic Air Command, spent most of his time working on the military staff of the United Nations. General Leslie Groves—the military director of the Manhattan Project, who was staunchly anti-Communist and anti-Soviet—argued that the atomic bomb's "very existence should make war unthinkable." He favored international control of nuclear weapons and tough punishments for nations that tried to make them. Without such a system, he saw only one alternative for the United States. "If there are to be atomic bombs in the world," Groves argued, "we must have the best, the biggest, and the most."

AT A CABINET MEETING on September 21, 1945, members of the Truman administration had debated what to do with this powerful new weapon. The issue of international control was complicated by another question: Should the secrets of the atomic bomb be given to the Soviet Union? The Soviets were a wartime ally, lost more than twenty million people fighting the Nazis, and now possessed a military stronger than that of any other country except the United States. Canada and Great Britain had been invited to join the Manhattan Project, while the Soviets hadn't even been informed of its existence. In a memo to President Truman, Henry Stimson, the outgoing secretary of war, worried that excluding the Soviets from the nuclear club would cause "a secret armament race of a rather desperate character." He proposed a direct approach to the Soviet Union, outside of any international forum, that would share technical information about atomic energy as a first step toward outlawing the atomic bomb. Otherwise, the Soviets were likely to seek nuclear weapons on their own. Stimson thought that a U.S.-Soviet partnership could ensure a lasting peace. "The only way you can make a man trustworthy," he told the president, "is to trust him."

Stimson's proposal was strongly opposed by Secretary of the Navy James Forrestal. "We tried that once with Hitler," Forrestal said. "There are no returns on appeasement." The meeting ended with the Cabinet split on whether to share atomic secrets with the Soviet Union. A few weeks later, George F. Kennan, one of the State Department's Soviet experts, gave his opinion in a telegram from Moscow, where he was posted at the U.S. embassy. "There is nothing—I repeat nothing," Kennan wrote, "in the history of the Soviet regime which could justify us in assuming that the men who are now in power in Russia, or even those who have chances of assuming power within the foreseeable future, would hesitate for a moment to apply this [atomic] power against us if by doing so they thought that they might materially improve their own power position in the world." In the absence of formal guarantees or strict controls, it would be "highly dangerous" to give the Soviets any technical information about how to make an atomic bomb. President Truman reached the same conclusion, and the matter was soon dropped.

The United States had good reason to distrust the Soviet Union. In 1939 the Soviet nonaggression pact with Germany was followed by the

Nazi invasions of Poland, Belgium, and France. Two years later the Soviet neutrality pact with Japan was followed by the Japanese attack on Pearl Harbor. During the war, the Soviet Union launched its own surprise attacks on Finland, the Baltic states, and Poland—and then executed tens of thousands of their citizens. After encouraging Japanese diplomats to believe it would mediate a peace agreement with the United States, the Soviet Union attacked and occupied Manchuria in the closing days of the war, causing the deaths of perhaps three hundred thousand Japanese soldiers and civilians. The ideology of the Soviet Union sought the overthrow of capitalist governments like that of the United States. And the Soviet leader, Joseph Stalin, was not only paranoid and megalomaniacal, but had already killed almost as many Russians as the Nazis had.

The Soviets had reason to distrust the United States, too. It had intervened militarily in the Russian civil war, using American troops to fight the Red Army until 1920. It had withheld diplomatic recognition of the Soviet Union until 1933. It had suffered vastly fewer casualties fighting the Nazis during the Second World War and yet claimed an equal role in the administration of occupied Germany. The United States government had a long history of opposing almost every form of socialism and communism. Armed with nuclear weapons, it was now the greatest impediment to Soviet influence in Europe, Asia, and the Middle East.

President Truman decided that a domestic policy on atomic energy had to be adopted before the issue of international control could be addressed. The War Department favored the May-Johnson bill, which would give the military a prominent role in atomic matters. The bill was also backed by J. Robert Oppenheimer, who'd become a celebrity since the end of the war, renowned as "the father of the atomic bomb." But the legislation was vehemently opposed by most of the young scientists who'd worked on the Manhattan Project. For years they had resented the strict, compartmentalized secrecy imposed by General Groves. Few of the Manhattan Project scientists had been allowed to know how the atomic bomb would be used. Many now regretted that both Hiroshima and Nagasaki had been destroyed. They considered themselves far more qualified than anyone in the Army to make decisions about atomic energy—and warned that passage of the

May-Johnson bill could turn the United States into a secretive, totalitarian state. Some still had an idealized vision of the Soviet Union and thought that the War Department's bill would endanger world peace. At the heart of the debate were fundamentally different views of who should control the atomic bomb: civilians or the military.

Physicists representing groups like the Federation of American Scientists and the Association of Los Alamos Scientists traveled to Washington, D.C., testified before Congress, wrote editorials, gave impassioned speeches, and publicly attacked General Groves. An ambitious first-term senator from Connecticut, Brien McMahon, soon embraced their cause, asserting that the atomic bomb was too important to be left in the hands of "a militaristic oligarchy." He was particularly upset that General Groves would not tell anyone in Congress how many atomic bombs the United States possessed or where they were kept—and that Groves refused to share that information with Cabinet members, the Joint Chiefs of Staff, or even the secretary of war. President Truman backed the Army's insistence that details of the atomic stockpile should remain top secret, for the sake of national security. But he sided with the young scientists on the issue of civilian control and threw his support to legislation sponsored by Senator McMahon.

McMahon's bill, the Atomic Energy Act of 1946, was passed by Congress in a somewhat amended form and signed into law by the president. It created an Atomic Energy Commission (AEC) run by civilians and a Joint Committee on Atomic Energy that provided congressional oversight. Members of the military could serve on a liaison committee that advised the AEC, but they could not determine the agency's policies.

The president was given the sole authority to decide how many atomic bombs the United States should have, when they should be handed over to the military, and whether they should be used against an enemy. One person now had the power to end the lives of millions, with a single command. All of the laboratories, reactors, processing plants, fissile material, and atomic bomb parts belonging to the Manhattan Project were transferred to the AEC. Civilian control of the atomic bomb was now an American principle firmly established by law—but that did not prevent the military, almost immediately, from seeking to undermine it.

"WE ARE HERE TO MAKE a choice between the quick and the dead," Bernard Baruch told a gathering of United Nations delegates on June 14, 1946, at the Hunter College gymnasium in the Bronx. "We must elect World Peace or World Destruction." Baruch was an elegant, silver-haired financier in his midseventies who'd been asked by President Truman to offer a proposal for international control of the atomic bomb. The "Baruch plan" called for the creation of a new agency, affiliated with the U.N., that would own or control "all atomic-energy activities potentially dangerous to world security." The agency would have the power to inspect nuclear facilities throughout the world, so that any attempt to make nuclear weapons could be discovered and severely punished. The new system of international control would be imposed in stages—and would eventually outlaw the manufacture, possession, or use of atomic bombs. The United States was willing to hand over its "winning weapons," Baruch said, but would require "a guarantee of safety" stronger than mere words.

The selection of Bernard Baruch to help formulate the American plan had been controversial within the Truman administration. Many liberals criticized Baruch for being too old, too ignorant about atomic weaponry, and too suspicious of the Soviet Union. The Baruch plan was attacked by Oppenheimer, among others, for not being bold enough—for emphasizing inspections and punishments instead of cooperation with the Soviets. Oppenheimer favored a scheme that would share technical information about atomic energy and promote goodwill. On June 19 the Soviet Union offered its own plan. Andrei Gromyko, the Soviet foreign minister, proposed that first the United States should destroy all of its nuclear weapons, and then an agreement should be reached on how to prevent other nations from obtaining them. The Soviet response confirmed liberal doubts about the Baruch plan—and conservative doubts about the Soviet Union.

During the summer of 1946, some form of international agreement to outlaw the atomic bomb still seemed within reach. Although the Soviets complained that the United States was trying to prolong its nuclear monopoly, America's defense policies were hardly those of an imperialist power

seeking world domination. In fact, the United States was quickly dismantling its armed forces. The number of soldiers in the U.S. Army soon
dropped from about 8 million to fewer than 1 million; the number of airplanes in the Army Air Forces fell from almost 80,000 to fewer than 25,000
and only one fifth of those planes were thought ready for action. Ships and
tanks were permanently scrapped, and the defense budget was cut by almost 90 percent.

American servicemen were eager to come home after the war and resume
their normal lives. When the pace of demobilization seemed too slow, they
staged protest marches in occupied Germany. The American people expressed little desire to build an empire or maintain a strong military
presence overseas. Although the War Department sought to acquire a wide
range of foreign bases, the likelihood of any military challenge to the
United States seemed remote. "No major strategic threat or requirement
now exists, in the opinion of our country's best strategists," Major General
St. Clair Street, the deputy commander of SAC, said in July 1946, "nor will
such a requirement exist for the next three to five years."

At the very moment when hopes for world government, world peace,
and international control of the atomic bomb reached their peak, the Cold
War began. Without the common enemy of Nazi Germany, the alliance
between the Soviet Union and the United States started to unravel. The
Soviet Union's looting of Manchuria, its delay in removing troops from
Iran, and its demand for Turkish territory along the Mediterranean coast
unsettled the Truman administration. But the roots of the Cold War lay in
Germany and Eastern Europe, where the Soviets hoped to create a buffer
zone against future invasion. Ignoring promises of free elections and self-
determination, the Soviet Union imposed a Communist puppet government in Poland. George Kennan told the State Department that the Soviets
were "fanatically" committed to destroying "our traditional way of life,"
and Winston Churchill warned that an "iron curtain" had descended
across Europe, along with the expansion of Communist, totalitarian rule.

By March 1947, American relations with the Soviet Union had grown
chilly. In a speech before Congress, President Truman offered economic aid
to countries threatened by a system relying on "terror and oppression, a

controlled press and radio, fixed elections, and the suppression of personal freedoms." Although the speech never mentioned the Soviet Union by name, the target of the Truman Doctrine was obvious. The United States now vowed to contain Soviet power throughout the world. The divide between east and west in Europe widened a few months later, when the Soviets prevented their allies from accepting U.S. aid through the Marshall Plan. In February 1948 the Communist overthrow of Czechoslovakia's freely elected government shocked the American public. The Soviet-backed coup revived memories of the Nazi assault on the Czechs in 1938, the timidity of the European response, and the world war that soon followed.

President Truman's tough words were not backed, however, by a military strategy that could defend Western Europe. During the early months of 1947, as Truman formulated his anti-Communist doctrine, the Pentagon did not have a war plan for fighting the Soviet Union. And the rapid demobilization of the American military seemed to have given the Soviets a tremendous advantage on the ground. The U.S. Army had only one division stationed in Germany, along with ten police regiments, for a total of perhaps 100,000 troops. The British army had one division there, as well. According to U.S. intelligence reports, the Soviet army had about one hundred divisions, with about 1.2 million troops, capable of invading Western Europe—and could mobilize more than 150 additional divisions within a month.

Instead of being outlawed by the U.N., the atomic bomb soon became integral to American war plans for the defense of Europe. In June 1947 the Joint Chiefs of Staff sent a top secret report, "The Evaluation of the Atomic Bomb as a Military Weapon," to President Truman. It contained the latest thinking on how nuclear weapons might be used in battle. The first postwar atomic tests, conducted the previous year at the Bikini atoll in the Marshall Islands, had demonstrated some of the weapon's limitations. Dropped on a fleet of empty Japanese and American warships, a Mark 3 implosion bomb like the one used at Nagasaki had missed its aiming point by almost half a mile—and failed to sink eighty-three of the eighty-eight vessels. "Ships at sea and bodies of troops are, in general, unlikely to be regarded as primary atomic bomb targets," the report concluded. "The bomb is pre-eminently a weapon for use against human life and activities in large urban and industrial areas." It was a weapon useful, most of all, for killing and terrorizing civilians. The report suggested that a nuclear attack would stir up "man's primordial fears" and "break the will of nations." The military significance of the atomic bomb was clear: it wouldn't be aimed at the military. Nuclear weapons would be used to destroy an enemy's morale, and some of the best targets were "cities of especial sentimental significance."

The Joint Chiefs did not welcome these conclusions, but assumed them to be true—the hard, new reality of strategy in the nuclear age. If other countries obtained atomic bombs, they might be used in similar ways against the United States. The destructive power of these weapons was so great that the logic of waging a preventive war, of launching a surprise attack upon an enemy, might prove hard to resist. Like a shootout in the Old West, a nuclear war might be won by whoever fired first. A country with fewer atomic bombs than its adversary had an especially strong incentive to launch an attack out of the blue. And for that reason, among others, a number of high-ranking American officers argued that the United States should bomb the Soviet Union before it obtained any nuclear weapons. General Groves thought that approach would make sense, if "we were ruthlessly realistic." General Orvil Anderson, commander of the Air University, publicly endorsed an attack on the Soviets. "I don't advocate preventive war," Anderson told a reporter. "I advocate the shedding of illusions." He thought that Jesus Christ would approve of dropping atomic bombs on the Soviet Union: "I think I could explain to Him that I had saved civilization." Anderson was suspended for the remarks.

Support for a first strike extended far beyond the upper ranks of the U.S. military. Bertrand Russell—the British philosopher and pacifist, imprisoned for his opposition to the First World War—urged the western democracies to attack the Soviet Union before it got an atomic bomb. Russell acknowledged that a nuclear strike on the Soviets would be horrible, but "anything is better than submission." Winston Churchill agreed, proposing that the Soviets be given an ultimatum: withdraw your troops from Germany, or see your cities destroyed. Even Hamilton Holt, lover of peace,

President Truman was given a briefing on HALFMOON and the atomic blitz in May 1948. He didn't like either of them. Truman told the Joint Chiefs to prepare a plan for defending Western Europe—without using nuclear weapons. He still hoped that some kind of international agreement might outlaw them. The Joint Chiefs began to formulate ERASER, an emergency war plan that relied entirely on conventional forces.

A month later the Soviets cut rail, road, and water access to the western sectors of Berlin. Truman now faced a tough choice. Defying the blockade could bring war with the Soviet Union. But backing down and abandoning Berlin would risk the Soviet domination of Europe. The U.S. military governor of Germany, General Lucius D. Clay, decided to start an airlift of supplies into the city. Truman supported the airlift, while the Joint Chiefs of Staff expressed doubts, worried that the United States might not be able to handle a military confrontation with the Soviets. Amid the Berlin crisis, work on ERASER was halted, Truman issued a series of directives outlining how nuclear weapons should be used—and the atomic blitz became the most likely American response to a Soviet invasion of Western Europe.

The new strategy was strongly opposed by George Kennan and others at the State Department, who raised questions about its aftermath. "The negative psycho-social results of such an atomic attack might endanger postwar peace for 100 years," one official warned. But the fiercest opposition to HALFMOON and the similar war plans that followed it—FLEETWOOD, DOUBLESTAR, TROJAN, and OFFTACKLE—came from officers in the U.S. Navy. They argued that slow-moving American bombers would be shot down before reaching Soviet cities. They said that American air bases overseas were vulnerable to Soviet attack. And most important, they were appalled by the idea of using nuclear weapons against civilian targets.

The Navy had practical, as well as ethical, reasons for opposing the new war plans. Atomic bombs were still too heavy to be carried by planes launched from the Navy's aircraft carriers—a fact that gave the newly independent U.S. Air Force the top priority in defense spending. For more than a century, naval officers had regarded themselves as the elite of the armed services. They now resented the aggressive public relations efforts of the Air

Force, the disparaging remarks about sea power, the books and articles claiming that long-range bombers had won the Second World War, the propaganda films like Walt Disney's *Victory Through Air Power*, with its jolly animated sequences of cities in flames and its tagline: "There's a thrill in the air!" The Navy thought the atomic blitz was the wrong way to defend the free world, and at the Pentagon a battle soon raged over how the next war in Europe should be fought.

Hoping to resolve the dispute, James Forrestal, who'd become secretary of defense, appointed an Air Force officer, General Hubert R. Harmon, to lead a study of whether a nuclear strike would defeat the Soviet Union. In May 1949 the Harmon Committee concluded that the most recent American war plan, TROJAN, would reduce Soviet industrial production by 30 to 40 percent. It would also kill perhaps 2.7 million civilians and injure an additional 4 million. Those were conservative estimates, not taking into account the fires ignited by more than one hundred atomic bombs. But TROJAN wouldn't prevent the Red Army from conquering Europe and the Middle East. Nor would it lead to the collapse of the Soviet Union. "For the majority of Soviet people," the committee noted, "atomic bombing would validate Soviet propaganda against foreign powers, stimulate resentment against the United States, unify these people and increase their will to fight." Nevertheless, Harmon saw no realistic alternative to the current war plan. The atomic blitz was "the only means of rapidly inflicting shock and serious damage" on the Soviet military effort, and "the advantages of its early use would be transcending."

On August 29, 1949, the Soviets detonated their first atomic device, RDS-1, at a test range in eastern Kazakhstan. The yield was about 20 kilotons, roughly the same as that of the bomb dropped on Nagasaki—and for good reason. RDS-1 was a copy of the Mark 3 implosion bomb. While American policy makers worried and fretted and debated whether to share classified atomic information with the Soviet Union, a network of Communist spies infiltrated Manhattan Project laboratories and simply took it. Soviet physicists like Yuli Borisovich Khariton were brilliant and inventive, but their task was made easier by the technical knowledge gained through espionage at Los Alamos, Hanford, and Oak Ridge.

The United States also provided the Soviet Union with the means for delivering an atomic bomb. In 1944, three American B-29 bombers were forced to make emergency landings in Siberia after attacking Japanese forces in Manchuria. The planes were confiscated by the Soviets, and one of them, the *General H. H. Arnold Special*, was carefully disassembled. Each of its roughly 105,000 parts was measured, photographed, and reverse engineered. Within two years the Soviet Union had its first long-range bomber, the Tupolev-4. The plane was almost identical to the captured B-29; it even had a metal patch where the *General Arnold* had been repaired.

News of the Soviet bomb arrived at an unfortunate moment. General Groves had assured the American people that the Soviet Union wouldn't develop an atomic bomb until the late 1960s. The United States had just signed the North Atlantic Treaty, promising to defend Western Europe— and America's nuclear monopoly was the basis for that promise. China was on the verge of falling to Mao Tse-tung's Communist army. And now, for the first time since the War of 1812, a devastating attack on the continental United States seemed possible. The rapid demobilization after the Second World War had, for more than a year, left North America without a single military radar to search for enemy planes. As late as 1949, the U.S. Air Defense Command had only twenty-three radars to guard the northeastern United States, and they were largely obsolete units that couldn't detect Soviet bombers flying at low altitudes. In the event of war, the safety of American cities would depend on the Air Force's Ground Observer Corps: thousands of civilian volunteers who would search the sky with binoculars.

The news of the Soviet bomb was made all the more ominous by a sense of disarray at the Pentagon. Overwhelmed by stress, lack of sleep, and fears of international communism, Secretary of Defense Forrestal had recently suffered a nervous breakdown and leaped to his death from a sixteenth floor window at Bethesda Naval Hospital. When the new secretary of defense, Louis A. Johnson, canceled plans to build the *United States,* an enormous aircraft carrier, angry naval officers spread rumors that the Air Force's new long-range bomber, the B-36, was deeply flawed. What began as an interservice rivalry over military spending soon became a bitter, public dispute about America's nuclear strategy, with top secret war plans being leaked to newspapers and war heroes questioning one another's patriotism.

At congressional hearings in October 1949, one high-ranking admiral after another condemned the atomic blitz, arguing that the bombing of Soviet cities would be not only futile but immoral. They advocated "precision" tactical bombing of Soviet troops and supply lines—using planes from American aircraft carriers. Admiral William F. Halsey compared the Air Force's new bomber to the siege weapons once used to destroy medieval castles and towns. "I don't believe in mass killings of noncombatants," Admiral Arthur W. Radford testified. "A war of annihilation might bring a pyrrhic military victory, but it would be politically and economically senseless." The harshest criticism of the Air Force came from Rear Admiral Ralph A. Ofstie, who'd toured the burned-out cities of Japan after the war. He described the atomic blitz as "random mass slaughter of men, women, and children." The whole idea was "ruthless and barbaric" and contrary to American values. "We must insure that our military techniques do not strip us of self-respect," Ofstie said.

The Navy's opposition to strategic bombing, soon known as "the revolt of the admirals," infuriated the Truman administration. A conventional defense of Europe seemed impossible. Congress had failed to renew the draft, defense spending was being cut, and even the Army, lacking sufficient manpower, supported the Air Force's bombing plans. The Navy's moral arguments were undercut by the main justification for building a supercarrier like the *United States:* it would be large enough to launch planes carrying atomic bombs. The head of the Joint Chiefs of Staff, General Omar Bradley, finally ended the revolt with a dramatic appearance before Congress. Bradley had earned enormous respect during the Second World War for his soft-spoken, humane leadership of the Army, and his reputation for fairness made his testimony all the more powerful. Bradley accused the Navy of being in "open rebellion" against the civilian leadership of the United States. The admirals were "Fancy Dans" and "aspiring martyrs" who just didn't like to take orders. As for the accusation that targeting cities was immoral, Bradley responded, "As far as I am concerned, war itself is immoral."

Although the Air Force and the Navy were willing to fight an ugly bureaucratic war over how atomic bombs should be used, the two services were in complete agreement about who should control them. David E. Lilienthal, the head of the Atomic Energy Commission, faced unrelenting pressure, from his first day in office, to hand over America's nuclear arsenal to the military. The Joint Chiefs of Staff repeatedly asserted that the nation's most powerful weapons should be kept securely in the custody of officers who might one day have to use them. At the height of the Berlin crisis, Secretary of Defense Forrestal asked President Truman to transfer the entire atomic stockpile to the Air Force, warning that a Soviet attack on AEC storage facilities could leave the United States defenseless. James Webb, one of Truman's advisers, wasn't persuaded by that argument and told Lilienthal: "The idea of turning over custody of atomic bombs to these competing, jealous, insubordinate Services, fighting for position with each other, is a terrible prospect." The president denied the military's request and publicly reaffirmed his support for civilian control of the atomic bomb. Privately, Truman explained that he didn't want "to have some dashing lieutenant colonel decide when would be the proper time to drop one."

WHITE HOUSE APPROVAL of the atomic blitz gave the Strategic Air Command a role of singular importance: SAC had the only planes that could drop atomic bombs. "Destruction is just around the corner for any future aggressor against the United States," an Air Force press release warned. "Quick retaliation will be our answer in the form of an aerial knock-out delivered by the Strategic Air Command." A wide gulf existed, however, between the rhetoric and reality. Demobilization had left SAC a hollow force, with a shortage of skilled pilots and mechanics. During one major exercise in 1948, almost half of SAC's B-29s failed to get off the ground and reach their targets. The public controversy surrounding the atomic blitz obscured a crucial point: the United States couldn't launch one. The nation's emergency war plans called for a counterattack against the Soviet Union with more than one hundred atomic bombs—but SAC had just twenty-six flight crews available to deliver them. Perhaps half of these crews would be shot down trying to reach their targets, while others would have to ditch their planes after running out of fuel. Although SAC's retaliation might still be devastating, it wouldn't be quick. An estimated thirty-five to forty-five days of preparation would be necessary before an all-out nuclear attack could be launched.

The problems at the Strategic Air Command extended from its enlisted personnel to its leading officers. General George Kenney, the head of SAC, had little prior experience with bombers, and his deputy commander hadn't served in a combat unit since the late 1920s. During the spring of 1948, as tensions with the Soviets increased, Charles A. Lindbergh was asked to provide a secret evaluation of SAC's readiness for war. Lindbergh found that morale was low, landings were rough, training was poor, equipment was badly maintained, and accidents were frequent. A month after Lindbergh's findings were submitted, General Kenney was relieved of command.

Kenney's replacement, General Curtis E. LeMay, was a bold, innovative officer who'd revolutionized bombing practices in both the European and Pacific campaigns of the Second World War. Admired, feared, honored as a war hero, considered a great patriot by his supporters and a mass murderer by his critics, LeMay soon transformed the Strategic Air Command into a model of lethal efficiency. He created a vast organization dedicated solely to nuclear combat and gave it a capacity for destruction unmatched in the history of warfare. The personality and toughness and worldview of Curtis LeMay not only molded an entirely new institutional culture at SAC, but also influenced American nuclear operations in ways that endure to the present day. And his nickname was "Iron Ass" for good reason.

Curtis LeMay was born in 1906 and raised mainly in Columbus, Ohio. His father was a laborer who held and then lost a long series of jobs, constantly moving the family to new neighborhoods in Ohio, to Montana, California, and Pennsylvania. His mother sometimes worked as a domestic servant. Again and again he was the new kid in school, shy, awkward, bullied. To counter the unsettled, anarchic quality of his family life, LeMay learned self-discipline and worked hard. At the age of nine, he got his first paying job: shooting sparrows for a nickel each to feed a neighbor's cat. He delivered newspapers and telegrams, excelled at academics but felt, in his own words, "cut off from normal life," earning and saving money while other kids played sports and made friends. He graduated from high school without ever having been to a dance. He'd saved enough, however, to make the first tuition payment at Ohio State University. For the next four years, LeMay attended college during the day, then worked at a steel mill from early evening until two or three in the morning, went home, slept for a few hours, and returned to campus for his nine o'clock class.

After studying to become a civil engineer, LeMay joined the Army Air Corps in 1929. Flying became his favorite thing to do—followed, in order of preference, by hunting, driving sports cars, and fishing. Socializing was far down the list. While other officers yearned to become fighter pilots, like the air aces of the First World War, LeMay thought that long-range bombers would prove decisive in the future. He learned to fly them, became one of the nation's finest navigators, and showed that planes could find and destroy battleships at sea. When LeMay led a bomber group from the United States to England in 1942, he was the only pilot among them who'd ever flown across an ocean.

Within days of arriving in Great Britain, LeMay began to question the tactics being used in daylight bombing runs against the Nazis. American B-17s zigzagged to avoid the heavy antiaircraft fire; the conventional wisdom held that if you flew straight and level for more than ten seconds, you'd be shot down. But the evasive maneuvers caused bombs to miss their targets. After some late-night calculations about speed, distance, and rate of fire, LeMay came up with a radically new approach. Planes flying straight went much faster than planes that zigzagged, he realized—and therefore would spend less time exposed to enemy fire. He devised a "combat box," a flight formation for eighteen to twenty-one bombers, that optimized their ability to drop bombs and defend against enemy fighters. When his men questioned the idea of heading straight into antiaircraft fire, LeMay told them that he'd fly the lead plane—the one most likely to be shot down.

On November 23, 1942, during the final approach to railway yards and submarine pens in Saint-Nazaire, France, the B-17s of LeMay's bombardment group flew straight and level for a full seven minutes. None was shot down by antiaircraft fire. Bombing accuracy was greatly improved. And within weeks the tactics that LeMay had adopted for his first combat mission became the standard operating procedure for every American bomber crew in Europe.

LeMay's greatest strength as a commander wasn't a subtle grasp of the historical, political, or psychological aspects of an enemy. It was his focus on the interplay between men and machines—a vision of war designed by an engineer. He also cared deeply about the safety and morale of his men. Strategic bombing required a particular form of courage. Unlike fighter pilots, who flew alone, free to roam the skies in pursuit of targets, bomber crews had to work closely with one another, follow a designated route, and stay in formation. The seven minutes from the initial aiming point to the target could induce feelings of helplessness and sheer terror, as flak exploded around the plane and enemy fighters tried to shoot it down. The death rate among American bomber crews was extraordinarily high: more than half would be killed in action before completing their tour of duty.

Curtis LeMay was hardly warm and cuddly. He was gruff, blunt, sarcastic, socially awkward, a man of few words, with a permanent frown left by a case of Bell's palsy and an unlit cigar perpetually stuck in his mouth. But he earned the deep loyalty of his men by refusing to tolerate incompetence and by doing everything possible to keep them alive. Instead of asking for bravery, he displayed it, flying the lead plane on some of the most dangerous missions of the war, like an old-fashioned cavalry officer leading the charge.

At the age of thirty-six, LeMay became the youngest general in the Army. During the summer of 1944, he was transferred from Europe to help fight Japan. Although incendiaries had been used on a small scale, it was LeMay who ordered the firebombing of Tokyo. "Japan would burn if we could get fire on it," one of his deputies explained.

LeMay was involved in almost every detail of the plan, from selecting the mix of bombs—magnesium for high temperatures, napalm for splatter—to choosing a bomb pattern that could start a firestorm. He hoped that the firebombing would break the will of the Japanese people, avoid an American invasion, end the war quickly, and save American lives.

The massive civilian casualties were unfortunate, LeMay thought, but pro-longing the war would cause even more. The destruction of Japanese cities, one after another, fit perfectly with his philosophy on the use of military force. "I'll tell you what war is about," LeMay once said. "You've got to kill people and when you kill enough of them, they stop fighting."

LeMay's managerial and logistical skills made him an ideal candidate to head the Strategic Air Command. His most recent assignment had been to organize the Berlin airlift. But he also knew a lot about the atomic bomb. He'd been involved with the preparations to drop Little Boy and Fat Man, later served as a military adviser to the Manhattan Project, supervised the aircraft during the atomic test at the Bikini atoll—and, as deputy chief of staff for research and development at the Air Force, helped to formulate the atomic blitz. LeMay recognized the destructive power of nuclear weapons but didn't feel the least bit intimidated by them. "We scorched and boiled and baked to death more people in Tokyo," he later recalled, "than went up in vapor at Hiroshima and Nagasaki combined." And he didn't lose any sleep over the morality of Truman's decision. Killing was killing, whether you did it with a rock, a rifle, or an atom bomb. LeMay's appointment to run SAC sent a clear message to the Soviets: if necessary, the United States would not hesitate to fight a nuclear war.

After arriving at SAC headquarters in Omaha, Nebraska, during the fall of 1948, LeMay was angered by what he found. Bomber crews had no idea what their targets would be, if war came. Navigators lacked up-to-date maps, and pilots rarely consulted checklists before takeoff. As an exercise, LeMay ordered every SAC crew in the country to stage a mock attack on Wright Field in Dayton, Ohio, at night, from high altitude, under heavy cloud cover, conditions similar to those they might encounter over the Soviet Union. Many of the planes didn't get anywhere near Ohio—and not a single one hit the target. The bombardiers who did simulate the dropping of an atomic bomb, aiming their radar at reflectors on the ground, missed Wright Field by an average of two miles. LeMay called it "about the darkest night in American military aviation history."

The top officers at SAC were let go, and LeMay replaced them with veterans of his bombing campaigns in Germany and Japan. He hoped to create a similar esprit de corps. Promotions weren't given to individuals, but to an entire crew, sometimes on the spot. And when one person screwed up, the rest of the crew also paid the price. Officers lost their jobs because of accidents and honest mistakes. "I can't afford to differentiate between the incompetent and the unfortunate," LeMay explained. "Standardization" became the watchword at SAC, repeated like a mantra and ruthlessly pursued, with manuals and checklists and numeric measures of success created for every job. Team players were rewarded, iconoclasts and prima donnas encouraged to go elsewhere. LeMay wanted SAC to function as smoothly as the intricate machinery of a modern bomber. "Every man a coupling or a tube; every organization a rampart of transistors, battery of condensers," he wrote in his memoir. "All rubbed up, no corrosion. Alert."

Within hours of the Japanese surrender, LeMay had flown low over cities that his planes destroyed. The experience confirmed his belief that America needed an Air Force so overwhelmingly powerful that no enemy would ever dare to launch a surprise attack. After Pearl Harbor it had taken years for the United States to mobilize fully for war. Nuclear weapons eliminated that option. If a counterattack couldn't be swift, it might never occur. LeMay wanted everyone at SAC to feel a strong sense of urgency, to be ready for war not next week or tomorrow but at any moment—to feel *"we are at war now."* His goal was to build a Strategic Air Command that could strike the Soviet Union with planes based in the United States and deliver every nuclear weapon at once. SAC bomber crews constantly trained and prepared for that all-out assault. They staged mock attacks on every city in the United States with a population larger than twenty-five thousand, practicing to drop atomic bombs on urban targets in the middle of the night. San Francisco was bombed more than six hundred times within a month.

One of LeMay's greatest concerns was the command and control of nuclear weapons—the system of rules and procedures that guided his men, the network of radars and sensors and communications lines that allowed information to travel back and forth between headquarters and the field, the mechanisms that prevented accidental detonations and permitted deliberate ones, all of it designed to make sure that orders could be properly given, received, and carried out. To retaliate against a surprise attack, you needed to know that one had been launched. You needed to share that news with your own forces and ensure they could immediately respond. Command and control had always been a crucial element in warfare. But in a nuclear war, where decisions might have to be made within minutes and weapons could destroy cities in an instant, the reliability of these administrative systems could be the difference between victory and annihilation. A breakdown in command and control could make it impossible to launch a nuclear attack—or could order one by mistake.

LeMay thought that the Strategic Air Command should control all of America's atomic bombs and select their targets. Such an arrangement would simplify things, creating a unified chain of command. It would give oversight and accountability to one military organization: his. The atomic arsenal should be viewed, according to SAC doctrine, as "a *single instrument*... directed, controlled, if need be, from a single source." The Army, the Navy, and other units in the Air Force didn't like that idea. As LeMay worked hard to gain control of America's nuclear weapons, his rivals at the Pentagon fought to get their own, expand their influence, and limit the power of the Strategic Air Command.

LOUIS SLOTIN WAS TICKLING the dragon in a laboratory at Los Alamos, carefully lowering a beryllium shell over the plutonium core of a Mark 3 implosion bomb. The beryllium served as a tamper; it reflected neutrons, increased the number of fissions, and brought the assembly closer to a chain reaction. The clicks of a Geiger counter gave an audible measure of how fast the fissions were multiplying. Slotin knew what he was doing. He'd assembled the core for the Trinity test and performed dozens of criticality experiments like this one. A coworker had asked to see how it was done and, on the spur of the moment, Slotin decided to show him. The core looked like an enormous gray pearl resting inside a shiny beryllium shell. Slotin used a screwdriver to lower the top half of that shell—and then, at about 3:20 in the afternoon on May 21, 1946, the screwdriver slipped, the shell shut, the core went supercritical, and a blue flash filled the room. Slotin immediately threw the top half of the tamper onto the floor, halting the chain reaction. But it was too late: he'd absorbed a lethal dose of radiation. And he, more than anyone else in the room, knew it.

Within hours Slotin was vomiting, his hands were turning red and swollen, his fingernails blue. General Groves flew Slotin's parents down from Winnipeg on a military plane to say good-bye. A week later, Slotin was gone, and his death was excruciating, like so many tens of thousands at Hiroshima and Nagasaki had been. It was recorded on film, with his consent, as a sobering lesson on the importance of nuclear safety. Three of the other seven men in the lab that day eventually died of radiation-induced illnesses. But Slotin had added years to their lives by thinking quickly and stopping the chain reaction. In the absence of any fast-acting safety mechanism at the laboratory, a report on the accident later concluded, "Slotin was that safety device."

The same plutonium core that took Slotin's life had already killed one of his assistants, Harry Daghlian. The previous August, while Daghlian was performing an experiment, alone in the laboratory at night, a small tungsten brick slipped from his hand. The brick landed near the core, which became supercritical for a moment, and Daghlian was dead within a month. Having taken the lives of two promising young physicists, it was nicknamed "the Demon Core," placed in a Mark 3 bomb, and detonated during a test at the Bikini atoll.

Slotin's mishap was the fourth criticality accident at Los Alamos within a year, raising concern about the management practices at America's nuclear weapon facilities. The reactors at Hanford were not only dangerous but largely incapable of making plutonium. Most of the famous scientists who'd worked on the Manhattan Project had left government service after the war. The manufacture of atomic bombs didn't seem to be a wise career choice, at a time when the world appeared ready to ban them.

In April 1947, David Lilienthal visited Los Alamos for the first time after becoming head of the Atomic Energy Commission. He was shocked by what he saw: rudimentary equipment; dilapidated buildings; poor housing; muddy, unpaved roads—and plutonium cores stored in cages at an old icehouse. Lilienthal was a liberal, one of the last New Dealers in the

Truman administration, and he'd seen a lot of rural poverty while running the Tennessee Valley Authority during the Great Depression. But that first day at Los Alamos, he later noted, was "one of the saddest days of my life." Nuclear weapons were now thought indispensable for the defense of the United States; Lilienthal had expected to find them neatly and safely stored for immediate use. "The substantial stockpile of atom bombs we and the top military assumed was there, in readiness, did not exist," Lilienthal subsequently wrote. "Furthermore, the production facilities that might enable us to produce quantities of atomic weapons . . . likewise did not exist."

The number of atomic bombs in the American arsenal was considered so secret that it could not be shared with the Joint Chiefs of Staff—or even recorded on paper. After visiting Los Alamos, Lilienthal met with President Truman in the Oval Office and told him how many atomic bombs would be available in the event of a war with the Soviet Union: at most, one. The bomb was unassembled but, in Lilienthal's view, "probably operable." The president was stunned. He'd just announced the Truman Doctrine before Congress, vowing to contain the worldwide spread of communism. Admirals and generals were fighting over the atomic stockpile, completely unaware that there wasn't one. "We not only didn't have a pile," Lilienthal recalled, "we didn't have a stock." The threat to destroy the Soviet Union, if it invaded Western Europe, was a bluff.

During his visit to New Mexico, Lilienthal also discovered a shortage of scientists trained to make atomic bombs. The physicists, chemists, and engineers who'd put together the bombs at the end of the Second World War were now scattered throughout the United States. The Mark 3 implosion bomb was, in Oppenheimer's words, a "haywire contraption," difficult and dangerous to assemble. But at least some of the scientists in Los Alamos still knew how to make one. Nobody had bothered to save all the technical drawings necessary for building another Little Boy, the uranium-based, gun-type bomb dropped on Hiroshima. The exact configuration of the various parts had never been recorded on paper—an oversight that, amid the current shortage of plutonium, created some unease. As files and storerooms at Los Alamos were searched for information about Little Boy's design, a machinist offered to demonstrate how one of the bomb's aluminum tubes had been forged. He'd wrapped the metal around a Coke bottle.

After the war, the Z Division at Los Alamos, which had designed the firing and fuzing mechanisms of both atomic bombs, was moved an hour and a half south to an old Army air base near Albuquerque. The Z Division's headquarters was soon renamed the Sandia Laboratory, and a new military outfit called the Armed Forces Special Weapons Project (AFSWP) was located at the base, too. When the production of Mark 3 bombs resumed, the work was now divided among three organizations: Los Alamos fabricated the cores and the explosive lenses; Sandia was responsible for the rest of the weapon; and the AFSWP trained military personnel how to complete the assembly in the field. Norris Bradbury, the director of Los Alamos, pushed for improved designs that would make atomic bombs simpler, smaller, lighter, and safer to handle. It would take years for such improvements to be made. Until then, the safety of America's nuclear weapons depended on checklists, standard operating procedures, and a laboratory culture with a low tolerance for mistakes.

Bradbury worried about what would happen if a B-29 bomber crashed in the United States while carrying a fully assembled Mark 3 bomb. The B-29 had a high accident rate—two had crashed and burned on the runways at Tinian while trying to take off the night before the bombing of Nagasaki. In 1947 the Armed Forces Special Weapons Project decided that the final assembly of Mark 3 bombs must always occur outside the United States. The reliability of the weapon's electronic, mechanical, and explosive components was unknown, and Bradbury thought that a crash during takeoff would pose "a very serious potential hazard to a large area in the vicinity."

The Mark 3 was considered too dangerous to be flown, fully assembled, over American soil. But no safety restrictions were imposed on flights of the bomb over Great Britain. Atomic bomb–making facilities were secretly constructed at two Royal Air Force bases, in Sculthorpe and Lakenheath. Before attacking the Soviets, American B-29s would leave the United States with partially assembled Mark 3s and land at the British bases. Plutonium cores would be inserted into the weapons there, and then the B-29s would head for their Soviet targets. If one of the B-29s crashed during takeoff, the RAF base, as well as neighboring towns, might be obliterated. Anticipating that possibility, the U.S. Air Force explored sites in the countryside of Norfolk and Suffolk where atomic bombs could be hidden, so that "if one blew, the others would survive."

During the AFSWP's first attempt to assemble an atomic bomb, it took a team of thirty-six men two weeks to finish the job. That did not bode well for a quick retaliation against a Soviet attack. Through constant practice, the assembly time was reduced to about a day. But the Mark 3 bomb had a number of inherent shortcomings. It was a handmade, complicated, delicate thing with a brief shelf life. The electrical system was powered by a car battery, which had to be charged for three days before being put into the bomb. The battery could be recharged twice inside the Mark 3, but had to be replaced within a week—and to change the battery, you had to take apart the whole weapon. The plutonium cores radiated so much heat that they'd melt the explosive lenses if left in a bomb for too long. And the polonium initiators inside the cores had to be replaced every few months. By the end of 1948, the United States had the necessary parts and cores to assemble fifty-six atomic bombs, enough for an atomic blitz. But the Armed Forces Special Weapons Project could deploy only one bomb assembly team overseas. It would take months for that team to put together so many atomic bombs—and a stray wire, some static electricity, or a little mistake could end the entire operation in a flash.

ROBERT PEURIFOY WAS A SENIOR at Texas A&M when a recruiter from Sandia visited the campus. America's nuclear weapons program was expanding, and it needed engineers. Peurifoy was intrigued. Unlike his father—a prominent civil engineer who designed roads, buildings, dams, and other concrete structures—Peurifoy was drawn to the study of electricity. Recent inventions like radar, television, the transistor, and the computer promised to transform American society. The typical A&M student with a degree in electrical engineering went to work for Dallas Power &

Light or other utility companies after graduation. Designing nuclear weapons at a mysterious, top secret laboratory sounded a lot more interesting to Peurifoy. And he was deeply patriotic. During the spring of 1952, the United States was at war. With the backing of Joseph Stalin and Mao Tse-tung, the Communist regime of North Korea had invaded South Korea two years earlier, starting a conflict that eventually killed more than two million civilians. The threat of Communist aggression was no longer hypothetical; young American soldiers were once again fighting and dying overseas. When Sandia offered Peurifoy a job, he eagerly accepted. It seemed like a good way to serve his country—and satisfy his curiosity.

Right after graduation, Peurifoy and his wife, Barbara, packed up their belongings in College Station and moved to a small rental house in Albuquerque, not far from the lab. He was twenty-one, ready to help the war effort, thrilled to be employed for $395 a month. But he was forced to work in Sandia's "leper colony" for the first ninety days, denied access to the classified areas at the lab. While the FBI conducted a background check, he spent six days a week recording weather information onto IBM computer cards with a pencil. It was not a thrilling job. In the fall of 1952, Peurifoy obtained a "Q clearance," allowing him access to top secret material and Tech Area I, the lab's research facilities. But his early work at Sandia didn't enable him to visit Tech Area II, a separate group of buildings surrounded by guard towers and a perimeter fence. It was America's first atomic bomb factory.

Tests conducted in the Marshall Islands a few years earlier had shown that "composite" cores made from a mix of plutonium and uranium would detonate, ending fears at the Pentagon about a potential shortage of fissile material. The United States would have more than enough for a large stockpile of atomic bombs. In 1949 full-scale production of a new implosion bomb had begun at Sandia: the Mark 4. It had a composite core. It could be assembled in a couple of hours, then stored for a couple of weeks. And it was much safer than previous designs. According to the final evaluation report, the Mark 4 had a variety of features to "prevent premature detonation under all predictable circumstances." The X-unit didn't charge until the bomb fell from the plane, greatly reducing the risk to the aircrew.

More important, the nuclear core was stored in the plane's cockpit during takeoff and inserted through a trap door into the nose of the bomb, mid-flight. As long as the core was kept physically separate from the rest of the bomb, it was impossible for a plane crash to cause a nuclear explosion.

The days of handmade nuclear weapons were over. At Sandia the Mark 4 was now being manufactured with standardized, interchangeable parts—and so was its replacement, the Mark 6, a lighter, sleeker weapon with a yield as much as ten times larger than that of the bomb that destroyed Hiroshima. Once a weapon was assembled at Tech Area II, it was shipped to Site Able, an AEC storage facility tunneled into the nearby Manzano Mountains, or to Site Baker in Killeen, Texas, or to Site Charlie in Clarksville, Tennessee. The storage sites were located near SAC bases, so that in an emergency bombs could be quickly retrieved and loaded onto planes.

The military's demand for nuclear weapons was so great that Sandia could no longer handle the production. An "integrated contractor complex" was being formed, with manufacturing increasingly outsourced to plants throughout the United States. Polonium initiators would be made by the Monsanto Chemical Company, in Miamisburg, Ohio; explosive lenses by the Silas Mason Company in Burlington, Iowa; electrical components by the Bendix Aviation Corporation in Kansas City, Missouri; and so on. What had begun as a handcrafted laboratory experiment was now the focus of a growing industrial system. And the idea of placing atomic bombs under international control, the idea of outlawing them, the whole notion of world government and world peace, now seemed like an absurd fantasy.

Bob Peurifoy was asked to help redesign the arming and fuzing mechanisms of the Mark 5 and the Mark 7, new bombs small enough to be carried by naval aircraft. Work had already begun on the Mark 12, the Mark 13, and the Mark 15, a bomb that promised to be more powerful than all the rest.

In Violation

J eff Kennedy had just gotten home from playing racquetball when the phone rang. It was about seven in the evening, and he was getting ready for dinner with his wife and their two small children. The call was from job control.

There's a problem out at 4-7, the dispatcher said. The Klaxons are going off, and a white cloud is rising from the exhaust vents. We think there's a fire in the silo.

Kennedy had dealt with fuel leaks, oxidizer leaks, and all sorts of mechanical breakdowns—but he'd never seen a fire at a Titan II complex.

Report immediately to the command post, job control said. We're going to chopper you out to the complex.

Things must be pretty bad, Kennedy thought. He'd been in the Air Force for years, and this was the first time somebody had offered him a ride in a helicopter. He knew Charles Heineman, the PTS team chief working at 4-7 that day. Heineman was good, Heineman could tell the difference between fuel, smoke, and oxidizer. Maybe there was a fire in the silo. That would be incredible.

Kennedy put on his uniform, said good-bye to his family, and headed for the command post. He was a quality control evaluator for the 308th Missile Inspection and Maintenance Squadron. More important than his official title was a fact widely acknowledged in the 308th. Kennedy was the best missile mechanic at the base. He understood the Titan II propulsion system better than just about anyone else. He knew how to fix it. And he seemed to embody the swagger and the spirit of the PTS crews. Kennedy was tough, outspoken, and fearless. He was six foot five and powerfully built, a leader among the enlisted men who risked their lives every day in the silos. Commanding officers didn't always like him. But they listened to him.

At Little Rock Air Force Base, Kennedy was briefed by Colonel John T. Moser, the wing commander, and Colonel James L. Morris, the head of the maintenance squadron. A large socket had been dropped in the silo, piercing the missile and causing a leak in the stage 1 fuel tank. The sprays were on, flooding the silo with water. The missile combat crew was trying to make sense of all the hazard lights flashing in the control center. The deputy commander, Al Childers, thought it was just a fuel leak. The missile systems analyst technician, Rodney Holder, thought there was a fire. The PTS team topside had reported seeing smoke—but then hurriedly left the scene and couldn't be reached. Nobody knew where they were. Pressure in the stage 1 fuel tank was falling. Pressure in the stage 1 oxidizer tank was rising. One was threatening to collapse, the other to burst.

Kennedy was surprised to hear how quickly the pressure levels had changed in the hour or so since the socket was dropped. The stage 1 fuel tank was now at 2.2 psi, about one fifth of what it should be; the stage 1 oxidizer was at 18.8 psi, almost twice as high as it should be. He'd never seen pressure levels change that fast.

Colonel Morris was preparing to leave for 4-7 by helicopter and wanted Kennedy to join him. The two men weren't particularly fond of each other. Morris was an officer in his midforties, cautious and by the book, just the sort of person that the PTS guys liked to ignore. He needed to know what was happening at the launch complex and thought Kennedy was the right man to find out. The Missile Potential Hazard Team had tentatively come up with a plan of action: enter the silo, determine the size of the hole in the missile, vent the fuel vapors, and try to stabilize the stage 1 fuel tank so that it wouldn't collapse. Of course, none of that would be possible if the silo was on fire. Was there smoke drifting from the exhaust vents, fuel vapor, or both? That was the critical question. Morris and Kennedy left the command post, went to the flight line, climbed into a chopper, and took off.

Kennedy had never been in an Air Force helicopter. His job focused largely on machinery that was underground—and like most of the PTS guys, his career in missile maintenance had come as a surprise, not as the fulfillment of a lifelong ambition. Kennedy was born and raised in South Portland, Maine. He played basketball in high school, graduated, got married, and worked as a deckhand on the Casco Bay Lines, a ferry service that linked Portland to neighboring islands. In 1976 he decided that being a deckhand just didn't cut it anymore. He had a one-year-old daughter and another child on the way. He needed to earn more money, and his brother suggested joining the military. Kennedy met with recruiters from the Navy, the Air Force, and the Marines. He chose the Air Force because its basic training was the shortest.

After enlisting, Kennedy hoped to become an airplane mechanic stationed in Florida or California. Instead, he soon found himself learning about missile propellant transfer at Chanute Air Force Base in Rantoul, Illinois. The training course did a fine job with the technical details of the missile system. But it didn't give a sense of how dangerous the work could be. The Titan II mock-up at Chanute was loaded with water, not oxidizer or fuel, and accidental spills didn't seem like a big deal. Kennedy learned about the risks through his on-the-job training with the 308th in Arkansas. During one of his first visits to a launch complex, the PTS team was doing a "recycle," removing oxidizer from the missile. An enormous propane tank, known as a "burn bot," sat near the silo door topside, burning excess propellant as it vented, roaring like a jet engine and shooting out a gust of flame. This sort of controlled burn was routine, like the flares at an oil field. Then the burn bot went out, the oxidizer leaked, a dirty orange cloud floated over the complex, and the sergeant beside Kennedy said, "You know that bullshit right there? You get that shit on your skin, it'll turn to nitric acid."

Kennedy thought, "Wow," and watched with some concern as the cloud drifted over the control trailer and the rest of the PTS team continued to work, hardly noticing it. He felt like running for the hills. Clearly, the text-books at Chanute didn't tell you what really happened in the field. Kennedy soon realized there was the way you were supposed to do things—and the way things got done. RFHCO suits were hot and cumbersome, a real pain in the ass to wear—and if a maintenance task could be accomplished quickly and without an officer noticing, sometimes the suits weren't worn. The PTS team would enter the blast lock, stash their RFHCOs against a blast door, and enter the silo unprotected. The risk seemed less important than avoiding the hassle. While disconnecting a vent hose in the silo, Kennedy once forgot to close a valve, inhaled some oxidizer, and coughed up nasty stuff for a week. On another occasion, oxidizer burned the skin off the top of his left hand. Working without a RFHCO violated a wide range of technical orders. But it forced you to think about the fuel and the oxidizer and the fine line between saving some time and doing something incredibly stupid.

Within a few years, Kennedy had become a PTS team chief. He loved the job and the responsibility that it brought. And he loved the Air Force. Where else could a twenty-five-year-old kid, without a college degree, be put in charge of complicated, hazardous, essential operations at a missile site worth hundreds of millions of dollars? The fact that a nuclear warhead was involved made the work seem even cooler. Over time, Kennedy had gained an appreciation for the Titan II, regarding it as a thing of beauty, temperamental but awe inspiring. He thought you had to treat the missile with respect, like you would a lady. Keeping the Titan IIs fueled and ready to go, ensuring the safety of his men—those were his priorities, and he enjoyed getting the work done.

The recycles were one of Kennedy's favorite parts of the job. They took weeks to prepare. The weather had to be just right, with at least three knots of wind and the outdoor temperature rising, so that a leak wouldn't linger over the complex. Once the valves were turned and the fuel or the oxidizer started to flow, the team chief was in charge of the operation, and the adrenaline kicked in. The danger was greatest when propellants were being loaded and off-loaded; that's when something bad was most likely to happen, something unexpected and potentially catastrophic. It always felt good to finish a recycle, pack up the tools, load up the trucks, and send the PTS team home to Little Rock at the end of a long day.

Some of the missile combat crew commanders were a pleasure to work with, Kennedy thought, and some of them were real pricks—officers who liked to meddle with things they didn't know anything about. The launch control center and the silo were only a few hundred feet apart, but the distance between the men who worked in them often felt like miles. Once, while Kennedy was learning the ropes, his team chief was criticized by a missile crew commander, over the radio, for skipping a few lines in a technical order. "Commander, if you want to tell me how to do my job," the team chief replied, "then you get your ass off your chair, and you come and sit your ass in my chair." Kennedy soon adopted a similar way of dealing with combat crew officers, most of whom seemed afraid of the propellants: just leave me alone, the work will get done the right way—and then I'll get the hell off your launch complex.

Most of all, Kennedy valued the intense loyalty among the PTS crews, a bond strengthened by the stress and the dangers of the job. They looked out for each other. At the end of a late-night shift, Kennedy's team members would sometimes flip a coin to see who'd babysit his kids. And then Kennedy's wife would dress in fatigues and sneak onto the base to join everybody for midnight chow in the cafeteria. The PTS crews didn't like it when someone couldn't take a joke. They didn't like it when someone couldn't work well with others. And they found all kinds of unofficial ways to impose discipline. At one missile complex a PTS team waited until an airman with a bad attitude put on his RFHCO. Then they grabbed him, stuck a hose down the neck of his suit, filled the suit with cold water, and left him lying on the ground, shouting for help, unable to stand up or take the RFHCO off, rolling around and looking like a gigantic water balloon. He got the message.

For the past year, Kennedy had served as a quality control evaluator, a job that required him to visit all the launch complexes and make sure that the work was being done properly. He'd been out to 4-7 many times. As the helicopter approached it, the command post radioed the latest pressure levels: the stage 1 oxidizer tank had climbed to 23.4 psi, and the stage 1 fuel had fallen to −0.7. The fuel reading unnerved Kennedy. The negative pressure meant a vacuum was forming inside the tank that supported the rest of the missile. The stage 1 fuel tank was like a tin can with the air getting sucked out of it—and a ten-pound can sitting on top of it. First the tank would crumple, then it would collapse. Word that the missile crew had just evacuated the control center pissed him off. That was chickenshit, Kennedy thought. That would make everything a lot more difficult. They would have been safe and sound behind those blast doors.

The chopper pilot circled the complex, shining a spotlight toward the ground. Amid the darkness, Kennedy could see a thick, white cloud rising from the exhaust vents. He told Colonel Morris that the cloud looked like fuel vapor, not smoke. It was a fuel leak, Kennedy thought, not a fire. And that meant maybe, just maybe, they could find a way to fix it.

AROUND THE SAME TIME that Kennedy got a call from job control, Jim Sandaker got one, too. Sandaker was a twenty-one-year-old PTS technician with a wife and a baby daughter, and the call reached him at home on the base. Job control said there was a fuel leak at 4-7 and asked him to round up a bunch of other PTS guys to head out there. Sandaker hung up, told his wife, "Well, I got to go," put on his uniform, and went to the barracks. He was good natured and well liked, low key and solid, a country boy from Evansville, Minnesota, who'd dropped out of high school in the eleventh grade and joined the Air Force at the age of seventeen. When he reached the barracks and asked for volunteers, saying that it was an emergency, nobody believed him. They all thought it was a prank.

"All right," Sandaker said. "You call job control and ask them."

Someone called and learned that Sandaker wasn't kidding. Airmen started throwing on their uniforms and hurrying to the PTS shop, not because they had to go, but because it felt like the right thing to do. Their buddies at 4-7 needed help. PTS Team B was assembled from a makeshift group of volunteers, the guys who were gung ho. They gathered things that might be needed at the site: RFHCO suits, air packs, dewars filled with liquid air, tool kits, radios. Their team chief, Technical Sergeant Michael

A. Hanson, told them to assume that nothing at 4-7 could be used and start from scratch. The PTS shop was a converted aircraft hangar, big enough to hold a few Titan IIs, with smaller rooms devoted to specialized tasks. The men of Team B loaded their gear onto half a dozen trucks, eager to leave, like reinforcements coming to the rescue.

In addition to the PTS team, a flatbed truck with about 450 gallons of bleach and a tractor trailer with about 5,000 gallons of mineral oil were sent to Damascus. The bleach could be used to neutralize rocket fuel and render it less explosive. The mineral oil, dumped by hose into the silo vents, might form a layer on top of the fuel, trapping the vapors. The "baby oil trailer," as some people called it, was brand new—and nobody had ever tried using baby oil to prevent an explosion at a Titan II missile site.

Elsewhere at Little Rock Air Force Base, the Disaster Response Force was getting ready to depart. Its commander, Colonel William A. Jones, was also the base commander and head of the 314th Combat Support Group, a squadron of cargo planes stationed there. Jones was new to Little Rock, having arrived just two months earlier. He had not yet taken a disaster control course and didn't have much experience with Titan II missiles. His cargo planes were part of the Military Airlift Command, the missiles were part of the Strategic Air Command—and although both commands shared the same base, their missions rarely intersected. The Disaster Response Force was supposed to handle any military emergency, large or small, that involved units at Little Rock. During his brief tenure as its commander, the only emergency that Jones had faced was a search for the missing tail gunner of a B-52 bomber. The tail gunner had ejected from the plane by mistake, afraid that it was about to crash. The B-52 landed safely, as did the tail gunner, whose parachute was easily spotted floating above the Arkansas River.

After hearing about the problem at 4-7, Jones decided not to recall the entire Disaster Response Force. In his view, a disaster hadn't happened yet. The force didn't pack any gas masks, toxic vapor detectors, radiation detectors, or firefighting equipment. Jones did, however, bring a press officer to deal with the media and a judge advocate general (JAG) to process any legal claims filed by neighbors of the missile site.

At about nine o'clock the dozen or so members of the force left the base in a small convoy. A few of them rode in the mobile command post, a pickup truck with two rows of seats and a camper shell. A bioengineer traveled in a van that carried equipment to monitor the vapor from a fuel leak. A physician and two paramedics followed in an ambulance. And the press officer joined Colonel Jones in the base commander's car, along with the JAG, who brought his disaster claims kit.

SID KING STOOD IN THE DARK beside the Live Ear. It was parked on the shoulder of Highway 65, overlooking the entrance to the missile complex. A camera crew from KATV was on the way, and reporters from the other Little Rock television stations and local newspapers weren't far behind. Nothing much seemed to be happening. The white cloud was still rising from the complex, but nobody appeared to be dealing with it. About a dozen men in Air Force fatigues were hanging around a blue pickup at the end of the access road. A security policeman sat in the cab, talking to the command post on the radio. And a helicopter hovered overhead, shining its spotlight toward the ground, looking for someplace to land.

The missile combat crew was glad to be outdoors, with a good half a mile between them and the silo. The night was warm, help was on the way, everybody had made it out of the complex safe and sound. The problem with the missile hadn't been solved, but the mood was calm. Then Rodney Holder looked up and saw that the helicopter was about to hit some power lines. The pilot couldn't see them in the dark, and the chopper was descending straight toward them. Holder started to yell and wave his arms, and then Mazzaro, his commander, noticed, too. "Tell the helicopter not to land," they both shouted, frantically, to the security officer in the pickup. "Tell it not to land!" In an instant, Holder had gone from feeling chilled and relaxed to being absolutely terrified, convinced that the chopper was going to hit the power lines, spin out of control, and explode. It didn't. At the last minute, the pilot saw the wires, dodged them, and landed safely in a field near a farmhouse on the other side of the highway.

Morris and Kennedy climbed from the copter and joined the men waiting on the access road. While Mazzaro spoke to the colonel about the accident, Kennedy and Holder discussed what should be done next. Kennedy didn't think much of Mazzaro and couldn't believe that his crew had abandoned the complex. But Kennedy got along with Holder. The two had taken some college classes together at the base and felt a mutual respect. They disagreed now, however, about whether there was a fire in the silo. Kennedy decided to see for himself. He asked Colonel Morris for permission to enter the site—and to bring David Powell, the airman who'd dropped the socket, with him.

Powell was one of Kennedy's closest friends in the Air Force. When Kennedy was a PTS team chief, Powell served as his right-hand man. Kennedy could count on Powell to do just about anything. He used Powell to train new PTS technicians, and Powell hoped to become a team chief himself, maybe a noncommissioned officer. Powell was always calm and reliable. But now he seemed anxious, agitated, upset. After the helicopter landed, Powell had run up to him and said, "Jeff, I fucked up like you wouldn't believe."

Powell added another detail: not only had he dropped the socket but he'd also used the wrong tool with it. A recent technical order said that a torque wrench always had to be used when tightening or loosening a fuel cap in the silo. The torque wrench ensured that a precise amount of pressure could be applied to the cap. Earlier that evening, Powell and Plumb had reached level 2 of the silo, fully dressed in their RFHCOs, before realizing that they'd left the torque wrench behind in their truck.

PTS Team A had already spent ten hours on the job that day. Everybody was tired, and instead of sending someone topside to get the torque wrench, wasting another ten or fifteen minutes, Powell grabbed the ratchet hanging on the wall near blast door 9. The socket fit on the ratchet, and for years PTS teams had used that ratchet instead of a torque wrench, without any problems. Powell had done it, Kennedy had done it, just about every PTS team had done it. This time the socket slipped off. And using the wrong tool could get Powell in even more trouble.

"Oh, David," Kennedy said. "David, David, David."

Colonel Morris liked Kennedy's idea. They could use a better look at what was coming out of the exhaust vents. But Morris didn't want anyone venturing too close to the silo. Captain Mazzaro approved the plan, as well. Technically, he was still in command of the launch complex. After arriving at the site that morning, he'd signed for the missile and the warhead—they were his responsibility—and he didn't want Kennedy and Powell to go near the complex unaccompanied. Mazzaro and his deputy, Al Childers, still wearing their handguns, would go with them. The two officers and the two enlisted men started down the access road in the darkness, carrying flashlights.

SAM HUTTO'S FAMILY HAD FARMED the same land for generations. The inscription on his great-great-grandfather's tombstone said: PIONEER OF VAN BUREN COUNTY AND FOUNDER OF DAMASCUS. The Huttos had come to Arkansas before the Civil War, and the town they settled had originally been called Huttotown—until another set of Sam's ancestors, the Browns, decided to find a name with a more biblical flavor. "Damascus" sounded like a place that would one day be important, a worthy rival to Jerusalem, Arkansas, about thirty miles to the west. For decades, life in Damascus remained largely the same, as farmers struggled on small land-holdings with thin topsoil. The poverty seemed as unchanging as the landscape. Even the Great Depression didn't leave much of a mark. "We went into, through, and out of the Depression," Hutto's father once said, "and never knew we had one."

Despite the challenges of rural life, Sam Hutto thought his childhood was perfect. He was born in 1954, the same year his father quit raising chickens and opened a feed mill in Damascus. Everybody in the community seemed to know one another and be related to one another, somehow. Their children roamed everybody's land and hunted pretty much wherever they liked. The feed mill was about two miles from Hutto's house, and his parents let him leave home in the morning with a fishing pole and slowly make his way to the mill, as long as he arrived by quitting time. Hutto went to school a couple of miles from the farm, left town to attend the University of Arkansas in Fayetteville, spent about a year or so there, dropped out, lasted a semester at Arkansas Tech University in Russellville, then came home. He had little use for the world beyond Damascus. Working at his father's mill gave him a chance to attend feed meetings and conferences throughout the United States—and Hutto never went anywhere that he didn't want to come home from.

For years, the Titan II sites in Van Buren County didn't attract much attention. Their construction had briefly provided some high-paying jobs, and the fire in the silo at Searcy had taken the lives of a few men from Damascus. But once the launch complexes were operational, most people never thought about them. Sam Hutto would occasionally see crews in their Air Force blue pickups, coming or going from the site near Damascus. Sometimes they'd stop at the little grocery store to buy sodas and candy. The launch complex was just another local landmark, useful for giving directions. You could tell somebody who wanted to visit Ralph and Reba Jo Parish: head north from Damascus on Highway 65 for a few miles, pass the access road to the missile base, and their house will be the first one on the left.

The oxidizer leak in January 1978 was the first sign that having a Titan II in the neighborhood might be a problem. Hutto was working in the barn when he heard about the leak. He was twenty-three years old, helping his father and his older brother, Tommy, run the farm. A few years earlier the family had sold the feed mill and gone into the dairy business. As a milk truck backed into the barn, the driver said something about passing through a bright orange cloud on the way over. Hutto stepped outside to take a look. Their farm was on a hillside about three quarters of a mile southeast of the launch complex, with Highway 65 running between them. Down below Hutto could see an orange cloud encircling the complex and slowly drifting south. He didn't think much of it and went back to work. His father, who was chopping wood about two miles due south of 4-7, thought the cloud tasted funny as it drifted past. It gave him a headache but didn't make him sick. When word spread that the orange fumes had killed some cattle and sent Sheriff Anglin to the hospital, the residents of Damascus began to wonder about the safety of the Titan II missile that sat about a mile from their elementary school. The Air Force response to the leak—the assurances that everything was under control and that the missile was perfectly safe—did not reassure them.

Sam Hutto was at home on the evening of September 18, 1980, with his pregnant wife and their one-year-old daughter. The baby was expected any day. Hutto's father called at about half past seven and told him to get out of the house. There was another leak or something at the missile site. Sheriff Anglin had gone out there to see what was happening, bumped into an Air Force security officer near the fence, and asked him whether there was any need to evacuate. Nope, everything is under control, the security officer had said. The sheriff got on his radio and ordered an evacuation of all the homes within a mile of the launch complex. The Parishes lived the closest to the site, less than half a mile from the missile itself, and perhaps twenty-five other homes were within the evacuation zone, mainly on the east side of the highway. To the west of the complex, woods and open fields stretched for hundreds of acres. Sheriff's deputies knocked on doors, and neighbors phoned one another to spread the word. Sam Hutto drove his family to his brother Tommy's house in Damascus, helped them get settled, and then left.

It was a bad night to evacuate the farm. The heat cycles of the heifers had been synchronized, and about twenty were ready to give birth. They were grazing in a field right across the highway from 4-7. Hutto wanted to make sure the cows and their calves were all right. He knew the back roads of Damascus pretty damn well and felt confident that he could safely make his way to the farm.

THE ARKANSAS OFFICE of Emergency Services had been notified by the Air Force, at 6:47 P.M., that there was a fuel leak and possibly a fire at the Titan II complex outside Damascus. For the rest of the evening, however, the Air Force provided few additional details about what was happening and whether the leak could pose a threat to public safety. Despite repeated calls to Little Rock Air Force Base, the Office of Emergency Services was told only that the problem was being addressed—and that more information would soon be forthcoming. Spokesmen at SAC headquarters in

Omaha were no more helpful, claiming that the Air Force didn't know what had caused the fuel leak, the white cloud rising from the silo wasn't toxic, and there was no danger of a nuclear incident.

State officials had good reason to be skeptical of reassuring words from the federal government. A few months earlier, when about fifty thousand gallons of radioactive water leaked at a nuclear power plant outside Russellville, the Nuclear Regulatory Commission (NRC) had waited five hours before telling the Office of Emergency Services about the accident. And then the NRC allowed radioactive gas to be vented from the reactor into the air above Pope County, ignoring objections by the Arkansas Department of Health.

The cultural differences between the Strategic Air Command and the Arkansas state government may have contributed to the feelings of mistrust. SAC's devotion to order, discipline, secrecy, and checklists was at odds with the looser, more irreverent spirit that guided policy making in Little Rock. Steve Clark, the Arkansas attorney general, was thirty-three years old. Paul Revere, the secretary of state, was also thirty-three. And William Jefferson Clinton, at thirty-four, was the youngest governor in the United States.

Educated at Georgetown University, Oxford University, and Yale Law School, Bill Clinton was an unlikely person for the Air Force to include in deliberations about the fate of a ballistic missile. He'd organized a demonstration against the Vietnam War, never served in the military, and supported the decriminalization of marijuana. During his gubernatorial campaign in 1978, the *New York Times* described Clinton as "tall, handsome, a populist-liberal with a style and speaking manner as smooth as Arkansas corn silk." His landslide victory that year seemed to mark a generational shift—the rise to power of a brilliant, charismatic representative of the 1960s youth counterculture. Many conservatives were disgusted by the idea of Clinton and his young, idealistic friends running the state government. "He was a punk kid with long hair," one Arkansas legislator said, "he had all those longhaired people working for him, and he was a liberal."

Governor Clinton began his two-year term in office with an ambitious agenda for one of America's most impoverished states. He gained passage of the largest spending increase for public education in Arkansas history. He created a Department of Energy to subsidize research on conservation, alternative fuels, and solar power. He proposed a rural health policy that would bring physicians and medical care to low-income communities. And he set out to fix the state's badly deteriorated highway system, promising infrastructure investments to create jobs and improve the lives of ordinary Arkansans. A number of Clinton's top aides and cabinet officers were recruited from out of state—sending a clear message that posts in his administration would be filled on the basis of merit, not as a reward for political favors. Instead of having a chief of staff, Clinton relied upon three close advisers who had long hair, beards, and an aversion to wearing jackets or ties. Nicknamed "the Three Beards," they looked like junior faculty members at Berkeley. Among Democratic officials nationwide, Little Rock was now considered a cool place to be, and the young governor became a frequent guest at the Carter White House.

By the second year of the Clinton administration, most of the enthusiasm and idealism was gone. Personal differences, political disputes, and feelings of betrayal had led two of the Three Beards to quit. Industry groups worked hard to block or dilute many of Clinton's reforms, and the governor's willingness to compromise alienated many of his allies. Instead of subsidizing road construction with higher taxes on the use of heavy trucks—a move opposed by the state's trucking companies and poultry firms—Clinton agreed to raise the taxes paid by the owners of old pickup trucks and cars. The lofty rhetoric and grand ambitions of the young governor lost much of their appeal, once people realized they'd have to pay more to renew their license plates. During the spring of 1980, a series of tornadoes struck Arkansas. During the summer, the state was hit by a heat wave and the worst drought in half a century. Hundreds of forest fires burned. Cuban refugees, detained by the federal government at an Army base in the state, started a riot. They tried to escape from the base and fought a brief skirmish with the Arkansas National Guard, terrifying residents in the nearby town of Barling. Each new day seemed to bring another crisis or a natural disaster.

Having gained almost two thirds of the popular vote in 1978, Bill Clinton now faced a tough campaign for reelection, confronting not only the anger and frustration in his own state but also the conservative tide rising across the United States. Frank White, the Republican candidate for governor, was strongly backed by the religious right and many of the industry groups that Clinton had antagonized. The White campaign embraced the candidacy of Ronald Reagan, attacked Clinton for having close ties to Jimmy Carter, ran ads that featured dark-skinned Cubans rioting on the road to Barling, raised questions about all the longhairs from out of state who seemed to be running Arkansas, and criticized the governor's wife, Hillary Rodham, for being a feminist who refused to take her husband's name.

While Lee Epperson, director of the Office of Emergency Services, tried to find out what was happening at the Titan II site in Damascus, Governor Clinton spent the evening in Hot Springs. The state's Democratic convention was about to open there, and Vice President Walter Mondale would be arriving in the morning to attend it. Hillary Rodham remained in Little Rock, where she planned to spend the weekend at the governor's mansion with their seven-month-old daughter, Chelsea.

JEFF KENNEDY WANTED a closer look at the white cloud drifting about two hundred feet away, on the other side of the perimeter fence.

"Captain Mazzaro, we have to get that propane tank off the complex," Kennedy said. A fire in the silo could ignite it. The tank was sitting on the hardstand, near the exhaust vents, attached to a pickup truck. Kennedy suggested that they enter the complex and drive the tank out of there.

Mazzaro thought that sounded like a good idea. But he and Childers had no desire to do it. They hadn't brought their gas masks, and the idea of running through clouds of fuel vapor without the masks didn't sound appealing. Kennedy and Powell seemed eager to move the tank; Mazzaro told them to go ahead. He and Childers would wait by the fence.

The gate was still locked, and so Kennedy and Powell had to leave the access road, circle the complex, and enter through the breakaway section of the fence. Kennedy wore combat boots and fatigues. Powell was still in long johns and the black vinyl boots from his RFHCO. They walked along the chain-link fence, looking for the gap.

Kennedy had no intention of moving the propane tank. He planned to enter the underground control center and get the latest pressure readings from the stage 1 tanks. That was crucial information. In order to save the missile, they had to know what was going on inside it. Mazzaro wouldn't have liked the plan, and that's why Kennedy didn't tell him about it. The point was to avert a disaster. "If Mazzaro hadn't abandoned the control center," Kennedy thought, "I wouldn't need to be doing this."

Fuel vapors swirled above the access portal, but the escape hatch looked clear. Kennedy ran for it, with Powell a few steps behind. During all the visits that Kennedy had made to Titan II complexes over the years, to fix one thing or another, he'd never been inside the escape hatch. The metal grate had been removed topside, and the two men climbed inside the air shaft, Kennedy going first.

"Stay here," Kennedy said.

"Hell no," Powell replied.

It'll be safer if I go down there alone, Kennedy said. I can get out of there quicker.

"I'll give you three minutes—and then I'm coming down."

Kennedy climbed down the ladder wearing his gas mask, then crawled through the narrow steel tunnel. He felt confident that the blast doors were sealed tight and that the control center hadn't been contaminated. But he didn't want to stay down there too long. The air in level 3 seemed clear, and the lights were still on. He got out of the escape hatch and ran up the stairs. Everything looked good; there was no sign that blast door 8 had been breached. Kennedy sat at the launch commander's console and pushed the buttons on the PTPMU. As the tank pressures flashed, he recorded them on a piece of paper.

"We're in some serious shit," Kennedy thought.

The pressure in the stage 1 oxidizer tank had risen to 29.6 psi. It was never supposed to exceed 17 psi. And the burst disk atop the tank was designed to pop at 50 psi. If the tank hadn't already ruptured by then, the burst disk would act like a safety valve and release oxidizer into the silo, relieving some of the pressure. Normally, that would be a good thing, but at the moment there were thousands of gallons of fuel in the silo.

The pressure in the stage 1 fuel tank had dropped to –2 psi. Kennedy had been told that the tank would probably rupture once it reached between –2 and –3. He was surprised that the pressure had fallen so much in the past hour.

I'm not even wearing a watch, Powell realized, moments after Kennedy disappeared down the hatch. After counting the seconds for a while, Powell figured that three minutes had passed. He climbed down the ladder to find Kennedy, made it about halfway, and then heard Kennedy yell, "There's not enough room for two people!" Kennedy was quickly climbing back up.

"Oh, God," Powell said, after hearing the latest tank pressures. They got out of the escape hatch, left the complex through the breakaway fence, and made their way back to the gate.

Kennedy told Mazzaro that they couldn't move the propane tank—and nothing more. The four of them walked down the access road to Highway 65. Colonel Morris was sitting in a pickup truck beside the road. Kennedy called him over and took him aside.

"Sir, this is what the tank readings are," Kennedy said.

Morris asked, "Where in hell did you get those?"

Kennedy told him about entering the control center. The situation was urgent. They needed to do something about the missile, immediately.

Morris was glad to have the new readings but upset about what Kennedy had just done.

Something has to be done, and right away, Kennedy said. Earlier in the evening, he'd thought that the tank pressures would stabilize, but they hadn't. He explained to Morris how precarious things had become. There was a major fuel leak, not a fire—and the stage 1 fuel tank wouldn't hold much longer. If something wasn't done soon, it would collapse like an accordion.

Colonel Morris asked Mazzaro if he knew what Kennedy had just done. After hearing about it, Mazzaro became furious.

Morris called the command post on the radio and provided the latest tank pressure readings, without revealing how he'd obtained them. Then Mazzaro got on the radio and told Little Rock that Kennedy had disobeyed orders and violated the two-man rule.

Kennedy didn't care about any of this bullshit. He wanted to save the missile. And he had a plan, a good plan that would work.

Morris agreed to hear it.

We need to open the silo door, Kennedy said. That would release a lot of the fuel vapor, lower the heat in the silo, and relieve the pressure on the stage 1 oxidizer tank. Then we need to drop the work platforms—all nine levels of them—to support the missile and keep it upright. The platforms could prevent the missile from collapsing or falling against the silo wall. And then we need to send a PTS team down there to stabilize the stage 1 fuel tank, to fill it with nitrogen and restore the positive pressure.

For Kennedy's plan to work, somebody would have to reenter the control center so that the platforms could be lowered and the silo door opened. Al Childers and Rodney Holder said they were willing to do it, if there was any chance of saving the missile.

Colonel Morris listened carefully and then spoke to the command post.

About fifteen minutes later, Morris told Kennedy the command post's response: nothing, absolutely nothing, was to be done without approval from SAC headquarters in Omaha. Lieutenant General Lloyd R. Leavitt, Jr., the vice commander in chief of the Strategic Air Command, was now in charge of the launch complex in Damascus. The problem with the missile and ideas about how to resolve it were being discussed. It was 9:30 P.M., almost three hours since the socket had been dropped. Until new orders came from Omaha, Morris said, everyone would have to sit tight.

Megadeath

Fred Charles Iklé began his research on bomb destruction as a graduate student at the University of Chicago. Born and raised in an alpine village near Saint Moritz, he'd spent the Second World War amid the safety of neutral Switzerland. In 1949, Iklé left his studies in Chicago and traveled through bombed-out Germany. The war hadn't touched his family directly, and he wanted to know how people coped with devastation on such a massive scale. One of the cities he visited, Hamburg, had suffered roughly the same number of casualties as Nagasaki—and had lost an even greater proportion of housing. A series of Allied bombing raids had killed about 3.3 percent of Hamburg's population and destroyed about half of its homes. Nevertheless, Iklé found, the people of Hamburg were resilient. They had not fled the city in panic. They'd tried to preserve the familiar routines of daily life and now seemed determined to rebuild houses, businesses, and stores at their original locations. "A city re-adjusts to destruction somewhat as a living organism responds to injury," Iklé later noted.

After returning to the United States, Iklé wrote a doctoral thesis that looked at the relationship between the intensity of aerial bombing and the density of a city's surviving population. The proponents of airpower, he suggested, had overestimated its lethal effects. Before the Second World War, British planners had assumed that for every metric ton of high-explosive bombs dropped on a city, about seventy-two people would be killed or injured. The actual rate turned out to be only fifteen to twenty casualties per ton. And the Royal Air Force strategy of targeting residential areas and "de-housing" civilians proved disappointing. The supply of urban housing was much more elastic than expected, as people who still had homes invited their homeless friends, neighbors, and family members to come and stay.

Iklé devised a simple formula to predict how crowded the houses of a bombed-out city might become. If P1 = the population of a city before destruction, P2 = the population of a city after destruction, H1 = the number of housing units before destruction, H2 = the number of housing units after destruction, and F = the number of fatalities, then "the fully compensating increase in housing density," could be expressed as a mathematical equation:

$$\frac{P1 - F}{H2} - \frac{P1}{H1}$$

Iklé was impressed by the amount of urban hardship and overcrowding that people could endure. But there were limits. The tipping point seemed to be reached when about 70 percent of a city's homes were destroyed. That's when people began to leave en masse and seek shelter in the countryside.

Iklé's dissertation attracted the attention of the RAND Corporation, and he was soon invited to join its social sciences division. Created in 1946 as a joint venture of the Army Air Forces and the Douglas Aircraft Company, Project RAND became one of America's first think tanks, a university without students where scholars and Nobel laureates from a wide variety of disciplines could spend their days contemplating the future of airpower. The organization gained early support from General Curtis LeMay, whose training as a civil engineer had greatly influenced his military thinking. LeMay wanted the nation's best civilian minds to develop new weapons, tactics, and technologies for the Army Air Forces.

RAND's first study, "Preliminary Design of an Experimental World-Circling Spaceship," outlined the military importance of satellites, more than a decade before one was launched. RAND subsequently conducted pioneering research on game theory, computer networking, artificial intelligence, systems analysis, and nuclear strategy. Having severed its ties to Douglas Aircraft, RAND became a nonprofit corporation operating under an exclusive contract to the Air Force. At the RAND headquarters in Santa Monica, California, not far from the beach, amid a freewheeling intellectual atmosphere where no idea seemed too outlandish to explore, physicists, mathematicians, economists, sociologists, psychologists, computer scientists, and historians collaborated on top secret studies. Behind the whole enterprise lay a profound faith in the application of science and reason to warfare. The culture of the place was rigorously unsentimental. Analysts at RAND were encouraged to consider every possibility, calmly, rationally, and without emotion—to think about the unthinkable, in defense of the United States.

While immersed in a number of projects at RAND, Fred Iklé continued to study what happens when cities are bombed. His book on the subject, *The Social Impact of Bomb Destruction*, appeared in 1958. It included his earlier work on the devastation of Hamburg and addressed the question of how urban populations would respond to nuclear attacks. Iklé warned that far more thought was being devoted to planning a nuclear war than to preparing for the aftermath of one. "It is not a pleasant task to deal realistically with such potentially large-scale and gruesome destruction," Iklé wrote in the preface. "But since we live in the shadow of nuclear warfare, we must face its consequences intelligently and prepare to cope with them."

Relying largely on statistics, excluding any moral or humanitarian considerations, and writing with cool, Swiss precision, Iklé suggested that the Second World War strategy of targeting civilians had failed to achieve its aims. The casualties were disproportionately women, children, and the elderly—not workers essential to the war effort. Cities adapted to the bombing, and their morale wasn't easily broken. Even in Hiroshima, the desire to fight back survived the blast: when rumors spread that San Francisco, San Diego, and Los Angeles had been destroyed by Japanese atomic bombs, people became lighthearted and cheerful, hoping the war could still be won.

A nuclear exchange between the United States and the Soviet Union, however, would present a new set of dilemmas. The first atomic bomb to strike a city might not be the only one. Fleeing to the countryside and re-

maining there might be the logical thing to do. Iklé conjured a nightmarish vision of ongoing nuclear attacks, millions of casualties, firestorms, "the
sheer terror of the enormous destruction," friction between rural towns-
people and urban refugees, victims of radiation sickness anxiously waiting
days or weeks to learn if they'd received a fatal dose. It was naive to think
that the only choice Americans now faced was "one world—or none." Nuclear weapons might never be abolished, and their use might not mean the
end of mankind. Iklé wanted people to confront the threat of nuclear war
with a sense of realism, not utopianism or apocalyptic despair. A nation
willing to prepare for the worst might survive—in some form or another.

Iklé had spent years contemplating the grim details of how America's cities could be destroyed. His interest in the subject was more than academic;
he had a wife and two young daughters. If the war plans of the United States
or the Soviet Union were deliberately set in motion, Iklé understood, as well
as anyone, the horrors that would be unleashed. A new and unsettling concern entered his mind: What if a nuclear weapon was detonated by accident?
What if one was used without the president's approval—set off by a technical glitch, a saboteur, a rogue officer, or just a mistake? Could that actually
happen? And could it inadvertently start a nuclear war? With RAND's support, Iklé began to investigate the risk of an accidental or unauthorized
detonation. And what he learned was not reassuring.

THE THREAT OF ACCIDENTS had increased during the past decade, as
nuclear weapons became more numerous, more widely dispersed—and
vastly more powerful. In the fall of 1949, American scientists had engaged in
a fierce debate over whether to develop a hydrogen bomb, nicknamed "the
Superbomb" or "the Super." It promised to unleash a destructive force
thousands of times greater than that of the bombs used at Hiroshima and
Nagasaki. While those weapons derived their explosive power solely from
nuclear fission (the splitting apart of heavy elements into lighter ones), the
hydrogen bomb would draw upon an additional source of energy, thermonuclear fusion (the combination of light elements into heavier ones). Fission
and fusion both released the neutrons essential for a chain reaction—but

fusion released a lot more. The potential yield of an atomic bomb was limited by the amount of its fissile material. But the potential yield of a thermonuclear weapon seemed limitless; it might only need more hydrogen as fuel. The same energy that powered the sun and the stars could be harnessed to make cities disappear.

The physicist Edward Teller had devoted most of his time during the Manhattan Project to theoretical work on the Super. But the problem of how to ignite and sustain fusion reactions had never been solved. After the Soviet Union detonated an atomic bomb in August 1949, Teller began to lobby for a crash program to build a hydrogen bomb. He was tireless, stubborn, brilliant, and determined to get his way. "It is my conviction that a peaceful settlement with Russia is possible only if we possess overwhelming superiority," Teller argued. "If the Russians demonstrate a Super before we possess one, our situation will be hopeless."

The General Advisory Committee of the Atomic Energy Commission discussed Teller's proposal and voted unanimously to oppose it. Headed by J. Robert Oppenheimer, the committee said that the hydrogen bomb had no real military value and would encourage "the policy of exterminating civilian populations." Six of the committee members signed a statement warning that the bomb could become "a weapon of genocide." Two others, the physicists Enrico Fermi and Isidor Rabi, hoped that the Super could be banned through an international agreement, arguing that such a bomb would be "a danger to humanity . . . an evil thing considered in any light."

David Lilienthal, the head of the AEC, opposed developing a hydrogen bomb, as did a majority of the AEC's commissioners. But one of them, Lewis L. Strauss, soon emerged as an influential champion of the weapon. Strauss wasn't a physicist or a former Manhattan Project scientist. He was a retired Wall Street financier with a high school education, a passion for science, and a deep mistrust of the Soviet Union. At the AEC, he'd been largely responsible for the monitoring system that detected the Soviet atomic bomb test. Now he wanted the United States to make a "quantum leap" past the Soviets, and "proceed with all possible expedition to develop the thermonuclear weapon."

Senator Brien McMahon, head of the Joint Committee on Atomic Energy, agreed with Strauss. A few years earlier, McMahon had been a critic of the atomic bomb and a leading opponent of military efforts to control it. But the political climate had changed: Democrats were under attack for being too "soft on Communism." The Soviet Union now loomed as a dangerous, implacable enemy—and McMahon was facing reelection. If the Soviets developed a hydrogen bomb and the United States didn't, McMahon predicted that "total power in the hands of total evil will equal destruction." The Air Force backed the effort to build the Superbomb, as did the Armed Forces Special Weapons Project and the Joint Chiefs of Staff—although its chairman, General Omar Bradley, acknowledged that the weapon's greatest benefit was most likely "psychological."

On January 31, 1950, President Truman met with David Lilienthal, Secretary of State Dean Acheson, and Secretary of Defense Louis Johnson to discuss the Superbomb. Acheson and Johnson had already expressed their support for developing one. The president asked whether the Soviets could do it. His advisers suggested that they could. "In that case, we have no choice," Truman said. "We'll go ahead."

Two weeks after the president's decision was publicly announced, Albert Einstein read a prepared statement about the hydrogen bomb on national television. He criticized the militarization of American society, the intimidation of anyone who opposed it, the demands for loyalty and secrecy, the "hysterical character" of the nuclear arms race, and the "disastrous illusion" that this new weapon would somehow make America safer. "Every step appears as the unavoidable consequence of the preceding one," Einstein said. "In the end, there beckons more and more clearly general annihilation."

Truman's decision to develop a hydrogen bomb had great symbolic importance. It sent a message to the Soviet leadership—and to the American people. In a cold war without bloodshed or battlefields, the perception of strength mattered as much as the reality. A classified Pentagon report later stressed the central role that "psychological considerations" played in nuclear deterrence. "Weapons systems in themselves tell only part of the necessary story," the report argued. The success of America's defense plans relied on an effective "information program" aimed at the public:

What deters is not the capabilities and intentions we have, but the capabilities and intentions the enemy thinks we have. The central objective of a deterrent weapons system is, thus, psychological. The mission is persuasion.

The usefulness of the Super wasn't the issue; the willingness to build it was. And that sort of logic would guide the nuclear arms race for the next forty years.

The debate over the hydrogen bomb strengthened the influence of the military in nuclear weapons policy, diminished the stature of the Atomic Energy Commission, and created a lasting bitterness among many of the scientists and physicists who'd served in the Manhattan Project. But all the passionate arguments about genocide and morality and the fate of mankind proved irrelevant. The Soviet Union had secretly been working on a hydrogen bomb since at least 1948. According to the physicist Andrei Sakharov, considered the father of the Soviet H-bomb, Joseph Stalin was determined to have such a weapon—regardless of what the United States did. "Any U.S. move toward abandoning or suspending work on a thermonuclear weapon would have been perceived either as a cunning, deceitful maneuver or as evidence of stupidity or weakness," Sakharov wrote in his memoirs. "In any case, the Soviet reaction would have been the same: to avoid a possible trap and to exploit the adversary's folly."

TWO WEEKS AFTER NORTH KOREAN TROOPS crossed the border and invaded South Korea, President Truman approved the transfer of eighty-nine atomic bombs to American air bases in Great Britain. The Joint Chiefs of Staff feared that the outbreak of war in Korea might be a prelude to a Soviet invasion of Western Europe. The Atomic Energy Commission readily agreed to hand over the bombs, minus one crucial component: the nuclear cores. They remained at storage facilities in the United States, ready to be airlifted overseas if war seemed imminent. The Department of Defense was still pushing hard for custody of America's nuclear arsenal. General Kenneth D. Nichols, head of the Armed Forces Special Weapons

Project, asserted that the military should not only control the atomic bombs but also design and manufacture them. Frustrated that so many Los Alamos scientists had opposed the Super, Edward Teller sought the creation of a new weapons laboratory, backed by the Air Force, in Boulder, Colorado.

The AEC fought against those proposals, while recognizing the need for military readiness. In August 1950, Truman approved the transfer of fifteen atomic bombs without cores to the *Coral Sea*, an aircraft carrier heading to the Mediterranean. The Air Force didn't like the precedent—and insisted that, in the future, all nuclear weapons stored on carriers should be under the formal control of the Strategic Air Command, not the Navy. The following year, as U.N. troops battled the Chinese army in Korea, the Air Force finally gained custody of atomic bombs and their nuclear cores. Allowing the military to have possession of them seemed, at the time, to be a momentous step. General Hoyt Vandenberg, the Air Force chief of staff, assumed personal responsibility for the nine weapons. They were shipped to an air base in Guam, ready for use, if necessary, against the Chinese.

By the end of 1950, the United States had about three hundred atomic bombs, and more than one third of them were stored, without nuclear cores, on aircraft carriers or at air bases overseas. The rest were kept at the AEC's American storage sites, ostensibly under civilian control. And yet that custody, required by the Atomic Energy Act, had in many respects become a legal fiction. For example, at Site Baker, the storage facility in Killeen, Texas, the AEC had eleven employees—and the military had five hundred, including all two hundred security personnel. The storage sites were well defended against saboteurs and intruders, but not against every kind of unauthorized use. General LeMay later admitted that special arrangements had been made at Site Able, the facility in the Manzano Mountains near Sandia:

Our troops guarded [the atomic bombs], but we didn't own them. . . . Civilian-controlled, completely. I remember sending somebody out . . . to have a talk with this guy with the key. I felt that under certain conditions—say we woke up some morning and there wasn't any Washington or something—I was going to take the bombs. I got no static from this man. I never had to do it or anything, but we had an understanding.

The arrangement seemed necessary, given the rudimentary nature of command and control in those days. "If I were on my own and half the country was destroyed and I could get no orders and so forth," LeMay explained, "I wasn't going to sit there fat, dumb, and happy and do nothing."

Work on the hydrogen bomb gained more urgency after it became clear that the Soviet Union was trying to build one. A few days after Truman's announcement that the United States would develop the Super, the British physicist Klaus Fuchs confessed to having spied for the Soviets. At Los Alamos, Fuchs had worked on the original design of the implosion bomb and conducted some of the early research on thermonuclear weapons. In January 1951, despite a year of intense effort, American scientists were no closer to creating a hydrogen bomb. Teller had proposed using a fission device to initiate the process of fusion. But he could not figure out how to contain the thermonuclear reaction long enough to produce a significant yield. The mathematician Stanislaw Ulam suggested a couple of new ideas: the hydrogen fuel should be compressed before being ignited, and the detonation of the bomb should unfold in stages. Teller was greatly inspired by Ulam's suggestions, and in March 1951 the two men submitted a paper at Los Alamos that laid out the basic workings of a thermonuclear weapon—"On Heterocatalytic Detonations I: Hydrodynamic Lenses and Radiation Mirrors." And then they applied for a patent on their H-bomb design.

Ulam had called his initial proposal "a bomb in a box." The Teller-Ulam design that emerged from it essentially placed two fission bombs in a box, along with hydrogen isotopes like deuterium and tritium to serve as thermonuclear fuel. Here is what would happen, if everything worked as planned: an implosion device would detonate inside a thick metal canister lined with lead. The X-rays emitted by that explosion would be channeled down the canister toward hydrogen fuel wrapped around a uranium-235 "spark plug." The fuel and the spark plug would be encased in a cylindrical layer of uranium-238, like beer inside a keg. The X-rays would compress the uranium casing and the hydrogen fuel. That compression would make the fuel incredibly dense—and then would detonate the uranium spark plug in the middle of it. Trapped between two nuclear explosions, the first one pressing inward, the second one now pushing outward, the hydrogen atoms would fuse. They would suddenly release massive amounts of neutrons, and that flood of neutrons would accelerate the fission of the uranium spark plug. It would also cause the uranium casing to fission. All of that would occur within a few millionths of a second. And then the metal canister holding everything together would blow apart.

The physics and the material science behind the Teller-Ulam design were highly complex, and there was no guarantee the bomb would work. It relied on a concept, "radiation implosion," that seemed plausible in theory but had never been accomplished. X-rays from the detonation of the first device, called the "primary," would have to be accurately focused and reflected onto the "secondary," the cylinder housing the fuel and the spark plug. Using X-rays to implode the secondary was a brilliant idea: the X-rays would move at the speed of light, traveling much faster than the blast wave from the primary. The difference in speed would prolong the fusion process—if the interaction of the various materials could be properly understood.

The steel, lead, plastic foam, uranium, and other solids within the bomb would be subjected to pressures reaching billions of pounds per square inch. They would be transformed into plasmas, and predicting their behavior depended on a thorough grasp of hydrodynamics—the science of fluids in motion. The mathematical calculations necessary to determine the proper size, shape, and arrangement of the bomb's components seemed overwhelming. "In addition to all the problems of fission . . . neutronics, thermodynamics, hydrodynamics," Ulam later recalled, "new ones appeared vitally in the thermonuclear problems: the behavior of more materials, the question of time scales and interplay of all the geometrical and physical factors." And yet the Teller-Ulam design had an underlying simplicity. Aside from the fuzing and firing mechanism that set off the primary, there were no moving parts.

In May 1951 a pair of nuclear tests in the South Pacific demonstrated that a nuclear explosion could initiate thermonuclear fusion. A device nicknamed "George," containing liquefied tritium and deuterium, produced the largest nuclear yield ever achieved: 225 kilotons, more than ten times that of the Nagasaki bomb. Although fusion was responsible for just a small part of that yield, radiation implosion did occur. The detonation of "Item" a few days later had a much lower yield, but enormous significance. It confirmed Teller's belief that fission bombs could be "boosted"—that their explosive force could be greatly magnified by putting a small amount of tritium and deuterium gas into their cores, right before the moment of detonation. When a boosted core imploded, the hydrogen isotopes fused and then flooded it with neutrons, making the subsequent fission explosion anywhere from ten to a hundred times more powerful. Boosted weapons promised to be smaller and more efficient than those already in the stockpile, producing larger yields with much less fissile material.

A full-scale test of the Teller-Ulam design took place on November 1, 1952. One of the world's first electronic, digital computers had been assembled at Los Alamos to perform many of the necessary calculations. The machine was called MANIAC (Mathematical Analyzer, Numerical Integrator, and Computer), and the device that it helped to create, "Mike," looked more like a large cylindrical whiskey still than a weapon of mass destruction. Mike was about twenty feet tall and weighed more than 120,000 pounds. The device was housed in a corrugated aluminum building on the island of Elugelab. When Mike detonated, the island disappeared. It became dust and ash, pulled upward to form a mushroom cloud that rose about twenty-seven miles into the sky. The fireball created by the explosion was three and a half miles wide. All that remained of little Elugelab was a circular crater filled with seawater, more than a mile in diameter and fifteen stories deep. The yield of the device was 10.4 megatons, roughly five hundred times more powerful than the Nagasaki bomb.

The Teller-Ulam design worked, and the United States now seemed capable of building hydrogen bombs. "The war of the future would be one in which man could extinguish millions of lives at one blow, demolish the great cities of the world, wipe out the cultural achievements of the past," President Truman said, a couple of months later, during his farewell address. Then he added, somewhat hopefully, "Such a war is not a possible policy for rational men."

THE THOUGHT OF USING nuclear weapons may have seemed irrational to Truman, but a credible threat to use them lay at the heart of deterrence. And planning for their use had become a full-time occupation for many of America's best minds. Fundamental questions of nuclear strategy still hadn't been settled. Project Vista, a top secret study conducted by the California Institute of Technology, revived the military debate about how to defend Western Europe from a Soviet invasion. In 1950 the North Atlantic Treaty Organization (NATO) had agreed to create an allied army with 54 divisions—enough to stop the Red Army, which was thought to have 175 divisions. The European members of NATO, however, failed to supply the necessary troops, and by 1952 the alliance seemed incapable of fielding anywhere near the requisite number. The small U.S. Army contingent in Western Europe served on the front line as a "trip wire," a "plate glass wall." American troops would be among the first to encounter a Soviet attack, and they'd be quickly overrun, forcing the United States to enter the war. The Strategic Air Command would respond by destroying most of the Soviet Union. But the Red Army would still conquer most of Europe, and civilian casualties would be extraordinarily high.

The prominent academics and military officers who led Project Vista, including Robert Oppenheimer, concluded that SAC's atomic blitz was the wrong response to a Soviet invasion. Bombing the cities of the Soviet Union might provoke a nuclear retaliation against the cities of Western Europe and the United States. Instead of relying on strategic bombing, the members of Project Vista urged NATO to replace manpower with technology, use low-yield, tactical atomic weapons against the advancing Soviet troops, and bring the "battle back to the battlefield." Such a policy might limit the scale of any nuclear war and save lives, *"preventing attacks on friendly cities."* The field officers of the U.S. Army and the fighter pilots of the U.S. Air Force's Tactical Air Command (TAC) wholeheartedly agreed with those conclusions, on humanitarian grounds. They also stood to benefit from any policy that reduced the influence of the Strategic Air Command.

As would be expected, Curtis LeMay hated the idea of low-yield tactical weapons. In his view, they were a waste of fissile material, unlikely to prove decisive in battle, and difficult to keep under centralized control. The only way to win a nuclear war, according to SAC, was to strike first and strike hard. "Successful offense brings victory; successful defense can now only lessen defeat," LeMay told his commanders. Moreover, an atomic blitz aimed at Soviet cities was no longer SAC's top priority. LeMay now thought it would be far more important to destroy the Soviet Union's capability to use its nuclear weapons. Soviet airfields, bombers, command centers, and nuclear facilities became SAC's primary targets. LeMay did not advocate preventive war—an American surprise attack on the Soviet Union, out of the blue. But the "counterforce" strategy that he endorsed was a form of preemptive war: SAC planned to attack the moment the Soviets seemed to be readying their own nuclear forces. Civilian casualties, though unavoidable, were no longer the goal. "Offensive air power must now be aimed at preventing the launching of weapons of mass destruction against the United States or its Allies," LeMay argued. "This transcends all other considerations because the price of failure might be paid with national survival."

The newly elected president, Dwight D. Eisenhower, had to reconcile the competing demands of his armed services—and develop a nuclear strategy that made sense. Eisenhower was well prepared for the job. He'd served as the supreme commander of Allied forces in Europe during the Second World War, as Army chief of staff after the war, and most recently as the supreme commander of NATO forces. He understood the military challenges of defending Western Europe and the revolutionary impact of nuclear weapons. The Manhattan Project had reported to him, until the AEC assumed its role. He had worked closely with LeMay for years and had been briefed by Oppenheimer on the findings of Project Vista. Eisenhower didn't like the Soviet Union but had no desire to fight a third world war. After being briefed on the details of how Mike had made an island disappear, he privately questioned the need "for us to build enough destructive power to destroy everything."

After replacing Truman's appointees to the Joint Chiefs of Staff, Eisenhower asked his national security team to take a "new look" at America's defense policies. He'd campaigned for the presidency vowing to lower taxes and reduce the size of the federal government. Despite his military background, he was eager to cut the defense budget, which had tripled in size during the Truman administration. In June 1953, while a wide range of proposals was being considered, the Soviets crushed a popular uprising in East Germany. Two months later they detonated RDS-6, a thermonuclear device. Although the yield of RDS-6 was relatively low and its design rudimentary, the test had ominous implications. Eisenhower was fully committed to preserving the freedom of Western Europe and containing the power of the Soviet Union—without bankrupting the United States. In his view, the simplest, most inexpensive way to accomplish those aims was to deploy more nuclear weapons. And instead of choosing between a strategy based on large thermonuclear weapons or one based on smaller, tactical weapons, Eisenhower decided that the United States should have both.

In the fall of 1953, the administration's national security policy was outlined in a top secret document, NSC 162/2. It acknowledged that the United States didn't have enough troops to protect Western Europe from a full-scale Soviet invasion. And it made clear that a Soviet attack would provoke an overwhelming response: "In the event of hostilities, the United States will consider nuclear weapons as available for use as other munitions."

During his State of the Union address in January 1954, President Eisenhower publicly announced the new policy, declaring that the United States and its allies would "maintain a massive capability to strike back." Five days later his secretary of state, John Foster Dulles, said that the security of the United States would depend on "a great capacity to retaliate, instantly, by means and at places of our own choosing." The two speeches left the impression that America would respond to any Soviet attack with an all-out nuclear strike, a strategy soon known as "massive retaliation."

The Air Force and the Strategic Air Command benefited the most from Eisenhower's "new look." SAC became America's preeminent military organization, its mission considered essential to national security, its commander reporting directly to the Joint Chiefs of Staff. While the other armed services faced cutbacks in spending and manpower, SAC's budget grew. Within a few years the number of personnel at SAC increased by almost one third, and the number of aircraft nearly doubled. SAC's demand for nuclear weapons soared as well, driven by the new focus on counterforce targets. The Soviet Union had far more airfields than major cities—and destroying them would require far more bombs. The Navy's shipbuilding budget stagnated, but the new look didn't inspire another revolt of the admirals. The Navy no longer seemed obsolete. It had gained approval for new aircraft carriers, every one of them equipped to carry nuclear weapons. The Navy also sought high-tech replacements for many conventional weapons: atomic depth charges, atomic torpedoes, atomic antiship missiles.

Although Eisenhower had served in the Army for nearly forty years, the Army suffered the worst budget cuts, quickly losing more than one fifth of its funding and about one quarter of its troops. General Matthew B. Ridgway, the Army chief of staff, became an outspoken critic of massive retaliation. Ridgway had demonstrated great leadership and integrity while commanding ground forces during the Second World War and in Korea. He thought that the United States still needed a strong Army to fight conventional wars, that an overreliance on nuclear weapons was dangerous and immoral, that Eisenhower's policy would needlessly threaten civilians, and that "national fiscal bankruptcy would be far preferable to national spiritual bankruptcy." Ridgway's unyielding criticism of the new look led to his early retirement. The Army, however, found ways to adapt. It lobbied hard for atomic artillery shells, atomic antiaircraft missiles, atomic land mines. During secret testimony before a congressional committee, one of Ridgway's closest aides, General James M. Gavin, later spelled out precisely what the Army required: 151,000 nuclear weapons. According to Gavin, the Army needed 106,000 for use on the battlefield and an additional 25,000 for air defense. The remaining 20,000 could be shared with America's allies.

AT LOS ALAMOS AND SANDIA, a crash program had been launched to make hydrogen bombs, long before it was clear that the Teller-Ulam design would even work. A six-day week became routine, and the labs were often busy on Sundays, as well. The goal was to produce a handful of H-bombs that the Air Force could use if Western Europe were suddenly invaded. Unlike the fission bombs being manufactured at factories across the United States, these "emergency capability" weapons would be assembled by hand at Sandia and then stored nearby at Site Able. Their components weren't required to undergo the same field testing as those used in the stockpile's other bombs. While Teller and Ulam wrestled with the theoretical issues of how to sustain thermonuclear fusion, the engineers at Sandia faced a more practical question: How do you deliver a hydrogen bomb without destroying the aircraft that carried it to the target?

The latest calculations suggested that an H-bomb would weigh as much as forty thousand pounds, and the only American bomber large enough to transport one to the Soviet Union, the B-36, was too slow to escape the blast. The Air Force investigated the possibility of turning the new, medium-range B-47 jet bomber into a pilotless drone. The B-47 would be fitted with a hydrogen bomb and carried to the Soviet Union by a B-36 mothership. Code-named Project Brass Ring, the plan was hampered by the cost and complexity of devising a guidance system for the drone.

Harold Agnew, a young physicist at Los Alamos, came up with a simpler idea. Agnew was an independent, iconoclastic thinker from Colorado who'd been present at some of the key moments in the nuclear age. As a graduate student at the University of Chicago, he'd helped Enrico Fermi create the first man-made nuclear chain reaction in 1942. Agnew subsequently worked on the Manhattan Project, flew as a scientific observer over Hiroshima when Little Boy was dropped, snuck his own movie camera onto the plane, and shot the only footage of the mushroom cloud. He'd helped to construct Mike and watched it detonate from a ship thirty miles away, amazed to see the island disappear. The heat from the blast kept growing stronger and stronger, as though it might never end. While thinking about how to deliver an H-bomb safely, Agnew remembered seeing footage of Nazi tanks being dropped from airplanes by parachute. He contacted a friend at the Air Force and said, "We've got to find out how they did that."

The Air Force had already taken an interest in those parachutes. Theodor W. Knacke, their inventor, had been brought to the United States after the Second World War as part of a top secret effort to recruit Nazi aerospace and rocket scientists. The program, known as Project Paperclip, had been run by Curtis LeMay, who later explained its aims: "rescue those able and intelligent Jerries from behind the barbed wire, and get them going in our various military projects, and feed them into American industry." Theodor Knacke now worked for the U.S. Navy at an air base in El Centro, California. Agnew promptly flew to California, met with Knacke, and asked, hypothetically, if he could design a parachute strong enough to bear the weight of something that weighed forty thousand pounds. "Oh yes," Knacke replied. "No problem."

Inspired by the German designs, Project Caucasian, a collaboration between the Air Force and Sandia, developed a three-parachute system that would slow the descent of a hydrogen bomb and give an American bomber enough time to get away from it. The bomb would be dropped by a B-36 at an altitude of about forty thousand feet. A small pilot chute would open immediately, followed by a slightly larger extraction chute. The first two chutes would protect the bomb from being jerked too violently, and then the third chute would open—an enormous ribbon parachute, Theodor Knacke's invention, with narrow gaps in the fabric that let air pass through it and prevented the whole thing from being torn apart. The hydrogen bomb would float gently downward for about two minutes, just a tiny little speck in the sky. And then it would explode, roughly a mile and a half above the ground.

Bob Peurifoy led the team at Sandia that designed the arming, fuzing, and firing mechanisms for the emergency capability weapons. Radar fuzes promised to be the most accurate means of detonating the bombs, but pinpoint accuracy wasn't essential for a weapon expected to have a yield of about 10 megatons. Klaus Fuchs had most likely given the Soviet Union information about the Archies and other radar fuzes used on atomic bombs, raising concern that the Soviets could somehow jam those radars and turn America's H-bombs into duds. A barometric switch or a mechanical timer seemed a more reliable way to trigger the X-unit, fire the detonators, and set off a thermonuclear explosion. Each of those fuzes, however, had potential disadvantages. If a mechanical timer was used and the main parachute failed, the bomb would plummet to the ground and smash to pieces before the timer ran out. But if a barometric switch was used and the main parachute failed, the bomb would fall to the designated altitude too fast and explode prematurely, destroying the B-36 before it had a chance to escape.

Peurifoy asked the Air Force to consider the risks of the two fuzes and then make a choice. One fuze might fail to detonate the bomb; the other might kill the crew. When the Air Force couldn't decide, Peurifoy ordered that both fuzes be added to the firing mechanism. The decision could be made before the bomb was loaded on the plane, with or without the crew's knowledge.

Sandia was no longer a small offshoot of Los Alamos. It now had more than four thousand employees, state-of-the-art buildings with blast walls for work on high explosives, and a year-round test site in the California desert. Plans were under way to open another division in Livermore, California, where the Atomic Energy Commission had recently established a new weapons laboratory to compete with Los Alamos. The University of California managed the labs at Livermore and Los Alamos, but Sandia was a nonprofit corporation operated by AT&T. The mix of public and private management, of academic inquiry and industrial production, helped to form a unique, insular culture at Sandia—rigorous, grounded, and pragmatic; eager to push the boundaries of technology, yet skeptical of wild and abstract schemes; highly motivated, collegial, and patriotic. Nobody took a job at Sandia in order to get rich. The appeal of the work lay in its urgency and importance, the technical problems to be solved, the sense of community inspired by the need to keep secrets. Most of the engineers, like Peurifoy, were young. They couldn't tell their friends, relatives, or even spouses anything about their jobs. They socialized at the Coronado Club inside the gates of Sandia, hiked and skied the nearby mountains, conducted experiments on new fuzes and detonators and bomb casings. They perfected America's weapons of mass destruction so that those weapons would never have to be used.

THE THERMONUCLEAR DEVICE that had vaporized Elugelab was too large to be delivered by plane. And that type of device presented a number of logistical challenges. Mike's thermonuclear fuel, liquefied deuterium, had to be constantly maintained at a temperature of −423 degrees Fahrenheit. Although the feasibility of liquid-fueled hydrogen bombs was being explored, weapons that used a solid fuel, such as lithium deuteride, would be much easier to handle. On March 1, 1954, a solid-fueled device named "Shrimp" was tested at a coral reef in the Bikini atoll. The code name of the test was Bravo, and the device worked. But miscalculations at Los Alamos produced a yield much larger than expected. The first sign that something had gone wrong was detected at the firing bunker on the island of Enyu, twenty miles from the explosion. While awaiting the blast wave, the lead scientist in the bunker, Bernard O'Keefe, grew concerned. He was hardly the nervous type. The night before the Nagasaki raid, he'd violated safety rules and secretly changed the plugs on Fat Man's master firing cable. In 1953, after an implosion device mysteriously failed to detonate at the Nevada Test Site, he'd climbed two hundred feet to the top of the shot tower and pulled out the firing cables by hand. Now he felt uneasy. About ten seconds after Shrimp exploded, the underground bunker seemed to be moving. But that didn't make any sense. The concrete bunker was anchored to the island, and the walls were three feet thick.

"Is this building moving or am I getting dizzy?" another scientist asked.

"My God, it is," O'Keefe said. "It's moving!"

O'Keefe began to feel nauseated, as though he were seasick, and held on to a workbench as objects slid around the room. The bunker was rolling and shaking, he later recalled, "like it was resting on a bowl of jelly." The shock wave from the explosion, traveling through the ground, had reached them faster than the blast wave passing through the air.

Shrimp's yield was 15 megatons—almost three times larger than what its designers had predicted. The fireball was about four miles wide, and about two hundred billion pounds of coral reef and the seafloor were displaced, much of it rising into a mushroom cloud that soon stretched for more than sixty miles across the sky. Fifteen minutes after the blast, O'Keefe and the eight other men in his firing crew tentatively stepped out of the bunker. The island was surrounded by a dull, gray haze. Trees were down, palm branches were scattered everywhere, all the birds were gone—twenty miles from ground zero. O'Keefe noticed that the radioactivity level on his do-simeter was climbing rapidly. A light rain of white ash that looked like snowflakes began to fall. Then pebbles and rocks started dropping from the sky. The men ran back into the bunker, slammed the door shut, detected high levels of radioactivity within the bunker, and after a few moments of confusion, turned off the air-conditioning unit. Inside, the radiation levels quickly fell, but outside they continued to rise. The men were trapped.

The dangers of radioactive fallout had been recognized since the days of the Manhattan Project but never fully appreciated. A nuclear explosion produces an initial burst of gamma rays—the source of radiation poisoning at Hiroshima and Nagasaki. The blast also creates residual radiation, as fission products and high-energy neutrons interact with everything engulfed by the fireball. The radioactive material formed by the explosion may emit beta particles, gamma rays, or both. The beta particles are relatively weak, unable to penetrate clothing. The gamma rays can be deadly. They can pass through the walls of a house and kill the people inside it.

Some elements become lethal after a nuclear explosion, while others remain harmless. For example, when oxygen is bombarded by high-energy neutrons, it turns into a nitrogen isotope with a half-life of just seven seconds—meaning that within seven seconds, half of its radioactivity has been released. That's why a nuclear weapon exploded high above the ground—an airburst, like the detonations over Hiroshima and Nagasaki—doesn't produce much radioactive fallout. But when manganese is bombarded by high-energy neutrons, it becomes manganese-56, an isotope that emits gamma rays and has a half-life of two and a half hours. Manganese is commonly found in soil, and that's one of the reasons that the ground-burst of a nuclear weapon can create a large amount of deadly fallout. Rocks, dirt, even seawater are transformed into radioactive elements within the fireball, pulled upward, carried by the wind, and eventually fall out of the sky.

The "early fallout" of a nuclear blast is usually the most dangerous. The larger particles of radioactive material drop from the mushroom cloud within the first twenty-four hours, landing wherever wind or rain carries them. On the ground, radiation levels steadily increase as the fallout accumulates. Unlike the initial burst of gamma rays from a nuclear explosion, the residual radiation can remain hazardous for days, months, or even years. A dose of about 700 roentgens is almost always fatal to human beings—and that dose need not be received all at once. Radiation poisoning, like a sunburn, can occur gradually. Gamma rays are invisible, and radioactive dust looks like any other dust. By the time a person feels the effects of the radiation damage, nothing can be done to reverse it.

"Delayed fallout" poses a different kind of risk. Minute particles of radioactive material may be pulled into the upper atmosphere and travel thousands of miles from the nuclear blast. Most of the gamma rays are emitted long before this fallout lands. But a number of radioactive isotopes can emit beta particles for long periods of time. Strontium-90 is a soft metal, much like lead, with a radioactive half-life of 29.1 years. It is usually present in the fallout released by thermonuclear explosions. When strontium-90 enters the soil, it's absorbed by plants grown in that soil— and by the animals that eat those plants. Once inside the human body, strontium-90 mimics calcium, accumulates in bone, and continues to emit radiation, often causing leukemia or bone cancer. Strontium-90 poses the greatest risk to children and adolescents, whose bones are still growing. Along with cesium-137, a radioactive isotope with a half-life of 30 years, it may contaminate agricultural land for generations.

In 1952, Mike's thermonuclear explosion had deposited high levels of fallout in the ocean near the test site. The following year, New York milk tainted with strontium-90 was linked to the detonation of fission devices at the Nevada Test Site. But the unanticipated size of Shrimp's yield, the volume of coral reef and seafloor displaced, and the stronger-than-expected winds combined to produce an amount of fallout that surprised everyone involved with the Bravo test. Thousands of scientists and military personnel, watching the detonation from ships thirty miles away, were forced to head belowdecks and remain there for hours amid stifling heat. O'Keefe and his men had to be rescued by helicopter. They taped bedsheets over every inch of their bodies before fleeing the bunker, trying to avoid any contact with the fallout.

Seaplanes evacuated an Air Force weather station 153 miles from ground zero, and two days after the blast, the Navy removed scores of villagers from the island of Rongelap in the Marshall Islands. The villagers had seen the brilliant explosion 115 miles in the distance but had no idea the white dust that later fell from the sky might be harmful. It settled on their skin and in their hair. They walked barefoot in it for hours. About eighty of them got radiation sickness. Many also developed burns, lesions, and discolored pigment from beta particles emitted by the fallout on their skin. And Rongelap was blanketed with so much of the white dust that the island's residents weren't allowed to return there for three years.

The dangers of fallout were inadvertently made public when a Japanese fishing boat, the *Lucky Dragon,* arrived at its home port of Yaizu two weeks after the Bravo test. The twenty-three crew members were suffering from radiation poisoning. Their boat was radioactive—and so was the tuna they'd caught. The *Lucky Dragon* had been about eighty miles from the detonation, well outside the military's exclusion zone. One of the crew died, and the rest were hospitalized for eight months. The incident revived memories of Hiroshima and Nagasaki, sparking protests throughout Japan. When Japanese doctors asked for information about the fallout, the American government refused to provide it, worried that details of the blast might reveal the use of lithium deuteride as the weapon's fuel. Amid worldwide outrage about the radiation poisonings, the Soviet Union scored a propaganda victory. At the United Nations, the Soviets called for an immediate end to nuclear testing and the abolition of all nuclear weapons. Although sympathetic to those demands, President Eisenhower could hardly agree to them, because the entire national security policy of the United States now depended on its nuclear weapons.

THE FATE OF THE *LUCKY DRAGON* was soon forgotten. But the Bravo test led to an alarming realization at the weapons laboratories, the Pentagon, and the White House: fallout from a hydrogen bomb was likely to kill far more people than the initial blast. At the Atomic Energy Commission, the fallout pattern from the Bravo test was superimposed on a map of the northeastern United States, with Washington, D.C., as ground zero. According to the map, if a similar 15-megaton groundburst hit the nation's capital, everyone in Washington, Baltimore, and Philadelphia could receive a fatal dose of radioactivity. Residents of New York City might be exposed to 500 roentgens, enough to kill more than half of them. People as far north as Boston or even the Canadian border might suffer from radiation poisoning.

The British prime minister, Winston Churchill, was disturbed by the results of the Bravo test. Churchill had been an early proponent of defending Western Europe with nuclear weapons, not conventional forces. In 1952, Great Britain detonated a fission device, and its first atomic bomb, the "Blue Danube," had recently been transferred to the Royal Air Force. The Blue Danube, with a yield of about 16 kilotons, now appeared minuscule and obsolete. "With all its horrors, the atomic bomb did not seem unmanageable as an instrument of war," Churchill told the House of Commons a month after the Bravo test. "But the hydrogen bomb carries us into dimensions which . . . have been confined to the realms of fancy and imagination." A small, densely populated nation would be especially vulnerable to such a weapon. Churchill asked William Strath, an official at the Central War Plans Secretariat, to lead a top secret study of what a thermonuclear attack would do to the United Kingdom.

Strath submitted his report in the spring of 1955, and its findings were grimly apocalyptic. According to the latest intelligence, a Soviet assault on the United Kingdom would have three main objectives: destroy the airfields hosting U.S. or British bombers, destroy the British government, and "render the UK useless as a base for any form of military operations." That would be relatively easy to accomplish. "The heat flash from one hydrogen bomb," the Strath report noted, "would start in a built-up area anything up to 100,000 fires, with a circumference of between 60 to 100 miles." If the Soviets detonated ten hydrogen bombs along the west coast of the United Kingdom, the normally prevailing winds would blanket most of the country with fallout. Almost one third of the British population would be killed or wounded immediately. Most of the nation's farmland would be rendered unusable for two months, some of the most productive land might "be lost for a long time," and supplies of drinking water would be contaminated. In a section entitled "Machinery of Control," the report warned that society

would collapse in much of the United Kingdom. Local military commanders would be granted "drastic emergency powers," and civil order might
have to be restored through the use of "rough and ready methods." Strath
urged the government to release accurate information about the hydrogen
bomb so that families could build fallout shelters, store canned foods, and
prepare for the worst.

The Strath report was kept secret, its plea for greater openness ignored.
Instead, Prime Minister Churchill ordered the BBC not to broadcast news
about the hydrogen bomb that might discourage the public. Telling the
truth about nuclear weapons, the British government feared, would weaken
popular support for a defense policy that required them. Churchill had already chosen a different sort of response to the threat of thermonuclear
war. "Influence depended on possession of force," he told advisers, not long
after the Bravo test. Great Britain would develop its own hydrogen bombs.
Once again, the appeal of the H-bomb lay in its symbolism. "We must do
it," Churchill explained. "It's the price we pay to sit at the top table."

The Eisenhower administration also struggled with how to handle public fears of the hydrogen bomb. The head of the Atomic Energy Commission, Lewis Strauss, waited almost a year to acknowledge that the Bravo
test had spread lethal fallout across thousands of square miles. While
Strauss tried to limit publicity about the dangers of fallout, the Federal
Civil Defense Administration (FCDA) conveyed a different message. Val
Peterson, the head of the FCDA, advised every American family to build
an underground shelter "right now." Once the Soviets deployed their hydrogen bombs, Peterson added, "we had all better dig and pray."

The FCDA had argued for years that people could survive a nuclear
attack by seeking some form of shelter. An animated character, Bert the
Turtle, urged America's schoolchildren to "duck and cover"—to hide under
classroom tables or desks as soon as they saw the flash of an atomic bomb.
And a widely distributed civil defense pamphlet, "Survival Under Atomic
Attack," provided useful and encouraging household tips:

YOUR CHANCES OF SURVIVING AN ATOMIC ATTACK ARE
BETTER THAN YOU MAY HAVE THOUGHT. . . . EVEN A LITTLE

MATERIAL GIVES PROTECTION FROM FLASH BURNS, SO BE
SURE TO DRESS PROPERLY. . . . WE KNOW MORE ABOUT
RADIOACTIVITY THAN WE DO ABOUT COLDS. . . . KEEP A
FLASHLIGHT HANDY. . . . AVOID GETTING WET AFTER
UNDERWATER BURSTS. . . . BE CAREFUL NOT TO TRACK
RADIOACTIVE MATERIALS INTO THE HOUSE. . . .

The destructive power of the hydrogen bomb forced civil defense planners to alter their recommendations. Suburban families were advised to remain in underground shelters, windowless basements, or backyard trenches for four or five days after a thermonuclear blast. Urban families were told to leave their homes when an attack seemed likely. Eisenhower's plans for an interstate highway system were justified by the need to evacuate American cities during wartime. Val Peterson called for concrete pipelines to be laid alongside the new roads, so that refugees could sleep inside them and avoid fallout. "Duck and cover," one journalist noted, was being replaced by a new civil defense catchphrase: "Run for the hills."

Hoping to boost morale and demonstrate that a nuclear war would not mean the end of the world, the FCDA staged Operation Alert 1955 during June of that year. It was the largest civil defense drill in the nation's history. During a mock attack, sixty-one cities were struck by nuclear weapons, ranging in yield from 20 kilotons to 5 megatons. As air-raid sirens warned that Soviet bombers were approaching, fifteen thousand federal employees were evacuated from Washington, D.C. The president and members of his Cabinet were driven to secret locations and remained there for three days. Throughout the United States, families climbed into shelters or rehearsed their escape routes. In New York City, everyone was cleared from the streets and kept indoors for ten minutes, bracing for the arrival of a Soviet hydrogen bomb—whose ground zero, for some reason, would be the corner of North 7th Street and Kent Avenue in Williamsburg, Brooklyn.

Administration officials called Operation Alert a great success. The secretary of the Treasury, George M. Humphrey, said that the exercise demonstrated the United States would "be able to take it" and "recover surprisingly rapidly." Out of a U.S. population of about 165 million, only 8.2 million people would be killed and 6.6 million wounded—and more than half of those casualties would be in New York City. If everybody took the right precautions, Val Peterson assured reporters, "we might—ideally—escape without losing any lives from fall-out."

In a public statement, Eisenhower said the drill had brought him "great encouragement." But at a Cabinet meeting, he summed up his feelings in one word: "staggering." On the first day of Operation Alert, the president had declared martial law, transferring power from the state governments to half a dozen Army field commands. The casualty figures released to the press vastly understated the likely impact of a thermonuclear war. A new word had entered the lexicon of nuclear war planning: megadeath. It was a unit of measurement. One megadeath equaled one million fatalities—and the nation was bound to suffer a great many megadeaths during a thermo-nuclear war. On January 23, 1956, President Eisenhower recorded in his diary the results of a top secret study on what would really happen after a Soviet attack:

> The United States experienced practically total economic collapse, which could not be restored to any kind of operative conditions under six months to a year. . . . Members of the Federal government were wiped out and a new government had to be improvised by the states. . . . It was calculated that something on the order of 65% of the population would require some sort of medical care, and in most instances, no opportunity whatsoever to get it. . . .

Eisenhower was infuriated by the Army's constant requests for more troops to help defend Western Europe. "It would be perfect rot to talk about ship-ping troops abroad when fifteen of our cities were in ruins," he told an aide. The Army would be needed at home to deal with the chaos. "You can't have this kind of war," Eisenhower said at a national security meeting a couple of years later. "There just aren't enough bulldozers to scrape the bodies off the streets."

PART THREE

ACCIDENTS
WILL HAPPEN

Acceptable Risks

Three weeks after winning an Oscar for best actor in *The Philadelphia Story*, Jimmy Stewart enlisted in the Army. It was the spring of 1941, long before Pearl Harbor, but Stewart thought the United States would soon be at war and wanted to volunteer his skills as a pilot. The previous year he'd failed an Army physical for being ten pounds underweight. This time he passed, just barely, and at the age of thirty-two entered the Army Air Corps as a private. By 1944, Major Jimmy Stewart was flying the lead plane in bombing runs over Germany. While other Hollywood stars like Ronald Reagan and John Wayne managed to avoid combat during the Second World War, Stewart gained a reputation in the Eighth Air Force as a "lucky" commander who always brought his men back from dangerous missions. He flew dozens of those missions, shunned publicity about his wartime exploits, and never discussed them with his family. "He always maintained a calm demeanor," a fellow officer recalled. "His pilots had absolute faith in him and were willing to follow him wherever he led."

After the war, Colonel Jimmy Stewart returned to Hollywood and starred in a series of well-received films—*It's a Wonderful Life, Harvey, Rear Window*—while serving in the Air Force Reserve. Deeply concerned about the Soviet threat, he decided to make a movie about the importance of America's nuclear deterrent. Stewart visited SAC headquarters in 1952 to discuss the idea with General Curtis LeMay. The two had met in England, while serving in the Eighth Air Force. LeMay gave the project his blessing, worked closely with the screenwriter Beirne Lay, Jr., and allowed the film to be shot at SAC air bases.

Strategic Air Command was released in 1955. It tells the story of a major league infielder, Dutch Holland, whose baseball career is interrupted when the Air Force returns him to active duty. For most of the film, Holland, played by Jimmy Stewart, is torn between his desire to enjoy civilian life and his duty to protect the United States from a Soviet attack. *Strategic Air Command* focuses on the hardships endured by SAC crews, the dangers of their job, the sacrifices that overseas assignments imposed on their families. Even the bubbly, upbeat cheer of the actress June Allyson, playing Stewart's wife, is briefly deflated by the challenges of being married to a SAC officer. Shot in Technicolor and wide-screen VistaVision, featuring spectacular aerial photography and a rousing score, the film offers an unabashed celebration of American airpower. "She's the most beautiful thing I've ever seen in my life," Stewart says, at his first glimpse of a new B-47 bomber.

More compelling than the film's plot, the onscreen chemistry between Allyson and Stewart, or the footage of SAC bombers midflight was the performance of actor Frank Lovejoy as General Ennis C. Hawkes. Gruff, unsentimental, fond of cigars, unwilling to tolerate mistakes, and ready at a moment's notice to unleash a massive retaliation, the character was a flattering, barely fictionalized portrait of Curtis LeMay. It was another demonstration of SAC's skill at public relations. LeMay had already become a national celebrity, a living symbol of American might. *Life* magazine described him as the "Toughest Cop of the Western World" and repeated an anecdote about his boundless self-confidence. Warned that if he didn't put out his cigar, the bomber he was sitting in might explode, LeMay replied: "It wouldn't dare."

The premiere of *Strategic Air Command* was held in New York's Times Square, with searchlights piercing the sky and more than three thousand guests, including Air Force generals, politicians, businessmen, Hollywood starlets, and Arthur Godfrey in the lobby of the Paramount Theatre, broadcasting the event live on television. Godfrey was a popular radio and television personality, as well as a good friend of LeMay's, who frequently promoted SAC during his shows. *Strategic Air Command* was one of the highest-grossing films of 1955. It fit the national mood. And a few years later Jimmy Stewart, as a member of the Air Force Reserve, was appointed deputy director of operations at SAC, one of the top jobs at the command.

Behind the public facade of invincibility, questions were secretly being raised at the Pentagon about whether SAC could survive a Soviet attack. LeMay had spent years building air bases overseas—in Greenland, Great Britain, Spain, Morocco, Saudi Arabia, and Japan—where his planes would begin and end their bombing missions against the Soviet Union. But a study by the RAND analyst Albert Wohlstetter suggested that a surprise attack on those bases could knock SAC out of the war with a single blow, leaving the United States defenseless. LeMay felt confident that sort of thing would never happen, that his reconnaissance planes, flying daily missions along the borders of the Soviet Union, would detect any unusual activity. Nevertheless, he accelerated SAC's plans to base most of its aircraft in the United States and to refuel them en route to Soviet targets. And LeMay continued to demand perfection from his officers. "Training in SAC was harder than war," one of them recalled. "It might have been a relief to go to war."

The town of Rhinelander, Wisconsin, became one of SAC's favorite targets, and it was secretly radar bombed hundreds of times, thanks to the snow-covered terrain resembling that of the Soviet Union. By 1955, the SAC battle plan called for 180 bombers, most of them departing from the United States, to strike the Soviet Union within twelve hours of receiving an emergency war order from the president. But constant training and the radar bombing of Wisconsin could not guarantee how aircrews would perform in battle with real weapons. During tests at the Bikini atoll in May 1956, the Air Force got its first opportunity to drop a hydrogen bomb from a plane. The 3.8-megaton weapon was carried by one of SAC's new, long-range B-52 bombers, with the island of Namu as its target. The B-52 safely escaped the blast—but the bombardier had aimed at the wrong island, and the H-bomb missed Namu by four miles.

Withdrawing most of SAC's planes from overseas bases did not, however, eliminate the threat of a surprise attack. The continental United States—code-named the "zone of the interior" (ZI)—was also considered highly vulnerable to Soviet bombers. During Operation Tailwind, 94 SAC bombers tested the air defense system of the ZI by approaching from Canada, flying at night, and using electronic countermeasures to simulate a Soviet raid. Only 7 of the planes were spotted by radar and "shot down." The failure to intercept the other 87 planes raised the possibility of a devastating attack on the United States. Now that the Soviets had hydrogen bombs and jet bombers, the Joint Chiefs of Staff recommended a large investment in America's air defense and early-warning system. General LeMay strongly disagreed with that proposal, arguing that in the nuclear age it made little sense to waste money "playing defense." If the Soviets launched an attack with 200 bombers and American forces somehow managed to shoot down 90 percent of those planes, the United States would still be hit by at least 20 H-bombs, if not more.

Instead of air defense, LeMay wanted every available dollar to be spent on more bombs and more bombers for the Strategic Air Command—so that Soviet planes could be destroyed before they ever left the ground. His stance gained support in Congress after the Soviet Union demonstrated its new, long-range jet bomber, the Bison, at Moscow's "Aviation Day" in 1955. Ten Bisons flew past the reviewing stand, turned around, flew past it again in a new formation—and tricked American observers into thinking that the Soviet Air Force had more than 100 of the planes. The CIA predicted that within a few years the Soviets would be able to attack the United States with 700 bombers. Democrats in the Senate, led by presidential hopeful Stuart Symington, claimed that the Soviets would soon have more long-range bombers than the United States, raised fears of a "bomber gap," and accused the Eisenhower administration of being weak on defense. "It is clear that the United States and its allies," Symington warned, "may have lost control of the air." Defying Eisenhower, Congress voted to appropriate an extra $900 million for new B-52s. The Soviet Union's bluff had an unintentional effect: it widened the bomber gap, much to the benefit of the United States. By the end of the decade, the Soviet Union had about 150 long-range bombers—and the Strategic Air Command had almost 2,000.

DESPITE SERIOUS DOUBTS THAT the United States could ever be protected against a nuclear attack, work began on an air defense and early-warning system. At the very least, the Joint Chiefs concluded, such a system would "provide a reasonable degree of protection for the essential elements of the war-making capacity"—SAC bases, naval bases, command centers, and nuclear weapon storage sites in the ZI. The Army erected batteries of Nike antiaircraft missiles to defend military installations and American cities. The Navy obtained radar-bearing "picket ships" and built "Texas towers" to search for Soviet bombers approaching over the ocean. The picket ships lingered about five hundred miles off the coast of the United States; the Texas towers were moored to the seafloor, like oil platforms, closer to shore. The Air Force assembled squadrons of jet fighter-interceptors, like the F-89 Scorpion, and developed its own antiaircraft missile, the BOMARC—infuriating the Army, which had traditionally controlled the nation's antiaircraft weapons.

More important, the Air Force started to build a Distant Early Warning (DEW) Line of radar stations two hundred miles north of the Arctic Circle. Stretching from the Aleutian Islands off Alaska, across Canada, to Greenland, the DEW Line was supposed to scan the polar route from the Soviet Union and provide at least two hours' warning of an attack. It was later extended west to Midway Island in the Pacific and east to Mormond Hill in Scotland, a distance of about twelve thousand miles. Its construction required the transport of almost half a million tons of building material into the Arctic, where thousands of workers labored in temperatures as low as –70 degrees Fahrenheit. A sense of urgency pervaded the effort; the United States seemed completely unprotected against Soviet planes carrying hydrogen bombs. Begun in February 1955, construction of the DEW Line's fifty-seven Arctic radar stations—some of them featuring radio antennae forty stories high, airstrips more than a mile long, and housing for the civilian and Air Force personnel who manned the facilities around the clock—was largely completed in about two and a half years.

Through an agreement with the Canadian government, the North

American Air Defense Command (NORAD) was organized in 1957, with its headquarters in Colorado Springs, Colorado. NORAD's mission was to provide early warning of an attack and mount a defense against it. If Soviet bombers were detected approaching North American airspace, fighter-interceptors would be sent to shoot them down as far as possible from the United States. Antiaircraft missiles would be fired at enemy planes that managed to get past the interceptors—first BOMARC missiles, then Nike. Coordinating the many elements of the system during an attack would be an extraordinarily complex task. Signals would be arriving from picket ships, Texas towers, DEW Line sites, airborne radars. Hundreds of Soviet bombers might have to be spotted and followed, their positions sent to antiaircraft batteries and fighter bases separated by thousands of miles. During the Second World War, Army radar operators had tracked enemy planes and used shared information about their flight paths verbally. That sort of human interaction would be impossible if large numbers of high-speed bombers approached the United States from different directions. The Air Force proposed a radical solution: automate the system and transfer most of its command-and-control functions to machines.

"The computerization of society," the technology writer Frank Rose later observed, was essentially a "side effect of the computerization of war." America's first large-scale electronic digital computer, ENIAC, had been built during the 1940s to help the Army determine the trajectory of artillery and antiaircraft shells. The war ended before ENIAC was completed, and its first official use was to help Los Alamos with early calculations for the design of a thermonuclear weapon. Los Alamos later relied on the more advanced MANIAC computer and its successor, MANIAC II, for work on the hydrogen bomb. Driven by the needs of weapon designers and other military planners, the U.S. Department of Defense was soon responsible for most of the world's investment in electronic computing.

At the Massachusetts Institute of Technology (MIT), researchers concluded that the Whirlwind computer, originally built for the Navy as a flight simulator, could be used to automate air defense and early-warning tasks. Unlike computers that took days or weeks to perform calculations, the Whirlwind had been designed to operate in real time. After extensive testing by the Air Force, an updated version of the Whirlwind was chosen to serve as the heart of the Semi-Automatic Ground Environment (SAGE)—a centralized command-and-control system that linked early-warning radars directly to antiaircraft missiles and fighter-interceptors, that not only processed information in real time but also transmitted it, that replaced manpower with technology on a scale reminiscent of pulp science fiction. It was the first computer network.

Built during roughly the same years as the DEW Line, SAGE consisted of twenty-four "direction centers" and three "combat centers" scattered throughout the United States. The direction centers were enormous four-story, windowless blockhouses that housed a pair of AN/FSQ-7 computers, the first mainframes produced by IBM. They were the largest, fastest, and most expensive computers in the world. Each of them contained about 25,000 vacuum tubes and covered about half an acre of floor space.

Analog signals from early-warning radar sites were converted into digital bits and sent via AT&T's telephone lines to SAGE direction centers, where the huge computers decided whether an aircraft was friend or foe. If it appeared to be an enemy bomber, the computers automatically sent details about its flight path to the nearest missile batteries and fighter planes. Those details were also sent to NORAD headquarters. Human beings would decide whether or not to shoot down the plane. But that decision would be based on information gathered, sorted, and analyzed by machines. In many respects SAGE created the template for the modern computer industry, introducing technologies that would later become commonplace: analog to digital conversion, data transmission over telephone lines, video monitors, graphic displays, magnetic core memory, duplexing, multiprocessing, large-scale software programming, and the light gun, a handheld early version of the mouse. The attempt to create a defense against Soviet bombers helped to launch a technological revolution.

Although dubious about the usefulness of SAGE, General LeMay thought that SAC's command-and-control system needed to be improved, as well. He wanted to know where all his planes were, at all times. And he wanted to speak with all his base commanders at once, if war seemed imminent. It took years to develop those capabilities.

When SAC's Strategic Operational Control System (SOCS) was first unveiled in 1950, its Teletype messages didn't travel from one base to another with lightning speed. During one early test of the system, they were received almost five hours after being sent. And it could take as long as half an hour for the American Telephone and Telegraph Company to make the SOCS circuits operable. That sort of time lag would make it hard to respond promptly to a Soviet attack. Transmission rates gradually improved, and the system enabled LeMay to pick up a special red telephone at SAC headquarters in Omaha, dial a number, gain control of all the circuits, and make an announcement through loudspeakers at every SAC base in the United States. The introduction of single-sideband radio later allowed him to establish voice communications with SAC's overseas base commanders—and with every one of its bomber pilots midair. The amount of information constantly streaming into SAC headquarters, from airplanes and air bases throughout the world, led to the creation of an automated command-and-control system that used the same IBM mainframes developed for SAGE. The system was supposed to keep track of SAC's bombers, in real time, as they flew missions. But until the early 1960s, the information displayed at SAC headquarters stubbornly remained anywhere from an hour and a half to six hours behind the planes.

All of these advances in command and control could prove irrelevant, however, if SAC's commander didn't survive a Soviet first strike. General LeMay's attitude toward civil defense was much the same as his view of air defense. "I don't think I would put that much money into holes in the ground to crawl into," he once said. "I would rather spend more of it on offensive weapons systems to deter war in the first place." Nevertheless, the plans for SAC's new headquarters building included an enormous command bunker. It extended three levels underground and could house about eight hundred people for a couple of weeks. One of its most distinctive features was a wall about twenty feet high, stretching for almost fifty yards, that was covered by charts, graphs, and a map of the world. The map showed the flight paths of SAC bombers. At first, airmen standing on ladders moved the planes by hand; the information was later projected onto movie screens. A long curtain could be opened and closed by remote control, hiding or revealing different portions of the screens. It gave the underground command center a hushed, theatrical feel, with rows of airmen sitting at computer terminals beneath the world map and high-ranking officers observing it from a second-story, glass-enclosed balcony.

While ordinary families were encouraged to dig fallout shelters in their backyards, America's military and civilian leadership was provided with elaborate, top secret accommodations. Below the East Wing at the White House, a small bomb shelter had been constructed for President Roosevelt during the Second World War, in case the Nazis attacked Washington, D.C. That shelter was expanded by the Truman administration into an underground complex with twenty rooms. The new bunker could survive the airburst of a 20-kiloton atomic bomb. But the threat of Soviet hydrogen bombs made it seem necessary to move America's commander in chief someplace even deeper underground. At Raven Rock Mountain in southern Pennsylvania, about eighty miles from the White House and six miles from Camp David, an enormous bunker was dug out of solid granite. Known as Site R, it sat about half a mile inside Raven Rock and another half a mile below the mountain's peak. It had power stations, underground water reservoirs, a small chapel, clusters of three-story buildings set within vast caverns, and enough beds to accommodate two thousand high-ranking officials from the Pentagon, the State Department, and the National Security Council. Although the bunker was huge, so was the competition for space in it; for years the Air Force and the other armed services disagreed about who should be allowed to stay there.

The president could also find shelter at Mount Weather, a similar facility in the Blue Ridge Mountains, near the town of Berryville, Virginia. Nicknamed "High Point," the bunker was supposed to ensure the "continuity of government." It would house Supreme Court justices and members of the Cabinet, as well as hundreds of officials from civilian agencies. In addition to making preparations for martial law, Eisenhower had secretly given nine prominent citizens the legal authority to run much of American society after a nuclear war. Secretary of Agriculture Ezra Taft Benson had agreed to serve as administrator of the Emergency Food Agency; Harold Boeschenstein, the president of the Owens Corning Fiberglas Company, would lead the Emergency Production Agency; Frank Stanton, the president of CBS, would head the Emergency Communications Agency; and Theodore F. Koop, a vice president at CBS, would direct the Emergency Censorship Agency. High Point had its own television studio, from which the latest updates on the war could be broadcast nationwide. Patriotic messages from Arthur Godfrey and Edward R. Murrow had already been prerecorded to boost the morale of the American people after a nuclear attack.

Beneath the Greenbrier Hotel in White Sulphur Springs, West Virginia, a bunker was built for members of the Senate, the House of Representatives, and hundreds of their staff members. Known as Project Greek Island, it had blast doors that weighed twenty-five tons, separate assembly halls in which the House and Senate could meet, decontamination showers, and a garbage incinerator that could also serve as a crematorium. A bunker was later constructed for the Federal Reserve at Mount Pony, in Culpeper, Virginia, where billions of dollars in currency were stored, shrink-wrapped in plastic, to help revive the postwar economy. NATO put its emergency command-and-control center inside the Kindsbach Cave, an underground complex in West Germany with sixty-seven rooms. The cave had previously served as a Nazi military headquarters for the western front.

The British government had planned to rely on a series of deep underground shelters built in London during the Second World War. But the Strath report suggested the need for an alternate seat of government far from the capital. In the Wiltshire countryside, about a hundred miles west of London, a secret abandoned aircraft engine factory hidden inside a limestone mine was turned into a Cold War bunker larger than any in the United States. Known at various times by the code names SUBTERFUGE, BURLINGTON, and TURNSTYLE, it was large enough to provide more than one million square feet of office space and house almost eight thousand people. Although the original plans were scaled down, the completed bunker had miles of underground roads, accommodations for the prime minister and hundreds of other officials, a BBC studio, a vault where the Bank of England's gold reserves could be stored, and a pub called the Rose & Crown.

DURING THE CLOSING MONTHS of the Truman administration, the Joint Chiefs of Staff had once again asked for control of America's nuclear weapons. And once again, their request had been denied. But the threat of Soviet bombers and the logistical demands of the new look strengthened the arguments for military custody. By keeping the weapons at half a dozen large storage sites, the Atomic Energy Commission maintained centralized, civilian control of the stockpile. The arrangement minimized the risk that an atomic bomb could be stolen or misplaced. Those AEC sites, however, had become an inviting target for the Soviet Union—and a surprise attack on them could wipe out America's nuclear arsenal. The Joint Chiefs argued that nuclear weapons should be stored at military bases and that time-consuming procedures to authorize their use should be scrapped. Civilian custody was portrayed as a grave threat to readiness and national security. A democratic principle that seemed admirable in theory could prove disastrous in an emergency.

According to the AEC's rules, if the Strategic Air Command wanted to obtain the nuclear cores of atomic bombs, the president of the United States would have to sign a directive. Local field offices of the AEC and the Department of Defense would have to be notified about that directive. Representatives of those field offices would have to contact the AEC storage sites. Once the proper code words were exchanged, keys would have to be retrieved, storerooms unlocked, nuclear cores carried outside in their metal containers. At best, SAC would get the cores in about twelve minutes. But the process could take a lot longer. Local officials might have to be tracked down on vacation or awakened in the middle of the night. They might have to be persuaded that this was the real thing, not a test.

In June 1953, President Eisenhower approved the shipment of nuclear cores to American naval vessels and overseas bases where the other components of atomic bombs were already stored—and where foreign governments had no authority to dictate how the bombs might be used. Cores were removed from the AEC stockpile, placed under military control, and shipped to sites that met those criteria: American naval vessels and the island of Guam. The following year the Joint Chiefs of Staff asked for permission to store bomb components and nuclear cores at SAC bases. Dispersing the weapons to multiple locations, the Pentagon argued, would make the stockpile much less vulnerable to attack. The AEC didn't object to handing over more nuclear cores. The chairman of the commission, Lewis Strauss, agreed with most of LeMay's strategic views. And the new general manager of the AEC, General Kenneth Nichols, had not only argued for years that the military should control America's atomic bombs, he'd pushed hard for dropping them on Chinese troops during the Korean War.

President Eisenhower allowed the Army, the Navy, and the Air Force to start moving nuclear cores to their own storage sites, both in the United States and overseas. But his faith in military custody had its limits. Eisenhower insisted that the AEC retain control of the cores for all of the nation's hydrogen bombs, even during an emergency. "No active capsule will be inserted in any high yield weapon," the new rules stated, "except with the expressed approval of the AEC custodian and in the custodian's presence." Civilian employees of the Atomic Energy Commission were posted on aircraft carriers, ammunition ships, and air bases where H-bombs were stored. These AEC custodians were supposed to keep the cores securely locked away and hold on to the keys, until the president ordered them to do otherwise. But the Joint Chiefs considered this arrangement inconvenient, largely symbolic, and an insult to the military. Secretary of Defense Charles Wilson agreed, and in 1956 the AEC custodians were withdrawn from ships and air bases. Instead, President Eisenhower allowed the captains of those Navy ships and the commanders of those Air Force bases to serve as "Designated Atomic Energy Commission Military Representatives." And they were given the keys to the nuclear storerooms.

Legally, the hydrogen bombs were still in civilian custody. But in reality, after nearly a decade of unrelenting effort, the military had gained control of America's nuclear weapons. The Navy carried them on ships in the Atlantic, the Pacific, and the Mediterranean. The Strategic Air Command stored them at air bases in the ZI and overseas—at Homestead in Florida and Ellsworth in South Dakota, at Carswell in Texas and Walker in New

Mexico, at Plattsburgh in New York and Castle in California; at Whiteman in Missouri, Schilling in Kansas, and Pease in New Hampshire; at Fairford, Lakenheath, Greenham Common, Brize Norton, and Mildenhall in Great Britain; at Nouasseur, Ben Guerir and Sidi Slimane in French Morocco; at Torrejón and Morón and Zaragoza in Spain; at Kadena in Okinawa; and at least nineteen other locations. Atomic bombs and hydrogen bombs had been liberated from civilian oversight and scattered throughout the world, ready to be assembled by military personnel.

For safety reasons, the nuclear cores and the bomb components were stored separately. On naval vessels they were kept in different rooms. At SAC bases they were kept in different bunkers, shielded by earthen berms and walls ten feet thick. The storage bunkers, known as "igloos," were located near runways, by order of the Joint Chiefs, "to provide rapid availability for use" and reduce "the possibility of capture."

In addition to gaining custody of nuclear weapons, the military also assumed a much larger role in their design. The AEC's authority had been diminished by a revision of the Atomic Energy Act in 1954 and by an agreement signed the previous year with the Department of Defense. A civilian agency that had once enjoyed complete control over the stockpile became, in effect, a supplier of nuclear weapons for the military. The Army, Navy, and Air Force were now customers whose demands had to be met. The AEC labs at Livermore and Los Alamos aggressively competed for weapon contracts, giving the armed services even greater influence over the design process. The rivalry between the two labs became so intense that at times their dislike for each other seemed to exceed their animosity toward the Soviet Union. When Livermore's first three designs for hydrogen bombs proved to be duds, it was an expensive setback to America's weapons program, but a source of much amusement at Los Alamos.

AS THE NUMBER OF storage sites multiplied, so did the need for weapons that were easy to assemble and maintain. Ordinary enlisted men would now be handling hydrogen bombs. The weapons in the stockpile during the mid-1950s were much simpler than the first generation of atomic bombs, and yet they still required a good deal of maintenance. Their batteries were large and bulky and could hold a charge for only about a month. When a battery died, the bomb had to be taken apart. After the battery was recharged, the bomb had to be reassembled, and its electrical system had to be checked. One of the final steps was a test to make sure that all the detonators had been properly connected. If the detonators didn't work, the bomb would be a dud—but if they were somehow triggered by the maintenance procedure, the bomb could go off. On at least three different occasions during the 1950s, the bridgewire detonators of nuclear weapons were set off by mistake during tests of their electrical systems. These accidents occurred during training exercises, and none resulted in the loss of life. But they revealed a worrisome design flaw. An error during routine maintenance or hurried preparations for war could detonate an atomic bomb.

Bob Peurifoy led a team at Sandia that was trying to create a "wooden bomb"—a nuclear weapon that wouldn't require frequent maintenance or testing, that could sit on a shelf for years, completely inert, like a plank of wood, and then be pulled from storage, ready to go. Peurifoy had heard about a new kind of battery that didn't need to be recharged. "Thermal batteries" had been invented by a Nazi rocket scientist, Georg Otto Erb, for use in the V-2 missiles that terrorized Great Britain during the Second World War. Erb revealed how the batteries worked during an interrogation by American intelligence officers after the war. Instead of employing liquid electrolytes, a thermal battery contained solid ones that didn't generate any electricity until they reached a high internal temperature and melted. Peurifoy thought that thermal batteries would be an ideal power source for a nuclear weapon. They were small, rugged, and lightweight. They had a shelf life of at least twenty-five years, if not longer. And they could produce large amounts of current quickly, after being ignited by an electric pulse. The main drawback of a thermal battery, for most civilian applications, was that it couldn't be reused or recharged. But Peurifoy didn't consider that to be much of a problem, since the batteries in a nuclear weapon needed to work only once.

At about the same time that thermal batteries were being added to America's atomic and hydrogen bombs, another important design change was being developed at Los Alamos. A weapon "boosted" by tritium and deuterium gas would use much less fissile material to produce a large explosion. Right before the moment of detonation, these hydrogen gases would be released into the weapon's core. When the core imploded, the gases would fuse, release neutrons, multiply the number of fissions, and greatly increase the yield. And because the fissile core would be hollow and thin, a lesser amount of explosives would be needed to implode it. As a result, boosted weapons could be light and small. The first widely deployed hydrogen bomb, the Mark 17, was about twenty-five feet long and weighed roughly forty thousand pounds. The Mark 17 was so big and heavy that the Air Force's largest bomber could carry only one of them. The Strategic Air Command hoped to replace it eventually with the Mark 28, a boosted weapon. The Mark 28 was eight to twelve feet long, depending on its configuration, and weighed just two thousand pounds. It was small enough and light enough to be delivered by a fighter plane—and a single B-52 could carry at least four of them.

The military advantages of boosted weapons were obvious. But the revolutionary new design raised a number of safety concerns. The nuclear core of a boosted weapon wouldn't be stored separately. It would be sealed inside the weapon, like the pit within a plum. Boosted, "sealed-pit" weapons would be stored fully assembled, their cores already surrounded by high explosives, their thermal batteries ready to ignite. In many respects, they'd be wooden bombs. And that is what could make them, potentially, so dangerous during an accident.

The first sealed-pit weapon scheduled to enter the stockpile was the Genie, a rocket designed for air defense. Conventional antiaircraft weapons seemed inadequate for destroying hundreds of Soviet bombers during a thermonuclear attack. Failing to shoot down a single plane could mean losing an American city. The Air Force believed that detonating atomic warheads in the skies above the United States and Canada would offer the best hope of success—and that view was endorsed in March 1955 by James

R. Killian, the president of MIT, who headed a top secret panel on the threat of surprise attack. At the height of American fears about a bomber gap, atomic antiaircraft weapons promised to counter the Soviet Union's numerical advantage in long-range bombers, much the same way tactical nuclear weapons were supposed to compensate for the Red Army's greater troop strength in Europe. The Genie would be carried by Air Force fighter-interceptors. It had a small, 1.5-kiloton warhead and a solid-fueled rocket engine. Unlike conventional air defense weapons, it didn't need a direct hit to eliminate a target. And it could prove equally useful against a single Soviet bomber or a large formation of them.

Once the enemy was spotted, the fire-control system of the American fighter plane would calculate the distance to the attacker and set the timer of the Genie's warhead. The fighter pilot would launch the Genie, its rocket motor would burn for about two seconds, and the weapon would shoot toward the target at about three times the speed of sound. The Genie's nuclear warhead would detonate when the timer ran out. The ensuing fireball would destroy any aircraft within about one hundred yards, and the blast wave would cause severe damage at an even greater distance. But the burst of radiation released by the explosion would pose the most deadly threat to Soviet aircrews. The Genie could miss its target badly and still prove effective. It had a "lethal envelope" with a radius of about a mile, and the "probability of kill" (PK) within that envelope was likely to be 92 percent. The Soviet aircrew's death from radiation might take as long as five minutes—a delay that made it even more important to fire the Genie as far as possible from urban areas. Detonated at a high altitude, the weapon produced little fallout and didn't lift any debris from the ground to form a mushroom cloud. After the bright white flash, a circular cloud drifted from the point of detonation, forming an immense smoke ring in the sky.

The Air Force wanted the Genie to be deployed by January 1, 1957. But first the Atomic Energy Commission had to determine whether the weapon was safe. Thousands of Genies would be stored at American airfields. Moreover, thousands of Nike missiles, as well as hundreds of BOMARCS, armed with small nuclear warheads, would soon be deployed in and around dozens of American cities. All of these weapons had been designed to explode in the skies above North America; their detonation on the ground would be catastrophic. "The Department of Defense has a most urgent need for information pertaining to the safety of nuclear weapons," an AEC official wrote in a top secret memo, as the Genie's deployment date approached. In the decade or so since the first atomic bomb was dropped, the subject of nuclear weapon safety had received little attention. The bombs had always been stored and transported without their nuclear cores. What would a fuel fire, a high-speed collision, or shrapnel from a nearby explosion do to a sealed-pit weapon? The AEC hurriedly began a series of tests to find out.

Project 56 was the code name for an AEC safety investigation of sealed-pit weapons secretly conducted in a remote valley at the Nevada Test Site. Computers still lacked the processing power to simulate the behavior of a nuclear weapon during an accident, and so actual devices had to be used. Under normal conditions, a sealed-pit weapon would fully detonate when all the explosive lenses surrounding its core went off at once, causing a symmetrical implosion. The AEC's greatest concern was that an imperfect, asymmetrical implosion—caused, for example, by a bullet setting off some of the high explosives—could produce a nuclear yield.

The Project 56 tests focused on what would happen if one of the explosive lenses were set off at a single point. It was thought almost impossible for more than one bullet or more than one piece of shrapnel to strike a weapon at different points, simultaneously, during an accident. The velocity of these high explosives was so fast that a lens would go off within microseconds of being struck, allowing no time for something else to hit. If the weapon's high explosives went off at a single point, the nuclear core might simply blow to pieces, without producing any yield. That's what the scientists of Project 56 hoped to observe: weapons that were "one-point safe." But the core might also implode just enough to cause a nuclear detonation.

Between November 1955 and January 1956, the nuclear components of four weapon designs underwent safety tests in the Nevada desert. Each device was placed inside a small wooden building—and then a single detonator was set off. Three of the designs passed the test; a one-point detonation didn't produce any yield. The fourth design failed the test, surprising everyone with a substantial detonation. The Genie's warhead was among those pronounced one-point safe. But Project 56 revealed that a nuclear detonation wasn't the only danger that a weapon accident might pose. The core of the Genie contained plutonium—and when it blew apart, plutonium dust spread through the air.

The risks of plutonium exposure were becoming more apparent in the mid-1950s. Although the alpha particles emitted by plutonium are too weak to penetrate human skin, they can destroy lung tissue when plutonium dust is inhaled. Anyone within a few hundred feet of a weapon accident spreading plutonium can inhale a swiftly lethal dose. Cancers of the lung, liver, lymph nodes, and bone can be caused by the inhalation of minute amounts. And the fallout from such an accident may contaminate a large area for a long time. Plutonium has a half-life of about twenty-four thousand years. It remains hazardous throughout that period, and plutonium dust is hard to clean up. "The problem of decontaminating the site of [an] accident may be insurmountable," a classified Los Alamos report noted a month after the Genie's one-point safety test, "and it may have to be 'written off' permanently."

The AEC debated whether to remove plutonium from the Genie's core and use highly enriched uranium instead. In one respect, uranium-235 seemed to be safer. It has a half-life of about seven hundred million years—but emits radiation at a much lower rate than plutonium, greatly reducing the inhalation hazard. And yet a Genie with a uranium core had its own risks. Norris Bradbury, the director of Los Alamos, warned the AEC that such a core was "probably <u>not</u> safe against one-point detonation." Given the choice between an accident that might cause a nuclear explosion and one that might send a cloud of plutonium over an American city, the Air Force preferred the latter. Handmade, emergency capability Genies were rushed into production, with cores that contained plutonium.

Once Soviet bombers were within range, air defense weapons like the Genie had to be fired immediately. Any delay in authorizing their use could allow some planes to reach their targets. Toward the end of 1955, the Joint Chiefs of Staff sought permission to use atomic air defense weapons—

without having to ask the president. They argued that if such authority was "predelegated," the military could respond instantly to an attack. Secretary of Defense Wilson backed the Joint Chiefs, arguing that it was "critical" for the Air Force to have some sort of advance authorization.

Harry Truman had insisted, repeatedly, that the president of the United States should be the only person allowed to order the use of a nuclear weapon. But the nature of the Soviet threat had changed, and President Eisenhower had more faith in the discipline of the American military. In April 1956, Eisenhower signed a predelegation order that authorized the use of atomic weapons for air defense within the United States and along its borders. The order took effect the following December, after rules of engagement were approved by the secretary of defense. Those rules allowed American planes to fire Genies at any Soviet aircraft that appeared "hostile." Air Force commanders were granted wide latitude to decide when these nuclear weapons could be used. But the Joint Chiefs demanded "strict command control [sic] of forces engaged in air defense." The Genies had to be kept locked away in storage igloos, never to be flown over the United States, until the nation was under attack.

For years the Department of Defense had refused to discuss where America's nuclear weapons were deployed. "We will neither confirm nor deny" was the standard response whenever a journalist asked if atomic or hydrogen bombs were kept at a specific location. The policy was justified by the need for military secrecy—and yet the desire to avoid controversy and maintain good public relations was just as important. When atomic bombs were first transferred to SAC bases in French Morocco, the French government wasn't told about the weapons. But the deployment of Genies at air bases throughout the United States was announced in an Air Force press release. According to a secret Pentagon memo, publicity that stressed the safety and effectiveness of the new weapon "should have a positive effect on national morale." And information about the Genie's lethal radius might be discouraging for Soviet aircrews.

"The possibility of any nuclear explosion occurring as a result of an accident involving either impact or fire is virtually non-existent," Secretary of Defense Wilson assured the public. His press release about the Genie didn't mention the risk of plutonium contamination. It did note, however, that someone standing on the ground directly beneath the high-altitude detonation of a Genie would be exposed to less radiation than "a hundredth of a dose received in a standard (medical) X-ray." To prove the point, a Genie was set off 18,000 feet above the heads of five Air Force officers and a photographer at the Nevada test site. The officers wore summer uniforms and no protective gear. A photograph, taken at the moment of detonation, shows that two of the men instinctively ducked, two shielded their eyes, and one stared upward, looking straight at the blast. "It glowed for an instant like a newborn sun," *Time* magazine reported, "then faded into a rosy, doughnut-shaped cloud."

IN JANUARY 1957 THE SECRETARY of the Air Force, Donald A. Quarles, visited Sandia to attend briefings on the latest sealed-pit weapons. Quarles left the meetings worried about the safety of the Genie, and he was unusually qualified to pass judgment. He'd served for two years as assistant secretary of defense for research and development, helping to select new weapon systems, guiding the Pentagon's investment in new technologies, and contemplating the future of warfare. He'd also spent a year as president of Sandia, immersed in the minutiae of atomic bombs. Small, wiry, brilliant, and intense, a high school graduate at the age of fifteen who later studied math and physics at Yale, Quarles felt the weight of his job, his place at the very epicenter of the arms race. He rarely took vacations and could often be found at his Pentagon office, late into the night, six or seven days a week. Only a handful of people understood, as well as Quarles did, how America's nuclear weapons worked—and how the military planned to use them.

Within weeks of the briefings for Quarles at Sandia, the Armed Forces Special Weapons Project created a safety board to scrutinize the design of every sealed-pit weapon in development. The Air Force soon commissioned wide-ranging studies of whether a nuclear weapon could be detonated by accident. And in July 1957, Quarles asked the Atomic Energy Commission to conduct the nation's first comprehensive inquiry into the possibilities for increasing the safety of nuclear weapons. The AEC agreed to do it, and a team of Sandia engineers was given the lead role.

One of the inquiry's first tasks was to compile a list of the accidents that had already occurred with nuclear weapons. The list would be useful for predicting not only what might happen to the new sealed-pit designs in the field but also the frequency of mishaps. The Department of Defense didn't always notify the AEC about nuclear weapon accidents—and a thorough accounting of them proved difficult to obtain. The Air Force eventually submitted a list of eighty-seven accidents and incidents that had occurred between 1950 and the end of 1957. Sandia found an additional seven that the Air Force had somehow neglected to include. Neither the Army nor the Navy submitted a list; they'd failed to keep track of their nuclear accidents. More than one third of those on the Air Force list involved "war reserve" atomic or hydrogen bombs—weapons that could be used in battle. The rest involved training weapons. And all of the accidents shed light on the many unforeseeable ways that things could go wrong.

An accident might be caused by a mechanical problem. On February 13, 1950, a B-36 bomber took off from Eielson Air Force Base, about thirty miles south of Fairbanks, Alaska. The crew was on a training mission, learning how to operate from a forward base near the Arctic. The weather at Eielson was windy and snowy, and the ground temperature had risen in the previous few hours. It was about –27 degrees Fahrenheit. Captain Harold L. Barry and sixteen crew members had been fully briefed on the mission: fly to Montana, turn around, go to Southern California, turn again, head north to San Francisco, simulate the release of a Mark 4 atomic bomb above the city, and then land at a SAC base in Fort Worth, Texas. The mission would take about twenty hours.

In the middle of the night, as the B-36 reached an altitude of fifteen thousand feet, it started to lose power. Ice had accumulated on the engines, as well as on the wings and propellers. The crew couldn't see the ice—visibility was poor, due to the darkness, cloud cover, and frost on the windows. But they could hear chunks of ice hitting the plane. It sounded like a hailstorm.

Ice clogged the carburetors, three of the six engines caught fire, and the bomber rapidly lost altitude. Captain Barry managed to guide the plane over the ocean not far from Princess Royal Island, in British Columbia, Canada. He ordered a copilot to open the bomb bay doors and dump the Mark 4. The doors were stuck and wouldn't open. The copilot tried again, the doors opened, and the Mark 4 fell from the plane. Its high explosives detonated three thousand feet above the water, and a bright flash lit the night sky. The bomb did not contain a nuclear core.

Navigating solely by radar, Captain Barry steered the plane back toward land and ordered the crew to bail out. One of the copilots, Captain Theodore Schreier, mistakenly put on a life jacket over his parachute. He was never seen again. The first four men to jump from the plane also vanished, perhaps carried by the wind into the ocean. Captain Barry, the last to go, parachuted safely onto a frozen lake, hiked for miles through deep snow to the coast, and survived, along with the rest of his crew. The abandoned B-36 somehow flew another two hundred miles before crashing on Mount Kologet in British Columbia.

An accident could occur during the loading, unloading, or movement of weapons. On at least four occasions, the bridgewire detonators of Mark 6 atomic bombs fired when the weapons were improperly removed from aircraft. They were training weapons, and nobody got hurt. But with the new sealed-pit weapons, that sort of mistake would cause a full-scale nuclear detonation. At least half a dozen times, the carts used to carry Mark 6 bombs broke away from the vehicles towing them. During one incident, the cart rolled into a ditch; had it rolled in another direction, a classified report noted, "a live Mk6 weapon" would have "plunged over a steep embankment." Dropping a nuclear weapon was never a good idea. Impact tests revealed that when the Genie was armed, it didn't need a firing signal to detonate. The Genie could produce a nuclear explosion just by hitting the ground.

An accident could be made worse by the response. In the early days of the Korean War, amid fears that Japan and Taiwan might be attacked, a B-29 bomber prepared to take off from Fairfield-Suisun Air Force Base in California. It was ten o'clock at night. The mission was considered urgent, its cargo top secret—one of the nine Mark 4 atomic bombs being transferred

to Guam, at President Truman's request. The cores would be airlifted separately. Brigadier General Robert F. Travis sat in the cockpit as a high-level
escort for the weapon. Travis had displayed great courage during the Second World War, leading thirty-five bombing missions for the Eighth Air
Force. As the B-29 gained speed, one of its engines failed near the end of
the runway. The bomber lifted off the ground, and then a second engine
failed.

The pilot, Captain Eugene Steffes, tried to retract the landing gear and
reduce drag, but the wheels were stuck, and the plane was heading straight
toward a hill. He put the B-29 into a steep 180-degree turn, hoping to land
at the base. The plane began to stall, with a trailer park directly in its path.
Steffes banked to the left, narrowly missing the mobile homes. The B-29
hit the ground, slid through a field, caught on fire, and broke into pieces.
When it came to a stop, the crew struggled to get out, but the escape
hatches were jammed.

Sergeant Paul Ramoneda, a twenty-eight-year-old baker with the Ninth
Food Service Squadron, was one of the first to reach the bomber. He helped
to pull Steffes from the cockpit. General Travis was found nearby, unconscious on the ground. Ambulances, fire trucks, and police cars soon arrived
at the field, along with hundreds of enlisted men and civilians, many of
them awakened by the crash, now eager to help out or just curious to see
what was going on. The squadron commander, Ray Holsey, told everyone
to get away from the plane and ordered the firefighters to let it burn. Flares
and .50 caliber ammunition had begun to go off in the wreckage, and Holsey was afraid that the five thousand pounds of high explosives in the atomic
bomb would soon detonate. The crowd and the firefighters ignored him.
Holsey, the highest-ranking officer on the scene, ran away as fast as he could.

Sergeant Ramoneda wrapped his baker's apron around his head for protection from the flames and returned to the burning plane, searching for
more survivors. Moments later, the high explosives in the Mark 4 detonated. The blast could be heard thirty miles away. It killed Ramoneda and
five firefighters, wounded almost two hundred people, destroyed all of the
base's fire trucks, set nearby buildings on fire, and scattered burning fuel
and pieces of molten fuselage across an area of about two square miles.

Captain Steffes and seven others on the plane escaped with minor injuries. Twelve crew members and passengers died, including General Travis, in whose honor the base was soon renamed. The Air Force told the press that the B-29 had been on "a long training mission," without mentioning that an atomic bomb had caused the explosion.

An accident could involve more than one weapon. On July 27, 1956, an American B-47 bomber took off from Lakenheath Air Base in Suffolk, England. It was, in fact, on a routine training flight. The plane did not carry a nuclear weapon. Captain Russell Bowling and his crew were scheduled to perform an aerial refueling, a series of touch-and-go landings, and a test of the B-47's radar system. The first three touch-and-go landings at Lakenheath went smoothly. The plane veered off the runway during the fourth and slammed into a storage igloo containing Mark 6 atomic bombs. A SAC officer described the accident to LeMay in a classified telegram:

> The B-47 tore apart the igloo and knocked about 3 Mark Sixes. A/C [aircraft] then exploded showering burning fuel overall. Crew perished. Most of A/C wreckage pivoted on igloo and came to rest with A/C nose just beyond igloo bank which kept main fuel fire outside smashed igloo. Preliminary exam by bomb disposal officer says a miracle that one Mark Six with exposed detonators sheared didn't go. Fire fighters extinguished fire around Mark Sixes fast.

The cores were stored in a different igloo. If the B-47 had struck that igloo instead, tearing it open and igniting it, a cloud of plutonium could have floated across the English countryside.

THE ENGINEERS AT SANDIA knew that nuclear weapons could never be made perfectly safe. Oskar Morgenstern—an eminent Princeton economist, military strategist, and Pentagon adviser—noted the futility of seeking that goal. "Some day there will be an accidental explosion of a nuclear weapon," Morgenstern wrote. "The human mind cannot construct something that is infallible . . . the laws of probability virtually guarantee such an accident." Every nation that possessed nuclear weapons had to confront the inherent risk. "Maintaining a nuclear capability in some state of readiness is fundamentally a matter of playing percentages," a Sandia report acknowledged. In order to reduce the danger, weapon designers and military officials wrestled with two difficult but interconnected questions: What was the "acceptable" probability of an accidental nuclear explosion? And what were the technical means to keep the odds as low as possible?

The Army's Office of Special Weapons Developments had addressed the first question in a 1955 report, "Acceptable Military Risks from Accidental Detonation of Atomic Weapons." It looked at the frequency of natural disasters in the United States during the previous fifty years, quantified their harmful effects according to property damage and loss of life—and then argued that accidental nuclear explosions should be permitted on American soil at the same rate as similarly devastating earthquakes, floods, and tornadoes. According to that formula, the Army suggested that the acceptable probability of a hydrogen bomb detonating within the United States should be 1 in 100,000 during the course of a year. The acceptable risk of an atomic bomb going off was set at 1 in 125.

After Secretary of the Air Force Quarles expressed concern about the safety of sealed-pit weapons, the Armed Forces Special Weapons Project began its own research on acceptable probabilities. The Army had assumed that the American people would regard a nuclear accident no differently from an act of God. An AFSWP study questioned the assumption, warning that the "psychological impact of a nuclear detonation might well be disastrous" and that "there will likely be a tendency to blame the 'irresponsible' military and scientists." Moreover, the study pointed out that the safety of nuclear weapons already in the American stockpile had been measured solely by the risk of a technical malfunction. Human error had been excluded as a possible cause of accidents; it was thought too complex to quantify. The AFSWP study criticized that omission: "The unpredictable behavior of human beings is a grave problem when dealing with nuclear weapons."

In 1957 the Armed Forces Special Weapons Project offered a new set of acceptable probabilities. For example, it proposed that the odds of a hydrogen bomb exploding accidentally—from all causes, while in storage, during the entire life of the weapon—should be one in ten million. And the lifespan of a typical weapon was assumed to be ten years. At first glance, those odds made the possibility of a nuclear disaster seem remote. But if the United States kept ten thousand hydrogen bombs in storage for ten years, the odds of an accidental detonation became much higher—one in a thousand. And if those weapons were removed from storage and loaded onto airplanes, the AFSWP study proposed some acceptable probabilities that the American public, had it been informed, might not have found so acceptable. The odds of a hydrogen bomb detonating by accident, every decade, would be one in five. And during that same period, the odds of an atomic bomb detonating by accident in the United States would be about 100 percent.

All of those probabilities, acceptable or unacceptable, were merely design goals. They were based on educated guesses, not hard evidence, especially when human behavior was involved. The one-point safety of a nuclear weapon seemed like a more straightforward issue. It would be determined by phenomena that were quantifiable: the velocity of high explosives, the mass and geometry of a nuclear core, the number of fissions that could occur during an asymmetrical implosion. But even those things were haunted by mathematical uncertainty. The one-point safety tests at Nevada Test Site had provided encouraging results, and yet the behavior of a nuclear weapon in an "abnormal environment"—like that of a fuel fire ignited by a plane crash—was still poorly understood. During a fire, the high explosives of a weapon might burn; they might detonate; or they might burn and then detonate. And different weapons might respond differently to the same fire, based on the type, weight, and configuration of their high explosives. For firefighting purposes, each weapon was assigned a "time factor"—the amount of time you had, once a weapon was engulfed in flames, either to put out the fire or to get at least a thousand feet away from it. The time factor for the Genie was three minutes.

Even if a weapon could be made fully one-point safe, it might still detonate by accident. A glitch in the electrical system could potentially arm a bomb and trigger all its detonators. Carl Carlson, a young physicist at Sandia, came to believe that the design of a nuclear weapon's electrical system was the "real key" to preventing accidental detonations. The heat of a fire might start the thermal batteries, release high-voltage electricity into the X-unit, and then set off the bomb. To eliminate that risk, heat-sensitive fuses were added to every sealed-pit weapon. At a temperature of 300 degrees Fahrenheit, the fuses would blow, melting the connections between the batteries and the arming system. It was a straightforward, time-honored way to interrupt an electrical circuit, and it promised to ensure that a high temperature wouldn't trigger the detonators. But Carlson was still worried that in other situations a firing signal could still be sent to a nuclear weapon by accident or by mistake.

A strong believer in systems analysis and the use of multiple disciplines to solve complex questions, Carlson thought that adding heat-sensitive fuses to nuclear weapons wasn't enough. The real safety problem was more easily stated than solved: bombs were dumb. They responded to simple electrical inputs, and they had no means of knowing whether a signal had been sent deliberately. In the cockpit of a SAC bomber, the T-249 control box made it easy to arm a weapon. First you flicked a toggle switch to ON, allowing power to flow from the aircraft to the bomb. Then you turned a knob from the SAFE position either to GROUND or to AIR, setting the height at which the bomb would detonate. That was all it took—and if somebody forgot to return the knob to SAFE, the bomb would remain armed, even after the power switch was turned off. Writing on behalf of Sandia and the other weapon labs, Carlson warned that an overly simplistic electrical system increased the risk of a full-scale detonation during an accident: "a weapon which requires only the receipt of intelligence from the delivery system for arming will accept and respond to such intelligence whether the signals are intentional or not."

The need for a nuclear weapon to be safe and the need for it to be reliable were often in conflict. A safety mechanism that made a bomb less likely to explode during an accident could also, during wartime, render it more likely to be a dud. The contradiction between these two design goals was succinctly expressed by the words "always/never." Ideally, a nuclear weapon would always detonate when it was supposed to—and never detonate when it wasn't supposed to. The Strategic Air Command wanted bombs that were safe and reliable. But most of all, it wanted bombs that worked. A willingness to take personal risks was deeply embedded in SAC's institutional culture. Bomber crews risked their lives every time they flew a peacetime mission, and the emergency war plan missions for which they trained would be extremely dangerous. The crews would have to elude Soviet fighter planes and antiaircraft missiles en route to their targets, survive the blast effects and radiation after dropping their bombs, and then somehow find a friendly air base that hadn't been destroyed. They would not be pleased, amid the chaos of thermonuclear warfare, to learn that the bombs they dropped didn't detonate because of a safety device.

Civilian weapon designers, on the other hand, were bound to have a different perspective—to think about the peacetime risk of an accident and err on the side of *never*. Secretary of the Air Force Quarles understood the arguments on both sides. He worried constantly about the Soviet threat. And he had pushed the Atomic Energy Commission to find methods of achieving "a higher degree of nuclear safing." But if compromises had to be made between always and never, he made clear which side would have to bend. "Such safing," Quarles instructed, "should, of course, cause minimum interference with readiness and reliability."

The Optimum Mix

A super long-distance intercontinental multistage ballistic rocket was launched a few days ago," the Soviet Union announced during the last week of August 1957. The news didn't come as a surprise to Pentagon officials, who'd secretly monitored the test flight with help from a radar station in Iran. But the announcement six weeks later that the Soviets had placed the first man-made satellite into orbit caught the United States off guard—and created a sense of panic among the American people. *Sputnik 1* was a metallic sphere, about the size of a beach ball, that could do little more than circle the earth and transmit a radio signal of "beep-beep." Nevertheless, it gave the Soviet Union a huge propaganda victory. It created the impression that "the first socialist society" had surpassed the United States in missile technology and scientific expertise. The successful launch of *Sputnik 2*, on November 3, 1957, seemed even more ominous. The new satellite weighed about half a ton; rocket engines with enough thrust to lift that sort of payload could be used to deliver a nuclear warhead. *Sputnik 2* also carried the first animal to orbit the earth, a small dog named Laika—evidence that the Soviet Union was planning to put a man in space. Although the Soviets boasted that Laika lived for a week in orbit, wearing a little space suit, housed in a pressurized compartment with an ample supply of food and water, she actually died within a few hours of liftoff.

Democrats in Congress whipped up fears of Soviet missiles and attacked the Eisenhower administration for allowing the United States to fall behind. The Democratic Advisory Council said that President Eisenhower had "weakened the free world" and "starved the national defense." Henry "Scoop" Jackson, a Democratic senator from Washington, called *Sputnik* "a devastating blow to U.S. prestige." Lyndon Baines Johnson, the Senate majority leader, scheduled hearings to investigate what had gone wrong with America's defense policies. Johnson's staff director, George Reedy, urged him "to plunge heavily" into the missile controversy, suggesting that it could "blast the Republicans out of the water, unify the Democratic Party, and elect you President." Another Democratic senator, John F. Kennedy, later accused Eisenhower of putting "fiscal security ahead of national security" and made the existence of a "missile gap" one of the central issues in his presidential campaign.

The Democratic effort to create anxiety about a missile gap was facilitated by Nikita Khrushchev, first secretary of the Communist Party of the Soviet Union. In a series of public comments over the next few years, Khrushchev belittled the American military and bragged about his nation's technological achievements:

The United States does not have an intercontinental missile, otherwise it would also have easily launched a satellite of its own. . . . Now we are capable of directing a rocket to any part of the earth and, if need be, with a hydrogen warhead . . . it is not a mere figure of speech when we say we have organized serial production of intercontinental ballistic rockets . . . let the people abroad know it, I am making no secret of this—that in one year 250 missiles with hydrogen warheads came off the assembly line in the factory we visited. . . . The territory of our country is immense. We have the possibility of dispersing our rocket facilities, of camouflaging them well. . . . Two hundred rockets are sufficient to destroy England, France, and Germany; and three hundred rockets will destroy the United States. At the present time the USSR has so many rockets that mass production has been curtailed and only the newest models are under construction.

Khrushchev had condemned Stalin's crimes in 1956, released political prisoners, gained a reputation as a reformer, and proposed a ban on nuclear weapons in central Europe. But he'd also ordered Soviet troops to invade Hungary and overthrow its government. More than twenty thousand Hungarian citizens were killed by the Red Army, and hundreds more were later executed. The thought of Khrushchev in command of so many long-range missiles seemed chilling.

President Eisenhower tried to calm the hysteria about Soviet missiles and address the criticism that his administration had become passive, timid, and out of touch. He felt confident that large increases in defense spending were unnecessary—and that the Strategic Air Command had more than enough nuclear weapons to deter the Soviet Union. He was particularly irritated by a secret report submitted to him during the first week of November. A high-level committee led by H. Rowan Gaither, a former president of the Ford Foundation, called for tens of billions of dollars to be spent on new missile programs and a nationwide system of fallout shelters. Eisenhower thought that the Gaither committee had an exaggerated view of the Soviet threat. In a televised speech on November 7, 1957, Eisenhower stressed that there was no reason to panic: the military strength of the free world was much greater than that of the Communists. "It misses the whole point to say that we must now increase our expenditures on all kinds of military hardware and defense," he said, with frustration.

The speech had little effect. On the morning of November 25, Lyndon Johnson opened the Senate hearings by asserting that "we have slipped dangerously behind the Soviet Union in some very important fields," and an influential newspaper columnist described the Gaither report as "just about the grimmest warning" in American history. While working in the Oval Office that day, Eisenhower had a stroke and suddenly found himself unable to speak. A week and a half later, a Vanguard rocket carrying America's first man-made satellite was launched at Cape Canaveral, Florida, before hundreds of reporters and a live television audience. The Vanguard rose about four feet into the air, hesitated, fell back to the launchpad, and exploded.

The Pentagon had good reason to be concerned about the Soviet Union's long-range missiles, regardless of the actual number. A Soviet bomber would approach the United States at about five hundred miles per hour—and the warhead of a Soviet missile would come at about sixteen thousand miles per hour. With luck, a bomber might be shot down. But no technology yet existed to destroy a nuclear warhead, midflight. And a missile attack would give the United States little time to prepare its response. Soviet bombers would take eight or nine hours to reach the most important American targets; Soviet missiles could hit them in thirty minutes or less. Early warning of a ballistic missile attack would be necessary to protect the nation's leadership and ensure that SAC's retaliatory force could get off the ground. That sort of warning, however, might never come. The DEW Line radars had been designed to track enemy aircraft, not missiles, and the Pentagon had no means of detecting ICBMs once they'd been launched.

After *Sputnik*, the Air Force gained swift approval to construct the Ballistic Missile Early Warning System (BMEWS), three huge radars that would spot Soviet missiles heading toward the United States. One of the radars would be built at Thule Air Base, Greenland; another at Clear Air Force Base, Alaska; and the third in the North Yorkshire Moors, England. Until the BMEWS was completed, however, the first sign of a Soviet missile attack would probably be mushroom clouds rising above SAC bases and American cities. Work immediately began on a bomb alarm system that would instantly let the president know when cities and air bases were being destroyed. Hundreds of small, innocuous-looking metal canisters were placed atop buildings and telegraph poles throughout the United States. Optical sensors inside the canisters, according to a classified account of the system, would detect the characteristic flash of a nuclear explosion, "locate precise blast locations, and indicate the intensity and pattern of the attack." At SAC headquarters, green lights dotting a map of the United States would turn red to display each nuclear detonation. The amount of warning time that the Bomb Alarm System could provide was far from ideal, especially if the Soviets managed to synchronize their missile launches, so that all the warheads landed at once—but it seemed better than nothing.

General LeMay had been concerned for years about the threat that missiles could pose to the Strategic Air Command. In 1956, SAC had begun to test a plan that would keep some of its bombers constantly on alert and get them airborne half an hour after being warned of an attack. The logistics of such a "ground alert" were daunting. Crews would need to sleep near the runways and run for their planes the moment that a Klaxon sounded. Bombers would be parked fully loaded with nuclear weapons and fuel; the planes were said to be "cocked," like the hammer of a pistol. Tankers for aerial refueling would be loaded as well and prepared for takeoff. By the fall of 1957, ground alerts had become routine at SAC bases in the United States, Great Britain, and Morocco. And the Strategic Air Command hoped that, within a year, at least one third of its bombers would always be parked beside runways, ready to get off the ground within fifteen minutes.

The successful launch of the two *Sputnik*s created the possibility that, during a missile attack, SAC might not have fifteen minutes to launch the ground alert planes. LeMay had recently been promoted to serve as the vice chief of staff at the Air Force, and his replacement at SAC, General Thomas S. Power, pushed hard for approval of an even bolder tactic: the "airborne alert." Power was widely considered, among fellow officers at SAC, to be a mean son of a bitch. Born in New York City and raised in Great Neck, Long Island, he'd dropped out of high school, worked in construction, returned to high school at the age of twenty, earned a degree, and joined the Army Air Corps in 1928. He later flew the lead plane during the firebombing of Tokyo and served as vice commander at SAC. He often played the role of LeMay's "hatchet man," firing people, enforcing discipline, and making sure that orders were carried out. The two men shared a strategic outlook but had different management styles. LeMay expressed disapproval with a stony silence or a few carefully chosen words; Power yelled and swore at subordinates. The warmth behind LeMay's gruff exterior, the intense devotion to the well-being of his men, was harder to find in his successor. Even LeMay admitted that Power was a sadist, "sort of an autocratic bastard"—and yet "he got things done." Kindness, sensitivity, and a genial disposition were not essential traits for a commander planning to win a nuclear war.

The basic premise of SAC's airborne alert was hard to refute: planes that were already in the air wouldn't be destroyed by missiles that hit bases on the ground. Keeping a portion of the bomber fleet airborne at all times would allow the United States to retaliate after a surprise attack. During an airborne alert, American bombers would take off and fly within striking distance of the Soviet Union. If the planes failed to receive a "Go" code, they'd turn around at a prearranged spot, circle for hours, and then return to their bases. The plan erred on the side of safety—a breakdown in communications between SAC headquarters and one of the bombers would end its mission without any bombs being dropped. The mission would "fail safe," an engineering term for components designed to break without causing harm. The fail-safe measures of an airborne alert could reduce the effectiveness of SAC's nuclear retaliation, once America was at war: bombers that didn't receive a Go code would circle and then return home, leaving their targets untouched. But the alternative—an airborne alert in which crews were ordered to fly to the Soviet Union and bomb it, unless they received some sort of "Don't Go" code from headquarters—could easily start a war by mistake. That sort of mission was bound, at some point, to "fail deadly."

"DAY AND NIGHT, I HAVE a certain percentage of my command in the air," General Power told the press, the week after the second *Sputnik* launch. "These planes are bombed up and they don't carry bows and arrows." The message to the Soviet Union was unmistakable: SAC's ability to retaliate wouldn't be diminished by intercontinental ballistic missiles. But Power was bluffing. The airborne alert existed only on paper, and the United States didn't keep bombers in the air, day and night, ready to strike. Carrying nuclear weapons over populated areas was still considered too dangerous. Designers at the weapons labs had been surprised to hear about SAC's ground alert. Aside from the occasional training exercise, the Atomic Energy Commission had always assumed that hydrogen bombs and atomic bombs would be safely locked away in igloos until the nation was at war. The idea of parking bombers near runways, loaded with nuclear weapons and fuel, had been proposed by LeMay, backed by the Joint Chiefs, and approved by President Eisenhower without input from Los Alamos or Sandia.

An airborne alert would be much riskier. The safety questions about the new sealed-pit weapons hadn't been resolved. And if older weapons were used during an airborne alert, their nuclear cores would have to be placed, before takeoff, into an "in-flight insertion" mechanism. It held the core about a foot outside the sphere of explosives, while the plane was en route to the target—and then pushed the core all the way inside the sphere, using a motor-driven screw, when the bomb was about to be dropped. The contraption made the weapon safer to transport, but not much. Once the core was placed into this mechanism, according to a Sandia report, "nuclear safety is not 'absolute,' it is nonexistent." The odds of a nuclear detonation during a crash or a fire would be about one in seven.

Weapon safety became an ongoing point of contention between the Strategic Air Command and the Atomic Energy Commission. General Power not only wanted to start an airborne alert as soon as possible, he also wanted SAC's ground-alert bombers to take off and land with fully assembled weapons during drills. When the AEC suggested that dummy weapons could be used instead, the Air Force came up with a series of arguments for why that would be "operationally unsuitable." During an emergency, having dummy weapons onboard would "degrade the reaction time to an unacceptable degree," SAC's director of operations argued. They'd hurt "crew morale and motivation," and they were hard to obtain. The typical air base had only seven dummy weapons, SAC claimed, a scarcity that made it necessary to train with real ones. Although the Atomic Energy Commission no longer retained physical possession of the hydrogen bombs stored at SAC bases, it still had legal custody. The AEC refused to allow any fully assembled bombs to be flown on SAC bombers. That prohibition applied to sealed-pit weapons and to older weapons with their cores attached. Crews were permitted, however, to train with fully assembled bombs and to load them onto planes—so long as the planes never left the ground.

SAC's arguments on behalf of an airborne alert were strengthened by the apparent shortcomings in the American missile program. A week be-

fore the launch of *Sputnik 1*, an Atlas long-range missile had failed spec-
tacularly in the sky above Cape Canaveral, Florida. It was the second Atlas
failure of the year. Near the end of the Second World War, the United
States and the Soviet Union had fiercely competed to recruit Nazi rocket
scientists. Although the three leading figures in Germany's V-2 program—
Wernher von Braun, Arthur Rudolph, and Walter Dornberger—were
secretly brought to the United States and protected from war crimes trials,
for almost a decade after the war the Air Force showed little enthusiasm for
long-range missiles. The V-2 had proven to be wildly inaccurate, more effective at inspiring terror in London than hitting specific targets. An intercontinental ballistic missile with the same accuracy as the V-2, fired at the
Soviet Union from an American launchpad, was likely to miss its target by
about one hundred miles. Curtis LeMay thought bombers were more reliable than missiles, more versatile and precise. He wanted SAC to develop
nuclear-powered bombers, capable of remaining airborne for weeks. But as
thermonuclear weapons became small enough and light enough to be
mounted atop a missile, accuracy became less of an issue. An H-bomb
could miss a target by a wide margin and still destroy it. Even LeMay
admitted that an accurate intercontinental ballistic missile would be "the
ultimate weapon."

During the fall of 1957, the United States had six different strategic missiles in development, with rival bureaucracies fighting not only for money
but also for a prominent role in the emergency war plan. On behalf of the
Army, Wernher von Braun's team was developing an intermediate-range
missile, the Jupiter, that could travel 1,500 miles and hit Soviet targets
from bases in Europe. The Air Force was working on an almost identical
intermediate-range missile, the Thor, as well as three long-range missiles—
Atlas, Titan, and Minuteman. The Navy was pursuing its own intermediate-
range missile, the Polaris, having decided not to deploy the Army's Jupiter
in submarines. The interservice rivalry over missiles was exacerbated by the
competition among the defense contractors hoping to build them. The
General Dynamics Corporation lobbied aggressively for Atlas; the Martin
Company, for Titan; Boeing, for Minuteman; Douglas Aircraft, for Thor;
Chrysler, for Jupiter; and Lockheed, for Polaris. President Eisenhower

planned to fund two or three of these missile programs and cancel the rest, based on their merits and the nation's strategic needs. Amid Democratic accusations of a missile gap, Eisenhower agreed to fund all six.

The *Sputnik* launches also complicated America's relationship with its NATO allies. The Soviet Union appeared to have gained a technological advantage, and the United States no longer seemed invincible. NATO ministers began to wonder if an American president really would defend Berlin or Paris, when that could mean warheads landing in New York City within an hour. Khrushchev's boasts about long-range missiles were accompanied by a Soviet "peace campaign" that called for nuclear disarmament and an end to nuclear weapon tests. For years, the World Peace Council, backed by the Soviet Union and Communist China, had been promoting efforts to "Ban the Bomb." The slogan had a strong resonance in Great Britain, Germany, the Netherlands, and France, countries that felt trapped in the middle of an arms race between the superpowers, that had already endured two world wars and now rebelled against preparations for a third. While public opinion in Western Europe increasingly turned against nuclear weapons, the leadership of NATO sought an even greater reliance on them. The French, in particular, had long argued that the United States should cede control of its nuclear weapons based in Europe. Giving the weapons to NATO would allow the alliance to use them quickly in an emergency— and prevent an American president from withholding them, regardless of any last-minute doubts. It would demonstrate that the fate of Europe and the United States were inextricably linked.

In December 1957, President Eisenhower traveled to a NATO summit in Paris, only weeks after his stroke, and announced that the United States would provide its European allies with access to nuclear weapons. He offered to create a separate nuclear stockpile for NATO and build intermediate-range missile sites in NATO countries. The offer stopped short of actually handing over missiles and bombs. The Atomic Energy Act prohibited the transfer of nuclear weapons to a foreign power; custody of the NATO stockpile would have to remain with the United States. The Eisenhower administration tried to strike a balance between physical control and legal custody, between sharing the weapons with allies in a meaningful way and obeying the will of Congress. As plans emerged to put intermediate-range missiles in Great Britain, Italy and Turkey, to store atom bombs and hydrogen bombs and atomic artillery shells at NATO bases throughout Europe, the tricky issue of command and control was resolved with a technical solution. The launch controls of the missiles and the locks on the weapon igloos would require at least two keys—and an American officer would keep one of them.

THE MARK 36 was a second-generation hydrogen bomb. It weighed about half as much as the early thermonuclears—but ten times more than the new, sealed-pit bombs that would soon be mass-produced for SAC. It was a transitional weapon, mixing old technologies with new, featuring thermal batteries, a removable core, and a contact fuze for use against underground targets. The nose of the bomb contained piezoelectric crystals, and when the nose hit the ground, the crystals deformed, sending a signal to the X-unit, firing the detonators, and digging a very deep hole. The bomb had a yield of about 10 megatons. It was one of America's most powerful weapons.

A B-47 bomber was taxiing down the runway at a SAC base in Sidi Slimane, Morocco, on January 31, 1958. The plane was on ground alert, practicing runway maneuvers, cocked but forbidden to take off. It carried a single Mark 36 bomb. To make the drill feel as realistic as possible, a nuclear core had been placed in the bomb's in-flight insertion mechanism. When the B-47 reached a speed of about twenty miles an hour, one of the rear tires blew out. A fire started in the wheel well and quickly spread to the fuselage. The crew escaped without injury, but the plane split in two, completely engulfed in flames. Firefighters sprayed the burning wreckage for ten minutes—long past the time factor of the Mark 36—then withdrew. The flames reached the bomb, and the commanding general at Sidi Slimane ordered that the base be evacuated immediately. Cars full of airmen and their families sped into the Moroccan desert, fearing a nuclear disaster.

The fire lasted for two and a half hours. The high explosives in the Mark 36 burned but didn't detonate. According to an accident report, the hydrogen bomb and parts of the B-47 bomber melted into "a slab of slag material weighing approximately eight thousand pounds, approximately six to eight feet wide and twelve to fifteen feet in length with a thickness of ten to twelve inches." A jackhammer was used to break the slag into smaller pieces. The "particularly 'hot' pieces" were sealed in cans, and the rest of the radioactive slag was buried next to the runway. Sidi Slimane lacked the proper equipment to measure levels of contamination, and a number of airmen got plutonium dust on their shoes, spreading it not just to their car but also to another air base.

The Air Force planned to issue a press release about the accident, stressing that the aircraft fire hadn't led to "explosion of the weapon, radiation, or other unexpected results." The State Department thought that was a bad idea; details about the accident hadn't reached Europe or the United States. "The less said about the Moroccan incident the better," one State Department official argued at a meeting on how much information to disclose. A public statement might be distorted by Soviet propaganda and create needless anxiety in Europe. The Department of Defense agreed to keep the accident secret, although the king of Morocco was informed. When an American diplomat based in Paris asked for information about what had happened at Sidi Slimane, the State Department told him that the base commander had decided to stage a "practice evacuation."

Two weeks after an accident that could have detonated a hydrogen bomb in Morocco, the Department of Defense and the Atomic Energy Commission issued a joint statement on weapon safety. "In reply to inquiries about hazards which may be involved in the movement of nuclear weapons," they said, "it can be stated with assurance that the possibility of an accidental nuclear explosion . . . is so remote as to be negligible."

Less than a month later, Walter Gregg and his son, Walter Junior, were in the toolshed outside their home in Mars Bluff, South Carolina, when a Mark 6 atomic bomb landed in the yard. Mrs. Gregg was inside the house, sewing, and her daughters, Helen and Frances, aged six and nine, were playing outdoors with a nine-year-old cousin. The Mark 6 had a variable yield of anywhere from 8 to 160 kilotons, depending on the type of nuclear core that was used. The bomb that landed in the yard didn't contain a core.

But the high explosives went off when the weapon hit the ground, digging a crater about fifty feet wide and thirty-five feet deep. The blast wave and flying debris knocked the doors off the Gregg house, blew out the windows, collapsed the roof, riddled the walls with holes, destroyed the new Chevrolet parked in the driveway, killed half a dozen chickens, and sent the family to the hospital with minor injuries.

The atom bomb had been dropped by a B-47 en route from Hunter Air Force Base near Savannah, Georgia, to Bruntingthorpe Air Base in Leicestershire, England. The locking pin had been removed from the bomb before takeoff, a standard operating procedure at SAC. Nuclear weapons were always unlocked from their bomb racks during takeoff and landing—in case the weapons had to be jettisoned during an emergency. But for the rest of the flight they were locked to the racks. Bombs were locked and unlocked remotely on the B-47, using a small lever in the cockpit. The lever was attached by a lanyard to the locking pin on the bomb. As the B-47 above South Carolina climbed to an altitude of about fifteen thousand feet, a light on the instrument panel said that the pin hadn't reengaged. The lever didn't seem to be working. The pilot told the navigator, Captain Bruce Kulka, to enter the bomb bay and insert the locking pin by hand.

Kulka couldn't have been thrilled with the idea. The bomb bay wasn't pressurized, the door leading to it was too small for him to enter wearing a parachute, and he didn't know where the locking pin was located, let alone how to reinsert it. Kulka spent about ten minutes in the bomb bay, looking for the pin, without success. It must be somewhere above the bomb, he thought. The Mark 6 was a large weapon, about eleven feet long and five feet in diameter, and as Kulka tried to peek above it, he inadvertently grabbed the manual bomb release for support. The Mark 6 suddenly dropped onto the bomb bay doors, and Kulka fell on top of it. A moment later, the eight-thousand-pound bomb broke through the doors. Kulka slid off it, got hold of something in the open bomb bay, and held on tight. Amid the gust and roar of the wind, about three miles above the small farms and cotton fields of Mars Bluff, he managed to pull himself back into the plane. Neither the pilot nor the copilot realized the bomb was gone until it hit the ground and exploded.

The accident at Mars Bluff was impossible to hide from the press. Although Walter Gregg and his family had no idea what destroyed their home, the pilot of the B-47, unable to communicate with Hunter Air Force Base, told controllers at a nearby civilian airport that the plane had just lost a "device." News of the explosion quickly spread. The state police formed checkpoints to keep people away from the Gregg property, and an Air Force decontamination team arrived to search for remnants of the Mark 6. Unlike the accident at Sidi Slimane, this one couldn't have produced a nuclear yield—and yet it gained worldwide attention and inspired a good deal of fear. "Are We Safe from Our Own Atomic Bombs?" the *New York Times* asked. "Is Carolina on Your Mind?" echoed London's *Daily Mail*. The Soviet Union claimed that a nuclear detonation had been prevented by "sheer luck" and that South Carolina had been contaminated by radioactive fallout.

The Strategic Air Command tried to counter the Soviet propaganda with the truth: there'd never been a risk of nuclear detonation, nor of harmful radioactivity. But SAC also misled reporters. During a segment entitled "'Dead' A-Bomb Hits U.S. Town," Ed Herlihy, the narrator of a popular American newsreel, repeated the official line, telling nervous movie audiences that this was "the first accident of its kind in history." In fact, a hydrogen bomb had been mistakenly released over Albuquerque the previous year. Knocked off balance by air turbulence while standing in the bomb bay of a B-36, the plane's navigator had steadied himself by grabbing the nearest handle—the manual bomb release. The weapon broke through the bomb doors, and the navigator held on to the handle for dear life. The H-bomb landed in an unpopulated area, about one third of a mile from Sandia. The high explosives detonated but did not produce a nuclear yield. The weapon lacked a core.

The Air Force grounded all its bombers after the accident at Mars Bluff and announced a new policy: the locking pins wouldn't be removed from nuclear weapons during peacetime flights. But the announcement failed to dampen a growing antinuclear movement in Great Britain. General Power had inflamed public opinion by telling a British journalist, who'd asked whether American aircraft routinely flew with nuclear weapons above

England, "Well, we did not build these bombers to carry crushed rose pet-als." Members of the opposition Labour Party criticized Prime Minister Harold Macmillan for allowing such flights and demanded an end to them. Macmillan was in a difficult position. For security reasons, SAC wouldn't allow him to reveal that the bombs lacked cores—and wouldn't even let him know when American planes were carrying nuclear weapons in British airspace.

Within weeks of the accident at Mars Bluff, a newly formed organiza-tion, the Campaign for Nuclear Disarmament (CND), led thousands of people on a protest march from London's Trafalgar Square to the British nuclear weapon factory at Aldermaston. The CND rejected the whole con-cept of nuclear deterrence and argued that nuclear weapons were "morally wrong." In preparation for the four-day march, the artist Gerald Holtom designed a symbol for the antinuclear movement. "I drew myself," Holtom recalled, "the representative of an individual in despair, with palms out-stretched outwards and downwards in the manner of Goya's peasant before the firing squad." He placed a circle around the self-portrait, an elongated stick figure, and created an image later known as the peace sign.

The Soviet Union worked hard to focus attention on the dangers of SAC's airborne alert and the possibility of an accidental nuclear war. "Imag-ine that one of the airmen may, even without any evil intent but through nervous mental derangement or an incorrectly understood order, drop his deadly load on the territory of some country," Khrushchev said during a speech. "Then according to the logic of war, an immediate counterblow will follow." Arkady A. Sobolev, the Soviet representative to the United Na-tions, made a similar argument before the Security Council, warning that the "world has yet to see a foolproof system" and that "flights of American bombers bring a grave danger of atomic war." The Soviet concerns may have been sincere. But they also promoted the idea that American bombers were the greatest threat to world peace—not the hundreds of Soviet medium-range missiles aimed at the capitals of Western Europe. Bertrand Russell, among others, had changed his view about whom to blame. Hav-ing once called for the United States to launch a preventive war on the Soviet Union with atomic bombs, Russell now argued that the American air bases in England should be shut down and that Great Britain should unilaterally get rid of its nuclear weapons.

The mental instability of SAC officers became a recurrent theme in Soviet propaganda. According to a Pentagon report obtained by an East German newspaper and discussed at length on Radio Moscow, 67.3 percent of the flight personnel in the United States Air Force were psychoneurotic. The report was a Communist forgery. But its bureaucratic tone, its account of widespread alcoholism, sexual perversion, opium addiction, and marijuana use at SAC seemed convincing to many Europeans worried about American nuclear strategy. And the notion that a madman could deliberately start a world war became plausible, not long after the forgery appeared, when an American mechanic stole a B-45 bomber from Alconbury Air Force Base in England and took it for a joyride. The mechanic, who'd never received flight training, crashed the jet not long after takeoff and died.

A former Royal Air Force officer, Peter George, captured the new zeitgeist about nuclear weapons, the widespread fear of an accidental war, in a novel published amid the debate over SAC's airborne alert. Pulp fiction like *One of Our H Bombs Is Missing* had already addressed some of these themes. But more than 250,000 copies of George's novel *Red Alert* were sold in the United States, and it subsequently inspired a classic Hollywood film. Writing under the pseudonym "Peter Bryant," George described how a deranged American general could single-handedly launch a nuclear attack. The madman's views were similar to those expressed by Bertrand Russell a decade earlier: the United States must destroy the Soviet Union before it can destroy the West. "A few will suffer," the general believes, "but millions will live."

Once the scheme is uncovered, the general's air base is assaulted by the U.S. Army. The president of the United States tries without success to recall SAC's bombers, and the Soviets question whether the impending attack really was a mistake. As an act of good faith, SAC discloses the flight paths of its B-52s so that they can be shot down. After negotiations between the leaders of the two nations and revelations about "the ultimate deterrent"—doomsday weapons capable of eliminating life on earth, to be triggered if the Soviets are facing defeat—all but one of the SAC bombers are shot down or recalled. And so a deal is struck: if the plane destroys a

Soviet city, the president will select an American city for the Soviets to destroy in retaliation. The president chooses Atlantic City, New Jersey. The lone B-52 drops its hydrogen bomb over the Soviet Union—but the weapon misfires and misses its target. Although Atlantic City is saved and dooms-day averted, *Red Alert* marked an important cultural shift. The Strategic Air Command would increasingly be portrayed as a refuge for lunatics and warmongers, not as the kind of place where you'd find Jimmy Stewart.

General Power was unfazed by protest marches in Great Britain, apoca-lyptic fears, criticism in the press, freak accidents, strong opposition at the AEC, President Eisenhower's reluctance, and even doubts about the idea expressed by LeMay. Power wanted an airborne alert. The decision to au-thorize one would be made by Eisenhower. The phrase "fail safe" had been removed from Air Force descriptions of the plan. The word "fail" had the wrong connotations, and the new term didn't sound so negative: "positive control." With strong backing from members of Congress, SAC proposed a test of the airborne alert. B-52s would take off from bases throughout America, carrying sealed-pit weapons. At a White House briefing in July 1958, Eisenhower was told that "the probability of any nuclear detonation during a crash is essentially zero." The following month, he gave tentative approval for the test. But the new chairman of the AEC, John A. McCone, wanted to limit its scale. McCone thought that the bombers should be per-mitted to use only Loring Air Force Base in Maine—so that an accident or the jettison of a weapon would be likely to occur over the Atlantic Ocean, not the United States. During the first week of October, President Eisen-hower authorized SAC to take off and land at Loring, with fully assembled hydrogen bombs. The flights secretly began, and SAC's airborne alert was no longer a bluff.

FRED IKLÉ COMPLETED HIS RAND REPORT, "On the Risk of an Accidental or Unauthorized Nuclear Detonation," two weeks after Eisen-hower's decision. Iklé's top secret clearance had gained him access to the latest safety studies by Sandia, the Armed Forces Special Weapons Project, and the Air Force Special Weapons Center. He'd read accident reports, met with bomb designers at Sandia, immersed himself in the technical literature on nuclear weapons. He'd discussed the logistical details of SAC's airborne alert, not only with the officers who would command them but also with the RAND analysts who'd come up with the idea in 1956. Iklé's report was the first thorough, wide-ranging, independent analysis of nuclear weapon safety in the United States—and it did not confirm the optimistic assurances that President Eisenhower had just been given.

"We cannot derive much confidence from the fact that <u>no</u> unauthorized detonation has occurred to date," Iklé warned: "the past safety record means nothing for the future." The design of nuclear weapons had a learning curve, and he feared that some knowledge might come at a high price. Technical flaws and malfunctions could be "eliminated readily once they are discovered . . . but it takes a great deal of ingenuity and intuition to prevent them beforehand." The risk wasn't negligible, as the Department of Defense and the Air Force claimed. The risk was impossible to determine, and accidents were likely to become more frequent in the future. During Air Force training exercises in 1957, an atomic bomb or a hydrogen bomb had been inadvertently jettisoned once every 320 flights. And B-52 bombers seemed to crash at a rate of about once every twenty thousand flying hours. According to Iklé's calculations, that meant SAC's airborne alert would lead to roughly twelve crashes with nuclear weapons and seven bomb jettisons every year. "The paramount task," he argued, "is to learn enough from minor incidents to prevent a catastrophic disaster."

Even more worrisome than the technical challenges were the risks of human error and sabotage. Iklé noted that the Air Force's shortage of trained weapon handlers "sometimes makes it necessary to entrust unspecialized personnel with complex tasks on nuclear weapons." A single mistake—or more likely, a series of mistakes—could cause a nuclear detonation. Safety measures like checklists, seals that must be broken before knobs can be turned, and constant training might reduce the odds of human error. But Iklé thought that none of those things could protect against a threat that seemed like the stuff of pulp fiction: deliberate, unauthorized attempts to detonate a nuclear weapon. The technical safeguards currently in use could be circumvented by "someone who knew the workings of the fuzing and firing mechanism." On at least one occasion, a drunken enlisted man had overpowered a guard at a nuclear storage site and attempted to gain access to the bombs. "It can hardly be denied that there is a risk of unauthorized acts," Iklé wrote—and figuring out how to stop them remained "one of the most baffling problems of nuclear weapon safety."

With help from the psychiatrist Gerald J. Aronson, Iklé outlined some of the motivations that could prompt someone to disobey orders and set off a nuclear weapon. The risk wasn't hypothetical. About twenty thousand Air Force personnel worked with nuclear weapons, and in order to do so, they had to obtain a secret or a top secret clearance. But they didn't have to undergo any psychiatric screening. In fact, "a history of transient psychotic disorders" no longer disqualified a recruit from joining the Air Force. A few hundred Air Force officers and enlisted men were annually removed from duty because of their psychotic disorders—and perhaps ten or twenty who worked with nuclear weapons could be expected to have a severe mental breakdown every year.

In an appendix to the report, Aronson offered "a catalogue of derange-ment" that seemed relevant to nuclear safety. The most dangerous disorders involved paranoia. Aronson provided a case history of the type of officer who needed to be kept away from atomic bombs:

> A 23-year-old pilot, a Lieutenant, had difficulty in maintaining social contacts, fearful of disapproval and anxious to please. A few hours after he had to say "Sir" to someone, he was overwhelmed with fantasies of tearing that person apart. . . . He felt like exploding when in crowded restaurants; this feeling lessened when hostile fantasies of "tearing the place apart" occurred. He suffered anxiety attacks every two weeks or so in connection with hostile or sexual thoughts. To him flying was excit-ing, rewarding in its expression of hostility and power.

In another case history, Aronson described an Air Force captain who devel-oped full-blown paranoid schizophrenia at the age of thirty-three. His behavior became "grandiose, inappropriate, and demanding." He considered himself the real commander of his unit and gave orders to a superior officer. At the height of these delusions, the captain nevertheless managed to log "eight hours on the B-25 [bomber] with unimpaired proficiency."

Aronson thought that an unauthorized nuclear detonation would have a unique appeal to people suffering from a variety of paranoid delusions— those who were seeking fame, who believed themselves "invested with a special mission that sets them apart from society," who wanted to save the world and thought that "the authorities . . . covertly wish destruction of the enemy but are uncomfortably constrained by outmoded convention." In addition to the mentally ill, officers and enlisted men with poor impulse control might be drawn to nuclear weapons. The same need for immediate gratification that pyromaniacs often exhibited, "the desire to see the tangible result of their own power as it brings about a visual holocaust," might find expression in detonating an atomic bomb. A number of case histories in the report illustrated the unpredictable, often infantile nature of impulse-driven behavior:

[An] assistant cook improperly obtained a charge of TNT in order to blast fish. He lighted it with a cigarette. As he was examining it to make sure it was ignited, the explosion took place. The man was blown to pieces.

"Private B and I each found a rifle grenade. We carried them back to our tent. Private K told us that we had better not fool with the grenades and to get rid of them. Private B said, 'What will happen if I pull this pin?' Then the grenade exploded."

A Marine found a 37-millimeter dud and turned it in to the Quartermaster tent. Later, a sergeant came into the tent and saw the dud. In disregard of orders and safety, he aimed the shell at a hole in the wooden floor of the tent and dropped it. He commented that he would make "a pretty good bombardier." He dropped the shell at least six times. Finally, inevitably, it exploded. The sergeant was killed and 2 others were injured.

Even relatively harmless motives—such as the urge to defy authority, the desire to show off, and "the kind of curiosity which does not quite believe the consequences of one's own acts"—could cause a nuclear detonation.

The unauthorized destruction of a city or a military base would be disastrous, and Iklé addressed the question of whether such an event could precipitate something even worse. Nikita Khrushchev had recently claimed that "an accidental atomic bomb explosion may well trigger another world war." The scenario seemed far-fetched but couldn't be entirely dismissed. Amid the chaos following an explosion, it might not be clear that the blast had been caused by a technical malfunction, human error, a madman, or saboteurs. The country where the detonation occurred might think that a surprise attack had begun and retaliate. Its adversary, fearing that sort of retaliation, might try to strike first.

Iklé believed that, at the moment, the risk of accidental war was small. He thought the leadership of both the United States and the Soviet Union would carefully investigate the cause of a single detonation before launching an all-out attack. And he felt confident that America could withstand the loss of a major city without much long-term social or economic upheaval. But an unauthorized detonation in the United States or Western Europe could have "unfortunate political consequences." It could fuel support for disarmament and neutrality, increase opposition to American bases overseas, weaken the NATO alliance, and facilitate "a peaceful expansion of the Soviet sphere of influence." Indeed, the military and political benefits to the Soviet Union would be so great that it might be tempted to sabotage an American weapon.

"The U.S. defense posture could be substantially strengthened by nuclear weapon safeguards that would give a nearly absolute guarantee against unauthorized detonations," Iklé concluded. He urged that more research be conducted on nuclear weapon safety, that new safety mechanisms be added to warheads and bombs, that Air Force personnel be screened more thoroughly for psychiatric problems. And he offered one solution to the problem of unauthorized use that seemed obvious, yet hadn't been tried: put combination locks on nuclear weapons. That way they could be detonated only by someone who knew the right code. None of these measures, however, could make weapons perfectly safe, and the United States had to be prepared for accidental or unauthorized detonations.

In a subsequent RAND report, Iklé offered suggestions on how to minimize the harm of an accidental nuclear explosion:

> If such an accident occurred in a remote area, so that leakage to the press could be prevented, no information ought to be made public. . . . If the accident has been compromised and public statements become necessary, they should depict the accident as an occurrence which has no bearing on the safety of other weapons. In some circumstances it might be treated as if it had been an experiment. . . . Internally, of course, information about the accident should not be suppressed.

An official "board of inquiry" should be established, headed by military experts and prominent politicians, as an "important device for temporizing." Ideally, the board would take a few months to reach any conclusions:

> During this delaying period the public information program should provide the news media with all possible news about rehabilitation and relief. There is always a strong and continued interest in such news after a disaster. Within a relatively short time the interest in rehabilitation tends to crowd out reports about destruction and casualties.

If an American bomber launched an unauthorized attack on the Soviet Union, Iklé argued that the United States should "avoid public self-implication and delay the release of any details about the accident." Then it should begin secret diplomatic negotiations with the Soviets. Amid the tensions of the Cold War, thanks to a military strategy that made the United States and its NATO allies completely dependent on nuclear weapons, Iklé's thinking reached a perverse but logical conclusion. After the accidental detonation of an atomic bomb, the president might have a strong incentive to tell the Soviet Union the truth—and lie to the American people.

FRED IKLÉ'S REPORTS ON nuclear weapon safety were circulated at the highest levels of the Air Force and the Department of Defense. But his work remained unknown to most weapon designers and midlevel officers. In 1958, Bob Peurifoy was a section supervisor at Sandia, working on the electrical system of the W-49 warhead. Development of the W-49 was considered urgent; lightweight and thermonuclear, the warhead would be mounted atop Atlas, Thor, and Jupiter ballistic missiles. During the rush to bring it into production, Peurifoy was surprised to read some of the language in a preliminary safety study of the W-49. "This warhead, like all other warheads investigated, can be sabotaged, i.e., detonated full-scale," the Air Force study mentioned, in passing. "Any person with knowledge of the warhead electrical circuits, a handful of equipment, a little time, and the intent, can detonate the warhead." Peurifoy hadn't spent much time thinking about nuclear weapon safety; his job at Sandia was making sure that bombs would explode. But the ease with which someone could intentionally set off a W-49 seemed incredible to him. It was unacceptable. And so was the Air Force's willingness to rely on physical security—armed guards, perimeter fences, etc.—as the only means of preventing an unauthorized detonation.

Peurifoy decided that the warhead should have an internal mechanism to prevent sabotage or human error from detonating it. Plans were already being made to incorporate a trajectory-sensing switch into the new Mark 28 bomb, and Peurifoy thought that the W-49 should contain one, too. The switch responded to changes in gravitational force. It contained an accelerometer—a small weight atop a spring, enclosed in a cylinder. As g-forces increased, the weight pushed against the spring, like a passenger pushed back against the seat of an accelerating car. When the spring fully compressed, an electrical circuit closed, allowing the weapon to be detonated. In the Mark 28 bomb, the switch would be triggered by the sudden jerk of the parachutes opening. Peurifoy wanted to use the strong g-forces of the warhead's descent to close the circuit. A trajectory-sensing switch would prevent the weapon from going off while airmen handled or serviced it, since the necessary g-forces wouldn't be present on the ground. A skilled technician could circumvent the switch, but its placement deep within the warhead would make an act of sabotage trickier and more time consuming.

The Army didn't like Peurifoy's idea. A switch that operated as the W-49 warhead fell to earth, the Army contended, might somehow make the weapon less reliable. The Army also didn't like what Sandia engineers called the switch: a "handling safety device" or a "goof-proofer." Both terms implied that Army personnel were capable of making mistakes. Peurifoy thought that sort of thinking was sheer stupidity. But the Army ran the Jupiter missile program and had the final say on its fuzing and firing system. Under enormous pressure to complete the design of the warhead's electrical system, Peurifoy said "to hell with it" and simply reversed the direction of the tiny springs. Now the switch would respond to the g-forces of the missile soaring upward—not those of the warhead coming down—and the Army couldn't complain that its control of the fuzing and firing system was being challenged. To avoid any hurt feelings, Sandia renamed the switch, calling it an "environmental sensing device."

At Los Alamos, the issue of one-point safety gained renewed attention as SAC began to fly planes with fully assembled weapons. A young physicist, Robert K. Osborne, began to worry that a number of the bombs carried during airborne alerts might not be one-point safe. Among those raising the greatest concern was the Mark 28, a hydrogen bomb with a yield of about 1 megaton. Any problem with the Mark 28 would be a big problem. The Air Force had chosen it not only to become the most widely deployed bomb in the Strategic Air Command, but also to serve as a "tactical" weapon for NATO fighter planes. In December 1957 the Fission Weapon Committee at Los Alamos had struggled to define what "one-point safe" should mean, as a design goal. If the high explosives of a weapon detonated at a single point, some fission was bound to occur in the core before it blew apart—and so "zero yield" was considered unattainable.

A naval officer at the Armed Forces Special Weapons Project suggested that the yield of a nuclear weapon accident should never exceed the explosive force produced by four pounds of TNT. The four-pound limit was based on what might happen during an accident at sea. If a nuclear detonation with a yield larger than four pounds occurred in the weapon storage area of an aircraft carrier, it could incapacitate the crew of the engine room and disable the ship. Los Alamos proposed that the odds of a yield greater than four pounds should be one in one hundred thousand. The Department of Defense asked for an even stricter definition of one-point safety: odds of one in a million.

The likelihood of a Mark 28 producing a large detonation during a plane crash or a fire, Osborne now thought, was uncomfortably high. The one-point safety tests conducted in Nevada had assumed that the most vulnerable place on a weapon was the spot where a detonator connected to a high-explosive lens. That's why the tests involved setting off a single lens with a single detonator. But Osborne realized that nuclear weapons had an even more vulnerable spot: a corner where three lenses intersected on the surface of the high-explosive sphere. If a bullet or a piece of shrapnel hit one of those corners, it could set off three lenses simultaneously. And that might cause a nuclear detonation a lot larger than four pounds of TNT.

A new round of full-scale tests on the Mark 28 would be the best way to confirm or disprove Osborne's theory. But those tests would be hard to perform. Ignoring strong opposition from the Joint Chiefs of Staff, President Eisenhower had recently declared a moratorium on American nuclear testing. He was tired of the arms race and seeking a way out of it. He increasingly distrusted the Pentagon's claims. "Testing is essential for weapons development," General Charles H. Bonesteel had argued, succinctly expressing the military's view, "and rapid weapons development is essential for keeping ahead of the Russians." But Eisenhower doubted that the United States was at risk of falling behind. The Air Force and the CIA had asserted that the Soviet Union would have five hundred long-range ballistic missiles by 1961, outnumbering the United States by more than seven to one. Eisenhower thought those numbers were grossly inflated; top secret flights over the Soviet Union by U-2 spy planes had failed to detect anywhere near that number of missiles.

Despite the Democratic attacks on his administration and dire warnings of a missile gap, President Eisenhower thought it was more important to preserve the secrecy of America's intelligence methods than to refute his critics. The nuclear test ban was voluntary, but he hoped to make it permanent. In the words of one adviser, Eisenhower had become "entirely preoccupied by the horror of nuclear war." The harsh criticism of his policies—not just by Democrats but also by defense contractors—led Eisenhower to believe in the existence of a "military-industrial complex," a set of powerful interest groups that threatened American democracy and sought new weapons regardless of the actual need.

The Air Force was in a bind. The hydrogen bomb scheduled to become its workhorse, deployed at air bases throughout the United States and Europe, might be prone to detonate during a plane crash. And full-scale tests of the weapon would violate the nuclear moratorium that Eisenhower had just promised to the world. While the Air Force and the Atomic Energy Commission debated what to do, the Mark 28 was grounded.

Norris Bradbury, the director of Los Alamos, recommended that a series of tests be secretly conducted. The tests would be called "hydronuclear experiments." Mark 28 cores containing small amounts of fissile material would be subjected to one-point detonations—and more fissile material would be added with each new firing, until a nuclear yield occurred. The largest yield that might be produced would be roughly equivalent to that of one pound of TNT. None of these "experiments" would be done without the president's approval. Eisenhower was committed to a test ban, disarmament, and world peace—but he also understood the importance of the Mark 28. He authorized the detonations, accepting the argument that they were "not a nuclear weapon test" because the potential yields would be so low. At a remote site in Los Alamos, without the knowledge of most scientists at the laboratory, cores were detonated in tunnels fifty to one hundred feet beneath the ground. The tests confirmed Osborne's suspicions. The Mark 28 wasn't one-point safe. A new core, with a smaller amount of plutonium, replaced the old one. And the bomb was allowed to fly again.

FOUR YEARS AFTER ANNOUNCING the policy of massive retaliation, Secretary of State John Foster Dulles was having doubts. "Are we becoming prisoners of our strategic concept," he asked at a meeting of Eisenhower's military advisers, "and caught in a vicious circle?" A defense policy that relied almost entirely on nuclear weapons had made sense in the early days of the Cold War. The alternatives had seemed worse: maintain a vast and expensive Army or cede Western Europe to the Communists. But the Soviet Union now possessed hydrogen bombs and long-range missiles—and the American threat of responding to every act of Soviet aggression, large or small, with an all-out nuclear attack no longer seemed plausible. It could force the president to make a "bitter choice" during a minor conflict and risk the survival of the United States. Dulles urged the Joint Chiefs of Staff to come up with a new strategic doctrine, one that would give the president a variety of military options and allow the United States to fight small-scale, limited wars.

General Maxwell D. Taylor, the Army's chief of staff, wholeheartedly agreed with Dulles. For years Taylor had urged Eisenhower to spend more money on conventional forces and adopt a strategy of "flexible response." The Army hated the idea of serving merely as a trip wire in Europe; it still wanted to bring the battle back to the battlefield. The need for a more flexible policy was backed by RAND analysts and by a young Harvard professor, Henry A. Kissinger, whose book *Nuclear Weapons and Foreign Policy* had become an unlikely bestseller in 1957. Kissinger thought that a nuclear war with the Soviet Union didn't have to end in mutual annihilation. Rules of engagement could be tacitly established between the superpowers. The rules would forbid the use of hydrogen bombs, encourage a reliance on tactical nuclear weapons, and declare cities more than five hundred miles from the battlefield immune from attack. Unlike massive retaliation, a strategy of "graduated deterrence" would allow the leadership on both sides to "pause for calculation," pull back from the abyss, and reach a negotiated settlement. Kissinger believed that in a limited war—fought with a decentralized command structure that let local commanders decide how and when to use their nuclear weapons—the United States was bound to triumph, thanks to the superior "daring and leadership" of its officers.

The Navy had also begun to question the thinking behind massive retaliation. It was about to introduce a new weapon system, the Polaris submarine, that might revolutionize how nuclear wars would be fought.

The sixteen missiles carried by each Polaris were too inaccurate to be aimed at military targets, such as airfields. But their 1-megaton warheads were ideal for destroying "soft" targets, like cities. The Polaris would serve best as a retaliatory, second-strike weapon—leading the Navy to challenge the whole notion of striking the Soviet Union first.

Admiral Arleigh Burke, the chief of naval operations, became an outspoken proponent of "finite deterrence." Instead of maintaining thousands of strategic weapons on Air Force bombers and land-based missiles to destroy every Soviet military target—a seemingly impossible task—Burke suggested that the United States needed hundreds, not thousands, of nuclear warheads. They could be carried by the Navy's Polaris submarines, hidden beneath the seas, invulnerable to a surprise attack. And they would be aimed at the Soviet Union's major cities, in order to deter an attack. Placing the nation's nuclear arsenal on submarines would eliminate the need for split-second decision making during a crisis. It would give the president time to think, permit the United States to apply force incrementally, and reduce the threat of all-out nuclear war. Burke argued that a strategy of massive retaliation no longer made sense: "Nobody wins a suicide pact." A decade earlier the Navy had criticized the Air Force for targeting Soviet cities, calling the policy "ruthless and barbaric." Now the Navy claimed that was the only sane and ethical way to ensure world peace.

As the debate over nuclear strategy grew more heated within the Eisenhower administration and in the press, General Curtis LeMay showed absolutely no interest in limited war, graduated deterrence, finite deterrence—or anything short of total victory. The United States should never enter a war, LeMay felt, unless it intended to win. And a counterforce policy that targeted the Soviet Union's nuclear assets was far more likely to prevent a war than a strategy that threatened its cities. Unlike "the public mind" that feared a nuclear holocaust, he argued, "the professional military mind" in both nations worried more about preserving the ability to fight, about losing airfields, missile bases, command centers. SAC claimed that a counterforce strategy was also "the most humane method of waging war . . . since there was no necessity to bomb cities." But that argument was somewhat disingenuous. In order to hit military targets, LeMay acknowledged, "weapons must be delivered with either very high accuracy or very high yield, or both." Because the accuracy of a bomb was less predictable than its yield, he favored the use of powerful weapons. They could miss a target and still destroy it, or destroy multiple targets at once. They would also, unavoidably, kill millions of civilians. LeMay wanted SAC to deploy a hydrogen bomb with a yield of 60 megatons, a bomb more than four thousand times more powerful than the one that destroyed Hiroshima.

BY THE LATE 1950S, the absence of a clear targeting policy and the size of America's stockpile had created serious command-and-control problems. The Army, the Navy, and the Air Force all planned to attack the Soviet Union with nuclear weapons but had done little to coordinate their efforts. Until 1957 the Strategic Air Command refused to share its target list with the other armed services. When the services finally met to compare war plans, hundreds of "time over target" conflicts were discovered—cases in which, for example, the Air Force and the Navy unwittingly planned to bomb the same target at the same time. These conflicts promised to cause unnecessary "overkill" and threaten the lives of American aircrews. The Joint Chiefs of Staff soon recognized that the chaos of war would be bad enough, without competing nuclear war plans to make it worse. They decided that the United States had to develop "atomic coordination machinery"—an administrative system to control what targets would be attacked, who would attack them, which weapons would be used, and how those attacks would be timed. The decision prompted the Army, Navy, and Air Force to battle even more fiercely over who would control that system.

The Air Force wanted a single atomic war plan, run by a centralized command. SAC would head that command—and take over the Navy's Polaris submarines. The Navy was outraged by that idea and joined the other services in offering a counterproposal: the Navy, the Air Force, and NATO should retain separate war plans but coordinate them more efficiently. The issues at stake were fundamental, and basic questions needed to be addressed—should the command structure be centralized or decentralized, should the attack be all out or incremental, should the strategy be counterforce or city busting? The president of the United States, once again, had to decide the best way not only to fight the Soviet Union but also to settle a dispute over nuclear weapons at the Pentagon.

During a meeting at the White House in 1956, President Eisenhower had listened patiently to General Taylor's arguments on behalf of a flexible response. Eisenhower wasn't persuaded that a war could be won without hydrogen bombs. "It was fatuous to think that the U.S. and the U.S.S.R. would be locked into a life and death struggle," he told Taylor, "without using such weapons." Eisenhower thought both sides would use them at once. Four years later, his views remained largely unchanged. If NATO forces were attacked, he said during another White House discussion of limited war, "an all-out strike on the Soviet Union" would be the only "practical" choice. Pausing to negotiate a diplomatic settlement seemed unrealistic; that sort of thing happened only in novels like *Red Alert*. Confronted with the choice between destroying Soviet military targets or cities, Eisenhower decided that the United States should destroy both. The new targeting philosophy combined elements of Air Force and Navy doctrine. It was called the "optimum mix."

In August 1960, General Nathan Twining, chairman of the Joint Chiefs of Staff, resolved the dispute over how a nuclear war would be planned and controlled. A Joint Strategic Target Planning Staff would be formed. Most of the officers would be drawn from the Air Force, although the other services would be represented. The targeting staff would be based at SAC headquarters in Omaha and led by SAC's commander. The Navy could keep its Polaris submarines, but the aiming points of their missiles would be chosen in Omaha. Twining ordered that a Single Integrated Operational Plan (SIOP) be completed by the end of the year. The SIOP would serve as America's nuclear war plan. The SIOP would spell out precisely when, how, and by whom every enemy target would be struck. And the SIOP would be inflexible. Twining had instructed that "atomic operations must be pre-planned for automatic execution to the maximum extent possible."

The Navy was furious about the new arrangement. Admiral Burke thought it represented a power grab by the Air Force and later accused the Strategic Air Command of using "exactly the same techniques . . . the methods of control" favored by the Communists. And he warned that once the SIOP was adopted, it would be hard to change. "The systems will be laid," Burke told William B. Franke, the secretary of the Navy:

> The grooves will be dug. And the power will be there because the money will be there. The electronic industry and all of those things. We will wreck this country. If we are not careful.

President Eisenhower was unfazed by Burke's critique of the SIOP, its underlying strategy, and its command-and-control machinery. "This whole thing has to be on a completely integrated basis," Eisenhower said. "The initial strike must be simultaneous."

The strategic planning staff gathered in Omaha to write the first SIOP, under tremendous pressure to complete it within four months. Their process would be as rational, impersonal, and automated as possible. The first step was to create a National Strategic Target List. They began by poring through the Air Force's *Bombing Encyclopedia*, a compendium of more than eighty thousand potential targets located throughout the world. The book gave a brief description of each target, its longitude and latitude and elevation, its category—such as military or industrial, airfield or oil refinery—and its "B.E. number," a unique, eight-digit identifier. From that lengthy inventory, twelve thousand candidates in the Soviet Union, the Eastern bloc, and China were selected. A "target weighing system" was adopted to measure their relative importance. Every target was assigned a certain number of points; those with the most points were deemed the most essential to destroy; and the National Strategic Target List, as a whole, was given a total value of five million points. All of this data, the B.E. numbers, the target locations, and the numerical points were fed into SAC's latest IBM computer. What emerged was a series of "desired ground zeros," containing multiple targets, at which America's nuclear weapons would be aimed.

Once the target list was complete and the ground zeros identified, the planners calculated the most efficient way to destroy them. A wide assortment of variables had to be taken into account, including: the accuracy and reliability of different weapon systems, the effectiveness of Soviet air defenses, the impact of darkness or poor weather, and the rate at which low-flying aircraft were likely to crash due to unknown causes, known as the "clobber factor." The Joint Chiefs specified that the odds of a target being destroyed had to be at least 75 percent, and for some targets, the rate of damage assurance was put even higher. Achieving that level of assurance required cross-targeting—aiming more than one nuclear weapon at a single ground zero. After the numbers were crunched, the SIOP often demanded that a target be hit by multiple weapons, arriving from different directions, at different times. One high-value target in the Soviet Union would be hit by a Jupiter missile, a Titan missile, an Atlas missile, and hydrogen bombs dropped by three B-52s, simply to guarantee its destruction.

The SIOP would unfold in phases. The "alert force" would be launched within the first hour, the "full force" in waves over the course of twenty-eight hours. And then the SIOP ended. The Strategic Air Command was responsible for striking most of the ground zeros. "Tactics programmed for the SIOP are in two principal categories," the head of the Joint Chiefs later explained, "the *penetration phase* and the *delivery phase*." SAC would attack the Soviet Union "front-to-rear," hitting air defenses along the border first, then penetrating more deeply into the nation's interior and destroying targets along the way, a tactic called "bomb as you go."

Great Britain's strategic weapons were controlled by the SIOP, as well. The Royal Air Force showed little interest in SAC's ideas about counterforce. The British philosophy of strategic bombing had changed little since the Second World War, and the RAF's Bomber Command wanted to use its nuclear weapons solely for city busting. The SIOP respected the British preference, asking Bomber Command to destroy three air bases, six air defense targets, and forty-eight cities.

George Kistiakowsky, the president's science adviser, visited SAC headquarters in November 1960 to get a sense of how work was proceeding on the SIOP. Kistiakowsky was hardly a peacenik. He'd fled the Soviet Union as a young man, designed the high-explosive lenses for the Trinity device, and later shared the Air Force's concerns about a missile gap. But he was shocked by the destructiveness of the SIOP. The damage levels caused by the alert force alone would be so great that any additional nuclear strikes seemed like "unnecessary and undesirable overkill." Kistiakowsky thought that the full force would deliver enough "megatons to kill 4 and 5 times over somebody who is already dead" and that SAC should be allowed to take "just one whack—not ten whacks" at each Soviet target. Nevertheless, he told Eisenhower, "I believe that the presently developed SIOP is the best that could be expected under the circumstances and that it should be put into effect."

At the beginning of the effort to devise a new war plan, Eisenhower had expressed opposition to any strategy that required "a 100 percent pulverization of the Soviet Union." He could still remember when the Pentagon said the Soviets had no more than seventy targets worth destroying. "There was obviously a limit," he told his national security staff, "a human limit—to the devastation which human beings could endure." On December 2, 1960, Eisenhower approved the SIOP, without requesting any changes.

The SIOP would take effect the following April. It featured 3,729 targets, grouped into more than 1,000 ground zeros, that would be struck by 3,423 nuclear weapons. The targets were located in the Soviet Union, China, North Korea, and Eastern Europe. About 80 percent were military targets, and the rest were civilian. Of the "urban-industrial complexes" scheduled for destruction, 295 were in the Soviet Union and 78 in China. The SIOP's damage and casualty estimates were conservative. They were based solely on blast effects. They excluded the harm that might be caused by thermal radiation, fires, or fallout, which were difficult to calculate with precision. Within three days of the initial attack, the full force of the SIOP would kill about 54 percent of the Soviet Union's population and about 16 percent of China's population—roughly 220 million people. Millions more would subsequently die from burns, radiation poisoning, exposure. The SIOP was designed for a national emergency, when the survival of the United States was at stake, and the decision to launch the SIOP would carry an almost unbearable weight. Once the SIOP was set in motion, it could not be altered, slowed, or stopped.

The SIOP soon became one of the most closely guarded secrets in the United States. But the procedures for authorizing a nuclear strike were kept even more secret. For years the Joint Chiefs had asked not only for custody of America's nuclear weapons but also for the authority to use them. In December 1956 the military had gained permission to use nuclear weapons in air defense. In February 1959 the military had gained custody of all the thermonuclear weapons stored at Army, Navy, and Air Force facilities. The Atomic Energy Commission retained custody of only those kept at its own storage sites. And in December 1959 the military had finally won the kind of control that it had sought since the end of the Second World War. Eisenhower agreed to let high-ranking commanders decide whether to use nuclear weapons, during an emergency, when the president couldn't be reached. He had wrestled with the decision, well aware that such advance authorization could allow someone to do "something foolish down the chain of command" and start an all-out nuclear war. But the alternative would be to let American and NATO forces be overrun and destroyed, if communications with Washington were disrupted.

At first, Eisenhower told the Joint Chiefs that he was "very fearful of having written papers on this matter." Later, he agreed to sign a predelegation order, insisting that its existence never be revealed. "It is in the U.S. interest to maintain the atmosphere that all authority [to use nuclear weapons] stays with the U.S. President without delegation," he stressed. Eisenhower's order was kept secret from Congress, the American people, and NATO allies. It made sense, as a military tactic. But it also introduced an element of uncertainty to the decision-making process. The SIOP was centralized, inflexible, and mechanistic. The predelegation order was exactly the opposite. It would rely on individual judgments, made in the heat of battle, thousands of miles from the White House. Under certain circumstances, a U.S. commander under attack with conventional weapons would be allowed to respond with nuclear weapons. Eisenhower knew all too well that delegating presidential authority could mean losing control of whether, how, and why a nuclear war would be fought. He understood the contradictions at the heart of America's command-and-control system—but couldn't find a way to resolve them during his last few weeks in office.

Breaking In

Colonel John T. Moser and his wife had just finished dinner, and they were getting ready to leave the house for a concert, when the phone rang.

There's a problem at Launch Complex 374-7, the controller said. It could be a fire.

Moser told his wife to go without him, put on his uniform, got in his car, and headed to the command post. They lived on the base, and the drive didn't take long. On the way, Moser radioed ahead, telling the controller to assemble the Missile Potential Hazard Team. It was six forty in the evening, about ten minutes after a mysterious white cloud had appeared in the silo.

The command post of the 308th Strategic Missile Wing resembled an executive boardroom, with a long conference table in the middle, communications equipment, and a chalkboard. It could accommodate twenty-five or thirty people. Moser was the wing commander, and when he arrived at the post, it was still largely empty, and the status of the missile, unclear. The sprays were on, dumping water into the silo. Stage 1 fuel pressure was falling, while the oxidizer pressure was rising. Flashing red lights in the control center at 4-7 warned there was a fuel leak, an oxidizer leak, a fire in the silo—three things that couldn't be happening at once. Adding to the confusion, Captain Mazzaro and Lieutenant Childers, the crew commander and deputy commander at the site, had both called the command post, using separate lines, one mentioning a fuel leak, the other a fire. Now Mazzaro was on the speakerphone, reporting the missile's tank pressures. His crew was going through checklists, trying to make sense of it all.

Moser was a great believer in checklists. After graduating from Franklin & Marshall College in 1955, he'd joined the Strategic Air Command. Two years later he became the navigator of a KC-97 Stratotanker, an aircraft that refueled B-47 bombers midair. The Stratotanker was a propeller plane, and the B-47 a jet, prone to stalling at low speeds. The two had to rendezvous at a precise location, with the bomber flying behind and slightly below the tanker. At an altitude of eighteen thousand feet, they would connect via a hollow steel boom and fly in unison for twenty minutes, entering a shallow dive so that the tanker could keep up with the bomber. Aerial refueling was a delicate, often dangerous procedure. The crew of the Stratotanker had to coordinate every step carefully, not just with the crew of the B-47 but also with one another. Spontaneous or improvised maneuvers would not be appreciated. Moser later flew as a navigator on KC-135 tankers that refueled B-52s during airborne alerts. The success of these missions depended on checklists. Every move had to be standardized and predictable, as two large jets flew about forty feet apart, linked by a boom, one plane carrying thermonuclear weapons, the other unloading a thousand gallons of jet fuel a minute, day or night, through air turbulence and rough weather.

Colonel Moser asked Mazzaro if the PTS team had done anything in the silo that could have caused the problem. Mazzaro got off the line and returned with an explanation: Airman Powell had dropped a socket into the silo, and the socket had pierced a hole in the stage 1 fuel tank. Mazzaro put the airman on the phone and made him describe what had happened, an unusual decision that violated the chain of command. Hearing the details silenced everyone in the room. Moser realized this was a serious accident that called for an urgent response. He activated the Missile Potential Hazard Net, a conference call that would connect him with SAC headquarters in Omaha, the Ogden Air Logistics Center in Utah, and the headquarters of the Eighth Air Force in Louisiana. But the communications equipment wasn't working properly, and for the next forty minutes the controller in Little Rock tried to set up the call.

Members of the hazard team were now filling the command post, officers and enlisted men who'd spent years working with the Titan II and its propellants. The missile wing's chief of safety sat at the conference table, along with the head of its technical engineering branch, a bioenvironmental engineer, an electrical engineer, and the K crew. The "K" stood for "on-call," and the four-man crew—a commander, a deputy commander, a missile facilities technician, and a missile systems analyst—served as backup to the launch crew at 4-7. The K crew could help interpret the data coming from the site, pore through the *Dash-1* and other operating manuals, offer a second opinion. The skills of everyone in the room focused on the question of how to save the missile. SAC didn't have a checklist for the problem they now faced, and so they would have to write one.

Moser needed all the technical assistance he could get. He was new to the job, having been in Little Rock for about three months. During that brief time, he'd come to be regarded as smart, fair, and open minded—as someone who was willing to listen. For a SAC wing commander, he was well liked. But Moser didn't know very much about Titan II missiles. He'd previously served as deputy director of missile maintenance at SAC headquarters and as the commander of missile maintenance at Whiteman Air Force Base in Missouri. Those assignments, however, had required an extensive knowledge of Minuteman missiles—a completely different weapon system. The Minuteman used solid fuel, not liquid propellants. It was smaller than a Titan II, with a less powerful warhead. And each Minuteman complex had ten missiles, not one, with silos dispersed as far as seventeen miles from the launch control center. A Minuteman crew could go months without visiting a silo. The Titan II was the only ballistic missile in the American arsenal that relied on liquid fuel and a combat crew living down the hall. It was a rare, exotic "bird." Of the more than one thousand long-range missiles that SAC controlled, only fifty-four were Titan IIs.

Moser didn't pretend to be an expert on the Titan II and, from his first day in Little Rock, had shown an eagerness to learn. Three or four mornings a week, he attended predeparture briefings for the launch crews and the PTS teams. He vowed to spend time at every launch complex, before the end of the year. But some of the complexes were a long way from Little Rock, and he still hadn't visited them all.

WHEN COLONEL JAMES L. MORRIS arrived at the command post, around 7 P.M., he already knew what had happened at the silo. Morris was the deputy commander for maintenance, and about half an hour earlier, he'd overheard Captain Mazzaro on the radio, sounding excited about something. Morris told job control to call 4-7 and ask Charles Heineman, the head of PTS Team A, what was going on there. Heineman said that Powell had dropped a socket into the silo and poked a hole in the missile. He said that Powell saw a lot of fuel vapor, but no fire. Morris absorbed the news, told job control to track down Jeff Kennedy, and ordered the dispatcher not to contact the launch complex again.

Within an hour of the accident, the pressure in the stage 1 fuel tank had dropped by about 80 percent. A vacuum was forming inside it, as fuel poured out. If the pressure continued to drop, the tank might collapse. After Jeff Kennedy joined Morris in the command post, Colonel Moser briefed them on the situation and instructed them to head to 4-7 by helicopter. Morris would serve as the on-site commander, and Kennedy would help him find out what was happening, whether there was a fire, and what needed to be done. Before leaving Little Rock, Kennedy asked job control to call the launch complex and tell them to get a RFHCO suit ready for him. We've been ordered not to call the complex, the dispatcher said, bring your own. Kennedy didn't have time to gather the necessary gear—a helmet, a fresh air pack, a RFHCO suit the right size—and left the base without it.

The hazard team had come up with a plan: PTS technicians would reenter the silo, vent the stage 1 fuel tank, equalize the pressure, and prevent the missile from collapsing. Time was of the essence, and the reentry had to be done as soon as possible. The PTS men topside had RFHCOs and air packs and a full set of equipment in their trucks. Ideally, they'd go into the complex. But nobody knew where they were. After leaving the complex, they'd probably driven beyond the range of the radios in their helmets. And their trucks didn't have radios that could contact the base. If they wanted to speak with the command post, they'd have to drive to Damascus and use a pay phone, or call from a nearby house.

The PTS crew that had taken refuge in the control center would have to do the job, wearing the RFHCOs left behind in the blast lock. Because their socket was now lying somewhere at the bottom of the silo, they'd have to remove the pressure cap on the stage 1 fuel tank with pliers. And if that didn't work, they might have to push open the tank's poppet valve with a broom handle.

Before Colonel Moser could approve the plan and set it in motion, SAC headquarters joined the discussion via speakerphone. It was about quarter to eight, the Missile Potential Hazard Net was finally up and running, and Lieutenant General Lloyd Leavitt, the vice commander in chief of the Strategic Air Command, was on the line. Leavitt made it clear that, from now on, nothing would be done in the launch control center, the silo, or anywhere else on the complex without his approval. And he would not authorize any specific action until a consensus had been reached that it was the right thing to do.

Leavitt was in his early fifties, short, compact, and self-confident. He'd been a member of the first class to enter West Point after the Second World War. While the heroism of that war was celebrated in popular books and films, his classmates were soon risking their lives in a conflict that was largely ignored by the public. Leavitt became a fighter pilot and flew one hundred combat missions during the Korean War. He routinely encountered enemy planes and antiaircraft fire. During one mission, his F-84 was hit by flak and suffered an electrical failure; Leavitt had to fly 250 miles without flight instruments or a radio, before landing safely at an American base. During another, his plane spun out of control amid a snowstorm; Leavitt had to bail out at eight thousand feet and felt lucky to be found by South Korean troops, not Communist guerrillas. He later flew 152 combat missions in Vietnam. The two conflicts, as well as training flights, took the lives of many good friends. Of the 119 West Pointers who graduated from flight school with Leavitt, 7 were killed in Korea, 2 in Vietnam, and 13 in airplane accidents. The odds of being killed on the job, for his classmates, was about one in six.

Some of Leavitt's most dangerous missions occurred during peacetime. From 1957 to 1960, he flew U-2 spy planes. The U-2 was designed to fly long distances and take photographs at an altitude of seventy thousand feet, without being detected or shot down. In order to do so, the plane had to be kept as light as possible. And the small size of the pilot's survival kit imposed certain restrictions. Before leaving on a mission to photograph Soviet airfields and radar sites in Siberia, Leavitt was given a choice: bring a life raft or a warm parka. He wasn't allowed to bring both. Leavitt chose the parka, figuring that if he had to bail out over the Bering Sea, he'd freeze to death—with or without the raft. U-2 pilots flew alone, in a tiny cockpit, wearing cumbersome pressure suits and maintaining complete radio silence, for as long as nine hours. The plane was difficult to fly. It was fragile and stalled easily. Strong g-forces could break it apart midair. To save weight, it had only two sets of landing gear, one in the front and the other in the back. "Landing the U-2," Leavitt wrote in his memoir, "was like landing a bicycle at 100 mph." Of the thirty-eight U-2 pilots with whom he trained, eight died flying the plane.

The Missile Potential Hazard Net was rarely activated, and the commander of SAC usually led it. But General Richard H. Ellis was out of town—and so Leavitt, the second in command, took his place. Leavitt got on the net from the balcony of SAC's underground command post, overlooking the world map. Although he'd flown B-52s for a year, worked at the Pentagon, commanded an Air Force training center, and served on the staff of a NATO general, Leavitt still had the manner of an old-fashioned fighter pilot: cocky, decisive, self-reliant. He did not, however, have firsthand experience working with Titan II missiles. Nor did Colonel Russell Kennedy, the director of missile maintenance at SAC headquarters, who joined Leavitt on the balcony. They would have to rely on the advice and the expertise of others.

THE PRESENCE OF A WHITE hazy cloud on the other side of blast door 8 was ominous. Regardless of whether it was fuel vapor or smoke, it shouldn't have been there when Gregory Lester opened the door, hoping to grab the RFHCOs. That meant blast door 9, leading to the cableway and the silo, had somehow been breached. That meant blast door 8 was all that stood between the men in the launch control center and a cloud of toxic, perhaps explosive fumes. The plan to reenter the silo was scrapped. Captain Mazzaro had already asked for permission to evacuate. Now he asked for it again, and Heineman, speaking on behalf of his PTS crew, wholeheartedly backed the request.

At the Little Rock command post, the hazard team debated what to do next. For the moment, their options were limited. The PTS team topside was still missing. Colonel Morris and Jeff Kennedy were en route in the helicopter but hadn't brought along air packs and RFHCOs. Rodney Holder, the missile systems analyst technician at 4-7, was getting ready to power down the missile so that a stray electrical spark wouldn't ignite fuel vapor in the silo. Once the main circuit breakers were shut off, the men in the control center could do little more than stare at the changing tank pressures on the PTPMU.

The K crew worried about the safety of their counterparts at 4-7. Captain Jackie Wells, a member of the K crew, thought that if the missile collapsed, the fuel vapor that had leaked into the blast lock might ignite and rupture blast door 8. Even if the door held, debris from a large explosion might trap everyone in the control center. The blast doors and the escape hatch were supposed to ensure the crew's survival, even after a nuclear detonation. But a Titan II complex had not yet faced that sort of test, and Wells thought the risks of leaving people in the control center outweighed any potential benefit.

The K crew advised Colonel Moser to order an evacuation. Sergeant Michael Hanson—the chief of PTS Team B, who was in the command post, preparing to lead a convoy to the site—agreed. He didn't think the control center would survive a blast. And he wanted his buddies to get out of there, right away.

Captain Charles E. Clark, the wing's chief technical engineer, said that the crew should stay right where they were. He had faith in the blast doors. And he warned Colonel Moser that if the crew left, the command post would have no way of knowing the tank pressures inside the missile and no means of operating the equipment within the complex. Clark argued that the crew should remain in the control center, monitor the status of the missile—and open the massive silo door above it. Opening the door would dilute the fuel vapor with air, making the vapor less flammable. The temperature in the silo would drop, and as the oxidizer tanks cooled, they'd become less likely to burst. Opening the door wouldn't pose much of a threat to Damascus. Unlike the oxidizer, the fuel would dissipate rapidly in the atmosphere. It wouldn't travel for miles, sickening people and killing cattle. First Lieutenant Michael J. Rusden, the bioenvironmental engineer, had calculated that with the winds prevailing at the moment, a toxic corridor would extend only four hundred to six hundred feet beyond the silo.

After consulting with SAC headquarters, Colonel Moser ordered everyone to evacuate the control center. And he asked SAC if the crew should open the silo door before they left.

That door was not to be opened under any circumstances, General Leavitt said. The idea wasn't even worth discussing. Leavitt wanted the fuel vapors fully contained in the silo. He did not want a cloud of Aerozine-50 floating over nearby houses and farms. More important, he didn't want to risk losing control of a thermonuclear weapon. Leavitt felt absolutely certain that if the missile blew up, the warhead wouldn't detonate. He'd been around nuclear weapons for almost thirty years. In 1952 he'd been secretly trained to deliver atomic bombs from a fighter plane, in case they were needed during the Korean War. He had complete faith in the safety mechanisms of the W-53 warhead atop the Titan II. But nobody could predict how far the warhead would travel, if the missile exploded with the silo door open. Leavitt didn't want a thermonuclear weapon landing in a backyard somewhere between Little Rock and St. Louis. Maintaining control of the warhead was far more important, he thought, than any other consideration.

The K crew waited tensely to hear if the men had made it out of the control center. Before abandoning the complex, the launch crew had left the phone off the hook—and when the intruder alarm suddenly went off at 4-7, the sound could be heard over the phone in the command post. That meant someone topside had opened the door to the escape hatch. More time passed without any word, and then Sergeant Brocksmith was on the radio, saying that he had everyone in his pickup truck.

Sergeant Hanson left the command post and went to the PTS shop, where Sandaker and the other volunteers were gathering their equipment. The Disaster Response Force left the base at about nine o'clock, but PTS Team B needed more time to get ready. Once they arrived at 4-7, Hanson thought the plan would go something like this: two men would put on RFHCOs, enter the complex through the access portal, open the blast doors, walk down the long cableway to the silo, and try to vent the missile. Perhaps they'd also turn on the purge fan to clear vapors from the silo.

Unsure of what equipment was available at 4-7, Hanson decided that PTS Team B had to bring everything it needed. They had to gather the gear, load it into five trucks, stop at two other missile complexes, and pick up items that the shop didn't have. Although PTS Team B wanted to get to 4-7 as quickly as possible, logistical problems delayed them, including an unexpected stop for water. Hanson's truck was the only one with a radio. Whenever he needed to communicate with the others, the entire convoy would have to pull over to the side of the road, and someone would get out of the truck to explain their next move.

The Little Rock command post continued to have communications difficulties, as well. Once the control center was evacuated, the radio in Sergeant Brocksmith's truck became the only way to speak with people at the missile site. Unfortunately, the radio transmissions from his truck weren't scrambled or secure. Anyone who knew the right frequency could listen to them, and the sound quality was less than ideal. Major Joseph A. Kinderman—the head of the wing's security police, who manned the radio at the command post—found that conversations were sometimes garbled and difficult to understand.

At about half past nine, Major Kinderman reported the latest set of tank pressures, and a sergeant added them to the chalkboard. For a moment, everyone focused on the pressure in the stage 1 fuel tank. During the hour since the last reading, it had fallen from -0.7 to -2 psi. Those numbers were disturbing, they suggested the tank was on the verge of collapse—and then a member of the K crew wondered, how the hell does anyone know what the tank pressures are? The control center had been evacuated at about half past eight. Kinderman asked Colonel Morris where those numbers came from.

Morris had provided the numbers, but didn't answer the question. He was sitting in Brocksmith's security police truck, parked at the end of the access road, off Highway 65.

Kinderman waited for a reply, and then Captain Mazzaro got on the radio and said that Kennedy had reentered the control center, without permission, violating the two-man rule.

Members of the K crew couldn't believe what Kennedy had just done. Colonel Moser was more upset than angry, and he wasn't thrilled about telling SAC headquarters. But the information that Kennedy obtained was extremely useful. Moser shared the numbers with everyone on the net and described Kennedy's unauthorized behavior. General Leavitt seemed unperturbed. Although one of SAC's cardinal rules had just been broken, Leavitt appreciated the importance of having the latest tank pressures—and the personal risk that Kennedy had taken to get them.

Colonel Morris was told not to allow any further actions at the launch complex without the approval of SAC headquarters. And while the PTS convoy drove to 4-7, the discussion on the net turned to whether the power at the complex should be completely shut off. The crew had turned off everything they could before leaving, but the water pumps on level 8 of the silo were still running, as were a series of fans, motors, and relays connected to the air-conditioning and ventilation systems. General Leavitt worried that a spark from one of these motors or the slightest bit of electrical arcing could ignite the fuel vapor in the silo. The command post called the Petit

Jean Electric Company, the local utility in Damascus, and asked it to send over workers who could climb the poles and disconnect the jacks from power lines leading to the complex.

The majority of the hazard team in Little Rock wanted to leave the power on. If the power were cut, the phone in the control center would go dead, and they wouldn't be able to monitor the vapor detector left behind there. The sound of the detector going off would signal that fuel vapor had seeped past blast door 8. Anyone who reentered the complex to save the missile would find the job more difficult, without power. You wouldn't be able to check tank pressures, turn on the purge fan, or do anything in the silo, aside from removing the pressure cap by hand and venting the stage 1 fuel tank.

The workers from Petit Jean were told to stand by, and for the time being, the power stayed on. An executive from Martin Marietta, the manufacturer of the Titan II, had joined the net, giving estimates of the tank pressures at which the stage 1 fuel tank was likely to collapse and the oxidizer tank to burst. The situation felt grim. Nevertheless, members of the hazard net debated how PTS Team B should proceed, step by step, upon their arrival at 4-7. First, everyone had to reach a consensus on the proper course of action—and then they had to write a checklist for it. The audio quality of the conference call was mediocre, and with so many people involved in the discussion, at half a dozen locations, it was often hard to figure out who was saying what.

One of the most authoritative voices had a strong Texan accent. It belonged to Colonel Ben Scallorn, the deputy chief of staff for missiles at Eighth Air Force headquarters in Louisiana. Moser had served under Scallorn at Whiteman Air Force Base and phoned him right after hearing about the accident in Damascus, wanting to get his opinion, privately, of how bad it sounded. Scallorn didn't sugar the pill; he thought it sounded really bad. He knew the Titan II as well as just about anyone else at SAC. He'd worked long hours in silos wearing a RFHCO and seen firsthand how dangerous the missile could be. During the discussions on the Missile Potential Hazard Net, he was blunt about what needed to be done at 4-7, regardless of whether anyone would listen.

WHEN BEN SCALLORN FIRST REPORTED to Little Rock Air Force Base in 1962, the Titan II silos there were still being dug. The missile maintenance department consisted of three people: a first lieutenant who ran it, a sergeant who served as his clerk, and a secretary. The 308th Strategic Missile Wing had not yet been activated, and the Air Force was eager to get the Titan IIs into the ground. Scallorn was glad to be in Little Rock, preparing to study missile maintenance. His previous assignment in the Air Force had been "recreational services." For years he'd managed softball fields, swimming pools, movie theaters, and service clubs at SAC bases everywhere from Mississippi to Morocco. He was thirty-three, with a wife and three small boys. Helping to deploy America's largest ballistic missile, at the dawn of the missile age, promised to be a more rewarding career path. He was sent to Sheppard Air Force Base in Wichita Falls, Texas, to learn how the Titan II worked—and six weeks later returned to Little Rock as chief of maintenance training at the 308th.

Scallorn visited the launch complexes around Little Rock as they were being constructed. Each one was a massive endeavor, requiring about 4.5 million pounds of steel and about 30 million pounds of concrete. Elaborate water, power, and hydraulic systems had to be laid underground. The silo door was too heavy to be transported by road; it arrived in eight pieces for assembly at the site. In order to bring missiles on alert as quickly as possible, the Air Force relied on a management practice known as "concurrency": work began on the Titan II complexes long before a Titan II missile had flown. Both would be completed at roughly the same time.

The Air Force also used concurrency to speed the deployment of other ballistic missiles. Led by the Army Corps of Engineers, tens of thousands of workers dug hundreds of silos to hide missiles beneath the landscape of rural America. It was one of the largest construction projects ever undertaken by the Department of Defense. In addition to Arkansas, underground launch complexes were placed in Arizona, California, Colorado, Idaho, Kansas, Missouri, Nebraska, New Mexico, New York, Oklahoma, South Dakota, Texas, Washington, and Wyoming. Between Malmstrom Air

Force Base in Montana and Minot Air Force Base in North Dakota, missile silos were dispersed across an area extending for thirty-two thousand square miles.

About an hour north of Santa Barbara, along a stretch of the central California coast with forty miles of pristine beaches and rocky cliffs, the Air Force built a missile research center and the first operational missile site. Later known as Vandenberg Air Force Base, it provided a clear shot to target sites at Eniwetok and Kwajalein in the Marshall Islands. Like the missile complexes in America's heartland, Vandenberg was rushed to completion. Within a few years of its opening in 1957, the base had launchpads, silos, underground control centers, storage facilities, administrative buildings, and a population of about ten thousand.

Although concurrency sped the introduction of new weapons, it also created problems. A small design change in a missile could require costly changes in silo equipment that had already been installed. The prototype of a new airplane could be flight-tested repeatedly to discover its flaws—but a missile could be flown only once. And missiles were expensive, limiting the number of flight tests and the opportunity to learn what could go wrong. A successful launch depended on an intricate mix of human and technological factors. Design errors were often easier to correct than to anticipate. As a result, the reliability of America's early missiles left much to be desired. "Like any machine," General LeMay noted, with understatement, "they don't always work."

The first intercontinental missile deployed by the United States, the Snark, had wings, a jet engine, and a range of about six thousand miles. It was a great-looking missile, sleek and futuristic, painted a fiery red. But the Snark soon became legendary for landing nowhere near its target. On long-distance flights, it missed by an average of twenty miles or more. During one test launch from Cape Canaveral, Florida, a Snark that was supposed to fly no farther than Puerto Rico just kept on going, despite repeated attempts by range safety officers to make it self-destruct. When the slow-moving missile passed Puerto Rico, fighter planes were scrambled to shoot it down, but they couldn't find it. The Snark eventually ran out of fuel and crashed somewhere in the Amazonian rain forests of Brazil. Air Force tests later suggested that during wartime, only one out of three Snarks would leave the ground and only one out of ten would hit its target. Nevertheless, dozens of Snarks were put on alert at Presque Isle Air Force Base in Maine. The missile carried a 4-megaton warhead.

Again and again, the symbolism of a missile seemed more important than its military usefulness. The Army's Redstone missile was rushed into the field not long after the Soviet Union launched *Sputnik*. Designed by Wernher von Braun and his team of German rocket scientists at the Redstone Arsenal in Huntsville, Alabama, the missile was a larger, more advanced version of the Nazi V-2. The Redstone often carried a 4-megaton warhead but couldn't fly more than 175 miles. The combination of a short range and a powerful thermonuclear weapon was unfortunate. Launched from NATO bases in West Germany, Redstone missiles would destroy a fair amount of West Germany.

The intermediate-range missiles that President Eisenhower offered to NATO were also problematic. The Thor missiles sent to Great Britain were stored aboveground, lying horizontally. They had to be erected and then fueled before liftoff. It would take at least fifteen minutes to launch any of the missiles in a Thor squadron and even longer to get them all off the ground. The missiles' lack of physical protection, lengthy countdown procedures, and close proximity to the Eastern bloc guaranteed that they'd be among the first things destroyed by a Soviet attack. The four-minute warning provided by Great Britain's radar system wouldn't offer much help to the RAF officers in charge of a Thor squadron that might need as much as two days to complete its mission. They might not have time to launch any Thors. The missiles would, however, be useful for a surprise attack against the Soviet Union—a fact that gave the Soviets an even greater incentive to strike first and destroy them. Instead of deterring an attack on Great Britain, the Thors seemed to invite one.

The military value of the Jupiter missiles offered to Italy and Turkey was equally dubious. Jupiters were also slow to launch, stored aboveground, and exposed to attack. Unlike the Thors, they stood upright, encircled by launch equipment hidden beneath metal panels. When the panels opened outward before liftoff, a Jupiter looked like the pistil of a huge, white, sinister flower. Sixty feet high, topped by a 1.4-megaton warhead, and deployed in the countryside, the missiles were especially vulnerable to lightning strikes.

In the days and months following *Sputnik*, the Atlas missile loomed as America's great hope, its first ICBM, designed to hit Soviet targets from bases in the United States. But producing a missile that could reliably reach the Soviet Union took much longer than expected. An Air Force missile expert later described its propellant system as a "fire waiting to happen." Liquid oxygen (LOX), the missile's oxidizer, was dangerously unstable. About twenty thousand gallons of LOX had to be stored in tanks outside the Atlas, at a temperature of −297 degrees Fahrenheit—and then pumped into the missile during the countdown. The margin for error was slim. During a series of dramatic, well-publicized mishaps at Vandenberg, Atlas missiles exploded on the launchpad, veered wildly off course, or never left the ground. Nevertheless, the first Atlas went on alert in 1959. At a top secret hearing two years later, an Air Force official admitted to Congress that the odds of an Atlas missile hitting a target in the Soviet Union were no better than fifty-fifty. General Thomas Power, the head of SAC, who much preferred bombers, thought the odds were closer to zero.

Developed as a backup to Atlas, the Titan missile incorporated a number of new technologies. It had a second stage that ignited in the upper atmosphere, enabling the launch of a heavier payload. Although it relied on the same propellants as the Atlas, the Titan would be based in an underground silo, gaining some protection from a Soviet attack. The missile would be filled with propellants underground, about fifteen minutes before launch, and then would ride an elevator to the surface before ignition. The elevator was immense, capable of lifting more than half a million pounds. But it didn't always work. During a test run of the first Titan silo, overlooking the Pacific at Vandenberg, a control valve in the elevator's hydraulic system broke. The elevator, the Titan, and about 170,000 pounds of liquid oxygen and fuel fell all the way to the bottom of the silo. Nobody was hurt by the explosion, though debris from it landed more than a mile away. The silo was destroyed and never rebuilt.

While Atlas and Titan missiles were being prepared for their launch complexes, the Air Force debated whether to deploy another liquid-fueled, long-range missile: the Titan II. It would be more accurate and reliable, carry a larger warhead, store propellants within its airframe, launch from inside a silo, and lift off in less than a minute. Those were compelling arguments on behalf of the Titan II, and yet critics of the missile asked a good question—did the Air Force really need four different types of ICBM? It had already committed to the development of the Minuteman, a missile that would be small, solid-fueled, mass-produced, and inexpensive.

Donald Quarles was one of the leading skeptics at the Pentagon, eager to cut costs and avoid the unnecessary duplication of weapon systems. No longer secretary of the Air Force, he was the second-highest-ranking official at the Pentagon, rumored to be Eisenhower's choice to become the next secretary of defense. And then Quarles suddenly died of a heart attack, amid the long hours and great stress of his job. Funding of the Titan II was soon approved, largely due to the size of its warhead. General LeMay didn't care much for the Atlas, Titan, or Minuteman—missiles whose only strategic use was the annihilation of cities. But the Titan II, with its 9 megatons, was the kind of weapon he liked. It could destroy the deep underground bunkers where the Soviet leadership might hide, even without a direct hit.

One of the many challenges that the designers of the Titan II faced was how to bring the warhead close to its target. The Titan II's rocket engines burned for only the first five minutes of flight. They provided a good, strong push, enough to lift the warhead above the earth's atmosphere. But for the remaining half hour or so of flight, it was propelled by gravity and momentum. Ballistic missiles were extraordinarily complex machines, symbols of the space age featuring thousands of moving parts, and yet their guidance systems were based on seventeenth-century physics and Isaac Newton's laws of motion. The principles that determined the trajectory of a warhead were the same as those that guided a rock thrown at a window. Accuracy depended on the shape of the projectile, the distance to the target, the aim and strength of the toss.

Early versions of the Atlas and Titan missiles had a radio-controlled guidance system. After liftoff, ground stations received data on the flight path and transmitted commands to the missile. The system eventually proved to be quite accurate, landing about 80 percent of the warheads within roughly a mile of their targets. But radio interference, deliberate jamming, and the destruction of the ground stations would send the missiles off course.

The Titan II was the first American long-range missile designed, from the outset, to have an inertial guidance system. It didn't require any external signals or data to find a target. It was a completely self-contained system that couldn't be jammed, spoofed, or hacked midflight. The thinking behind it drew upon ancient navigational rules: if you know exactly where you started, how long you've been traveling, the direction you've been heading, and the speed you've been going the whole time, then you can calculate exactly where you are—and how to reach your destination.

"Dead reckoning," in one form or another, had been used for millennia, especially by captains at sea, and the key to its success was the precision of each measurement. A poor grasp of dead reckoning may have led Christopher Columbus to North America instead of India, a navigational error of about eight thousand miles. On a ship, the essential tools for dead reckoning were a compass, a clock, and a map. On a missile, accelerometers measured speed in three directions. Spinning gyroscopes kept the system aligned with true north, the North Star, as a constant reference point. And a small computer counted the time elapsed since launch, calculated the trajectory, and issued a series of instructions.

The size of the guidance computer had been unimportant in radio-controlled systems, because it was located at the ground station. But size mattered a great deal once the computer was going to be carried by the missile. The Air Force's demand for self-contained, inertial guidance systems played a leading role in the miniaturization of computers and the development of integrated circuits, the building blocks of the modern electronics industry. By 1962 all of the integrated circuits in the United States were being purchased by the Department of Defense, mainly for use in missile guidance systems. Although the Titan II's onboard computer didn't rely on integrated circuits, at only eight pounds, it was still considered a technological marvel, one of the most powerful small computers ever built. It had about 12.5 kilobytes of memory; many smart phones now have more than five million times that amount.

The short-range V-2 had been the first missile to employ an inertial guidance system, and the Nazi scientists who invented it were recruited by the Army's Redstone Arsenal after the Second World War. They later helped to give the Jupiter missile an impressive Circular Error Probable—the radius of the circle around a target, in which half the missiles aimed at it would land—of less than a mile. But the longer a missile flew, the more precise its inertial guidance system had to be. Small errors would be magnified with each passing minute. The guidance system had to take into account factors like the eastward rotation of the earth. Not only would the target be moving toward the east as the world turned, but so would the point from which the missile was launched. And at different latitudes, the earth rotates at slightly different speeds. All these factors had to be measured precisely. If the missile's velocity were miscalculated by just 0.05 percent, the warhead could miss its target by about twenty miles.

The accuracy of a Titan II launch would be determined early in the flight. The sequence of events left no room for error. Fifty-nine seconds after the commander and the deputy commander turned their keys, the Titan II would rise from the silo, slowly at first, almost pausing for a moment above the open door, before shooting upward, trailed by flames. About two and a half minutes after liftoff, at an altitude of roughly 47 miles, the thrust chamber pressure switch would sense that most of the oxidizer in the stage 1 tank had been used. It would shut off the main engine, fire the staging nuts, send stage 1 of the missile plummeting to earth, and ignite the stage 2 engine. About three minutes later, at an altitude of roughly 217 miles, the guidance system would detect that the missile had reached the correct velocity. The computer would shut off the stage 2 engine and fire small vernier engines to make any last-minute changes in speed or direction. The vernier engines would fire for about fifteen seconds. And then the computer would blow the nozzles off them and detonate an explosive squib to free the nose cone from stage 2. The nose cone, holding the warhead, would continue to rise into the sky, as the rest of the missile drifted away.

About fourteen minutes later, the nose cone would reach its apogee, its maximum height, about eight hundred miles above the earth. Then it would start to fall, rapidly gaining speed. It would fall for another sixteen minutes. It would reach a velocity of about twenty-three thousand feet per second, faster than a speeding bullet—a lot faster, as much as ten to twenty times faster. And if everything had occurred in the right order, at the right time, precisely, the warhead would detonate within a mile of its target.

In addition to creating an accurate guidance system, missile designers had to make sure that a warhead wouldn't incinerate as it reentered the atmosphere. The friction created by a falling body of that size, at those speeds, would produce surface temperatures of about 15,000 degrees Fahrenheit, hotter than the melting point of any metal. In early versions of the Atlas missile, the nose cone—also called the "reentry vehicle" (RV)—contained a large block of copper that served as a heat sink. The copper absorbed heat and kept it away from the warhead. But the copper also added a lot of weight to the missile. The Titan II employed a different technique. A thick coating of plastic was added to the nose cone, and during reentry, layers of the plastic ablated—they charred, melted, vaporized, and absorbed some of the heat. The cloud of gases released by ablation became a buffer in front of the nose cone, a form of insulation, reducing its temperature even further.

The nose cone not only protected the warhead from heat, it also contained the weapon's arming and fuzing system. On the way up, a barometric switch closed when it reached a specific altitude, allowing electricity to flow from the thermal batteries to the warhead. On the way down, an accelerometer ignited the thermal batteries and armed the warhead. If the warhead had been set for an airburst, it exploded at an altitude of fourteen thousand feet when a barometric switch closed. If the warhead had been set for a groundburst—or if, for some reason, the barometric switch malfunctioned—it exploded when the piezoelectric crystals in the nose cone were crushed upon impact with the target. Instead of being vaporized by reentry, the warhead was kept cool and intact long enough to vaporize everything for miles around it.

Three strategic missile wings were formed to deploy the Titan II, each with eighteen missiles, located in Arkansas, Kansas, and Arizona. The Air Force felt confident that the Titan II would be more reliable than its predecessors. At first, perhaps 70 to 75 percent of the missiles were expected to hit their targets, and as crews gained experience, that proportion would rise to 90 percent. Newspapers across the country heralded the arrival of the Titan II, America's superweapon, "the biggest guns in the western world." The missile would play a dual, patriotic role in the rivalry with the Soviet Union. It would carry SAC's deadliest warhead—and also serve, in a slightly modified form, as the launch vehicle to send NASA's Gemini astronauts into space. At Little Rock Air Force Base, the introduction of the Titan II was greeted with a nervous enthusiasm. The first launch crews had to train with cardboard mock-ups of equipment, and the number of operational launch complexes in Arkansas soon exceeded the number of crews qualified to run them. Vital checklists were still being written and revised as the missiles were placed on alert.

Ben Scallorn became a site maintenance officer for the 308th Strategic Missile Wing, eventually overseeing half a dozen Titan II launch complexes. He liked the new job and didn't hesitate to wear a RFHCO and work long hours beside his men. Launch Complex 373-4 in Searcy was one of his sites. After the fire killed fifty-three workers there, he was part of the team that pulled the missile from the silo. It was a sobering experience. Thick black soot covered almost everything. But handprints could still be seen on the rungs of ladders, and the bodies of fallen workers had left clear outlines on the floor. Scallorn could make out the shapes of their arms and legs, the positions of their bodies as they died, surrounded by black soot. All that remained of them were these pale, ghostly silhouettes.

JEFF KENNEDY WAS FURIOUS. They were just sitting there in the dark, at the end of the access road, with their thumbs up their asses, doing nothing, while the missile got ready to blow. Colonel Morris said they'd been ordered to wait for further instructions—period. The decisions were being made elsewhere, and nothing, nothing was to be done without the approval of SAC headquarters. Morris hadn't shared Kennedy's latest plan with the command post, and nobody had asked to hear it. In fact, none of the PTS guys or launch crew members on the scene had been asked to give an opinion of what should be done.

Kennedy thought that was bullshit. They were there. They were ready to go. They had all the knowledge and experience you needed. What were they waiting for? Every minute they waited to do the job would make the job more dangerous.

At about 10:15, almost four hours after the accident, the Disaster Response Force arrived. But its commander, Colonel William Jones, had no authority at the site—a disaster hadn't occurred yet. The five vehicles in his convoy pulled off Highway 65 and parked along the access road. Members of his team got out of their trucks, introduced themselves, and distributed C-rations and cans of water.

Colonel Morris asked the flight surgeon who'd come with the ambulance, Captain Donald P. Mueller, to do him a favor. Mueller had never worked with the Disaster Response Force before. He was twenty-eight years old and happened to be the doctor on call at the base hospital that night. Morris asked him to speak with Mazzaro, the missile crew commander. Morris was concerned about Mazzaro: he didn't look well. He seemed anxious and tense. Mueller spent about forty-five minutes with Mazzaro, who admitted to feeling worried about his pregnant wife. Mazzaro wanted someone to call his wife and tell her that he was safe. Mueller assured him that she'd already been contacted—and that Fuller's wife, who was also pregnant, had been contacted, too. Both women knew their husbands were safe. The news made Mazzaro feel better, and he lay down in the back of the ambulance to rest.

SERGEANT BROCKSMITH WAS HAVING TROUBLE supervising the evacuation of local residents. Colonel Jones and Colonel Morris would periodically sit in his truck and use his radio to speak with the command post. When one of them was on the Security Police Net, Brocksmith's officers couldn't communicate with each other. And his officers didn't have maps of the area. And they didn't have an evacuation plan or any formal guidance about how an evacuation should proceed. The only map that Brocksmith had in his truck showed the location of nearby Titan II complexes. But it didn't show where any houses, farms, schools, or even streets were located.

The Missile Potential Hazard Team instructed Brocksmith to post officers in a roughly three-quarters-of-a-mile radius around 4-7. Two Missile Alarm Response Teams were available for the job, and a couple of Mobile Fire Teams (MFTs) had been sent from Little Rock. That gave Brocksmith ten military police officers to secure the area. The MARTs were trained to guard Titan II sites, the MFTs to defend the air base from sabotage and attack, using machine guns, grenade launchers, and M-16 rifles. The MFTs—most of whom had never seen a Titan II complex—left their machine guns and grenade launchers in Little Rock. Brocksmith established roadblocks on Highway 65 and stationed officers on County Roads 836 and 26, a pair of dirt roads that crossed the highway north and south of the missile complex. The officers on County Road 836 were forced to stop short of their assigned position. They'd encountered an old wooden bridge, and they were afraid to drive their truck over it.

The military police had no legal jurisdiction on civilian property and couldn't order anyone to evacuate. As officers knocked on doors in the middle of the night, carrying flashlights and M-16s, they found that most of the houses were empty. Sheriff Anglin or the state police had already been there. The handful of residents who'd refused to leave their homes generally fell into two categories: some were stubborn and defiant, while others, like Sam Hutto, were sneaky. Hutto kept returning to his farm, on back roads, to look after the cows.

The roughly two hundred officers in the security police squadron had been recalled to Little Rock Air Force Base. Sergeant Donald V. Green was serving as a referee at a football game when he heard about the recall. Green quickly went home, changed into his uniform, and reported for duty. He was in his early thirties, born and raised in Old Town, Florida, a small rural community about forty miles west of Gainesville. He lived on the base with his wife and six-year-old son. And he loved being a military police officer, despite how most people viewed the job. Being a cook or a cop, those were the only two jobs at SAC that nobody seemed to want. Too often, he thought, guys who'd flunked out of every technical school in the Air Force would be assigned to the military police. But the camaraderie among the officers was strong, their work interesting and important—even if it was rarely appreciated.

Green was the noncommissioned officer in charge of training at the 308th. He taught MART teams everything they needed to know about the Titan II. The teams escorted warheads to and from launch sites, kept an eye on warheads as they were being mated to missiles, and responded whenever an alarm went off. Officers learned how to deal with antiwar protesters, saboteurs, and all sorts of false alarms. A bird flying past the tipsies could set them off, and then a two-man MART team would have to visit the site and investigate what had tripped them—because the complexes didn't have security cameras topside. A missile crew had no way of knowing whether the tipsies had been set off by a squirrel or a squad of Soviet commandos. A MART team usually stayed overnight at a launch control center in each sector, using that "home complex" as a base to oversee security at three or four neighboring sites.

Four-seven often served as a home complex, and one of Sergeant Green's teams had pointed out a major security breach there, just a few weeks before the accident. Green had been amazed by their discovery: you could break into a Titan II complex with just a credit card. Once the officers showed him how to do it, Green requested permission to stage a black hat operation at 4-7—an unannounced demonstration of how someone could sneak into the launch control center undetected. SAC had a long history of black hatting to test the security at its facilities. Black hat teams would plant phony explosives on bombers, place metal spikes on runways, infiltrate a command post and then hand a letter to the base commander that said, "You're dead." General LeMay liked to run these tests and to punish officers who failed them. After Green received the go-ahead to stage a black hat at 4-7, his men secretly practiced the break-in.

On the day of the exercise, Green and two of his officers, Donald G. Mowles, Jr., and Larry Crowder, began the subterfuge by setting off the tipsies at Launch Complex 374-8—about ten miles from Damascus, in the town of Little Texas. When the alarm sounded there, the MART team stationed at 4-7 got a call and drove off to see what was wrong. Green and his men hurried to Damascus, jumped the perimeter fence at 4-7, carefully avoided the radar beams that set off the tipsies, and entered the access portal. Green picked up the phone and told the missile crew commander that "General Wyatt"—a fictitious, high-ranking officer—needed to see a schematic drawing in one of the technical manuals. When the crew commander hesitated, Green demanded his name and warned him the general would be unhappy with that response. The commander said he'd look for the drawing right away.

Taking advantage of the distraction, Crowder and Mowles jimmied the lock on the outer steel door with an ID card, ran down the stairs, and within seconds jimmied the door at the entrapment area, too. The men ran past the only security camera at the launch complex. But the missile crew wasn't looking at the television monitor—they were probably searching for that tech drawing—and the entrapment area didn't have a microphone to capture the sounds of a break-in.

Green ran back to the perimeter fence, climbed over it, got into his truck, drove a safe distance from the launch complex, and parked.

Crowder and Mowles hid outside blast door 6, waiting. When the MART team returned from the false alarm at the other launch site, it was given permission to reenter 4-7. The team was buzzed through the first two doors and walked downstairs to blast door 6—where it was surprised to hear a voice say, "You're dead."

One of Green's men picked up the phone there and said, "Security team at blast door six."

The door was opened, as were blast doors 7 and 8. Crowder and Mowles walked into the control center, feeling awfully pleased.

Steel plates were soon welded to the outer doors at Titan II sites so that intruders would need more than a credit card.

THE DRIVE TO DAMASCUS SEEMED to be taking forever, as the PTS convoy picked up equipment at two launch complexes, made three stops, and obeyed the speed limit.

"I've got a bad feeling about this," Senior Airman David Livingston said. "Somebody's going to die out there tonight."

The other members of Team B didn't like hearing Livingston talk that way. He wasn't a fearful or high-strung type. He was one of the most easygoing, laid-back guys at the base. If anything, Livingston was too laid back. He'd become legendary for his ability to sleep just about anywhere, anytime—and once he was out, it was almost impossible to wake him. Jeff Kennedy would sometimes have to bang on Livingston's door in the morning and yell at him and literally drag him out of bed. But nobody really minded, because once he was awake and alert, Livingston worked hard. He knew how to fix things. He was constantly tinkering with mechanical objects in his spare time—with citizens band radios, lawn mower engines, transmissions, and the old VW Beetle that he'd bought a few years earlier, right after graduating from high school. He loved to ride motorcycles and could pop a wheelie, lean back in the seat, and cruise.

During the previous summer, Livingston had visited his family in Heath, Ohio, a small town surrounded by cornfields in the central part of the state, where his father drove a truck and his mother worked as a clerk at a nearby Air Force base. He'd ridden his motorcycle there and back for a long weekend, a round trip of about fifteen hundred miles. He lived off base in a double-wide trailer, planned to ask his landlord's niece to marry him, and couldn't decide whether to move with her to California or sign on for another four years with SAC. The hardest part about leaving the Air Force, Livingston thought, would be saying good-bye to his loud, rowdy PTS buddies. They felt like family.

Senior Airman Greg Devlin was riding next to Livingston in the truck. At first he thought Livingston was joking about the bad vibes and the premonition of death. But it wasn't funny. And then Livingston said it again.

"Somebody's going to die tonight, I can feel it."

"Don't even be kidding around with stuff like that," Devlin said. "Don't even be talking about that."

Devlin wasn't very superstitious. He just didn't like to dwell on bad things. The job was full of risks, and if something dangerous had to be done, his attitude was: okay, let's go do it. There was no use talking about it or thinking about it too much. He was the type of person who instinctively ran toward a fire, not from it. And he didn't like to waste time worrying about it first.

Devlin, like Livingston, had grown up in Ohio, graduated from high school in 1977, and joined the Air Force that year. Devlin had to miss his high school graduation; it was held the day after he reported for duty. During basic training, he was seventeen years old. His father and his uncles had been Marines, but Devlin was drawn to the Air Force. He wanted to become a pilot or an airplane mechanic. The Air Force decided, instead, that he would become a Titan II propellant transfer system technician. At training school, he desperately missed his high school sweetheart, Annette Buchanan. With her mother's blessing, they soon got married, and Annette joined him in Arkansas. She was sixteen. The newlyweds started out in a small trailer and then made a down payment on their first house, when Devlin turned nineteen. The house was in Jacksonville, not far from Little Rock Air Force Base. His friends didn't like to throw parties in the dormitories, because they always had to worry about the dorm monitors and the dorm guards. And so almost every weekend, the parties were held at Devlin's house. A fair amount of alcohol was consumed. And if a party got a little out of hand, Devlin knew how to deal with it. He was friendly, courteous, even tempered—and a Golden Gloves boxer, just like his father, his uncles, and one of his grandfathers had been. Devlin trained at a local gym. He fought as a junior middleweight and had recently scored five straight knockouts. When he asked people to quiet down at a party, they generally did.

AT THE COMMAND POST, a checklist was slowly being prepared. Each step had to be discussed on the Missile Potential Hazard Net and then approved by General Leavitt. Colonel Moser spoke on behalf of his team, after listening to the recommendations of the K crew and everyone else on the net. At about eleven o'clock, a consensus seemed to have emerged, and Moser read the latest plan aloud:

1. An airman in a RFHCO suit would carry a portable vapor detector to one of the silo's exhaust vents, place the detector's probe into the white cloud rising from the vent, and measure the amount of fuel vapor. The measurement would give them a sense of whether the silo was safe to enter. At a level of about 18,000 parts per million (ppm), the RFHCO would start to melt. At 20,000 ppm, the fuel vapor could spontaneously combust, without any exposure to a spark or flame, just from the friction caused by the movement of air. Waving your hand through the fuel vapor, at that concentration, could ignite it. The portable vapor detector—a blue rectangular steel box that weighed about twelve pounds, with a round gauge on top—wasn't an ideal instrument for the task. It "pegged out" and shut off when the vapor level reached a maximum of 250 ppm. But it was the best they had.

2. If the proportion of fuel vapor rising from the exhaust shaft was lower than 200 ppm, a couple of airmen in RFHCOs would enter the launch complex through the access portal. Everybody on the hazard net agreed that the escape hatch was too narrow for someone in a RFHCO suit to fit through it.

3. After proceeding through the two outer doors, the airmen would open blast doors 6 and 7 manually with a portable hydraulic pump. Using electricity to open the blast doors might create a spark.

4. The airmen would enter the blast lock and look at the readout from the Mine Safety Appliance. It would tell them the vapor level in the silo. If the level was below 200 ppm, the men would open blast door 9, walk down the long cableway, enter the silo, and vent the stage 1 fuel tank.

5. The airmen would bring a portable vapor detector with them. And if it registered a vapor level higher than 200 ppm at any point during those first four steps, the men would get out of the launch complex as quickly as possible, leaving the doors open behind them.

Colonel Scallorn wasn't happy with part of the plan. He was concerned about the rising heat in the silo, the risk that an oxidizer tank would rupture from the heat, and the huge explosion that would follow. Working outdoors with PTS teams, he'd seen how sensitive the oxidizer could be to small increases in temperature. On a cold, clear day at a launch site in Arkansas, the stainless steel mesh of an oxidizer hose could get warm enough, just from lying in the sun, to blow off a poppet. He thought it would be foolish to enter the silo without knowing the tank pressures inside the missile. It wasn't worth the risk. It would put these young men in harm's way. Over the years, he'd found that some people at SAC headquarters treated maintenance crews and PTS guys like they were expendable.

Scallorn suggested, on the net, that the two airmen should enter the launch control center first, check the tank pressures on the PTPMU, and turn on the purge fan to clear fuel vapor from the silo. They could always go into the silo later.

General Leavitt didn't appreciate the suggestion. "Scallorn, just be quiet and stop telling people what to do," he snapped. "We're trying to figure this thing out."

"Roger, General," Scallorn replied. "You got that, Moser?"

It was an awkward moment. Nobody liked to hear one of SAC's leading Titan II experts being told to shut up.

Not long afterward, Charles E. Carnahan, a vice president at Martin Marietta, who'd been quietly listening to the discussion, spoke up.

"Little Rock, this is Martin-Denver," Carnahan said. "Are you interested in any of our judgments in this matter?"

Of course, Leavitt told him, go ahead.

"If it was us, we would seriously consider not moving into the silo area for some number of hours."

Carnahan was asked if he meant the silo or the entire launch complex.

"I am talking about the launch complex," he said. "It is entirely possible that the leak is still leaking. It is our judgment that while the leak continues, the vapor content in the silo and the general area will continue to rise. The potential for a monopropellic explosion increases as the vapor content increases. Once the leak has leaked out, if you have no explosion, it is our judgment that the vapor content in the area will decrease. We are unclear as to the gain that is expected from an early entry, or an entry at this point in time, into the complex area."

After hours of debating what to do, the Missile Potential Hazard Team now had to ponder the advice of the company that built the missile: do nothing.

A SMALL GROUP OF REPORTERS stood along Highway 65, watching the Air Force trucks roll up. It was about half past eleven, and Sid King was impressed by all the Air Force personnel and equipment that suddenly appeared. Crews from the local television stations in Little Rock pointed their lights and cameras at the vehicles, as military police tried to keep the press off the access road. A cattle guard about thirty feet from the highway served as the line that civilians were prohibited to cross. The questions shouted by reporters were ignored. Sergeant Joseph W. Cotton, the public affairs officer who'd arrived with the Disaster Response Force, had already told the press that there was a fuel leak and it was under control. Cotton refused to say anything more. And he gave reporters the phone number of SAC headquarters in Omaha, in case they had any further questions.

King and his friend Tom Phillips thought about sneaking closer to the launch complex to see what was happening. King knew Ralph and Reba Jo Parish, who owned the farm to the north of the missile site. Although the Parishes had been evacuated, King was sure they wouldn't mind his entering the property and heading west through their fields toward the silo. King and Phillips quietly discussed the plan, feeling confident they wouldn't get caught. It was dark out there. But they wondered what would happen if they were caught—and decided, for the time being, to stay put.

PTS Team B unloaded their gear just past the cattle guard, along the road to the launch complex, relying on flashlights to see what they were doing. The television crews had better lights.

Man, those look like space suits, Sid King thought, as the RFHCOs and their helmets were unpacked. He was struck by how young the airmen appeared. He'd expected to see gray-haired scientists and high-ranking Air Force officers coming to fix the missile. These guys were younger than him. They were kids.

Once the RFHCOs were laid out, the air packs filled, and everything ready to go, Sergeant Hanson walked over to Colonel Morris. He told Morris that a couple of people would be sent through the access portal into the silo.

Colonel Morris hadn't heard anything about a plan to reenter the complex.

"Hey, wait a minute," Morris said. "We're not doing anything until I get directions."

Morris got on the radio to the command post and asked, what's the plan? He was told to stand by, they were still working on it.

COLONEL MOSER ASKED SAC headquarters if they should follow Martin Marietta's advice.

"Well, let's go over what we've got here," General Leavitt said.

About half an hour earlier, Leavitt had called Governor Clinton in Hot Springs. Their conversation was brief and polite. He told Clinton that a team was about to reenter the complex and that the situation was under control. Clinton thanked him for the update and went to bed.

But Leavitt had changed his mind. He decided that they should wait and allow the fuel vapor to dissipate before sending anyone near the missile. And he asked everyone on the net to discuss what had happened at 4-7, from the moment the socket was dropped.

JEFF KENNEDY LAY ON THE GRASS atop a low hill. Silas Spann, a member of PTS Team B, sat beside him. Spann was one of the few African Americans who worked in missile maintenance, and he stood out in this part of rural Arkansas. Whenever he walked into one of the local shops, people looked surprised. Kennedy and Spann could see the launch complex down below. A thick white cloud still floated from the vents. The two men wondered what would happen if the missile exploded. Would the blast doors and the silo door hold, would they fully contain the blast? Both agreed that the doors would. They had faith in those big fucking doors. It was a warm, beautiful night with a slight breeze and plenty of stars in the sky.

DON GREEN WAS AT LITTLE ROCK Air Force Base, guarding the weapons storage area, around midnight, when a new set of officers came on duty. Green was told that he could go home. Before leaving, he stopped by central security control to see if anybody needed help. He bumped into another security officer, Sergeant Jimmy Roberts, who'd come there for the same reason. Roberts worked across the hall from Green, and the two were friends. They both felt like being useful; it was a busy night. A third security officer walked into the office and asked for a map. He was supposed to escort a flatbed truck carrying an all-terrain forklift to Launch Complex 374-7 but didn't know how to get there. The job sounded pretty urgent: they needed the forklift to haul light-all units onto the complex, so that the PTS team could see what they were doing.

Green and Roberts said they'd be glad to escort the flatbed. They knew the way and could get the forklift out there fast. Instead of going home and getting into bed, they got into a pickup and headed to Damascus.

COLONEL MOSER LEFT the Missile Potential Hazard Net and used the Security Police Net to speak directly with Morris. It was almost one in the morning, and a decision had been made. He told Morris that three airmen should put on RFHCO suits. A checklist had been prepared, and Moser wanted him to copy it down, word for word.

Morris grabbed a piece of paper and a pencil and, while sitting in the front seat of Brocksmith's truck, copied down the instructions.

It was the same checklist that the command post had prepared two hours earlier, except that the 200 ppm fuel vapor limit had been raised to 250 ppm.

Morris spent fifteen minutes listening carefully and writing down exactly what Moser said. They finished—and then Moser paused, told him to stand by, and signed off.

Morris sat in the truck, waiting. Twenty minutes later, Colonel Moser was on the radio again. There was a slight change of plan: instead of entering the silo, the two airmen in RFHCOs should enter the control center. Moser stressed that the men should avoid passing through any fuel vapor. He didn't want anyone to get hurt. And he passed along General Leavitt's instructions that no electrical switch should be turned on or off without permission from SAC headquarters.

Colonel Morris left the truck, gathered the members of PTS Team B, and read them the final checklist. He went through every step. And he said, we don't want any heroes out there. We'll do exactly what's on the paper, and that's all, and then we're all going to come back.

"Colonel, this is unreal," Jeff Kennedy said. Kennedy could not believe that this was the plan. It was insane. It made absolutely no sense to send men into the launch complex through the access portal, instead of the escape hatch. The access portal was a much more dangerous route. If you went through the escape hatch, the trip to the control center would be quick and direct, and you wouldn't have to open any blast doors with a goddamn hand pump. If you went through the escape hatch, you'd be protected by the blast doors, not impeded by them. And the escape hatch was on the opposite side of the complex from the missile. The access portal was a lot closer to the missile. Why send anyone in there? Of course you'd have to sample for fuel vapor every step of the way; you'd be in danger every step of the way. To reach the control center, the men would have to pass through the blast lock—and it was full of fuel vapor six hours ago, when PTS Team A opened the door a crack, took a peek, and then had to slam it shut. Why send anyone down the longest, most dangerous, most likely to be contaminated route? Kennedy thought this checklist must have been written by somebody who'd never set foot on a Titan II complex. Of course you can fit a man in RFHCO through the escape hatch, Kennedy argued. He'd just been through the escape hatch, so he ought to know.

Kennedy, this is the plan, Morris said. This is the plan that's come down, and that's it. End of discussion.

Sergeant Hanson had selected the three men who'd enter the complex and the three who would wait in RFHCOs, halfway down the access road, as backup. Kennedy wasn't one of them. Kennedy and Hanson didn't get along. Hanson wished Kennedy had returned to the base with the rest of PTS Team A. As team chief, Hanson was in charge of this operation. He didn't think you could fit through the escape hatch in a RFHCO. He liked the checklist, and if Kennedy didn't, that was too bad.

David Livingston, Greg Devlin, and Rex Hukle, a farm boy from Kansas, climbed into the back of a pickup truck, wearing their RFHCOs. Colonel Morris got into the front seat, along with Hanson and Captain George Short, chief of the field maintenance branch at the 308th. Before the truck drove down the road to the complex, Jeff Kennedy jumped into the back.

Outside the gate, Livingston, Devlin, and Hukle drew straws to see who would be the first to go in. Walking over to the exhaust vent, alone, as fuel vapor poured out of it, seemed like a brave thing to do. All of them were willing, but this felt like the best way to choose.

David Livingston drew the short straw.

Before anyone could enter the launch complex, a hole had to be cut in the chain-link fence. The gate was still locked, nobody had the key, and climbing over the fence in a RFHCO could tear the suit. Morris, Hanson, and Short spent about fifteen minutes making a hole with bolt cutters. They finished at two in the morning. Livingston put on his helmet and his air pack and prepared to go in. Although the pack was designed to hold an hour's worth of air, the command post had instructed that it should be used for just half an hour. The air packs were considered unreliable—and running out of air amid a thick cloud of fuel vapor could kill you.

Hanson and Morris got into the front seat of the truck. Morris would stay in touch with the command post on the Security Police Net, and Hanson would talk to Livingston on the radio network at the launch complex. The two radio systems were incompatible. If General Leavitt wanted to give Livingston an order, Leavitt would have to tell Moser, who would have to tell Morris, who would have to tell Hanson, who would have to tell Livingston. Although Hanson had brought along a repeater to strengthen the signal, reception on the complex was spotty.

Carrying a flashlight and a vapor detector, Livingston went through the hole in the fence. He saw a cloud of white vapor streaming from the silo's exhaust vents, like steam from a boiling kettle. He entered the complex, crossed the gravel near the hardstand, and approached one of the vents. Hanson had told him to get the vapor detector as close as possible to the cloud, without getting engulfed in it if the wind shifted. Livingston stuck the probe into the mist, and the needle on the gauge shot all the way to the right.

The portable vapor detector has pegged out, Livingston said.

Hanson told Morris, who informed the command post. The news was shared with everyone on the net.

Colonel Scallorn thought the mission was over—the detector had pegged out.

Sergeant Hanson told Livingston to put his hand over the vent and try to get a sense of the vapor temperature. Hanson had meant to bring a thermometer from the base but had forgotten it.

Scallorn kept expecting someone on the net to call it off and bring this boy back to the truck. He didn't understand why they were sending anyone into the complex at two in the morning. They'd already waited more than seven hours to do something. It seemed too late now.

Livingston put his hand over the metal grate. He could feel the heat through his glove.

Colonel Morris told the command post that he was bringing Livingston back.

Livingston returned from the complex, took off his helmet, and leaned against the bed of the pickup.

"It's hot as hell over there," he said.

At the command post, members of the K crew assumed that the mission was over. The fuel vapor hadn't dissipated—like Martin Marietta had suggested it would—and the portable vapor detector couldn't reveal how high the level really was. It was at least 250 ppm, the cutoff mark that everyone had agreed upon. SAC headquarters ordered Devlin and Hukle to enter the launch complex.

The men put on their helmets and air packs and grabbed their equipment. They had a lot more gear than Livingston. Between the two of them, Devlin and Hukle carried a portable vapor detector, flashlights, the hydraulic hand pump, and a tool bag holding screwdrivers, Crescent wrenches, and pliers. They also brought a couple of crowbars.

The outer steel door and the door at the bottom of the entrapment area were locked—and could no longer be jimmied open with a credit card. Devlin and Hukle would have to break into the launch complex with crowbars. Nobody knew how difficult that would be since nobody there had ever done it.

The two young airmen in RFHCO suits, holding their flashlights and crowbars and tools, went through the hole in the fence.

Part Four

OUT OF CONTROL

Decapitation

On January 23, 1961, a B-52 bomber took off from Seymour Johnson Air Force Base in Goldsboro, North Carolina, for an airborne alert. The flight plan was a long, circular route along the East Coast. At the end of the first loop, the B-52 met its tanker a couple of minutes early and refueled. At the end of the second loop, after more than ten hours in the air, the bomber refueled again. It was almost midnight. Amid the darkness, the boom operator of the tanker noticed fuel leaking from the B-52's right wing. Spray from the leak soon formed a wide plume, and within two minutes about forty thousand gallons of jet fuel had poured from the wing. The command post at Seymour Johnson told the pilot, Major Walter S. Tulloch, to dump the rest of the fuel in the ocean and prepare for an emergency landing. But fuel wouldn't drain from the tank inside the left wing, creating a weight imbalance. At half past midnight, with the flaps down and the landing gear extended, the B-52 went into an uncontrolled spin.

Major Tulloch heard a loud explosion and ordered his crew to bail out, as the plane started to break apart at an altitude of ten thousand feet. Four of the men ejected safely, including Tulloch. First Lieutenant Adam C. Mattocks managed to jump through the escape hatch, while the bomber was upside down, and survived. Major Eugene Shelton ejected but suffered a fatal head injury. The radar navigator, Major Eugene H. Richards, and Technical Sergeant Francis R. Barnish died in the crash.

The B-52 was carrying two Mark 39 hydrogen bombs, each with a yield of 4 megatons. As the aircraft spun downward, centrifugal forces pulled a lanyard in the cockpit. The lanyard was attached to the bomb release mechanism. When the lanyard was pulled, the locking pins were removed from one of the bombs. The Mark 39 fell from the plane. The arming wires were yanked out, and the bomb responded as though it had been deliberately released by the crew above a target. The pulse generator activated the low-voltage thermal batteries. The drogue parachute opened, and then the main chute. The barometric switches closed. The timer ran out, activating the high-voltage thermal batteries. The bomb hit the ground, and the piezoelectric crystals inside the nose crushed. They sent a firing signal. But the weapon didn't detonate.

Every safety mechanism had failed, except one: the ready/safe switch in the cockpit. The switch was in the SAFE position when the bomb dropped. Had the switch been set to GROUND or AIR, the X-unit would've charged, the detonators would've triggered, and a thermonuclear weapon would have exploded in a field near Faro, North Carolina. When Air Force personnel found the Mark 39 later that morning, the bomb was harmlessly stuck in the ground, nose first, its parachute draped in the branches of a tree.

The other Mark 39 plummeted straight down and landed in a meadow just off Big Daddy's Road, near the Nahunta Swamp. Its parachutes had failed to open. The high explosives did not detonate, and the primary was largely undamaged. But the dense uranium secondary of the bomb penetrated more than seventy feet into the soggy ground. A recovery team never found it, despite weeks of digging.

The Air Force assured the public that the two weapons had been unarmed and that there was never any risk of a nuclear explosion. Those statements were misleading. The T-249 control box and ready/safe switch, installed in every one of SAC's bombers, had already raised concerns at Sandia. The switch required a low-voltage signal of brief duration to operate—and that kind of signal could easily be provided by a stray wire or a short circuit, as a B-52 full of electronic equipment disintegrated midair.

A year after the North Carolina accident, a SAC ground crew removed four Mark 28 bombs from a B-47 bomber and noticed that all of the weapons were armed. But the seal on the ready/safe switch in the cockpit was intact, and the knob hadn't been turned to GROUND or AIR. The bombs had not been armed by the crew. A seven-month investigation by Sandia found that a tiny metal nut had come off a screw inside the plane and lodged against an unused radar-heating circuit. The nut had created a new electrical pathway, allowing current to reach an arming line—and bypass the ready/safe switch. A similar glitch on the B-52 that crashed near Goldsboro would have caused a 4-megaton thermonuclear explosion. "It would have been bad news—in spades," Parker F. Jones, a safety engineer at Sandia, wrote in a memo about the accident. "One simple, dynamo-technology, low-voltage switch stood between the United States and a major catastrophe!"

With strong northerly winds, the groundburst of that 4-megaton bomb in Goldsboro would have deposited lethal fallout over Washington, D.C., Baltimore, Philadelphia, and New York City. And the timing would have been unfortunate: the new president of the United States, John F. Kennedy, had delivered his inaugural address only three days earlier, promising renewal and change, vowing to "pay any price, bear any burden, meet any hardship, support any friend, oppose any foe, to assure the survival and the success of liberty." The spirit of youthful optimism sweeping the United States would have been dimmed by the detonation of a hydrogen bomb in North Carolina and an evacuation of the nation's capital.

The Goldsboro accident, far from being an isolated or improbable event, was a portent of the nuclear threats that the Kennedy administration would have to confront. Robert S. McNamara, the new secretary of defense, learned about the accident during his third day on the job. The story scared the hell out of him. McNamara knew remarkably little about nuclear weapons. The previous month, when Kennedy had asked him to head the Department of Defense, McNamara was the president of the Ford Motor

Company. He was a young, supremely self-confident businessman devoted to systems analysis and efficiency. At the Harvard Business School, he'd taught accounting. Aside from a three-year stint in the Army Air Forces—where he'd served in the Office of Statistical Control and helped General LeMay calculate optimal fuel use for the bombing of Japan—McNamara had no military experience. And he'd spent little time thinking about military strategy or procurement. Determined to shake things up at the Pentagon, McNamara found himself, instead, feeling profoundly shaken during his first week on the job.

The B-52 crash in North Carolina wasn't the only accident that involved fully assembled, sealed-pit weapons—and McNamara soon learned about others. A B-47 carrying a Mark 39 bomb had caught fire while taking off at Dyess Air Force Base, near Abilene, Texas. At an altitude of about two hundred feet, the pilot realized the plane was on fire, banked to avoid a populated area, and ordered the crew to bail out. Three of the four crew members got out in time. The plane entered a vertical dive, hit the ground, and vanished in a fireball. The high explosives of the hydrogen bomb detonated but didn't produce a nuclear yield. A few weeks later a B-47 carrying a Mark 39 bomb caught fire on the runway at Chennault Air Force Base in Lake Charles, Louisiana. The crew escaped, and the weapon didn't explode. It melted into radioactive slag.

In the skies above Hardinsburg, Kentucky, a B-52 carrying two hydrogen bombs collided with a tanker while attempting to refuel. The crew of the B-52 heard a "crunching sound," all the lights went out, the cabin rapidly decompressed, and the plane began to disintegrate. Four of the crew ejected safely. The other four were killed, as were all four members of the tanker's crew. The wreckage of the two planes covered an area of roughly twenty-seven square miles. The hydrogen bombs were torn open by the crash. The nuclear cores of their primaries were discovered, intact, resting on piles of broken high explosives.

At an air defense site in Jackson Township, New Jersey, a helium tank ruptured near a BOMARC missile, starting a fire. A pair of explosions soon followed inside the concrete shelter that housed the missile. Fifty-five other BOMARCs lay in similar shelters, beneath corrugated steel roofs, nearby. When emergency personnel arrived, the fire was out of control. They put fire hoses in the entrances to the burning shelter and fled the area. An Air Force security officer called the state police and mistakenly reported that a nuclear weapon had exploded at the site—spreading panic throughout central New Jersey and prompting civil defense authorities to go on full alert in New York City, seventy miles to the north. Fallout from the BOMARC's 10-kiloton warhead, it was feared, could reach Trenton, the state capital, Princeton, Newark—and, possibly, Manhattan. Firefighters returned to the missile site about an hour and a half after the initial explosions and put out the fire. The warhead had fallen out of the nose cone. The high explosives had burned, instead of detonating, and the nuclear core had melted onto the floor. The shelter contained most of the radioactivity. But water from the fire hoses had swept plutonium residue under the doors, down the street, and into a drainage ditch.

The accidents in North Carolina and Texas worried Robert McNamara the most. In one crash, the failure of a single mechanical switch could have led to a full-scale, thermonuclear explosion; in the other, the detonation of the Mark 39's high explosives was the sort of one-point safety test that you never want to conduct in the real world. The Mark 39 had passed the test—this time. It wasn't something that McNamara wanted to see repeated. The lapses in weapon safety seemed to be part of a much larger problem: a sense of disarray and mismanagement at the Pentagon, extending from the budget process to the planning for nuclear war. In his view, the Department of Defense had been saddled with the previous administration's intellectual "bankruptcy in both strategic policy and in the force structure." McNamara was determined to bring order, rational management, and common sense to the workings of the Pentagon, as quickly as possible.

DURING THE 1960 CAMPAIGN, John F. Kennedy had repeatedly attacked President Eisenhower for allowing the Soviet Union to surpass the United States in military power. "The Communists will have a dangerous lead in intercontinental missiles through 1963," the platform of the Democratic Party declared, and "the Republican administration has no plans to catch up." Kennedy argued that Eisenhower's strategy of massive retaliation had left the United States in a helpless position, unable to prevent the Soviets from subverting and overthrowing governments friendly to the West. An overreliance on nuclear weapons had made American promises to defend the free world seem hollow. "We have been driving ourselves into a corner where the only choice is all or nothing at all, world devastation or submission," Kennedy warned.

General Maxwell Taylor's book, *The Uncertain Trumpet*, and its call for a nuclear strategy of flexible response had greatly impressed Kennedy. He agreed with Taylor's central thesis: in a crisis, the president should have a wide range of military options. Kennedy wanted the ability to fight limited wars, conventional wars—and a nuclear war with the Soviets that could be stopped short of mutual annihilation. "Controlled response" and "controlled escalation" and "pauses for negotiation" became buzzwords in the Kennedy administration. If the American military had the means to prevail in a variety of different ways, with or without nuclear weapons, the United States could resist Soviet influence throughout the world. "The record of the Romans made clear," Kennedy later told his national security staff, "that their success was dependent on their will and ability to fight successfully at the edges of their empire."

Despite the harsh, personal attacks during the presidential campaign, Eisenhower helped the new administration with its reappraisal of nuclear strategy. His science adviser's memo on the shortcomings of the Single Integrated Operational Plan was forwarded to McNamara and Kennedy. The memo supported many of the arguments against the SIOP made by General Taylor and leading officers in the Navy. The chief of naval operations, Admiral Arleigh Burke, warned that such a large, undiscriminating attack on the Soviet Union would deposit lethal fallout not only on American allies like South Korea and Japan but also on the U.S. Navy's Pacific fleet. A reappraisal of the nation's entire military stance now seemed urgent, and President Kennedy asked McNamara to lead it—to raise fundamental questions about how weapons were procured, what purpose they served, and whether they were even necessary.

Although a year older than the president, McNamara, at forty-four, was the youngest person, thus far, to head the Department of Defense. And he recruited a group of cocky and iconoclastic young men to join the administration, academics from Harvard and MIT, RAND analysts, economists, Rhodes scholars. Henry Rowen, a graduate of Harvard and Oxford who soon played a large role in nuclear planning, was thirty-six. Harold Brown, chosen to guide Pentagon research on new weapon systems and technology, was thirty-three. Alain Enthoven, an economist who rigorously applied cost-benefit analysis to the defense budget, was thirty. Later depicted as "whiz kids," "defense intellectuals," "the best and the brightest," McNamara's team was determined to transform America's nuclear strategy and defense spending.

Three days after the Goldsboro accident, McNamara met with members of the Pentagon's Weapons Systems Evaluation Group (WSEG). It had recently completed a study, WSEG Report No. 50, that described the Soviet forces the United States would most likely face by the mid-1960s and compared the merits of different tactics to oppose them. Eisenhower's secretary of defense, Thomas B. Gates, had seen the report a few months earlier and thought McNamara should know about it. McNamara's briefing on WSEG Report No. 50, scheduled to last a few hours, wound up occupying a full day. The authors of the report had measured the economic efficiency of various American weapon systems—explaining, for example, that the annual operating costs of keeping a B-52 bomber on ground alert was about nine times larger than the annual maintenance costs of a Minuteman missile. That was just the sort of data that Robert McNamara craved. But the authors of WSEG R-50 had also reached a conclusion that nobody in the Kennedy administration wanted to hear: America's command-and-control system was so complex, outdated, and unreliable that a "controlled" or "flexible" response to a Soviet attack would be impossible. In fact, the president of the United States might not be able to make any response; he would probably be killed during the first moments of a nuclear war.

By launching a surprise attack on five targets—the White House, the Pentagon, Camp David, Site R, and High Point—the Soviet Union had a good chance of wiping out the civilian leadership of the United States.

None of the bunkers at those locations would survive the blast from a multimegaton weapon. And two of the emergency command posts, Site R and High Point, weren't regularly staffed with high-ranking officers. By hitting nine additional targets, the Soviet Union could eliminate America's military leadership. The destruction of America's command-and-control system could be achieved, with a 90 percent chance of success, through the use of only thirty-five Soviet missiles. Four would be aimed at the White House and five at Camp David, to ensure that the president was killed. "Under surprise attack conditions, there can be little confidence," the report concluded, "that the Presidential decision would be made and military execution orders be received by the combat elements of the strategic nuclear forces before the high command is disrupted."

Moreover, the command bunkers built during the Eisenhower years lacked the communications equipment that would allow the controlled escalation of a nuclear war or pauses for negotiation with the Soviets—even if the president survived the initial attack. The high-frequency radio system used to communicate with SAC's bombers and the very-low-frequency system used to contact the Navy's Polaris submarines relied on a handful of terminals that could easily be destroyed. According to one classified account, the Eisenhower administration had installed "a one-shot command, control, and communication system." It hadn't been designed to fight a limited or prolonged nuclear war. The SIOP required only that a Go code be transmitted, and after that, nothing needed to be said—because nothing could be done to change or halt the execution of the war plan. The underground command posts were little more than hideouts, where military and civilian leaders could ride out a nuclear attack and then emerge, perhaps, to rebuild the United States.

America's early-warning systems were also woefully inadequate. The DEW Line of radar stations stretching across the Arctic, the SAGE direction centers, the mighty IBM computers—built with great urgency, at enormous expense—had been designed to track Soviet bombers. They could not detect Soviet missiles. The Ballistic Missile Early Warning System, created for that task, was just becoming operational. At best, the BMEWS could spot missiles launched from the Soviet Union roughly fifteen minutes before they hit the United States. But if the missiles were launched from Soviet submarines off the coast, the warning time would be zero. The BMEWS couldn't detect missiles approaching at such a low altitude. And the reliability of the system, McNamara learned, still left much to be desired.

DURING A TOUR OF NORAD headquarters in Colorado Springs, Colorado, a few months earlier, Peter G. Peterson, the executive vice president of the Bell & Howell Company, had been allowed to sit in the commander's chair. Peterson was visiting the facility with Bell & Howell's president, Charles H. Percy, and Thomas J. Watson, Jr., the president of IBM. The first BMEWS radar complex, located at Thule Air Base, Greenland, had come online that week, and the numerical threat levels of the new warning system were being explained to the businessmen.

If the number 1 flashed in red above the world map, unidentified objects were traveling toward the United States. If the number 3 flashed, the threat level was high; SAC headquarters and the Joint Chiefs of Staff had to be notified immediately. The maximum threat level was 5—a computer-generated warning, with a 99.9 percent certainty, that the United States was under attack. As Peterson sat in the commander's chair, the number above the map began to climb. When it reached 4, NORAD officers ran into the room. When it reached 5, Peterson and the other executives were quickly escorted out and put in a small office. The door was closed, and they were left there believing that a nuclear war had just begun.

The vice commander of NORAD, Air Marshal C. Roy Slemon, a dapper Canadian with a small mustache, managed to track down the head of NORAD, General Laurence S. Kuter, who was in an Air Force plane above South Dakota.

"Chief, this is a hot one," Slemon said.

The BMEWS indicated that the Soviets had launched an all-out missile attack against North America. The Joint Chiefs of Staff were on the phone, awaiting confirmation. The United States had only minutes to respond.

"Where is Khrushchev?" Slemon asked his officers.

Khrushchev's in New York today, at the United Nations, NORAD's chief of intelligence said.

Slemon immediately felt relieved. The Soviet Union was unlikely to launch an attack that would kill the first secretary of its Communist Party. Twenty minutes passed, and no Soviet missiles landed. The three businessmen were let out of the small office, glad to be alive. When news of the false alarm leaked to the press, the Air Force denied that the missile warning had ever been taken seriously. Percy, who later became a Republican senator from Illinois, disputed that account. He recalled a sense of panic at NORAD. A subsequent investigation found the cause of the computer glitch. The BMEWS site at Thule had mistakenly identified the moon, slowly rising over Norway, as dozens of long-range missiles launched from Siberia.

Both of America's early-warning systems were deeply flawed—and, as a result, the most reliable indicator of a Soviet attack might be the destruction of those systems by nuclear blasts. Bomb Alarm System sensors would be placed at the SAGE direction centers and at Thule. By the time those bomb sensors went off, however, the president might already be dead. Of the fourteen potential successors, as specified by Congress, only the vice president and the secretary of defense would have any familiarity with the SIOP. If all fourteen were in Washington, D.C., during a surprise attack, they would probably be killed or incapacitated.

Amid the confusion, it might be impossible to determine who was America's commander in chief. Everyone on the presidential succession list had been given a phone number to call, in case of a national emergency. The call would put them in touch with the Joint War Room at the Pentagon. But telephone service was bound to be disrupted by a nuclear attack, the Pentagon might no longer exist—and even if it did, the first person to call the war room might be named president of the United States, regardless of whether he or she was next on the list. WSEG Report No. 50 outlined the problem:

There is no mechanism for nor organization charged with locating, identifying, and providing essential defense communications to the senior, non-incapacitated member of that list in the event of a nuclear attack presumed to have removed the President from control. . . . The possibility exists that the man to wield Presidential authority in dire emergency might in fact be selected by a single field grade military officer.

The idea of a "decapitation" attack, aimed at America's military and civilian leadership, didn't seem entirely far-fetched. Indeed, it was the most plausible scenario for a Soviet attack on the United States. And it had the best chance of success. "No other target system can at present offer equal potential returns from so few weapons," the report said.

McNamara subsequently discovered that the command-and-control problems were hardly limited to the United States. "We have been concerned with the vulnerability of our defense machine in the U.S.," a Pentagon task force informed him, "but it is nothing compared with the situation in Europe." All of NATO's command bunkers, including the operations center inside the Kindsbach Cave, could easily be destroyed, even by an attack with conventional weapons. Although NATO maintained fighter planes on a ground alert, ready to take off within fifteen minutes, it lacked an early-warning system that could detect Soviet missiles. It also lacked a bomb alarm system. At best, NATO commanders might receive five or ten minutes of warning that a Soviet attack had begun—not enough time to get those planes off the ground. And that warning would most likely never be received, because the NATO communications system was completely unprotected. Its destruction would prevent NATO from transmitting messages not only within Europe but also between Europe and the United States. Once the fighting began, the president could not expect to reach any of NATO's high-ranking officers or to give them any orders. And they wouldn't be able to communicate with one another.

The Pentagon task force found that NATO had done little to prepare for the devolution of command in wartime:

It is imperative that each commander knows when a higher headquarters has been erased or isolated from command; that he knows his own responsibilities as the situation degrades; that he knows the status of similar commands at his level elsewhere; and that he knows the status of lower echelons, and what responsibilities they can assume. It appears that this is not the case in Europe today.

The absence of early-warning capabilities, the poor communications, and the lack of any succession plan at NATO posed a grave, immediate risk. "Not only could we initiate a war, through mistakes in Europe," McNamara was told, "but we could conceivably precipitate Soviet pre-emptive action because of a loose C & C [command and control] in Europe." The situation was made even more dangerous by the predelegation authority that Eisenhower had secretly granted to the military. NATO units under attack were permitted to use their nuclear weapons, without awaiting presidential approval. The new national security adviser, McGeorge Bundy, succinctly explained the rules to President Kennedy: "A subordinate commander faced with a substantial Russian military action could start the thermonuclear holocaust on his own initiative if he could not reach you (by failure of the communication at either end of the line)."

Any use of nuclear weapons in Europe, McNamara now believed, would quickly escalate to an all-out war. And the more he learned about America's nuclear deployments in Europe, the more he worried about such a catastrophe. Three weeks after the Goldsboro accident, Congress's Joint Committee on Atomic Energy sent Kennedy and McNamara a top secret report, based on a recent tour of NATO bases. It warned that the risk of an accidental or unauthorized nuclear detonation in Europe was unacceptably high—not just in wartime, but also during routine NATO maneuvers. NATO's command-and-control problems were so bad, the bipartisan committee found, that in many respects the United States no longer had custody of its own nuclear weapons. Within months the NATO stockpile would include atomic bombs, hydrogen bombs, thermonuclear warheads, nuclear artillery shells, nuclear depth charges, nuclear land mines, and the Davy Crockett, a recoilless rifle, carried like a bazooka by an infantryman, that fired small nuclear projectiles. But none of these weapons, except the land mines—formally known as Atomic Demolition Munitions—had any sort of lock to prevent somebody from setting them off without permission. And the three-digit mechanical locks on the land mines, like those often found on gym lockers, were easy to pick. According to one adviser, when Secretary of Defense McNamara heard that hundreds of American nuclear weapons stored in Europe were poorly guarded, vulnerable to theft, and unlocked, "he almost fell out of his chair."

THE JOINT COMMITTEE on Atomic Energy had been concerned for almost a year that NATO's custody arrangements were inadequate—and in violation of American law. The Atomic Energy Act of 1946 strictly prohibited the transfer of nuclear weapons, as well as classified information about them, to foreign countries. The act was amended in 1954 so that NATO forces could be trained to use tactical weapons. After the launch of *Sputnik*, President Eisenhower asked Congress to change the law again and allow the creation of a NATO atomic stockpile. "I have always been of the belief that we should not deny to our allies," Eisenhower said, "what your potential enemy already has." His proposal was opposed by many in Congress, who feared that it might be difficult to retain American control of nuclear weapons based in Europe. The Soviet Union strongly opposed the idea, too. Hatreds inspired by the Second World War still lingered—and the Soviets were especially upset by the prospect of German troops armed with nuclear weapons. In order to gain congressional approval, the Eisenhower administration promised that the weapons would remain, at all times, under the supervision of American military personnel. The nuclear cores would be held by the United States until the outbreak of war, and then the cores would be handed over to NATO forces. Secretary of State Christian A. Herter assured the Soviet Union that "an essential element" of the NATO stockpile would be that "custody of atomic warheads remains exclusively with the United States."

On January 1, 1960, General Lauris Norstad, the supreme allied commander in Europe, placed all of NATO's nuclear-capable units on a fifteen-minute alert, without consulting Congress. Every NATO air squadron was ordered to keep at least two fighter planes loaded with fuel and a nuclear weapon, parked near a runway. And thermonuclear warheads were mated to the intermediate-range Jupiter missiles in Italy and the Thor missiles in

Great Britain. The new alert policy had the full support of President Eisenhower, who thought that NATO should be able to respond promptly to a Soviet attack. Eisenhower had faith in the discipline of NATO forces. And he had, most likely, a private understanding with Norstad similar to the one made with LeMay—granting the permission to use nuclear weapons, if Washington, D.C., had been destroyed or couldn't be reached during a wartime emergency. The supreme commander of NATO reported directly to the president, not to the Joint Chiefs of Staff, and Norstad was fiercely protective of his authority. He disliked General Thomas Power, the head of the Strategic Air Command, and wanted to preserve NATO's ability to destroy the Soviet Union without any help from SAC. The thermonuclear warheads atop NATO's Jupiter missiles were aimed at Soviet cities. With those missiles, and the hundreds of other nuclear weapons under NATO command, Norstad could conceivably fight his own war against the Soviets, on his own terms.

Members of the Joint Committee on Atomic Energy visited fifteen NATO bases in December 1960, eager to see how America's nuclear weapons were being deployed. The group was accompanied by Harold Agnew, the Los Alamos physicist who'd come up with the idea of attaching parachutes to hydrogen bombs and later helped to develop one-point safety standards. Agnew was an expert on how to design bombs—and how to handle them properly. At a NATO base in Germany, Agnew looked out at the runway and, in his own words, "nearly wet my pants." The F-84F fighter planes on alert, each carrying a fully assembled Mark 7 bomb, were being guarded by a single American soldier. Agnew walked over and asked the young enlisted man, who carried an old-fashioned, bolt-action rifle, what he'd do if somebody jumped into one of the planes and tried to take off. Would he shoot at the pilot—or the bomb? The soldier had never been told what to do. The wings of the fighters were decorated with the Iron Cross, a symbol that powerfully evoked two world wars. Agnew realized there was little to prevent a German pilot from taking a plane, flying it to the Soviet Union, and dropping an atomic bomb.

The custody arrangements at the Jupiter missile sites in Italy were even more alarming. Each site had three missiles topped with a 1.4-megaton warhead—a weapon capable of igniting firestorms and flattening every brick structure within thirty square miles. All the security was provided by Italian troops. The launch authentication officer was the only American at the site. Two keys were required to launch the missiles; one was held by the American, the other by an Italian officer. The keys were often worn on a string around the neck, like a dog tag.

Congressman Chet Holifield, the chairman of the joint committee, was amazed to find three ballistic missiles, carrying thermonuclear weapons, in the custody of a single American officer with a handgun. "All [the Italians] have to do is hit him on the head with a blackjack, and they have got his key," Holifield said, during a closed-door committee hearing after the trip. The Jupiters were located near a forest, without any protective covering, and brightly illuminated at night. They would be sitting ducks for a sniper. "There were three Jupiters setting there in the open—all pointed toward the sky," Holifield told the committee. "Over $300 million has been spent to set up that little show and it can be knocked out with 3 rifle bullets."

Foreign personnel weren't supposed to enter the nuclear weapon igloos at NATO bases. But little had been done to stop them. A lone American soldier manned the entrance to the igloos, serving as a custodian of the weapons, not as an armed guard. Once again, security was provided by troops from the host nation, who also moved weapons in and out of the storage facilities. Senator Albert A. Gore, Sr., could hardly believe the arrangement: "Non-Americans with non-American vehicles are transporting nuclear weapons from place to place in foreign countries." It was one thing to entrust these weapons to the Strategic Air Command, with its strict operating procedures and rigorous devotion to checklists. But the competence of NATO troops varied considerably. And their level of professionalism wasn't the most important consideration, when it came to guarding America's nuclear weapons. "The prime loyalty of the guards, of course, is to their own nation, and not to the U.S.," the joint committee said.

A nuclear weapon might be stolen by a deranged or psychotic NATO soldier; by a group of officers seeking political power; or by the government of a host nation, for use against an enemy other than the Soviet Union. These scenarios were, unfortunately, plausible. A pair of NATO countries,

Greece and Turkey, despised each other and would soon go to war over the island of Cyprus. Right-wing officers had staged two coups d'état in Turkey during the previous year, and Jupiter missiles were scheduled for deployment there in the fall of 1961. Covertly funded by the Soviet Union, the Italian Communist Party had strong support in the region where Jupiter missiles were based. Members of the party might seek to sabotage or steal a nuclear weapon. Concerns about theft weren't absurd or far-fetched. A few months after the joint committee's visit to NATO bases, a group of dissident French officers sought to gain control of a nuclear device in Algeria, as part of a coup. At the time, Algeria was the site of French nuclear tests—and a French colony fighting for independence. A nuclear test codenamed *"Gerboise verte"* was promptly conducted in the Sahara desert so that the officers attempting to overthrow President Charles de Gaulle couldn't get hold of a nuclear device. "Refrain from detonating your little bomb," General Maurice Challe, one of the coup leaders, had urged the head of the special weapons command. "Keep it for us, it will always be useful."

In addition to being loosely controlled by the United States, the nuclear weapons in the NATO stockpile were often old and poorly maintained. According to the joint committee's report, NATO had been turned into "the dumping ground for obsolete warheads and weapon systems" that were, nevertheless, placed "in an 'alert' position of 15 minutes readiness without adequate safety precautions." Congressman Holifield estimated that about half of the Jupiters wouldn't take off, if the order to launch was ever given. The missiles were complicated, liquid fueled, and leaky. The chairman of the Joint Chiefs of Staff admitted that, from a military standpoint, the Jupiters were useful mainly for increasing the number of targets that the Soviet Union would have to hit during a first strike. "It would have been better to dump them in the ocean," Eisenhower later said of the missiles, "instead of trying to dump them on our allies."

The Mark 7 atomic bombs carried by NATO fighters had been rushed into production during the Korean War, almost a decade earlier. The nickel cadmium batteries of a Mark 7 constantly had to be recharged, and its nuclear core had to be carefully placed into an in-flight insertion mechanism before takeoff. The bombs were not designed for use during an alert. Once the core was inserted, a Mark 7 wasn't one-point safe. And the bomb had to undergo at least twenty different diagnostic tests, increasing the odds of a mistake during assembly and disassembly. It was plagued by mechanical problems and seemed to invite human error.

Harold Agnew was amazed to see a group of NATO weapon handlers pull the arming wires out of a Mark 7 while unloading it from a plane. When the wires were pulled, the arming sequence began—and if the X-unit charged, a Mark 7 could be detonated by its radar, by its barometric switches, by its timer, or by falling just a few feet from a plane and landing on a runway. A stray cosmic ray could, theoretically, detonate it. The weapon seemed to invite mistakes. A rocket-propelled version of the Mark 7 was unloaded, fully armed, with its X-unit charged, from a U.S. Navy plane in the spring of 1960. The ground crew had inadvertently yanked out the arming wires. An incident report noted defects in another Mark 7:

> During initial inspection after receipt of a War Reserve Mk 7 Mod 5 bomb, it was observed that the safing and arming wires were in reversed locations in the Arm/Safe Retainer assembly, i.e., the arming wires were in the safing wire location and the safing wires were in the arming wire location. Four screws were missing from the assembly.

And a Mark 7 sometimes contained things it shouldn't. A screwdriver was found inside one of the bombs; an Allen wrench was somehow left inside another. In both bombs, the loose tools could have caused a short circuit.

The risk of a nuclear accident at a European base was increased by the fact that the training and operating manuals for the Mark 7—indeed, for all the weapons in the NATO atomic stockpile—were written in English. But many of the NATO personnel who handled the weapons could not read or speak English. And few of them knew what to do if something went wrong. "In many areas we visited," the joint committee found, "little or no Explosive Ordnance Disposal (EOD) capability was available in the

event of accidental radioactive contamination resulting from fire, careless-
ness, or accident, or in the event of threat to custody and security of the
weapon requiring emergency disposal." Western Europe was more densely
populated than the United States, and a cloud of plutonium, released by a
nuclear weapon, could threaten a large number of people. The possibility of
such an accident was "far from remote," according to the joint committee.
It cited a mishap on January 16, 1961, just a few days before Kennedy's inauguration. The underwing fuel tanks of a U.S. Air Force F-100D fighter
were mistakenly jettisoned when the pilot started the engines. The plane
was on alert at the Lakenheath air base in Suffolk, England. The fuel tanks
hit the runway and ruptured, some fuel ignited, and a Mark 28 hydrogen
bomb mounted beneath the plane was engulfed in flames. Firefighters
managed to extinguish the blaze before the weapon's high explosives could
detonate or ignite. Because the accident occurred at a military base, away
from the scrutiny of the press and the public, neither the American government nor the British would acknowledge that it happened.

THE JOINT COMMITTEE on Atomic Energy unanimously agreed that
the Jupiter missiles should be removed from Italy—and should never be
deployed in Turkey. The missiles seemed to pose more of a threat to NATO,
one way or another, than to the Soviets. And placing missiles with thermonuclear warheads in Turkey, a politically unstable country that bordered
the Soviet Union, might be viewed as a provocation at the Kremlin. The
joint committee also recommended that the Mark 7 bomb either be removed from the NATO stockpile or fitted with a trajectory-sensing switch,
so that a mistake by a ground crew would be less likely to cause an accidental detonation. Moreover, the current "fictional" custody arrangements had
to be replaced with measures that gave the United States "real" possession
and control of its nuclear weapons in Europe. A lone American sentry, ordered to stand on a runway for eight hours at a time, was bound to start
"goofing off." The committee wanted at least two American soldiers keeping an eye on the igloos, the missiles, the fighter planes on alert. It wanted
American vehicles and troops, at every major NATO base, capable of evac-

uating or destroying nuclear weapons that an enemy or an ally might want to seize. And most of all, the committee wanted some kind of mechanical device added to NATO's weapons so that unauthorized personnel couldn't detonate them.

Harold Agnew had recently met with Donald R. Cotter, a supervisor at Sandia, about the best way to install use controls on a nuclear weapon. Cotter mentioned an electromechanical lock that Sandia was developing for atomic land mines. The weapons were, essentially, time bombs that NATO troops could arm and then leave behind to destroy buildings, bridges, airfields, or units of an invading Red Army. The new lock had originally been conceived as a safety device. Because these weapons wouldn't be dropped from a plane or launched by a missile, a trajectory-sensing switch wouldn't help to prevent accidental detonations. The g-forces that a land mine would normally experience before being armed would be the same as those of the soldier carrying it. And the weapon might sit for hours or days before exploding. But a motor-driven lock inside the mine, connected by a long cable to a handheld decoder, would allow troops to arm the weapon from a safe distance. Agnew thought that sort of lock would solve many of the custody problems at NATO. A coded switch, installed in every nuclear weapon, would block the crucial arming circuits. It would make a clear distinction between the physical possession of a weapon and the ability to use one. It would become a form of remote control. And the power to exert that control, to prohibit or allow a nuclear detonation, would remain with whoever had the code.

Agnew brought an early version of the electromechanical locking system to Washington, D.C., for a closed-door hearing of the joint committee, putting the switch and the decoder in the seat next to him on a commercial flight from Albuquerque. The coded switch that went inside a weapon weighed about a pound; the decoder weighed about forty. It was a black box with knobs, numbers, and a series of colored lights on it, powered by a large internal battery. To unlock a nuclear weapon, a two-man custodial team would attach a cable to it from the decoder. Then they'd turn the knobs on the decoder to enter a four-digit code. It was a "split-knowledge" code—each custodian would be given only two of the four numbers. Once the correct code was entered, the switch inside the weapon would take any-where from thirty seconds to two and a half minutes to unlock, as its little gears, cams, and cam followers whirred and spun. When Agnew and Cot-ter showed the committee how the new lock worked, it didn't. Something was wrong. But none of the senators, congressmen, or committee staff members realized that it wouldn't unlock, no matter how many times the proper code was entered. The decoder looked impressive, the colored lights flashed, and everyone in the hearing room agreed that it was absolutely essential for national security.

The American military, however, vehemently opposed putting any locks on nuclear weapons. The Army, the Navy, the Air Force, the Marines, the Joint Chiefs of Staff, General Power at SAC, General Norstad at NATO—all of them agreed that locks were a bad idea. The always/never dilemma lay at the heart of military's thinking. "No single device can be expected to increase both safety and readiness," the Joint Chiefs of Staff argued. And readiness was considered more important: the nuclear weapons in Europe were "adequately safe, within the limits of the operational requirements imposed on them."

Although the description "adequately safe" was hardly reassuring, the possibility of America's nuclear weapons being rendered useless during war-time, when their locks somehow malfunctioned, was more worrisome to the Joint Chiefs. Even if the locking and unlocking mechanisms worked flawlessly, use of the weapons would depend on effective code manage-ment. If only a few people were allowed to know the code, then the death of those few or an inability to reach them in an emergency could prevent the weapons from being unlocked. But if the code was too widely shared, the locks would offer little protection against unauthorized use. The joint committee's desire for stronger use controls threatened to add complexity and uncertainty to the command and control of nuclear weapons. A State Department official summarized the military's position: "all is well with the atomic stockpile program and there is no need for any changes."

The Kennedy administration was far more receptive to the committee's proposals. The former RAND analysts at the Pentagon were familiar with Fred Iklé's work and his recommendation, two years earlier, that locks should be put on nuclear weapons. Jerome Wiesner, the president's science adviser, met with Agnew and agreed that something had to be done about NATO's atomic stockpile. Wiesner was deeply concerned about the risk of an unauthorized or accidental detonation. He had trained as an electrical engineer, briefly worked at Los Alamos, and advised Eisenhower on nuclear issues. Wiesner supported placing locks on the weapons but had no illusions that locks would completely solve the problem. A skilled technician could open a stolen nuclear weapon and unlock it within a few hours. But Wiesner thought that the locks might help "to buy time" after a weapon had been taken, stop "individual psychotics," and prevent "unauthorized use by military forces holding the weapons during periods of high tension or military combat."

For Secretary of Defense McNamara, the locks were part of a larger effort to regain not only American control but also civilian control of nuclear weapons. He felt adamant that the president of the United States should have the sole authority to order a weapon's use. The military had gained far too much power over the nuclear arsenal since the days of Harry Truman, McNamara thought—and the lack of civilian oversight at NATO was chilling. The Davy Crockett recoilless rifle was especially problematic. Its atomic projectiles weighed about fifty pounds and would be easy to steal. They were small enough to fit in a duffle bag or a backpack. After reading the joint committee's report, President Kennedy halted the dispersal of nuclear weapons among America's NATO allies. Studies on weapon safety and command and control were commissioned. At Sandia, the development of coded, electromechanical locks was begun on a crash basis. Known at first as "Prescribed Action Links," the locks were given a new name, one that sounded less restrictive, in the hopes of appeasing the military. "Permissive Action Links" sounded more friendly, as did the acronym: PALs.

WITHIN SEVEN WEEKS of President Kennedy's inauguration, the broad outlines of his defense policies were set. Spending on conventional forces would increase. More Polaris submarines would be built. And intercontinental ballistic missiles would largely replace bombers. Missiles were thought to be faster, cheaper, and less likely to be destroyed in a surprise attack. The Atlases, Titans, Jupiters, and Thors, so recently rushed into service, would be decommissioned as soon as possible. Less expensive, solid-fueled missiles would replace them. McNamara and his team had come to believe that nuclear weapons with a lower yield were more cost effective. The Minuteman missile carried a 1-megaton warhead, and calculations suggested that five of them would inflict more damage than a single 9-megaton warhead carried by a Titan II. Nevertheless, a relatively small number of Titan II missiles would be retained, for the time being. They would be useful for destroying naval bases, missile complexes, and underground command centers.

The Polaris submarine seemed like the ideal weapon system for the Kennedy administration's strategic goals. The sixteen missiles on each sub would serve as a powerful deterrent to the Soviets, greatly increasing the odds that the United States could offer some sort of nuclear response after a surprise attack. Safely hidden beneath the ocean, the submarines could also give the president more time to think or negotiate during a crisis. In 1958 the Navy had requested a dozen Polaris subs; facing intense pressure from Congress, Eisenhower later agreed to deploy 19. Kennedy decided to build 41. The 656 missiles of the Polaris fleet would be aimed solely at "countervalue" targets—at civilians who lived in the major cities of the Soviet Union.

The Air Force didn't like most of the Pentagon's new spending priorities, which seemed to favor the Army and the Navy. The B-47 bomber—long the mainstay of the Strategic Air Command and the favorite ride of Colonel Jimmy Stewart—was to be taken out of service. No additional B-52 bombers would be built. The fate of a supersonic replacement for the B-52 was suddenly uncertain, and plans for a nuclear-powered bomber were scrapped. McNamara had concluded that bombers were not only too costly to operate but increasingly vulnerable to Soviet air defenses. The B-47 and the B-52 had been designed for high-altitude bombing; they would now have to attack at low altitudes to avoid Soviet radar. And the Soviets were beginning to put atomic warheads on their antiaircraft missiles, as well. During an attack on the Soviet Union, about half of SAC's bomber crews, if not more, were expected to lose their lives.

General Curtis LeMay, the second in command at the Air Force, had little use for McNamara and his whiz kids. Few of them had served in the armed forces, let alone seen combat—yet they acted like military experts. They seemed arrogant and clueless. General Thomas D. White, the Air Force chief of staff, had similar misgivings, later criticizing the "pipe-smoking, tree-full-of-owls type of so-called professional 'defense intellectu-als' who have been brought into this nation's capital." LeMay was convinced that long-range bombers were still the best weapons for strategic warfare. The Pentagon had never allowed SAC to test-launch a ballistic missile with a live nuclear warhead, despite many requests. Such a launch, with a flight path over the United States, was considered too risky. Dummy warheads were successfully tested instead, on missiles fired from Vandenberg—and the same fuzing and firing mechanisms would presumably detonate a real one. But LeMay didn't want the survival of the United States to depend on a weapon that had never been fully tested. And the idea of a "limited war" still seemed ridiculous to him. The phrase was an oxymoron. If you won't fight to win, LeMay argued, then you damn well shouldn't fight. His protégé at SAC, General Power, felt the same way and continued to push for a counterforce strategy, aiming at military targets. For that task, Polaris missiles—relatively inaccurate and impossible to launch simultaneously, as one massive salvo—were useless.

To placate the Air Force and gain additional security against a surprise attack, McNamara raised the proportion of SAC bombers on ground alert from one third to one half. The number of bombers on airborne alert was increased, as well. Twelve B-52s were soon in the air at all times, loaded with thermonuclear weapons, as part of Operation Chrome Dome. Every day, six of the bombers would head north and circumnavigate the perime-ter of Canada. Four would cross the Atlantic and circle the Mediterranean. And two would fly to the ballistic missile early-warning facility in Thule, Greenland, and orbit it for hours, maintaining visual or radio contact with the base—just to make sure that it was still there. Thule would probably be hit by Soviet missiles during the initial stage of a surprise attack. Known as the "Thule monitor," the B-52 assured SAC, more reliably than any bomb alarm system, that the United States was not yet at war.

Feuds between the Army, the Navy, and the Air Force continued, despite McNamara's vow that the Pentagon would have "one defense policy, not three conflicting defense policies." Interservice rivalries once again complicated the effort to develop a rational nuclear strategy. The Joint Chiefs of Staff had been instructed to alter the SIOP so that President Kennedy would have a number of options during a nuclear war. Studies were under way to make that possible. But the nuclear ambitions of the Army, the Navy, and the Air Force still seemed incompatible—and, at times, incomprehensible.

General Maxwell Taylor had contended in his bestselling book that the Army needed more money to fight conventional wars, an argument that helped to make him the principal military adviser to President Kennedy. Nevertheless, with Taylor's support, the Army was now seeking thirty-two thousand nuclear weapons for use on the battlefield. Even the little Davy Crockett was portrayed as an indispensable weapon, despite the risk of theft. The handheld atomic rifles were as urgently needed, the Army claimed, as intercontinental ballistic missiles. McNamara still couldn't understand the rationale for battlefield nuclear weapons and challenged the Army to answer a series of questions about them: Is the purpose of our tactical weapons to prevent the Soviets from using their tactical weapons? Can the Army defend Europe with them, without destroying Europe? And how will our own troops survive the fallout? The maximum range of the Davy Crockett was so short—about a mile and a half—that the soldiers who fired it stood a good chance of being killed by it.

In response to McNamara's questions, the Army admitted that its request for thirty-two thousand nuclear weapons might "appear to be unreasonably high." But General Taylor insisted that tactical weapons would serve as a valuable first step on the ladder of nuclear escalation. They would demonstrate American resolve—and the United States obviously needed to have them "if the enemy does."

The latest intelligence reports on the Soviet Union added a new twist to the debate over America's nuclear strategy. Within weeks of taking office, President Kennedy found out that the missile gap did not exist. Like the bomber gap, it was a myth. For years it had been sustained by faulty assumptions, Soviet deception, and a willingness at the Department of Defense to believe the worst-case scenario—especially when it justified more spending on defense. The CIA had estimated that the Soviet Union might have five hundred long-range ballistic missiles by the middle of 1961. Air Force Intelligence had warned that the Soviets might soon have twice that number. But aerial photographs of the Soviet Union, taken by U-2 spy planes and the new *Discoverer* spy satellite, now suggested that those estimates were wrong. The photos confirmed the existence of only four missiles that could reach the United States.

Instead of deploying long-range missiles to attack the United States, the Soviets had built hundreds of medium- and intermediate-range missiles to destroy the major cities of Western Europe. The strategy had been dictated, in large part, by necessity. Khrushchev's boasts—that his factories were turning out 250 long-range missiles a year, that the Soviet Union had more missiles than it would ever need—were all a bluff. For years the Soviet missile program had been plagued with engineering and design problems. Medium-range missiles were less technologically demanding. It wasn't easy to build a weapon that could fly six thousand miles and put a warhead near its target. And on October 24, 1960, the Soviet program had secretly endured a major setback.

Like the Atlas, the first Soviet long-range missiles used liquid oxygen as a propellant, and they required a lengthy fueling process before launch. A new Soviet missile, the R-16, used hypergolic propellants stored separately within its airframe, like the Titan II. The R-16 would be able to lift off within minutes. It was the largest missile that had ever been built, and Khrushchev was eager for its inaugural flight to take place before November 7, the anniversary of the Bolshevik Revolution. Marshal Mitrofan Ivanovich Nedelin, head of the Soviet Strategic Rocket Forces, traveled to Kazakhstan and supervised preparations for the launch of an R-16 at the Baikonur Cosmodrome.

As the giant missile sat on the launchpad, full of oxidizer and fuel, a series of malfunctions occurred. Angry about the delay, under tremendous pressure from the Kremlin, and eager to know what was wrong, Nedelin drove to the pad. Half an hour before the scheduled launch, a crew of technicians was working on the missile when its second-stage engine started without warning. Flames from the engine shot downward and ignited the fuel tank of the first stage. Marshal Nedelin was sitting in a chair about fifty feet from the missile when it exploded. He was killed, along with many of the Soviet Union's top rocket scientists and about one hundred other people. The chief designer of the R-16, Mikhail Yangel, happened to be taking a cigarette break in an underground bunker and survived the explosion. Movie cameras set up to record the launch instead captured some horrific images—men running for their lives, as an immense fireball pursues and then engulfs them; men falling to the ground, their clothes on fire; everywhere, clouds of deadly smoke with a reddish glow. The following day, TASS, the official Soviet news agency, announced that Nedelin had been killed in a plane crash.

Far from being grounds for celebration, the absence of a missile gap became a potential source of embarrassment for the Kennedy administration. Many of the claims made by the Democrats during the recent presidential campaign now seemed baseless. Although General Power still insisted that the Soviets were hiding their long-range missiles beneath camouflage, the United States clearly had not fallen behind in the nuclear arms race. Public knowledge of that fact would be inconvenient—and so the public wasn't told. When McNamara admitted that the missile gap was a myth, during an off-the-record briefing with reporters, President Kennedy was displeased.

At a press conference the following day, Kennedy stressed that "it would be premature to reach a judgment as to whether there is a gap or not a gap." Soon the whole issue was forgotten. Political concerns, not strategic ones, determined how many long-range, land-based missiles the United States would build. Before *Sputnik*, President Eisenhower had thought that twenty to forty would be enough. Jerome Wiesner advised President Kennedy that roughly ten times that number would be sufficient for deterrence. But General Power wanted the Strategic Air Command to have ten thousand Minuteman missiles, aimed at every military target in the Soviet

Union that might threaten the United States. And members of Congress, unaware that the missile gap was a myth, also sought a large, land-based force. After much back and forth, McNamara decided to build a thousand Minuteman missiles. One Pentagon adviser later explained that it was "a round number."

WHILE DISAGREEMENTS OVER NUCLEAR STRATEGY continued at the White House and the Pentagon, the need for an improved command-and-control system was beyond dispute. For McNamara, it was the most urgent national security issue that the United States faced, "a matter of transcendent priority." A few weeks after his briefing on WSEG R-50 and the threat of a surprise attack, McNamara outlined the problem to Kennedy:

> The chain of command from the President down to our strategic offensive and defensive weapon systems is highly vulnerable in almost every link. The destruction of about a dozen sites, most of which are soft, none of which is adequately hardened, would deprive U.S. forces of all high-level command and control. . . . Without the survival of at least some of these sites (including the one containing the President, his successor, or designated replacement) with their communications, there can be no authorized response in the event of a nuclear attack on the U.S.

The Soviet Union might not need a thousand missiles to prevail in a nuclear war; twenty or thirty might do. And the relative weakness of the Soviets, the small size of their missile arsenal, had oddly become a source of anxiety. It might encourage the Soviet Union to strike first. A decapitation attack, launched without warning, like a "bolt out of the blue," might be the Kremlin's only hope of achieving victory.

A centralized, effective command-and-control system would ensure that the United States could retaliate—and that the order to do so would be given by the president. The demands placed on such a system would be enormous, if the Soviets attacked. The system would have to "classify the attack, as large or small," a Pentagon report later noted, "accidental or deliberate, selective or indiscriminate, against cities or not, against high command or not . . . in order to support a decision as to an 'appropriate' retaliatory response." The system had to do those things in real time. And it had to maintain communications between the president, the Joint Chiefs of Staff, and military commanders throughout a nuclear war.

After commissioning a number of studies on command and control, McNamara approved the creation of a new entity: the World Wide Military Command and Control System (WWMCCS). It would combine the radars, sensors, computers, and communications networks of the different armed services into a single integrated system. The challenges were formidable. Making the system work would require not only technological and administrative changes but also new ways of thinking about command. The task was further complicated by the efforts of the Army, the Navy, and the Air Force to retain as much authority as possible over their own facilities and resist any centralized system run by civilians.

Although the bureaucratic struggle between the demands of centralization and decentralization proved difficult to resolve at the Pentagon, Paul Baran, a researcher at RAND, came up with an ingenious method of harmonizing the two within a digital communications network. Centralized and even decentralized networks—like those traditionally used to broadcast radio or television, to send messages by telegraph or telephone—could be shut down by the destruction of a few crucial nodes. Any hierarchical network would remain vulnerable at its apex, at the point where all the lines of communication converged. "The first duty of the command and control system is to survive," Baran argued, proposing a distributed network with hundreds or thousands of separate nodes connected through multiple paths. Messages would be broken into smaller "blocks," sent along the first available path, and reassembled at their final destination. If nodes were out of service or destroyed, the network would automatically adapt and send the data along a route that was still intact. Baran's work later provided the conceptual basis for the top secret communications networks at the Pentagon, as well as their civilian offshoot, the Internet.

The survival of America's military and civilian leadership would be harder to achieve. As a subset of the World Wide Military Command and Control System, a new administrative structure was established. The National Military Command Center replaced the Joint War Room at the Pentagon. It would serve as the nation's military headquarters during a nuclear war. Since the Pentagon was likely to be destroyed at the beginning of that war, an Alternate National Military Command Center was formed at Site R, inside Raven Rock Mountain. It would have the data-processing and communications equipment necessary to manage the SIOP. It would be staffed year-round, twenty-four hours a day, awaiting the arrival of the president and the Joint Chiefs during an emergency. But fixed sites now seemed like easy targets for Soviet missiles. McNamara thought that the United States also needed mobile command centers that would be difficult to find and destroy. The Air Force wanted these command centers to be located on airplanes. SAC already had a plane, nicknamed "Looking Glass," in the air at all times as a backup to its headquarters in Omaha. The Navy wanted the command centers to be located on ships. McNamara decided to do both, creating the National Emergency Airborne Command Post and the National Emergency Command Post Afloat.

None of these command posts would matter if there were no means of transmitting the Go code after a nuclear attack on the United States. The Navy began work on an airborne system for contacting its Polaris submarines. Take Charge and Move Out (TACAMO) planes would quickly get off the ground, climb steeply, and send an emergency war order on a very-low-frequency radio, using an antenna five miles long. SAC began to develop a Post Attack Command and Control System. It would rely on airborne command posts, a command post on a train, a command post at the bottom of an abandoned gold mine in Cripple Creek, Colorado, and a command post, known as The Notch, inside Bare Mountain, near Amherst, Massachusetts. The bunker in Cripple Creek was never constructed; airborne facilities were less expensive, and more likely to survive, than those underground. The Emergency Rocket Communications System provided another layer of redundancy. If SAC's airborne command posts somehow failed to send the Go code, it could be sent by radio transmitters installed in a handful of Minuteman missiles. A prerecorded voice message, up to ninety seconds long, would be broadcast to bomber crews and launch crews, as the specially equipped missiles flew over SAC bases.

The most intractable problem was finding a way to keep the president alive. The National Emergency Airborne Command Post was placed on full-time alert at Andrews Air Force Base near Washington, D.C. But the plane would need at least ten or fifteen minutes to take off. And it would need another ten minutes to fly beyond the lethal range of a thermonuclear explosion. At least half an hour of warning might be necessary for the president to reach Andrews, get into the airborne command post, and escape the blast. Traveling by helicopter to the National Emergency Command Post Afloat, a Navy cruiser kept off the coast, would take even longer. And a Soviet missile attack might come with little or no warning.

After considering a variety of options, Secretary of Defense McNamara and Secretary of State Dean Rusk supported the construction of the National Deep Underground Command Center. McNamara described the bunker as a "logical, survivable node in the control structure . . . a unified strategic command and control center under duly constituted political authorities." It would be located beneath the Pentagon, at a depth of 3,500 feet. High-speed elevators, a light-rail system, and horizontal tunnels more than half a mile underground would link it to the White House. It would hold anywhere from fifty to three hundred people, depending on whether Kennedy chose to build an "austere" version or one of "moderate size." It was designed to "withstand multiple direct hits of 200 to 300 MT [megaton] weapons bursting at the surface or 100 MT weapons penetrating to depths of 70-100 feet." If the Soviets attacked on that scale and the new bunker met those design goals, the president and his staff could expect to be the only people still alive in Washington, D.C.

Amid all the consideration of how to protect the president and the Joint Chiefs, how to gather information in real time, how to transmit war orders, how to devise the technical and administrative means for a flexible response, little thought had been given to an important question: how do you end a nuclear war? Thomas Schelling—a professor of economics at Harvard, a RAND analyst, proponent of game theory, and adviser to the

Kennedy administration—began to worry about the issue early in 1961. While heading a committee on the risk of war by accident, miscalculation, or surprise, he was amazed to learn that there was no direct, secure form of communications between the White House and the Kremlin. It seemed almost unbelievable. Schelling had read the novel *Red Alert* a few years earlier, bought forty copies, and sent them to colleagues. The book gave a good sense of what could go wrong—and yet the president's ability to call his Soviet counterpart on a "hot line" existed only in fiction. As things stood, AT&T's telephone lines and Western Union's telegraph lines were the only direct links between the United States and the Soviet Union. Both of them would be knocked out by a thermonuclear blast, and most radio communications would be, as well. The command-and-control systems of the two countries had no formal, reliable means of interacting. The problem was so serious and so obvious, Schelling thought, everybody must have assumed somebody else had taken care of it. Pauses for negotiation would be a waste of time, if there were no way to negotiate. And once a nuclear war began, no matter how pointless, devastating, and horrific, it might not end until both sides ran out of nuclear weapons.

The Brink

Mankind must put an end to war—or war will put an end to mankind," President John F. Kennedy told a gathering of world leaders at the United Nations, on September 25, 1961. Dag Hammarskjöld, the beloved secretary-general of the United Nations, had recently died in a plane crash, and to honor his memory Kennedy gave a speech that called for world peace and stressed the U.N.'s central role as a peacekeeper. He also revived the hope that nuclear weapons could be outlawed through an international agreement:

> Today, every inhabitant of this planet must contemplate the day when this planet may no longer be habitable. Every man, woman and child lives under a nuclear sword of Damocles, hanging by the slenderest of threads, capable of being cut at any moment by accident or miscalculation or by madness. The weapons of war must be abolished before they abolish us. . . . The events and decisions of the next ten months may well decide the fate of man for the next ten thousand years. There will be no avoiding those events. There will be no appeal from those decisions. And we in this hall shall be remembered either as part of the generation that turned this planet into a flaming funeral pyre or the generation that met its vow "to save succeeding generations from the scourge of war."

Instead of an arms race, Kennedy challenged the Soviets to join the United States in a "peace race," a series of steps that would lead to "general and complete disarmament" under the supervision of the U.N. He proposed a ban on nuclear testing, an end to the production of fissile material for use in nuclear weapons, a prohibition on the transfer of nuclear weapons to other countries, and the destruction of all nuclear weapons, as well as their delivery systems. Kennedy had no illusions about the perfectibility of mankind, only a desire for its survival:

> Such a plan would not bring a world free from conflict or greed—but it would bring a world free from the terrors of mass destruction. It would not usher in the era of the super state—but it would usher in an era in which no state could annihilate or be annihilated by another.

The abolition of nuclear weapons couldn't be postponed any longer. "Together we shall save our planet," he said, "or together we shall perish in its flames."

During the same week that Kennedy appealed for an end to the arms race at the United Nations, he met with a handful of military advisers at the White House to discuss launching a surprise attack on the Soviet Union. General Thomas Power encouraged him to do it. According to notes of the meeting, held on September 20, Power warned that the United States now faced the greatest danger, ever, of a Soviet nuclear attack. "If a general atomic war is inevitable," he argued, "the U.S. should strike first." Power was not the only high-ranking officer having such thoughts. Kennedy had just received a memo from General Maxwell Taylor, summarizing how an American first strike might proceed. Taylor didn't recommend it—or rule it out. "There are risks as well as opportunities in this approach," he wrote.

The United States and the Soviet Union were, at the time, engaged in their most serious confrontation since the Berlin airlift of 1948. And once again, Berlin was at the center of the crisis. Sixteen years after the defeat of the Nazis, the city was still divided among four occupying powers: the

British, French, and Americans in the West; the Soviets in the East. The division was economic, as well as political. While Communist East Berlin stagnated, capitalist West Berlin thrived. But it was a fragile prosperity. Located deep within East Germany, linked to West Germany only by air and a 110-mile stretch of highway, the free sectors of Berlin were surrounded by troops from the Soviet bloc. NATO forces in the city were vastly outnumbered. America's nuclear weapons were all that protected West Berlin from being overrun.

Since 1958 the Soviet Union had been threatening to sign a treaty with East Germany, hand over the eastern part of the city to its Communist ally—and block NATO access to West Berlin. The threat was forcefully repeated at a summit meeting between President Kennedy and Nikita Khrushchev in June 1961. The Soviet Union seemed ascendant, having recently launched the first man into space. And Kennedy's stature had been greatly diminished by the Bay of Pigs invasion, a failed attempt to overthrow the Communist government of Cuba. Khrushchev thought the new president was young and inexperienced, perhaps too timid to provide air support for the CIA-backed army pinned down on the beaches of Cuba. Kennedy had hoped that the summit would lead to warmer relations between the two superpowers. Instead, Khrushchev confronted him with an ultimatum: if the United States did not agree to the creation of a "free" and demilitarized Berlin, the Soviets would sign a treaty with East Germany by the end of the year and severely limit NATO's rights in the city. When Kennedy made clear that would be unacceptable, the Soviet leader didn't back down.

"It is up to the United States to decide whether there will be war or peace," Khrushchev said.

"Then it will be a cold winter," Kennedy replied.

DURING THE EISENHOWER ADMINISTRATION, the Joint Chiefs of Staff seemed to have few options if the Soviets tried to close the autobahn to Berlin. A convoy of American troops would most likely depart from West Germany on the road—and if they were attacked, the United States would be under great pressure to launch a massive nuclear strike on the Soviet Union. Secretary of Defense McNamara hoped that a subtler response could be devised. He wanted a plan that would permit the gradual escalation of a conflict, and delay the use of nuclear weapons for as long as possible. But the French president, Charles de Gaulle, and the British prime minister, Harold Macmillan, had little confidence that West Berlin could be defended with conventional weapons. Any suggestion that the United States might not use nuclear weapons immediately, they worried, could weaken deterrence and encourage the Soviets to take risks.

General Lauris Norstad, the supreme allied commander of NATO, agreed with the British and the French. Norstad thought that once the fighting began, the escalation wouldn't be gradual. It would be "explosive," and NATO had to be ready for all-out nuclear war. After the Bay of Pigs fiasco, Norstad had persuaded McNamara to keep the Jupiter missiles in Turkey and Italy. "This is the time to create strength," Norstad said, "not reduce it."

As Khrushchev continued to make public threats against West Berlin and raise the specter of war, President Kennedy followed the advice of former Secretary of State Dean Acheson. "If a crisis is provoked," Acheson had suggested, "a bold and dangerous course may be the safest." The United States should raise the stakes, send more conventional forces to Germany, and show a willingness to fight. On July 25, Kennedy gave a televised address on the Berlin crisis. The Soviet Union had no right to restrict NATO's presence in West Berlin, Kennedy asserted, "and we have given our word that an attack upon that city will be an attack upon us all." He proposed a call-up of reservists and National Guard units, an expansion of the draft, the addition of more than 100,000 troops to the Army, a delay in the retirement of the Strategic Air Command's B-47 bombers—and a plan to build more civilian bomb shelters in the United States. Angered by the speech, Khrushchev asked John McCloy, a White House adviser who was visiting Russia, to pass along a message: "Tell Kennedy that if he starts a war, then he would probably become the last President of the United States."

Although Kennedy and McNamara now understood the urgency of America's command-and-control problems, little had been done to rectify them. Barely six months had passed since the inauguration, and much more time would be needed to make fundamental changes in the system. As the Berlin crisis deepened, the commanders of NATO units were ordered not to use their nuclear weapons without the explicit approval of General Norstad. But locks had not been installed in those weapons—and McNamara soon agreed to equip American troops on the front line with Davy Crockett atomic rifles. They were likely to be the first weapons fired at an invading Red Army.

More important, the SIOP remained the same. It had officially become the nuclear war plan of the United States in mid-April, although Kennedy hadn't even received a formal briefing on it. His national security adviser, McGeorge Bundy, thought that an alternative to the SIOP was needed, now that a war with the Soviets seemed like a real possibility. "[T]he current strategic war plan is dangerously rigid," Bundy informed the president, "and, if continued without amendment, may leave you with very little choice as to how you face the moment of thermonuclear truth." One of Bundy's aides, Carl Kaysen, was given the task of quickly preparing a new war plan. During the Second World War, Kaysen had selected bomb targets in Germany. He later worked at RAND and served as a professor of economics at Harvard. Kaysen thought that NATO should rely increasingly on conventional weapons and that Germany should eventually become a nuclear-free zone. Nevertheless, he enlisted help from one of McNamara's aides, Henry Rowen, to come up with a nuclear war plan that the president might actually use. The "spasm war" demanded by the current SIOP, they agreed, was a "ridiculous and unworkable notion."

Just after midnight, on August 13, without any warning, East German troops began to string a barbed wire fence between East and West Berlin. For weeks, thousands of people had fled East Germany through the city, the last stretch of the border that hadn't been militarized. NATO troops now watched helplessly as the fence became a wall.

After an initial, tentative response, on August 18 President Kennedy ordered a battle group of 1,500 soldiers to travel the autobahn from West Germany to Berlin. McNamara had opposed the move, afraid that it might start a nuclear war. The Soviets didn't challenge the convoy. When it arrived in West Berlin, the American troops were greeted by hundreds of thousands of cheering Germans and Vice President Lyndon B. Johnson, who felt relieved. Twelve days later, the Soviet Union surprised the Kennedy administration again, unilaterally ending the moratorium on nuclear tests. As a show of strength, within the next month, the Soviets detonated twenty-six nuclear weapons.

Carl Kaysen's war plan was ready by the first week of September. It was designed for use during the Berlin crisis. "We should be prepared to initiate general war by our own first strike," Kaysen wrote. "We should seek the smallest possible list of targets, focusing on the long-range striking capacity of the Soviets, and avoiding, as much as possible, casualties and damage in Soviet civil society." If President Kennedy launched the current SIOP, the United States would have to kill more than half of the people in the Soviet Union—and millions more in Eastern Europe and China—just to maintain the freedom of West Berlin. Doing so would be not only morally questionable but impractical. The scale of the military operations required by the SIOP was so large, it would "inevitably" tip off the Soviets that a nuclear strike was coming. It would give them time to retaliate. Kaysen proposed a surprise attack that would use just forty-one American bombers, approaching at low altitude, to destroy roughly twice that number of long-range missile and bomber bases in the Soviet Union. The whole thing would be over "no more than fifteen minutes" after the first bomb dropped.

Following the attack, Kaysen suggested, "we should be able to communicate two things to Khrushchev: first, that we intend to concentrate on military targets unless he is foolish enough to hit our cities; secondly, that we are prepared to withhold the bulk of our force from the offensive . . . provided that he accepts our terms." Instead of killing hundreds of millions, the raid would probably kill "less than 1,000,000 and probably not much more than 500,000."

General Lyman Lemnitzer, head of the Joint Chiefs of Staff, was not overly impressed by the plan. At a meeting the following week, Lemnitzer told President Kennedy that the United States still lacked the command-and-control capabilities for a limited nuclear attack. Any forces withheld from a first strike might never be available for a second one. And there was no guarantee that Khrushchev would understand, amid the chaos of nuclear war, that only his military targets had been attacked. Kaysen's plan left the Soviet Union's medium-range and intermediate-range missiles untouched—and if Khrushchev didn't get the message and capitulate, Great Britain and most of Europe would be destroyed. Lemnitzer opposed any changes to the SIOP:

> The plan is designed for execution as a whole, and the exclusion of attack of any category or categories of target would, in varying degree, decrease the effectiveness of the plan.

General Curtis LeMay wholeheartedly agreed with Lemnitzer. Indeed, if war came, LeMay thought the Soviet Union should be hit by more nuclear weapons, not fewer, to guarantee that every strategic target was eliminated. Despite strong political and philosophical differences, President Kennedy had recently promoted LeMay to Air Force chief of staff, out of respect for his operational skills. "If you have to go, you want LeMay in the lead bomber," Kennedy later explained. "But you never want LeMay deciding whether or not you have to go."

The underlying logic of both nuclear war plans was inescapable: kill or be killed. General Lemnitzer said that regardless of how the SIOP was executed, "some portion of the Soviet . . . nuclear force would strike the United States." By the fall of 1961, the Soviet Union had about 16 long-range missiles, 150 long-range bombers, and 60 submarine-based missiles that could hit North America. It would be hard to find and destroy every one of them. Kaysen estimated that the number of American deaths stemming from his plan, "while small percentage wise—between three and seven percent [of the total U.S. population]," would nevertheless range between 5 million and 13 million. Just a handful of high-yield weapons, landing on New York City and Chicago, could produce that many deaths. "In thermonuclear warfare," Kaysen noted, "people are easy to kill." But the alternative to launching a surprise attack on the Soviet Union might be a lot worse. A Soviet first strike could kill as many as 100 million Americans.

PRESIDENT KENNEDY WAS WRESTLING WITH these issues in the days leading up to his U.N. speech. The recommendations of the young civilians at the Pentagon seemed, in many ways, to contradict those of the Joint Chiefs of Staff. The president would have to decide who was right. Neither superpower wanted a nuclear war. But neither wanted to back down, alienate its allies, or appear weak. Behind the scenes, all sorts of formal and informal contacts were being made between the two governments, including a secret correspondence between Kennedy and Khrushchev. And yet their positions seemed irreconcilable, especially with a deadline approaching. For the Soviet leader, West Berlin was a "rotten tooth which must be pulled out," a center of American espionage, a threat to the future of East Germany. For Kennedy, it was an outpost of freedom, surrounded by totalitarian rule, whose two million inhabitants couldn't be abandoned. The Berlin Wall, at least, had preserved the status quo. "It's not a very nice solution," Kennedy said, the day the barbed wire went up, "but a wall is a hell of a lot better than a war."

On September 19, the day before the White House meeting on whether to launch a surprise attack, Kennedy sent a list of questions to General Power:

> Berlin developments may confront us with a situation where we may desire to take the initiative in the escalation of the conflict from the local to the general war level. . . . Could we achieve surprise (i.e., 15 minutes or less warning) under such conditions by examining our current plan? . . . How would you plan an attack that would use a minimum-sized force against Soviet long-range striking power only, and would attempt to achieve tactical surprise? How long would it take to develop such a plan? . . . Is this idea of a first strike against the Soviets' long-range striking power a feasible one? . . . I assume I can stop the strategic attack at any time, should I receive word the enemy has capitulated. Is this correct?

The president also wanted to know if the missiles aimed at Europe could be destroyed by an American first strike. During the meeting on the twentieth, General Power expressed concern that Khrushchev was hiding many of his long-range missiles. Without better intelligence, a limited strike on the Soviet Union would be too risky. The choice was all or nothing—and Power advocated an attack with the full SIOP.

"The Western Powers have calmly resolved," Kennedy said at the United Nations a few days later, "to defend, by whatever means are forced upon them, their obligations and their access to the free citizens of West Berlin." The following week, Secretary of Defense McNamara told the press that the United States would not hesitate to use nuclear weapons "whenever we feel it necessary to protect our vital interests." And he confidently added that America's nuclear stockpile was much larger than that of the Soviet Union. The administration now found it useful to deflate the myth of the missile gap. Details about SAC's ability to destroy the Soviet Union were provided to NATO officials—so that Soviet intelligence officers who'd infiltrated NATO would share the information with the Kremlin. Perceptions of American military strength were important, as tensions rose in Europe. Soviet fighter planes buzzed commercial airliners heading to West Berlin and dropped chaff to disrupt their navigational systems. Border guards in East Berlin shot at civilians trying to get past the wall. Police officers in West Berlin responded by firing clouds of tear gas to help the refugees escape—and fought a gun battle with East German police.

Although negotiations with the Soviets quietly continued, on October 10, President Kennedy, the secretary of state, the secretary of defense, the head of the Joint Chiefs, and a few other advisers met at the White House to finalize plans for a military defense of West Berlin. Everyone agreed about the first three phases, a gradually escalating set of responses with conventional weapons. But a disagreement arose over Phase IV, the point at which nuclear weapons would be introduced. McNamara said that tactical weapons should be used first, to protect NATO troops and show the Soviets that America wasn't afraid to fight a nuclear war. Paul H. Nitze—a McNamara aide and an advocate not only of containing, but of overthrowing, Communist regimes throughout the world—thought the use of tactical weapons would be a mistake. According to notes of the meeting, Nitze said that Phase IV should begin with the United States launching an all-out first strike against the Soviet Union, because "with such a strike, we could in some real sense be victorious." Neither side could be confident of winning a nuclear exchange, McNamara argued—and the consequences would be devastating for both. The meeting ended with the issue unresolved.

When President Kennedy later sent instructions for the defense of West Berlin to General Norstad, Phase IV was made up of three parts:

A. Selective nuclear attacks for the primary purpose of demonstrating the will to use nuclear weapons.

B. Limited tactical employment of nuclear weapons. . . .

C. General nuclear war.

Although Norstad was supposed to try A and B before proceeding to C, the behavior of the Soviets could prompt the United States to begin with C.

Norstad had already received these orders on October 27, when Soviet and American tanks confronted one another at Checkpoint Charlie, the last border crossing in Berlin. An American diplomat had been detained by East German border guards the previous week, and a dispute arose over the process of gaining access to East Berlin. American tanks were sent to Checkpoint Charlie as a show of strength. Soviet tanks appeared there at about five in the evening on the twenty-seventh. The British soon deployed two antitank guns to support the Americans, while all the French troops in West Berlin remained safely in their barracks. For the first time since the Cold War began, tanks belonging to the U.S. Army and the Red Army pointed their guns at one another, separated by about a hundred yards. General Norstad had ordered his tank commanders to tear down the Berlin Wall, if East German guards blocked the rightful passage of American civilians. Amid the armored standoff at the border, Secretary of State Rusk had those orders rescinded. A miscalculation by either side, a needless provocation, could lead to war.

The Soviet foreign minister met with the American ambassador in Moscow to discuss the situation. Attorney General Robert F. Kennedy, the president's younger brother, had a secret, late-night meeting with Georgi Bolshakov, a Soviet intelligence officer, in Washington, D.C. The negotiations were successful. Sixteen hours after arriving at the border, the Soviet tanks turned around and left. The American tanks departed half an hour later.

Khrushchev had already backed away from his ultimatum that NATO troops must leave West Berlin by the end of the year—and withdrawing the tanks first seemed like another sign of weakness. Two days later, Khrushchev made a blunt, defiant statement. Above an island in the Arctic Sea, the Soviet Union detonated Tsar Bomba, "the King of Bombs"—the most powerful nuclear weapon ever built. It had a yield of 50 megatons. The mushroom cloud rose about forty miles into the sky, and the fireball could be seen more than six hundred miles from ground zero. The shock waves circled the earth three times with enough force to be detected in New Zealand.

The Berlin crisis eased somewhat. But Khrushchev did not let go of his central demands, Kennedy distrusted the Soviets, and the city still threatened to become a flash point where a third world war would begin. McGeorge Bundy later recalled, "There was hardly a week in which there were not nagging questions about what would happen if. . . ." On November 6, a tear-gas battle erupted between East German and West German police officers. On November 20, a crowd of fifty thousand gathered to protest the wall, and the demonstration ended in chaos, with about a thousand people battling police. And on November 24, just before dawn, SAC headquarters in Omaha lost contact with the Ballistic Missile Early Warning System radar in Thule, Greenland. A SAC controller picked up the phone and called NORAD headquarters in Colorado Springs to find out what was wrong. The line was dead.

The odds of a communications breakdown simultaneously extending east and west from Omaha seemed low. SAC's entire alert force was ordered to prepare for takeoff. At air bases worldwide, Klaxons sounded and pilots climbed into hundreds of planes. A few minutes later the order was rescinded. The B-52 circling Thule had made contact with the base. It had not been destroyed by the Soviets. An investigation subsequently found that the failure of a single AT&T switch in Black Forest, Colorado, had shut down all the ballistic missile early warning circuits, voice communications between the SAC and NORAD command posts, and the "hot line" linking SAC's commander to NORAD headquarters. AT&T had neglected to provide redundant circuits for some of the nation's most important communications links, despite assurances that it had done so. When news of the "Black Forest incident" leaked, Radio Moscow claimed the false alarm was proof that "any maniac at a US military base can, in a panic, easily throw mankind into the abyss of a nuclear war."

THE BERLIN CRISIS LED Secretary of Defense McNamara to believe, even more strongly, that NATO's reliance on tactical nuclear weapons increased the threat of a nuclear holocaust. During the first week of May 1962, at a meeting of NATO ministers in Athens, Greece, McNamara urged America's European allies to spend more money on their own defense. Despite having a larger population than the Soviet Union and much larger economies, the European members of NATO refused to pay for conventional forces that could stop the Red Army. In his top secret speech, McNamara warned that NATO should never be forced to choose between suffering a military defeat or starting a nuclear war. "Highly dispersed nuclear weapons in the hands of troops would be difficult to control centrally," he said. "Accidents and unauthorized acts could well occur on both sides."

In addition to greater spending on conventional weapons, McNamara proposed a new nuclear strategy. Later known as "no cities," it was similar to Kaysen's plan, influenced by RAND—and like Henry Kissinger's early work, hopeful that a nuclear war could be fought humanely. Its goal was to save the lives of civilians. "Our best hope lies in conducting a centrally controlled campaign against all of the enemy's vital nuclear capabilities," McNamara said. Attacking only military targets would give the Soviets a strong incentive to do the same. The centralized control of nuclear weapons was essential for this strategy—and the control would ultimately lie with the president of the United States. McNamara's remarks were partly aimed at the French, who planned to keep their nuclear weapons outside of NATO's command structure. By acting alone during a conflict with the Soviet Union, France could threaten the survival of everyone else. The independent actions of one country, McNamara explained, could "lead to the destruction of our hostages—the Soviet cities—just at a time at which our strategy of coercing the Soviets into stopping their aggression was on the verge of success." Without the centralized command and control of nuclear weapons, NATO might suffer "the catastrophe which we most urgently wish to avoid."

The following month, McNamara repeated many of these themes during a commencement speech at the University of Michigan, in his hometown of Ann Arbor. The speech was poorly received. McNamara's plan to save civilian lives—without the classified information that supported its central argument—sounded like a boast that the United States could fight and win a nuclear war. Great Britain and France publicly repudiated the strategy. In their view the threat of total annihilation was a better deterrent than a more limited and more expensive form of warfare, fought with conventional weapons. And America's NATO allies suspected that a "no cities" approach would primarily spare the cities of the United States. Nikita Khrushchev didn't like the speech, either. "Not targeting cities—how aggressive!" Khrushchev told the Presidium of the Supreme Soviet of the Soviet Union. He suggested that McNamara's remarks had a sinister aim: "To get the population used to the idea that nuclear war will take place."

Although the United States and the Soviet Union publicly supported peace, diplomacy, and a settlement of their differences through negotiation, both countries behaved less nobly in secret. During the summer of 1962, the Kennedy administration was trying to overthrow the government of Cuba and assassinate its leader, Fidel Castro. Robert Kennedy guided the CIA's covert program Operation Mongoose enlisting help from Cuban exiles and the Cosa Nostra. Robert McNamara supervised the planning for a full-scale invasion of the island, should Operation Mongoose succeed. Meanwhile, Khrushchev approved a KGB plan to destabilize and overthrow the governments of El Salvador, Guatemala, and Nicaragua.

More important, he decided to turn Cuba into a military outpost of the Soviet Union, armed with nuclear weapons.

If Khrushchev's scheme worked, by the end of 1962, the Soviets would have twenty-four medium-range ballistic missiles, sixteen intermediate-range ballistic missiles, forty-two bombers, a fighter wing, a couple of tank battalions, antiaircraft missiles, and about 50,000 personnel in Cuba. The medium-range missiles would be able to strike targets as far north as Washington, D.C.; the intermediate-range, to destroy SAC bases in the West and the Midwest. The Cuban deployment would triple the number of Soviet land-based missiles that could hit the United States. Throughout the summer, Soviet merchant ships secretly transported the weapons to Cuba, hidden belowdecks, along with troops dressed in civilian clothes. Once the Cuban missile sites were operational, Khrushchev planned to announce their existence during a speech at the United Nations. And then he would offer to remove them—if NATO agreed to leave West Berlin. Or he would keep them in Cuba, just a hundred miles from Florida, and build a naval base on the island for ballistic-missile submarines.

"We have no bases in Cuba, and we do not intend to establish any," Khrushchev had assured Kennedy in a personal note. That promise was later repeated by the Soviet ambassador, Anatoly Dobrynin, during a meeting with Robert Kennedy. On September 11, TASS issued a flat-out denial: "Our nuclear weapons are so powerful in their explosive force and the Soviet Union has such powerful rockets to carry these nuclear warheads, there is no need to search for sites for them beyond the boundaries of the Soviet Union." A month later photographs taken by an American U-2 spy plane revealed Soviet missile sites under construction in the countryside near San Cristobal, about fifty miles west of Havana. Kennedy had warned the Soviets that the United States would not tolerate the deployment of ballistic missiles in Cuba. Now he had to figure out what to do about them.

FOR THE NEXT THIRTEEN DAYS, the Kennedy administration debated how to respond, worried that a wrong move could start a nuclear war. Many of the crucial discussions were secretly recorded; the president and his brother were the only ones at the meetings who knew that a tape recorder was running. At first, President Kennedy thought that the Soviet missiles had to be destroyed before they became operational. Most of his advisers felt the same way. They disagreed mainly on the issue of how large the air strike should be—confined solely to the missiles or expanded to include Cuban air bases and support facilities. As the days passed, doubts began to intrude. A surprise attack had the best chance of success; but it might anger America's allies in Europe, especially if Khrushchev used it as a pretext to seize West Berlin. A small-scale attack might not destroy every missile and nuclear weapon on the island; but getting them all might require a full-scale invasion. And a blockade of the island would prevent the Soviets from delivering more weapons to Cuba; but it might have little effect on the weapons already there.

The Joint Chiefs of Staff unanimously agreed that the Soviet missiles had to be attacked at once, without any warning. Like the Jupiters in Italy and Turkey, the missiles in Cuba weren't protected by concrete silos. From a strictly military point of view, they were useful only for a Soviet first strike. And their strategic purpose seemed to be a decapitation attack against the military and civilian leadership of the United States. The Ballistic Missile Early Warning System was oriented to the north and the east, not the south. Missiles launched from Cuba might not be detected until their thermonuclear warheads hit American targets three or four minutes later. The Joint Chiefs recommended a massive air strike against the Soviet missiles, planes, and weapons in Cuba. A limited strike would not only be more dangerous, they argued, it might be worse than doing nothing at all. Missiles that survived the attack would probably be hidden or launched—and the one opportunity to destroy them, lost.

The strategic implications of the missiles meant less to President Kennedy than the intangible threat they posed. "It doesn't make any difference if you get blown up by an ICBM flying from the Soviet Union or one that was ninety miles away," he said the day after the missiles were discovered. Failing to destroy them or to force their removal would make America look weak. It might encourage the Soviets to move against Berlin. But attacking the missiles brought a whole new set of risks. At a meeting with the Joint

Chiefs of Staff on October 19, four days into the crisis, after the president and his brother and his national security advisers had gone back and forth discussing what sort of action to take, the stark differences between America's civilian and military leadership were exposed.

"If we attack Cuba, the missiles, or Cuba, in any way then it gives [the Soviets] a clear line to take Berlin," President Kennedy said.

General LeMay disagreed.

"We've got the Berlin problem staring us in the face anyway," LeMay said. "If we don't do anything to Cuba, then they're going to push on Berlin and push *real hard* because they've got us on the run."

LeMay thought the Strategic Air Command was so overwhelmingly powerful, and America's nuclear superiority was so great, that the Soviets wouldn't dare to attack Berlin or the United States. Anything short of an air strike on Cuba, he told Kennedy, would be "almost as bad as the appeasement at Munich" that led to the Second World War. The remark was especially pointed: Kennedy's father had long been criticized for supporting that appeasement of Hitler. An extraordinary exchange soon occurred between America's commander in chief and one of its most prominent generals:

LeMay: I think that a blockade and political talk would be considered by a lot of our friends and neutrals as being a pretty weak response to this. And I'm sure a lot of our own citizens would feel the same way. In other words, you're in a pretty bad fix at the present time.

President Kennedy: What did you say?

LeMay: You're in a pretty bad fix.

President Kennedy: You're in there with me. [*Slight laughter, a bit forced.*] Personally.

When the meeting ended, Kennedy left the Cabinet Room, unsure about what to do. The tape recorder was still running. General David Shoup, commandant of the Marine Corps, turned to LeMay. "I just agree with you," Shoup said. "I agree with you a hundred percent."

On the evening of October 22, America's television networks interrupted their regularly scheduled programming to broadcast a special message from the president. Appearing somber and grim behind his desk in the Oval Office, Kennedy informed the nation that Soviet missiles had been spotted in Cuba. He called upon Khrushchev to "eliminate this clandestine, reckless and provocative threat to world peace." He reminded viewers that a policy of appeasement, of allowing aggressive conduct to go unchallenged, had led to the Second World War. And he declared that the United States was imposing a modified blockade, a "quarantine," on the shipment of offensive weapons to Cuba. The Soviet missiles had to be removed, and Khrushchev had to "move the world back from the abyss of destruction." Otherwise, Kennedy said, the United States would take further, unspecified actions.

The Joint Chiefs of Staff had established five defense readiness conditions (DEFCON) for the armed forces. DEFCON 5 was the state of military readiness during normal peacetime operations; DEFCON 1 meant that war was imminent. As Kennedy spoke to the nation, the Joint Chiefs ordered American forces to DEFCON 3. Polaris submarines left their ports and headed for locations within range of the Soviet Union. Fighter-interceptors patrolled American airspace with Genies and Falcons, atomic antiaircraft rockets, in case Soviet planes tried to attack from Cuba. Nearly two hundred B-47 bombers left SAC bases and flew to dozens of civilian airports throughout the United States—to Portland, Spokane, and Minneapolis; to Chicago and Detroit; to Birmingham, Philadelphia, and Tulsa. Dispersing the bombers from SAC bases made them less vulnerable to a Soviet missile attack. Aircrews slept on the ground beside their planes, which were loaded with hydrogen bombs, as commercial airliners took off and landed on nearby runways.

The number of B-52s on airborne alert was increased more than five-fold. Every day about sixty-five of the bombers circled within striking distance of the Soviet Union. Each of them carried a Hound Dog missile with a thermonuclear warhead, as well as two Mark 39 or four Mark 28 hydrogen bombs. On October 24, when the quarantine of Cuba took effect, the Strategic Air Command was placed on DEFCON 2 for the first time in its history. "I am addressing you for the purpose of reemphasizing the seriousness of the situation this nation faces," General Power said in a message transmitted to all his commanders worldwide. "We are in an advanced state of readiness to meet any emergencies. . . . I expect each of you to maintain strict security and use calm judgment during this tense period." Sent by radio, without any encryption, his announcement that SAC was ready for war could also be heard by the Soviets.

One quarter of a million American troops prepared for an invasion of Cuba. Secretary of Defense McNamara worried that, with thousands of nuclear weapons on high alert, something could go wrong. President Kennedy had recently approved the installation of permissive action links. But his executive order applied only to weapons in the NATO atomic stockpile—and none of the locks had been installed yet. U.S. Air Force units in Europe were kept at DEFCON 5, and the readiness of NATO forces wasn't increased. Any sign of a mobilization in Europe might alarm the Soviets, creating another potential trigger for nuclear war. McNamara also worried that if the United States attacked the Soviet missiles in Cuba, the Soviet Union might retaliate by attacking the Jupiter missiles in Turkey. The American custodians of the Jupiters were ordered to render the missiles inoperable, somehow, if Turkish officers tried to launch them without Kennedy's approval.

The lack of direct, secure communications between the White House and the Kremlin, the distrust that Kennedy felt toward the Soviet leader, and Khrushchev's impulsive, unpredictable behavior complicated efforts to end the crisis peacefully. Khrushchev felt relieved, after hearing Kennedy's speech, that the president hadn't announced an invasion of Cuba. Well aware that the Soviet Union's strategic forces were vastly inferior to those of the United States, Khrushchev had no desire to start a nuclear war. He did, however, want to test Kennedy's mettle and see how much the Soviets could gain from the crisis. Khrushchev secretly ordered his ships loaded with missiles not to violate the quarantine. But in private letters to Kennedy, he vowed that the ships would never turn around, denied that offensive weapons had been placed in Cuba, and denounced the quarantine as "an act of aggression which pushes mankind toward . . . a world nuclear-missile war."

Bertrand Russell agreed with the Soviet leader and sent President Kennedy a well-publicized telegram. "Your action desperate," it said. "Threat to human survival. No conceivable justification. Civilized man condemns it. . . . End this madness." Khrushchev's first public statement on the missile crisis was a cordial reply to the British philosopher, proposing a summit meeting. While the Kennedy administration anxiously wondered if the Soviets would back down, Khrushchev maintained a defiant facade. And then on October 26, persuaded by faulty intelligence that an American attack on Cuba was about to begin, he wrote another letter to Kennedy, offering a deal: the Soviet Union would remove the missiles from Cuba, if the United States promised never to invade Cuba.

Khrushchev's letter arrived at the American embassy in Moscow around five o'clock in the evening, which was ten in the morning, Eastern Standard Time. It took almost eleven hours for the letter to be fully transmitted by cable to the State Department in Washington, D.C. Kennedy and his advisers were encouraged by its conciliatory tone and decided to accept the deal—but went to bed without replying. Seven more hours passed, and Khrushchev started to feel confident that the United States wasn't about to attack Cuba, after all. He wrote another letter to Kennedy, adding a new demand: the missiles in Cuba would be removed, if the United States removed its Jupiter missiles from Turkey. Instead of being delivered to the American embassy, this letter was broadcast, for the world to hear, on Radio Moscow.

On the morning of October 27, as President Kennedy was drafting a reply to Khrushchev's first proposal, the White House learned about his second one. Kennedy and his advisers struggled to understand what was happening in the Kremlin. Conflicting messages were now coming not only from Khrushchev, but from various diplomats, journalists, and Soviet intelligence agents who were secretly meeting with members of the administration. Convinced that Khrushchev was being duplicitous, McNamara now pushed for a limited air strike to destroy the missiles. General Maxwell Taylor, now head of the Joint Chiefs of Staff, recommended a large-scale attack. When an American U-2 was shot down over Cuba, killing the pilot, the pressure on Kennedy to launch an air strike increased enormously. A nuclear war with the Soviet Union seemed possible. "As I left the White

House . . . on that beautiful fall evening," McNamara later recalled, "I feared I might never live to see another Saturday night."

The Cuban Missile Crisis ended amid the same sort of confusion and miscommunication that had plagued much of its thirteen days. President Kennedy sent the Kremlin a cable accepting the terms of Khrushchev's first offer, never acknowledging that a second demand had been made. But Kennedy also instructed his brother to meet privately with Ambassador Dobrynin and agree to the demands made in Khrushchev's second letter— so long as the promise to remove the Jupiters from Turkey was never made public. Giving up dangerous and obsolete American missiles to avert a nuclear holocaust seemed like a good idea. Only a handful of Kennedy's close advisers were told about this secret agreement.

Meanwhile, at the Kremlin, Khrushchev suddenly became afraid once again that the United States was about to attack Cuba. He decided to remove the Soviet missiles from Cuba—without insisting upon the removal of the Jupiters from Turkey. Before he had a chance to transmit his decision to the Soviet embassy in Washington, word arrived from Dobrynin about Kennedy's secret promise. Khrushchev was delighted by the president's unexpected—and unnecessary—concession. But time seemed to be running out, and an American attack might still be pending. Instead of accepting the deal through a diplomatic cable, Khrushchev's decision to remove the missiles from Cuba was immediately broadcast on Radio Moscow. No mention was made of the American vow to remove its missiles from Turkey.

Both leaders had feared that any military action would quickly escalate to a nuclear exchange. They had good reason to think so. Although Khrushchev never planned to move against Berlin during the crisis, the Joint Chiefs had greatly underestimated the strength of the Soviet military force based in Cuba. In addition to strategic weapons, the Soviet Union had almost one hundred tactical nuclear weapons on the island that would have been used by local commanders to repel an American attack. Some were as powerful as the bomb that destroyed Hiroshima. Had the likely targets of those weapons—the American fleet offshore and the U.S. naval base at Guantánamo—been destroyed, an all-out nuclear war would have been hard to avoid.

Pushed to the brink, Kennedy and Khrushchev chose to back down. But Kennedy emerged from the crisis looking much tougher—his concession to the Soviets not only remained secret but was vehemently denied. LeMay, among others, suspected that some sort of deal had been struck. Asked at a Senate hearing whether the Jupiters in Turkey had been traded for the missiles in Cuba, McNamara replied, "Absolutely not . . . the Soviet Government did raise the issue . . . [but the] President absolutely refused even to discuss it." Secretary of State Rusk repeated the lie. In order to deflect attention from the charge, members of the administration told friendly journalists, off the record, that Adlai Stevenson, the American ambassador to the United Nations, had urged Kennedy to trade NATO missiles in Turkey, Italy, and Great Britain for the missiles in Cuba, but the president had refused—another lie. A reference to the secret deal was later excised from Robert Kennedy's diary after his death. And a virile myth was promoted by the administration: when the leaders of the two superpowers stood eye to eye, threatening to fight over Cuba, Khrushchev was the one who blinked.

Within the following year, President Kennedy gave a speech at American University that called for a relaxation of the Cold War and "genuine peace" with the Soviets. The United States, the Soviet Union, and Great Britain signed the Limited Test Ban Treaty, prohibiting nuclear detonations in the atmosphere, the ocean, and outer space. And a hot line was finally created to link the Kremlin and the Pentagon, with additional terminals at the White House and the headquarters of the Communist Party in Moscow. The Soviet Union welcomed the new system. At the height of the Cuban Missile Crisis, urgent messages from the Soviet ambassador in Washington had been encoded by hand and then given to a Western Union messenger who arrived at the embassy on a bicycle. "We at the embassy could only pray," Ambassador Dobrynin recalled, "that he would take it to the Western Union office without delay and not stop to chat on the way with some girl!"

Unlike the hot line frequently depicted in Hollywood films, the new system didn't provide a special telephone for the president to use in an emergency. It relied on Teletype machines that could send text quickly and

securely. Written statements were considered easier to translate, more deliberate, and less subject to misinterpretation than verbal ones. Every day, a
test message was sent once an hour, alternately from Moscow, in Russian,
and from Washington, in English. The system would not survive nuclear
attacks on either city. But it was installed with the hope of preventing them.

During the Cuban Missile Crisis, the Strategic Air Command
conducted 2,088 airborne alert missions, involving almost fifty thousand
hours of flying time, without a single accident. The standard operating
procedures, the relentless training, and the checklists introduced by LeMay
and Power helped to achieve a remarkable safety record when it was needed
most. Nevertheless, in the aftermath of the crisis, public anxieties about
nuclear war soon focused on the dangers of SAC's airborne alert. The great
risk—as depicted in the 1964 films *Fail-Safe* and *Dr. Strangelove*—wasn't
that a hydrogen bomb might accidentally explode during the crash of a
B-52. It was that an order to attack the Soviet Union could be sent without
the president's authorization, either through a mechanical glitch (*Fail-Safe*)
or the scheming of a madman (*Dr. Strangelove*).

The plot of both films strongly resembled that of the novel *Red Alert*. Its
author, Peter George, cowrote the screenplay of *Dr. Strangelove* and sued
the producers of *Fail-Safe* for copyright infringement. The case was settled
out of court. The threat of accidental nuclear war was the central theme of
the films—and *Strangelove*, although a black comedy, was by far the more
authentic of the two. It astutely parodied the strategic theories pushed by
RAND analysts, members of the Kennedy administration, and the Joint
Chiefs. It captured the absurdity of debating how many million civilian
deaths would constitute a military victory. And it ended with an apocalyptic metaphor for the arms race, conjuring a Soviet doomsday machine that's
supposed to deter an American attack by threatening to launch a nuclear
retaliation, automatically, through the guidance of a computer, without
need of any human oversight. The failure of the Soviets to tell the United
States about the contraption defeats its purpose, inadvertently bringing
the end of the world. "The whole point of the doomsday machine is lost,"

Dr. Strangelove, the president's eccentric science adviser, explains to the Soviet ambassador, "IF YOU KEEP IT A SECRET!"

The growing public anxiety about accidental war prompted a spirited defense of America's command-and-control system. Sidney Hook, a prominent conservative intellectual, wrote a short book dismissing the fears spread by Cold War fiction. "The probability of a mechanical failure in the defense system," Hook wrote in *The Fail-Safe Fallacy*, "is now being held at so low a level that no accurate quantitative estimate of the probability . . . can be made." Senator Paul H. Douglas, a Democrat from Illinois praised the book and condemned the misconception that America's nuclear deterrent was a grave danger to mankind, not "the Communist determination to dominate the world." And Roswell L. Gilpatric, one of McNamara's closest advisers, assured readers of the *New York Times* that any malfunction in the command-and-control system would make it "'fail safe,' not unsafe." Gilpatric also suggested that permissive action links would thwart the sort of unauthorized attack depicted in *Dr. Strangelove*.

In fact, there was nothing to stop the crew of a B-52 from dropping its hydrogen bombs on Moscow—except, perhaps, Soviet air defenses. The Go code was simply an order from SAC headquarters to launch an attack; bombers on airborne alert didn't have any technological means to stop a renegade crew. General Power had waged a successful bureaucratic battle against the installation of permissive action links in SAC's weapons. All of its bombs and warheads were still unlocked, as were those of the Navy. The effort to prevent the unauthorized use of nuclear weapons remained largely administrative. In 1962, SAC had created a Human Reliability Program to screen airmen and officers for psychological problems, drug use, and alcohol abuse. And a version of the two-man rule was introduced in its bombers. A second arming switch was added to the cockpit. In order to use a nuclear weapon, both the ready/safe switch and the new "war/peace switch" had to be activated by two different crew members. Despite these measures, an unauthorized attack on the Soviet Union was still possible. But the discipline, training, and esprit de corps of SAC's bomber crews made it unlikely.

As a plot device in novels and films, an airborne alert gone wrong could provide suspense. A stray bomber would need at least an hour to reach its target, enough time to tell a good story. But one of the real advantages of SAC's bombers was that their crews could be contacted by radio and told to abort their missions, if the Go code had somehow been sent by mistake. Ballistic missiles posed a far greater risk of unauthorized or accidental use. Once they were launched, there was no calling them back. Missiles being flight-tested usually had a command destruct mechanism—explosives attached to the airframe that could be set off by remote control, destroying the missile if it flew off course. SAC refused to add that capability to operational missiles, out of a concern that the Soviets might find a way to detonate them all, midflight. And for similar reasons, SAC opposed any system that required a code to enable the launch of Minuteman missiles. "The very existence of the lock capability," General Power argued, "would create a fail-disable potential for knowledgeable agents to 'dud' the entire Minuteman force."

After examining the launch procedures proposed for the Minuteman, John H. Rubel—who supervised strategic weapon research and development at the Pentagon—didn't worry about the missiles being duds. He worried about an entire squadron of them being launched by a pair of rogue officers. A Minuteman squadron consisted of fifty missiles, overseen by five crews housed underground at separate locations. Only two of the crews were necessary to launch the missiles—making it more difficult for the Soviet Union to disable a squadron by attacking its control centers. When both of the officers in two different centers turned their keys and "voted" for a launch, all of the squadron's missiles would lift off. There was no way to fire just a few of them: it was all or nothing. And a launch order couldn't be rescinded. After the keys were turned, fifty missiles would leave their silos, either simultaneously or in a "ripple order," one after another.

By requiring a launch vote from at least two crews, SAC hoped to prevent the launch of Minuteman missiles without proper authorization. But Rubel was surprised to learn that SAC had also installed a timer in every Minuteman control center. The timer had been added as a backup—an automated vote to launch—in case four of the five crews were killed during a surprise attack. When the officers in a control center turned their launch keys, the timer started. And when the timer ran out, if no message had been received from the other control centers, approving or opposing the order to launch, all the missiles lifted off. The problem with the timer, Rubel soon realized, was that a crew could set it to six hours, six minutes— or zero. In the wrong hands, it gave a couple of SAC officers the ability to wipe out fifty cities in the Soviet Union. An unauthorized attack on that scale, a classified history of the Minuteman program noted, would be "an accident for which a later apology might be inadequate."

In 1959, Rubel sent a copy of *Red Alert* to every member of the Pentagon's Scientific Advisory Committee for Ballistic Missiles. He thought that the Minuteman launch control system needed much stronger safeguards against unauthorized use, as well as some sort of "stop-launch" capability. The committee agreed with him. But the Air Force fought against any modifications of the system, arguing that they would be too expensive and that the Minuteman, America's most important land-based missile, was "completely safe."

Rubel's concerns were taken seriously by the Kennedy administration, and an independent panel was appointed to investigate them. The panel found that Minuteman missiles were indeed vulnerable to unauthorized use—and that an entire squadron could be launched, accidentally, by a series of minor power surges. Although that sort of mistake was unlikely, it was possible. Two young SAC officers might be sitting innocently at their consoles, on an ordinary day, their launch keys locked away in the safe, as small fluctuations in the electricity entering the control center silently mimicked the pulses required by the launch switch. The crew would be caught by surprise when fifty Minuteman missiles suddenly left the ground.

"I was scared shitless," said an engineer who worked on the original Minuteman launch control system. "The technology was never to be trusted." Secretary of Defense McNamara insisted that a number of command-and-control changes be made to the Minuteman, and the redesign cost about $840 million. The new system did not let the crew set the timer, allowed missiles to be launched individually, and prevented minor power surges from causing an accidental launch. Minuteman missiles became operational for the first time during the Cuban Missile Crisis. To err on the side of safety, the explosive bolts were removed from their silo doors. If one of the missiles were launched by accident, it would explode inside the silo. And if President Kennedy decided to launch one, some poor enlisted man would have to kneel over the silo door, reconnect the explosive bolts by hand, and leave the area in a hurry.

WHILE THE DEPARTMENT OF DEFENSE publicly dismissed fears of an accidental nuclear war, the Cuban Missile Crisis left McNamara more concerned than ever about the danger. At a national security meeting a few months after the crisis, he opposed allowing anyone other than the president of the United States to authorize the use of nuclear weapons. A secret memorandum on the meeting summarized his views:

> Mr. McNamara went on to describe the possibilities which existed for an accidental launch of a missile against the USSR. He pointed out that we were spending millions of dollars to reduce this problem, but we could not assure ourselves completely against such a contingency. Moreover he suggested that it was unlikely that the Soviets were spending as much as we were in attempting to narrow the limits of possible accidental launch. . . . He went on to describe the crashes of US aircraft, one in North Carolina and one in Texas, where, by the slightest margin of chance, literally the failure of two wires to cross, a nuclear explosion was averted. He concluded that despite our best efforts, the possibility of an accidental nuclear explosion still existed.

The supreme commander of NATO should not be granted any type of predelegation "to fire nuclear weapons," McNamara argued—and even the president should never order their use without knowing all the details of a nuclear explosion, whether it was deliberate or accidental, "whether or not it was Soviet launched, how large, where it occurred, etc." Secretary of State Rusk agreed with McNamara. But their views did not prevail. The head of NATO retained the authority to use nuclear weapons, during an emergency, on the condition that "every effort to contact the President must be made."

The elaborate nuclear strategies promoted by RAND and embraced by McNamara now seemed largely irrelevant. After the Cuban Missile Crisis, a "no cities" policy lost its appeal. Newspapers had criticized it, NATO allies had repudiated it, and the dispersal of SAC bombers to commercial airports had blurred the distinction between civilian and military targets. And as the Soviet Union built more long-range missiles, a counterforce strategy would require the United States to deploy more missiles to destroy them. The arms race would become never ending. The hope of eliminating the Soviet threat with a first strike and defending America from attack now seemed illusory. Thousands of new missiles, the construction of more bomb shelters, or even an antiballistic missile system couldn't change what appeared to be an unavoidable fact for both superpowers: launching any nuclear attack would be suicidal.

Within weeks of President Kennedy's assassination, McNamara formally endorsed a strategy of "Assured Destruction." The idealism and optimism that had accompanied Kennedy's inauguration were long gone. The new strategy was grounded in a sense of futility. It planned to deter a Soviet attack by threatening to wipe out at least "30% of their population, 50% of their industrial capacity, and 150 of their cities." McNamara's staff had calculated that the equivalent of 400 megatons, detonated above the Soviet Union, would be enough for the task. Anything more would be overkill. Informed by a reporter that the Soviets were hardening their silos to protect the missiles from an American attack, McNamara said, "Thank God." The move would improve "crisis stability." Once the Soviets felt confident that they could retaliate after being attacked, they'd feel much less pressure to strike first. Leaving the cities of the United States and the Soviet Union vulnerable to annihilation, McNamara now thought, would keep them safe. The strategy was soon known as MAD: "mutually assured destruction."

The strategic thinking at the White House and the Department of Defense, however, didn't correspond to the targeting policies at SAC headquarters in Omaha. The gulf between theory and practice remained vast. Although the SIOP had been revised during the Kennedy administration, General Power had blocked significant changes in weapon allocation.

The new SIOP divided the "optimum mix" into three separate target groups: Soviet nuclear forces, conventional military forces, and urban-industrial areas. The president could decide to attack only the first group, the first two groups, or all three. Moscow, China, and cities in the Eastern bloc could selectively be spared from destruction. The SIOP could be launched as a first strike or as retaliation. But all the attack options still required that the Soviet Union be hit by thousands of nuclear weapons, far more than were necessary for "assured destruction." The three target categories of the SIOP—Alpha, Bravo, Charlie—were the same as those in the attack plan proposed by SAC in 1950. And the new SIOP was almost as destructive, inflexible, and mechanistic as the previous one. A war plan that seemed too horrible to contemplate when Kennedy and McNamara first learned of its existence had become institutionalized.

By the time Robert McNamara retired from the Pentagon in February 1968, the command-and-control system of the United States had been improved. The new Missile Defense Alarm System—satellites with infrared sensors that could detect heat from the launch of missiles—promised to give as much as half an hour of warning, if the Soviets attacked. SAC's Looking Glass command post, airborne twenty-four hours a day, increased the likelihood that a Go code could be sent after the United States was hit. New computer and communications systems were being added to the World Wide Military Command and Control System. But many of the underlying problems hadn't been solved.

The number of nuclear weapons in the American arsenal had increased by more than 50 percent since the Eisenhower administration. The United States now had about thirty thousand of them, and each one could potentially be lost, stolen, sabotaged, or involved in an accident. Tactical weapons hadn't been removed from Europe. On the contrary, the number of tactical weapons had more than doubled, and they were no longer safely tucked away in igloos. Putting locks in NATO's weapons allowed them to be widely dispersed to units in the field—where they could be more easily stolen. And the question of how to keep the president alive and in command still didn't have a satisfactory answer. The plans for a Deep Underground Command Center were scrapped after Kennedy's death. The bunker had a good chance of surviving multiple hits from Soviet warheads. But its survival would prove meaningless. After an attack the president and his aides would most likely find themselves trapped two thirds of a mile beneath the rubble of the Pentagon, unable to communicate with the rest of the world or even get out of their bunker. The facility would serve primarily as a multimillion-dollar tomb.

Although McNamara's efforts to avoid a nuclear war were tireless and sincere, he left office as one of the most despised men in the United States. Half a million American soldiers were fighting in Vietnam, the war seemed unwinnable, and most Americans blamed the number-crunching secretary of defense and his Ivy League advisers for the fiasco. A centralized command-and-control system—so essential for managing a nuclear war— had proven disastrous when applied to a civil war in Southeast Asia. Distrusting the Joint Chiefs of Staff and convinced that victories on the battlefield could be gained through cost-benefit analysis, the secretary of defense micromanaged the Vietnam War. McNamara personally chose targets to be bombed and supervised air strikes from his office at the Pentagon. "I don't object to its being called McNamara's war," he said in 1964. "In fact I'm proud to be identified with it."

Four years later hundreds of thousands of Vietnamese civilians had been killed, tens of thousands of American servicemen had been killed or wounded, antiwar protests were spreading throughout the United States, and the Pentagon had become a symbol of bureaucratic malevolence and pointless slaughter. Known for his cool, detached manner, McNamara was now prone to bouts of sobbing in his office. While receiving the Presidential Medal of Freedom, the day before his retirement, he apologized for being unable to speak. President Lyndon Johnson put a hand on McNamara's shoulder, ended the ceremony, and guided him from the room.

Curtis LeMay withdrew from public life the same year, having left the Air Force in 1965. Once the darling of Hollywood and the media, he was now widely mocked and ridiculed. His well-publicized disputes with the Kennedy administration had given him a reputation for being a right-wing

Neanderthal. When a fictionalized version of General LeMay appeared in film, the character was no longer a heroic defender of freedom. He was a buffoon, like General Buck Turgidson in *Dr. Strangelove*, willing to sacrifice twenty million American lives for the sake of defeating the Soviet Union. Or he was a crypto-fascist, like General James Mattoon Scott in *Seven Days in May*, preferring a coup d'état in the United States to a disarmament treaty with the Soviets.

LeMay seemed to confirm those stereotypes in October 1968, when he agreed to serve as the vice presidential candidate for the American Independent Party. George C. Wallace, an outspoken racist and segregationist, was the presidential candidate. LeMay had played a leading role in integrating the Air Force, and his support for equal rights, labor unions, birth control, and abortion seemed out of place in the Wallace campaign. But LeMay's anger at how the Vietnam War was being fought—and his belief that both the Democratic and Republican candidates, Hubert H. Humphrey and Richard M. Nixon, were willing to appease the Communists—persuaded him to run. It was perhaps the worst decision of his life.

Tough and disciplined as a commander, LeMay was a supremely incompetent politician. At the press conference announcing his candidacy, he refused to rule out the use of nuclear weapons in Vietnam. The same implied threat that Eisenhower had made to end the Korean War sounded heartless and barbaric sixteen years later, as images of Vietnamese women and children burned by napalm appeared on the nightly news. LeMay had strongly opposed sending ground troops to Vietnam and disagreed with McNamara's strategy for fighting a limited war there. "War is *never* 'cost-effective,'" LeMay argued. "People are killed. To them the war is total." At the press conference he stressed that the United States should always try to avoid armed conflict, "but when you get in it, get in it with both feet and get it over with as soon as you can." The logic of his argument received less attention than the tone-deaf remark that preceded it: "We seem to have a phobia about nuclear weapons."

On the campaign trail, the general who'd risked his life countless times fighting the Nazis was jeered by protesters yelling, "*Sieg Heil*." He told reporters that the antiwar movement was "Communist-inspired," lost his job as an aerospace executive for running with Wallace, and largely faded into obscurity after their defeat. LeMay and McNamara, polar opposites who'd battled over a wide range of national security issues, each convinced that the other was dangerously wrong, now found themselves in much the same place. They ended 1968 in humiliation and disgrace, their views repudiated by the American people.

An Abnormal Environment

On March 13, 1961, at about half past eleven in the morning, a B-52 took off from Mather Air Force Base in California, not far from Sacramento. The plane was on a Chrome Dome mission, carrying two Mark 39 hydrogen bombs. Twenty minutes after takeoff, the pilot, Major Raymond Clay, felt too much hot air coming from the vents in the cockpit. He and one of the copilots, First Lieutenant Robert Bigham, tried to turn off the heat. The vents wouldn't close, and it became uncomfortably warm in the cockpit. Almost seven hours into the flight, the control tower at Mather instructed Clay to "continue mission as long as you can . . . if it gets intolerable, of course, bring it home." Before the second refueling, Clay guided the plane to a low altitude and depressurized the cabin to cool it. But it heated up again, as the bomber climbed to thirty thousand feet. Fourteen hours into the flight, the temperature in the cockpit had reached 160 degrees Fahrenheit—so hot that one of the pilot's windows shattered.

Clay descended to twelve thousand feet again and requested permission to end the mission. In addition to the broken window, a couple of the crew members were feeling sick. The cockpit had become so hot that Clay and his two copilots took turns flying the plane, going back and forth to the cabin below, where the temperature was a little cooler. Passing through overcast skies, the bomber flew off course, fell behind schedule by about half an hour, and lost another seven or eight minutes avoiding bad weather. Twenty-two hours into the flight, First Lieutenant Bigham realized that a gauge for one of the main fuel tanks was broken. The reading hadn't changed for at least ninety minutes—but nobody had noticed, amid the heat and the hassle of coming and going from the cockpit. Bigham asked the control tower to send a tanker; they were running low on fuel. Forty minutes later, while approaching the tanker, the B-52 ran out of gas. All eight engines flamed out at once.

At an altitude of seven thousand feet, the crew started to bail out. Major Clay stayed in the cockpit and banked the plane away from Yuba City, California, just forty miles short of their base. Confident that the bomber wouldn't hit the town, Clay ejected at an altitude of four thousand feet. The B-52 made a full 360-degree turn and then crashed nose first into a barley field. The high explosives of both hydrogen bombs shattered on impact and didn't burn or detonate. The weapons harmlessly broke into pieces. All eight members of the crew survived the crash. But an Air Force fireman, rushing to the scene, was killed when his truck overturned.

Fred Iklé had predicted that as the number of nuclear weapons and airborne alerts increased, so would the number of accidents. He was correct, and the aircraft involved in those accidents had few safeguards to protect weapons during a crash. The Air Force considered the performance of a bomber or a fighter—its speed, maneuverability, capacity, and range—more important than its structural integrity. The B-52 had been designed in the late 1940s, and its designers never anticipated that the bomber would be used for airborne or ground alerts. It wasn't built to carry fully assembled nuclear weapons during peacetime. When the weapons were attached to the underside of a plane, they were fully exposed to the effects of a crash. And when they were carried inside the bomb bay of a B-52, a Sandia report noted, they were located in "a weak point in the aircraft's structure, a point at which the aircraft is apt to break open, spewing weapons beyond the protection afforded by the fuselage."

On Johnston Island in the central Pacific, tests designed to measure the effects of high-altitude nuclear explosions served as a reminder that missiles and warheads didn't always behave in predictable ways. On June 3, 1962, a

Thor intermediate-range missile with a 400-kiloton warhead lifted off smoothly. But a radar tracking station failed, endangering ships in the area if the missile flew off course. The range safety officer decided to abort the flight. The command destruct mechanism blew up the missile, destroying its warhead. Two and a half weeks later, another Thor was launched, this time with a 1.4-megaton warhead. The missile's engine shut down after fifty-nine seconds, and the range safety officer decided, once again, to use the command destruct mechanism. The Thor exploded at an altitude of about thirty thousand feet. Pieces of the missile and the warhead, including plutonium from its core, fell on Johnston Island and the surrounding lagoon.

About a month later, another Thor missile with a 1.4-megaton warhead misfired on the launchpad. It never got off the ground. The range safety officer gave the command destruct order, and a massive explosion destroyed much of the launch complex, showering it with debris, burning fuel, and plutonium. The next two months were spent rebuilding the complex and decontaminating the island. On October 15, during the first use of the new launchpad, a Thor missile went off course about ninety seconds after liftoff. The command destruct order was given, the missile exploded, and more plutonium fell onto Johnston Island. Two thirds of the Thor missiles used in the tests—modified versions of the Thors deployed in Great Britain— had to be destroyed by remote control.

The mishaps on Johnston Island occurred during test launches carefully planned for months. But mundane, everyday tasks also caused nuclear weapon accidents. On November 13, 1963, three workers at an Atomic Energy Commission base in Medina, Texas, were moving partially assembled Mark 7 bombs into a storage igloo. The weapons were being decommissioned. Their high explosives would eventually be burned, their uranium recovered. Two explosive spheres most likely rubbed together while being unloaded, and one of them ignited. The three workers— Marvin J. Ehlinger, Hilary F. Huser, and Floyd T. Lutz—noticed the flames, ran out of the igloo, and jumped into a ditch across the road. The sphere burned for about forty-five seconds and then detonated, setting off approximately 123,000 pounds of high explosives in the building. The explosion did not produce a nuclear yield, although the mushroom cloud rising from the blast contained uranium dust. Shop windows were blown out in San Antonio, fourteen miles away. All that remained, where the igloo had once stood, was a crater twenty feet deep. The other igloos at the base were undamaged, the three workers unharmed. They were given the rest of the day off.

A few weeks later a B-52 encountered severe air turbulence while crossing the Appalachian Mountains. It was transporting two Mark 53 hydrogen bombs—an air-delivered version of the weapon carried by the Titan II missile, with a yield of 9 megatons. The pilot, Major Thomas McCormick, took the plane down to about twenty-nine thousand feet, looking for a smoother ride. But the turbulence got worse, and McCormick received permission to climb another few thousand feet. The crew heard a loud thud. The fifty-foot-high tail fin had snapped off the bomber. McCormick told everyone to bail out, as the plane rolled over and flew upside down for a moment before spiraling downward. Four crew members got out safely; the radar navigator, Major Robert Townley, didn't. The plane crashed into the side of Savage Mountain, about twenty miles from Cumberland, Maryland, during a heavy snowstorm. It was one thirty in the morning, and the temperature outdoors was about 0 degrees Fahrenheit.

Technical Sergeant Melvin Wooten, the gunner, landed in a field about half a mile from Salisbury, Pennsylvania. The lights of the town were visible in the distance, but Wooten died before reaching it. He'd suffered severe head, chest, and leg injuries. Major Robert Payne, the navigator, walked for hours in the darkness, through snowdrifts two to three feet deep. He fell into a stream and froze to death. Major McCormick and a copilot, Captain Parker Peedin, landed near trees, about three miles apart. They waited until daylight to seek help. McCormick found refuge in a farmhouse, after walking for two miles. Peedin was spotted by a search plane, and both men were hospitalized with minor injuries. The hydrogen bombs were found amid the wreckage of the B-52, partially buried in snow. Their high explosives had neither detonated nor burned.

Another accident with a Mark 53 bomb took place on December 8, 1964. During a training exercise at Bunker Hill Air Force Base, about a dozen miles north of Kokomo, Indiana, a B-58 bomber turned onto an icy runway. The plane carried five hydrogen bombs—four Mark 43s and the Mark 53—with a combined yield of perhaps 13 megatons. As the B-58 turned, the plane ahead revved its engines. The strong, sudden gust of exhaust hit the B-58. The bomber slid off the runway, and the landing gear beneath the right wing collapsed. The pilot, Captain Leary Johnson, saw a bright flash; fuel had leaked and ignited. Johnson gave the order to bail out, jettisoned his canopy, climbed over the nose of the plane, leaped through flames, and caught on fire. He rolled through snow and puddles of water to put out the flames, suffering only minor burns. The defensive systems operator, Roger Hall, jettisoned his canopy, noticed the left wing was on fire, climbed onto the right one, jumped off the engine, and briefly caught on fire, too. His burns were superficial. Instead of climbing out, the navigator, Manuel Cervantes, Jr., triggered his escape capsule, and a rocket blasted it into the air. The capsule landed about 150 yards from the burning plane, but Cervantes was killed by the impact. He had two young sons.

The five hydrogen bombs incurred varying degrees of damage: two were intact; one was scorched; another was mostly consumed by the fire; and the fifth completely melted into the tarmac. None of the high explosives detonated. Fire crews aggressively fought the blaze, long past the time factors of the bombs. The fire threatened not only a SAC base crowded with bombers and nuclear weapons but also the fifty thousand inhabitants of Kokomo. At one point firefighters dragged a burning hydrogen bomb fifty yards from the plane, dumped it into a trench, covered it with sand, and extinguished the flames.

During the same week as the Bunker Hill accident, a couple of young airmen, Leonard D. Johnson and Glenn A. Dodson, Jr., drove out to a Minuteman missile site at Ellsworth Air Force Base in South Dakota. A crew in the launch control center, about twenty miles away, had reported a problem with the security system around the silo. Johnson and Dodson were told to find out what was wrong. They entered the silo, opened the security alarm control box, and checked the fuses. Dodson had forgotten to bring a fuse puller, so he used a screwdriver instead. After removing each fuse, he'd put it back into place. You could hear the difference between a good fuse and one that had burned out. When a good fuse was inserted, it made a clicking sound. One of the fuses didn't make that "click." Dodson pulled it out again with the screwdriver, put it back, and heard a different kind of sound—a loud explosion.

The two airmen ran out of the launch duct and called the control center. Half an hour later, a Missile Potential Hazard Team ordered them to reenter the silo. They found it full of thick, gray smoke. One of the retrorockets atop the Minuteman had fired. The reentry vehicle, containing a W-56 thermonuclear weapon, had lifted a few inches into the air, flipped over, fallen nose first from the missile, bounced off the wall, hit the second-stage engine, and landed at the bottom of the silo. The warhead wasn't damaged, although its arming and fuzing package was torn off during the seventy-five-foot drop. An investigation later found that the retrorocket had been set off by a fault in an electrical connector—and by Dodson's screwdriver.

The weapon accidents often felt sudden and surreal. On December 5, 1965, a group of sailors were pushing an A-4E Skyhawk fighter plane onto an elevator aboard the USS *Ticonderoga*, an aircraft carrier about seventy miles off the coast of Japan. The plane's canopy was open; Lieutenant Douglas M. Webster, its pilot, strapped into his seat. The deck rose as the ship passed over a wave, and one of the sailors blew a whistle, signaling that Webster should apply his brakes. Webster didn't hear the whistle. The plane started to roll backward. The sailor kept blowing the whistle; other sailors yelled, "Brakes, brakes," and held on to the plane. They let go as it rolled off the elevator into the sea. In an instant, it was gone. The pilot, his plane, and a Mark 43 hydrogen bomb vanished. No trace of them was ever found; the ocean there was about three miles deep. The canopy may have closed after the plane fell, trapping Webster in his seat. He had recently graduated from Ohio State University, gotten married, and completed his first tour of duty over Vietnam.

BY THE MID-1960S, sealed-pit nuclear weapons had burned, melted, sunk, blown apart, smashed into the ground. But none had detonated accidentally. The B-52 crash in Goldsboro, North Carolina, had been an awfully close call, gaining the attention of engineers at Sandia. Nobody wanted that sort of thing to happen again—and yet during the Goldsboro crash, the weapons had failed safe. Now that nuclear testing had resumed, Los Alamos, Lawrence Livermore, and Sandia were busy designing new warheads and bombs for every branch of the armed services. The need for new safety devices was not apparent. Again and again, the existing ones worked.

President Kennedy and Secretary of Defense McNamara had taken a personal interest in nuclear weapon safety. A few months after Goldsboro, Kennedy gave the Department of Defense "responsibility for identifying and resolving health and safety problems connected with the custody and storage of nuclear weapons." The Atomic Energy Commission was to play an important, though subsidiary, role. Kennedy's decision empowered McNamara to do whatever seemed necessary. But it also reinforced military, not civilian, control of the system. At Los Alamos, Livermore, and Sandia, the reliability of nuclear weapons continued to receive far greater attention than their safety. And a dangerous way of thinking, a form of complacency later known as the Titanic Effect took hold among weapon designers: the more impossible an accidental detonation seemed to be, the more likely it became.

The military's distrust of use control and safety devices was encouraged by some of the early models. The first permissive action links—Category A PALs—did not always operate flawlessly. The batteries in their decoders had a tendency to run down without warning. When that happened, the weapons couldn't be unlocked. And the gears in the Category A PALs were too loud. During a black hat exercise at Sandia, an engineer listened carefully to the sounds of a PAL, deciphered its code, and picked the lock.

The W-47 warhead had a far more serious problem. Designed at Lawrence Livermore in the late 1950s and rushed into production amid the anxiety about *Sputnik,* the warhead sat atop every missile in Polaris submarines. Its primary had a revolutionary new core—small and egg shaped, with only two detonators—that could generate a large yield for a weapon so compact. But the W-47 wasn't one-point safe, by a significant margin.

And the moratorium on nuclear testing, during Eisenhower's last two years in office, prevented the sort of tests that could make it one-point safe. Edward Teller, now the director of Lawrence Livermore, considered using a more traditional core designed at Los Alamos, even though the two labs had competed fiercely for this contract with the Navy. Each Polaris submarine would have sixteen missiles, aligned closely together in two rows. An unsafe warhead could threaten the sub's 150 crew members—and the port cities where it docked.

To avoid the embarrassment of relying on a Los Alamos design, Teller used Livermore's new core but added a mechanical safing device to it. A strip of cadmium tape coated with boron was placed in the center of the core. Cadmium and boron absorb neutrons, and the presence of the tape would stop a chain reaction, making a nuclear detonation impossible. During the warhead's arming sequence, the tape would be pulled out by a little motor before the core imploded. It seemed like a clever solution to the one-point safety problem—until a routine examination of the warheads in 1963 found that the tape corroded inside the cores. When the tape corroded, it got stuck. And the little motor didn't have enough torque to pull the tape out. Livermore's mechanical safing device had made the warheads too safe. A former director of the Navy's Strategic Systems Project Office Reentry Body Coordinating Committee explained the problem: there was "almost zero confidence that the warhead would work as intended." A large proportion of W-47 warheads, perhaps 75 percent or more, wouldn't detonate after being launched. The Polaris submarine, the weapon system that McNamara and Kennedy considered the cornerstone of the American arsenal, the ultimate deterrent, the guarantor of nuclear retaliation and controlled escalation and assured destruction, was full of duds. For the next four years, Livermore tried to fix the safety mechanism of the W-47, without success. The Navy was furious, and all the warheads had to be replaced. The new cores were inherently one-point safe.

The Strategic Air Command's safety procedures had become so effective that the risks of its airborne alert were easily overlooked. During the first five years of the program, SAC conducted tens of thousands aerial refuelings—with only one fatal accident. But the laws of probability couldn't be escaped. On January 17, 1966, at about ten fifteen in the morning, a B-52 on a Chrome Dome mission prepared for its second refueling, a couple of miles inland from the southern coast of Spain. It had left Goldsboro, North Carolina, the previous evening and needed more fuel, after seventeen hours of flight, for the trip home. The B-52 approached the tanker too quickly, flew into the fuel boom, and started to break apart. Flames traveled straight through the boom. The tanker exploded, incinerating its four-man crew.

Major Larry G. Messinger, a copilot who was flying the B-52 at the time, bailed out first. His ejection seat cleared the plane, his parachute opened, and high winds carried him out to sea. The morning sky was clear enough for him to watch the coast of Spain receding in the distance. Messinger landed in the ocean, eight miles from shore, and inflated a life raft. Captain Ivans Buchanan, the radar navigator, left the plane, passed through a fireball, couldn't get out of his ejection seat—and couldn't get his parachute to open. Stuck in the chair as it plummeted and spun, Buchanan removed the parachute from the pack by hand. The chute finally opened, but the weight of the seat caused a hard landing. It hurt his back, broke his shoulder, and knocked him unconscious. Captain Charles J. Wendorf, the pilot, broke an arm ejecting from the plane. Although his parachute caught on fire, it deposited him safely in the ocean, about three miles out.

Lieutenant Michael J. Rooney, another copilot, was sitting below the cockpit, reading a book, when the two planes collided. He wasn't near an ejection seat. The g-forces of the falling bomber delayed his exit for a few long minutes, tossing him against the walls, the roof, the floor. He managed to crawl out through the navigator's escape hatch and opened his parachute. A burning engine pod flew right past him, close enough to singe hair. Rooney landed in the ocean, not far from Wendorf, and started to swim.

Rooney and Wendorf were picked up by fishing boats within half an hour, and Messinger was rescued about fifteen minutes later. Residents of Palomares, a nearby village, discovered Buchanan sitting in a field, strapped into the ejection seat, still unconscious. They took him to a hospital. Sergeant Ronald Snyder, the gunner, and Lieutenant George Glesner, the electronic warfare operator, died in the plane. Lieutenant Stephen Montanus, the navigator, bailed out, fell thirty thousand feet in his ejection seat, and hit the ground. For some reason, the parachute hadn't opened. Montanus was the youngest member of the crew, just twenty-three, and his wife was only nineteen.

The B-52 carried four Mark 28 hydrogen bombs. None of the crew knew what had happened to them. A full-scale nuclear explosion clearly hadn't occurred, and yet beyond that, little was known. A Disaster Control Team from the SAC base in Torrejón, Spain, arrived in the afternoon and started to look for the bombs. Debris from the B-52 littered the ground for miles; much of it had fallen in and around Palomares. The village was so poor and remote that it didn't appear on most maps of southern Spain. The roughly two thousand inhabitants lacked electricity until 1958 and still didn't have running water.

At dusk, members of the Spanish federal police led the Disaster Control Team to the first bomb, which had landed southeast of Palomares, about three hundred yards from the beach. The weapon was remarkably intact. One of the parachutes had opened, dropping the Mark 28 onto soft, clay soil. Air Force sentries were left there to guard it overnight. A group of experts from Los Alamos, Sandia, and the Atomic Energy Commission, assembled by the Joint Nuclear Accident Coordinating Center in Albuquerque, were supposed to arrive the next morning.

The second bomb was spotted from a helicopter, almost twenty-four hours after the crash. What was left of the weapon lay in the hills above the local cemetery. Its parachutes hadn't opened. And its high explosives had partially detonated, digging a crater twenty feet wide, scattering bomb parts, and spreading plutonium across the hills. The third bomb was found about an hour later. It had struck the base of a stone wall, amid a vegetable garden on the outskirts of Palomares. The hydrogen bomb had missed a farmhouse by about seventy-five feet. One of its parachutes had deployed, and some of the high explosives had gone off. Pieces of the weapon, charred explosives, and a cloud of plutonium had been blown into nearby tomato fields.

The fourth bomb couldn't be found. Long lines of troops walked for miles, shoulder to shoulder, looking for it. Planes and helicopters looked for it. Hundreds of abandoned mine shafts, wells, and other holes in the ground were carefully explored for it. A month and a half after the crash, the Mark 28 was still missing, and the search of the countryside near Palomares was called off.

The little village had been overrun by reporters from around the world. At first, the Air Force refused to confirm or deny that nuclear weapons were involved in the accident. But the sight of "450 airmen with Geiger counters looking for nuclear material," as Reuters reported, soon made the subject hard to avoid. Three days after the accident, the Air Force admitted that the B-52 had been carrying "unarmed nuclear armament," stressed that "there is no danger to public health or safety as a result of this accident," and failed to disclose that a bomb had been lost. As a small armada of American ships searched for it, headlines conveyed the growing anger and doubts about the official story: "SECRECY SHROUDS URGENT HUNT FOR MISSING A-WEAPON," "MADRID POLICE DISPERSE MOB AT U.S. EMBASSY," "NEAR CATASTROPHE FROM U.S. BOMB, SOVIETS SAY; 'NUCLEAR VOLCANO' IN SEA OFF SPAIN." After weeks of bad publicity, the Pentagon finally acknowledged that a nuclear weapon was missing. The news brought to mind the plot of the latest James Bond film, *Thunderball,* and its underwater search for stolen hydrogen bombs.

The governments of Spain and the United States denied that the plutonium released by the two weapons posed any threat to the public. "There is not the slightest risk in eating meat, fish, vegetables from the [impact] zone, or of drinking milk from there," Spain's Nuclear Energy Board declared. The truth was somewhat more complex. Little research had been done on plutonium dispersal or the proper methods of decontamination. And the alpha particles emitted by plutonium were hard to detect outside of a laboratory. They traveled about an inch and could be blocked by a blade of grass or even a thin film of dew—making it almost impossible, with the available equipment, to determine exactly how much land was contaminated around Palomares. The Air Force had been caught unprepared for a weapon accident that spread plutonium. Portable alpha detectors had to be rushed to Spain from bases in other NATO countries, the United States, and North Africa. And the detectors often didn't work.

Nevertheless, traces of plutonium were detected in the mile-long strip of land between the two spots where bombs had landed. The contamination extended through the village of Palomares into nearby tomato fields. Residents weren't evacuated from these areas, and hazard control lines weren't established, a report by the Defense Nuclear Agency (DNA) later explained, because of "the politics of the situation."

The United States promised to decontaminate Palomares. But guidelines for removing plutonium after a weapon accident didn't exist. Nor did criteria for determining safe levels of plutonium in the environment. Almost four thousand truckloads of contaminated beans, cabbages, and tomatoes were harvested with machetes and burned. About thirty thousand cubic feet of contaminated soil were scraped from the ground, packed into steel drums, sent to an AEC facility in Aiken, South Carolina, and buried. The soldiers who cleared the fields and filled the drums were given surgical masks. According to the DNA report, the masks offered no protection against radiation hazards and served mainly as a placebo—"a psychological barrier to plutonium inhalation." To reassure the public and encourage tourists to visit southern Spain, the American ambassador brought his family to the beach near Palomares, put on a bathing suit, invited the press to join him, and took a well-publicized swim in the ocean, not far from where the hydrogen bomb had landed.

Randall C. Maydew, head of the aerodynamics department at Sandia, was recruited to help look for the missing bomb. His group had designed the parachutes and casing of the Mark 28. Before Maydew left for Spain, his friend Bob Peurifoy gave him a tool to aid with the search: a forked stick, like the divining rods used by dowsers to find water. Maydew and his team tried to ascertain where in the sky the two planes had collided. They performed reverse trajectory calculations—based on where the three bombs and the B-52's engines had hit the ground—and decided that the crash had happened somewhere within a circular, mile-wide patch of the sky, two miles from the coast, at an altitude of fifteen thousand feet. Given that location, the prevailing winds at the time of the accident, the discovery of the missing bomb's tail plate on the beach, and an assumption that its parachutes had opened, Maydew's team pointed to an eight-square-mile area in the Atlantic where it had most likely landed. A few days later, their conclusions were supported by a Spanish fisherman, who claimed to have seen a "stout man," attached to a large parachute, fall into the water there.

Ships, planes, helicopters, underwater television platforms, more than one hundred deep-sea divers, and four manned submersibles—*Deep Jeep, Cubmarine, Aluminaut,* and *Alvin*—searched the ocean for weeks, as Soviet vessels lingered nearby. "It isn't like looking for a needle in a haystack," Rear Admiral William S. Guest, the commander of the operation, said. "It's like looking for the eye of a needle in a field full of haystacks in the dark." On March 15, the crew of the *Alvin* spotted the bomb, wrapped in a parachute, at a depth of roughly half a mile. Nine days later, while it was being pulled from the sea, the line snapped—and the bomb disappeared again. The search resumed, another week passed, and *Alvin* found the bomb a second time. Aside from a small dent on the nose, it looked fine. The second attempt to recover it went smoothly. Having endured two and a half months of bad press, the Pentagon invited reporters aboard Admiral Guest's ship to show off the weapon, which sailed past them on the deck of another ship, proudly displayed like a prizewinning fish that had just been caught. Although the United States had deployed thousands of hydrogen bombs during the previous decade, this was the first time the American people were allowed to see one.

AFTER THE PALOMARES ACCIDENT, the government of Spain prohibited American planes from carrying nuclear weapons in its airspace. The SAC base in Torrejón was handed over to NATO, and members of President Lyndon Johnson's administration debated whether to end the airborne alert. It now seemed risky, expensive, outdated, and unnecessary. The kind of surprise attack that Pentagon officials had feared in 1960 no longer seemed likely. And as a nuclear deterrent, the twelve B-52s on airborne alert weren't as intimidating to the Soviets as the roughly 1,600 ballistic missiles in American silos and submarines. But the Joint Chiefs of Staff and the new commander of SAC, General John Dale Ryan, insisted that the airborne alert was crucial for the national defense. President Johnson decided to continue the alert for the time being, but reduced the number of daily flights to four.

"The possibility of an accidental nuclear explosion taking place is essentially negligible," the director of nuclear safety at Kirtland Air Force Base told CBS News. The Atomic Energy Commission said much the same thing to the *New York Times*, claiming the odds were "so remote that they can be ruled out completely." But a number of scientists and engineers at Sandia didn't share that degree of optimism. Bob Peurifoy felt uneasy that a simple, low-voltage signal, lasting a few seconds, was still being used to arm hydrogen bombs. That kind of signal dated back to the days of Thomas Edison—and it could come from a lot of places as a B-52 fell apart. It could come from a short circuit during an otherwise uneventful flight. Peurifoy thought that a more complicated signal—a unique series of electrical pulses—could prevent a bomb from being armed accidentally. Transmitted between the ready/safe switch in the cockpit and the nuclear weapon in the bomb bay, it would operate much like a secret code, alternating long and short pulses in a pattern that fate, bad luck, or even Mother Nature couldn't randomly generate.

Another engineer, Thomas Brumleve, criticized the air of overconfidence at Sandia, the overemphasis on reliability, the faith that an accidental detonation could never happen. "But suppose some important aspect of nuclear safety has been overlooked," Brumleve wrote in a 1967 report. "The nation, and indeed the world, will want to know who was responsible, how it could have happened, and why it wasn't prevented."

On January 21, 1968, a B-52 was serving as the Thule monitor. For hours it flew a "bowtie" pattern at thirty-five thousand feet, heading back and forth above the ballistic missile early warning complex in western Greenland. One of the copilots, Major Alfred D'Amario, Jr., had stuffed three cloth-covered, foam-rubber cushions beneath the instructor navigator's seat, and someone later put a fourth one under it, keeping the cushions wedged in place with a small metal box. The cushions might ease the discomfort of a long, tedious mission. About five hours into the flight, the crew noticed that the heat wasn't working properly. The cockpit felt too cold, and so D'Amario turned on a system that pulled air from the engine manifold into the cabin. The air was hot, about 428 degrees Fahrenheit. It ignited the cushions, which were blocking a vent under the seat.

The radar navigator, Major Frank F. Hopkins, thought he smelled something burning. It smelled like burning rubber. The crew looked for the source of the smoke, found it, sprayed the cushions with fire extinguishers, but couldn't put out the fire. The pilot, Captain John Haug, asked the control tower at Thule for permission to conduct an emergency landing. As Haug started the descent, Hopkins opened the sextant port, a small hole in the fuselage, to let out smoke. The navigator, Captain Curtis R. Criss, tried to smother the burning cushions with a duffle bag. But the flames spread, and the smoke in the cockpit became so thick that Haug could barely see the instrument panel. He told Thule that the fire was out of control. Moments later, the plane lost all its power.

The crew would have to bail out into some harsh weather. The temperature that day in western Greenland was −23 degrees Fahrenheit; the windchill made it feel like −44. Haug wanted to get as close as possible to Thule and increase the odds of his crew's survival—without crashing the B-52 into the base. Although their mission was simply to keep an eye on Thule and make sure that it still existed, the plane carried four Mark 28 bombs.

Haug stayed with the plane until everyone was out and then ejected, just four miles short of the runway. The B-52 passed right over Thule, made a 180-degree turn, flew another few miles, and slammed into the ice of Bylot Sound. The explosion caught most of the men on the base by surprise, shaking the buildings and lighting up the sky. It was about four thirty in the afternoon but completely dark outside. The sun hadn't been seen in Thule for almost two months, since late November. Except for a brief period of dim light in the afternoon, the snow-covered landscape around the base seemed dark as night. SAC headquarters was notified, for the first time, about the fire on the plane, the crash, and the explosion. The command post at Thule had no idea if there were any survivors. And then Major D'Amario walked into one of the aircraft hangars and asked to use a phone. His parachute had deposited him near a runway. D'Amario told the base commander that at least six of the seven crew members had bailed out. Security police officers split into teams and got into trackmasters to find them, driving the large vehicles out of the base. Helicopters soon joined the search. In the Arctic weather, every minute counted: uncovered skin could become frostbitten within two.

Haug parachuted onto the base as well, and made his way to a different hangar. He and D'Amario had suffered only scrapes and bruises. About an hour after the crash, the gunner, Sergeant Calvin Snapp, was found in good shape near the dump. A couple of parachutes and ejection seats were spotted from a helicopter, three miles from Thule, along with footprints in the snow. Security police followed them to the base of a nearby mountain, where Major Hopkins and a copilot, Captain Richard Marx, had gone looking for help. Marx had bruises and abrasions; Hopkins, a broken arm. The body of Captain Leonard Svitenko, another copilot, was discovered at around midnight. He'd died leaving the plane. And almost a full day after the crash, the last remaining crew member, the navigator, Captain Criss, was found wrapped in his parachute, six miles from the base, suffering from frostbite, hypothermia, a dislocated shoulder. Criss was forty-three years old and eventually lost both of his feet. But he later worked as a postmaster in Maine, kept playing golf, and lived for another forty years.

The B-52 had struck the ice at a speed of almost six hundred miles per hour, about seven miles west of Thule. The high explosives of the four hydrogen bombs fully detonated upon impact, and roughly 225,000 pounds of jet fuel created a large fireball. For five or six hours, the fire burned, until being extinguished by the ice. When the first Explosive Ordnance Disposal team arrived at the site two days later, using flashlights and traveling from Thule on a dogsled, they found a patch of blackened ice about 720 yards long and 160 yards wide. Pieces of the bombs and the plane were scattered across an area of three square miles. The pieces were small—and highly radioactive. Tiny particles of plutonium had bonded with metal and plastic debris, mixed with jet fuel, water, and ice. Plutonium had risen in the smoke from the fire and traveled through the air for miles.

The one-point safety tests of the Mark 28's core, performed secretly at Los Alamos during the Eisenhower administration, had been money well spent. If the Mark 28 hadn't been made inherently one-point safe, the bombs that hit the ice could have produced a nuclear yield. And the partial detonation of a nuclear weapon, or two, or three—without any warning, at the air base considered essential for the defense of the United States—could have been misinterpreted at SAC headquarters. Nobody expected the Thule monitor to destroy Thule. Instead, the Air Force had to confront a less dangerous yet challenging problem: how to decontaminate about three square miles of ice, about seven hundred miles north of the Arctic Circle, during the middle of winter, in the dark.

Generators, floodlights, a helicopter pad, sleds, tracked vehicles, and half a dozen prefabricated buildings were brought to the crash site. New roads from the base were cut through the snow. A "Hot Line" was drawn around the contaminated area, with restrictions on who could enter it and decontamination control points for everyone who left it. Once again hundreds of young airmen walked shoulder to shoulder, looking for bomb parts and pieces of a B-52. Most of the debris was small, ranging from the size of a dime to that of a cigarette pack. Some of it had fallen through a gash in the ice, cut by the crash, that later refroze. The ice was about two feet thick; the water below it six hundred feet deep. Pieces of the bomb and the plane were carried away by the current or settled on the bottom of Bylot Sound.

Arctic storms with high winds complicated the recovery and cleanup efforts, spreading plutonium dust and hiding it beneath the snow. But the levels of contamination were more accurately measured at Thule than at Palomares. A new device, the Field Instrument for the Detection of Low-Energy Radiation (FIDLER), looked for the X-rays and gamma rays emitted by plutonium, instead of the alpha particles. Those rays traveled a longer distance and passed through snow. Over the next eight months, the top two inches of the blackened ice within the Hot Line were removed, trucked to the base, condensed, packed in containers, shipped to Charleston, South Carolina, and then transported by rail to the AEC facility in Aiken. The radioactive waste from Thule filled 147 freight cars.

During the summer of 1968, after Bylot Sound thawed, a Navy submersible searched for part of a Mark 28 bomb. The plutonium cores of the primaries in all four weapons had been blown to bits, and most of the uranium from their secondaries had been recovered. But a crucial piece of one

bomb was still missing, most likely the enriched uranium spark plug necessary for a thermonuclear blast. It was never found—and the search later
inspired erroneous claims that an entire hydrogen bomb had been lost beneath the ice.

The Air Force did a much better job of handling the press coverage
at Thule than at Palomares. It helped that the B-52 had crashed near one of
the most remote military installations in the world, far from any cities,
towns, or tourists. An accident that contaminated three square miles of a
large metropolitan area would have gained more attention. The Air Force
admitted, from the outset, that nuclear weapons had been involved in the
crash. Dozens of journalists were flown to Thule within days of the accident and supplied with a good deal of information. Few had the desire to
remain in the Arctic for long. And a couple of other news stories—the seizure of the USS *Pueblo* by North Korea and the Tet offensive in Vietnam—
quickly pushed Thule off the front page.

The Air Force account of the accident, however, was deliberately misleading. Denmark had imposed a strict ban on nuclear weapons, and its
NATO allies were forbidden to bring them into Danish territory or airspace. For more than a decade, the Strategic Air Command had routinely
violated that prohibition at Thule. The B-52 that crashed onto the ice, the
Pentagon told reporters, had been on a "training flight" and had radioed
that it was preparing to make an emergency landing. A handful of people
within the Danish government and its military were no doubt aware that
B-52s had been flying nuclear weapons over Danish territory every day for
almost seven years. But they may not have known that atomic bombs were
stored in secret underground bunkers at Thule as early as 1955. Hydrogen
bombs were deployed there the following year. Before the introduction of
SAC's airborne alert, Thule was a convenient spot for American bombers to
land, refuel, and pick up their weapons en route to the Soviet Union. The
early hydrogen bombs were so heavy that prepositioning them in Greenland would allow SAC's planes to make the long round-trip flight to Russia
over the North Pole. Dozens of antiaircraft missiles with atomic warheads
were later placed at Thule to defend the base from a Soviet attack. But none
of these facts were shared with the Danish people.

The airborne alert program was terminated the day after the Thule accident. The risks no longer seemed justifiable, and many B-52s were now being used to bomb Vietnam. SAC's ground alert was unaffected by the new policy. Hundreds of planes, loaded with hydrogen bombs, still sat beside runways all over the United States, ready to take off within minutes. And a B-52 secretly continued to fly back and forth above Thule, day and night, without nuclear weapons, just to make sure it was still there.

TWENTY-THREE YEARS AFTER Sandia became a separate laboratory, it created a nuclear weapon safety department. An assistant to the secretary of defense for atomic energy, Carl Walske, was concerned about the risks of nuclear accidents. He had traveled to Denmark, dealt with the aftermath of the Thule accident, and come to believe that the safety standards of the weapons labs were based on a questionable use of statistics. Before a nuclear weapon could enter the stockpile, the odds of its accidental detonation had to be specified, along with its other "military characteristics." Those odds were usually said to be one in a million during storage, transportation, and handling. But the dimensions of that probability were rarely defined. Was the risk one in a million for a single weapon—or for an entire weapon system? Was it one in a million per year—or throughout the operational life of a weapon? How the risk was defined made a big difference, at a time when the United States had about thirty thousand nuclear weapons. The permissible risk of an American nuclear weapon detonating inadvertently could range from one in a million to one in twenty thousand, depending on when the statistical parameters were set.

Walske issued new safety standards in March 1968. They said that the "probability of a premature nuclear detonation" should be no greater than one in a billion, amid "normal storage and operational environments," during the lifetime of a single weapon. And the probability of a detonation amid "abnormal environments" should be no greater than one in a million. An abnormal environment could be anything from the heat of a burning airplane to the water pressure inside a sinking submarine. Walske's safety standards applied to every nuclear weapon in the American stockpile. They demanded a high level of certainty that an accidental detonation could never occur. But they offered no guidelines on how these strict criteria could be met. And in the memo announcing the new policy, Walske expressed confidence that "the adoption of the attached standards will not result in any increase in weapon development times or costs."

A few months later, William L. Stevens was chosen to head Sandia's new Nuclear Safety Department. Stevens had earned a degree in electrical engineering at Virginia Polytechnic Institute, served as an officer in the Army, and spent a few years in Baton Rouge, Louisiana, working for an oil company. He joined Sandia in 1957, at the age of twenty-eight. Bob Peurifoy had hired him, and the two worked together on the electrical system of the W-49 warhead, the first one to contain a trajectory-sensing switch as a safety device. When Stevens was assigned to lead the new safety department, he wasn't convinced that nuclear weapon accidents posed a grave threat to the United States. But he'd been closer to a nuclear detonation than most scientific observers—and seen firsthand how unpredictable one could be.

While serving in the Army, Stevens had been trained to assemble the warheads of tactical weapon systems. In May 1953 members of his battalion participated in the test of an atomic cannon. Its shells could travel twenty miles and produce a yield equivalent to that of the bomb that destroyed Hiroshima. For the test in the Nevada desert, all sorts of things were placed near ground zero to study the weapon's effects: trucks, tanks, railroad cars, aircraft panels, oil drums and cans of gasoline, household goods and materials—denim, flannel, rayon curtains, mops and brooms— a one-story brick structure, steel bridges, buildings that resembled motels, one hundred tall pine trees, field crops, flowers, insects, cages full of rats and mice, fifty-six dogs tethered inside aluminum tubes, forty-two pigs dressed in U.S. Army uniforms whose skin would respond to thermal radiation in a manner similar to that of human skin, and more than three thousand soldiers, including Bill Stevens, who huddled in a trench about three miles from ground zero.

The troops were part of an ongoing study of the psychological effects of nuclear warfare. They'd been ordered to climb out of their trenches and march toward the mushroom cloud after the blast. The Army Field Forces Human Research Unit hoped to discover how well they would follow the order, whether they'd obey it or come unglued at the sight of a large nuclear explosion. The atomic shell would fly directly over the heads of Stevens and the other soldiers. They were told to crouch in their trenches until the weapon detonated, then rise in time to brace against the blast wave and watch the explosion. At eight thirty in the morning, a great fireball lit up the desert, about ninety miles from Las Vegas.

As the troops stood, a powerful shock wave blew past, catching them by surprise. It was a "precursor wave," a weapon effect that hadn't been predicted. Highly compressed air had come down from the fireball, hit the ground, and spread outward, traveling faster than the blast wave. When Stevens and his unit climbed from the trenches to march toward ground zero, they were engulfed by a cloud of dirt and dust. Their lead officer couldn't read the radiation dosage markers and led them closer to ground zero than planned. After returning to their base in Albuquerque, Stevens shook the dirt out of his uniform and saved some of it in a can. Twenty years later, he had the dirt tested at Sandia—and it was still radioactive.

After becoming the head of the nuclear safety department at the lab, Stevens looked through the accident reports kept by the Defense Atomic Support Agency, the Pentagon group that had replaced the Armed Forces Special Weapons Project. The military now used Native American terminology to categorize nuclear weapon accidents. The loss, theft, or seizure of a weapon was an Empty Quiver. Damage to a weapon, without any harm to the public or risk of detonation, was a Bent Spear. And an accident that caused the unauthorized launch or jettison of a weapon, a fire, an explosion, a release of radioactivity, or a full-scale detonation was a Broken Arrow. The official list of nuclear accidents, compiled by the Department of Defense and the AEC, included thirteen Broken Arrows. Bill Stevens read reports that secretly described a much larger number of unusual events with nuclear weapons. And a study of abnormal environments commissioned by Sandia soon found that at least 1,200 nuclear weapons had been involved in "significant" incidents and accidents between 1950 and March 1968.

The armed services had done a poor job of reporting nuclear weapon accidents until 1959—and subsequently reported about 130 a year. Many of the accidents were minor: "During loading of a Mk 25 Mod O WR Warhead onto a 6X6 truck, a handler lost his balance . . . the unit tipped and fell approximately four feet from the truck to the pavement." And some were not: "A C-124 Aircraft carrying eight Mk 28 War reserve Warheads and one Mk 49 Y2 Mod 3 War Reserve Warhead was struck by lightning. . . . Observers noted a large ball of fire pass through the aircraft from nose to tail. . . . The ball of fire was accompanied by a loud noise."

Reading these accident reports persuaded Stevens that the safety of America's nuclear weapons couldn't be assumed. The available data was insufficient for making accurate predictions about the future; a thousand weapon accidents were not enough for any reliable calculation of the odds. Twenty-three weapons had been directly exposed to fires during an accident, without detonating. Did that prove a fire couldn't detonate a nuclear weapon? Or would the twenty-fourth exposure produce a blinding white flash and a mushroom cloud? The one-in-a-million assurances that Sandia had made for years now seemed questionable. They'd been made without much empirical evidence.

Instead of basing weapon safety on probabilistic estimates, Stevens wanted to ground it in a thorough understanding of abnormal environments—and how the components of a nuclear weapon would behave in them. During a single accident a weapon might be crushed, burned, and struck by debris, at a wide range of temperatures and velocities. The interplay among those factors was almost impossible to quantify or predict, and no two accidents would ever be exactly the same. But he thought that good engineering could invent safety devices that would always respond predictably.

Bill Stevens hired half a dozen staff members to explore how to make nuclear weapons safer. Stan Spray was one of the first Sandia engineers to be recruited, and he soon led the research on abnormal environments. Spray had been concerned about weapon safety for years. While visiting the Naval Ordnance Test Station near Cape Canaveral, Florida, he'd watched a bent pin nearly detonate an atomic bomb during a routine test. The accident could have obliterated a large stretch of the Florida coast. In the early

1960s Spray investigated a series of electrical faults in nuclear weapons, analyzing more than a dozen anomalous events prompted by crashes, handling mistakes, and design errors. He had a rare ability to focus intently on a problem for hours, to the exclusion of almost everything around him, until it was solved.

Spray and his team began to gather components from existing weapons and subject them to every kind of abuse that might be encountered in an abnormal environment. It helped that Sandia had the world's largest lightning simulator. Ever since Donald Hornig babysat the first nuclear device during a lightning storm, the night before the Trinity test, various forms of electromagnetic radiation had been considered a potential trigger of accidental detonations. The Navy tested many of its weapons by placing them, unarmed, on the deck of an aircraft carrier, turning on all the ship's radars and communications equipment, and waiting to see if anything happened. The electroexplosive squibs of a Navy missile detonated during one of those shipboard tests—and similar squibs were used in some nuclear weapons. By 1968 at least seventy missiles with nuclear warheads had already been involved in lightning accidents. Lightning had struck a fence at a Mace medium-range missile complex, traveled more than a hundred yards along the fence, damaged three of the eight missiles, and knocked out the power to the site. Each missile carried a Mark 28 thermonuclear warhead.

Four Jupiter missiles in Italy had also been hit by lightning. Some of their thermal batteries fired, and in two of the warheads, tritium gas was released into their cores, ready to boost a nuclear detonation. The weapons weren't designed to sit atop missiles, exposed to the elements, for days at a time. They lacked safety mechanisms to protect against lightning strikes. Instead of removing the warheads or putting safety devices inside them, the Air Force surrounded its Jupiter sites with tall metal towers to draw lightning away from the missiles.

Stan Spray's group ruthlessly burned, scorched, baked, crushed, and tortured weapon components to find their potential flaws. And in the process Spray helped to overturn the traditional thinking about electrical circuits at Sandia. It had always been taken for granted that if two circuits were kept physically apart, if they weren't mated or connected in any way—like separate power lines running beside a highway—current couldn't travel from one to the other. In a normal environment, that might be true. But strange things began to happen when extreme heat and stress were applied.

When circuit boards were bent or crushed, circuits that were supposed to be kept far apart might suddenly meet. The charring of a circuit board could transform its fiberglass from an insulator into a conductor of electricity. The solder of a heat-sensitive fuse was supposed to melt when it reached a certain temperature, blocking the passage of current during a fire. But Spray discovered that solder behaved oddly once it melted. As a liquid it could prevent an electrical connection—or flow back into its original place, reconnect wires, and allow current to travel between them.

The unpredictable behavior of materials and electrical circuits during an accident was compounded by the design of most nuclear weapons. Although fission and fusion were radically new and destructive forces in warfare, the interior layout of bombs hadn't changed a great deal since the Second World War. The wires from different components still met in a single junction box. Wiring that armed the bomb and wiring that prevented it from being armed often passed through the same junction—making it possible for current to jump from one to the other. And the safety devices were often located far from the bomb's firing set. The greater the distance between them, Spray realized, the greater the risk that stray electricity could somehow enter an arming line, set off the detonators, and cause a nuclear explosion.

By 1970 the Nuclear Safety Department had come up with an entirely new approach to preventing accidental nuclear detonations. Three basic safety principles had been derived from its research—and each would be assured by a different mechanism or component inside a weapon. The first principle was incompatibility: there had to be a unique arming signal that couldn't be sent by a short circuit or a stray wire. The second principle was isolation: the firing set and the detonators had to be protected behind a physical barrier that would exclude fire, electricity, and electromagnetic energy, that couldn't be easily breached, and that would allow only the unique arming signal to enter it. The third principle was inoperability: the firing set had to contain a part that would predictably and irreversibly fail in an abnormal environment. That part was called a "weak link." The hardened barrier was called a "strong link," and combined with a unique arming signal, they promised a level of nuclear weapon safety that would meet or exceed Walske's one-in-a-million standard.

Another Sandia safety effort was being concluded at roughly the same time. Project Crescent had set out to design a "supersafe" bomb—one that wouldn't detonate "under any conceivable set of accident conditions" or spread plutonium, even after being mistakenly dropped from an altitude of forty thousand feet. At first, the Air Force was "less than enthusiastic about requiring more safety in nuclear weapons," according to a classified memo on the project. But the Air Force eventually warmed to the idea; a supersafe bomb might permit the resumption of the Strategic Air Command's airborne alert. After more than two years of research, Project Crescent proposed a weapon design that—like a concept car at an automobile show—was innovative but impractical. To prevent the high explosives from detonating and scattering plutonium after a plane crash, the bomb would have a thick casing and a lot of interior padding. Those features would make it three to four times heavier than most hydrogen bombs. The additional weight would reduce the number of nuclear weapons that a B-52 could carry—and that's why the supersafe bomb was never built.

BOB PEURIFOY BECAME THE DIRECTOR of weapon development at Sandia-Albuquerque in September 1973. He'd closely followed the work of engineers in the safety department and shared many of their frustrations with the bureaucratic mind-set at the lab. Nothing had been done about the problems that they'd discovered. Bill Stevens had traveled to Washington, D.C., three years earlier, briefed the Military Liaison Committee to the AEC on the dangers of abnormal environments, and described the weak link/strong link technology that could minimize them. The committee took no action. The Department of Defense was preoccupied with the war in Vietnam, a Broken Arrow hadn't occurred since Thule, and a familiar complacency once again settled upon the whole issue of nuclear weapon safety.

After taking the new job, Peurifoy made a point of reading the classified reports on every Broken Arrow and major weapon accident, a lengthy catalog of fires, crashes, and explosions, of near misses and disasters narrowly averted. The fact that an accidental detonation had not yet happened, that a major city had not yet been blanketed with plutonium, offered little comfort. The probabilities remained unknown. What were the odds of a screwdriver, used to repair an alarm system, launching the warhead off a missile, the odds of a rubber seat cushion bringing down a B-52? After reading through the accident reports, Peurifoy reached his own conclusion about the safety of America's nuclear weapons: "We are living on borrowed time."

Peurifoy had recently heard about an explosive called 1,3,5-triamino-2,4, 6-trinitrobenzene (TATB). It had been invented in 1888 but had been rarely used since then—because TATB was so hard to detonate. Under federal law, it wasn't even classified as an explosive; it was considered a flammable solid. With the right detonators, however, it could produce a shock wave almost as strong as the high explosives that surrounded the core of a nuclear weapon. TATB soon became known as an "insensitive high explosive." You could drop it, hammer it, set it on fire, smash it into the ground at a speed of 1,500 feet per second, and it still wouldn't detonate. The explosives being used in America's nuclear weapons would go off from an impact one tenth as strong. Harold Agnew was now the director of Los Alamos, and he thought using TATB in hydrogen bombs made a lot more sense—as a means of preventing plutonium dispersal during an accident—than adding two or three thousand extra pounds of steel and padding.

All the necessary elements for nuclear weapon safety were now available: a unique signal, weak link/strong link technology, insensitive high explosives. The only thing missing was the willingness to fight a bureaucratic war on their behalf—and Bob Peurifoy had that quality in abundance. He was no longer a low-level employee, toiling away on the electrical system of a bomb, without a sense of the bigger picture. As the head of weapon development, he now had some authority to make policy at Sandia. And he planned to take advantage of it. Three months into the new job, Peurifoy told his superior, Glenn Fowler, a vice president at the lab, that all the nu-clear weapons carried by aircraft had to be retrofitted with new safety de-vices. Peurifoy didn't claim that the weapons were unsafe; he said their safety could no longer be presumed. Fowler listened carefully to his argu-ments and agreed. A briefing for Sandia's upper management was sched-uled for February 1974.

The briefing did not go well. The other vice presidents at Sandia were indifferent, unconvinced, or actively hostile to Peurifoy's recommendations. The strongest opponents of a retrofit argued that it would harm the lab's reputation—it would imply that Sandia had been wrong about nuclear weapon safety for years. They said new weapons with improved safety features could eventually replace the old ones. And they made clear that the lab's research-and-development money would not be spent on bombs already in the stockpile. Sandia couldn't force the armed services to alter their weapons, and the Department of Defense had the ultimate responsi-bility for nuclear weapon safety. The lab's upper management said, essen-tially, that this was someone else's problem.

In April 1974, Peurifoy and Fowler went to Washington and met with Major General Ernest Graves, Jr., a top official at the Atomic Energy Com-mission, whose responsibilities included weapon safety. Sandia reported to the AEC, and Peurifoy was aiming higher on the bureaucratic ladder. Graves listened to the presentation and then did nothing about it. Five months later, unwilling to let the issue drop and ready to escalate the bat-tle, Peurifoy and Fowler put their concerns on the record. A letter to Gen-eral Graves was drafted—and Glenn Fowler placed his career at risk by signing and sending it. The "Fowler Letter," as it was soon called, caused a top secret uproar in the nuclear weapon community. It ensured that high-level officials at the weapons labs, the AEC, and the Pentagon couldn't hide behind claims of plausible deniability, if a serious accident happened. The letter was proof that they had been warned.

"Most of the aircraft delivered weapons now in stockpile were designed to requirements which envisioned . . . operations consisting mostly of long periods of igloo storage and some brief exposure to transportation environ-ments," the Fowler letter began. But these weapons were now being used in ways that could subject them to abnormal environments. And none of the weapons had adequate safety mechanisms. Fowler described the "possibility of these safing devices being electrically bypassed through charred organic plastics or melted solder" and warned of their "premature operation from stray voltages and currents." He listed the weapons that should immediately be retrofitted or retired, including the Genie, the Hound Dog, the 9-megaton Mark 53 bomb—and the weapons that needed to be replaced, notably the Mark 28, SAC's most widely deployed bomb. He said that the secretary of defense should be told about the risks of using these weapons during ground alerts. And Fowler recommended, due to "the urgency associated with the safety question," that nuclear weapons should be loaded onto aircraft only for missions "absolutely required for national security reasons."

The scope of the Fowler Letter had deliberately been limited to the weapons whose safety devices were Sandia's responsibility—mainly bombs carried by airplanes. The Army, the Navy, and the Air Force were responsible for the arming and fuzing mechanisms of the nuclear warheads carried by their missiles. And the safety of those warheads in an abnormal environment was even more questionable than the safety of the bombs. The batteries, accelerometers, barometric switches, and safety devices weren't located inside the warhead of a ballistic missile. They were in an adaptation kit a few feet beneath it—which meant the arming wires traveled a good distance to the detonators. That distance made it easier for stray voltage to enter the wires. And the missile was constantly linked to sources of electrical power inside the silo. In 1974 the oldest nuclear warhead deployed on a ballistic missile was also the most powerful, the W-53 atop the Titan II, designed in the late 1950s. Tucked away inside a silo, the W-53 was less likely to encounter abnormal environments than a bomb. But how the warhead would respond to them was less clearly understood.

PART FIVE

DAMASCUS

Balanced and Unbalanced

During the summer of 1979, James L. "Skip" Rutherford III was working in the Little Rock office of Senator David H. Pryor. Rutherford was twenty-nine years old. He'd grown up in Batesville, Arkansas, a small town in the northern part of the state, attended the University of Arkansas, and edited the student newspaper there. After graduation he did public relations work for a bank in Fayetteville. The job introduced him to Pryor, who was running for a seat in the United States Senate, after two terms as the governor of Arkansas. Pryor was a new breed of southern Democrat, an opponent of racism and segregation, a supporter of women's rights, a progressive who greatly enjoyed meeting with voters, rich or poor, in every corner of the state. Rutherford worked as a volunteer for the campaign and joined Pryor's staff after the election, representing the senator at events throughout Arkansas. And then one day Rutherford took a call from someone at Little Rock Air Force Base, a young airman who wanted to meet with Pryor confidentially. The airman sounded nervous. When Rutherford asked what this was about, the airman said: "It's about the Titan missiles."

Skip Rutherford didn't consider himself an expert on intercontinental ballistic missiles. But he'd served in the Arkansas Air National Guard for six years, spending one weekend a month at Little Rock Air Force Base. He knew a lot of people at the base and felt comfortable there. The airman agreed to meet with Rutherford at the federal building in Little Rock, after hours, to avoid being seen—and brought a couple of other guys who worked with the Titan II. They were about Rutherford's age. They didn't want their names used as the source of any information. They were scared about getting into trouble. And most of all they were scared about what was happening at the Titan II silos in Arkansas.

The missiles were old, the airmen said, and most of them leaked. The portable vapor detectors and the vapor detectors in the silos often didn't work. Spare parts were hard to find. The Propellant Transfer System crews were overworked, sometimes spending fifteen or sixteen hours on the job. And many of the young PTS technicians weren't adequately trained for the tasks they were being ordered to perform. After that first meeting, Rutherford secretly met with other airmen from the base and took their calls from pay phones late at night. He spoke to roughly a dozen members of the 308th Strategic Missile Wing, promising not to reveal their identities to the Air Force. And they all said basically the same thing: the Titan II was a disaster waiting to happen.

Rutherford told Senator Pryor about the meetings. Pryor was disturbed by the information and decided that something had to be done. He wrote to Dr. Hans S. Mark, the secretary of the Air Force, asking for details about the staff shortages and training deficiencies at Little Rock Air Force Base. And Pryor learned that other members of Congress were concerned about the Titan II. Representative Dan Glickman, a Democrat, and Senator Bob Dole, a Republican, had already asked the Air Force to launch a formal investigation of safety problems with the Titan II. Glickman and Dole were both from Kansas, where some of the missile's flaws had been revealed during an accident the previous summer.

AT LAUNCH COMPLEX 533-7, about an hour southeast of Wichita, Kansas, the final stages of a missile recycle were being completed. A Titan II had been removed from 3-7 and returned to McConnell Air Force Base, where it would undergo routine maintenance checks. A replacement missile had been lowered into the silo. On the morning of August 24, 1978, a PTS crew arrived at the complex to pump oxidizer into the tanks. The fuel would be added the following day, and then the warhead would be placed atop the Titan II, finishing the recycle. On the main floor of the control center, the head of the PTS crew, Staff Sergeant Robert J. Thomas, briefed the missile combat crew commander, First Lieutenant Keith E. Matthews, about the work that would be done that day. A trainee, Airman Mirl Linthicum, would be acting as PTS team chief, supervising the procedure from the control trailer topside.

Oxidizer lines were attached to the stage 1 and stage 2 tanks, and both were full in about an hour. The lines were thick, heavy hoses through which the propellant flowed. Airman Erby Hepstall and Airman Carl Malinger put on RFHCO suits and entered the silo to disconnect the lines. Malinger had never been inside a Titan II silo before. He was nineteen years old and new to the Air Force, accompanying Hepstall that day for on-the-job training. The removal of the stage 2 lines, near the top of the missile, went smoothly. Hepstall and Malinger rode the elevator down to disconnect the lines from stage 1. Standing on a platform near the bottom of the missile, they unscrewed one of them. A powerful stream of oxidizer, like water suddenly released from a fire hydrant, hit Malinger's chest and the faceplate of his helmet and knocked him down. Hepstall tried to reconnect the line, but it wouldn't screw back on. Oxidizer poured from the missile, fell into the *W* below it, and then rose as a thick, reddish brown cloud of vapor.

Inside the top level of the control center, Lieutenant Matthews was preparing his lunch when a Klaxon sounded. Down below, the deputy commander, Second Lieutenant Charles B. Frost, sat at the launch control console. Frost wore a headset and monitored the PTS team on the radio. He pushed a button on the console and turned off the Klaxon, assuming that a puff of oxidizer had set it off when the lines were disconnected. That happened all the time. The Klaxon sounded again, and Frost heard screams over the radio.

"Oh my God, the poppet."

"What was the poppet?" Frost said into his headset. "What's wrong?"

Matthews came down the stairs as warning lights flashed on the console: OXI VAPOR LAUNCH DUCT, VAPOR SILO EQUIP. AREA, VAPOR OXI PUMP ROOM.

"Get out of here, let's get out," a voice yelled over the radio.

"Where are you?" Frost asked. The sounds on the radio were chaotic. People were talking at the same time, they were shouting and screaming and drowning one another out. Frost pushed the override button, blocking everybody else's radio transmission, and ordered: "Come back to the control center."

"I can't see," somebody said.

Lieutenant Matthews walked over to the blast door protecting the control center. He tried to open the door and see what was going on. The blast door wouldn't open. And Matthews got a whiff of something that smelled a lot like Clorox bleach. It smelled like oxidizer.

In the control trailer topside, Airman Linthicum, the trainee running his first recycle, heard the shouting on the radio but couldn't understand what was being said. Linthicum ran out of the trailer, trying to get better reception on a portable headset, and saw a reddish cloud rising from the exhaust vents. Another member of the PTS crew left the trailer, found Sergeant Thomas—the most experienced technician at the site—and told him something had gone wrong. Thomas was twenty-nine years old. He saw the oxidizer, ran to the access portal, and asked the control center for permission to enter the launch complex.

Lieutenant Frost granted the permission, unlocking the outer steel door for Thomas and then the door at the bottom of the entrapment area. All the hazard lights on Frost's console seemed to be flashing at once, including FUEL VAPOR LAUNCH DUCT, which made no sense. Frost kept asking the PTS team chief where they were in the checklist when the accident happened, hoping to find the right emergency checklist for dealing with it. But the radio still didn't work properly. Frost pulled out different tech manuals and flipped through their pages. He wasn't sure what they were supposed to do.

"Hey, I smell Clorox," Matthews said. He told the missile crew to set up a portable vapor detector in front of the door, to close the blast valve and the blast damper, protecting the air supply of the control center.

The missile facilities technician, Senior Airman Glen H. Wessel, placed a vapor detector near the blast door. He could smell oxidizer. The detector quickly registered one to three parts per million; somehow the stuff was getting into the control center. Wessel told his commander that the room was being contaminated with oxidizer. They both tried to open the blast door, but it wouldn't budge. The crew was locked inside the control center.

The two PTS technicians waiting in the blast lock, serving as backup, had no idea what was happening in the silo. They could hear screams on the radio, but nobody would answer them. And then the door from the long cableway suddenly swung open, and Hepstall appeared. Oxidizer had turned the faceplate of his helmet white. It was so opaque you couldn't see his face.

Hepstall pulled off the helmet. He was sobbing. He said Malinger's still down there, we have to go and get him out. If anything happens to Malinger, he said, I'll never forgive myself.

Hepstall had left his trainee in the silo, amid a thick cloud of oxidizer, found his way to the elevator, and ridden it five levels to the long cableway.

The door to the blast lock opened, and Sergeant Thomas walked inside. He saw Hepstall sobbing, heard that Malinger was missing, and put on one of the backup team's RFHCO suits. Without a moment's hesitation, Thomas had decided to search for Malinger.

Hepstall offered to go with him and grabbed a fresh helmet. Wearing the RFHCOs, they opened the door and headed down the long cableway toward the silo. The air was becoming thick with oxidizer.

The PTS backup team waited anxiously in the blast lock. Moments later, the door swung open. Hepstall stumbled inside and fell to the ground coughing. He hadn't made it very far. The new helmet leaked, and oxidizer was getting into his RFHCO. Hepstall took off the suit, got into another one, and left for the silo again.

On the bottom floor of the control center, Wessel was amazed by how hard it was to open the escape hatch. The ratchet that you needed to use felt really heavy. He and the ballistic missile analyst technician, Danford M. Wong, took turns with it, wearing their gas masks. They were highly motivated. The blast door still wouldn't open, and this looked like their only way out.

Lieutenant Frost was still attempting, without success, to reach the PTS team in the silo, Sergeant Thomas, and the PTS guys in the trailer, using the telephone and the radio. It wasn't easy with a gas mask on. Frost would pull off the mask momentarily, speak, put the mask back on, and listen for some response. Nobody answered him. And then, clear as a bell, he heard Malinger shouting over the radio.

"My God, help us, help us, we need help."

"Hey, door eight is locked, we're locked in, you guys get out," Frost told him.

Malinger kept repeating that he needed help, and Frost tried to make him understand that the blast door was stuck.

The emergency phone rang, and Frost answered it. Someone was outside blast door 8, asking for help.

"Hey, you guys, get out of here, get out of here now," Frost said, "just get out, door eight is locked, so you guys get out."

Wessel and Wong could hear the commotion on the floor above them and cranked the ratchet on the escape hatch as fast they could.

Blast door 8 swung open, and Malinger ran into the control center, carrying his helmet, yelling that Sergeant Thomas was dead. A cloud of oxidizer followed him, and then Hepstall came in, without a helmet, and collapsed onto the floor. He landed near the stairs, as Malinger kept screaming. None of it made sense to the missile crew.

Commander Matthews said, "Come help me," to Frost, and they entered the blast lock. Sergeant Thomas lay unconscious on the floor. They picked him up, carried him into the control center, and shut the door. Thomas was having convulsions, his head nodding side to side in the RFHCO helmet. Malinger took off the helmet and started to give him mouth-to-mouth.

"This is three-seven," Frost told the command post at McConnell Air

Force Base. "The locks are on the safe and the keys are in it. We got one man possibly down and we're evacuating now."

Thomas died on the floor, staring at the ceiling.

"Where's the dep, where's the dep?" Wessel shouted, calling for Frost, their deputy commander. They were getting tired, and they needed his help to open the escape hatch. The light grew dimmer as the control center filled with oxidizer.

Malinger didn't want to leave Thomas behind. It seemed wrong. After getting knocked down by the powerful stream of oxidizer, Malinger had gotten lost in the silo, near the base of the missile, unable to see more than a few feet, unaware that Hepstall had taken the elevator and left him down there. Sergeant Thomas had found him and brought him out, and now Malinger didn't want to leave Thomas on the floor.

"We'll get him later," Frost said, heading downstairs to work on the hatch.

Matthews helped Malinger and Hepstall down the stairs and then helped them take off their RFHCO suits. They said their skin was burning. "My God, please help me," Hepstall said. "It's in here with me, it's with me."

Matthews went back upstairs and checked the other two levels of the control center, looking for stragglers, just in case. The cloud of oxidizer was now so thick that he couldn't see more than two or three feet ahead.

The escape hatch was open, finally. Wessel went into it first, crawled through the tunnel, and climbed the ladder as fast as he could. It felt like climbing up a chimney full of smoke, as the oxidizer filled the narrow air shaft. At the top, Wessel pulled the pins and then pushed the metal grating open with his head. Wong was right behind him, and then Frost, who'd paused every few rungs to pull Hepstall up the ladder. Frost wanted to help him—and didn't want him falling onto Malinger. Lieutenant Matthews went last, closing the hatch behind him to trap the oxidizer in the control center.

The missile crew carried the two injured PTS technicians to the emergency showers on the hardstand to rinse them off. The showers didn't work.

"Get them under the fire hydrant," Matthews said.

The crew put Hepstall and Malinger in front of the hydrant and turned it on. Water poured out, and then after a few seconds the hydrant sputtered air and quit. They had to get these men rinsed off, immediately. But the gate to the launch complex was locked. No one had remembered to unlock it before abandoning the control center, and the trucks were parked on the other side of the fence. With help from some of the PTS technicians, the missile crew carried Hepstall and Malinger through the breakaway panel in the fence and placed them in the bed of a pickup.

The crew drove to a nearby farmhouse, and warned the occupants that deadly fumes were rising from the silo. Wong said to leave the area at once—and Frost asked to use their phone. Wessel found a garden hose in the backyard. After spraying the two airmen with water, they drove Hepstall and Malinger to the nearest hospital.

A cloud of oxidizer floated from the launch complex, extending for about a mile and drifting toward the town of Rock, Kansas. The cloud looked like a dark, ominous thunderhead. Local residents didn't know what it was, and the cars and trucks on Highway 77 drove right through it. Air Force security police soon evacuated the roughly two hundred inhabitants of Rock.

Sergeant Thomas had been left behind, and none of the PTS crew members felt right about that. Even though he was gone, they thought, he shouldn't be lying down there, alone. Two men volunteered to get him: Mirl Linthicum, the team chief trainee, and Airman John G. Korzenko. They returned to the launch complex and put on RFHCO suits. Linthicum climbed into the escape hatch first, followed by Korzenko. Within seconds, Korzenko had climbed out; oxidizer was leaking into his suit. Linthicum came back moments later; he wasn't getting enough air in his helmet.

Another PTS team arrived from McConnell, with fresh RFHCO suits and air packs. They wanted to get Thomas out, too. Airman Middland R. Jackson put on a RFHCO and climbed into the escape hatch. He came right back; his helmet was leaking. Jackson grabbed another helmet, tried the escape hatch again, and climbed the ladder all the way to the bottom in his RFHCO. But he'd never been in the escape hatch before, and the oxidizer was so thick down there he couldn't find the entrance to the control center. He climbed back up the ladder, frustrated and yet determined not to quit.

A few minutes later, Jackson and two other PTS technicians in RFHCOs, Technical Sergeant John C. Mock and Airman Michael L. Greenwell, tried to enter the control center through the access portal. They wandered underground through dense clouds of oxidizer, literally feeling their way down the stairs and through blast doors. They could not see more than a foot or so ahead—and had to stick together because none of their radios worked. They made it to the control center, found Sergeant Thomas on the floor, and carried his body onto the elevator. But no matter how many times they pushed the buttons, the elevator wouldn't work. They decided to carry Thomas up the stairs. His body was heavy, their suits felt heavy, and it was hot down there. After a few minutes, they couldn't carry him any farther and had to leave his body on the stairs. Two more PTS technicians in RFHCOs, Sergeant James Romig and Airman Gregory W. Anderson, went down and carried him, then had to quit, because of the heat. The five men took turns going into the complex and carrying Thomas as far as they could. As soon as one group got tired, the other would step in. It took two hours to get Thomas up the stairs and out of the complex.

An investigation of the accident later found the cause of the leak. Someone hadn't put a filter inside the oxidizer line. But the small rubber O-ring designed to hold the filter had been left inside the line. The O-ring blocked the poppet valve from closing fully, allowing oxidizer to pour out. Nobody accepted responsibility for failing to insert the filter. Oxidizer flowed more quickly without a filter in place—and someone may have deliberately omitted the filter to save time and load the tank quickly.

The blast door leading to the control center wouldn't open because someone had propped open the blast door across from it with a bungee cord—and both doors couldn't be open at the same time. Hepstall had used the manual override to unlock blast door 8, and by entering the control center, he'd contaminated it with oxidizer.

Robert J. Thomas was killed by a leak in his RFHCO, most likely at the spot where it intersected with the left glove. Oxidizer may have poured into the suit as he tried to reconnect the line to the missile. The Air Force recommended, in the future, that black vinyl electrical tape be used to seal the interface between the glove and the RFHCO suit more securely. Thomas left a widow and two young sons.

Erby Hepstall died a week and a half later, at the age of twenty-two, his lungs destroyed by oxidizer. His son had just turned two. A small tear in the left leg of Hepstall's RFHCO suit, about seven eighths of an inch long, had allowed oxidizer to enter it.

Carl Malinger had a stroke, went into a coma, suffered lung and kidney damage, lost the use of his left arm, and spent the next several months in the hospital. He'd enlisted to get training as an automobile mechanic, and his mother later felt enormous anger at the Air Force. Its report on the accident said that Hepstall and Malinger had failed to "comply with [Technical Order] 21M-LGM25C-2-12 which states 'if disconnect starts to leak . . . screw disconnect to fully connected position immediately.'" The report suggested that Malinger—never trained for the task and working in a Titan II silo for the first time—was somehow to blame for what happened.

General Curtis LeMay had created an institutional culture at the Strategic Air Command that showed absolutely no tolerance for mistakes. People were held accountable not only for their behavior but for their bad luck. "To err is human," everyone at the command had been told, "to forgive is not SAC policy."

BLAMING YOUNG ENLISTED MEN for the accident at Rock, Kansas, didn't eliminate the problems with the Titan II. The Pentagon had announced in 1967 that the Titan II was no longer needed and would be decommissioned, with the first missiles coming off alert in 1971. But every year the Air Force successfully battled to keep the Titan II. Its warhead was more than seven times more powerful than the warhead carried by the Minuteman II. The United States had about one thousand land-based missiles—and the fifty-four Titan IIs represented roughly one third of their total explosive force. SAC didn't want to lose all that megatonnage without getting new weapons to replace it. As the Titan II aged, however, its ability to reach the Soviet Union became more uncertain. The last test-launch of a Titan II occurred in 1976, and no more were planned, due to a shortage of missiles and parts.

When Senator Pryor and Skip Rutherford visited a Titan II site in Arkansas, the place looked impressive. But one of Rutherford's confidential sources later told him that there'd been an oxidizer leak at a nearby launch complex that day—and that the vapor detectors in thirteen of the state's eighteen silos were broken. Pryor came up with a relatively inexpensive plan for protecting rural communities from fuel and oxidizer leaks at Titan II missile sites: install a siren, at every complex, that would blare whenever the crew turned on the red warning beacon topside. The siren could easily be mounted on the same pole. It would warn neighboring homes and farms of a leak. The Air Force opposed the idea, arguing that a siren "might cause people to leave areas of safety and evacuate into or through areas containing propellant fumes." Colonel Richard D. Osborn told Pryor that during those rare occasions when civilians needed to be alerted, the combined efforts of Air Force personnel and local law enforcement officers would ensure public safety. Pryor nevertheless decided to seek funding for the sirens through an amendment to a Senate bill.

The Titan II missile wasn't the only Air Force weapon system having maintenance problems. Amid the defense cutbacks following the Vietnam War, the purchase of new planes and missiles had a much higher priority than buying spare parts for the old ones. During the late 1970s, on a typical day, anywhere from one half to two thirds of the Air Force's F-15 fighters were grounded for mechanical reasons. The Strategic Air Command had lost more than half of its personnel since 1961. Some of its B-52 bombers were twenty-five years old. And SAC's aura of invincibility had taken a beating. The highest-ranking officers in the Air Force tended to be "bomber generals" who'd risen through the ranks at SAC—and many of the pilots who flew bombing missions in Vietnam resented their insistence on rigid, centralized control. Tactics designed for executing the SIOP proved ineffective during combat in Vietnam, where the targets were often mobile and flying in a rigid formation could get you shot down. American pilots began to disobey orders, ignore their designated targets, bomb those that seemed more urgent, and lie about it in their reports.

Chuck Horner—who flew more than a hundred missions in Vietnam and later commanded the U.S. and allied air campaign during the first Gulf War—resented the inflexible, "parent-child relationship" that SAC's bomber generals often demanded. He felt a tremendous anger, shared by many other young officers, about how the Air Force leadership had behaved during the Vietnam War:

> I didn't hate them because they were dumb, I didn't hate them because they had spilled our blood for nothing, I hated them because of their arrogance . . . because they had convinced themselves that they actually knew what they were doing and that we were too minor to understand the "Big Picture." I hated my own generals, because they covered up their own gutless inability to stand up to the political masters in Washington and say, "Enough. This is bullshit. Either we fight or we go home."

Horner vowed that he would "never again be a part of something so insane and foolish." After the war, thousands of young officers left the Air Force, profoundly disillusioned. Many of those who stayed were determined to change things. And the influence of the Strategic Air Command gradually diminished, as a younger generation of "fighter generals," who rejected centralization and standardization and rigid planning, who had firsthand experience in real combat and little interest in abstract theories about nuclear war, rose to power.

During the years following the Vietnam War, antimilitary sentiment in the United States became stronger, perhaps, than at any other time in the nation's history. Vietnam veterans were routinely depicted in books and films as racists, stoners, nutcases, and baby killers. Morale throughout the armed services suffered—and illegal drug use soared. By 1980, according to the Pentagon's own surveys, about 27 percent of all military personnel were using illegal drugs at least once a month. Marijuana was by far the most popular drug, although heroin, cocaine, and LSD were being used, too. Among the armed services, the Marines had the highest rate of drug use: about 36 percent regularly smoked pot. About 32 percent of Navy personnel used marijuana at least once a month; the proportion of Army personnel was about 28 percent. The Air Force had the lowest rate, about 14 percent. It also had the most powerful warheads and bombs. The surveys by the Department of Defense most likely understated the actual amount of drug use. Random urine tests of more than two thousand sailors at naval bases in Norfolk, Virginia, and San Diego, California, found that almost half had recently smoked pot. Although nuclear weapons and marijuana had recently become controversial subjects in American society, inspiring angry debates between liberals and conservatives, nobody argued that the two were a good combination.

Donald Meyer served as a corporal with the 74th United States Field Artillery Detachment in Germany during the early 1970s. His detachment kept Pershing missiles on alert, ready to fire within fifteen minutes. Each missile carried an atomic warhead ten to twenty times more powerful than the bomb that destroyed Hiroshima. Meyer told the *Milwaukee Journal* that almost every one of the more than two hundred men in his unit regularly smoked hashish. They were often high while handling secret documents and nuclear warheads. A survey found that one out of every twelve members of the United States Army in Germany was smoking hashish every day. "You get to know what you can handle," Meyer said. "Too much hash and you would ruin a good thing."

At Homestead Air Force Base in Florida, thirty-five members of an Army unit were arrested for using and selling marijuana and LSD. The unit controlled the Nike Hercules antiaircraft missiles on the base, along with their nuclear warheads. The drug use at Homestead was suspected after a fully armed Russian MiG-17 fighter plane, flown by a Cuban defector, landed there unchallenged, while Air Force One was parked on a nearby runway. Nineteen members of an Army detachment were arrested on pot charges at a Nike Hercules base on Mount Gleason, overlooking Los Angeles. One of them had been caught drying a large amount of marijuana on land belonging to the U.S. Forest Service. Three enlisted men at a Nike

Hercules base in San Rafael, California, were removed from guard duty for psychiatric reasons. One of them had been charged with pointing a loaded rifle at the head of a sergeant. Although illegal drugs were not involved in the case, the three men were allowed to guard the missiles, despite a history of psychiatric problems. The squadron was understaffed, and its commander feared that hippies—"people from the Haight-Ashbury"—were trying to steal nuclear weapons.

More than one fourth of the crew on the USS *Nathan Hale*, a Polaris submarine with sixteen ballistic missiles, were investigated for illegal drug use. Eighteen of the thirty-eight seamen were cleared; the rest were discharged or removed from submarine duty. A former crew member of the *Nathan Hale* told a reporter that hashish was often smoked when the sub was at sea. The Polaris base at Holy Loch, Scotland, helped turn the Cowal Peninsula into a center for drug dealing in Great Britain. Nine crew members of the USS *Casimir Pulaski*, a Polaris submarine, were convicted for smoking marijuana at sea. One of the submarine tenders that docked at the base, the USS *Canopus,* often carried nuclear warheads and ballistic missiles. The widespread marijuana use among its crew earned the ship a local nickname: the USS *Cannabis.*

Four SAC pilots stationed at Castle Air Force Base near Merced, California, were arrested with marijuana and LSD. The police who raided their house, located off the base, said that it resembled "a hippie type pad with a picture of Ho Chi Minh on the wall." At Seymour Johnson Air Force Base in Goldsboro, North Carolina, 151 of the 225 security police officers were busted on marijuana charges. The Air Force Office of Special Investigations arrested many of them leaving the base's nuclear weapon storage area. Marijuana was discovered in one of the underground control centers of a Minuteman missile squadron at Malmstrom Air Force Base near Great Falls, Montana. It was also found in the control center of a Titan II launch complex about forty miles southeast of Tucson, Arizona. The launch crew and security officers at the site were suspended while investigators tried to determine who was responsible for the "two marijuana cigarettes."

The true extent of drug use among American military personnel with access to nuclear weapons was hard to determine. Of the roughly 114,000 people who'd been cleared to work with nuclear weapons in 1980, only 1.5 percent lost that clearance because of drug abuse. But the Personnel Reliability Program's 98.5 percent success rate still allowed at least 1,728 "unreliable" drug uses near the weapons. And those were just the ones who got caught.

Before assuming command of the 308th Strategic Missile Wing at Little Rock Air Force Base, Colonel John Moser had supervised a major drug bust at Whiteman Air Force Base, near Knob Noster, Missouri. More than 230 airmen were arrested for using and selling drugs there. Many were responsible for guarding and maintaining nuclear weapons. Some admitted to using marijuana, cocaine, and LSD on the job. Two of the three officers who were arrested had highly sensitive jobs at the base: they entered target information into the guidance systems of Minuteman missiles. When Moser arrived at Little Rock to assume command of the 308th, another drug bust was unfolding. Marijuana had been found in the control center at a Titan II complex. But the arrests didn't end the drug use. The Strategic Air Command wasn't immune to larger social forces, in an era before mandatory urine tests. Although launch officers rarely condoned illegal drug use, they spent alerts underground, without video cameras to reveal what was happening throughout a launch site. Their ability to command and control had its limits. Every so often, PTS crews would sit outside at a Titan II complex, light up a joint, crack open a few beers, and unwind at the end of a long day.

HENRY KISSINGER HAD TRIED TO get rid of the Titan II. He considered the missile "inaccurate and unreliable." It was a weapon system, he later explained, "which the Pentagon had been wanting to scrap for years and I had kept in service for trading purposes." In 1972, while serving as the national security adviser to President Richard M. Nixon, Kissinger had offered a deal to the Soviet Union: the United States would decommission its Titan II missiles, if the Soviets agreed to retire their SS-9 missiles. The deal would eliminate a powerful threat to Moscow. And the Soviet missile was similar in a number of respects to the Titan II, employing the same type of fuel and oxidizer. But the SS-9 was also newer, larger, and capable of delivering a much heavier payload. The Soviet Union declined the offer. The Nixon administration was stuck with the Titan II—getting rid of fifty-four ballistic missiles, without getting anything in return from the Soviets, made little sense in the midst of an arms race.

The failed attempt to decommission an aging weapon system reflected the new balance of power. Robert McNamara had assumed that once the Soviet Union felt confident about its ability to destroy the United States in any nuclear exchange, it would stop building new missiles. But the Soviets didn't share McNamara's faith in mutually assured destruction. After the humiliation of the Cuban Missile Crisis, one of their diplomats had told an American counterpart, "You Americans will never be able to do this to us again." In a rivalry where a nation's power was measured numerically in warheads and bombs, the Soviet Union now sought to gain the upper hand. Within a decade of removing strategic weapons from Cuba, the Soviet Union increased the number of its long-range, land-based missiles from about 56 to more than 1,500. Its arsenal of submarine-based missiles rose from about 72 to almost 500. By the early 1970s, the Soviets had more long-range missiles than the United States. An elaborate antiballistic missile system had been created to defend Moscow. And a network of underground bunkers had been constructed beneath the city to protect the leadership of the Communist Party. Linked by secret subway lines, the bunkers could house thousands of people.

Although the United States possessed fewer ballistic missiles than the Soviet Union, it still had more nuclear weapons. McNamara had imposed a limit on the number of missiles that the United States would deploy—but not on the number of warheads that each missile could carry. Before leaving office, he'd approved the development of "multiple independently targetable reentry vehicles" (MIRVs). Publicly justified as a method of overwhelming a Soviet antiballistic missile system—adding more warheads to a single missile was less expensive than building more missiles—MIRVs also increased the number of Soviet targets that the United States could destroy in a first strike.

The Minuteman III missile, introduced in 1970, carried three warheads. They were housed on a post-boost vehicle, nicknamed the "bus," that had its own rockets and guidance system. The bus separated from the missile and released each warhead over a different target, delivering them one after another, like a school bus dropping off children after school. The Poseidon missile, first deployed on American submarines in 1971, could carry fourteen warheads.

Kissinger was considered one of America's leading authorities on nuclear strategy. For more than a decade his writing had helped to shape the national debate on the subject. He had served as an adviser to the Kennedy administration during the Berlin crisis. He knew as much as any civilian about the competing theories of nuclear warfare. And yet Kissinger was astonished by his first formal briefing on the SIOP. The smallest attack option would hit the Soviet Union with almost two thousand weapons; the largest with more than three thousand. The vast scale and inflexibility of the SIOP led Kissinger to describe it as a "horror strategy." At a national security meeting in the Situation Room of the White House, he later wondered "how one rationally could make a decision to kill 80 million people." President Nixon was equally appalled.

Most of the targets in the SIOP were still part of the Soviet war machinery—missile sites, air bases, command centers, ports. But the desire for assured destruction of the Soviet economy inspired calculations that made Fred Iklé's theories about urban bombing seem like a relic of the Stone Age. RAND had developed a computer model to provide speedy estimates of the casualties and deaths that would be caused by different nuclear attacks. It was called QUICK COUNT. The types of weapons to be used in an attack, their targets, the prevailing winds, and the density of the local population were entered into an IBM-7090 computer—and then QUICK COUNT produced graphs, charts, and summaries of the potential carnage. It predicted the consequences of various attacks not only on the Soviet Union, but also on Eastern Europe, Western Europe, and the United States. And it included, as a bonus, an "Urban DGZ Selector" that helped war planners maximize the destruction of cities, allowing them to select the desired ground zeros likely to kill the most people.

A government report later outlined the "obstacle course to recovery" that victims of such nuclear attacks would have to navigate:

Time After Attack	Attack Effect
1–2 days	Blast and thermal
2–20 days	Lethal fallout
2–7 days	Trapped; no medical treatment
5–50 days	Life support inadequacies (food, water, shelter)
2 weeks–1 year	Epidemics and diseases
1–2 years	Economic breakdown
5–20 years	Late radiation effects
10–50 years	Ecological effects
2–several generations	Genetic effects

Although the human toll would be grim, the authors of the report were optimistic about the impact of nuclear detonations on the environment. "No weight of nuclear attack which is at all probable could induce gross changes in the balance of nature that approach in type or degree the ones that human civilization has already inflicted on the environment," it said. "These include cutting most of the original forests, tilling the prairies, irrigating the deserts, damming and polluting the streams, eliminating certain species and introducing others, overgrazing hillsides, flooding valleys, and even preventing forest fires." The implication was that nature might find nuclear warfare a relief.

Kissinger had once thought that Western Europe could be defended with tactical nuclear weapons, confining the damage to military targets and avoiding civilian casualties. But that idea now seemed inconceivable, and the refusal of America's NATO allies to build up their conventional forces ensured that a military conflict with the Soviet Union would quickly escalate beyond control. During a meeting in the White House Situation Room, Kissinger complained that NATO nuclear policy "insists on our destruction before the Europeans will agree to defend themselves."

Nixon's administration soon found itself in much the same position as

Kennedy's, urgently seeking alternatives to an all-out nuclear war with the Soviet Union. "I must not be—and my successors must not be—limited to the indiscriminate mass destruction of enemy civilians as the sole possible response," President Nixon told Congress. Phrases like "flexible response" and "graduated escalation" and "pauses for negotiation" seemed relevant once again, as Kissinger asked the Joint Chiefs of Staff to develop plans for limited nuclear war. But the Joint Chiefs still balked at making changes to the SIOP—and resisted any civilian involvement in target selection. The debacle in Vietnam had strengthened their belief that once the United States entered a war, the military should determine how to fight it. When Kissinger visited the headquarters of the Strategic Air Command to discuss nuclear war plans, General Bruce K. Holloway, the head of SAC, deliberately hid "certain aspects of the SIOP" from him. The details about specific targets were considered too important and too secret for Kissinger to know.

The Pentagon's reluctance to allow civilian control of the SIOP was prompted mainly by operational concerns. A limited attack on the Soviet Union might impede the full execution of the SIOP—and provoke an immediate, all-out retaliation by the Soviets. A desire to fight humanely could bring annihilation and defeat. More important, the United States still didn't have the technological or administrative means to wage a limited nuclear war. A 1968 report by the Weapons Systems Evaluation Group said that within five to six minutes of launching a submarine-based missile, the Soviet Union could "with a high degree of confidence" kill the president of the United States, the vice president, and the next fourteen successors to the Oval Office. The World Wide Military Command and Control System had grown to encompass eight warning systems, sixty communications networks, one hundred command centers, and 70,000 personnel. But the ground stations for its early-warning satellites could easily be destroyed by conventional weapons or sabotage, eliminating the ability to detect Soviet missile launches.

The National Emergency Airborne Command Post—a converted Boeing 747, designed to take off, whisk the president away from Washington safely, and permit the management of nuclear warfare in real time—

did not have a computer. The officers manning the plane would have to record information about a Soviet attack by hand. And the entire command-and-control system could be shut down by the electromagnetic pulse and the transient radiation effects of a nuclear detonation above the United States. Communications might be impossible for days after a Soviet attack.

The system had already proven unreliable in conditions far less demanding than a nuclear war. In 1967, during the Six Day War, urgent messages warning the USS *Liberty* to remain at least one hundred miles off the coast of Israel were mistakenly routed to American bases in the Philippines, Morocco, and Maryland. The spy ship was attacked by Israeli planes almost two days after the first urgent warning was sent—and never received. The following year, when the USS *Pueblo* was attacked by North Korean forces, its emergency message calling for help took more than two hours to pass through the WWMCCS bureaucracy and reach the Pentagon. The American naval commander in Japan who managed to contact the *Pueblo* couldn't establish direct communications with the Pentagon, the Situation Room at the White House, or commanders in the Pacific whose aircraft might have defended the ship.

During a conflict with the Soviet Union, messages would have to be accurately relayed within moments of an attack. A decade after the Kennedy administration recognized the problem, despite the many billions of dollars that had been spent to fix it, the command-and-control system of the United States was still incapable of managing a nuclear war. "A more accurate appraisal," a top secret WSEG study concluded in 1971, "would seem to be that our warning assessment, attack assessment, and damage assessment capabilities are so limited that the President may well have to make SIOP execution decisions virtually in the blind, at least so far as real time information is concerned." A few years later another top secret report said that the American response to a nuclear attack would be imperfect, poorly coordinated, and largely uncontrolled, with "confused and frightened men making decisions where their authority to do so was questionable and the consequences staggeringly large."

As the Soviet Union added multiple warheads to its ballistic missiles, Pentagon officials began to worry about the vulnerability of America's nuclear forces. A Soviet surprise attack might wipe out not only the nation's command-and-control facilities but also its land-based missiles. To deter such an attack, the Strategic Air Command considered a new retaliatory option, known as "launch on warning" or "launch under attack." As soon as a Soviet attack was detected—and before a single warhead detonated— the United States would launch its land-based missiles, saving them from destruction. A launch-on-warning policy might dissuade the Kremlin from attempting a surprise attack. But it would also place enormous demands on America's command-and-control system.

Missiles launched from Soviet submarines could hit Minuteman and Titan II bases in the central United States within about fifteen minutes; missiles launched from the Soviet Union would arrive in about half an hour. The president would have no more than twenty minutes to decide whether to retaliate—and would probably have a lot less time than that. With each passing minute, the pressure to "use it or lose it" would grow stronger. And the time constraints would increase the risk of errors. The reliability of America's early-warning system attained an existential importance. If the sensors failed to detect a Soviet attack, the order to launch might never be given. But if they issued an attack warning erroneously, millions of people would be killed by mistake.

The Pentagon decision to provide the United States with a nuclear hair trigger, capable of being fired at a moment's notice, oddly coincided with the warmest relations between the two superpowers since the end of the Second World War. The Soviet invasion of Czechoslovakia in 1968 hadn't raised tensions between the two Germanys, inspired massive demonstrations against the Soviet Union, or provoked much European revulsion toward communism. On the contrary, the overthrow of a moderate Czech government had encouraged Willy Brandt, the foreign minister of West Germany at the time, to seek closer ties with the Soviet Union. The status quo in Europe, the division between East and West, would not be challenged.

Within a few years, a series of international agreements clarified the legal status of Berlin, recognized the sovereignty of both German governments, promised to reduce the threat of nuclear war, and established a working relationship between the United States and the Soviet Union known as détente. The two countries signed the Anti-Ballistic Missile Treaty, allowing each side to defend two locations from attack; the Threshold Test Ban Treaty, limiting the size of underground detonations to 150 kilotons; and an Interim Agreement on Certain Measures with Respect to the Limitation of Strategic Offensive Arms, freezing the number of land-based ballistic missiles and permitting the deployment of new submarine-based missiles only when old ones were retired.

The advent of détente did not, however, end the nuclear arms race. The United States and the Soviet Union continued to modernize weapon systems and improve their accuracy. More than ever, nuclear weapons seemed important as totems of status and world power. Not long after taking office, President Nixon tried to end the Vietnam War by threatening the use of nuclear weapons, convinced that Eisenhower had employed a similar tactic to end the war in Korea. "I call it the Madman Theory, Bob," Nixon told his chief of staff, H. R. Haldeman. "I want the North Vietnamese to believe that I've reached the point where I might do anything to stop the war." The secretary of state, the secretary of defense, and the Joint Chiefs of Staff thought it was a bad idea. But Nixon and Kissinger thought the plan might work. Ignoring the safety risks, the Strategic Air Command secretly resumed its airborne alert for two weeks. B-52s loaded with hydrogen bombs took off from bases in the United States and flew circular routes along the coast of the Soviet Union. Neither the Soviets nor the Vietcong was fooled by the bluff.

A few years later, at the height of the 1973 Arab-Israeli War, nuclear weapons were once again utilized as a diplomatic tool. Concerned that the Soviet Union might send troops to Egypt, Secretary of State Kissinger and Secretary of Defense James R. Schlesinger placed American military forces throughout the world at DEFCON 3. The elevated level of readiness was a signal to the Soviet Union, implying that the United States was willing to fight a nuclear war over the issue. The Soviets didn't intervene in the Mideast conflict, and Kissinger later attributed their reluctance to the administration's bold diplomacy. Great leaders sometimes need to appear unbalanced, he thought: "What seems 'balanced' and 'safe' in a crisis is often the most risky."

Fred Iklé served as the head of the U.S. Arms Control and Disarmament Agency during the Nixon and Ford administrations. Iklé brought to the job an extensive knowledge of nuclear weapons, deterrence theory, and the workings of the command-and-control system. He argued against the adoption of a launch-on-warning policy, worried that it could inadvertently prove to be disastrous. Nevertheless, the policy had a strong military and psychological appeal. "Launching the ICBM force on attack assessment is probably the simplest and most cost-effective way to frustrate a [Soviet] counterforce attack," a classified RAND report noted. "But as a *declared* policy, we believe it would be vigorously opposed as both dangerous and unstable (an accident could theoretically precipitate a nuclear war)."

At a meeting of the National Security Council, Iklé expressed his opposition to launch on warning, calling it "accident-prone." Secretary of State Kissinger disagreed, praising its usefulness as a deterrent. Kissinger felt confident that the command-and-control system could handle it and stressed that "the Soviets must never be able to calculate that you plan to rule out such an attack." The national security adviser, Brent Scowcroft, agreed with Kissinger. Reason now played a diminished role in nuclear strategy. "It is not to our disadvantage," Scowcroft said, "if we appear irrational to the Soviets in this regard."

Too much madness, however, could be dangerous. Since the days of Harry Truman, the president of the United States had been entrusted with the sole authority to order the use of nuclear weapons. It gave one human being the ability to destroy cities, nations, entire civilizations. The president was accompanied everywhere by a military aide carrying the "football"—a briefcase that held the SIOP Decisions Handbook, a list of secret command bunkers throughout the United States, and instructions on how to operate the Emergency Broadcast System. The SIOP Decisions

Handbook outlined various attack options, using cartoonlike illustrations to convey the details quickly. It was known as the Black Book.

Eager to defend the civilian control of nuclear weapons from military encroachment, John F. Kennedy and Robert McNamara had fought hard to ensure that only the president could make the ultimate decision. But they hadn't considered the possibility that the president might be clinically depressed, emotionally unstable, and drinking heavily—like Richard Nixon, during his final weeks in office. Amid the deepening Watergate scandal, Secretary of Defense Schlesinger told the head of the Joint Chiefs to seek his approval before acting on "any emergency order coming from the president." Although Schlesinger's order raised questions about who was actually in command, it seemed like a good idea at the time.

The Wrong Tape

One month after the inauguration of President Jimmy Carter, a member of his national security staff, General William E. Odom, attended briefings on the SIOP at the headquarters of the Strategic Air Command in Omaha. Odom was considered a staunch anti-Communist, one of the hard-liners in the new administration. He was a Soviet expert, fluent in Russian, who'd attended West Point and trained as a tactical nuclear targeting officer for the Army. His visit to SAC headquarters occurred in February 1977. Eight years had passed since Henry Kissinger began to push for more flexibility in the SIOP. Secretary of Defense Schlesinger had announced in 1974 that America's war plans were being revised, that they would soon include "Limited Nuclear Options" and "Regional Nuclear Options" using fewer weapons. And yet General Odom could find no trace of those changes in the SIOP. Like others before him, nuclear initiates granted a secret knowledge, Odom was stunned by the SIOP:

At times I simply could not believe what I was being shown and told, causing me to doubt my own comprehension. It was an unnerving experience for me personally. . . . It was just a huge mechanical war plan aimed at creating maximum damage without regard to the political context. I concluded that the United States had surrendered political control over nuclear weapons to a deterministic theory of war that . . . ensured an unprecedented devastation of both the Soviet Union and the United States. . . . And the president would be left with two or three meaningless choices that he might have to make within 10 minutes after he was awakened after a deep sleep late some night.

A policy of launch on warning was "absurd and irresponsible," and implementing the SIOP under any conditions would be "the height of folly." The SIOP now called for the Soviet Union to be hit with about ten thousand nuclear weapons. But what disturbed Odom the most about the Joint Strategic Target Planning Staff in Omaha was that they didn't seem to have any postattack plans: "Things would just cease in their world about 6 to 10 hours after they received the order to execute the SIOP."

President Carter was determined to end the arms race with the Soviet Union. And he knew more about nuclear weapons than any of his predecessors at the White House, except, perhaps, Eisenhower. Carter had attended the U.S. Naval Academy, served as an officer on submarines, and helped to design the first nuclear propulsion systems for the Navy. A few weeks before his inauguration, Carter had met with the Joint Chiefs of Staff and asked them an unexpected question: How long would it take to reduce America's nuclear arsenal to just one or two hundred ballistic missiles? The room fell silent—and no answer was given.

In that moment, President Carter had revealed himself to be an advocate of "minimum deterrence," a strategy that the Navy had endorsed in the late 1950s, as the Polaris submarine was being developed. He thought that one or two hundred missiles might be sufficient to deter the Soviets. And if both superpowers reduced their strategic forces to those levels, neither could launch a successful first strike. During his inaugural address, Carter spoke about his ultimate goal: "the elimination of all nuclear weapons from this Earth." To make sure the issue was never far from his mind, he kept wooden miniatures of Soviet and American missiles on his desk in the Oval Office.

The Joint Chiefs of Staff regarded Carter with suspicion. The new president not only supported minimum deterrence, he also sought a ban on all nuclear testing. He proposed large cuts in military spending. He sincerely wanted new arms control agreements, world peace, friendship with the Soviet Union. And he appointed Harold Brown—one of McNamara's former whiz kids—to serve as secretary of defense. Brown thought that the United States hadn't fallen behind the Soviets and that new strategic weapons, like the B-1 bomber, weren't urgently needed. Within weeks of taking office, Carter found his plans opposed by most Republicans, many Democrats, the armed services—and even the Soviets. At the Kremlin, his proposal to accelerate the reduction of ballistic missiles seemed like an attempt to gain favorable publicity, and his criticism of human rights violations in the Soviet Union were regarded as insulting. The Soviet leadership much preferred dealing with Nixon and Kissinger, who never mentioned the repression of dissidents.

A new organization, the Committee on the Present Danger, soon attacked the Carter administration for being weak on defense and endangering the security of the United States. The group's membership included academics, defense intellectuals, former government officials, and retired military officers. They warned that within a few years the nation would face a "window of vulnerability," a period in which the Soviets might be able to launch a surprise attack that spared American cities but destroyed all of its land-based missiles. The president would then face an agonizing choice: accede to the demands of the Soviet Union and save American lives—or launch submarine-based missiles at Soviet cities and cause pointless, mutual annihilation. The committee's views were succinctly expressed in an essay by Richard Pipes, a history professor at Harvard and one of the group's founders: "Why the Soviet Union Thinks It Could Fight and Win a Nuclear War." The Soviets were violent, deceitful, authoritarian, and cunning, Pipes argued, and they'd already shown a willingness to commit mass murder on behalf of communism. The downfall of the United States now seemed within their grasp and would be pursued, regardless of the cost.

The window of vulnerability—like the bomber gap and the missile gap before it—provided a strong rationale for increased spending on defense.

And like those other scares, it was based more on fear than on facts. A successful surprise attack on America's land-based missiles wouldn't be easy to pull off. To achieve a 95 percent certainty of wiping them out, at least two Soviet warheads would have to be aimed at each silo. Those warheads would have to land in precisely timed intervals, so that the blast effects of one didn't destroy the other. And the Soviets would have to prevent the Strategic Air Command from launching its missiles on warning. Even if the surprise attack were successful, disabling every single Minuteman and Titan II, the fallout from the nuclear blasts would kill somewhere between two million and twenty million Americans. And the United States would still have thousands of nuclear warheads, mounted on submarine-based missiles, ready to seek revenge.

President Carter's idealistic vision soon collided with the reality of the late 1970s. He had to contend with gasoline shortages, high unemployment, and inflation; anxieties about the decline of American power; the arms buildup in the Soviet Union, its crackdown on dissidents, its use of Cuban troops as proxies in Ethiopia and Angola. The Senate refused to approve another arms control treaty, and détente became a thing of the past. Instead of cutting the defense budget, Carter increased it for the first time in more than a decade. Instead of adopting a strategy of minimum deterrence, he endorsed a "countervailing strategy" that would allow the president to use limited nuclear strikes in a variety of situations. Instead of eliminating strategic weapons, he backed the development of entirely new ones—the MX long-range missile, the Pershing II medium-range missile, cruise missiles that used jet engines instead of rockets to fly low and evade Soviet radar, the B-2 bomber, the Trident submarine.

The MX missile system embodied the strategic thinking of its time. To avoid destruction in a surprise attack, the MX would be mounted on a two-hundred-foot-long truck. The missile would constantly be moved between twenty-three protective concrete shelters, like a pea in an immense shell game. The Soviet Union would never know which shelter housed a missile. The shelters would be a mile apart. Twenty-two of them would contain fake missiles—and those decoys would also be moved constantly by truck. If the scheme worked, the Soviets would have to use at least forty-six warheads to destroy a single MX missile.

President Carter approved the deployment of two hundred MX missiles in the Great Basin area of Utah and Nevada. The missiles would be scattered across roughly fifteen thousand square miles of federal land, most of it closed to the public. Eight thousand miles of new roads would be built for access to the MX sites. About a hundred thousand workers would be required to construct the system and about half that number to run it. The total cost of the project was estimated to be at least $40 billion. The new weapon was designed not only to close the window of vulnerability for the United States but also to open one for the Soviet Union. Each MX would carry ten highly accurate warheads, thereby placing Soviet missiles at risk of destruction during an American first strike.

AT ABOUT ELEVEN O'CLOCK in the morning on November 9, 1979, the computers at the NORAD headquarters inside Cheyenne Mountain said that the United States was under attack. The huge screen in the underground command center at SAC headquarters showed that Soviet missiles had been launched from submarines off the West Coast. The same message was received by computers in the National Military Command Center at the Pentagon and the Alternate National Military Command Center at Site R inside Raven Rock Mountain. And then more missiles appeared on the screen, launched not only from submarines but also from sites within the Soviet Union. It was a massive attack, and warheads would begin to hit American targets within five or six minutes.

Whenever NORAD's early-warning sensors detected signs of a possible missile launch, a Missile Display Conference was held. It happened about four times a day; the infrared sensors on the Air Force satellites could be triggered by forest fires, volcanic eruptions, and other sources of heat. The officers on duty would discuss whether the threat seemed real or merely a false alarm. The commander in chief of NORAD would decide if a Threat Assessment Conference had to be arranged, bringing the head of SAC and the chairman of the Joint Chiefs of Staff into the discussion. That type of conference happened a few times a year. And if missiles truly seemed to be heading toward the United States, a Missile Attack Conference would be set up. It would give the president a chance to speak with senior officers, listen to their advice, and decide whether to launch missiles in retaliation. A Missile Attack Conference had never been held.

As the computer screens at NORAD filled with Soviet missiles, a Threat Assessment Conference was called. Although the pattern of the attack seemed to fit with the Pentagon's assumptions about Soviet war plans, its timing made little sense. Tensions between the superpowers weren't particularly high, and nothing in the news seemed to warrant a "bolt from the blue" attack on the United States. Duty officers at NORAD contacted the radar and ground stations whose sensors were relaying information about the launches. None of them had detected signs of any missiles. The NORAD computers seemed to be providing an erroneous—but highly realistic—account of a Soviet surprise attack.

As a precaution, the Klaxons were sounded at SAC bases nationwide. Bomber crews ran to their planes, and missile crews were put on heightened alert. Fighter-interceptors took off to look for signs of a Soviet attack. The National Emergency Airborne Command Post left Andrews Air Force Base—without President Carter on board. And air traffic controllers throughout the country prepared to clear America's airspace for military flights, warning every commercial airliner that it might soon have to land.

As the minutes passed without the arrival of Soviet warheads, it became clear that the United States wasn't under attack. The cause of the false alarm was soon discovered. A technician had put the wrong tape into one of NORAD's computers. The tape was part of a training exercise—a war game that simulated a Soviet attack on the United States. The computer had transmitted realistic details of the war game to SAC headquarters, the Pentagon, and Site R.

The computers at NORAD had been causing problems for more than a decade. Although they were perhaps the most important data-processing machines in the United States—responsible for compiling and assessing information from all its early-warning radars and satellites—the Honeywell 6060 computers were already obsolete when NORAD installed them within Cheyenne Mountain. A 1978 investigation by the General Accounting Office (GAO) found that budget cuts and bureaucratic inflexibility during the Nixon administration had forced NORAD to buy the computers—despite protests from the head of NORAD that they lacked sufficient processing power for crucial early-warning tasks. NORAD's computers were frequently out of commission, the GAO reported, "due to the lack of readily available spare parts." Many of the parts hadn't been manufactured by Honeywell for years.

The morale at NORAD, like its aging computers and software, left room for improvement. A couple of months after the false alarm, twenty-three security officers assigned to the Combat Operations Center inside Cheyenne Mountain were stripped of their security clearances. According to the Air Force Office of Special Investigations, the security force responsible for protecting the nerve center of America's command-and-control system was using LSD, marijuana, cocaine, and amphetamines.

"FALSE ALARM ON ATTACK SENDS FIGHTERS INTO SKY" was one of the headlines, when news of the training tape incident leaked. Pentagon officials denied that the missile warning had been taken seriously. But the technical and human errors at NORAD felt in keeping with the general mood of the country. An accidental nuclear war didn't sound inconceivable to most people—America seemed to be falling apart. A few months earlier a nuclear reactor at Three Mile Island in Pennsylvania had suffered a partial meltdown, largely because a worker at the plant had turned off an emergency cooling system by mistake.

At about two thirty in the morning on June 3, 1980, Zbigniew Brzezinski, the president's national security adviser, was awakened by a phone call from a staff member, General William E. Odom. Soviet submarines have launched 220 missiles at the United States, Odom said. This time a surprise attack wasn't implausible. The Soviet Union had recently invaded Afghanistan, confirming every brutal stereotype promoted by the Committee on the Present Danger. The United States was leading a boycott of the upcoming Moscow Olympics, and relations between the two superpowers were at their lowest point since the Cuban Missile Crisis. Brzezinski told Odom to call him back with confirmation of the Soviet attack and its intended targets. The United States would have to retaliate immediately; once the details of the attack were clear, Brzezinski would notify the president. Odom called back and said that 2,200 missiles were heading toward the United States—almost every long-range missile in the Soviet arsenal. As Brzezinski prepared to phone the White House, Odom called again. The computers at NORAD said that Soviet missiles had been launched, but the early-warning radars and satellites hadn't detected any. It was a false alarm. Brzezinski had allowed his wife to sleep through the whole episode, preferring that she not be awake when the warheads struck Washington.

SAC bomber crews had run to their planes and started the engines. Missile crews had been told to open their safes. The airborne command post of the Pacific Command had taken off. And then the duty officer at the Pentagon's National Military Command Center ended the Threat Assessment Conference, confident that no Soviet missiles had been launched. Once again, NORAD's computers and its early-warning sensors were saying different things. The problem was clearly in one of the computers, but it would be hard to find. A few days later NORAD computers warned SAC headquarters and the Pentagon for a third time that the United States was being attacked. Klaxons sounded, bomber crews ran to their planes—and another Threat Assessment Conference declared another false alarm.

This time technicians found the problem: a defective computer chip in a communications device. NORAD had dedicated lines that connected the computers inside Cheyenne Mountain to their counterparts at SAC headquarters, the Pentagon, and Site R. Day and night, NORAD sent test messages to ensure that those lines were working. The test message was a warning of a missile attack—with zeros always inserted in the space showing the number of missiles that had been launched. The faulty computer chip had randomly put the number 2 in that space, suggesting that 2 missiles, 220 missiles, or 2,200 missiles had been launched. The defective chip was replaced, at a cost of forty-six cents. And a new test message was written for NORAD's dedicated lines. It did not mention any missiles.

TOWARD THE END OF the Eisenhower administration, amid the fiery rhetoric of the missile gap, Bob Peurifoy became concerned that the Soviet Union might attack the United States. With help from his wife, Barbara, and a local contractor, Peurifoy built a bomb shelter underneath the garage at the family home in Albuquerque. Other engineers at Sandia added bomb shelters to their houses, too. The laboratory was a prime target for the Soviets, and the series of international crises during the first two years of the Kennedy administration made the decision seem wise. The Peurifoy shelter had food, water, a dosimeter to measure radiation levels, a door that could be sealed shut, a hand-cranked ventilation fan, a gun, and enough room for five people. He later viewed it as a youthful folly. When the family moved to another house in 1967, a few miles from the nuclear weapon storage facility at Site Able, he didn't bother to build another shelter. Peurifoy couldn't dig a hole deep enough to protect his family from the thermonuclear warheads likely to hit the neighborhood. And by the mid-1970s, he was preoccupied with a different threat. Although Peurifoy was conservative and anti-Communist, a Republican and a supporter of increased spending on defense, the nuclear weapons in the American arsenal were the ones keeping him up at night.

The Fowler Letter's only immediate effect was to raise the possibility that Glenn Fowler would lose his job. His urgent safety warning didn't persuade the Air Force to remove nuclear weapons from its bombers on ground alert. At the Department of Defense and the Atomic Energy Commission, the anger provoked by the letter was intense. High-ranking officials from both organizations flew from Washington, D.C., to meet with the head of Sandia. In preparation for the meeting, Peurifoy asked Stan Spray to put together an exhibit of weapon components that had been subjected to abnormal environments. Perhaps seeing would be believing: the melted solder on charred circuit boards seemed like irrefutable evidence that nuclear weapons could behave unpredictably during a fire. Spray's presentation was soon known as the Burned Board briefing. Donald R. Cotter, the assistant to the secretary of defense for atomic energy, and Major

General Ernest Graves, the AEC official to whom Fowler's letter had been sent, weren't impressed. They found the evidence unconvincing. And they were outraged that Sandia had put these claims on the record. The American stockpile contained dozens of different types of nuclear weapons, and the Fowler Letter didn't assert there was a minor safety problem with one of them. It suggested that none were demonstrably safe.

Don Cotter was particularly upset. He knew Peurifoy and Bill Stevens well. Before going to the Pentagon, Cotter had worked at Sandia for years. He'd designed the electrical systems of nuclear weapons, championed early safety devices, and helped Fred Iklé prepare the RAND report on weapon safety. Cotter was offended by the Fowler Letter. His response to it was blunt: "It's our stockpile. We think it's safe. Who do you guys think you are?" Peurifoy's team had challenged not only the conventional wisdom about weapon design but also the readiness of some NATO units and the Strategic Air Command.

Fowler kept his job. But the recommendations in his letter weren't followed. No air-delivered weapons were taken out of service or retrofitted with new safety mechanisms. Instead, a series of government studies was commissioned to explore the issue of nuclear weapon safety, a classic bureaucratic maneuver to delay taking any action. The Department of Defense argued that "the magnitude of the safety problems is not readily apparent"—and it now had unprecedented influence over the nuclear stockpile. The Atomic Energy Commission was disbanded in 1975. It was replaced by the Energy Research and Development Administration, an agency that lasted only two years, before being subsumed into the Department of Energy. The Joint Committee on Atomic Energy—which had served for three decades as a powerful civilian counterweight to the military—was abolished in 1977. The Pentagon wielded largely unchecked power over the management of nuclear weapons, and its Defense Nuclear Agency had a set of priorities that differed from Bob Peurifoy's. "The safety advantages gained by retrofitting existing stockpile weapons . . . will be a costly program that in all probability will reduce funds available for future weapons," the DNA said.

The Air Force deployed most of the weapons that Peurifoy wanted to fix. And it supported the use of new safety devices, so long as they didn't require:

1. Modification of any current operational aircraft
2. Additional crew actions and
3. Expenditure of Air Force money.

The Air Force also continued to have little interest in permissive action links or other forms of use control. The latest PALs were far more sophisticated and reliable than the ones provided to NATO in the early 1960s. The new Category D PALs had a six-digit code with a million possible combinations, a limited-try feature that permanently locked the weapon if the wrong numbers were entered, and the capability to store multiple codes. The president could now choose to unlock some nuclear weapons, but not others, by selecting a certain code. The system promised centralized, secure command and control. But the Strategic Air Command continued to resist installing PALs inside its warheads and bombs.

After the accident at Thule, the Pentagon had ordered SAC to impose some form of use control. Instead of relying on PALs, during the early 1970s the Air Force put a coded switch in the cockpit of every bomber that carried nuclear weapons. The switch permitted an arming signal to be sent to the bomb bay when the right code was entered. The lock had been placed on the bomber, not inside the bombs—and a stolen weapon could still be detonated with a simple DC signal. SAC was far more worried about its weapons being rendered inoperable during wartime than about someone stealing them or using them without proper authorization. During the late 1970s, a coded switch was finally placed in the control center of every SAC ballistic missile. It unlocked the missile, not the warhead. And as a final act of defiance, SAC demonstrated the importance of code management to the usefulness of any coded switch. The combination necessary to launch the missiles was the same at every Minuteman site: 00000000.

Peurifoy was undaunted by the many layers of bureaucratic opposition. The issue at stake wasn't trivial, and he was determined to persuade others in the defense community that the danger was real. The cost of adding weak links and strong links and a unique signal mechanism was about $100,000 per weapon. The Office of Management and Budget estimated that the installation of those safety devices in the two most widely used Air Force bombs, the Mark 28 and the B-61, would cost about $360 million. Peurifoy realized that was a good deal of money—but a nuclear weapon accident could be a hell of a lot more expensive. The amount of money needed for that retrofit was roughly 1 percent of what the Air Force planned to spend driving around MX missiles in the Utah and Nevada desert. The Pentagon's fixation on obtaining new weapons, instead of properly maintaining older ones, would be hard to overcome. But the fight seemed worthwhile. A friend sent Peurifoy a cartoon that showed a member of the Supreme Court speaking from the bench. It conveyed Peurifoy's general attitude, when the facts were on his side. "My dissenting opinion will be brief," the justice said. "You're all full of crap."

The role of the weapons laboratories had become mainly advisory. They competed for contracts from the Department of Defense—and felt reluctant to criticize their largest customer. Peurifoy had no authority to demand changes in weapon systems that the armed services already possessed. But he refused to sign the Sandia major assembly release of any new bombs or warheads that didn't have the new safety devices. And without his approval, those weapons couldn't enter the stockpile. In 1977, almost four years after gaining some real authority at the lab, Peurifoy signed the release papers on a modification of the B-61 bomb. It was the first nuclear weapon to feature weak link/strong link technology.

As the dispute with the Pentagon dragged on, Peurifoy learned that the armed services were no longer telling him about nuclear weapon accidents. Broken Arrows would be difficult to hide, but the more commonplace mishaps—short circuits, bombs falling off loading carts, weapon carriers overturned—weren't being reported to him. Peurifoy would often hear about them through other sources. The sense of denial at the upper levels of the Air Force and the Department of Defense had a ripple effect throughout both institutions. The bomber crews, the missile crews, the technicians who routinely handled warheads and bombs, the maintenance teams and firefighters—they were told the weapons were perfectly safe. The misinformation placed them at greater risk. It was also a form of disrespect toward young servicemen and women who were already risking their lives. And it encouraged careless behavior around nuclear weapons. In many ways, denying the safety problems only made them worse.

While Peurifoy fought the bureaucratic wars, Bill Stevens and the rest of the nuclear safety department continued to study how to make nuclear weapons less likely to detonate by accident, spread plutonium, or fall into the wrong hands. During the late 1960s, Stevens had begun to worry about a terrorist attempt to steal a weapon, and the massacre at the 1972 Munich Olympics demonstrated that the threat was real. The weapons inside NATO storage igloos seemed the most vulnerable to theft, not only by potential terrorists but also by rogue elements of an allied army or enemy troops. If an igloo seemed on the verge of being overrun, NATO forces were supposed to "spike the guns"—to attach a shaped explosive charge to each weapon and blow it up. A nuclear detonation wouldn't occur. But the collateral damage could be enormous, and a great deal of plutonium dust might be spread. Stevens thought that better ways of keeping weapons out of the wrong hands needed to be found and that the risk of plutonium dispersal had to be taken most seriously.

Changes were soon made to the storage practices at NATO igloos and to the emergency procedures for destroying weapons. Antiterrorism research at Sandia led to the development of new perimeter control technologies, such as motion detectors, and innovative methods for stopping intruders who somehow managed to get past the door of an igloo. Nozzles on the walls would rapidly fill the place with sticky foam, trapping intruders and preventing the removal of nuclear weapons. The foam looked ridiculous, like a prop from a Three Stooges film, but it worked.

Peurifoy and Stevens also looked at how nuclear weapons should be rendered safe after an accident. The civilians at Sandia and the military personnel in Explosive Ordnance Disposal units often had conflicting notions about what should be done. It was another dispute that pitted scientists in white lab coats against men in uniform. Air Force bomb squads were accustomed to dealing with conventional weapons. And they were trained to get the job done quickly—during wartime, an unexploded bomb near a runway could prevent essential aircraft from taking off. The EOD guys liked to approach a weapon, tear it down fast, and get rid of it. Peurifoy and Stevens thought that wasn't a good idea with nuclear weapons. A hydrogen bomb that survived an accident reasonably intact could still detonate if someone handled it improperly. Even if it didn't produce a nuclear yield, the high explosives could spread plutonium and harm anyone nearby.

After the B-52 crash near Cumberland, Maryland, an Air Force EOD team started to remove the weapons from the wreckage of the plane, using improvised heavy machinery—until a representative from Sandia intervened and asked them to stop. The bombs weren't moved until their condition had been assessed. A naval bomb disposal team began to disassemble the Mark 28 bomb recovered from the ocean near Palomares—until another Sandia nuclear safety specialist made clear that a ship, rolling over swells, might not be the best place for the task. Peurifoy and Stevens thought that, most of the time, there was no need to rush. "Don't move someone who's hurt before you know the extent of the injuries," a basic rule of first aid, also applied to nuclear weapons. Ease of disassembly had never been a top priority among weapon designers. In fact, it was rarely considered when weapons were on the drawing board. Inside the metal casing, parts were tightly welded or glued together. If you weren't careful, thermal batteries could be ignited, high explosives set off. Peurifoy took an EOD course and gained tremendous respect for the soldiers and airmen who put on bomb suits to render bombs safe. They were fearless. But the weapons they typically handled might kill them and injure people within about a quarter of a mile. Peurifoy didn't want anyone to feel hurried or gung ho while trying to dismantle a thermonuclear warhead.

The need to retrofit and retire older weapons in the stockpile became more urgent after a discovery about the Mark 28 hydrogen bomb. Stan Spray found that one of the bomb's internal cables was located too close to its skin. If the weapon was exposed to prolonged heat, the insulation of the cable would degrade—and the wires inside it could short circuit. One of those wires was connected to the ready/safe switch, another to the thermal battery that charged the X-unit. It was a serious problem. The heat from a fire could arm a Mark 28 bomb, ignite its thermal battery, charge its

X-unit, and then fully detonate the high explosives. Depending on the particular model of the Mark 28, a blast of anywhere from 70 kilotons to 1.5 megatons would immediately follow.

The problem with the Mark 28 was more significant than the safety flaws in other weapons. Mark 28 bombs were routinely carried by B-52 bombers on ground alert. And those B-52s sometimes caught on fire, even when they never left the ground. The bomber carried more than 300,000 pounds of highly flammable JP-4 jet fuel, a mix of gasoline and kerosene. In preparation for a typical B-52 flight, the crew would spend at least an hour in the plane, going through checklists, before starting the engines—and then the engines would be started one after another, until all eight were running. It could take an hour and a half for the pilot to get a B-52 into the air. But planes on ground alert were expected to be airborne within ten or fifteen minutes, the maximum time available for a "base escape." Explosive cartridges on the four engine pods would be detonated by the copilot, as soon as he climbed into the plane, spinning the turbines rapidly and starting all eight engines in about a minute. A "cartridge start" was a memorable sight—a series of small explosions, B-52s filling the runway with clouds of smoke—and crews on ground alert practiced it regularly. And yet it could also start a fire.

The combination of Mark 28 bombs and B-52 bombers on alert was increasingly dangerous. Peurifoy doubted it was worth the risk. Both were aging weapon systems; many of the B-52s were older than their pilots. And most of the planes would probably never reach their targets, let alone return safely from a mission. After a 1975 briefing on the role of the Strategic Air Command's bombers in executing the SIOP, the head of the CIA, William Colby, expressed surprise that "our B-52s are planned for one-way missions." Once an emergency war order was transmitted, the bombers on ground alert would quickly take off from their bases in the United States, fly eight to ten hours toward Soviet targets—and find what? The Soviet Union would have already been hit by thousands of warheads delivered by American missiles. Targets that hadn't been destroyed were likely to be surrounded by antiaircraft missiles, and dust clouds of unimaginable scale would blanket the landscape. Each B-52 was assigned a poststrike base in

Europe or the Middle East where it was supposed to land, refuel, and pick up more nuclear weapons for another run at the Soviets. Would any of those bases still exist, if bombers somehow managed to survive their first passage through Soviet airspace? Most B-52 crews didn't count on it.

Stan Spray added components from the Mark 28 bomb to his Burned Board briefing, along with a dramatic flourish: when the bomb's wires short-circuited, a flashbulb went off. The briefing was given to hundreds of officials—with little immediate effect. A study of all the nuclear weapons in the American arsenal was completed by one of Peurifoy's deputies in 1977. It provided the Department of Defense with a list of the weapons posing the greatest threat and a timetable for retiring them or improving their safety. The Mark 28 bomb was at the top of the list, followed by the W-25 warhead of the Genie antiaircraft missile. Despite being the oldest sealed-pit weapon in the stockpile, vulnerable to lightning, and fitted with an outdated accelerometer, the Genie was still being loaded onto fighter planes. On the list of weapons requiring urgent attention, the only strategic warhead was the W-53 atop the Titan II missile. It needed a "retrofit for Enhanced Electrical Safety."

In 1979 the Department of Defense finally accepted some of the recommendations that Sandia's safety department had been making for years—but didn't want to pay for them. The Pentagon agreed to schedule retrofits of weapons like the Mark 28, so long as the cost wouldn't interfere with the acquisition of new weapons. And until the funds were obtained, the Mark 28 could still be carried by B-52s on ground alert. Although the Air Force balked at devoting a few hundred million dollars to improve the safety of hydrogen bombs, it planned to spend at least $10 billion to equip B-52s with cruise missiles. Instead of trying to penetrate Soviet airspace, the bombers would launch cruise missiles a thousand miles from their targets, turn around, and come home. Until those cruise missiles were available, B-52s were loaded with Short-Range Attack Missiles (SRAMs), carried in a rotary rack. It turned as each missile was fired, like the cylinder of a revolver shooting bullets. The SRAMs were designed to fly a hundred miles or so, destroy Soviet air defenses, and give the B-52 a better chance of reaching its target. The missiles had a destructive force of as much as 200 kilotons, and a single B-52 could carry a dozen of them.

Peurifoy was frustrated by the delays. Even the retrofit of the Mark 28, top on the list, kept getting pushed back. Through a friend in the Air Force, Peurifoy arranged for General Howard W. Leaf to visit Sandia on June 13, 1980. Leaf would be given the Burned Board briefing. The safety problems with the Mark 28 would be outlined in detail, as well as the history of nuclear weapon accidents and the development of weak link/strong link devices. Leaf had an important job, inspector general of the Air Force, with the authority to cut through red tape. The false alarm caused by a faulty computer chip at NORAD, ten days earlier, had brought renewed attention to the importance of command and control, the limits of technology, the risks of human error. After lengthy meetings at Sandia, General Leaf returned to Washington, D.C.—and commissioned another study on the safety of the Mark 28 bomb.

ON SEPTEMBER 15, 1980, Jeffrey A. Zink was pulling an alert at Grand Forks Air Force Base in North Dakota. Zink was the navigator of a B-52. Once a month he and the rest of his crew would sleep in a building at the end of a runway, with a tunnel leading to their plane. Four or five other B-52 crews would stay there, too, along with the crews of their tankers. In some respects it felt like being confined in a prison. The alert quarters were surrounded by concertina wire, motion detectors, and security police carrying M-16s. Zink and his friends spent most of their time being bored. They would eat, sleep, read books, take naps, watch crap like *The Love Boat* on TV. But Zink always thought boredom, in this case, was good. Boredom meant that deterrence still worked. So long as these fifty young men were stuck there doing nothing, America's nuclear strategy was a success. About once a week, however, the Klaxons would sound, and life would suddenly become more interesting.

Zink had never intended to join the Air Force. In the mid-1970s he was a long-haired, true-blue hippie attending the University of Pittsburgh and planning to go to law school. One day he walked into an Air Force recruiter's office, thinking it would be cool to fly planes. The recruiter told Zink that his eyes weren't good enough to become a pilot—but he could become a navigator. Zink put aside law school and joined the Air Force in 1977, right after graduation. His hippie girlfriend was stunned, and their relationship soon ended. At first, Zink didn't fit into the tough, regimented culture of the Strategic Air Command. "What have I gotten myself into?" he wondered. "I don't think I like these people." But his feelings gradually changed, and he eventually became a lieutenant colonel.

The navigator of a B-52 sat at a desktop in the "chin" of the plane, a lower level beneath the pilot. Beside the navigator sat the bombardier. They both had ejection seats that fired downward. Their compartment was small, cramped, and windowless, with a ceiling about five feet high. Training flights lasted six to eleven hours, and they could be rough. The eight engines were so loud that the navigator and the bombardier, seated a foot or two from each other, couldn't shout loud enough to have a conversation. They had to speak on the intercom. And most of the time they'd wear earplugs. The B-52 had originally been designed to attack the Soviet Union at an altitude of about 50,000 feet. But Soviet air defenses now forced the bomber to approach at a low altitude—very low. For three to four hours during a training flight, Zink's plane would fly 150 to 350 feet off the ground. At that altitude, especially in the summer months, the air turbulence was terrible. The hot sun would send thermals of air swirling upward from the ground. Sitting in his little windowless compartment, getting bounced so hard that things would slide off the desk, Zink often felt airsick. But he also felt too busy to get sick. "I'll throw up later," he'd tell himself. "I have too much to do right now."

The navigator would be in constant communication with the pilot, warning of the terrain that was approaching. The B-52's navigational tools were rudimentary. Its avionics still relied on vacuum tubes, instead of integrated circuits, and data was entered into the bombing computer with IBM punch cards. At low altitudes, the B-52 was an extraordinary sight, a huge plane with a wingspan about sixty yards wide, hugging the terrain, casting a long shadow, traveling seven or eight miles a minute. Zink's crew often flew through the Rocky Mountains, and the one time that Zink sat in the cockpit, it was fun to watch the pilot bank around hills and drop into alpine valleys. But sitting down below, without any frame of reference other than his radar screen, the experience could be terrifying. On more than one nighttime flight, Zink thought, "we're going to die," as the pilot ignored his warning that a mountain was dead ahead and waited an extra moment to climb.

During low-altitude practice runs, Zink's crew would radar bomb targets throughout the American West, hitting SAC radar huts in places like Sheridan, Wyoming; Bismarck, North Dakota; and La Junta, Colorado. And before a training mission ended, the pilot would spend an hour or two doing "pattern work," landing the plane, rolling down the runway, and then taking off again. Zink found these touch-and-go landings even harder to endure than heavy turbulence. At the end of every training flight, he felt like someone had just pummeled him for hours.

The Klaxons sounded about once a week during ground alerts. The drills were supposed to be "no-notice" and come as a total surprise. But by the late 1970s, SAC was taking some precautions. Whenever Zink and his buddies saw three fire trucks and the wing commander's car park on the alert pad, they'd know a drill was about to begin. They'd stand in the tunnel, waiting, making bets on how many seconds would pass before the Klaxons went off. And then they'd run to their planes. As navigator, Zink would decode the message from SAC headquarters. It usually called for an engine start or a "mover," an exercise that involved taxiing the bomber to the end of the runway, turning around, and returning to the alert pad. Once the drills were completed, the crew would spend about three hours reconfiguring the plane for the next alert.

A few months earlier, during the first week of June, Zink had been fast asleep at about twelve thirty in the morning when the Klaxons sounded. He jumped out of bed, looked out the window—and didn't see any fire trucks or the wing commander's car. He and the bombardier thought, "Oh my God, it's the real thing." Drills were never held late at night. Hearts pounding, they ran to the plane. Zink decoded the message and felt profoundly relieved that it didn't contain an emergency war order. The whole episode felt strange, and it wasn't until weeks later that they learned NORAD had experienced a false alarm. The gunner on Zink's crew, a young staff sergeant, was so shaken by the experience that he quit the Air Force. All of a sudden, the meaning of their wartime mission had become clear, and he realized, "I can't do this." Zink believed strongly in the value of nuclear deterrence and tried not to dwell on what would happen if deterrence failed. He knew that any attack on the Soviet Union by his crew would be not only murderous but suicidal. And yet he never thought about those things while crawling around the Mark 28s and Short-Range Attack Missiles in the bomb bay, checking their serial numbers before an alert.

Zink and his crew were expecting the drill on September 15, 1980. It was about eight thirty in the evening, and out the window you could see the fire trucks and the wing commander's car. The Klaxons sounded. They ran to the plane. Zink put on his headphones and turned the crew volume low, so he could hear the code from SAC headquarters over the radio.

"Alpha, Charlie, Delta . . ." he heard, copying each letter down. And then his pilot's voice was shouting over the intercom.

"Terminate, terminate, terminate."

For some reason, the pilot was ending the drill. Zink felt scared for a moment, wondering why the pilot was yelling. He and the bombardier looked at each other. They couldn't see outside, had no idea what was happening—and then heard a loud bang. Something big had struck the right side of the plane. The lights went out, the cabin became pitch black, and Zink knew it was time to evacuate. The navigator was supposed to open the hatch for the rest of the crew and leave the plane first. But the gunner, who sat upstairs, had already jumped down, landed on the floor, and opened the hatch. And without a word, the gunner leaped through the hatch to the tarmac below. Zink's seat was closest to the hatch, yet four of the five other crew members managed to get out of the plane before him, like rats from a sinking ship. Through the open hatch, Zink could see a bright orange glow—not a good sign.

Zink didn't bother with the ladder. He jumped the five feet to the runway, landed in a crouch, saw that the right wing of the bomber was on fire, and ran as fast as he could. Now he understood why the crew was in such a hurry. A B-52 had caught fire on the runway a few weeks earlier, at Warner Robins Air Force Base, near Macon, Georgia. Within minutes the plane had exploded, and it literally melted into the ground. But that B-52 hadn't been carrying nuclear weapons. This one was loaded with eight SRAMs and four Mark 28 bombs.

Zink ran for about three hundred yards, expecting to get knocked down at any second by an explosion. The wing commander's car pulled up beside him. A window rolled down, and the wing commander said, "Get in." Zink was glad to obey that order. He turned around and saw that the plane's number five engine was shooting flames like a blowtorch. It was the engine on the right wing closest to the fuselage, and the fire was cascading down the length of the aircraft. The wing commander was calling firemen on the radio, trying to solve the problem, well aware that not only the plane, but his career at SAC, might be going up in flames.

The nose of the B-52 was pointing toward the southeast, and a wind with gusts of up to thirty-five miles per hour was blowing in that direction. The wind swept from the tail straight down the fuselage, keeping the fire away from the fuel tanks in the wings and away from the bomb bay. Although the power had been shut off on the plane, gravity continued to feed jet fuel into the number five engine. It had become a gigantic flamethrower. Fire trucks sprayed foam on the engine, and yet the steady supply of fuel kept the fire burning. For the moment, the strong wind was pushing the flames away from the B-52. But the wind could change direction, the plane was getting hotter, and its tanks still held another few hundred thousand pounds of fuel.

TIM GRIFFIS WAS AT HOME with his family in Alvarado, Minnesota, a rural town with a population of about four hundred, when the phone rang. Griffis was a civilian fire inspector at Grand Forks Air Force Base, about forty-five miles to the south. His job mainly involved teaching the public about fire hazards and looking at blueprints to make sure that new buildings complied with the fire code. His wife was a schoolteacher at the base. They had a six-year-old son and an eleven-year-old daughter. The kids had gone to bed.

George VanKirk, the fire chief at Grand Forks, was on the phone. The two men were good friends, and they both lived in Alvarado. A B-52 caught fire near the runway about forty minutes ago, VanKirk said. Did Griffis want to come along and help out? Griffis said yes. The two sped to the base as fast as they could in VanKirk's Ford Fiesta.

By the time Griffis and VanKirk arrived, the fire had been burning for about an hour and a half. The strong wind was still blowing the flames away from the bomber. But the fire trucks couldn't put out the fire. Some of the hoses were now being used to cool the wings and the fuselage. The copilot had admitted that he might have made a mistake before leaving the plane. Two of the steps in the emergency checklist may have been performed in the wrong order. The checklist said to pull the fire suppression handle for the number five engine, shutting off the fuel—and then turn the emergency battery switch off, cutting the power. The copilot may have turned off the battery first. Without any power, the fire suppression system wouldn't work, and fuel would continue to flow. Firefighters climbed into the plane twice, entering the cockpit and attempting to perform the steps in the correct order. But nothing happened.

SAC headquarters was on the radio, along with representatives from Boeing, trying to figure out what to do. By quarter to midnight, the fire had been burning for almost three hours. The right wing and the doors of the bomb bay were starting to blister. The fuel tank inside the wing would soon get hot enough to ignite. Boeing's recommendation was simple: pull the firefighters from the area, abandon the plane, and let it burn. The safety mechanisms on the nuclear weapons would prevent them from detonating, and nobody would get hurt. For some reason, SAC headquarters didn't seem to like that idea.

VanKirk looked at Griffis and said, "What do you think?"

Griffis knew what the question really meant: somebody should make one last attempt to shut off the fuel.

"Yeah, let me try it," he replied.

Although Griffis's current job was fairly sedate, he'd worked for years as a firefighter at Castle Air Force Base in California, where many B-52 pilots were trained. He'd served as the crew chief of a rescue squad, a post that required him to lead men into burning planes as everyone else was leaving them. The interior layout of a B-52 had become awfully familiar, and Griffis thought he could find his way through one blindfolded. But just in case, he wanted Gene Rausch, one of his fire inspectors, to climb into the plane with him—and bring a flashlight.

Their conversation was brief.

"Gene, you want to go with me?"

"Yeah."

Griffis conferred with the wing commander, going over diagrams of the console and the position of switches in the cockpit. Griffis and Rausch borrowed "silvers," hooded firefighting suits, from one of the trucks. The boots were two sizes too big for Griffis, and he had to grip the insoles with his toes to walk in them. He stuffed a handheld radio in his hood to communicate with VanKirk, and their conversation was recorded.

"Chief, that engine is getting pretty hot," Griffis said, five minutes before midnight, "it's starting to pop, if we're going to go in, we've got to do it now."

"Yeah, go."

Griffis and Rausch ran to the plane, entered through the bottom hatch, and climbed into the cockpit. Griffis realized he didn't need Rausch with him after all. The cockpit was so bright from the flames right outside the window that a flashlight was completely unnecessary. Rausch could have stayed outside in the truck. Griffis had been in burning planes before, but never in one where the fire was cascading with such force. He had no idea if the fuel could be shut off. But he'd give it a try—and if it didn't work, they'd get their asses out of there. He saw that the fire suppression handle had already been pulled. All he had to do was plug it in. He switched on the emergency battery, and the fire went out, like the burner of a gas cooktop that had just been turned off. And then Griffis and Rausch heard everyone cheering outside.

As Griffis walked from the plane, VanKirk handed him a radio and said, "Here, somebody wants to talk to you."

It was General Richard Ellis, the commander in chief of the Strategic Air Command.

"Mr. Griffis, I want to thank you," Ellis said.

Griffis was impressed that the head of SAC knew his name. He subsequently received a Civilian Medal of Valor. But he didn't consider himself much of a hero. Climbing into a B-52 that was on fire, without power, in the middle of the night, loaded with nuclear weapons, was no big deal. If you're an Air Force firefighter, he thought, that's what you do.

During a closed Senate hearing, Dr. Roger Batzel, the director of the Lawrence Livermore National Laboratory, subsequently testified that if the B-52 had caught on fire, the nuclear weapons inside it could have scattered plutonium over sixty square miles of North Dakota and Minnesota. The city of Grand Forks, with a population of about sixty thousand, would have been directly in the path of the radioactive plume. Batzel failed to mention that one of the Mark 28 bombs could have detonated. It would have destroyed Grand Forks and deposited lethal fallout on Duluth, Minnesota, or Minneapolis–Saint Paul, depending on the high-altitude winds. An Air Force investigation discovered the cause of the fire in engine number five: someone had forgotten to screw a nut onto the fuel strainer. The missing nut was smaller than a penny.

Jeffrey Zink and his crew were taken to the hospital, given drug tests, and kept there until three in the morning. They later resented the obsession, among local newspapers, with the question of whether nuclear weapons had been on the plane. The Air Force would neither confirm nor deny it. The crew focused on a more immediate issue: how easily they could have lost their lives. Some of the bombers on alert that night were parked facing west. Had the nose of their B-52 faced west, the fire would have entered the plane the moment the hatch was opened. They would have been incinerated, and the flames would've quickly reached the SRAMs and the Mark 28 bombs. The difference between life and death was their parking space.

Not long after the accident, Zink and his wife were having a romantic, candlelit dinner. They were newlyweds. When his napkin brushed the candle and caught on fire, Zink came unglued. All the feelings that had been suppressed hit him at once. He lost it, he felt like a complete basket case. He didn't have post-traumatic stress disorder or anything really debilitating, just a sudden realization that was hard to express, without sounding trite. Zink was twenty-five years old, and something abstract had become real. These planes are dangerous, he thought. People die in them.

THE DAY AFTER THE B-52 fire at Grand Forks, Senator David Pryor once again introduced an amendment to a Senate bill, calling for the installation of warning sirens at every Titan II launch complex. The commander of the 308th Strategic Missile Wing, Colonel Moser, had informed Pryor that at least nine accidents or propellant leaks had occurred at Titan II missile sites in Arkansas during the previous year. At a launch complex near Heber Springs, a steel rod had fallen onto a circuit breaker, starting a fire and endangering the missile. More than one third of the entire Titan II force had been patched for leaks. Pryor's amendment was cosponsored by Senator Bob Dole, among others, but it was still opposed by the Air Force. "We have a responsibility to protect the civilians living in the communities and on the farms surrounding these missile sites," Pryor said during the Senate debate. "Accidents have occurred in the past, and we must take steps to reduce their recurrence and provide for the best course of action in case an accident should occur."

The Air Force had recently submitted a lengthy report to the House and Senate armed services committees, addressing their concerns about the safety of the Titan II. The report acknowledged that the RFHCO suits and the silo's communications system could be improved. It also noted that the portable vapor detectors did a poor job of detecting fuel vapor and should be replaced. But the Air Force contended that the accident rate at Titan II sites was lower than the rate at most American workplaces, that current maintenance procedures "provide a high level of safety," and that the physical condition of the missile was "considered by many to be better now than when it was new." The safety record of the W-53 warhead was "commendable," the report said—without mentioning that even the Pentagon thought it needed a retrofit to be safe in abnormal environments. The Air Force argued that the risk of a major propellant leak was low, because the Titan II's fuel tanks and oxidizer tanks were so well maintained. "Airframe rupture," the report concluded, "therefore does not constitute a viable concern."

The Air Force report was useful not only to the Strategic Air Command, which hoped to keep the Titan II on alert, but also to the defense contractors responsible for the missile, like Martin Marietta. They were being sued by Airman Carl Malinger and other victims of the oxidizer leak at Rock, Kansas. But the report didn't help the Air Force in the Senate. Pryor's amendment was approved on September 16, 1980, almost a year after it had first been introduced.

Skip Rutherford and his wife were at home, having dinner with an old friend, a couple of days later, when the phone rang. Rutherford got up, took the call, and returned to the table looking white as a ghost.

His wife asked what was wrong.

Somebody dropped a socket in a Titan II silo near Damascus, Rutherford said. The skin of the missile has been pierced, and fuel's leaking out. The guy who just called says the missile's going to explode.

Rutherford phoned Senator Pryor, who was in Hot Springs, Arkansas, for the state Democratic convention, along with Governor Bill Clinton and Vice President Walter Mondale.

"This is serious," Rutherford told the senator.

"Well, how serious?"

"They tell me it's going to explode."

"You're kidding me."

Outside Rutherford's house, cars were driving past, kids were playing in yards—and none of them seemed to know that a nuclear disaster might be unfolding, just fifty miles away. Rutherford thought the whole thing was surreal. If the missile did explode, would the warhead detonate? Was the state of Arkansas really about to be wiped off the map? After the conversation with Senator Pryor, the phone at the house kept ringing. The calls were from other staff members, journalists, and the airmen who'd secretly been warning him about the Titan II for months. They said the missile was going to explode, and they hadn't been wrong yet.

The television was on in the living room, and Rutherford noticed that a good friend of his, Frank Thomas, a twenty-seven-year-old correspondent for Channel 7, was standing across the road from the Titan II site in Damascus. He was repeating the Air Force claim that everything was under control. Rutherford picked up the phone and called Bob Steele, the news director at Channel 7.

"Bob, listen to me," Rutherford said. "This is totally off the record, but you tell Frank to get the hell out of there."

"What?"

"Tell Frank to get the hell out of there. He is a friend of mine, and that missile, Bob, is going to explode."

"How do you know?"

"You have your sources, I have mine," Rutherford said, beginning to feel a little frantic. "And I'm just telling you, I'm sitting over here watching my friend Frank Thomas on your station standing right before a death trap. And I don't have a way to get to him, but you all do, and you've got to get him out of there."

Steele got the message. But Thomas was about to leave Damascus, anyway.

Like Hell

The outer door was a real bitch.

The entrance to Launch Complex 374-7 wasn't protected by high-tech security devices, invented at a top secret weapons lab—just by a heavy steel door, with an electromagnetic lock. And it was hard to open with a crowbar. Greg Devlin and Rex Hukle took turns, one holding the flashlight, the other trying to pry the door open. Nobody had told them how to do it. There wasn't a checklist for breaking into a Titan II complex, and so the two airmen improvised. They used brute force. Devlin was in pretty good shape from boxing, but the air pack and the RFHCO suit made the work more difficult.

Hukle felt uneasy. They'd walked beneath a thick cloud of fuel vapor to reach the access portal. Now the outer door wouldn't open. And once they got past this door, they'd have to go downstairs, break open the door in the entrapment area, and open three blast doors with a hand pump to reach the control center. All of that would have to be accomplished within half an hour; their air packs were considered too unreliable after that point. It was about five after two in the morning. They were the only people on the complex. Hukle figured anything could happen and prepared himself for the worst.

Devlin wasn't having dark thoughts. He just wanted to open the damn door. He felt focused and alert, ready for whatever may come. Devlin's attitude was: somebody's got to do this, so it might as well be me.

After fifteen minutes of pulling and prying, the steel door swung open. Devlin and Hukle broke through the entrapment door in about thirty seconds. They left crowbars in both doorjambs to prevent the doors from closing, went down the stairs, and got to work on the first blast door, attaching hoses to its hydraulic valves. Neither of the men had ever used the emergency hand pump before—and the blast door wouldn't open, no matter how hard they pumped. The fine threads on the hoses were tricky to connect in the dark while wearing rubber gloves. And the pump was an elaborate contraption that didn't seem to do anything, no matter what they tried. Another fifteen minutes passed, and the blast door was still shut. Their time limit was up. Over the radio, Sergeant Michael Hanson ordered them to quit. Feeling frustrated and defeated, they left the pump beside the door, climbed the stairs, and walked back to the hole in the fence.

Sergeant Hanson, the chief of PTS Team B, led the effort to reenter the control center. He told Devlin and Hukle to read the instructions for the hand pump, grab fresh air packs, go back down there, and try the door again.

Jeff Kennedy thought the whole plan was idiotic. They should be going through the escape hatch, not the access portal. They should have done it at ten o'clock in the evening, not at two in the morning. Almost eight hours had passed since the skin of the missile was pierced. Entering the complex was much more dangerous now—and if something went wrong underground, Devlin and Hukle would be close to the missile, surrounded by fuel vapors, vulnerable to all kinds of bad things.

Let me do it, Kennedy said. I know how to work the pump.

Hanson had tried to send Kennedy back to Little Rock a few hours earlier. He hadn't asked Kennedy to put on a RFHCO suit; and he hadn't invited Kennedy to join them at the complex gate. The two men didn't get along. But Kennedy sure knew a lot about the missile, and he was volunteering.

I'll go with him, David Livingston said.

Hanson told them to get ready.

While Livingston and Kennedy checked their radios and air packs, Major Wayne Wallace, Sergeant Archie James, and Sergeant Silas Spann left to set up a decontamination area in front of the water treatment building, at the northeast corner of the complex, just outside the fence. When they got to the building, the door was locked, and the combination they'd been given didn't work. Wallace had to break into the place. Inside, they found a short rubber garden hose. It wasn't ideal—Livingston and Kennedy would have to walk about a hundred yards to get rinsed off. But it was better than nothing. Spann and James drove over a light-all unit and began to set it up so that the men wouldn't have to be decontaminated in the dark.

Sergeant Ronald W. Christal showed Livingston and Kennedy the tech order for the emergency hand pump. Christal was a missile pneudraulics technician. He often worked on the blast doors and knew a few tricks to open them that weren't in the book.

Livingston and Kennedy planned to communicate with each other using hand signals instead of the radios in their RFHCO suits. Only one person at a time could speak on the launch complex radio system—and they wanted to keep the line open as much as possible. One of them would speak to Hanson on the launch complex radio; Hanson would relay the information to Colonel Morris, who'd be right next to him at the pickup truck near the gate. Using the radio in the truck, Morris would speak to Colonel Moser, who was at the command post in Little Rock; Moser would talk to SAC headquarters in Omaha. And, hopefully, as the words passed from one person to another, nothing would be garbled or misunderstood.

At about ten minutes before three, Kennedy and Livingston reached the first blast door. Christal read the instructions for the hand pump to Hanson, who conveyed them over the radio.

The blast door opened.

Livingston took an air sample with a portable vapor detector. They'd been told to check the fuel vapor level every step of the way. If the level

exceeded 250 parts per million, they were supposed to leave the complex. The vapor level was 65 ppm in front of the first blast door. As they
walked through the door and entered the large blast lock, the level rose to
181 ppm.

At the command post in Little Rock, Sergeant Jimmy D. Wiley heard
the vapor level and thought that Kennedy and Livingston should get out of
there immediately. Wiley was part of the K crew, the backup team assembled to advise Colonel Moser. Another member of the K crew, Lieutenant
David Rathgeber, agreed—if the vapor level was that high after the first
blast door, it was bound to be even higher after the second one, as the men
got closer to the missile. Wiley and Rathgeber told Colonel Moser that the
reentry should be terminated, that the men should be withdrawn from the
complex.

The issue was discussed with SAC headquarters. Livingston and Kennedy were ordered to proceed. If they could reach the next blast lock—the
small area between the door to the control center and the long cableway to
the silo—they could check a panel on the wall that displayed readings from
the Mine Safety Appliance. The panel showed the vapor levels in the silo.
Kennedy removed the breathing nuts from the second blast door and inserted the probe of the vapor detector through a small hole in the door.
Sticking the probe through the door would give a preview of what awaited
them on the other side.

The fuel vapor level was about 190 ppm. SAC headquarters told Livingston and Kennedy to open the door, enter the next blast lock, and check
the readings on the panel. They opened the door. The room was so full of
fuel vapor that they could barely see inside. It looked like a steam room.
The portable vapor detector pegged out—the vapor level was far beyond
250 ppm.

Kennedy walked over to the panel. For the first time, he was scared. The
blast lock had eight emergency lights, some of them bright red, and he
could barely see them. The cloud of fuel vapor floating around them was
highly flammable. The slightest spark could ignite it. The RFHCO suits
and tools abandoned by PTA Team A were lying on the floor. This is the

kind of place you don't want to be in, Kennedy thought. He looked at the panel, and the needles on the gauges were pointing all the way to the right. They'd pegged out. The gauges said the fuel vapor level in the silo now exceeded 21,000 ppm—high enough to melt their RFHCO suits.

Back out, Hanson said, back out.

Livingston and Kennedy left the blast lock, hurried through the two blast doors, and went up the stairs.

Hanson had an idea: maybe they should turn on a ventilation fan to clear out some of the fuel vapor. The switch for the fan was on the wall of the access portal, at the bottom of the first flight of stairs.

Livingston and Kennedy were almost out of the complex when they heard Hanson say, turn on the fan. They looked at each other. Livingston patted himself on the chest, signaling that he would go down and do it.

Kennedy reached the top of the stairs and stepped into the night air. It felt good to be out of there. That cloud of fuel vapor was insane, he'd never seen anything like it. Kennedy was tired. He decided to sit for a moment on the concrete curb outside the access portal. It had been a hell of a night.

Livingston switched on the fan and came back up the stairs. He was a foot or two behind Kennedy when the Titan II exploded.

At the command post in Little Rock, the radio went dead. And the open phone line from the control center at 4-7 became silent. The sound of the tipsies—the intruder alarm that had been ringing ever since the missile crew left—was gone. Nobody at the launch site could be reached on the radio. For the next eight minutes, the command post did not hear a word from anyone in Damascus. Colonel Moser thought the warhead had detonated.

SID KING AND HIS SALES REP, Tom Phillips, were sitting on the hood of Sheriff Anglin's squad car, talking with some of the reporters who'd gathered at the access road to the complex, off Highway 65. Nobody seemed worried about the situation. The Air Force had denied there was a serious problem and said everything was under control. But Van Buren

County didn't get a lot of big news stories, and King was willing to hang around a little longer just to see what happened.

A bright white flash lit the sky, and King felt the air around him being sucked toward the missile site. An instant later, a gust blew it back, and a loud sustained roar came from behind the trees, like the sound of a rocket being launched. A column of fire rose hundreds of feet into the air, tall as a skyscraper and towering overhead. The blast briefly turned night into day, pulled the launch complex apart, and lifted the debris into a mushroom cloud. King saw the flames and felt heat on his face and dove to the ground, terrified, as rocks and pieces of concrete began to rain down.

People were screaming, "Get out of here, get out of here," and a scene that had been calm and quiet a moment earlier became sheer chaos. King and Phillips hid under the taillights of the squad car, trying to avoid falling rocks—and then the taillights came on. Sheriff Anglin was backing out, and he didn't know they were behind the car. They leaped out of the way as Anglin floored it and pulled onto the road. State officials, highway patrolmen, Air Force officers, cameramen, and reporters were getting into their cars and speeding south toward Damascus. The scene had a primordial feel: every man for himself.

Just a few minutes earlier, Lou Short, the cameraman for Channel 4, had been showing off his brand-new, state-of-the-art, $30,000 RCA video camera. When the debris started to fall, King saw him toss the camera into the back of a truck like an old piece of wood and drive off. None of the news photographers got a picture of the explosion. Getting away from it seemed a lot more important. Larry Ellis, the cameraman for Channel 11, captured the only images of the blast—ten seconds of blurry footage, shot in 16mm, after the eyepiece of his camera was blown off. And ten seconds was long enough for Ellis, who stopped filming, jumped into the truck driven by his reporter, and joined the panicked exodus to Damascus.

King and Phillips headed the other way in the Live Ear, driving north on Highway 65 toward the radio station in Clinton. King had his foot to the floor, praying that his little Dodge Omni could outrun the radioactive fallout and whatever else had been released into the air. They knew the missile had a nuclear warhead, no matter what the Air Force said. But they had no idea if that warhead had detonated. About half a mile up the road, an Air Force security officer stood in the middle of the highway, wearing a gas mask and holding an M-16.

Sheriff Anglin was ahead of them, driving erratically, going ninety miles an hour, slowing down to fifty, and then speeding up again. The cord of Anglin's police radio had gotten wrapped around his right leg, and every time he lifted the handset to speak into it, the cord pulled his foot off the gas. The sheriff stopped at the truck stop in Bee Branch, about six miles north of Damascus, and told everyone to get out of there, right away. Nobody argued with him. The place emptied, and big eighteen-wheelers peeled onto the highway.

Driving through Choctaw, King realized that neither he, nor Phillips, had spoken since the explosion.

"We just left a bunch of dead people back there," King said.

"Yeah, I know."

SAM HUTTO WAS COMING HOME to milk the cows when the missile blew. He was just north of Damascus, on a stretch of Highway 65 that looked down on the launch complex, about two miles away. The blast rattled his pickup. He saw the bright flash, the flames shooting upward like a Roman candle. And then he saw a little sparkly thing fly out of the fire, soar above it briefly, and fall to the ground. He decided not to milk the cows, turned the pickup around, and drove to his brother's house. And his father, who was spending the night there, seemed curious about what had just happened

"Hop in here," Hutto said to his dad, "and let's go up to the top of the hill so you can see."

Hutto drove to the top of the hill and saw another incredible sight: the headlights of vehicles speeding toward them, bumper to bumper, filling both lanes of the two-lane highway. It looked like a NASCAR restart. As Hutto and his father sat in the pickup beside the road, a couple of state police cars flew past them, followed by news trucks and all sorts of Air Force vehicles—even an ambulance. Nobody stopped, slowed down, or told them to evacuate. Once the vehicles were gone, the road was empty and still again, like it always was at three in the morning. But a fire was burning brightly in the silo.

BOB PEURIFOY WAS FAST ASLEEP when he got the call. A Titan II just blew up in Arkansas, Stan Spray told him. There was a lot of confusion about the details—and no word on the warhead. Of course, it hadn't detonated full scale. If it had, much of Arkansas would be gone. An Accident Response Group was being assembled, and they wanted Peurifoy to be part of it. A plane would soon land at Kirtland Air Force Base to take him and the rest of the group to Little Rock. Peurifoy got out of bed, thinking about that warhead.

THE DECISION TO EVACUATE the missile site was made by Colonel William Jones, the commander not only of Little Rock Air Force Base but also of its Disaster Response Force. He didn't have any authority at Launch Complex 374-7 until a disaster occurred. The explosion qualified as one, and Jones briefly conferred with Richard English, the chief of the Disaster Preparedness Division, about what to do. They both thought that everyone at the launch complex was dead and that the air drifting toward Highway 65 was probably full of toxic fumes. Jones knew very little about Titan II missiles and their propellants. He belonged to the Military Airlift Command, which flew transport planes, not the Strategic Air Command.

"Evacuate, evacuate," English shouted repeatedly, over the loudspeaker of the mobile command post.

Members of the Disaster Response Force were among the first to leave the scene of the disaster.

MICHAEL MAZZARO, the missile crew commander at 4-7, was resting in the back of the ambulance when the missile blew up. Al Childers, the deputy commander, sat beside Ronald Fuller, the missile facilities technician, in the security police pickup that had carried them away from the complex hours before. The truck was parked at the entry control point, about thirty feet down the access road from Highway 65. They were listening to Livingston and Kennedy on the radio. Rodney Holder, the crew's missile systems analyst technician, was in a truck a few hundred feet closer to the launch complex. None of them thought that the missile was about to explode. Holder hoped that somebody would arrive the next morning, figure out what to do, and fix the problem. They were just sitting there, waiting for that somebody to arrive.

Childers was surprised by the bright white flash. The sun seemed to have appeared in the sky. He knew the warhead hadn't detonated—and yet, somehow, felt it had.

Fuller opened the door and dove into a ditch.

Holder saw the flash and ducked, heard things hitting the truck, waited a few seconds, took a deep breath, and found it remarkable that he was still alive. Then he got out of the truck and ran toward the highway.

Childers, Holder, and Fuller bumped into one another at the back of the security police pickup. They'd all had the same thought, at the same time: grab the gas mask that you wore out of the launch complex. But the masks were gone, and security police officers were now wearing them. The missile crew members climbed into the backseat of the truck, as the loudspeaker called for everyone to evacuate. Sergeant Thomas Brocksmith, who'd picked them up after they left the control center, got into the driver's seat. The sky had turned deep red, and Holder worried that a cloud of oxidizer was about to engulf them.

"I need to get the hell out of here before the oxidizer starts falling," Holder thought. "Everybody at the complex is dead, and Rodney has no need to be here."

Vehicles were pulling out haphazardly, people were running around in the dark, the evacuation seemed chaotic, and Childers became worried that someone might get hurt. He got out of the pickup truck to direct traffic. It was a thoughtful, well-intended thing to do. Brocksmith drove off without him. Cars and trucks sped past him. Everyone ignored him, and yet somehow nobody got hurt.

About fifty Air Force officers and airmen were at the Titan II site when the missile exploded. Most of them drove to Damascus at high speed. But none of the PTS crew members left. Jim Sandaker had started the night at the barracks, recruiting volunteers to help save the missile. He expressed the PTS point of view, bluntly, when an officer told him to evacuate.

"Screw you," Sandaker said. "I'm not leaving until I have my friends or their bodies."

OUTSIDE THE WATER TREATMENT BUILDING, Major Wallace and Sergeant James hid beneath one of the light-all units after the missile blew. As rocks and concrete and little pieces of molten steel landed all around them, James thought: I just want everything to stop falling. The debris lacerated one of his elbows, burned the other, and tore up his left leg. But James was able to stand, and Wallace helped him put on a gas mask. Wallace hadn't even been scratched. They both wondered what had happened to Silas Spann, who'd been a few feet away from them, seconds before. Now there wasn't a trace of him.

THE MOMENT THE MISSILE EXPLODED, Silas Spann began to run. He didn't need to see what was happening—he knew what was happening and instinctively bolted. Hiding under the light-all unit would have made more sense, but running away from the explosion felt a lot better. Spann ran toward the entry control point as fast as he could.

COLONEL MORRIS WAS REACHING for the radio inside his pickup truck when the explosion blew out the windshield. The truck was parked near the gate to the complex and the hole they'd cut in the fence. Morris felt like laughing, as the truck shook and got pounded with debris. It seemed comical: he was sprawled across the front seat and couldn't get his legs inside the truck, no matter how hard he tried. The door slammed hard onto his left leg. And then he lay there, waiting for something big to hit the pickup.

Morris looked up, saw the immense pillar of fire rising from the silo, and put his head back onto the seat.

Hukle was sitting on the tailgate. He managed to crawl across the bed of the truck and hide behind the cab, keeping his eyes tightly shut, amid the roar. Through his eyelids he saw a brilliant red blur. His hands got burned, and something shattered his right kneecap.

Hanson was standing next to the door of the pickup, right beside Colonel Morris. Hanson saw two explosions. The first one shot flames twenty-five feet high out of the exhaust vents, and the second obliterated the silo. The blast wave inflated Hanson's uniform like a balloon, lifted him off his feet, tossed him down the road, and sent enormous steel beams flying past him.

Christal was standing next to Hanson. He saw the first explosion, missed seeing the second one, flew into the air, and landed twenty feet away. Christal covered his head as the debris fell, got up, looked around, thanked God for sparing his life, and checked to see if all his hair had been burned off. It hadn't. But the left side of his face and both of his hands were burned.

Greg Devlin was standing about two feet from the gate, facing the silo. The blast wave knocked the wind out of him, like a punch to the stomach, picked him up, threw him onto his back, and slid him fifty feet down the asphalt road. Devlin felt completely under the control of some powerful, malevolent force, unable to move or resist it, propelled by air that seemed to have become rock solid. As Devlin slid down the road on his back, he saw molten steel and pieces of concrete flowing by him like lava.

"Oh shit, you ain't gonna live through this," Devlin thought. "I just hope it's not painful."

Seconds after the explosion, Devlin was lying in the road, feeling dazed and bleary, like he'd been coldcocked in a boxing match. And then he heard a loud voice in his ear yelling, *Run, run!* The voice scared the shit out of him. He didn't see anybody, anywhere nearby. Devlin got up, ran for about five steps—and got knocked down again by steel rebar that had just fallen from the sky. It struck his right ankle, tearing the Achilles tendon. The rebar hung from a block of concrete about fifteen feet high and thirteen feet wide. The concrete was part of the silo door abutment. It had landed in the middle of the road, and if he hadn't gotten up and started to run, it would have landed on him. When Devlin opened his eyes, he saw the shadow of this huge block of concrete, thought the Titan II had landed right next to him, and said to himself, "Oh, my God."

COLONEL MORRIS LOOKED UP AGAIN, when debris stopped falling onto the truck, and saw that flames were still rising from the silo. He figured it was time to leave. He got out of the truck, and the silhouette of something enormous in the middle of the road made him feel disoriented. Morris heard someone call for help. It was Hukle, sitting in the bed of the pickup, with his RFHCO suit pulled down to his knees. One of the knees was torn open, and Hukle said that he couldn't walk. Morris pulled the RFHCO suit off him, picked him up, put him over a shoulder, and carried him around the piece of concrete, big as a mobile home, that was blocking the access road.

Devlin saw Colonel Morris and yelled, "Please help, I can't move."

Morris carried Hukle for about one hundred yards, lay him down in a field, and then ran back for Devlin. He picked up Devlin and put him over a shoulder.

Devlin could not believe the strength of Colonel Morris. The two were about the same size, and yet Morris was running while carrying him. The man was forty-two years old. Devlin couldn't stop looking at his face. Blood was pouring down it. Morris looked like he'd been shot in the head.

"I have to put you down," Morris said. "I have to get to the end of the road, or they'll leave without us."

Morris lay Devlin in the field beside Hukle and ran off.

AT THE ACCESS CONTROL POINT, two members of the Disaster Response Force, Richard English and David Rossborough, were preparing to leave for Damascus. Mazzaro was on the radio to the Little Rock command post. Childers was standing nearby when he saw Silas Spann on the access road, sprinting toward them. Spann said there were still people alive on the complex; he'd just helped Hanson and Christal find their way onto the road.

A PTS maintenance officer, Captain George Short, drove up in a station wagon with Colonel Morris, whom he'd seen staggering at the top of the hill.

Colonel Morris wanted to go back for Hukle and Devlin. But Morris looked terrible, and the other men didn't want him to go. Morris and Short started to do a head count, trying to figure out who was left on the complex. Hanson and Christal appeared, suffering from cuts and burns but strong enough to walk.

Childers grabbed Mazzaro's gas mask. He didn't want Mazzaro to be heroic and take any foolish risks—Mazzaro's wife was about to have a baby. Childers climbed into the station wagon with Rossborough and English. Silas Spann got behind the wheel, and they drove back into the thick of it.

English was the only civilian in the Disaster Response Force. He'd spent twenty years in the Air Force, serving as a navigator in SAC bombers and helping to manage early tests of the Titan II. He retired in 1967, sold insurance for a year, hated it, and got a job at Little Rock Air Force Base that involved a lot of action—training people how to handle disasters, responding to disasters, advising the base commander what to do about disasters. He was fifty-seven, an old man by Air Force standards, and yet greatly admired by his men, who always addressed him as "Colonel." Far from being over the hill, English was athletic and fit and looked a lot like William Holden, a 1950s movie star.

Rossborough was thirty-two, a sergeant from upstate New York. He'd been at a bowling alley when the Disaster Response Force was recalled. And that explained why, at quarter past three in the morning, on a burning missile site, in the middle of a Broken Arrow, Rossborough was wearing a red bowling shirt.

When the station wagon reached the top of the hill overlooking the complex, the road was littered with debris, and Rossborough told Spann to stop.

The reentry vehicle may have blown apart, Rossborough said, and pieces of the warhead could be scattered everywhere. You don't want to drive over, or step onto, any of it.

Childers could barely recognize the place that he'd left just hours before. It looked like a war zone. The silo was on fire, the grass was on fire, the hills to the west of the complex and the woods to the north were on fire.

They reached the field where Morris had left Devlin and Hukle. Jim Sandaker was already there, with a fellow member of PTS Team B, Buddy Boylan. They were putting two injured men, Wallace and James, into a pickup truck.

Gene Schneider, another member of the PTS team, had run into the field and picked up Devlin. Schneider carried Devlin in his arms, like a child, as Devlin screamed in pain. His RFHCO suit was dragging along the ground, and every time it got caught on a piece of debris, it applied pressure to his wounded ankle. Schneider would stop for a moment, and Devlin would tell him to keep going. And then Schneider couldn't carry him any farther. Rossborough and Childers ran over, grabbed Devlin, and placed him in the back of a large truck that Captain Short had driven over. Joseph Tallman, another PTS technician, carried Hukle to the station wagon.

Childers thought he saw the reentry vehicle near the road. Spann was standing right beside it.

"Get away from there," Childers yelled.

Spann obeyed the order, and when all of the injured had been loaded into vehicles, Childers asked him if anybody was unaccounted for.

Only Livingston and Kennedy, Spann said.

"Let's go, let's get out of here," people shouted.

Nobody was wearing a gas mask. Clouds of oxidizer seemed to be floating above the complex. A large object by the side of the road was loudly hissing; if it was the propane tank, it could explode at any moment. The place did not look or feel remotely safe. Everyone piled into the vehicles, drove off, and returned to the entry control point. Livingston and Kennedy had been left for dead.

COLONEL MORRIS TRIED TO CONTACT the ambulance, using a radio in one of the security police trucks. But the radio in the ambulance was part of the hospital net. It operated on a different frequency. A radio on the security police net couldn't communicate with a radio on the hospital net. And the radio in the ambulance wasn't working properly. Captain Donald Mueller—the physician assigned to the Disaster Response Force, who was in the ambulance—could speak to the hospital at Little Rock Air Force Base on the radio. But Mueller couldn't hear anything that the hospital said in response.

MANY OF THE SECURITY POLICE officers and most of the Disaster Response Force were now in the parking lot of the Sharpe-Payne grocery store in Damascus. It seemed like a good place to regroup. Colonel Jones knew that injured airmen had just been found at the launch complex—but he couldn't contact the ambulance, either. Speaking to Colonel Morris over the radio, Jones suggested that the injured should be brought to the grocery store.

CAPTAIN SHORT WAS FURIOUS THAT everyone had left the PTS crews at the site, that the ambulance and the security police were nowhere to be seen. Devlin was in great pain. He kept yelling for water, saying his skin was on fire. Devlin's friends cut the RFHCO suit off him and tried to ease the pain. They didn't have any painkillers or a medical kit. They emptied a cooler and covered Devlin in water and ice.

"Well, at least I've still got the hair on my arms," Sergeant James said to Childers, "but what's my face look like?"

Childers thought it wasn't looking too good. It was burned so badly that most of the skin had peeled away.

Fed up with waiting, Major Wallace said the men should be taken to the nearest hospital. Almost half an hour had passed since the explosion. The injured were placed into a station wagon, a pickup, and a large ton-and-a-half PTS truck. They headed for Damascus.

As the trucks sped south on Highway 65, they passed the ambulance, which was heading north. The PTS truck carrying Devlin and Hukle turned around and drove back to the access road so that a doctor could determine how badly they'd been hurt. Sandaker, driving the pickup, just kept going.

Hukle was put on a stretcher next to the ambulance, and Devlin was examined while lying in the back of the truck. Dr. Mueller thought the injuries didn't look too serious. But the diagnosis didn't satisfy Childers or the members of PTS Team B. They took the station wagon and the PTS truck, departed for the hospital in Conway, about twenty-five miles to the south—and, amid the confusion, left Hukle on the stretcher beside the ambulance.

NEAR THE TOWN OF GREENBRIER, about ten miles south of Damascus, Sandaker spotted a couple of security police officers. He stopped the pickup and left two injured men—Hanson and Archie James—with the officers. Then Sandaker did a U-turn and drove north. He wanted to get back to the missile site.

THE HOSPITAL IN CONWAY REFUSED to admit the injured men, claiming that it lacked the authority to treat Air Force personnel. Childers demanded that they be treated and took full responsibility for their care. On the way to the hospital, while sitting in the backseat of the station wagon, Joseph Tallman—the PTS technician who'd carried Hukle from the field—had gone into shock. The refusal to admit these injured young airmen, at four in the morning, about half an hour away from another hospital, seemed in keeping with the spirit of the entire night. The hospital finally agreed to treat them, and Childers called the command post in Little Rock to say where they were.

———

A FEW HOURS EARLIER, at about one in the morning, after escorting a flatbed truck with light-all units to Launch Complex 374-7, Jimmy Roberts and Don Green had asked if there was anything else they could do to help. They were security police officers with a pickup truck. Devlin and Hukle had not yet broken into the complex with crowbars. Everybody was still waiting for instructions from SAC headquarters.

Sergeant Thomas Brocksmith, the commander of the security police at the site, asked Roberts and Green to drive along the roads surrounding the complex and check on the security officers who were manning the roadblocks. Brocksmith wanted to make sure that all the officers knew how to use their gas masks—in case anything went wrong. Roberts and Green got into their truck and drove along the roads surrounding 4-7. They chatted with security officers at the roadblocks, showing them how to use the masks. Most of the officers didn't know anything about the Titan II or the danger of its propellants.

At about three o'clock, Roberts and Green were on a road about half a mile southwest of the silo.

The sky lit up.

"Man, ain't that pretty," Roberts said, not realizing what had just happened.

A moment later the blast wave shook the pickup so hard it almost went off the road. Roberts and Green quickly put on their gas masks. They had a clear view of the launch complex, and it looked like the fireball extended all the way to Highway 65. They couldn't reach anybody on the radio and thought that everyone at the complex was dead.

We may be the only two left, Green said.

They decided to evacuate nearby homes—and then heard Sergeant Brocksmith on the radio, calling from the grocery store in Damascus. He told them to evacuate the homes south of the launch complex. They drove east, reached Highway 65, got out of the truck, banged on the doors of small farmhouses and mobile homes, told people to leave at once. Despite the disturbing, early-morning sight of two men in battle fatigues and gas masks standing at the front door, most of the homeowners were grateful for the warning. But one man opened the door, pointed a handgun at them, and said, "I'm not going to leave." They didn't argue with him.

Roberts and Green were about a mile north of Damascus when they heard the following exchange over the radio:

"Help! Help me. Help me! Can anybody read me?"

"Yes, we can hear you."

"Help me!"

"Where are you?"

"This is Sergeant Kennedy."

"Where are you, Jeff?"

"Colonel Morris, I'm down here by your truck, please help me . . . my leg's broke and I'm bleeding."

"Where are you?"

"I'm down here in your truck!"

Roberts and Green had assumed that they were the only people anywhere near the launch complex. Neither of them had ever met Jeff Kennedy, and they didn't even know who he was. But they weren't going to leave him out there. Green turned the pickup truck around and floored it, driving all out, pedal to the metal.

About a minute later, the pickup died right in the middle of Highway 65. It had run out of gas. They got out and pushed it to the side of the road. A passing Air Force truck refused to stop for them, even after they chased it, yelling and waving their arms. The driver of a civilian vehicle swore at them and kept going, when they tried to flag it down. Roberts spotted a Cadillac parked in the driveway of a nearby home, ran over to it, broke one of the windows with a rock, and started to hot-wire the car.

Green was impressed, but not surprised, that Roberts knew how to do that.

A pickup truck approached at high speed from Damascus. Roberts and Green left the Cadillac and stood in the highway, blocking both lanes. They figured: if the truck runs us over, to hell with it.

The truck stopped, and they commandeered it. The driver, Jim Sandaker, insisted on coming with them to the launch complex.

They said, Fine, but get in the backseat.

Green floored it, and the three set out to find Jeff Kennedy.

ONE MOMENT KENNEDY HAD BEEN looking at the ground in front of the access portal, getting ready to sit on the curb. And the next moment he was soaring through the air, spinning head over heels, like an acrobat from a trapeze. And then he blacked out.

When Kennedy opened his eyes, he was lying on his back, and his legs were pointing toward the sky, propped against a chain-link fence. Fires burned all around him. He screamed and yelled for help. But nobody answered.

After lying in that position for a few minutes, wedged against the fence, something inside Kennedy clicked. The choice became clear: he could get up and go—or stay there and die.

Kennedy pulled his legs off the fence, stood up, and immediately fell down. He saw that his right leg was broken, and the rest of him felt bruised and cut up. His helmet was gone. His face was bleeding. After falling down, Kennedy said to himself, "I am not going to die on this complex."

Using the fence for support, Kennedy pulled himself up and tried to get his bearings. The launch complex was nothing but rubble and flames. It took a little while, but he figured out where he was. The blast had hurled Kennedy about 150 feet through the air. He'd landed upside down against the fence in the southwest corner of the complex. He decided to follow the fence east, toward Highway 65, and then north, hoping to find the hole they'd cut in it. The fence gave Kennedy some physical support and a sense of direction, but it also imprisoned him inside the complex. He couldn't climb over it, with a broken leg. Until he could find a way out, he was trapped there amid the fires and debris and toxic smoke.

Every few steps, Kennedy fell down. The RFHCO suit was heavy and cumbersome, and without the helmet, it no longer served a useful purpose. It was slowing him down. Kennedy sat on the ground, took off the air pack, and got his arms out of the RFHCO. But he couldn't pull the suit off his broken leg. He searched the ground, found a jagged piece of metal, and cut the RFHCO suit off above his boots.

Kennedy walked and fell, walked and fell, tripping over debris, looking for the hole in the fence. From somewhere in the darkness, he heard Livingston's voice, crying out.

"Oh, my God, help me. Please, somebody help me. Please, God, help me."

"Livy, I'm going for help," Kennedy shouted.

Livingston didn't seem to hear him.

"Oh, my God, help me," Livingston repeated. "Please, somebody help me."

Kennedy had no idea where Livingston was. The only sign of him was his voice, calling out.

"Please, somebody help me."

Kennedy kept walking, falling, and getting back up, aware that both of their lives were now at stake. The pain in his leg became excruciating, and he didn't think he could walk any farther. He started to panic. He thought about his children, his wife. He didn't want to die on this launch complex. He shouted for help, but nobody answered. And then he told himself to shut up and walk.

In the distance, Kennedy spotted the flashing hazard lights of the pickup truck that Colonel Morris had parked near the gate. The truck was about a hundred yards away—on the other side of the fence. But it gave Kennedy a target, a goal, a destination to reach. Walking and falling, walking and falling, he got close enough to hear chatter on the truck's radio.

The explosion had knocked over a section of the fence. Kennedy lay on top of it and rolled over it to the other side. He got to the truck and picked up the radio.

COLONEL MORRIS AND CAPTAIN SHORT were sitting in the mobile command post, parked at the end of the access road, talking to Little Rock on the radio. The mobile command post was a pickup truck with two rows of seats in the cab and a camper shell over the back. They both heard a voice on the radio say, "Help," and then realized it was Kennedy's.

English and Rossborough jumped into the backseat of the truck, and it took off. Short was driving, Morris giving the directions. He knew exactly where Kennedy was.

The four men in the mobile command post were the last ones at the site who could retrieve Kennedy—and Colonel Morris looked like hell. Dr. Mueller and a medic, Reginald Gray, were in the ambulance on Highway 65, taking care of Hukle. Everyone else was apparently at the grocery store in Damascus, manning roadblocks or en route to the hospital in Conway. English was eager to go back and find this young airman. Rossborough seemed fearless, but this was only his second visit to a Titan II launch complex. His first, about fifteen minutes earlier, had been to rescue Hukle and Devlin.

Short navigated around a deep crater in the road and then stopped the truck. The road was blocked by the slab of concrete that had almost crushed Devlin. They found Kennedy in the battered pickup near the fence and carried him out. He told them that Livingston was still alive, somewhere on the complex, and then asked Short to do him a favor.

"Captain," Kennedy said, "you have to call my wife."

Short promised that he would.

Kennedy looked pale. His face was covered with blood. He was having trouble breathing. None of the men were wearing gas masks, and they could smell oxidizer in the air. They had to get Kennedy out of there before searching for Livingston. They lifted Kennedy into the back of the pickup and drove back toward the highway.

A security police truck came toward them on the access road. Short slowed down but didn't stop. He stuck his head out the window and yelled, we've got Kennedy, Livingston is still on the complex, go down there and try to find him.

Roberts and Green had no idea who was in the truck, yelling at them. They didn't know what Livingston looked like or where he might be. But they were willing to look for him. Green thought about his six-year-old

boy, fast asleep at home, completely unaware of what his father was doing
right now.

As they neared the complex, a large cylindrical object appeared in
the road.

Well, damn, there's the warhead, Green thought. He carefully drove
around it.

Green stopped the truck, and they walked to the northeast section of
the complex, looking for a way to get through the fence. They didn't have
a flashlight. Green climbed onto a light-all unit and tried to point it toward
the fence, hoping to find a hole. It wouldn't budge.

The light-all unit was attached to a Dodge Power Wagon, and Green
had an idea: I'll drive this big pickup right through that fence.

Green climbed into the driver's seat. Someone had left the motor running. He put the engine into first gear and floored it. The truck smashed
into the fence, but the fence held. He backed up and tried again—still, no
luck. The fence was too strong, and the truck felt kind of sluggish. He got
out of the cab and noticed that all four tires had been blown out by the
explosion. It was running on rims.

Green thought that Roberts must have returned to their pickup truck.
He walked over to it, but nobody was there. He started the truck and followed the southern section of the fence, looking for a hole big enough to
drive through. But he couldn't find one, and the pickup got stuck on some
large pieces of cement. After ditching the truck, Green found a small hole
in the fence, entered the complex on foot, and started calling for Livingston and Roberts. Nobody replied. It was hard to see anything, with all
the smoke and dust. The lenses of his gas mask fogged up. He kept tripping over debris and falling down. He worried that something terrible had
happened, that Roberts had fallen into a hole and gotten badly hurt. Green
shouted for Livingston and Roberts and realized that he was lost.

JIM SANDAKER HAD BEEN DROPPED OFF at the access control point by
the two security officers, and he didn't plan to remain there for long. The
men who'd just returned with Kennedy said that Livingston was still alive

but the fumes were pretty strong at the complex. Sandaker looked around for a RFHCO suit, found one, and started to get into it.

Under the Category I rules, you needed at least one other person in RFHCO, as backup, whenever you put on the suit. Colonel Morris objected to Sandaker reentering the complex by himself.

Given the circumstances, Sandaker thought those rules were total bullshit. He was going to look for Livingston.

I'll go with you, Richard English said, claiming to have been trained to wear the suit.

Sandaker had a feeling that English was lying. He couldn't believe this old guy was going to put on a RFHCO suit. He worried that English would have a heart attack. Doing anything in a RFHCO was hard work; the whole outfit, with the air pack, weighed almost sixty pounds. The two men had never met, but Sandaker was glad not to be heading into the complex alone.

Colonel Jimmie D. Gray had returned to the site, after looking for water at a nearby farmhouse. Gray had started the night at the Little Rock command post, drove to 4-7 with food and supplies before the explosion, and stuck around after it. He helped Sandaker and English get into the RFHCO suits, and Rossborough drove them to the complex in the mobile command post. This time, he wore a gas mask.

Sandaker and English rode on the back of the truck, dangling their legs over the taillights. Rossborough dropped them off. The communications system on the complex no longer worked, and the two men wouldn't be able to talk to each other with the headsets inside their helmets. They agreed to signal with their flashlights if one of them got into trouble. They found the hole in the fence and walked through it. From a distance they looked like astronauts exploring a hostile planet.

JIMMY ROBERTS HADN'T SEEN or heard Green slamming the Dodge Power Wagon into the fence. He'd wandered off, searched through Colonel Morris's battered pickup for a flashlight, failed to find one, and stumbled upon a hole in the fence. Roberts climbed through it and, within minutes, felt completely lost. A couple of thoughts entered his mind: he didn't want to fall into a hole, and he didn't want that propane tank, hissing beside the road, to catch on fire and explode. He shouted for Livingston and Green, but got no response. He kept shouting their names—and then he heard someone reply.

"Okay, keep on yelling," Roberts said, "and I'll come to your voice."

About twenty feet from the access portal, Roberts found David Livingston lying on the ground. His face was bloody, and he had a wound in his abdomen. But Livingston was conscious and alert.

Roberts picked him up and started to carry him toward the fence. It wasn't easy to carry someone while breathing through a gas mask. Roberts started to feel dizzy, and his mask clouded up with sweat.

AT THE ACCESS CONTROL POINT, Don Green suddenly appeared in a pickup truck. Green got out of the truck, looking distraught, and said that Roberts was missing, that he may have fallen into a deep hole. Green needed a new gas mask, he needed to go back to the complex and find Roberts. The others thought Green was delirious, but he felt like they just didn't understand. His gas mask was clogged, he had to get a new one and find Roberts. Mueller gave Green a shot of Benadryl and persuaded him to sit down for a moment.

WALKING THROUGH THE COMPLEX, Sandaker felt scared. He'd been told to watch out for the warhead and its high explosives. Debris was scattered everywhere, and in the darkness you couldn't tell what any of it was. The explosion had stripped the concrete off steel rebar, and the rebar had been twisted into all kinds of strange shapes, looming out of the smoke. Sandaker had worked at 4-7 many times, but now nothing seemed familiar. The RFHCO helmet prevented him from calling out for English and Livingston. Within minutes, he was lost.

———

ROBERTS COULDN'T CARRY LIVINGSTON ANYMORE and put him on the ground.

Livingston pleaded with Roberts not to leave him.

"Look, we're going to make it out of here," Roberts said. "I'm going to have to carry you on my back."

Roberts carried Livingston on his back for a while, but then had to put him down again, unable to carry him another step. Roberts said that he'd go find help and promised to come right back.

"Please don't leave me," Livingston said.

Roberts picked him up again and put him on his back.

SANDAKER WANDERED THROUGH THE COMPLEX, looking for the access portal, but couldn't find it. He felt odd being lost in a place that he knew like the back of his hand. Sandaker spotted English, about thirty feet away. He was turning his flashlight on and off. That meant trouble.

English couldn't walk any farther in the RFHCO suit. He was exhausted and signaled to Sandaker that he was running out of air.

They turned around and tried to find their way out.

ROBERTS FEARED HE WAS ABOUT to pass out. He put Livingston down near the fence and promised to come back for him. He made his way to the battered pickup near the gate and saw two men in the distance wearing RFHCO suits. He flashed the headlights and honked the horn, but they didn't see him. And then Roberts saw another truck parked nearby. Someone was sitting in the front seat.

The door of the truck opened, and a man got out, with a flashlight. He was wearing a gas mask and a red bowling shirt.

Roberts thought, "Great."

Rossborough and Roberts reentered the complex, found Livingston, picked him up, and carried him out. They carried him through bushes and around debris. It felt like running an obstacle course in the dark. They got tired and had to put Livingston down.

As Sandaker and English took off their RFHCOs, they saw Rossborough and Roberts about twenty yards away. They ran over to help, carried Livingston to the truck, and gently lowered him into the back. Sandaker rode with his friend, while the others sat in the cab.

Livingston asked Sandaker not to tell his mother what had happened.

"Please don't tell my mother," he said, again and again.

ABOUT AN HOUR after the explosion, Colonel Jones and the rest of the Disaster Response Force returned to the access control point. Jones had been listening to Colonel Morris on the radio and suddenly thought: if he sounds OK back there, what am I doing in Damascus?

Mueller did the best he could to treat Kennedy in the ambulance. Kennedy was pale and thirsty and having difficulty breathing. Mueller started him on an IV and gave him some medicine to prevent pulmonary edema— an excess of fluid in the lungs that could be caused by oxidizer exposure. Kennedy also had a big hole in his right leg. His long johns reeked of rocket fuel, and Mueller cut them off.

Livingston arrived in the back of the pickup, and Mueller examined him there. In some ways, Livingston seemed to be in better shape than Kennedy. His face wasn't as pale, and he hadn't passed out. But the wound in his abdomen was deep. Pieces of concrete were lodged in there, and you could see his intestines. Mueller wanted to give him an IV but couldn't. The ambulance only had one.

Colonel Jones had already requested a helicopter to take Kennedy to the hospital. The command post in Little Rock said that the chopper was on its way. But there was no sign of it.

The helicopter had not yet departed from Little Rock Air Force Base. Its crew had been instructed to bring portable vapor detectors to 4-7. Nobody could find any, and the chopper sat there and waited, for more than half an hour, while people looked for the vapor detectors.

Jones couldn't understand why the helicopter hadn't arrived yet.

Kennedy and Livingston were in rough shape, and the ambulance wasn't equipped to deal with their injuries. Livingston needed an IV, right away. Jones told Colonel Morris that he was taking them to the hospital in Conway.

Hukle and Kennedy rode in the ambulance. Livingston remained in the back of the pickup truck with Sandaker, who kept him talking. And Colonel Jones led the way in a station wagon. The convoy had to drive slowly because Livingston was in so much pain.

The helicopter finally took off from Little Rock—without any vapor detectors, because none could be found. The pilot was told to meet the convoy at Launch Complex 374-6, near the town of Republican. But Jones and the others mistakenly drove past it. Instead they met the chopper at Launch Complex 374-5, outside Springhill. The chief of aerospace medicine at the base, another physician, and four medics immediately got to work on the injured men. Kennedy was given a shot of morphine, and Livingston finally got an IV. Sandaker said good-bye to them both, and the helicopter took off for Little Rock. It was five in the morning.

A couple of security police officers picked up Colonel Morris at the access control point and drove him to the hospital.

Colonel Jimmie Gray was the only person left at the site. He waited there, alone, as dawn approached, fires still burned, and the warhead lay somewhere in the dark.

Confirm or Deny

At the Redstone Arsenal in Huntsville, Alabama, Matthew Arnold was taught how to deactivate chemical and biological weapons. "Chlorine is your friend," the instructor told the class. The principal ingredient in household bleach would render almost every deadly pathogen, nerve agent, and blister agent harmless. That's good to know, Arnold thought. Although Redstone was an Army facility, he'd been sent there by the Air Force. The three-week course at Redstone was the first step toward becoming an Explosive Ordnance Disposal technician. Students were no longer exposed to nerve gas and then told to inject themselves with atropine—an exercise to build confidence that the antidote would work during a chemical attack. Instead, they were shown footage of a goat being exposed to a nerve agent and given an injection. The goat lived. But the film and the lectures at Redstone suggested how dangerous the work of an EOD technician could be, and a number of people dropped out.

The attrition rate was even higher among those students who, like Arnold, reached the next step—seven months of training, six days a week, at the Naval Explosive Ordnance Disposal School in Indian Head, Maryland. About one third of the students typically flunked out or quit, and only one fifth completed the course on his or her first try. The classes at Indian Head focused mainly on conventional weapons. EOD trainees were required to study every kind of ordnance used by every military in the world. The render safe procedures were similar for most munitions, regardless of their national origin: remove the fuze if it could easily be done, or just attach a small explosive charge to the weapon, retreat a safe distance, and blow it up.

Unlike the bomb squads run by law enforcement agencies, the Air Force EOD teams usually didn't care about preserving evidence. They were trained to get rid of the hazard, as quickly as possible, and then get out of the way. Arnold learned how to render safe all the conventional warheads, rockets, artillery shells, and bombs in the American arsenal. He also learned how to defuse the sort of handmade, improvised explosive devices used by terrorists groups like the Red Brigades and the Palestine Liberation Front. The handmade stuff could be tricky and unpredictable; the military ordnance, simpler but more powerful. An EOD technician had to approach both kinds with the same mental attitude—disciplined, thoughtful, patient, and calm.

Arnold performed well enough to enter Division Six, the program at Indian Head that taught students how to dismantle a nuclear weapon. The course began with a lesson on the dangers of radioactivity. Every class was shown the film of Louis Slotin dying from radiation sickness in 1946, after his criticality accident at Los Alamos. It was hard to watch. Slotin had been fully conscious and in enormous pain, as his skin swelled, changed color, blistered, and peeled away.

After learning how to use radiation detectors and calculate safe exposure times, the trainees became familiar with various nuclear weapon designs. At the time, the United States had about twenty-five different types—missiles, rockets, warheads, and bombs; artillery shells, depth charges, torpedoes, and mines; large weapons and small ones, atomic and thermonuclear. The most powerful were the Mark 53 bomb, delivered by aircraft, and the W-53 warhead carried by the Titan II. The least powerful was the Mark 54 Special Atomic Demolition Munition (SADM), with a yield of less than 1 kiloton. The SADM weighed only sixty pounds. It was known as a "suitcase bomb" or a "backpack bomb" because of the preferred methods of delivery. One person would carry the SADM and place it in the right spot. Another would set the timer, and then they'd both leave in a hurry.

The instructors at Division Six offered some basic tips on how to deal with a nuclear weapon that's been in an accident. The first thing you want to do, they said, is find out whether the case of the weapon has been compromised and whether any components have shifted inside it. If your gamma ray detector is showing high levels of radiation, you've got a serious problem. Gamma rays will pass right through your protective gear. If you can detect gamma rays from a distance, back away immediately. The weapon may have partially detonated—or it may be about to detonate. But if lives are at stake, calculate how long you can work at the accident site without getting too much gamma radiation.

Always wear a bunny suit, they said, when you walk up to the weapon for the first time. It's the yellow jumpsuit with the hood. And keep an eye on your alpha and beta meters. If they detect anything, that probably means the weapon's case has been compromised. The alphas are emitted by the nuclear core, the betas by the tritium gas used to boost it. Your bunny suit will block them, and the respirator will prevent you from inhaling them. And remember: never take off your mask, even if there's no sign of radiation, until you're sure that the "skull" of the weapon is intact. The skull is the beryllium reflector around the core. Inhaling beryllium dust can be worse than inhaling plutonium. Both of them can be lethal.

In addition to an alpha meter, a beta meter, a gamma meter, and a tritium meter, an EOD team relied on more prosaic tools to handle a nuclear weapon accident—screwdrivers, ratchets, wrenches, and pliers. The tools were made with metal alloys unlikely to create a spark. If the weapon looked capable of detonating, an EOD technician would open its case with a screwdriver. The most important goal, by far, was to isolate the power sources and ensure that electricity could not reach the detonators. The best way to do that was simply to disconnect the batteries and yank them out. Capacitors that had already charged could be short-circuited with the touch of a screwdriver. But if the X-unit had already charged, an EOD technician had to be very careful. A wrong move could trigger it and detonate the weapon.

Arnold practiced the render safe procedures on dummy weapons that were identical to the real thing—except for the high explosives and fissile material, which were fake. The job was a meticulous process of disassembly. You took the weapon apart, wrapped the parts in plastic, boxed them up, and got them ready for return shipment to the manufacturer. After months of training, Arnold passed all the tests at Indian Head and joined an EOD unit at Barksdale Air Force Base, outside Shreveport, Louisiana. He had learned how to defuse car bombs and biological weapons, to handle Broken Arrows and dismantle nuclear warheads. He was twenty years old.

WHEN SID KING GOT TO CLINTON, he hurried into the radio station and turned on the transmitter. KGFL was licensed to broadcast only during the daylight hours, but the Federal Communications Commission allowed a sunset station to go on the air during an emergency. King thought the explosion of an intercontinental ballistic missile qualified as one. Moments later, his wife arrived at the station, happy to see that he hadn't been killed. King described the blast to his listeners, and callers to the station shared what they'd seen. Soon the little studio at KGFL was crammed with people, as friends and neighbors gathered there, eager to find out what was going on.

The Air Force was refusing to disclose any information about the explosion. It would not explain what had just happened. It would not discuss the potential danger from toxic fumes. It would neither confirm nor deny that the Titan II was carrying a nuclear warhead. Journalists who called Little Rock Air Force Base were told to phone the headquarters of the Strategic Air Command in Omaha—and nobody at SAC headquarters would answer their questions. SAC headquarters wouldn't even tell Frank Wilson, the director of environmental services at the Arkansas Department of Health, if the accident had spread radioactive contamination. SAC wouldn't tell him anything. And so Wilson called a Department of Energy office in Albuquerque. An official there asked him to describe the explosion. Wilson mentioned the fireball and the sparkly thing that seemed to emerge from it. The DOE representative said that the missile probably did carry a nuclear warhead—and it sounded like the high explosives of the weapon had detonated, spreading fissile material. Unable to get any confirmation from SAC, the state of Arkansas sent employees to Van Buren County with radiation detectors.

The Air Force's silence helped to sow panic and confusion. More than a thousand people left their homes, got into their cars, and fled the area around Damascus. One caller to KGFL said that he was leaving town to stay with family in Fairfield, Illinois, about four hundred miles away. Other callers told of windows being blown out, doors knocked off hinges, an ominous dark cloud that passed over their homes. The cloud smelled like rotten eggs, burned their eyes, and made them cough. The refusal to acknowledge that the missile carried a nuclear weapon made the Air Force seem foolish. One of KGFL's listeners phoned the station and said that he'd found the radio frequency that SAC was using at the missile site. The conversations with the Little Rock command post weren't being scrambled. And the whereabouts of "the warhead" were being discussed.

AFTER TELLING THE TRUCKERS in Bee Branch to hit the road, Sheriff Anglin got back into his squad car and drove south on Highway 65 toward Damascus. He wanted to make sure that everybody within five miles of the silo had been evacuated. He stopped at a roadblock north of Launch Complex 374-7. The security police manning it were wearing gas masks.

"Hey, I need one of them masks," Anglin said.

"Oh, you don't need a mask," one of the officers replied, his voice muffled by the mask.

"Well, give me yours, if you don't need it."

Neither of them gave Anglin a gas mask, and he headed toward Damascus without one.

The chaos of the early-morning hours extended to the management of roadblocks. The Air Force had no legal authority to decide who could or couldn't drive on Arkansas roads. But SAC's failure to confer with state and local officials left a crucial question unanswered—who was in charge? At a roadblock south of 4-7, Air Force security officers refused to let journalists pass. Correspondents from the major television networks had arrived to cover the story, along with radio and newspaper reporters. Sheriff Anglin overruled the Air Force and allowed the media to park on the shoulder of Highway 65, across from the access road to the missile site. It was public property. Not long afterward a reporter for the Arkansas *Democrat* was stopped at the same roadblock by Air Force security officers and told that he couldn't drive any farther. The reporter pointed out that his newspaper's competitors had just been allowed up the road—and then drove around the roadblock without permission and headed toward 4-7, ignoring the soldiers with M-16s. An Air Force security truck pursued him at high speed but gave up the chase. And the correspondent for the *Democrat* joined the crowd of journalists near the access road, who were shouting questions at every Air Force vehicle that entered or left the site.

AFTER LOADING THE WOUNDED onto helicopters, Richard English and Colonel William Jones returned to 4-7. A convoy from Little Rock Air Force Base soon met them there. It brought specialized equipment and personnel that the Disaster Response Force lacked: portable vapor detectors, radiation detectors, bunny suits, fire trucks, firefighters, and an EOD unit.

A two-man radiation team traveled by helicopter to Launch Complex 374-6 and got a ride from a security police officer to 4-7, about ten miles away. Wearing protective gear, they walked down the access road in the dark, carrying alpha, beta, and gamma ray detectors. They went as far as the low hill overlooking the complex, found no evidence of radioactivity—a good sign—and walked back to the access control point near Highway 65.

English put on a bunny suit and prepared to search for the warhead. The suit was a lot lighter than the RFHCO he'd worn to find Livingston. English thought that he'd seen the warhead during one of his trips onto the complex. His second in command at Disaster Preparedness, Sergeant Franklin Moses, and the members of the EOD unit suited up, too. The half dozen members of the initial reconnaissance team, led by English, waited for permission from SAC headquarters to look for the weapon. The word came from Omaha: they could enter the complex at first light.

RODNEY HOLDER WAS STILL WEARING the T-shirt and old pants he'd put on to take a nap, just before the Klaxons sounded at 4-7. Almost twelve hours had passed since then, and it felt like a long night. Now Holder and Ron Fuller were sitting on the access road to Launch Complex 4-6, outside the town of Republican. They'd hitched a ride from a security police officer at the grocery store in Damascus, hoping to get back to the base in Little Rock. But the officer had gone to 4-6 to pick up a two-man radiation team. And the helicopter had taken off from 4-6 without waiting for Holder and Fuller. The chopper's departure left them with a couple of options. They could return to the scene of the accident with the radiation team—or stay on the access road at 4-6. The security officer lent Holder his coat and drove off. It was still dark, and the two men sat in the road, exhausted, waiting for someone to give them a ride.

At the Baptist Medical Center in Little Rock, doctors tried to save the lives of Jeff Kennedy and David Livingston. The two were put into the intensive care unit, placed on ventilators, and given high doses of corticosteroids. Oxidizer released by the blast had induced a dangerous form of respiratory distress. Both of the men were now suffering from pulmonary edema, as fluid filled their lungs. Kennedy's wife left their children with a friend and rushed to the hospital. A young woman came to see Livingston as well, telling one doctor that she was his wife, another that she was his sister. Colonel Michael J. Robertson—the chief of aerospace medicine at the base who'd treated the injured airmen aboard the helicopter—didn't care who she was. He was just glad that Livingston had someone there. The worst effects of the oxidizer would usually appear about five hours after exposure. Like the phosgene gas used as a chemical weapon during the First World War, the oxidizer could kill you in an extremely unpleasant way. It was known as "dry land drowning."

Matthew Arnold had been fast asleep when the phone rang at about half past three in the morning. The caller told him to report to the base: his EOD unit was heading into the field. The call came at a bad time. Arnold and his wife had just moved into a new apartment in Shreveport, and they'd stayed up late moving boxes. He'd gotten only a few hours of sleep. The place was full of boxes that still needed to be unpacked, and he didn't feel like going to work at three in the morning. When Arnold arrived at Barksdale, his squadron commander said that they were going to Arkansas—and nothing more. As the unit loaded its gear into a couple of pickup trucks and prepared to leave, Arnold felt guilty about leaving his wife to deal with the mess at home. He wouldn't be able to call her, tell her where he was going, or let her know how long he'd be gone.

The EOD team at Barksdale was part of the Strategic Air Command, and it responded to every accident involving SAC nuclear weapons in the eastern half of the United States. During Arnold's two and a half years as an EOD technician, the unit had spent most of its time on mundane assignments. When unexploded ordnance was found in the marshes surrounding the air base, his EOD squad would defuse it. Every so often, when a plane crashed, they'd render safe the bombs, starter cartridges, flare packages, rounds of ammunition, and ejection-seat rocket motors found in the wreckage. And when nothing else was happening, they'd practice taking apart and reassembling dummy weapons. But on a few occasions, Arnold responded to accidents that involved the real thing.

Twice at Barksdale, a load cart collapsed while transporting a rotary launcher full of Short-Range Attack Missiles. Each launcher held eight SRAMs, and the load carts had telescoping arms to lift the missiles into the bomb bay of a B-52. During both accidents, the telescoping arms broke, dropping the rotary launcher and the SRAMs about five feet to the ground. At least two warheads and half a dozen missiles were damaged. A manufacturing defect or corrosion seemed the most likely explanation for the collapse of the telescoping arms. But an Air Force investigation later found a different cause: maintenance crews had been goofing around with the load carts, out of sheer boredom, and using them to lift B-52 bombers off the ground.

In April 1979, Arnold's unit responded to a nuclear weapon accident a few miles north of Fort Worth, Texas. The accident was considered serious enough to require their presence urgently, in the middle of the night, and so they flew there in the only aircraft that was available: the base commander's C-135. The big jet was a lot plusher than the planes that usually carried Arnold's team. At Carswell Air Force Base, someone on a loading crew had ignored a tech order and pulled a handle too hard in the cockpit of a B-52. Instead of opening the bomb bay doors, he'd inadvertently released a B-61 hydrogen bomb. It fell about seven feet and hit the runway. When members of the loading crew approached the weapon, they saw that its parachute pack had broken off—and that a red flag had appeared in a little window on the casing. The bomb was armed. Arnold's team arrived at the base, removed a small panel from the casing, and rotated a switch with a wrench. A green flag replaced the red one in the little window; the bomb was safed. The whole procedure took about an hour, and Arnold's unit flew back to Barksdale on their usual means of air transportation, a cargo plane.

The prospect of having to render safe a W-53 warhead didn't make Arnold nervous. The core of the W-53 contained highly enriched uranium, not plutonium, largely eliminating the inhalation hazard and the risk of radioactive contamination. He'd visited Titan II launch complexes, practiced on dummy versions of the weapon. And at Indian Head, he'd been taught that nuclear weapons were almost impossible to detonate accidentally. The safety mechanisms had always worked, even during plane crashes and fires; the high explosives were said to pose the greatest threat to EOD teams. Arnold's unit handled nuclear weapons all the time, and they rarely thought about the destructive force that could be unleashed. EOD technicians sat on nuclear weapons, casually leaned against them, used them as tables during lunch breaks. But one of Arnold's commanders was too cocky and nonchalant. He once removed a dummy weapon from a storage bunker in broad daylight, put it into the back of his pickup truck, covered it with a tarp, drove right past security, and disassembled it in front of his girlfriend. Arnold thought the move was stupid and irresponsible, as well as a major breach of security. Inside the bunker, the dummy weapons were stored beside the real ones.

THE RECONNAISSANCE TEAM LEFT the access control point just after sunrise. The search for the warhead didn't take long. Richard English led them to a spot, about two hundred yards east of the silo, where he thought he'd seen the weapon's outline in the dark. And there it was, lying in a shallow ditch, right next to the access road. The pickup trucks driving back and forth after the accident, the men stumbling in the darkness, had passed within a few feet of it.

Alpha radiation was detected directly on top of the weapon, but nowhere else on the complex.

The ensuing conversation between Air Force personnel at the site and the Little Rock command post could be overheard by anyone with a shortwave radio:

"It's laying in a ditch beside, you know, it's not even up close. It blew out. It's laying in a ditch. It's all exposed, and all we need to do is go in and get it."

"Okay, I'd recommend that we wait for those people that are going to arrive in about an hour."

"Fine with me."

IN A HOT SPRINGS HOTEL ROOM, Senator David Pryor and Vice President Walter Mondale were briefed on the Titan II accident. The Democratic Party's state convention began later that morning, and the vice president was scheduled to give the opening speech. Reporters would be asking questions about the accident, and Mondale wanted to be prepared. Three SAC officers who'd come from Little Rock described the dropping of the socket, the piercing of the missile's skin, the long wait through the night, the futile attempt to reenter the control center, the explosion. But they refused to disclose whether the Titan II had been carrying a warhead. SAC headquarters had instructed them neither to confirm nor deny the presence of a nuclear weapon.

Mondale picked up the phone and called the secretary of defense, Harold Brown—who wouldn't tell him, either.

"Goddamn it, Harold, I'm the vice president of the United States," Mondale said.

Brown told him the missile had a nuclear warhead.

BEFORE TAKING A HELICOPTER to the launch complex, Bob Peurifoy and the rest of the Accident Response Group met with SAC officials at Little Rock Air Force Base. General James E. Light, Jr., had already seen the warhead. Light was the deputy chief of staff for logistics at SAC headquarters. He'd flown to Arkansas, taken a chopper to the accident site, inspected the damage, and returned to the Little Rock command post for this meeting. Light said that the reentry vehicle was remarkably intact, given the size of the explosion.

Peurifoy didn't like hearing that bit of information. The W-53's arming and fuzing system, along with its batteries, were attached to the base of the reentry vehicle. And if they were intact, the weapon still had the potential to detonate.

General Light also said that the EOD unit from Barksdale had arrived at the scene, dug a hole under the warhead, wrapped a chain around it, and planned to yank it out of the ditch. But Light had told them not to do anything until the scientists from Los Alamos and Sandia gave their approval.

Peurifoy and William Chambers, who was representing Los Alamos, knew right away that they'd like General Light. He'd made the correct decision. The Air Force was eager to get the weapon out of that ditch as quickly as possible. A crowd of journalists had assembled near the access road on Highway 65, and a small plane carrying a photographer had already flown over the launch complex. But Peurifoy and Chambers thought there was no need to rush the dismantling of America's most powerful thermonuclear warhead. Chambers knew a fair amount about the subject. He'd responded to the Broken Arrow at Palomares, advised the recovery effort at Thule, written EOD manuals for nuclear weapons, and helped to create the Nuclear Emergency Search Team (NEST), a secretive group that handled threats of nuclear terrorism within the United States. None of the work at Los Alamos and NEST had made Chambers feel anxious—not the weapon accidents, not the ransom note warning of a 20-kiloton bomb in Manhattan, not the warning of a terrorist attack on America's bicentennial celebrations in 1976. He'd served with General George S. Patton's Third

Army during the Second World War, and the genuine horrors that he saw on the battlefield tempered his fear of hypothetical ones.

From the air, the launch complex looked like it had been hit by a bomb. The Accident Response Group traveled to the site by helicopter, and Peurifoy wondered about the condition of the warhead's electrical system, his area of expertise. The moment he saw the weapon, Peurifoy thought: Well, my job here is done. General Light had used the wrong term to describe what was lying in the ditch. The "reentry vehicle" wasn't intact—it was gone, nowhere to be seen, no doubt blown to pieces by the explosion. The warhead lay there by itself, stripped of the electrical power source necessary for a nuclear detonation. But that W-53 was looking pretty good, considering what it had been through. It was still, essentially, in one piece. The outer cover of the primary had been torn off—you could see the detonator cables, the high explosives, the tubing, wiring, capacitors. And the secondary was loose; it no longer sat directly below the primary, like a metal garbage can under a silver basketball. The damage was impressively slight, however, for an object that had flown through a fireball, climbed more than a thousand feet into the air, and hit the ground without a parachute.

Chambers walked over to a nearby Pettibone crane, a mobile all-terrain vehicle that was ready to lift the weapon from the ditch, and drained hydraulic fluid from it. He poured the oil into the holes and cracks of the warhead, coating the high explosives and making them less likely to be set off by a random spark—the kind of spark that might be generated by a chain wrapped around the metal casing of a nuclear warhead. Chambers wanted to know exactly what had happened inside the warhead before anyone tried to move it or take it apart. An X-ray would reveal the amount of damage, but the Accident Response Group hadn't brought a portable X-ray unit to Arkansas. Until the damage could be properly assessed, Chambers said that nothing should be done. The Air Force had suffered enough embarrassment already. Another accident with this weapon could kill people and spread radioactive tritium, with a pack of journalists literally down the road.

When Matthew Arnold heard about the decision to do nothing until the weapon was X-rayed, he thought it was ridiculous. It was bullshit. It meant his unit would have to sit around in Arkansas for at least another day or two. These civilians don't know what they're talking about, he thought. They're being overly cautious. The warhead doesn't look that bad, and the render safe procedures wouldn't be complicated. They were right out of the book.

We're ready to rock-and-roll, Arnold told his EOD commander. This is what we train for, day after day. These eggheads should just get out of the way and let us go to work. Let's get the weapon out of here and go home.

Arnold wasn't allowed anywhere near the warhead. Instead, he was sent onto the launch complex to look for the remnants of retrorockets and other explosives carried by the Titan II. He'd lost his cool, and he knew it. Someone else should do the render safe, Arnold agreed—his mind was too preoccupied with the recent move, the unpacked boxes, the mess waiting for him at home. He wasn't on top of his game. And much as Arnold hated to admit it, the guy from Los Alamos was probably right.

IN THE PARKING LOT of the hospital at Little Rock Air Force Base, Al Childers was told to take off his clothes. He was contaminated with radiation, according to the alpha detector being used to screen everyone who'd been at 4-7. One of the detectors at the hospital didn't work at all, and the other kept finding traces of alpha particles. A line of naked men stood in front of Childers, preparing for a rudimentary form of decontamination. They were sprayed with cold water from a garden hose before being allowed into the emergency room. Childers got angry. He'd just come from the hospital in Conway, after making sure that the injured airmen would receive treatment there. He'd pulled a muscle in his back helping to carry Devlin from the field. He didn't think these alpha readings were accurate. And he couldn't believe that the hospital was forcing people to strip in the parking lot, while reporters and photographers stood nearby. Childers told the hospital staff to set up a screen or something for a little privacy. This was a harsh welcome home for men who'd had a rough night.

The water from the garden hose felt incredibly cold.

The doctors gave Childers a muscle relaxant for his back and admitted him to the hospital. He was planning to go home later that day, hug his wife, and get some sleep. Instead he was told to get dressed and return to the launch complex. The emergency war order checklists and other classified material had to be retrieved from the safe in the control center. Childers couldn't understand why his missile crew commander, Mazzaro, hadn't been asked to do it. But as deputy commander, Childers was responsible for the material, as well. Feeling a bit groggy and wearing the dirty uniform that had just been deemed radioactive, he was driven back to 4-7.

In the early-morning light Childers saw the scale of the destruction for the first time—and realized his life had been spared by sheer luck. The explosion had blown most of the debris toward the west, some of it landing almost half a mile from 4-7. Enormous pieces of steel and concrete lay in the fields of nearby farms. The silo door had been thrown more than two hundred yards, shearing off the tops of trees before crashing into the woods northwest of the complex. The door weighed about 150,000 pounds. Had the debris been blown to the east, toward Highway 65, it would have killed a lot of people.

Driving down the access road, Childers was amused when he saw where the warhead had landed. The object that he'd thought to be the warhead was actually a nitrogen accumulator—a large steel tank, tossed into the road, that looked like the weapon. While yelling for Silas Spann to get away from the tank, afraid that it was the warhead, Childers had been standing right next to the warhead.

Near the entrance to the complex, the road was blocked by debris. Childers and his escorts entered on foot. Smoke still drifted from the silo. The blast had obliterated its upper levels and widened the hole in the ground. What had once been a deep, concrete cylinder now looked like a huge funnel, with a rough edge of rocks and dirt. Security police officers seemed to be everywhere, guarding the site and searching through the wreckage. Childers entered through the access portal, walking down the stairs as Kennedy and Livingston had done earlier that morning. It was dark, and some of the walls and floors were charred. But Childers was impressed that you could still walk through the blast doors and blast locks, that the place was there at all.

The control center felt eerie, like a dark, abandoned basement. Everything was exactly as they'd left it. The Coke that Childers had been drinking was still in its cup. The tech orders and tech manuals were still in their plastic binders, propped open on the floor—none of them had been knocked over by the explosion. The door of the safe was still slightly open, and the classified documents inside it hadn't moved so much as an inch. Childers and Holder had been right. They'd been right. They could have stayed in the control center. They could have monitored the tank pressures, remained in touch with the command post, turned equipment on or off. And they would have been just fine.

IN THE ABSENCE OF ANY INFORMATION from the Air Force, officials from the Arkansas Department of Health and the Pollution Control and Ecology Department performed their own tests, looking for signs of radiation and oxidizer. About a dozen people in Guy, Arkansas, claimed to have been sickened by toxic fumes. Guy was about six miles from the missile complex. The small town hadn't been evacuated, and its mayor, Benny Mercer, was among those feeling ill. Everyone seemed to be angry about the federal government's response. "The Air Force wouldn't tell us a damn thing when it happened," a member of the Office of Emergency Services told the *Democrat*, "and they still won't." Gary Gray, the sheriff of nearby Pulaski County, said that he learned more from the radio than from the Air Force. Sam Tatom, the state's director of public safety, tried to enter the missile site and speak with the commanding officer there, but security police stopped Tatom on the access road, not far from Highway 65.

Governor Bill Clinton found himself in a difficult spot. He had to pacify his own officials, reassure the public, and limit his criticism of the Carter administration, six weeks before the presidential election. After taking a call from Sheriff Gus Anglin, who let him know how poorly everything had been handled, Clinton urged the Air Force to release more details about the accident—and praised its leadership for doing "the best they could." Vice President Mondale spoke to journalists at the Democratic convention in Hot Springs, accompanied by Governor Clinton, Senator Pryor, and Congressman Bill Alexander. Mondale would neither confirm nor deny the presence of a nuclear warhead. But Alexander was willing to state the obvious. "I assume they're armed," he said about the Titan IIs in Arkansas. "That's why they're here."

AT FOUR IN THE AFTERNOON, the secretary of the Air Force, Hans Mark, held a press conference at the Pentagon. Mark was a physicist, a nuclear engineer, and an expert in aerospace technology who'd previously led a research institute at NASA. Mark was the ideal person to explain the inner workings not only of the Titan II but also of the W-53 warhead. He'd been a rocket scientist and a weapon designer. As secretary of the Air Force, Mark provided the Carter administration's view of the accident.

"I believe that the Titan missile system is a perfectly safe system to operate, just as I believe that the 747 aircraft is a perfectly safe aircraft to operate," Mark told the press. "Accidents happen."

When reporters suggested that the Titan II was dangerous, obsolete, and poorly maintained, Mark said that the problem in Damascus hadn't been caused by equipment failure or a maintenance lapse—it was just an accident, and human error was solely to blame. He refused to answer any questions about the warhead, not even to correct an erroneous claim that plutonium might have been spread by the blast. The explosion was "pretty much the worst case" of what could happen at a Titan II site, he argued. Nobody was killed, no radioactive contamination had occurred, and the only people who got hurt were members of "the emergency teams whose job it is to take these risks." Unless a more detailed investigation proved otherwise, Mark thought that "the emergency procedures worked properly."

A COUPLE OF HOURS LATER, David Livingston died at Baptist Medical Center in Little Rock. He'd celebrated his twenty-second birthday the previous week. He was planning to marry his girlfriend in the spring, perhaps leave the Air Force and move to California. She was at the hospital when he passed away; his parents were on an airplane, en route from Ohio, to see him. The official cause of death was pulmonary edema.

Jeff Kennedy remained in the intensive care unit, fighting for every breath.

THE CROWD OF JOURNALISTS in front of the access road swelled on September 20, a full day after the blast. Sid King was impressed by the large truck that a new television network had driven to Damascus. The Cable News Network (CNN) had gone on the air a few months earlier. It was the first television network to offer the news twenty-four hours a day, and the Titan II accident in Damascus was its first big, breaking story. The CNN truck, boasting a huge satellite dish, dwarfed the little Live Ear. CNN correspondent Jim Miklaszewski provided nonstop coverage from the missile site—and broadcast the only images of what appeared to be the warhead, lying on the ground, beneath a blue tarp. To get the shot, Miklaszewski and his cameraman borrowed a cherry picker from a local crew installing phone lines, and rode the cab fifty feet into the air. The Air Force tried, without success, to block their view.

The Titan II explosion fit perfectly with the media narrative inspired by the nuclear accident at Three Mile Island, the taking of American hostages in Iran, and the Carter administration's failed attempt to rescue those hostages. The United States seemed to have become weak, timid, incompetent. And the "official" version of events was never to be trusted. Although Pentagon rules allowed the disclosure of information about a nuclear weapon after an accident, "as a means of reducing or preventing widespread public alarm," the Air Force wouldn't release any details about the warhead in Damascus. When General Lloyd Leavitt threatened to end a press conference in Little Rock if anyone asked another question about the warhead, whose existence had already been televised on CNN, the whole issue became a joke. A newspaper cartoon depicted three Air Force officers: one covering his eyes, one plugging his ears, and one covering his mouth. "If you're on the military's side, you can claim that the system worked because the nuclear warhead didn't go off," columnist Art Buchwald wrote. "If you live in the area, you may find it hard to sell your house."

The Soviet Union claimed that the Titan II explosion could have been mistaken for a surprise attack and precipitated "a nuclear conflict." Senator Pryor and two Republican senators, Bob Dole and Barry Goldwater, demanded a new investigation of the Titan II missile system. "If it's not safe and effective, I don't know why you need it," Dole said.

THE ACCIDENT RESPONSE GROUP examined the interior of the warhead with the aid of a "pig"—a highly radioactive block of cobalt-60 in a lead box. A sheet of photographic film was placed on one side of the weapon, the pig was put on the other, and the box was opened briefly with a lanyard. Everyone stayed a respectful distance from the pig until the box was shut. The device offered a simple but effective means of taking an X-ray, and it revealed that the warhead was safe to move. Contrary to protocol, the EOD unit from Little Rock was asked to render safe the weapon. Matthew Arnold's team from Barksdale had to stand and watch as EOD technicians who didn't even belong to the Strategic Air Command separated the primary from the secondary at 4-7, hidden from CNN's cameras by a tent. The two sections of the warhead were loaded into separate jet engine containers filled with sand. The containers were lifted onto a flatbed truck, and the truck left the complex as part of a convoy early in the morning on September 22.

"Hey, Colonel, is that what you won't confirm or deny?" a reporter shouted at one of the passengers, as the truck turned onto Highway 65.

The officer smiled for the cameras and gave a thumbs-up.

The End

Ronald Reagan didn't feel despair about the future, suffer from a crisis of confidence, or doubt the greatness of the United States. His optimism had tremendous appeal to a nation that seemed in decline. Reagan soundly defeated Jimmy Carter in the presidential election, winning the popular vote by about 10 percent and receiving almost ten times the number of electoral votes. The Republican Party gained control of the Senate and drove four Democratic governors from office—including Bill Clinton, who lost a close race to his conservative opponent. At the age of thirty-four, Clinton became the youngest ex-governor in the United States. The election of 1980 marked a cultural shift, a rejection of liberalism, big government, and the self-critical, apologetic tone that had dominated American foreign policy since the end of the Vietnam War. The new sense of patriotism and nationalism appeared to have an immediate effect. As President Reagan concluded his inaugural address on January 20, 1981, the fifty-two Americans who'd been held hostage for more than a year were released by the government of Iran.

"Peace through strength" had been one of Reagan's campaign slogans, and his administration soon began the largest peacetime military buildup in the history of the United States. Over the next five years, America's defense budget would almost double. And the arms race with the Soviet Union would be deliberately accelerated—out of a belief that the United

States could win it. Reagan opposed not only détente, but every arms control agreement that the United States had signed with the Soviet Union. In a 1963 speech, he said that President Kennedy's foreign policy was "motivated by fear of the bomb" and that "in an all-out race our system is stronger, and eventually the enemy gives up the race as a hopeless cause." The following year Reagan described the Soviets as "the most evil enemy that has ever faced mankind." His views on the subject remained largely unchanged for the next two decades. He was the first president since Woodrow Wilson who sincerely believed that American military power could bring an end to communism in the Soviet Union.

Most of Reagan's foreign policy advisers belonged to the Committee on the Present Danger, and they pushed for bold nuclear policies. The counterforce strategy once proposed by Robert McNamara—long associated with RAND and the youthful self-confidence of the early Kennedy administration—was now embraced by conservative Republicans. But the word "counterforce" had become problematic. It sounded aggressive and implied the willingness to fight a nuclear war. Much the same strategy was now called "damage limitation." By launching a nuclear attack on Soviet military targets, the United States might "limit the damage" to its own territory and, perhaps, emerge victorious.

The new secretary of defense, Caspar "Cap" Weinberger, was, like McNamara, a businessman who'd served in the Army during the Second World War but knew little about nuclear weapons. As a result, his undersecretary of defense for policy, Fred Iklé, played an important role in the Reagan administration's strategic decisions. Iklé was still haunted by the possibility that deterrence might fail—through an accident, a miscalculation, the actions of a fanatic in the Kremlin. And if that happened, millions of Americans would die. Iklé considered the all-or-nothing philosophy of "assured destruction" to be profoundly immoral, a misnomer more accurately described as "assured genocide." Aiming nuclear weapons at civilian populations threatened a "form of warfare universally condemned since the Dark Ages—the mass killing of hostages." He pushed the Reagan administration to seek a nuclear strategy that would deter the Soviets from attacking or blackmailing the United States, maintain the ability to fight a "protracted nuclear war," limit American damage if that war occurred, and end the war on terms favorable to the United States. A blind faith in mutual deterrence, Iklé believed, was like a declaration of faith during the Portuguese Inquisition—"an *auto-da-fé,* an act that ends in a mass burning."

Two Air Force reports on the Titan II were released to the public in January 1981. One assessed the overall safety of the missile, and the other provided a lengthy account of the accident at Damascus. According to the Eighth Air Force Missile Accident Investigation Board, Launch Complex 374-7 and its Titan II were destroyed by three separate explosions. The first occurred when fuel vapor ignited somewhere inside the complex. The vapor could have been ignited by a spark from an electric motor, by a leak from the stage 1 oxidizer tank, or by the sudden collapse of the missile. A small explosion was followed by a much larger one, as the stage 1 oxidizer tank ruptured, allowing thousands of gallons of fuel and oxidizer to mix. The blast wave from this explosion tore apart the upper half of the silo, tossed the silo door two hundred yards, and launched the second stage of the Titan II into the air. The door was already gone by the time the missile left the silo. The second stage soared straight upward, carrying the warhead, and then briefly flew parallel to the ground. Its rocket engine had been shoved into its fuel tank by the blast. Fuel and oxidizer leaked, causing the third explosion, producing a massive fireball, and hurling the warhead into the ditch.

The accident investigation board determined the sequence of events by examining the fragmentation patterns of the missile and silo debris. Pieces of the second stage were found almost half a mile from the silo, while most of the first stage was scattered within three hundred feet of it. The narrative offered by the report was factual and thorough. But the Air Force seemed more interested in describing how the accident unfolded than in establishing why it happened. "It may not be important whether the immediate cause that initiated the explosive events is precisely known," the board argued, "since, over a period of time, there were so many potential ignition sources available. . . ."

The Titan II Weapon System Review Group report was prepared for members of Congress. The report contained a number of criticisms and a long list of recommendations for making the missile safer. It said that the vapor detectors in Titan II silos were broken 40 percent of the time, that the portable vapor detectors rarely worked, that the radio system at launch complexes was unreliable and needed to be replaced, that missile combat crews should be discouraged from evacuating the control center during an emergency, that the shortage of RFHCO suits often forced maintenance teams to be selected on the basis of who'd fit into the available suits instead of who knew how to do a particular job, that the suits and helmets were obsolete, that the air packs were obsolete, that some of the missile's spare parts were either hard to obtain or no longer manufactured, that security police officers should always be provided with maps, that lightning arrestors and other "modern safing features" should be added to the W-53 warhead so that it would meet "modern nuclear safety criteria for abnormal environments." The report also said that having a warning siren at every launch complex might be useful. The Titan II missile system was "potentially hazardous," the Air Force concluded, but "basically safe" and "supportable now and in the foreseeable future."

Jeff Kennedy was angered by both of the reports. He'd spent weeks in the hospital, battling the damage to his respiratory system, and credited a young pulmonologist, Dr. James S. Anderson—not the Air Force—for saving his life. Anderson had sat at Kennedy's bedside for almost forty hours straight, forcing him to cough up phlegm and clear his lungs. And Anderson had to improvise the treatment for nitrogen tetroxide exposure, since guidance in the medical literature was scarce and nobody from the Air Force would speak to him, for three days after the accident, about the oxidizer or its harmful effects.

The reports were part of a cover-up, Kennedy thought: the Air Force cared more about preserving the image of the Titan II missile than protecting the lives of its own men. The accident investigation board said that Kennedy and Livingston were never ordered to turn on the fan in the launch complex. "Do not operate the switch," Sergeant Michael Hanson told them over the radio, according to the accident report. "Just go to the switch and stand by."

Kennedy thought the report was wrong. He and Livingston had both heard the order to turn on the fan. Livingston had signaled that he'd go back down and do it; that was one of Kennedy's last memories before the explosion. Turning on the fan wasn't part of their original checklist. It was Hanson's idea. Hanson had suggested it earlier in the evening, while Kennedy and others were arguing that all the electricity should be shut off. And Kennedy had absolutely no doubt that a spark from the fan had caused the explosion. But now Hanson was saying that an order to turn on the fan had never been given, and Colonel Morris was backing Hanson, making the source of ignition seem like some great big mystery. You didn't need to be a rocket scientist, Kennedy thought, to figure out why the missile exploded. Livingston obeyed the order, turned on the fan—and seconds later the whole place blew up. And the man who was killed by the error was now being blamed for it.

Livingston's death deeply affected Kennedy. They were close friends, and his death seemed completely unnecessary. Kennedy thought that his commanders at SAC had made a series of mistakes—the decision to evacuate the control center, the refusal to open the silo door and vent the fuel vapor, the endless wait to reenter the complex, the insistence upon using the access portal instead of the escape hatch, the order to turn on the fan. Worst of all was the feeling that he and Livingston had risked their lives for nothing—and then been abandoned. Livingston had lain on the ground for more than an hour, without his helmet, inhaling oxidizer, before anyone came to help. And the delay in sending a helicopter was incomprehensible.

The morale among the PTS crews at Little Rock Air Force Base was terrible. Airman David Powell, who'd dropped the socket that hit the missile, blamed himself for Livingston's death. A number of PTS technicians refused to work on Titan II missiles, citing the danger of the job, and their security clearances were revoked. Drug and alcohol use increased. The commander of the 308th Strategic Missile Wing, Colonel John Moser, was abruptly reassigned to a desk job at Fort Ritchie in Maryland, overseeing the monthly replacement of computer tapes for the SIOP—a career-ending move. Moser was well liked, and he hadn't made the crucial decisions that led to the explosion. Nobody at SAC headquarters was fired. Many of the enlisted men in the 308th thought the Air Force was scapegoating the little guys in order to hide problems with the Titan II and protect the top brass.

A few weeks after the accident investigation board's report was made public, Jeff Kennedy was served with a formal letter of reprimand by the Air Force. It rebuked him for violating the two-man rule and entering the control center at 4-7 without permission. No mention was made of the valuable information he'd obtained there or the bravery he'd displayed trying to save the missile. Air Force regulations permitted a violation of the two-man rule during an emergency, if lives were at risk. But Kennedy wasn't granted an exemption from the rule. His punishment sent a clear message: the rowdy, hell-raising culture of the PTS crews would no longer be tolerated. They were held responsible for what had gone wrong, not aging equipment or the decisions made at SAC headquarters. And to enforce strict discipline, an officer now accompanied a PTS crew everywhere, like a babysitter, whenever it visited a missile site.

David Powell was given an Article 15 citation—"dereliction of duty"—for attaching the socket to the wrong tool. Powell thought that if he accepted the charge, he'd be admitting negligence and assuming responsibility for the accident. Powell refused to sign and faced the risk of a court-martial instead, where he could defend himself before a panel of military judges. The Air Force didn't seek a court-martial and gave him a lesser punishment.

Jeff Kennedy had planned to spend the rest of his career in the Strategic Air Command; now he desperately wanted to leave it. Kennedy applied for a medical discharge, hoping to return home and attend college in Maine. The Air Force balked at the request, despite his injuries. Kennedy was sent to Lackland Air Force Base in San Antonio, Texas, for a medical evaluation. He was placed in the psychiatric ward there—along with Greg Devlin, who was also pursuing a medical disability claim.

Devlin had torn his Achilles tendon, suffered burns on his face, neck, back, and hands. He spent ten days at a Little Rock hospital recovering from the skin grafts. But the Air Force was not pleased with Devlin. He'd spoken to reporters about the accident, without SAC's permission. And he'd filed a $1.5 million lawsuit against the manufacturer of the Titan II, Martin Marietta; members of the armed forces cannot sue the federal government for damages after an injury. David Livingston's family and Rex Hukle had also decided to sue Martin Marietta. One of the attorneys suing the defense contractor, Bill Carter, was an Air Force veteran and a former Secret Service agent who hoped to obtain compensation for his clients—and to establish in court that the Titan II missile system was unsafe. Carter owned a farm near Damascus and had represented a neighbor sickened by the oxidizer leak there in 1978. During that case, the surgeon general of the Air Force had denied that inhaling oxidizer was bad for you, claiming it was "a substance no more dangerous than smog."

Devlin could not believe that he and Kennedy had been confined in a mental ward, after everything they'd been through. The place was full of crazy people, like a scene from *One Flew Over the Cuckoo's Nest.* Devlin already felt shunned by the Air Force. After returning to duty, he'd been put to work selling hot dogs at the base—a job usually reserved for airmen caught with illegal drugs or facing a dishonorable discharge. But selling hot dogs was preferable to staying in a loony bin. Kennedy would have none of it. He told the staff to release them immediately and move them to a different wing at the hospital—or he'd contact the press. They were promptly transferred. After being examined by physicians, Kennedy was denied a medical discharge, and Devlin was denied a full medical disability. It would have allowed him to use Air Force hospitals for the rest of his life.

A few months later, at a ceremony in Little Rock, both men were given an Airman's Medal for Heroism, the highest peacetime honor that the Air Force can bestow. Kennedy didn't want to accept it. But his local congressman in Maine, David Emery, said that if he took the medal, the Air Force would allow him to leave. Kennedy was given the medal by Verne Orr, the secretary of the Air Force, in a room full of reporters. Airman's Medals were also given to Rex Hukle, Don Green, Jimmy Roberts, and David Livingston's father. Intended to boost morale, the award ceremony was dismissed by the PTS crews. They thought it was a public relations stunt—and couldn't understand why Jim Sandaker, who'd returned to the launch complex twice after the accident, didn't get the highest honor, too.

Jeff Kennedy was granted a "temporary medical leave by reason of disability" three days after receiving his medal. Although the Air Force could recall him to duty in the future, Kennedy's military career was essentially over. He moved back to Maine, sued Martin Marietta for $7.5 million, and settled out of court for a much smaller sum.

Greg Devlin also left the Air Force within days of receiving the Airman's Medal. His term of enlistment was over. And his lawsuit was settled out of court, as well. After attorney fees, court costs, and other charges were deducted, Devlin got a check for $6,400.

THE ACCIDENTS AT GRAND FORKS and Damascus had occurred during the same week, and Bob Peurifoy hoped that they would prompt a serious interest in weapon safety at the Pentagon. He traveled to Washington, D.C., and briefed a group of Air Force officials on the design flaws that could detonate a Mark 28 hydrogen bomb during a fire—and the need to retrofit the bombs with new safety mechanisms. The Air Force inspector general and the head of the Air Force Directorate of Nuclear Safety attended the meeting. But it had little effect. A study commissioned by the Air Force later questioned the possibility of an accidental detonation and argued that the Mark 28 didn't need to be removed from bombers on alert. The study did, however, urge the Air Force to "expedite the proposed retrofit of the 28 and, in the meantime, take extraordinary steps to prevent and ameliorate fires that might involve the unmodified 28s." Neither of those recommendations was followed.

The Department of Defense had made its spending priorities clear: safety modifications on older weapons like the Mark 28, while desirable, could wait. But Peurifoy was determined to keep fighting the nuclear bureaucracy—and he was willing to engage in a bit of devious behavior, on behalf of weapon safety. After almost twenty years of fierce resistance, the Strategic Air Command had finally agreed to put locks in its bombs. The installation of permissive action links would require new control boxes in the cockpits of SAC's bombers. Under a contract with the Department of Energy, those new control boxes would be produced by Sandia. Peurifoy quietly arranged for a unique signal generator to be installed in the boxes, along with the coded switch necessary to unlock the PALs. The officials at the Air Force Logistics Command who handled the contract may or may not have understood the purpose of this special, added feature. It allowed all of SAC's bombers to carry nuclear weapons employing the latest safety devices. The planes would soon be ready—and now Peurifoy had to find a way to get those devices into the weapons.

THE REAGAN ADMINISTRATION'S military buildup was expected to cost approximately $1.5 trillion during its first five years. About $250 billion would be spent on nuclear weapon systems. By the end of the 1980s, the United States would have about fourteen thousand strategic warheads and bombs, an increase of about 60 percent. The Navy would get new cruise missiles and Trident submarines. The Air Force would get new cruise missiles, two new strategic bombers, and one hundred long-range MX missiles, now renamed "the Peacemaker." The Carter administration's plan to hide MX missiles amid thousands of square miles in the American Southwest was soon abandoned. Instead, the missiles would be deployed in existing silos—defeating their original purpose and leaving them vulnerable to attack. The only military use of the Peacemaker would be a first strike on the Soviet Union.

The Army's Pershing II missiles and land-based cruise missiles were among the most controversial weapons proposed by the Reagan administration. They were to be placed in Western Europe, as a counterbalance to the SS-20 missiles recently deployed by the Soviet Union. The SS-20 was not considered a "strategic" weapon—and therefore not covered by existing arms control agreements—because its range was only three thousand miles. An SS-20 missile couldn't reach targets in the continental United States. But its three warheads could destroy NATO bases and European cities. The Army's cruise and Pershing II missiles were intended as a nuclear tit for tat. And yet the Soviet Union considered their deployment extremely provocative. The Pershing II had a range of about a thousand miles and an accuracy of about two hundred feet. From bases in West Germany the Pershing II could destroy command centers in Moscow within five or six minutes. It would give the United States the capability to launch a "super-sudden first strike."

The new missiles, bombers, and subs gained the most attention in the press. But the "highest priority element" of Reagan's strategic modernization program was the need to improve the command-and-control system. "This system must be foolproof in case of any foreign attack," Reagan said. A handful of limited-war options would finally be included in the SIOP, and the ability to fight a protracted nuclear war depended on the survival of command-and-control facilities for days, weeks, or even months. The Pentagon also sought greater "interoperability"—a system that could quickly transmit messages between civilian and military leaders, between the United States and NATO, even between different branches of the American armed services. General Richard Ellis, the head of SAC, told Congress that, at a bare minimum, the command-and-control system had "to recognize that we are under attack, to characterize that attack, get a decision from the President, and disseminate that decision to the forces prior to the first weapon impacting upon the United States."

The Reagan administration planned to make an unprecedented investment in command and control, spending about $18 billion on new early-warning radars and communications satellites, better protection against nuclear weapon effects and electromagnetic pulse, the creation of a Global Positioning System (GPS) to improve weapon guidance and navigation, upgrades of the bunkers at SAC headquarters in Omaha and at Site R within Raven Rock Mountain, and an expansion of Project ELF, the extremely low frequency radio system for sending an emergency war order message to submarines. Three new ELF antennae would be built in upper Michigan—one of them twenty-eight miles long, the others about fourteen miles long. Project ELF was a scaled-down version of SANGUINE, a plan that had been strongly backed by the Navy. It would have buried six thousand miles of antenna, four to six feet deep, across an area covering almost one third of the state of Wisconsin.

One of the principal goals of the new command-and-control system was to ensure the "continuity of government." The vice president would assume a larger role in the planning for nuclear war and would be swiftly taken to an undisclosed location at the first sign of a crisis, ready to serve as commander in chief. New hideouts for the nation's leadership would be built throughout the country. And mobile command centers, housed in tractor-trailer trucks and transported by special cargo planes, would provide a backup to the National Emergency Airborne Command Post.

During the Kennedy administration, the problems with America's command-and-control system were deliberately hidden from the public. But as President Reagan prepared to adopt an updated version of "flexible response," the issue of strategic command was discussed in newspapers, books, magazines, and television news reports. Desmond Ball, an Australian academic, made a strong case that a nuclear war might be impossible to control. John D. Steinbruner—who'd helped to write a top secret history of the nuclear arms race for the Pentagon in the 1970s—reached much the same conclusion, warning that a "nuclear decapitation" of America's leadership could be achieved with as few as fifty warheads. Steinbruner had read the classified studies on decapitation that so alarmed Robert McNamara, but did not mention them in his work. Bruce G. Blair, a former Minuteman officer, described how the command-and-control systems of the United States and the Soviet Union were now poised on a hair trigger, under tremendous pressure to launch on warning if war seemed likely. Paul Bracken, a management expert at Yale University, wrote about how unmanageable a nuclear exchange would be. And Daniel Ford, a former head of the Union of Concerned Scientists, revealed that, among other things, the destruction of a single, innocuous-looking building in Sunnyvale, California, located "within bazooka range" of Highway 101, could disrupt the operation of Air Force early-warning and communications satellites. Although many aspects of Reagan's strategic modernization program provoked criticism, liberals and conservatives agreed that a robust command-and-control system was essential—to wage nuclear war or to deter it.

In the fall of 1981, Secretary of Defense Weinberger announced the retirement of the Titan II. The missile was increasingly regarded as a relic of another nuclear era. Testifying about the Titan II before the Senate, Fred Iklé cited "its low accuracy and its accident-proneness." The enormous yield of a single W-53 warhead had become less important. The one hundred Peacemaker missiles scheduled for deployment would carry one thousand warheads—almost twenty times the number carried by the remaining Titan II missiles. And the secrets of the Titan II had recently been compromised. Christopher M. Cooke, a young deputy commander at a Titan II complex in Kansas, had been arrested after making three unauthorized visits and multiple phone calls to the Soviet embassy in Washington, D.C. Inexplicably, Cooke had been allowed to serve as a Titan II officer on alerts for five months after his first contact with the Soviet embassy was detected. An Air Force memo later said the information that Cooke gave the Soviets—about launch codes, attack options, and the missile's vulnerabilities—was "a major security breach . . . the worst perhaps in the history of the Air Force."

Despite the obsolescence of the Titan II, its decommissioning would proceed slowly. The last missile was scheduled to go off alert in 1987. In order to save money, the Air Force decided to cancel some of the modifications recommended by the Titan II review group after the accident in Damascus. Funding would not be provided for a new vapor detection system in the silo, additional video cameras within the complex, or a retrofit of the W-53 warhead with new safety mechanisms. Upgrading the warhead to meet "modern nuclear safety criteria for abnormal environments" would have cost about $400,000 per missile.

THE SOVIET INVASION OF AFGHANISTAN, the breakdown in détente, the tough rhetoric from the White House, and the impending arrival of cruise missiles and Pershing II missiles created widespread fear of nuclear war in Western Europe. The fear was encouraged by a Soviet propaganda campaign that sought to stop the deployment of America's new missiles. But the apocalyptic mood in Europe was real, not Communist inspired, and loose talk by members of the Reagan administration helped to strengthen it. Thomas K. Jones, an undersecretary of defense, played down the number of casualties that a nuclear war might cause, arguing that families would survive if they dug a hole, covered it with a couple of doors, and put three feet of dirt on top. "It's the dirt that does it," Jones explained. "Everyone's going to make it if there are enough shovels to go around."

In Great Britain, membership in the Campaign for Nuclear Disarmament soon increased tenfold. A quarter of a million CND supporters attended a demonstration in London's Hyde Park during the fall of 1981, and a well-publicized Women's Peace Camp grew outside the Royal Air Force Base Greenham Common, where American cruise missiles would soon be housed. In Bonn, a demonstration against the Pershing II missile also attracted a quarter of a million people. The sense of powerlessness and dread, the need to take some sort of action and halt the arms race, led to a nuclear version of the Stockholm syndrome. Throughout Western Europe, protesters condemned American missiles that hadn't yet arrived—not the hundreds of new Soviet missiles already aimed at them.

The *New Yorker* magazine ran a three-part article in February 1982 that catalyzed the antinuclear movement in the United States. Written by Jonathan Schell and later published as a book, *The Fate of the Earth* revived the notion that nuclear weapons confronted the world with a stark, existential choice: life or death. Schell tried to pierce the sense of denial that had seemingly gripped the United States since Hiroshima and Nagasaki, the refusal to face the threat of annihilation. "On the one hand, we returned to business as usual, as though everything remained as it always had been," Schell wrote. "On the other hand, we began to assemble the stockpiles that could blow this supposedly unaltered existence sky-high at any second." He called for the abolition of nuclear weapons, offered a chilling description of what a single hydrogen bomb would do to New York City, and presented the latest scientific evidence on how nuclear detonations could harm the ozone layer of the earth's atmosphere. Later that year the astronomer Carl Sagan conjured an even worse environmental disaster: nuclear winter. The vast amount of soot produced by burning cities would circle the earth after a nuclear exchange, block the sun, and precipitate a new ice age. Sagan warned that the effects of nuclear winter would make victory in a nuclear war impossible; a nation that launched a first strike would be committing suicide.

On June 12, 1982, perhaps three quarters of a million people gathered in New York's Central Park, demanding a different kind of freeze—a worldwide halt to the production of nuclear weapons. The *New York Times* called it "the largest political demonstration in American history." The Nuclear Weapons Freeze Campaign gained the support of mainstream groups like the U.S. Conference of Mayors, the National Council of Churches, and the Roman Catholic Church. Unlike the European antinuclear movement, it called upon both the United States and the Soviet Union to disarm. But the campaign threatened the Reagan administration's strategic modernization plans, and opponents of the freeze claimed that it was being orchestrated by "KGB leaders" and "Marxist leaning 60's leftovers." By the end of 1982, about 70 percent of the American people supported a nuclear freeze. And more than half worried that Reagan might involve the United States in a nuclear war.

NINETEEN EIGHTY-THREE PROVED TO BE one of the most dangerous years of the Cold War. The new leader of the Soviet Union, Yuri Andropov, was old, paranoid, physically ill, and staunchly anti-American. A former head of the KGB, Andropov had for many years played a leading role in the suppression of dissent throughout the Soviet bloc. The election of Ronald Reagan persuaded him that the United States might seek to launch a first strike. The KGB began an intensive, worldwide effort to detect American preparations for a surprise attack, code-named Operation RYAN. Andropov's concerns were heightened by the Reagan administration's top secret psychological warfare program, designed to spook and confuse the Kremlin. American naval exercises were staged without warning near important military bases along the Soviet coastline; SAC bombers entered Soviet airspace and then left it, testing the air defenses. The Soviet Union played its own version of the game, keeping half a dozen ballistic-missile submarines off the coast of the United States.

On March 8, 1983, at the annual convention of the National Association of Evangelicals, President Reagan called the Soviet Union "the focus
of evil in the modern world . . . an evil empire." Two weeks later, Reagan
announced his Strategic Defense Initiative, soon known as Star Wars, a
long-range plan to defend the United States by shooting down enemy missiles from outer space. The technology necessary for such a system did not
yet exist—and Reagan acknowledged that it might not exist for another
ten or twenty years. But Star Wars deepened the Kremlin's fears of a first
strike. An American missile defense system was unlikely to be effective
against an all-out Soviet attack. It might, however, prove useful in destroying any Soviet missiles that survived an American first strike. Andropov strongly criticized the plan and warned that it would start a new
arms race. "Engaging in this is not just irresponsible," Andropov said. "It is
insane."

The Pershing II missiles were supposed to arrive in West Germany at
the end of November, and anxieties about nuclear war increased throughout Europe as the date approached. On the evening of September 1, Soviet
fighter planes shot down a civilian airliner, Korean Airlines Flight 007, killing all 269 of its passengers. The Boeing 747 had accidentally strayed into
Soviet airspace, not far from a missile test site, and the airliner was mistaken for an American reconnaissance plane. The Kremlin denied that it
had anything to do with the tragedy—until the United States released
audio recordings of Soviet pilots being ordered to shoot down the plane.
President Reagan called the attack "an act of barbarism" and a "crime
against humanity [that] must never be forgotten."

A few weeks later alarms went off in an air defense bunker south of
Moscow. A Soviet early-warning satellite had detected five Minuteman
missiles approaching from the United States. The commanding officer on
duty, Lieutenant Colonel Stanislav Petrov, tried to make sense of the
warning. An American first strike would surely involve more than five
missiles—but perhaps this was merely the first wave. The Soviet general
staff was alerted, and it was Petrov's job to advise them whether the missile
attack was real. Any retaliation would have to be ordered soon. Petrov
decided it was a false alarm. An investigation later found that the missile

launches spotted by the Soviet satellite were actually rays of sunlight reflected off clouds.

During the third week of October, two million people in Europe joined protests against the introduction of Pershing II missiles—and a team of Army Rangers, Navy Seals, and U.S. Marines led an invasion of Grenada, a small island in the Caribbean. The invasion had ostensibly been launched to protect the lives of American citizens and restore order amid the aftermath of a military coup. It also achieved another goal: the overthrow of a Communist regime backed by the Soviet Union and Cuba. Nineteen American soldiers, twenty-five Cubans, and forty-five Grenadians were killed in the fighting. The Soviet Union condemned Operation Urgent Fury as a violation of international law. But it was enormously popular in the United States, boosting President Reagan's image as a strong, decisive leader. A long time had passed since Americans had been able to celebrate a military victory.

The invasion of Grenada, however, revealed a number of serious problems with the World Wide Military Command and Control System. The Army's radio equipment proved to be incompatible with that of the Navy and the Marines. According to a Pentagon report, at one point during the fighting, unable to contact the Navy for fire support, "a frustrated Army officer used his AT&T credit card on an ordinary pay telephone to call Ft. Bragg, NC [the headquarters of the 82nd Airborne Division] to have them relay his request."

The week after the invasion, NATO staged a command-and-control exercise, Able Archer 83. It included a practice drill for NATO's defense ministers, simulating the procedures to authorize the use of nuclear weapons. The KGB thought that Able Archer 83 might be a cover for a surprise attack on the Soviet Union. The timing of such an attack—a few weeks before the arrival of the Pershing IIs—seemed illogical. Nevertheless, "the KGB concluded that American forces had been placed on alert," a Soviet agent later wrote, "and might even have begun the countdown to war." A number of the Soviet Union's own war plans called for using military exercises as a cover for a surprise attack on Western Europe. While NATO played its war game, Soviet aircraft in Poland and East Germany prepared to counterattack. Able Archer 83 ended uneventfully on November 11—and NATO's defense ministers were totally unaware that their command-and-control drill had been mistaken for the start of a third world war.

On the evening of November 20, American fears of nuclear war reached their peak, as ABC broadcast *The Day After,* a made-for-television movie. Directed by Nicholas Meyer, starring Jason Robards, and set in Lawrence, Kansas, the film combined melodrama with a calm, almost documentary account of how the world might end in 1983. Some of the most powerful images in *The Day After* had nothing to do with mushroom clouds, radiation sickness, or the rubble of a major American city. When Minuteman missiles first appear above Kansas, launched from rural silos there and rising in the sky, the film conveyed the mundane terror of nuclear war, the knowledge that annihilation could come at any time, in the midst of an otherwise ordinary day. People look up, see the missiles departing, realize what's about to happen, and yet are powerless to stop it. About 100 million Americans watched *The Day After,* roughly half of the adult population of the United States. And unlike most made-for-television movies, it did not have a happy ending.

THE PERSHING II MISSILES ARRIVED in West Germany, and the Soviet Union's response was purely diplomatic. Its negotiators walked out of arms control talks and didn't return. The relationship between the two superpowers had reached its lowest point since the dangerous events of 1962. And while billions of dollars were being spent on new strategic weapons in the United States, the safety problems with older ones continued to go unaddressed. Earlier in the year, another B-52 had caught on fire on a runway at Grand Forks Air Force Base. It was undergoing a routine maintenance check, at 9:30 in the morning, when fuel suddenly ignited, created a large fireball, destroyed the plane, and killed five young maintenance workers. No nuclear weapons were involved in the accident. But similar B-52s were being loaded with Mark 28 bombs and Short-Range Attack Missiles every day.

A program to add new safety devices to the Mark 28—weak links and strong links and a unique signal switch—was begun in 1984. But the retrofits were halted a year later, because the program ran out of money. Thousands of the bombs remained unmodified. And the safety problems with the Short-Range Attack Missile were worse than originally thought. The high explosives used in the primary of the SRAM were found to be vulnerable to fire. As the missiles aged, they also became more hazardous. The propellant used by their rocket motors had to be surrounded at all times by a blanket of nitrogen gas. When the gas leaked, the propellant became a "contact-sensitive explosive" that could easily be set off by flames, static electricity, or physical shock. If the SRAMs were poorly maintained, simply dropping them on the ground from a height of five or six feet could make them explode—or take off. "The worst probable consequence of continuous degradation . . . is spontaneous ignition of the propellant in a way similar to a normally initiated burn," an Air Force nuclear safety journal warned. "Naturally, this would be a catastrophe." The journal advised its readers to "follow procedures and give the weapons a little extra care and respect."

Bill Stevens retired from Sandia in 1985. His job had been redefined during a management shake-up, and he lacked enthusiasm for bureaucratic infighting. He was disappointed that most of the weapons in the stockpile still didn't possess the safety devices his team had pioneered. But Stevens felt proud of his recent contribution to the safety of the Pershing II. Hoping to eliminate human error during launch exercises with the missile, the Army had decided to computerize the procedure. At Pershing II bases in West Germany, crews would install the warhead, erect the missile, remove the pin that locked the missile onto its launcher, run the countdown until one second before launch—and then stop the exercise. The countdown would be controlled by a computer. Stevens felt uncomfortable with the idea; in fact, he thought it was crazy. A software glitch could launch a Pershing II missile. And the Army's software, written in 1980, was unlikely to be bug free.

Stevens refused to sign off on the nuclear weapon system study of the Pershing II missile, citing the risk of a DUL—a deliberate, unauthorized launch. In response to his criticisms, a safety device was added to the first-stage rocket motor. It required a separate code, entered manually, before the missile could take off. The warhead atop the Pershing II contained a permissive action link and wouldn't have detonated after an accidental launch. But the Soviet Union wouldn't have known that fact, as the missile on their radar screens headed toward Moscow.

RONALD REAGAN, despite all his tough rhetoric, had long harbored a fear of nuclear war. His first years in the White House increased that fear. During a command-and-control exercise in March 1982, Reagan watched red dots spreading across a map of the United States on the wall of the Situation Room. Each dot represented the impact of a Soviet warhead. Within an hour the map was covered in red. Reagan was shaken by the drill and by how little could be done to protect America. Although some members of the administration viewed the Strategic Defense Initiative as a clever response to the growing antinuclear movement, an attempt to show America's aims were peaceful and defensive, Reagan's belief in the plan was sincere. He thought that a missile defense system might work, that it could save lives, promote world peace, render nuclear weapons "impotent and obsolete." Reagan had a sunny, cheerful disposition, but watching *The Day After* left even him feeling depressed. With strong encouragement from his wife, Nancy, he publicly called for the abolition of nuclear weapons. Reagan's criticism of the Soviet Union became less severe, and his speeches soon included this heartfelt sentiment: "A nuclear war cannot be won and must never be fought."

The deaths of Yuri Andropov and his successor, Konstantin Chernenko, brought Mikhail Gorbachev to power. Gorbachev represented a dramatic break from the past. He was youthful and dynamic, the first Soviet leader since Vladimir Lenin who'd attended a university. Although Gorbachev's attempts to change the Soviet Union were tentative at first, he was committed to reforming its stagnant economy, allowing freedom of speech and religion, ending the war in Afghanistan, rejecting the use of force against other nations, linking the Soviet bloc more closely to the rest of Europe, and abandoning the pursuit of nuclear superiority. Although many of his views were radical, compared to those of his predecessors, Gorbachev did not seek to betray the tenets of Marxism-Leninism. He hoped to fulfill them.

In age, temperament, background, education, political orientation, Gorbachev and Reagan could hardly have been more different. And yet they were both self-confident, transformational leaders, willing to defy expectations and challenge the status quo. During their first meeting, at a Geneva summit conference in November 1985, the two men established a personal rapport and discussed how to reduce the nuclear arsenals of both nations. Gorbachev left Geneva viewing Reagan not as a right-wing caricature, a puppet of the military-industrial complex, but as a human being who seemed eager to avoid a nuclear war.

A year later, at a summit in Reykjavik, Iceland, the discussion strayed onto a topic that alarmed many of Reagan's close advisers: huge reductions in the number of nuclear weapons. Secretary of State George P. Shultz was elated by the possibility. The recent accident at the Chernobyl nuclear power plant had deposited radioactive fallout across much of Europe and the Soviet Union, reminding the world of the far greater danger that nuclear weapons posed. Reagan and Gorbachev seemed on the verge of reaching an extraordinary agreement, as a transcript of their meeting shows:

> The President agreed this could be sorted out . . . cruise missiles, battlefield weapons, sub-launched and the like. It would be fine with him if we eliminated all nuclear weapons.
>   Gorbachev said we can do that. We can eliminate them.
>   The Secretary [of State] said, "Let's do it."

The euphoria that Reagan and Shultz felt didn't last long. Moments later Gorbachev insisted, as part of the deal, that all Star Wars testing must be confined to the laboratory. Reagan couldn't comprehend why a missile-defense system intended to spare lives—one that didn't even exist yet, that might never exist—could stand in the way of eliminating nuclear weapons forever. He refused to place limits on the Strategic Defense Initiative and promised to share its technology. The Soviet Union was conducting exactly the same research, he pointed out, and an antiballistic missile system had already been built to defend Moscow. Neither Gorbachev nor Reagan would budge from his position, and the meeting ended.

Despite the failure to reach an agreement on the abolition of nuclear weapons, the Reykjavik summit marked a turning point in the Cold War, the start of a process that soon led to the removal of all intermediate-range missiles from Europe and large cuts in the number of strategic weapons. The all-out nuclear arms race was over. Gorbachev now felt emboldened to pursue reform in the Soviet Union, confident that the United States did not seek to attack his country. And the hard-liners in the Reagan administration breathed a sigh of relief, amazed that their president had come so close to getting rid of America's nuclear weapons. Margaret Thatcher, the conservative prime minister of Great Britain, and François Mitterrand, the socialist president of France, were furious that Reagan had questioned the value of nuclear deterrence, a strategy that had kept the peace since the Second World War. Although European protest marches had focused mainly on the United States for the previous six years, it was the leadership of Western Europe who most strongly opposed creating a world without nuclear weapons.

BOB PEURIFOY HAD BECOME a vice president at Sandia, and his new status enabled him to lobby more effectively for nuclear weapon safety. By 1988 almost half of the weapons in the American stockpile were fitted with weak link/strong link devices, and the safety retrofit of Mark 28 bombs had finally resumed. But SAC was still loading about one thousand Short-Range Attack Missiles onto its bombers on alert. Those planes were parked on runways nationwide, ready to take off from bases in California, Kansas, Maine, Michigan, New Hampshire, New York, North Dakota, South Dakota, Texas, and Washington State. As tensions between the United States and the Soviet Union eased, the Air Force's willingness to risk an accident with a SRAM became harder to justify.

On February 26, 1988, Peurifoy wrote to the assistant secretary for defense programs at the Department of Energy and invited him to Sandia for a briefing on the dangers of the SRAM. The assistant secretary never replied to the letter. The following month, the president of Sandia raised the issue with another official at the DOE, who suggested that the secretary of energy and the secretary of defense should be briefed on the matter. But nothing was done. A few months later an independent panel was commissioned to look at management practices at the Department of Energy, and Peurifoy was asked to serve as a technical adviser. Headed by Gordon Moe, a former member of Henry Kissinger's national security staff, the panel wound up using the SRAM's safety problems as a case study in mismanagement. Moe was shocked by the lack of attention to nuclear weapon safety and its implications. Almost fifteen years had passed since concerns about the SRAM were first expressed—and yet no remedial action had been taken. "The potential for a nuclear weapon accident will remain unacceptably high until the issues that have been raised are resolved," the Moe panel said in a classified report. "It would be hard to overstate the consequences that a serious accident could have for national security."

John H. Glenn, a former astronaut and a Democratic senator from Ohio, visited Sandia on April 26, 1989. Peurifoy took the opportunity to give Glenn a briefing on nuclear weapon safety—and handed him a copy of the Moe panel's report. Glenn wanted to know more about the subject and asked whom he should contact at the Department of Energy to discuss it.

Peurifoy suggested that he skip the midlevel bureaucrats and raise the issue with the secretary of energy, James D. Watkins.

Glenn said that he'd be seeing Watkins the following week.

The bureaucratic logjam was broken. A well-respected senator—a national hero—planned to raise the issue of nuclear weapon safety with someone who could actually do something about it.

Secretary Watkins and his staff met with Senator Glenn, read the Moe panel report, got worried about the safety of older weapons in the stockpile, and contacted the secretary of defense, Dick Cheney, about the issue. Instead of taking the weapons off alert, the Pentagon commissioned two more studies of the SRAM. One would be conducted by the Air Force, the other by Gordon Moe—who was rehired by the Department of Energy to repeat his earlier work.

Almost another year passed. The Berlin Wall had fallen. Mikhail Gorbachev had visited the White House; signed major arms agreements; removed hundreds of thousands of Soviet troops from Eastern Europe; allowed Poland, Hungary, Czechoslovakia, East Germany, Romania, Latvia, Estonia, and Lithuania to leave the Soviet bloc. By any rational measure, the Cold War was over. But every day, across the United States, Short-Range Attack Missiles continued to be loaded into B-52s on ground alerts.

During the spring of 1990, R. Jeffrey Smith, a reporter at the *Washington Post*, learned about the safety problems with some American nuclear weapons. The *Post* ran a series of his articles, bringing public attention to the SRAM's flaws and to the W-79 atomic artillery shells' lack of one-point safety. Smith didn't divulge any classified information, but he did suggest that bureaucratic rivalries and inertia were creating unnecessary risks. A Pentagon spokesman defended the SRAM, claiming that the "weapon meets all our current safety standards." Secretary of Defense Cheney met with Air Force officials, Secretary of Energy Watkins, the heads of the three weapons laboratories, and General Colin Powell, the chairman of the Joint Chiefs of Staff, to discuss the SRAM. On June 8, 1990, Cheney said that the SRAMs posed "no safety hazards to the public"—but that they would immediately be removed from bombers on alert, until another safety study was completed.

The House Armed Services Committee had already appointed a panel of three eminent physicists to investigate the safety of America's nuclear weapons. Charles H. Townes was a Nobel laureate who had advised the Department of Defense for many years. John S. Foster, Jr., was a former director of the Lawrence Livermore Laboratory who'd served in high-level posts at the Pentagon during the Johnson and Nixon administrations—an expert not only on nuclear weapon technology but also on targeting strategies. Sidney Drell, the chairman of the panel, was a theoretical physicist, long associated with the Stanford Linear Accelerator, who for many years had served as a JASON—a civilian granted a high-level security clearance to help with sensitive defense matters. Drell, Foster, and Townes didn't always agree on nuclear weapon policies. Drell had opposed the MX missile; Foster had supported it. But they shared a mutual respect, and their expertise in the field was unsurpassed. Peurifoy was asked to serve as a technical adviser.

The Drell Panel on Nuclear Weapons Safety submitted its report to the House Armed Services Committee in December 1990. The report confirmed what Bill Stevens and Bob Peurifoy had been saying for almost twenty years: America's nuclear arsenal was not as safe as it should be. Recent improvements in computing power, the report noted, had led to "a realization that unintended nuclear detonations present a greater risk than previously estimated (and believed) for some of the warheads in the stockpile." The Drell panel recommended that every nuclear weapon should be equipped with weak link/strong link devices, that every weapon carried by an airplane should contain insensitive high explosives and fire-resistant nuclear cores—and that the Pentagon should "affirm enhanced safety as the top priority of the U.S. nuclear weapons program."

A separate study on nuclear weapon safety was requested by the House Foreign Affairs Committee. The study was conducted by Ray E. Kidder, a Lawrence Livermore physicist, and released in 1991. It gave a safety "grade" to each nuclear weapon in the American stockpile. The grades were based on their potential risk of accidental detonation or plutonium scattering. Three weapons received an A. Seven received a B. Two received a C plus. Four received a C. Two received a C minus. And twelve received a D, the lowest grade.

ON JANUARY 25, 1991, General George Lee Butler became the head of the Strategic Air Command. During his first week on the job, Butler asked the Joint Strategic Target Planning Staff to give him a copy of the SIOP. General Colin Powell and Secretary of Defense Dick Cheney had made clear that the United States needed to change its targeting policy, now that the Cold War was over. As part of that administrative process, Butler decided to look at every single target in the SIOP, and for weeks he carefully scrutinized the thousands of desired ground zeros. He found bridges and railways and roads in the middle of nowhere targeted with multiple warheads, to assure their destruction. Hundreds of nuclear warheads would hit Moscow—dozens of them aimed at a single radar installation outside the city. During his previous job working for the Joint Chiefs, Butler had dealt with targeting issues and the damage criteria for nuclear weapons. He was hardly naive. But the days and weeks spent going through the SIOP, page by page, deeply affected him.

For more than forty years, efforts to tame the SIOP, to limit it, reduce it, make it appear logical and reasonable, had failed. "With the possible exception of the Soviet nuclear war plan, this was the single most absurd and irresponsible document I had ever reviewed in my life," General Butler later recalled. "I came to fully appreciate the truth . . . we escaped the Cold War without a nuclear holocaust by some combination of skill, luck, and divine intervention, and I suspect the latter in greatest proportion."

Butler eliminated about 75 percent of the targets in the SIOP, introduced a targeting philosophy that was truly flexible, and decided to get rid of the name SIOP. The United States no longer had a single, integrated war plan. Butler preferred a new title for the diverse range of nuclear options: National Strategic Response Plans.

MIKHAIL GORBACHEV WAS ON VACATION in the Crimea on August 18, 1991, when a group calling itself the "State Committee for the State of Emergency" entered his house and insisted that he declare martial law or resign. After refusing to do either, Gorbachev was held hostage, and the communications lines to his dacha were shut down by the KGB. His military aides, carrying the nuclear codes and the Soviet equivalent of a "football," were staying at a guesthouse nearby. Their equipment stopped functioning—and the civilian leadership of the Soviet Union lost control of its nuclear weapons.

Two other Soviet officials possessed nuclear codes and footballs: the minister of defense and the chief of the general staff. Both of them supported the coup d'état. It has never been conclusively established who controlled the thousands of nuclear weapons in the Soviet arsenal during the next few days. The head of the air force later claimed that he, the head of the navy, and the head of the Strategic Rocket Forces took over the command-and-control system, preventing anyone else from launching missiles at the United States. After the coup failed on August 21, communications were restored to Gorbachev's dacha, and the football carried by his military aides became operable once again.

Eager to reduce the risk of an accidental war and encourage deeper cuts in the Soviet arsenal, President George H. W. Bush announced a month later that the United States would unilaterally make large reductions in its nuclear deployments. It would remove all of the Army's tactical weapons from Europe, destroy half of the Navy's tactical weapons and place the rest in storage, take 450 Minuteman II missiles off alert—and end the Strategic Air Command's ground alert. For the first time since 1957, SAC's bombers wouldn't be parked near runways, loaded with fuel and hydrogen bombs, as their crews waited for the sound of Klaxons.

The Soviet Union ceased to exist on Christmas Day, 1991. The following June, the Strategic Air Command disappeared, as well. General Powell and General Butler thought that SAC had outlived its original purpose. The recent war against Iraq had demonstrated the importance of close collaboration between the armed services—and future wars were likely to be fought with conventional, not nuclear, weapons. The Strategic Air Command and its institutional culture no longer seemed relevant. SAC's aircraft were divided among various Air Force units. America's land-based missiles and ballistic-missile submarines were assigned to a single, unified command—to be headed, alternately, by an officer from the Air Force or the Navy. The fierce interservice rivalry to control America's nuclear weapons largely vanished, as those weapons played an increasingly minor role in the Pentagon's war plans. But many SAC veterans were outraged that what had once been the most powerful organization in the American military was being disbanded. They thought it was a mistake, regarded General Butler as a turncoat, and felt that the legacy of Curtis LeMay was being dishonored.

President Bush told members of his administration not to brag or gloat about the downfall of the Soviet Union, an event with myriad causes that Mikhail Gorbachev had unintentionally but peacefully overseen. General Colin Powell ignored those instructions at the ceremony in Omaha marking the end of the Strategic Air Command. "The long bitter years of the Cold War are over," Powell said. "America and her allies have won—totally, decisively, overwhelmingly."

Epilogue

The sociologist Charles B. Perrow began his research on dangerous technologies in August 1979, after the partial meltdown of the core at the Three Mile Island nuclear power plant. In the early minutes of the accident, workers didn't realize that the valves on the emergency coolant pipes had mistakenly been shut—one of the indicator lights on the control panel was hidden by a repair tag. Perrow soon learned that similar mistakes had occurred during the operation of other nuclear power plants. At a reactor in Virginia, a worker cleaning the floor got his shirt caught on the handle of a circuit breaker on the wall. He pulled the shirt off it, tripped the circuit breaker, and shut down the reactor for four days. A lightbulb slipped out of the hand of a worker at a reactor in California. The bulb hit the control panel, caused a short circuit, turned off sensors, and made the temperature of the core change so rapidly that a meltdown could have occurred. After studying a wide range of "trivial events in nontrivial systems," Perrow concluded that human error wasn't responsible for these accidents. The real problem lay deeply embedded within the technological systems, and it was impossible to solve: "Our ability to organize does not match the inherent hazards of some of our organized activities." What appeared to be the rare exception, an anomaly, a one-in-a-million accident, was actually to be expected. It was normal.

Perrow explored the workings of high-risk systems in his book *Normal*

Accidents, focusing on the nuclear power industry, the chemical industry, shipping, air transportation, and other industrial activities that could harm a large number of people if something went wrong. Certain patterns and faults seemed common to all of them. The most dangerous systems had elements that were "tightly coupled" and interactive. They didn't function in a simple, linear way, like an assembly line. When a problem arose on an assembly line, you could stop the line until a solution was found. But in a tightly coupled system, many things occurred simultaneously—and they could prove difficult to stop. If those things also interacted with each other, it might be hard to know exactly what was happening when a problem arose, let alone know what to do about it. The complexity of such a system was bound to bring surprises. "No one dreamed that when X failed, Y would also be out of order," Perrow gave as an example, "and the two failures would interact so as to both start a fire and silence the fire alarm."

Dangerous systems usually required standardized procedures and some form of centralized control to prevent mistakes. That sort of management was likely to work well during routine operations. But during an accident, Perrow argued, "those closest to the system, the operators, have to be able to take independent and sometimes quite creative action." Few bureaucracies were flexible enough to allow both centralized and decentralized decision making, especially in a crisis that could threaten hundreds or thousands of lives. And the large bureaucracies necessary to run high-risk systems usually resented criticism, feeling threatened by any challenge to their authority. "Time and time again, warnings are ignored, unnecessary risks taken, sloppy work done, deception and downright lying practiced," Perrow found. The instinct to blame the people at the bottom not only protected those at the top, it also obscured an underlying truth. The fallibility of human beings guarantees that no technological system will ever be infallible.

AFTER SERVING AS A CONSULTANT to the Joint Chiefs of Staff on strategic nuclear policy, Scott D. Sagan applied "normal accident" theory to the workings of the American command-and-control system during the

Cuban Missile Crisis. According to Sagan, now a professor of political science at Stanford University, the crisis was the most severe test of that system during the Cold War, "the highest state of readiness for nuclear war that U.S. military forces have ever attained and the longest period of time (thirty days) that they have maintained an alert." Most historians attributed the peaceful resolution of the crisis to decisions made by John F. Kennedy and Nikita Khrushchev—to the rational behavior of leaders controlling their military forces. But that sense of control may have been illusory, Sagan argued in *The Limits of Safety*, and the Cuban Missile Crisis could have ended with a nuclear war, despite the wishes of Khrushchev and Kennedy.

With hundreds of bombers, missiles, and naval vessels prepared to strike, the risk of accidents and misunderstandings was ever present. At the height of the confrontation, while Kennedy and his advisers were preoccupied with the Soviet missiles in Cuba, an Atlas long-range missile was test-launched at Vandenberg Air Force Base, without the president's knowledge or approval. Other missiles at Vandenberg had already been placed on alert with nuclear warheads—and the Soviet Union could have viewed the Atlas launch as the beginning of an attack. The Jupiter missiles in Turkey were an issue of great concern to Secretary of Defense Robert McNamara throughout the crisis. McNamara ordered American troops to sabotage the missiles if Turkey seemed ready to launch them. But he was apparently unaware that nuclear weapons had been loaded onto fighter planes in Turkey. The control of those weapons was "so loose, it jars your imagination," Lieutenant Colonel Robert B. Melgard, the commander of the NATO squadron, told Sagan. "In retrospect," Melgard said, "there were some guys you wouldn't trust with a .22 rifle, much less a thermonuclear bomb."

During one of the most dangerous incidents, Major Charles Maultsby, the pilot of an American U-2 spy plane, got lost and inadvertently strayed into Soviet airspace. His mistake occurred on October 27, 1962—the same day as the Atlas missile launch and the shooting down of a U-2 over Cuba. Maultsby was supposed to collect air samples above the North Pole, seeking radioactive evidence of a Soviet nuclear test. But the flight path was new, the aurora borealis interfered with his attempt at celestial navigation, and Maultsby soon found himself flying over Siberia, pursued by Soviet fighter planes. The U-2 ran out of fuel, and American fighters took off to escort Maultsby back to Alaska. Under the DEFCON 3 rules of engagement, the American fighter pilots had the authority to fire their atomic antiaircraft missiles and shoot down the Soviet planes. A dogfight between the two air forces was somehow avoided, the U-2 landed safely—and McNamara immediately halted the air sampling program. Nobody at the Pentagon had considered the possibility that these routine U-2 flights could lead to the use of nuclear weapons.

America's command-and-control system operated safely during the crisis, Sagan found, and yet "numerous dangerous incidents . . . occurred despite all the efforts of senior authorities to prevent them." He'd long believed that the risk of nuclear weapon accidents was remote, that nuclear weapons had been "a stabilizing force" in international relations, reducing the risk of war between the United States and the Soviet Union. "Nuclear weapons may well have made *deliberate* war less likely," Sagan now thought, "but the complex and tightly coupled nuclear arsenal we have constructed has simultaneously made *accidental* war more likely." Researching *The Limits of Safety* left him feeling pessimistic about our ability to control high-risk technologies. The fact that a catastrophic accident with a nuclear weapon has never occurred, Sagan wrote, can be explained less by "good design than good fortune."

THE TITAN II EXPLOSION at Damascus was a normal accident, set in motion by a trivial event (the dropped socket) and caused by a tightly coupled, interactive system (the fuel leak that raised the temperature in the silo, making an oxidizer leak more likely). That system was also overly complex (the officers and technicians in the control center couldn't determine what was happening inside the silo). Warnings had been ignored, unnecessary risks taken, sloppy work done. And crucial decisions were made by a commanding officer, more than five hundred miles from the scene, who had little firsthand knowledge of the system. The missile might have exploded no matter what was done after its stage 1 fuel tank began to leak. But to blame the socket, or the person who dropped it, for that explosion is to misunderstand how the Titan II missile system really worked. Oxidizer leaks and other close calls plagued the Titan II until the last one was removed from a silo, northwest of Judsonia, Arkansas, in June 1987. None of those leaks and accidents led to a nuclear disaster. But if one had, the disaster wouldn't have been inexplicable or hard to comprehend. It would have made perfect sense.

The nuclear weapon systems that Bob Peurifoy, Bill Stevens, and Stan Spray struggled to make safer were also tightly coupled, interactive, and complex. They were prone to "common-mode failures"—one problem could swiftly lead to many others. The steady application of high temperature to the surface of a Mark 28 bomb could disable its safety mechanisms, arm it, and then set it off. "Fixes, including safety devices, sometimes create new accidents," Charles Perrow warned, "and quite often merely allow those in charge to run the system faster, or in worse weather, or with bigger explosives." Perrow was not referring to the use of sealed-pit weapons during SAC's airborne alerts. But he might as well have been. Promoted as being much safer than the weapons they replaced, the early sealed-pit bombs posed a grave risk of accidental detonation and plutonium scattering. Normal accident theory isn't a condemnation of modern technological systems. But it calls for more humility in how we design, build, and operate them.

The title of an influential essay on the role of technology in society asked the question: "Do Artifacts Have Politics?" According to its author, Langdon Winner, the answer is yes—the things that we produce are not only shaped by social forces, they also help to mold the political life of a society. Some technologies are flexible and can thrive equally well in democratic or totalitarian countries. But Winner pointed to one invention that could never be managed with a completely open, democratic spirit: the atomic bomb. "As long as it exists at all, its lethal properties demand that it be controlled by a centralized, rigidly hierarchical chain of command closed to all influences that might make its workings unpredictable," Winner wrote. "The internal social system of the bomb must be authoritarian; there is no other way."

Secrecy is essential to the command and control of nuclear weapons. Their technology is the opposite of open-source software. The latest warhead designs can't be freely shared on the Internet, improved through anonymous collaboration, and productively used without legal constraints. In the years since Congress passed the Atomic Energy Act of 1946, the design specifications of American nuclear weapons have been "born secret." They are not classified by government officials; they're classified as soon as they exist. And intense secrecy has long surrounded the proposed uses and deployments of nuclear weapons. It is intended to keep valuable information away from America's enemies. But an absence of public scrutiny has often made nuclear weapons more dangerous and more likely to cause a disaster.

Again and again, safety problems were hidden not only from the public but also from the officers and enlisted personnel who handled nuclear weapons every day. The strict, compartmentalized secrecy hid safety problems from the scientists and engineers responsible for weapon safety. Through the Freedom of Information Act, I obtained a document that listed the "Accidents and Incidents Involving Nuclear Weapons" from the summer of 1957 until the spring of 1967. It was 245 pages long. It gave brief accounts of the major Broken Arrows during that period. It also described hundreds of minor accidents, technical glitches, and seemingly trivial events: a Genie antiaircraft missile released from a fighter plane by mistake and dropped onto a weapon trailer; a Boar missile crushed by the elevator of an aircraft carrier; a Mark 49 warhead blown off a Jupiter missile when explosive bolts detonated due to corrosion; smoke pouring from a W-31 warhead atop a Nike missile after a short circuit; the retrorockets of a Thor missile suddenly firing at a launch site in Great Britain and startling the crew; a Mark 28 bomb emitting strange sounds, for reasons that were never discovered. I shared the document with Bob Peurifoy and Bill Stevens—who'd never seen it. Both were upset after reading it. The Defense Atomic Support Agency had never told them about hundreds of accidents.

The United States was often more successful at keeping secrets from its own weapon designers than at keeping them from the Soviet Union. Beginning with the Soviet infiltration of the Manhattan Project, through the John Walker spy ring—which from the late 1960s until 1985 provided about a million documents on the Pentagon's war plans, codes, and submarine technology to the Soviets—the leadership in the Kremlin knew a lot more about the nuclear capabilities of the United States than the American people were ever allowed to know. One of the most important secrets of the Cold War was considered so secret that the president of the United States wasn't allowed to know it. Harry Truman was deliberately never told that Army cryptologists had broken Soviet codes and deciphered thousands of messages about espionage within the United States. But the Soviet Union learned the secret, when one of its spies, the British double agent Kim Philby, was given a tour of the Army's Signal Intelligence Service headquarters.

The need to protect national security has long been used as a justification for hiding things to avoid embarrassment. "Secrecy is a form of government regulation," a Senate commission, headed by Daniel Patrick Moynihan, said in 1997. "What is different with secrecy is that the public cannot know the extent or the content of the regulation." To this day, the classification decisions at the Department of Defense and the Department of Energy have an arbitrary, often Kafkaesque quality. Cold War documents that were declassified in the 1990s were later reclassified—making it illegal to possess them, even though the federal government once released them.

In many of the documents that I obtained through the Freedom of Information Act, the redactions by government censors made little sense. Exactly the same information would be supplied in one document, yet blacked out in another. The government still won't reveal the yield of the Titan II's warhead—even though the weapon hasn't been in the American arsenal for almost a quarter of a century, the Soviet Union no longer exists, and Soviet espionage discovered everything remotely interesting about the missile.

The operational details of nuclear weapons might seem like the kind of information that should always be kept secret. And yet throughout the Cold War, news reports about Broken Arrows and other nuclear weapon problems forced the Pentagon to adopt new safety measures. Bad publicity influenced the decision to lock hydrogen bombs securely inside bombers during takeoffs and landings, to end SAC's airborne alert, retire the Titan II missile, remove Short-Range Attack Missiles from aircraft on ground alert. Too much secrecy often threatened the national security far more than revelations about America's nuclear arsenal.

A detailed account of the nuclear weapon accidents in the Soviet Union has never been published. The absence of a free press no doubt contributed to the many large-scale industrial accidents and widespread environmental devastation that occurred in the Soviet bloc. Chelyabinsk-65, the site of a nuclear weapon facility in central Russia, has been called "arguably the most polluted spot on the planet." A massive explosion there in 1957 contaminated hundreds of square miles with highly radioactive fallout. Countless accidents occurred at the plant, and tens of thousands of people were exposed to harmful levels of radiation. Soviet nuclear technology was, for the most part, inferior to that of the West. But the authoritarian rule of the Soviet Union was especially well suited to the demands of nuclear command and control. Unlike the president of the United States—who predelegated the authority to use nuclear weapons not only to SAC generals and Air Force fighter pilots but also to NATO officers in Europe—the leadership of the Communist Party and the Soviet general staff strictly retained that sort of power. Locks of various kinds were placed on Soviet weapons, and the permission to unlock them came only from the top. According to Bruce Blair, a leading command-and-control expert, Soviet safeguards against unauthorized use were "more stringent than those of any other nuclear power, including the United States."

The rigidly centralized command structure, however, made the Soviet Union quite vulnerable to a decapitation attack. Despite all the underground bunkers and secret railways built in and around Moscow, Soviet leaders constantly worried about their ability to retaliate after an American first strike. Instead of loosening their control of nuclear weapons and shifting authority further down the chain of command, they automated the decision to use nuclear weapons. In 1974, little more than a decade after the release of *Dr. Strangelove*, the Soviet Union began work on the "Perimeter" system—a network of sensors and computers that could order the launch of intercontinental ballistic missiles automatically. Completed in 1985, it was known as the "dead hand." The Soviet general staff planned to activate Perimeter if an American attack seemed imminent. The system would decide when to retaliate, instructing launch crews to fire their missiles if it detected nuclear explosions on Russian soil. Perimeter greatly reduced the pressure to launch on warning at the first sign of an American attack. It gave Soviet leaders more time to investigate the possibility of a false alarm, confident that a real attack would trigger a computer-controlled, devastating response. But it rendered American plans for limited war meaningless; the Soviet computers weren't programmed to allow pauses for negotiation. And the deterrent value of Perimeter was wasted. Like the doomsday machine in *Dr. Strangelove*, the system was kept secret from the United States.

IN MARCH 1991, three months after the Drell panel submitted its report to Congress, Bob Peurifoy retired from Sandia. He had no more tolerance for the bureaucratic warfare and petty slights, the disrespect from Sandia's upper management. More important, his goals had been achieved. Congress, the weapons laboratories, the Pentagon, and the Department of Energy all agreed that the safety of America's nuclear weapons had to be improved. Weak link/strong link devices were put into every nuclear weapon. And other safety technologies—insensitive high explosives, nuclear cores encased in a fire-resistant shell—were to be included in every new design. The changes in the stockpile that Peurifoy had sought for decades, once dismissed as costly and unnecessary, were now considered essential. Building a nuclear weapon without these safety features had become inconceivable.

Sidney Drell regards Bob Peurifoy as one of the leading, though largely unacknowledged, figures in the history of nuclear technology. He thinks that Peurifoy's achievements rank alongside those of Admiral Hyman G. Rickover, who pioneered the safe use of nuclear propulsion for the U.S. Navy. And yet Peurifoy told me, on many occasions, that he regrets not having been braver, especially about the safety problems with the Mark 28 bomb. He'd chosen to work within the system, despite his strong opposition to many of its practices. Although he was critical of the way in which official secrecy has been used to cover up mistakes, he'd honorably obeyed its code. As we sat in the sunroom of Peurifoy's modest home, with a lovely view of the Texas hill country, talking for hours about his work to improve nuclear weapon safety, his wife, Barbara, listened attentively. Despite a close, loving marriage that had lasted for sixty years, he'd kept these details to himself, never sharing the weight of that dark knowledge with Barbara or their children.

Within a year of Peurifoy's retirement, the nuclear weapon community that had long ignored, dismissed, and opposed him became outspoken in defense of his cause. The Comprehensive Nuclear Test Ban Treaty was being discussed at the United Nations. The treaty prohibited the sort of underground nuclear detonations that the United States and other countries needed to develop new weapons. A ban on these tests was, in many respects, a ban on new weapons—since no military would place its faith in a warhead or bomb that had never been proven to work. During a Senate debate on the treaty in August 1992, the opponents of a test ban came up with a novel rationale for continuing to detonate nuclear weapons.

"Why is testing of nuclear weapons so important?" asked one senator, a close ally of the Pentagon and the weapons laboratories. "It is so important because nuclear weapons, even today's nuclear weapons, represent a great danger to the American public and to the world because of the lack of safety of their devices." He then put a list of Broken Arrows into the Congressional Record. Another senator opposing the treaty claimed that "we already know that science and technology cries out for safety modifications." A third attacked the Department of Energy for its negligence on safety issues over the years, warning: "A vote to halt nuclear testing today is a vote to condemn the American people to live with unsafe nuclear weapons in their midst for years and years—indeed, until nuclear weapons are eliminated."

In 1996 the United States became the first country to sign the Comprehensive Nuclear Test Ban Treaty, and since then more than 180 other nations have signed it, too. But the U.S. Senate voted against ratifying the treaty in 1999. Once again, the treaty's opponents argued that nuclear tests might be necessary to ensure that the American stockpile remains safe and reliable. During the administration of President George W. Bush, the Pentagon and the weapons laboratories supported the development of a new nuclear weapon, the Reliable Replacement Warhead (RRW). It would be safer, more secure, and more reliable than current weapons, the administration promised. The RRW would also be the first "green" nuclear weapon—designed to avoid the use of beryllium, a toxic environmental contaminant.

Bob Peurifoy has been bemused by the newfound passion for nuclear weapon safety and security among his former critics. He sees no need for more weapon tests, supports the test ban treaty, and thinks it would be highly irresponsible to add a new weapon like the RRW to the stockpile without having detonated it first. The plans to develop new warheads and bombs, Peurifoy says, are just "a money grab" by the Pentagon and the weapons laboratories. The yield-to-weight ratio of America's nuclear weapons became asymptotic—approached their mathematical upper limit—around 1963. New designs won't make detonations any more efficient. And a study by JASON scientists concluded that the cores of existing weapons will be good for at least another hundred years. Although the boosting gas and neutron generators within the weapons deteriorate with age, they can be replaced through programs currently managed by the Department of Energy. Harold Agnew, the former head of Los Alamos who championed one-point safety and permissive action links, agrees with Peurifoy. Agnew says that the idea of introducing a new weapon without testing it is "nonsense." And he opposes any additional tests.

The only weapons in today's stockpile that trouble Peurifoy are the W-76 and W-88 warheads carried by submarine-launched Trident II missiles. The Drell panel expressed concern about these warheads more than twenty years ago. Both of them rely on conventional high explosives, instead of insensitive high explosives. The Navy had insisted upon use of the more dangerous explosive to reduce the weight of the warheads, increase their range, and slightly increase their yield. The decision was unfortunate from a safety perspective, because the multiple warheads of a Trident II don't sit on top of the missile. They surround the rocket motor of its third stage, as a space-saving measure. And the Navy chose a high-energy propellant for the rocket motor that's much more likely to explode in an accident—simply by being dropped or struck by a bullet—than other solid fuels. A Trident submarine has as many as twenty-four of these missiles, each carrying between four to five warheads. An accident with one missile could detonate the third-stage propellant, set off the high explosives of the warheads, and spread a good deal of plutonium around the ports in Georgia and Washington State where Trident submarines are based.

For years the Navy has resisted changing the third-stage rocket propellant of the Trident II missile or using the W-87 warhead—which is almost identical to the W-88 but employs a safer insensitive high explosive. Using a less energetic propellant would decrease the missile's range by perhaps 4 percent, and the W-87 warhead has a slightly lower yield. Parochial concerns may also be a factor in the Navy's attachment to the W-88. That warhead was designed for the Navy by Los Alamos; the W-87, by Lawrence Livermore for the Air Force.

The best way to load a Trident II missile onto a submarine is one of the few areas of disagreement between Sidney Drell and Bob Peurifoy. Drell endorses the Navy's current method: load the missile first, then attach the warheads. Peurifoy prefers another method: put fully assembled missiles into the launch tubes. The difference between the two opinions may seem esoteric, and yet the potential consequences of an accident are beyond dispute: a missile explosion inside a submarine with as many as 144 nuclear warheads.

TODAY'S UNITED STATES AIR FORCE bears little resemblance to the Air Force of the 1970s. The arms buildup during the Reagan administration greatly increased spending on new aircraft, new weapons, spare parts, and better training. Morale improved and illegal drug use plummeted, thanks to widespread testing. A cultural shift occurred, as well. While serving as head of the Tactical Air Command from 1978 until 1984, General Wilbur

L. Creech had the same sort of lasting influence on the Air Force that Curtis LeMay once exerted. But Creech promoted a fundamentally different type of leadership—the adaptive, decentralized, independent thinking of the fighter pilot. By the early 1980s the bomber generals had been driven from power, and the leading staff positions at the Air Force were filled with fighter generals. The new tactics, equipment, and esprit de corps transformed its performance in battle. During the Vietnam War, 1,737 Air Force planes were shot down. During the past quarter century of air campaigns over Iraq, Kuwait, Kosovo, Libya, and Afghanistan, the Air Force has lost fewer than 30 planes to enemy fire.

The Air Force's focus on tactical warfare, however, led to severe neglect of its strategic mission. Nuclear weapons seemed largely irrelevant after the Cold War, and ambitious officers wanted nothing to do with them. The United States Strategic Command not only combined the nuclear arsenals of the Air Force and the Navy, it also assumed control of numerous conventional missions: missile defense, intelligence and reconnaissance, space operations, cyber warfare. After the Strategic Air Command was dismantled, the Air Force no longer had an organization solely devoted to maintaining nuclear weapons and planning for their use. The no-notice inspections and black hat exercises that LeMay thought indispensable were ended. Nuclear weapon units were now given seventy-two hours of warning before an inspection. And instead of a four-star general commanding the Air Force's strategic assets, a captain or a colonel became the highest-ranking officer in charge of daily nuclear operations. The lack of interest in the subject began to show.

In 2003 half of the Air Force units responsible for nuclear weapons failed their safety inspections—despite the three-day advance warning. In August 2006 the nose-cone fuze assemblies of four Minuteman III missiles were inadvertently shipped from Hill Air Force Base in Utah to Taiwan. Workers at the Defense Logistics Agency thought they were helicopter batteries. The top secret nuclear-weapon fuzes sat in unopened boxes for two years, until Taiwanese officials discovered the error. On August 29, 2007, six cruise missiles armed with nuclear warheads were mistakenly loaded onto a B-52 bomber named Doom 99 at Minot Air Force Base in North

Dakota. The plane sat on the tarmac at Minot overnight without any armed guards, took off the next morning, flew almost fifteen hundred miles to Barksdale Air Force Base in Louisiana—violating the safety rule that prohibits nuclear weapons from being transported by air over the United States—landed at Barksdale, and sat on the tarmac there for nine hours, unguarded, until a maintenance crew noticed the warheads. For a day and a half, nobody in the Air Force realized that half a dozen thermonuclear weapons were missing.

The Defense Science Board later conducted an investigation of the safety and security lapses at Minot. It found a serious breakdown in command and control. Cruise missiles armed with nuclear warheads were being stored in the same bunker as those armed with conventional or training warheads. Verification checklists were routinely ignored to save time. On the day of the incident, the breakout crew that initially entered the bunker, the convoy crew that drove the cruise missiles to the B-52, the load crew that placed them on the bomber, and the aircrew that flew the plane were all supposed to check whether the missiles were carrying nuclear warheads. None of the crews did. After interviewing them, the Defense Science Board noted a basic lack of understanding about who had the authority to remove weapons from the bunker—and "significant confusion about delegation of responsibility and authority for movement of nuclear weapons." Nobody seemed to know who was in charge. And nobody was ever asked to sign a piece of paper recording the movement of nuclear weapons or acknowledging the transfer of custody from one Air Force unit to another. Paper would be necessary for that sort of record keeping— unlike packages shipped by Federal Express, the weapons had serial numbers that had to be written down, not bar codes that could be scanned.

On May 28, 2008, the Air Force discovered another safety problem. A maintenance team arrived at a Minuteman III silo near F. E. Warren Air Force Base in Wyoming and found the walls covered with soot. A fire had started in an equipment room, melting a shotgun case, part of a shotgun, and the shotgun shells stored there. Heat from the flames had damaged one of the electrical cables attached to the Minuteman III. The fire had extinguished itself—but hadn't been detected by the smoke alarm at the site. The launch crew in its control center miles away never received any indication that the missile might be at risk. The fire was most likely caused by a lightning strike or an improperly installed battery charger. And it may have occurred five days before the maintenance team noticed the soot.

The Global Strike Command was created in 2009 to improve the management of the Air Force's nuclear weapons. The command assumed responsibility for the remaining Minuteman III missiles, as well as the B-2 and B-52 bombers that still have nuclear missions. It is a successor to the Strategic Air Command, though smaller and less influential, with the same narrow focus on maintaining deterrence and fighting a nuclear war. Among other reforms, the new command has recently introduced "unique identifiers" for its nuclear weapons—bar codes that will allow them to be tracked. The Global Strike Command hopes to instill the same sort of dedication, motivation, and attention to detail that SAC long possessed. But the Air Force emphasis on tactical warfare has left the new command with aging and expensive weapon systems. Each of its twenty B-2 bombers costs $2 billion, and no more will be produced. Its Minuteman III missiles were first deployed in 1970. And its B-52 bombers haven't been manufactured since John F. Kennedy was president. The B-52s are scheduled to remain in service through the year 2040.

The age of these strategic weapons raises doubts about whether the Air Force will have a significant nuclear role in the future. At the moment, funding for new long-range missiles and bombers has not been approved. But the command-and-control mechanisms used by the Air Force, the Global Strike Command, and the other armed services are continually being upgraded. The World Wide Military Command and Control System was deactivated in 1996. Its mainframe computers had become hopelessly out of date. The WWMCCS was replaced by the Global Command and Control System and its various subsets: the Secret Internet Protocol Router Network, the Pentagon Global Information Grid, the Army LandWarNet, the Air Force Constellation Net, the Navy FORCENet, the Minimum Essential Communications Network, and the Defense Improved Emergency Message Automatic Transmission System Replacement Command

and Control Terminal System. Known by the acronym DIRECT, it sends and receives the war order to use nuclear weapons. A DIRECT terminal looks like a desktop PC, circa 2003, with a round slot on the front for a metal key.

All of these military computer networks are far more technologically advanced than the gold telephone that used to connect General LeMay to the White House. But sometimes they experience a glitch. In October 2010 a computer failure at F. E. Warren Air Force Base knocked fifty Minuteman III missiles offline. For almost an hour, launch crews could not communicate with their missiles. One third of the Minuteman IIIs at the base had been rendered inoperable. The Air Force denied that the system had been hacked and later found the cause of the problem: a circuit card was improperly installed in one of the computers during routine maintenance. But the hacking of America's nuclear command-and-control system remains a serious threat. In January 2013, a report by the Defense Science Board warned that the system's vulnerability to a large-scale cyber attack had never been fully assessed. Testifying before Congress, the head of the U.S. Strategic Command, General C. Robert Kehler, expressed confidence that no "significant vulnerability" existed. Nevertheless, he said that an "end-to-end comprehensive review" still needed to be done, that "we don't know what we don't know," and that the age of the command-and-control system might inadvertently offer some protection against the latest hacking techniques. Asked whether Russia and China had the ability to prevent a cyber attack from launching one of their nuclear missiles, Kehler replied, "Senator, I don't know."

Operation Neptune Spear, the raid that killed Osama bin Laden, was an extraordinarily complex military operation, and much of its success can be attributed to the Global Command and Control System. Personnel belonging to the Army, the Navy, the Air Force, and the CIA, as well as unmanned drones, secretly communicated with one another in real time. And details of the raid in Pakistan were simultaneously shared with President Barack Obama at the White House; CIA director Leon Panetta at the agency's headquarters in Langley, Virginia; and Admiral William H.

McRaven at a special operations base in Jalalabad, Afghanistan. The effectiveness of a command-and-control system in launching an attack, however, reveals little about how it will perform when under attack.

The *9/11 Commission Report* offers a sobering account of the confusion, miscommunication, and parallel decision making that occurred at the highest levels of the government during an attack on the United States that lasted about seventy-eight minutes. President George W. Bush did not board Air Force One until almost an hour after the first hijacked airliner struck the World Trade Center. His calls to the Pentagon and the White House underground bunker were constantly dropped. Continuity of government measures weren't implemented until more than an hour after the initial attack. Vice President Cheney ordered Air Force fighter planes to shoot down any hijacked airliners over Washington, D.C., and New York City, but the order was never received. The only fighter planes that got an authorization to fire their weapons belonged to the District of Columbia Air National Guard—and they were ordered into the air by a Secret Service agent, acting outside the chain of command, without Cheney's knowledge. A command-and-control system designed to operate during a surprise attack that could involve thousands of nuclear weapons—and would require urgent presidential decisions within minutes—proved incapable of handling an attack by four hijacked airplanes.

As of this writing, the United States has approximately 4,650 nuclear weapons. About 300 are assigned to long-range bombers, 500 are deployed atop Minuteman III missiles, and 1,150 are carried by Trident submarines. An additional 200 or so hydrogen bombs are stored in Turkey, Belgium, Germany, Italy, and the Netherlands for use by NATO aircraft. About 2,500 nuclear weapons are held in reserve, mainly at the Kirtland Underground Munitions Maintenance and Storage Complex near Albuquerque, New Mexico. America's current nuclear war plan, now known as the Operations Plan (OPLAN) 8010, has two official aims: "Strategic Deterrence and Global Strike." Both seek to prevent an attack with weapons of mass destruction against the United States—one, with an implied threat;

the other with an American first strike. While the attack options of the SIOP focused primarily on targets in the Soviet Union, the OPLAN enables the president to use nuclear weapons against Russia, China, North Korea, Syria, and Iran. "Adaptive planning" allows targets in other countries to be chosen at the last minute.

The United States now plans to spend as much as $180 billion, over the next twenty years, to maintain its nuclear weapons, run its weapon laboratories, and upgrade its uranium-processing facilities. The world's other nuclear powers are behaving in much the same way. Russia has about 1,740 deployed strategic weapons and perhaps 2,000 tactical weapons. It plans to introduce a new long-range missile by the end of the decade. France is adding new aircraft and submarines to carry its roughly 300 weapons. The United Kingdom plans to obtain new Trident submarines for its approximately 160 warheads. China is thought to have about 240 nuclear weapons. It is building new cruise missiles, long-range missiles, and submarines to carry them. It has also constructed an "underground Great Wall"— thousands of miles of deeply buried tunnels, large enough to fit cars, trucks, and trains—in which to hide them. The size of China's arsenal is not limited by any arms control treaties. After vowing for decades that nuclear weapons would be used only for retaliation after an enemy attack, China may be abandoning its "no-first-use" pledge. And a more aggressive Chinese strategy would increase the number of ballistic missiles, worldwide, that are ready to be fired at a moment's notice—as well as the risk of mistakes.

The number of nuclear weapons possessed by Israel has never been revealed. Israel recently purchased submarines from Germany to deploy some of them and hopes in the near future to place others on long-range missiles. The nuclear programs of North Korea and Iran remain shrouded in mystery. Both may be seeking to deploy long-range missiles with nuclear warheads. North Korea may already have half a dozen nuclear weapons. Despite well-publicized threats to launch a nuclear attack on American cities, North Korea may not have the capability to destroy targets thousands of miles away. The technical proficiency of the world's aspiring nuclear powers remains unknown. The yield of North Korea's first weapon test was less than 1 kiloton. And Iraq's nuclear weapon program, before it was halted, may have posed a greater threat to Baghdad than to Saddam Hussein's enemies. "It could go off if a rifle bullet hit it," one United Nations inspector said about the Iraqi weapon design. "I wouldn't want to be around if it fell off the edge of this desk."

The United States and Russia still maintain thousands of missiles on alert, ready to be launched within minutes. As tensions between the two countries have eased, the risk of an accidental war has diminished; but it has not disappeared. The targets of American missiles are no longer preprogrammed. They are transmitted right before launch, and the default setting of the missiles would send their warheads into the nearest ocean. The command-and-control systems of both countries, however, are still profoundly important. Russia has become far more dependent on land-based missiles than the United States—and, as a result, more vulnerable to a first strike. Any sign of a surprise attack must be taken seriously at the Kremlin. The ballistic-missile submarines in the Russian fleet are old, poorly maintained, and rarely leave their ports. The subs have become easy targets and no longer provide a secure retaliatory threat. The odds of the United States launching an all-out surprise attack on Russia's nuclear forces are infinitesimal. But the pressure to maintain a launch-on-warning policy may be stronger now in Moscow than it was thirty years ago. And the reliability of the Russian early-warning system has declined considerably since the end of the Cold War.

On January 25, 1995, the launch of a small research rocket by Norway prompted a warning at the Kremlin that Russia was under attack by the United States. Russian nuclear forces went on full alert. President Boris Yeltsin turned on his "football," retrieved his launch codes, and prepared to retaliate. After a few tense minutes, the warning was declared a false alarm. The weather rocket had been launched to study the aurora borealis, and Norway had informed Russia of its trajectory weeks in advance.

The greatest risk of nuclear war now lies in South Asia. The United States and the Soviet Union, for all their cultural differences, were separated by thousands of miles. Their animosity was more theoretical and geopolitical than personal. Pakistan and India are neighbors, embittered by religious and territorial disputes. Both countries have nuclear weapons. The flight time of a missile from one to the other may be as brief as four or five minutes. And the command-and-control facilities on both sides are not hardened against an attack. During a crisis, the pressure to launch first would be enormous.

Much like China, India for many years embraced a strategy of minimum deterrence, building a small arsenal of weapons and vowing to use them only in retaliation. But India may be moving toward a more aggressive strategy, too. Pakistan has doubled the size of its arsenal since 2006. It now has about 100 nuclear weapons. It is the only nuclear power whose weapons are entirely controlled by the military. And the Pakistan army has not ruled out using them first, even in response to an Indian attack with conventional weapons. To make that sort of deterrent credible, the authority to use tactical nuclear weapons has probably been given to lower-level Pakistani officers, much like the United States once predelegated it to NATO commanders on the front lines.

Instead of making a war between India and Pakistan less likely, nuclear weapons may have the opposite effect. For most of the Cold War, the status quo in Europe, the dividing line between East and West, was accepted by both sides. The border dispute in South Asia is far more volatile, with Pakistan seeking to dislodge India from Kashmir. Pakistan's nuclear weapons have allowed it to sponsor terrorism against India, a much larger and more powerful nation, without fear of retaliation. Since the early 1990s the two countries have come close to nuclear war about half a dozen times, most recently in November 2008, after suicide attacks on India's largest city, Mumbai.

The security of Pakistan's nuclear arsenal is now threatened not only by an attack but also by radical Islamists within the country seeking to steal weapons. The internal and external threats place competing demands on Pakistan's command-and-control system. To protect against theft, the weapons should be stored at a handful of well-guarded locations. But to safeguard against an Indian surprise attack, the weapons should be dispersed to numerous storage sites. Pakistan has most likely chosen the latter approach. Although the warheads and bombs are said to be stored without their nuclear cores, the dispersal of Pakistan's weapons makes it a lot easier for terrorists to seize one.

Islamic militants staged a bold attack on the headquarters of the Pakistan army in October 2009. They wore military uniforms, used fake IDs, penetrated multiple layers of security, and held dozens of hostages for almost a full day. The head of the Strategic Forces Command, responsible for Pakistan's nuclear arsenal, worked at that headquarters. Another attack penetrated a naval aviation base outside Karachi in May 2011. Most of Pakistan's nuclear weapon storage facilities were built in the northwestern part of the country, as far as possible from India, to extend the warning time of a missile attack and to make a conventional attack on them more difficult. Unfortunately, that means the nuclear storage sites are located near the border with Afghanistan, Pakistan's lawless tribal areas, and the heart of its radical Islamist movement.

MOST OF THIS BOOK has been devoted to stories of accidents, miscalculations, and mistakes, tempered by a great deal of personal heroism. But one crucial fact must be kept in mind: none of the roughly seventy thousand nuclear weapons built by the United States since 1945 has ever detonated inadvertently or without proper authorization. The technological and administrative controls on those weapons have worked, however imperfectly at times—and countless people, military and civilian, deserve credit for that remarkable achievement. Had a single weapon been stolen or detonated, America's command-and-control system would still have attained a success rate of 99.99857 percent. But nuclear weapons are the most dangerous technology ever invented. Anything less than 100 percent control of them, anything less than perfect safety and security, would be unacceptable. And if this book has any message to preach, it is that human beings are imperfect.

A retired Strategic Air Command general told me about the enormous, daily stress of his job during the Cold War. It involved, among other things, managing the nuclear command-and-control system of the United States. New codes had to be regularly obtained from the National Security Agency and distributed to missile sites, bombers, submarines. False alarms from NORAD had to be considered and dismissed, Soviet military transmissions carefully analyzed, their submarines off the coast tracked. Thousands of things seemed to be happening in the system at once, all over the world, subtly interconnected, and at any moment something could go terribly wrong. He compared the job to holding an angry tiger by the tail. And like almost every single Air Force officer, weapon designer, Pentagon official, airman, and missile maintenance crew member whom I interviewed about the Cold War, he was amazed that nuclear weapons were never used, that no major city was destroyed, that the tiger never got loose.

The challenges that the United States has faced in the management of its arsenal should give pause to every other nation that seeks to obtain nuclear weapons. This technology was invented and perfected in the United States. I have no doubt that America's nuclear weapons are among the safest, most advanced, most secure against unauthorized use that have ever been built. And yet the United States has narrowly avoided a long series of nuclear disasters. Other countries, with less hard-earned experience in the field, may not be as fortunate. One measure of a nation's technological proficiency is the rate of industrial accidents. That rate is about two times higher in India, three times higher in Iran, and four times higher in Pakistan than it is in the United States. High-risk technologies are easily transferred across borders; but the organizational skills and safety culture necessary to manage them are more difficult to share. Nuclear weapons have gained allure as a symbol of power and a source of national pride. They also pose a grave threat to any country that possesses them.

In recent years an international movement to abolish nuclear weapons has arisen from an unlikely source: the leadership of America's national security establishment during the Cold War. In January 2007, two former Republican secretaries of state—George Shultz and Henry Kissinger—along with two prominent Democrats—former Secretary of Defense William J. Perry and Sam Nunn, the former chairman of the Senate Armed Services Committee—wrote an op-ed for the *Wall Street Journal* that spelled out their goal: "A World Free of Nuclear Weapons." Sidney Drell had given the group not only technical guidance but also encouragement to take a bold stance. "The world is now on the precipice of a new and dangerous nuclear era," they warned. The end of the Cold War, the threat of nuclear terrorism, and the spread of nuclear weapons to countries like North Korea rendered long-standing notions of deterrence obsolete. The use of nuclear weapons had become more, not less, likely. And the two nations that control about 90 percent of those weapons—the United States and Russia—had an obligation to remove their missiles from hair-trigger alert, minimize the risk of accidents, reduce the size of their arsenals, and pursue abolition with the collaborative spirit that reigned, briefly, at the 1986 Reykjavik summit.

The campaign to eliminate nuclear weapons was subsequently endorsed by a wide variety of former Cold Warriors, including Robert McNamara, Colin Powell, and George H. W. Bush. It became part of America's foreign policy on April 5, 2009. "Some argue that the spread of these weapons cannot be stopped, cannot be checked—that we are destined to live in a world where more nations and more people possess the ultimate tools of destruction," President Barack Obama said that day, during a speech before a crowd of twenty thousand people in Prague. "Such fatalism is a deadly adversary, for if we believe that the spread of nuclear weapons is inevitable, then in some way we are admitting to ourselves that the use of nuclear weapons is inevitable." Obama committed his administration to seeking "a world without nuclear weapons," warning that the threat of global nuclear war had gone down but the risk of a nuclear attack had gone up. Later that year, the United Nations Security Council voted to support abolition. The idealistic rhetoric at the U.N. has not yet been followed, however, by the difficult steps that might lead to the elimination of nuclear weapons: passage of the Comprehensive Nuclear Test Ban Treaty by the U.S. Senate; major reductions in the Russian and American arsenals; arms control talks that include China, India, Pakistan, North Korea, and Israel; strict rules on the production and distribution of fissile materials; and harsh punishments for countries that violate the new international norms.

In the United States, the nuclear abolition movement has failed to generate much popular support. The retired officials who jump-started the debate in 2007 had an average age of seventy-nine. Many of the issues at stake seem hypothetical and remote. Almost half of the American population were not yet born or were children when the Cold War ended. And support for the abolition of nuclear weapons is hardly universal. The administration of President George W. Bush not only sought to develop new warheads and hydrogen bombs but also broadened the scope of the OPLAN. Bush's counterforce strategy, adopted after 9/11, threatened the preemptive use of nuclear weapons to thwart conventional, biological, and chemical attacks on the United States. A pair of liberal Democrats, former Secretary of Defense Harold Brown and former director of the CIA John M. Deutch, criticized the "nuclear disarmament fantasy" from a different perspective. Nuclear weapons can never be un-invented, Brown and Deutch argued, and countries that secretly violate an international ban might achieve unchecked power. The temptation to cheat would be enormous. In their view, utopian proposals shouldn't distract attention from practical measures to reduce the nuclear threat and avoid armed conflicts: "Hope is not a policy, and, at present, there is no realistic path to a world free of nuclear weapons."

Between the extremes of a counterforce strategy requiring thousands of nuclear weapons always on alert and an agreement to abolish all nuclear weapons, there lies a third course. Promoted by the U.S. Navy in the late 1950s, when its submarine-based missiles were too inaccurate to hit military targets, the strategy of minimum deterrence has lately gained strong support, even in some unexpected places. In 2010 a group of high-ranking Air Force officials, including its chief of strategic planning, argued that the United States needed only 311 nuclear weapons to deter an attack. Any more would be overkill. The arsenal proposed by these Air Force strategists would contain almost 200 fewer weapons than the one recommended by the National Resources Defense Council and the Federation of American Scientists, a pair of liberal groups that also support minimum deterrence.

Bob Peurifoy advocates a similar strategy. He considers himself a realist and thinks that a world free of nuclear weapons is unattainable. He would like the United States to get rid of its land-based missiles, take all its weapons off alert, give up the notion that a counterforce strategy might work, and retain a few hundred ballistic missiles securely deployed on submarines. To avoid accidental launches and mistakes, the subs shouldn't be capable of firing their missiles quickly. And to dissuade foreign enemies from attacking the United States, Peurifoy would let them know in advance where America's warheads might land on their territory. That knowledge would deter any rational world leader. But the problems with a strategy of minimum deterrence have changed little in the past fifty years. It cannot defend the United States against an impending attack. It can only kill millions of enemy civilians after the United States has already been attacked.

LAUNCH COMPLEX 374-7 was never rebuilt. The underground passages were disassembled. The land around it was cleared of debris. Toxic waste was pumped from the silo, and then the silo was filled with gravel and dirt. The Air Force returned the land to Ralph and Reba Jo Parish, from whom it had been taken through eminent domain. Seeing the place today, you would never think that one of the most destructive weapons ever built once lay beneath the ground there. Nature has reclaimed the site. It's covered with grass, surrounded by woods and farmland. A large mound covers the spot where the missile stood. The paved access road is now dirt. Quiet, peaceful, bucolic—it could not feel more removed from international diplomacy, Washington politics, nuclear strategy. The only hints of what happened there are patches of concrete overgrown with weeds and a few scattered pieces of metal, lying on the ground, that have been bent and deformed by tremendous heat.

I first heard about the accident at Damascus in the fall of 1999, while visiting Vandenberg Air Force Base. I was interested in the future of warfare in space, the plans to build laser beam, particle beam, and directed energy weapons. The Air Force Space Command invited me to watch the launch of a Titan II missile, and it seemed like an opportunity that shouldn't be missed. The payload of the missile was a weather satellite. During the long delay of the scheduled launch, I spoke to officers who'd served on missile combat crews. They told me Cold War stories and showed me footage of warheads arriving at the Kwajalein Test Site in the South Pacific. A Peacekeeper missile had been fired from Vandenberg at night, and as one warhead after another fell from the sky and landed precisely within their target circles, it was an oddly beautiful sight. They looked like shooting stars.

The evening before the Titan II launch, I rode an elevator to the top of the tower and got to see the missile up close. I could just about reach out and touch it. The Titan II seemed a living, breathing thing, attached to all sorts of cables and wires, like an angry patient about to be released from intensive care. The tower hummed with the sound of cooling units. Looking down the length of the missile, I could hardly believe that anyone would be brave enough and crazy enough to sit on top of it, like the Gemini astronauts did, and ride it into space.

The next morning I signed a waiver, promising not to sue the Air Force for any injuries, and received training in the use of a Scott Air-Pak. I carried the breathing apparatus in case the Titan II misfired on the pad. The officer who served as my host had never been allowed to stand so close to a launch. When the missile left the ground, you could feel it in your bones. The blast, the roar, the sight of the flames slowly lifting the Titan II upward—they suddenly affected me. They were more visceral and more powerful than any Cold War story. I had grown up in the 1970s hearing about missiles and warheads, throw weights and megatons, half believing that none of those weapons really worked, that the fears of nuclear Armageddon were overblown and based on some terrible fiction. The Titan II hesitated for a moment and then really took off, like a ten-story silver building disappearing into the sky. Within moments, it was gone, just a tail of flame somewhere over Mexico.

Watching that launch, the imaginary became tangible and concrete for me. It rattled me. It pierced a false sense of comfort. Right now thousands of missiles are hidden away, literally out of sight, topped with warheads and ready to go, awaiting the right electrical signal. They are a collective death wish, barely suppressed. Every one of them is an accident waiting to happen, a potential act of mass murder. They are out there, waiting, soulless and mechanical, sustained by our denial—and they work.

ACKNOWLEDGMENTS

Jeff Kennedy was the first person whom I interviewed for this book. More than a decade ago, I visited him in Maine, listened with amazement to his stories about the Titan II, and learned the extraordinary details of what happened in Damascus, Arkansas. Over the years, Kennedy was helpful, encouraging—and never shy about telling me how or why I was completely wrong. I admired his honesty. And I admired the bravery he showed not only in trying to save the missile that night but also in sacrificing his Air Force career to speak out about the Titan II. Kennedy passed away in the fall of 2011, at the age of fifty-six. I regret not having finished this book in time for him to read it.

Bob Peurifoy spent countless hours speaking to me about nuclear weapons, explaining fine points of physics and engineering, hoping that I'd use the knowledge well. I am grateful to him and Barbara Peurifoy for all their hospitality and their friendship. Sidney Drell played a crucial role in opening my eyes to this hidden world. And Bill Stevens patiently answered the same technical questions of mine again and again. Peurifoy, Drell, and Stevens truly are public servants.

Al Childers and Greg Devlin similarly spent untold hours helping me to understand the events at Launch Complex 374-7. Rodney Holder, Jim Sandaker, and Don Green talked to me at length as well. I am grateful for all the time these men devoted to my research. Colonel John T. Moser was extremely gracious in answering questions about perhaps the worst experience of his long Air Force career. And I'm grateful to General Chris Adams—a prolific author as well as a former chief of staff at the Strategic Air Command—for his many insights about the role of the Air Force in the Cold War. Although our political views differ, I have great respect for the way General Adams has served his country.

David and Barbara Pryor, Phil and Annette Herrington, Sid King, Sam Hutto, and Skip Rutherford made my time in Arkansas a real pleasure. I'm grateful to Cindy English for telling me about her late father, Richard English; to David Rossborough, Jeffrey Zink, David Powell, and Jeffrey Plumb; to Colonel Ben Scallorn, Colonel Jimmie Gray, Major Vincent Maes, Colonel Ron Bishop; and to Mary Ann Dennis, whose memories of her late brother, David Livingston, served as a poignant reminder of how meaningless statistics can be—and how the loss of a single life is one too many.

Ann Godoff proved to be exactly what a great editor should be: blunt, fiercely intelligent, and seemingly afraid of nothing. Those are rare qualities in a literary world that's increasingly timid and homogenized.

Stefan McGrath, Helen Conford, and Rosie Glaisher could not have been more supportive, from the first to the last. And I am profoundly grateful.

Tina Bennett made this book happen. She urged me to write it, discussed it with me for almost ten years, and through thick and thin never wavered in her enthusiasm for it. Her advice was reliably on the mark. Every writer should have such a brilliant, forceful advocate.

A number of other people at William Morris Endeavor must be thanked: Tracy Fisher, Raffaela De Angelis, Annemarie Blumenhagen, Alicia Gordon. And Svetlana Katz is simply the best.

Ellis Levine proved himself, as always, to be a fine critic as well as a formidable legal mind. I am very lucky to have him on my side, not the other one.

I'm grateful to Sarah Hutson and Ryan Davies for their efforts to bring attention to my work.

Benjamin Platt deserves some sort of prize for how he handled the production of this book. I hope he gets it. Meighan Cavanaugh gave the book a clear, beautiful design. Deborah Weiss Geline's copyediting made me seem more eloquent; she's a wonderful practitioner of an unfortunately vanishing art. Lindsay Whalen, Michael McConnell, Nina Hnatov, Christina Caruccio, Melanie Belkin, and Denise Boyd all helped turn my manuscript into a book. And I'm grateful to Eamon Dolan for bringing me to The Penguin Press in the first place.

Jennifer Jerde and Scott Hesselink at Elixir Design came up with a memorable, original jacket. Gideon Kendall worked hard to capture every little detail in his very cool illustration of a Titan II missile complex. And I'm honored that the first words in this book were written by Leonard Cohen.

I did not employ researchers while writing *Command and Control*. But I later received invaluable help from a small team of people who did their best to ensure the book's accuracy. Bea Marr did a terrific job transcribing interview tapes, wading through all sorts of jargon—and immediately forgetting everything she heard. Jane Cavolina carefully scrutinized my quotations and assertions of fact. I am grateful for every single error that she found, from the trivial to the deeply embarrassing. Once again, Charles Wilson helped me get things right, reinterviewing many of the subjects in this book with sensitivity and skill. Ariel Towber helped to compile the bibliographic citations and made sure that my calculations actually had some basis in mathematics. Stephanie Simon, Jessica Bufford, and Aaron Labaree also worked on the citations—and I even recruited my poor children, Mica and Conor Schlosser, to help with the task. They no doubt hope my next book will be a novel. And I'm grateful to David Schmalz, Elizabeth Limbach, and Hilary McClellen for their fact-checking efforts. One of the central themes of *Command and Control* is the fallibility of all human endeavors. Sadly, that inescapable law applies to me as well. Any mistakes in this book are my fault. I hope that readers will kindly point them out to me.

A number of dear friends read the manuscript in full or in part, gave me good suggestions, and helped me to get through it: Michael Clurman, Dominic Dromgoole, Robby Kenner, Corby Kummer, Cullen Murphy, John Seabrook. The fact that I ignored some of those suggestions reflects poorly on me, not them. And Katrina vanden Heuvel has been a true friend throughout, a fellow student of the Cold War who helped me navigate the national security bureaucracy.

My greatest thanks go to my family: Mica, Conor, Dylan, Lena, Andrew, Austin, and Hillary; Lynn and Craig; James and Kyle; Matt and Amy; Bob and Bylle; Lola and George; my parents. I can't imagine what they've put up with these past six years. While writing this book, I have not been the life of the party.

Most of all, I feel love and gratitude and great compassion for Red, who's had to live beside this darkness. Without her, it would have been impossible.

NOTES

A NOTE ON SOURCES

Although I did a great deal of research for this book, I also benefited enormously from the writing, expertise, and firsthand experience of others. I've tried in these notes to acknowledge my debt to the many people whose work influenced mine. For the past six decades, the intense official secrecy surrounding nuclear weapons has presented an unusual challenge to journalists and scholars who write about the subject. Sometimes the only thing more difficult than obtaining accurate information is demonstrating to readers that it's true. I have done my best here not to cite or rely solely upon anonymous sources. Nevertheless, over the years, I've spoken to countless people who formulated or carried out America's nuclear weapon policies, including three former secretaries of defense, presidential advisers, heads of the Los Alamos and Lawrence Livermore laboratories, physicists and engineers once employed at those labs, Pentagon officials, Strategic Air Command generals, bomber pilots and navigators, missile crew commanders, missile repairmen and bomb squad technicians trained to handle weapons of mass destruction. Most of their names never appear in this book. And yet what they told me helped to ensure its accuracy. Any factual errors in these pages are entirely my own.

One of the primary sources for my narrative of the Damascus accident was a three-volume report prepared by the Air Force: "Report of Missile Accident Investigation: Major Missile Accident, 18–19 September 1980, Titan II Complex 374-7, Assigned to 308th Strategic Missile Wing, Little Rock Air Force Base, Arkansas," conducted at Little Rock Air Force Base, Arkansas, and Barksdale Air Force Base, Louisiana, December

14–19, 1980, Eighth Air Force Missile Investigation Board, December 1980. When I contacted the Air Force for a copy of this report, I was told that the Air Force no longer possessed one. I later found a copy among the congressional papers of Dan Glickman at Wichita State University. I am very grateful to Mary Nelson, a program consultant in the department of special collections there, who arranged for the report to be photocopied for me. Other copies, I subsequently learned, are held at the Titan Missile Museum in Sahuarita, Arizona, and at the Jacksonville Museum of Military History in Jacksonville, Arkansas.

The accident report contains more than a thousand pages of maps, charts, photographs, analysis, and testimony from ninety-two witnesses. The material was invaluable for reconstructing what happened that night in Damascus. Two other official reports on the Titan II were much less reliable but still worth reading, if only for what they failed to say about the missile: "Assessment Report: Titan II LGM 25 C, Weapon Condition and Safety," prepared for the Senate Armed Services Committee and House Armed Services Committee, May 1980; and "Titan II Weapon System: Review Group Report," December 1980.

David H. Pryor, who was a U.S. senator from Arkansas in 1980, helped me to understand the state's political culture at the time and shared his long-standing concerns about the Titan II. One of his former aides, James L. "Skip" Rutherford III, described his own investigation of the missile's safety and his secret meetings with airmen from Little Rock Air Force Base. I tracked down one of those airmen, who spoke to me, off the record, and confirmed Rutherford's account. At the University of Arkansas in Fayetteville, I found many useful memos and documents about the Titan II in the David H. Pryor Papers, especially in Group II, Boxes 244–84.

Most important, perhaps, I spoke to people who played leading roles in the Damascus accident and its aftermath. I am grateful to all those who shared their recollection of the events at Launch Complex 374-7, at Little Rock Air Force Base, at the underground command post of the Strategic Air Command in Omaha, the headquarters of the Eighth Air Force in Louisiana, and elsewhere. Some of the most useful details were provided by Jeffrey L. Plumb and David F. Powell, who were in the missile silo when the socket fell; Allan D. Childers and Rodney Holder, who were in the launch control center; Colonel John T. Moser, the head of the 308th Strategic Missile Wing, who was at the Little Rock command post; Major Vincent O. Maes, the maintenance supervisor at the 308th, who advised Moser that night; Colonel Jimmie D. Gray, the commander of the 308th Missile Inspection and Maintenance Squadron, who was at both the Little Rock command post and the accident site; Colonel Ben Scallorn, the deputy chief of staff for Missiles and Space Systems Support at headquarters, Eighth Air Force, a Titan II expert who spent hours on the Missile Potential Hazard Net; General Lloyd R. Leavitt, the vice commander in chief of the Strategic Air Command, who made many of the crucial decisions about what should be done; Colonel Ronald Bishop, who took over the 308th Strategic

the Titan II and the Damascus accident. Walter Pincus, a correspondent for the *Washington Post*, did a particularly fine job of investigating the missile system, ignoring Air Force denials, and seeking the facts. The *New York Times*, the *Arkansas Gazette*, and the *Arkansas Democrat* also covered the story well. I'm grateful to Randy Dixon, the former news director at KATV-TV in Little Rock, and to Albert Kamas, an attorney in Wichita, who helped me to find local television coverage of problems with the Titan II.

The literature about nuclear weapons is vast, and I tried to read as much of it as possible. A number of books stand apart from the rest; the quality of their thinking and prose match the importance of the subject matter. John Hersey's *Hiroshima* (New York: Knopf, 2003) is one of the greatest works of nonfiction ever written. Compassionate and yet tough minded, Hersey calmly describes the destruction of a city without hyperbole or sentimentality. Despite all the horrific imagery, the book is ultimately about the resilience of human beings, not their capacity for evil. *The Making of the Atomic Bomb* (New York: Simon & Schuster, 1986), by Richard Rhodes, is another classic. Rhodes skillfully conveys the drama and high stakes of the Manhattan Project, the clash of big egos and great minds. He also explains the science, physics, and technical details of the first nuclear weapons with admirable clarity. Much like *Uncle Tom's Cabin* and *The Jungle*, Jonathan Schell's *The Fate of the Earth* (New York: Knopf, 1982) had an electrifying effect when it was first published and helped to create a social movement. The book retains its power, more than thirty years later. An extraordinary biography by Kai Bird and Martin J. Sherwin—*American Prometheus: The Triumph and Tragedy of J. Robert Oppenheimer* (New York: Vintage Books, 2006)—uses the genius, idealism, contradictions, and hypocrisy of one man to shed light on an entire era of American history. Perhaps my favorite book about nuclear weapons is one of the most beautifully written and concise. John McPhee's *The Curve of Binding Energy* (New York: Farrar, Straus & Giroux, 1974) not only has great literary merit, it also prompted engineers at Sandia to confront the possibility that terrorists might try to steal a nuclear weapon. Martin J. Sherwin and John McPhee were both professors of mine a long time ago, and the integrity of their work, the scholarship and ambition, set a high standard to which I've aspired ever since.

A number of other writers and historians influenced my view of how nuclear weapons affected postwar America. Barton Bernstein, a professor of history at Stanford University, has written complex and persuasive essays about President Truman's decision to use the atomic bomb. Paul Boyer's *By the Bomb's Early Light: American Thought and Culture at the Dawn of the Atomic Age* (Chapel Hill, NC: University of North Carolina Press, 1994) shows how the euphoria that accompanied the end of the Second World War soon became a deep anxiety about nuclear war that endured for almost half a century. *The Wizards of Armageddon, The Untold Story of the Small Group of Men Who Have Devised the Plans and Shaped the Policies on How to Use the Bomb* (Stanford: Stanford University Press, 1991), by Fred Kaplan, explains how RAND analysts and brilliant theorists rationalized the creation of a nuclear arsenal with thousands of weapons. In *Whole World on*

Fire: Organizations, Knowledge & Nuclear Weapons Devastation (Ithaca: Cornell University Press, 2004), Lynn Eden delves into the mentality of war planners who excluded from their calculations one of the principal effects of nuclear weapons: the capability to ignite things. Lawrence Freedman's *The Evolution of Nuclear Strategy* (New York: Palgrave Macmillan, 2003) is the finest book on the subject, clear and authoritative—although the gulf between clever strategic theories and the likely reality of nuclear war has always been vast. The best overview of how nuclear weapons have affected American society is *Atomic Audit: The Costs and Consequences of U.S. Nuclear Weapons Since 1940* (Washington, D.C.: Brookings Insitution Press, 1998), edited by Stephen I. Schwartz. And since 1945, the *Bulletin of Atomic Scientists* has been publishing timely, informative, and reliable articles about the nuclear threat.

During my research for *Command and Control*, I spoke to Pentagon officials from every postwar administration, except that of President Harry Truman. But my understanding of the Cold War owes much to the work of historian John Lewis Gaddis, most notably his recent biography, *George F. Kennan: An American Life* (New York: Penguin Press, 2011), and his synthesis of more than thirty years studying the conflict, *The Cold War: A New History* (New York: Penguin Books, 2007). The opening of archives in the former Soviet Union has added a much-needed new perspective to events long narrowly viewed from the American side, and a number of books have supplanted earlier histories or added important new details. I learned much from Vojtech Mastny's *The Cold War and Soviet Insecurity: The Stalin Years* (New York: Oxford University Press, 1996) and from two excellent books by Alexsandr Fursenko and Timothy Naftali: *Khruschchev's Cold War: The Inside Story of an American Adversary* (New York: W. W. Norton, 2006) and *"One Hell of a Gamble": Khrushchev, Castro, and Kennedy, 1958–1964* (New York: W. W. Norton, 1997).

Some of the most compelling books about the Cold War have been written by people who helped to wage it. For the Truman years, I strongly recommend the deeply personal works of James Forrestal and David E. Lilienthal—Walter Millis, ed. *The Forrestal Diaries* (New York: Viking Press, 1951) and *The Journals of David E. Lilienthal, Volume II: The Atomic Energy Years, 1945–1950* (New York: Harper & Row, 1964). One of the most perceptive observers of President Eisenhower's strategic thinking was McGeorge Bundy. But his epic book—*Danger and Survival: Choices About the Bomb in the First Fifty Years* (New York: Random House, 1988)—is less trustworthy about the Kennedy administration in which Bundy served. I also learned a great deal from books by Kenneth D. Nichols, a strong proponent of nuclear weapons, and by Herbert F. York, a former head of the Lawrence Livermore Laboratory who came to doubt their usefulness. Nichols's memoir is *The Road to Trinity: A Personal Account of How America's Nuclear Policies Were Made* (New York: William Morrow, 1987), and York wrote two books about his experiences, *Race to Oblivion: A Participant's View of the Arms Race* (New York: Simon & Schuster, 1970) and *Making Weapons, Talking Peace: A Physicist's Odyssey from Hiroshima to Geneva*

(New York: Basic Books, 1987). Thomas C. Reed, a nuclear weapons designer and close adviser to Ronald Reagan, wrote a blunt, fascinating account of the Cold War's final chapter, *At the Abyss: An Insider's History of the Cold War* (New York: Ballantine Books, 2004). The Cold War memoir that I found to be the most interesting and revelatory was written by Robert M. Gates, the former secretary of defense and director of the CIA: *From the Shadows: The Ultimate Insider's Story of Five Presidents and How They Won the Cold War* (New York: Simon & Schuster, 2006).

Two classic texts offer a good introduction to the origins and explosive power of nuclear weapons: Henry DeWolf Smyth's *Atomic Energy for Military Purposes: The Official Report on the Development of the Atomic Bomb Under the Auspices of the United States Government 1940–1945:* (Princeton: Princeton University Press, 1945) and *The Effects of Nuclear Weapons* (Washington, D.C.: U.S. Government Printing Office, 1964), edited by Samuel Glasstone. More than twenty-five years after being published, *The Making of the Atomic Bomb* remains the definitive work on the Manhattan Project. I also learned a great deal about the development of the first nuclear weapons from *Critical Assembly: A Technical History of Los Alamos During the Oppenheimer Years, 1943–1945* (New York: Cambridge University Press, 1993), by Lillian Hoddeson, Paul W. Henriksen, Roger A. Meade, and Catherine Westfall. The weapons themselves are described with unparalleled accuracy in John Coster-Mullen's book, *Atom Bombs: The Top Secret Inside Story of Little Boy and Fat Man* (Waukesha, WI: John Coster-Mullen, 2009). David Samuels profiles Coster-Mullen and his indefatigable research methods in "Atomic John: A Truck Driver Uncovers Secrets About the First Nuclear Bombs," *The New Yorker,* December 15, 2008.

Chuck Hansen's *The Swords of Armageddon,* a digital collection released by Chuklea Publications in 2007, is by far the most impressive work on the technical aspects of nuclear weapons. Spanning seven volumes and more than three thousand pages, it is based almost entirely on documents that Hansen obtained through the Freedom of Information Act. Many of the documents are included verbatim, and they cover almost every aspect of nuclear weapon design. The only sources that I found to be more reliable than Hansen were people who'd actually designed nuclear weapons.

Sidney Drell introduced me to the issue of nuclear weapon safety, and I'm profoundly grateful for the assistance that he gave me with this book. Drell is a theoretical physicist who for many years headed the SLAC National Accelerator Laboratory at Stanford University, a founding member of JASON, a former adviser to both the Los Alamos and Lawrence Livermore laboratories, and a former member of the president's foreign intelligence advisory board. And he served, between 1990 and 1991, as the chairman of the House Armed Services Committee Panel on Nuclear Weapons Safety. Drell also introduced me to Bob Peurifoy, a former vice president at the Sandia National Laboratory—and through Peurifoy, I met Bill Stevens, the former head of nuclear safety at Sandia. More than anything else, these three men helped me understand the effort, pursued for decades, to ensure that nuclear weapons would never detonate accidentally or without proper authorization.

Through the Freedom of Information Act, I obtained some fascinating reports about nuclear weapon safety. Among the more useful were: "Acceptable Premature Probabilities for Nuclear Weapons," Headquarters Field Command, Armed Forces Special Weapons Project, FC/10570136, October 1, 1957 (SECRET/RESTRICTRED DATA/declassified); "A Survey of Nuclear Weapon Safety Problems and the Possibilities for Increasing Safety in Bomb and Warhead Design," prepared by Sandia Corporation with the advice and assistance of the Los Alamos Scientific Laboratory and the University of California Ernest O. Lawrence Radiation Laboratory, RS 3466/26889, February 1959 (SECRET/RESTRICTED DATA/declassified); "Accidents and Incidents Involving Nuclear Weapons: Accidents and Incidents During the Period 1 July 1957 Through 31 March 1967," Technical Letter 20-3, Defense Atomic Support Agency, October 15, 1967 (SECRET/RESTRICTED DATA/declassified); "Accident Environments," T. D. Brumleve, chairman, Task Group on Accidents Environments Sandia Laboratories, Livermore Laboratory, SCL-DR-69-86, January 1970 (SECRET/RESTRICTED DATA/declassified); and "A Review of the U.S. Nuclear Weapon Safety Program—1945 to 1986," R. N. Brodie, Sandia National Laboratories, SAND86-2955, February 1987 (SECRET/RESTRICTED DATA/declassified).

The best and most thorough history of nuclear weapons safety was written by Bill Stevens: "The Origins and Evolution of S²C at Sandia National Laboratories, 1949–1996," Sandia National Laboratories, SAND99-1308, September 2001 (OFFICAL USE ONLY). It has never been released to the public, but I managed to obtain a copy—and I did not get it from Stevens. In 2011 Sandia produced an informative two-hour documentary, *Always/Never: The Quest for Safety, Control & Survivability* that has also been classified OFFICIAL USE ONLY and never released to the public. Through an anonymous source, I got a copy of that, as well. It is absurd that these two historical works are not freely available. Neither contains classified information. And both illuminate subjects of enormous national importance.

I feel fortunate to have spent time with the late Fred Charles Iklé. Although our political views were in many ways quite different, I found him to be an eloquent, deeply patriotic opponent of nuclear war. And he spoke to me at length about his two pioneering studies on nuclear weapons safety and use control: one of them written with Gerald J. Aronson and Albert Madansky, "On the Risk of an Accidental or Unauthorized Nuclear Detonation," research memorandum, Project RAND, USAF, Santa Monica, California, October 15, 1958, RM-2251 (CONFIDENTIAL/RESTRICTED DATA/declassified), and the other written with J. E. Hill, "The Aftermath of a Single Nuclear Detonation by Accident or Sabotage: Some Problems Affecting U.S. Policy, Military Reactions, and Public Information," Research Memorandum, Project RAND, US Air Force, Santa Monica, California, May 8, 1959, RM-2364 (SECRET/RESTRICTED DATA/declassified). I am also grateful to Harold Agnew, a former director of the Los Alamos National Laboratory, for describing his work to assure the one-point safety of nuclear weapons, to place locks inside warheads and bombs, and to provide adequate security to American weapons deployed overseas. And I spoke to the late Robert McNamara about his determination, as secretary of defense, to make nuclear weapons safer and less vulnerable to unauthorized use.

Remarkably little has been published about nuclear weapon accidents, and I was glad to find two good books that addressed the potential dangers: *Nuclear Weapons Safety and the Common Defense,* by Joel Larus (Columbus, OH: Ohio State University Press, 1967), and Shaun R. Gregory's *The Hidden Cost of Deterrence: Nuclear Weapon Accidents* (Washington, D.C.: Brassey's, 1990). Both were written, however, without access to the accident reports that have been released through the Freedom of Information Act since the end of the Cold War. Two retired Air Force nuclear technicians, Michael H. Maggelet and James C. Oskins, have done a superlative job of obtaining information about weapon accidents from their former employer. And they've made documents on the subject available, largely unedited, in a couple of books that I found extremely useful: *Broken Arrow: The Declassified History of U.S. Nuclear Weapons Accidents* (Raleigh, NC: Lulu, 2007), and *Broken Arrow, Volume II: A Disclosure of Significant U.S., Soviet, and British Nuclear Weapon Incidents and Accidents, 1945–2008* (Raleigh, NC: Lulu, 2010). Maggelet and Oskins don't exaggerate the danger of the many bomber crashes and fires that involved nuclear weapons. In fact, they tend to understate the actual risk of an accidental detonation. But what they've uncovered is remarkable.

One of the most eye-opening documents that I read for this book was a study prepared for Secretary of Defense James R. Schlesinger: "The Evolution of U.S. Strategic Command and Control and Warning 1945–1972," written by L. Wainstein, C. D. Cremeans, J. K. Moriarity, and J. Ponturo, Study S-467, International and Social Studies Division, Institute for Defense Analyses, June 1975 (TOP SECRET/RESTRICTED DATA/declassified). It gave me the unmistakable feeling that, during the Cold War, things were never fully under control. Another fine study commissioned at about the same time—"History of the Strategic Arms Competition, 1945–1972," written by Ernest R. May, John D. Steinbruner, and Thomas W. Wolfe, Office of the Secretary of Defense, Historical Office, March 1981 (TOP SECRET/RESTRICTED DATA/declassified)—strongly reinforced that sense.

A number of articles and books on command and control, written before those two studies were declassified, conveyed how hard it would be to fight a limited nuclear war or pause one to negotiate with the enemy. Desmond Ball was one of the first scholars who publicly challenged the reigning strategic orthodoxy. His article—"Can Nuclear War Be Controlled?" Adelphi Paper #169, International Institute for Strategic Studies, 1981—raised some fundamental questions that have never adequately been answered. A series of fine books on the subject soon appeared: Paul Bracken's *The Command and Control of Nuclear Forces* (New Haven, CT: Yale University Press, 1983); Daniel Ford's *The Button: The Pentagon's Strategic Command and Control System* (New York: Simon & Schuster, 1985); Bruce Blair's *Strategic Command and Control: Redefining the Nuclear Threat*

(Washington, D.C.: Brookings Institution, 1985); and the most extensive study of the subject that has been published to date, *Managing Nuclear Operations* (Washington, D.C: Brookings Institution, 1987), edited by Ashton Carter, John D. Steinbruner, and Charles A. Zraket. Steinbruner is now a professor of public policy at the University of Maryland and director of the Center for International and Security Studies at Maryland. He read an early draft of my book, and I'm grateful for his comments and support. Blair is a former Minuteman launch officer who earned a graduate degree at Yale, later joined the Brookings Institution, and now heads Global Zero, an organization devoted to the abolition of nuclear weapons. He has continued to write about command-and-control issues, and I learned a great deal from his work, especially *The Logic of Accidental Nuclear War* (Washington, D.C.: Brookings Institution, 1993). A more recent book on command and control during the Cold War largely confirms what the others found: *The World Wide Military Command and Control System: Evolution and Effectiveness,* by David Pearson (Maxwell Air Force Base, AL: Air University Press, 2000).

The Australian scholar Desmond Ball was also responsible for groundbreaking research on American nuclear strategy and targeting. His study of how the alleged missile gap affected subsequent defense spending—*Politics and Force Levels: The Strategic Missile Program of the Kennedy Administration* (Berkeley: University of California Press, 1980)—shows how domestic concerns, not military necessity, established the number of ICBMs that the United States would deploy for the next thirty years. A book that Ball edited with Jeffrey Richelson, *Strategic Nuclear Targeting* (Ithaca: Cornell University Press, 1986), explains the thinking behind where those missiles were aimed. The work of another influential scholar, David Alan Rosenberg, reveals how the American nuclear arsenal became so much larger than it needed to be. Two of Rosenberg's essays—"The Origins of Overkill: Nuclear Weapons and American Strategy 1945–1960," *International Security,* vol. 7, no. 4 (1983), pp. 3–71, and "'A Smoking Radiating Ruin at the End of Two Hours': Documents on American Plans for Nuclear War with the Soviet Union, 1954–55," written with W. B. Morse, *International Security,* vol. 6, no. 3 (1981), pp. 3–38—show how little would have been left after an attack by the Strategic Air Command.

The ongoing dispute about the merits of civilian or military control of nuclear weapons is addressed throughout the official history of the Atomic Energy Commission: *The New World, 1939/1946: A History of the United States Atomic Energy Commission, Volume I* written by Richard G. Hewlett and Oscar E. Anderson, Jr. (University Park, PA: Pennsylvania State University Press, 1962); *Atomic Shield, 1947/1952: A History of the United States Atomic Energy Commission, Volume II, by* Richard G. Hewlett and Francis Duncan (University Park, PA: Pennsylvania State University Press, 1969); and *Atoms for Peace and War, 1953/1961: Eisenhower and the Atomic Energy Commission, a History of the United States Atomic Energy Commission, Volume III,* by Richard G. Hewlett and Jack M. Holl (Berkeley: University of California Press, 1989). A fascinating declassified report traces how the military gained the upper hand—"History of the Custody and Deployment of

Nuclear Weapons: July 1945 through September 1977," Office of the Assistant to the Secretary of Defense (Atomic Energy), February 1978 (TOP SECRET/RESTRICTED DATA/ FORMERLY RESTRICTED DATA/declassified). The best academic studies of the issue have been written, wholly or in part, by Peter D. Feaver, now a professor of political science and public policy at Duke University. In *Guarding the Guardians: Civilian Control of Nuclear Weapons in the United States* (Ithaca: Cornell University Press, 1992), Feaver explores not only the tension between civilian and military control, but also the always/ never dilemma governing how that control would be exercised. And in an earlier work written with Peter Stein, Feaver gave the first detailed account of why the Kennedy administration took such a strong interest in coded, electromechanical locks: *Assuring Control of Nuclear Weapons: The Evolution of Permissive Action Links* (Cambridge, MA: Center for Science and International Affairs, John F. Kennedy School of Government, Harvard University, and University Press of America, 1987).

One of the main themes of this book is the difficulty of controlling complex, high-risk technologies. I've never had much patience for theories of historical inevitability—and in recent years a number of scholars have applied a healthy skepticism to the traditional view that scientific inventions are somehow the logical, necessary result of some previous development. They have challenged a simplistic technological determinism, suggesting that every manmade artifact is created within a specific social context. Donald MacKenzie, a professor of sociology at Edinburgh University, greatly influenced my thinking about how and why new inventions are made. MacKenzie has edited, with Judy Wajcmann, a fine collection that explores some of these ideas: *The Social Shaping of Technology: Second Edition* (New York: Open University Press, 1999). MacKenzie has also written a brilliant, thought-provoking book on the ways in which American targeting decisions improved the likelihood that a warhead would hit its target—*Inventing Accuracy: A Historical Sociology of Nuclear Missile Guidance* (Cambridge, MA: MIT Press, 1993). His views on the process of scientific and technological change resonate strongly with one of my own long-standing beliefs: if things aren't inevitable, then things don't have to be the way they are. Without being utopian or overly optimistic, MacKenzie and Graham Spinardi applied that sort of thinking to weapons of mass destruction, after interviewing dozens of scientists at Los Alamos and Lawrence Livermore, in their essay "Tacit Knowledge and the Uninvention of Nuclear Weapons." It can be found in MacKenzie's book *Knowing Machines: Essays on Technical Change* (Cambridge, MA: MIT Press, 1998).

Many of the declassified documents cited in this book were found online. Two of the best sites for historical material are the Pentagon's Defense Technical Information Center, "Provider of DoD Technical Information to Support the WarFighter," and the U.S. Department of Energy's OpenNet. L. Douglas Kenney—the author of *15 Minutes: General Curtis LeMay and the Countdown to Nuclear Annihilation* (New York: St. Martin's Press, 2011)—has posted a few Strategic Air Command official histories online that I found quite useful. A Web site called the Black Vault also features a wide variety of declassified documents. And the Federation of American Scientists is an excellent online source for information about nuclear weapons.

I am especially grateful for the work of the National Security Archive, based at George Washington University, which for almost three decades has been obtaining documents through the Freedom of Information Act and suing federal agencies when they are denied—not only to reveal what the government has done but also to hold it accountable for that behavior. The archive is a national treasure. Its digital collection proved invaluable to my research. William Burr, the director of its nuclear project, has done an extraordinary job of uncovering and explaining some of the more significant documents. With the head of the archive, Thomas S. Blanton, and Stephen I. Schwartz, Burr wrote a fine essay that explains why freedom of information is so essential: "The Costs and Consequences of Nuclear Secrecy," in *Atomic Audit*, pages 433–483. Throughout my bibliography and endnotes I have used the acronym NSA to identify documents originally obtained by the National Security Archive.

Prior to the publication of this book, I gave a rough draft of it to a nuclear weapons expert who is not employed by the U.S. government and yet possesses a high-level clearance. I wanted to feel confident that nothing disclosed in these pages would pose any threat to national security. My unpaid but much appreciated reader found nothing that even remotely does—and I agree with him. A far greater threat has been posed, for the past sixty years, by official secrecy and misinformation about America's nuclear arsenal. The suppression of the truth has allowed a small and elite group of policy makers to wield tremendous, largely unchecked power. There are few issues more important than what nuclear weapons can do, where they are aimed, why they might be used, and who has the ability to order their use. I hope my book contributes, in some small way, to restoring a semblance of democracy to the command and control of the deadliest, most dangerous machines that mankind has ever invented.

PART ONE: THE TITAN

Not Good

3   *Senior Airman David F. Powell and Airman Jeffrey L. Plumb:* I spoke to Plumb and Powell about the accident. Plumb's statement before the Missile Accident Investigation Board can be found at Tab U-71 and Powell's at Tab U-73, "Report of Missile Accident Investigation: Major Missile Accident, 18–19 September 1980, Titan II Complex 374-7, Assigned to 308th Strategic Missile Wing, Little Rock Air Force Base, Arkansas," conducted at Little Rock Air Force Base, Arkansas, and Barksdale Air Force Base, Louisiana, December 14–19, 1980.

3   *10 feet in diameter and 103 feet tall:* According to the Titan II historian David K. Stumpf, the height of the missile was often erroneously described as "anywhere from 108 feet to 114 feet." The actual height was 103.4 feet. See "Table 3.2, Titan II ICBM Final Design Specifications," in David K. Stumpf, *Titan II: A History of a Cold War Missile Program* (Fayetteville: University of Arkansas Press, 2000), p. 49.

3   *a yield of 9 megatons*: The yields of American nuclear weapons remain classified, except for those of
     the bombs that destroyed Hiroshima and Nagasaki. But for decades government officials have
     discussed those yields, off the record, with journalists. Throughout this book, I cite the weapon
     yields published by a pair of reliable defense analysts. For some reason, the megatonnage of the
     warheads carried by the Titan and Titan II missiles was disclosed in a document obtained by the
     National Security Archive through the Freedom of Information Act. For the yields of the W-38
     warhead atop the Titan and the W-53 atop the Titan II, see "Missile Procurement, Air Force," U.S.
     Congress, House Committee on Appropriations, Subcommittee on Defense, May 16, 1961
     (SECRET/declassified), NSA, p. 523. For the yields of other American weapons, see Norman Polmar
     and Robert S. Norris, *The U.S. Nuclear Arsenal: A History of Weapons and Delivery Systems Since
     1945* (Annapolis, MD: Naval Institute Press, 2009), pp. 1–70.

3   *about three times the explosive force of all the bombs:* Although estimates vary, the American physicist
     Richard L. Garwin and the Russian physicist Andrei Sakharov both noted that the explosive force
     of all the bombs used during the Second World War was about 3 megatons. The United States was
     responsible for most of it. According to Senator Stuart Symington, who'd served as the first secre-
     tary of the Air Force after the war, the bombs dropped by the United States had a cumulative force
     of 2.1 megatons. Two thirds of that amount was employed against Germany, the rest against
     Japan. The enormous power of the Titan II's warhead seems hard to comprehend. Nine megatons
     is the equivalent of eighteen billion pounds of TNT—about four pounds of high explosives for
     every person alive in September 1980. Symington's estimates can be found in "Military Applica-
     tions of Nuclear Technology," Hearing Before the Subcommittee on Atomic Energy, 93rd Cong.,
     April 16, 1973, pt. 1, pp. 3–4. For the other estimates, see Richard L. Garwin, "New Weapons/
     Old Doctrines: Strategic Warfare in the 1980s," *Proceedings of the American Philosophical Society*,
     vol. 124, no. 4 (1980), p. 262; and Andrei Sakharov, "The Danger of Thermonuclear War," *Foreign
     Affairs,* Summer 1983, p. 1002.

4   *"hypergolic":* The word, according to rocket scientists, means "spontaneously ignitable." One of the
     advantages of using hypergolic propellants is that the propellants eliminate the need for an igni-
     tion system in a missile. One of the disadvantages is how dangerous they are. For a good introduc-
     tion to the subject, see B. M. Nufer, "A Summary of NASA and USAF Hypergolic Propellant
     Related Spills and Fires," National Aeronautics and Space Administration, NASA/TP-2009-
     214769, June 2009. For a more thorough examination, see the chapters "Liquid Propellant Rocket
     Engine Fundamentals" and "Liquid Propellants" in George P. Sutton and Oscar Biblarz, *Rocket
     Propulsion Elements*, 7th ed. (New York: Wiley, 2001), pp. 197–267.

4   *supersonic convergent-divergent nozzles:* Shaped like an hourglass, a convergent-divergent nozzle in-
     creases the velocity of a hot gas by forcing it through a narrow chamber.

4   *The fuel, Aerozine-50:* A brief overview of the Titan II's propellants and their hazards can be found
     in "Propellant Transportation Awareness Guide for Titan II Deactivation," Department of the Air
     Force, October 1, 1982. A more detailed account is offered in "Titan II Storable Propellant Hand-
     book," Revision B, Bell Aerosystems Company, Prepared for Air Force Ballistic Systems Division,
     March 1963.

5   *a Rocket Fuel Handler's Clothing Outfit (RFHCO):* For a description of the gear and its proper use,
     see "Missile Liquid Propellant Systems Maintenance Specialist: Volume 3, Propellant Transfer
     System," CDC 4551, Extension Course Institute, Air Training Command, February 1983,
     pp. 1–42.

6   *Electroexplosive devices were used:* For the various things that could explode in a Titan II silo and
     the potential risks, see "Nuclear Weapon Specialist: Volume 5, Rockets, Missiles, and Reentry
     Systems," CDC 46350, Extension Course Institute, Air Training Command, November 1980
     (FOR OFFICIAL USE ONLY), pp. 19–38.

7   *Technical Order 21M-LGM25C-2-12, Figure 2-18*: The relevant excerpt of the tech order can be
     found in "Titan II Class A Mishap Report: Serial Number 62-0006, 18 September 1980, Damas-
     cus, Arkansas," Eighth Air Force Mishap Investigation Board, October 30, 1980, p. 0-1.

7   *"Oh man," Plumb thought:* Interview with Jeffrey L. Plumb.

New Wave

8   *Second Lieutenant Allan D. Childers had gotten out of bed:* I spoke to Childers at length about that day. His testimony before the accident investigation board can be found in "Report, Major Missile Accident, Titan II Complex 374-7," Tab U-13.

11   *the* Dash-1: An abridged version has been published: *Technical Manual, USAF Model LGM-25C, Missile System Operation* (Tucson: Arizona Aerospace Foundation, 2005).

12   *"the hostile invasion . . . by the Iraqi regime":* Quoted in "Iran Criticizes Iraq for Ending '75 Pact," *New York Times*, September 19, 1980.

13   *the International Institute for Strategic Studies . . . issued a report:* The title of the report was "The Military Balance, 1980–1981." See Louis Nevin, "Soviets and Warsaw Pact Have Weapons Lead Over West," Associated Press, September 17, 1980.

13   *an unemployment rate of about 8 percent:* President Carter cited that figure while speaking to reporters on September 18, 1980. See "Transcript of the President's News Conference," *New York Times*, September 19, 1980.

13   *"a crisis in confidence":* For the complete speech, see "Text of President Carter's Address to the Nation," *Washington Post*, July 16, 1979.

13   *an official report on the failed rescue attempt:* See "Rescue Mission Report," Joint Chiefs of Staff, Special Operations Review Group, August 1980.

14   *77 percent of the American people disapproved:* President Nixon's disapproval rate never exceeded 71 percent. These ratings are cited in Donald M. Rothberg, "Carter Plunges in Polls, But Campaign Chief Insists He'll Win," Associated Press, July 30, 1980.

14   *"I refuse to accept [Carter's] defeatist and pessimistic view":* See "Transcript of Reagan Speech Outlining Five-Year Economic Program for the U.S.," *New York Times*, September 10, 1980.

14   *"four more years of weakness, indecision, mediocrity":* See "Text of Reagan's Speech Accepting Republicans' Nomination," *New York Times*, July 18, 1980.

14   *"a bumbler":* Quoted in "Interview with John B. Anderson," *BusinessWeek*, September 8, 1980.

14   *"People feel that the country is coming apart":* Quoted in ibid.

14   *a bestselling nonfiction book in late September:* See Edwin McDowell, "Behind the Best Sellers; 'Crisis Investing,'" *New York Times*, September 21, 1980.

15   *"In the last few years before the outbreak of war":* John Hackett, *The Third World War: August 1985* (New York: Macmillan, 1978), p. 316.

15   *Ronald Reagan later called* The Third World War: In 1983, President Reagan told the *New York Times* that *The Third World War* was the most important book that he'd read for work that year. See "Reading for Work and Pleasure," *New York Times*, December 4, 1983.

15   *the techno-thriller:* For Hackett's role in creating the new genre, see J. William Gibson, "Redeeming Vietnam: Techno-Thriller Novels of the 1980s," *Cultural Critique*, no. 19 (Fall 1991), pp. 179–202.

16   *"Life begins at forty":* Quoted in David Sheff, *All We Are Saying: The Last Major Interview with John Lennon and Yoko Ono*, ed. G. Barry Golson (New York: St. Martin's Griffin, 2000), p. 8.

16   *"Politics and rebellion distinguished the '60's":* Jerry Rubin, "Guess Who's Coming to Wall Street," *New York Times*, July 30, 1980.

16   *the highest-paid banker . . . earned about $710,000 a year:* Roger E. Anderson earned $710,440 in 1980, an income that would be roughly $2 million in today's dollars. A few years later, Anderson was forced to leave Continental Illinois, and the Federal Deposit Insurance Corporation subsequently took it over—at the time, the largest bank bailout in American history. For Anderson's salary, see L. Michael Cacage, "Who Earned the Most?," *American Banker* (May 29, 1981). The story of how Anderson's bank collapsed remains sadly relevant. See "Continental Illinois and 'Too Big to Fail,'" in *History of the Eighties: Lessons for the Future, Volume 1* (Washington, D.C.: Federal Deposit Insurance Corporation, Division of Research and Statistics, 1997), pp. 235–57.

17   *"There is a tidal wave coming":* Quoted in Ernest B. Furgurson, "Carter as Hoover, Reagan as F.D.R.? Socko!," *Los Angeles Times*, July 22, 1980.

No Lone Zones

19   *political, as well as military, considerations:* According to one historian, Congressman Wilbur D.
      Mills agreed to support a reduction in corporate taxes—and in return Arkansas got the Titan II
      bases. See Julian E. Zelizer, *Taxing America: Wilbur D. Mills, Congress, and the State, 1945–1975*
      (New York: Cambridge University Press, 2000), p. 187.

21   *It weighed roughly six thousand pounds:* Cited in Stumpf, *Titan II*, p. 118.

21   *steel doorjambs . . . weighed an additional thirty-one thousand pounds:* Ibid.

22   *Rodney Holder was once working in the silo:* Interview with Rodney L. Holder.

23   *Launch Complex 373-4 had been the site of the worst Titan II accident:* My account of the Searcy
      accident is based primarily on "Report of USAF Aerospace Safety Missile Accident Investigation
      Board, Missile Accident LGM-25C-62-006, Site 373-4," Little Rock Air Force Base, August 9,
      1965 (OFFICIAL USE ONLY); "Launch Operations and Witness Group Final Report," submitted to
      USAF Aerospace Safety Missile Accident Investigation Board, Missile Accident LGM-25C-62-006,
      Site 373-4, n.d., (OFFICIAL USE ONLY); and Charles F. Strang, "Titan II Launch Facility Accident
      Briefing, Little Rock Air Force Base, Arkansas," minutes of the Ninth Explosives Safety Seminar,
      Naval Training Center, San Diego, California, August 15–17, 1967 (NO FOREIGN WITHOUT THE
      APPROVAL OF THE ARMED SERVICES EXPLOSIVES SAFETY BOARD); and Stumpf, *Titan II*, pp. 215–21.

23   *(serial number 62-0006):* Cited in "Witness Group Final Report," p. 1.

23   You and the Titan II: Ibid., p. 11.

25   *an "explosive situation":* Ibid., p. 4.

26   *Gary Lay insisted that nobody had been welding:* See Linda Hicks, "Silo Survivor Tells His Story,"
      Searcy Daily Citizen, May 7, 2000.

27   *the launch checklist went something like this:* I have presented a somewhat abbreviated version of the
      checklist. For the complete one, see *Technical Manual, USAF Model LGM-25C, Missile System
      Operation* (Tucson: Arizona Aerospace Foundation, 2005). fig. 3-1, sheets 1–3.

32   *The missile's serial number was 62-0006:* See "Titan II Class A Mishap Report, Serial Number
      62-0006, 18 September 1980, Damascus Arkansas," Eighth Air Force Mishap Investigation
      Board, October 30, 1980, p. 0-1.

33   *"Dang," Holder thought:* Holder interview.

Spheres Within Spheres

35   *Sergeant Herbert M. Lehr had just arrived:* Interview with Herbert M. Lehr. I am grateful to Lehr
      for describing that historic day in New Mexico. His memory, at the age of ninety, seemed better
      than mine. An account of Lehr's work for the Manhattan Project can be found at the Library of
      Congress: Herbert Lehr Collection (AFC/2001/001/12058), Veterans History Project, American
      Folklife Center.

36   *the most expensive weapon ever built:* By the end of 1945, about $1.9 billion had been spent on the
      Manhattan Project—roughly $24.7 billion in today's dollars. See Richard G. Hewlett, and Oscar
      E. Anderson, Jr., *The New World: A History of the United States Atomic Energy Commission,
      Volume 1, 1939–1946* (University Park, PA: Pennsylvania State University Press, 1962), p. 723.

36   *Ramsey bet the device would be a dud:* For the yield predictions made by Ramsey, Oppenheimer,
      Teller, and other Manhattan Project scientists, see Richard Rhodes, *The Making of the Atomic
      Bomb* (New York: Simon & Schuster, 1986), p. 657.

36   *odds of the atmosphere's catching fire were about one in ten:* According to the physicist Victor Weiss-
      kopf, a fear that the atmosphere might ignite caused one of his colleagues at Los Alamos to have a
      nervous breakdown. See the interview with Weisskopf in Denis Brian, *The Voice of Genius: Conversa-
      tions with Nobel Scientists and Other Luminaries* (New York: Basic Books, 2001), pp. 74–75.

36   *"tickling the dragon's tail":* For the origins of the term, see Lillian Hoddeson, Paul W. Henriksen,
      Roger A. Meade, and Catherine Westfall, *Critical Assembly: A Technical History of Los Alamos Dur-
      ing the Oppenheimer Years, 1943–1945* (New York: Cambridge University Press, 1993), pp.
      346–48. For a firsthand account of the dangerous experiments, see Frederic de Hoffmann, "'All in

Our Time': Pure Science in the Service of Wartime Technology," *Bulletin of the Atomic Scientists,* January 1975, pp. 41–44.

37 *"So I took this heavy ball in my hand":* Quoted in James P. Delgado, *Nuclear Dawn: From the Manhattan Project to the Bikini Atoll* (Oxford: Osprey Publishing, 2009), p. 59.

37 the *"ultimate explosive":* H. G. Wells, *The World Set Free: A Story of Mankind* (New York: E. P. Dutton, 1914), p. 117.

37 *"carry about in a handbag:* Ibid., p. 118.

37 *"The catastrophe of the atomic bombs":* Ibid., p. 254. Wells was an early proponent of world government, and his complex, often contradictory views on the subject are explored in Edward Mead Earle, "H. G. Wells, British Patriot in Search of a World State," *World Politics,* vol. 2, no. 2 (January 1950), pp. 181–208.

37 *"it may become possible":* The full text of the letter, as well as Roosevelt's response to it, can be found in Cynthia C. Kelly, ed., *The Manhattan Project: The Birth of the Atomic Bomb in the Words of Its Creators, Eyewitnesses, and Historians* (New York: Black Dog & Leventhal, 2007), pp. 42–44.

37 *"extremely powerful bombs of a new type":* Ibid., p. 43.

38 *Conventional explosives, like TNT:* I am grateful to members of the New York Police Department Bomb Squad not only for teaching me how high explosives work but also for demonstrating some of them for me in the field. See Eric Schlosser, "The Bomb Squad," *Atlantic Monthly,* January 1994.

38 *similar to the burning of a log in a fireplace:* Ibid.

38 *temperatures reach as high as 9,000 degrees:* Cited in Samuel Glasstone, ed., *The Effects of Nuclear Weapons* (Washington, D.C.: U.S. Government Printing Office, 1964), p. 29. Glasstone's book is unsurpassed at explaining what nuclear weapons can do. The original edition appeared in 1950, the last edition in 1977—and the one cited here comes with a round, plastic "nuclear effects computer," similar to a slide rule, that allows you to calculate the maximum overpressures, wind speeds, and arrival times of various nuclear blasts, depending on how far you're standing from them.

38 *1.4 million pounds per square inch:* Cited in Schlosser, "The Bomb Squad."

38 *tens of millions degrees Fahrenheit:* See Glasstone, *Effects of Nuclear Weapons,* p. 24.

38 *many millions of pounds per square inch:* Ibid., p. 29.

39 *the largest building in the world:* Cited in Michael Kort, *The Columbia Guide to Hiroshima and the Bomb* (New York: Columbia University Press, 2007), p. 22.

40 *"the Introvert":* See Hoddeson et al., *Critical Assembly,* p. 86.

40 *"The more neutrons—the more fission":* "Survey of Weapon Development and Technology" (WR708), Sandia National Laboratories, Corporate Training and Development, February 1998 (SECRET/RESTRICTED DATA/declassified), p. 112.

40 *"We care about neutrons!":* Ibid.

40 *"precision devices":* For Kistiakowsky's thinking about how to create a symmetrical implosion, see George B. Kistiakowsky, "Reminiscences of Wartime Los Alamos," in Lawrence Badash, Joseph O. Hirschfelder, and Herbert P. Broida, eds., *Reminiscences of Los Alamos, 1943–1945* (Boston: D. Reidel Publishing, 1980), pp. 49–65. The reference to precision devices appears on page 54.

41 *the exploding-bridgewire detonator:* For the story behind the invention of this revolutionary new detonator, see Luis W. Alvarez, *Alvarez: Adventures of a Physicist* (New York: Basic Books, 1987), pp. 132–36. For a brief overview of the technology, see Ron Varesh, "Electric Detonators: Electric Bridgewire Detonators and Exploding Foil Initiators," *Propellants, Explosives, Pyrotechnics,* vol. 21 (1996), pp. 150–54.

43 *Hornig was instructed to "babysit the bomb":* Cited in Donald Hornig and Robert Cahn, "Atom-Bomb Scientist Tells His Story," *Christian Science Monitor,* July 11, 1995. For more details of that night atop the tower, see also "60th Anniversary of Trinity: First Manmade Nuclear Explosion, July 16, 1945," Public Symposium, National Academy of Sciences, July 14, 2005, pp. 27–28; and "Babysitting the Bomb: Interview with Don Hornig," in Kelly, *Manhattan Project,* pp. 298–99.

43 *This is what the end of the world will look like:* See James G. Hershberg, *James B. Conant: Harvard*

to *Hiroshima and the Making of the Nuclear Age* (Stanford, CA: Stanford University Press, 1993), p. 234.

43 *[Weisskopf] thought that his calculations were wrong:* See Brian, *Voice of Genius*, p. 75.

43 *"The hills were bathed in brilliant light":* See O. R. Frisch, "Eyewitness Account of 'Trinity' Test, July 1945," in Philip L. Cantelon, Richard D. Hewlett, and Robert C. Williams, eds., *The American Atom: A Documentary History of Nuclear Policies from the Discovery of Fission to the Present* (Philadelphia: University of Pennsylvania Press, 1992), p. 50.

44 *"The whole country was lighted by a searing light":* Quoted in "Appendix 6, War Department Release on New Mexico Test, July 16, 1945," in Henry DeWolf Smyth, *Atomic Energy for Military Purposes, 1940–1945: The Official Report on the Development of the Atomic Bomb Under the Auspices of the United States Government* (Princeton, NJ: Princeton University Press, 1945), p. 254.

44 *"Now we are all sons of bitches":* Bainbridge was disturbed by the immense explosion—but also exhilarated and relieved. Had the nuclear device failed to detonate, he would have been the first person to climb the tower and investigate what had gone wrong. See Kenneth T. Bainbridge, "A Foul and Awesome Display," *Bulletin of the Atomic Scientist* (May 1975), pp. 40–46. The "sons of bitches" line appears on page 46.

44 *the "inhuman barbarism" of aerial attacks:* The full text of Franklin Roosevelt's statement can be found in Bertram D. Hulen, "Roosevelt in Plea; Message to Russia, Also Sent to Finns, Decries 'Ruthless Bombing,'" *New York Times*, December 1, 1939.

44 *attacked the Spanish city of Guernica, killing a few hundred civilians:* The Basque government claimed that almost one third of the city's five thousand inhabitants were killed by the attack. The actual number was mostly likely two to three hundred. But most of Guernica's buildings were destroyed, and the aim of the attack was to terrorize civilians. See Jörg Diehl, "Hitler's Destruction of Guernica: Practicing Blietzkrieg in Basque Country," *Der Spiegel*, April 26, 2007.

44 *bombed and invaded . . . Nanking . . . killing many thousands:* More than seventy-five years later, the number of people killed in Nanking remains a controversial subject. Chinese scholars now assert that between three and four hundred thousand civilians were massacred while Japanese nationalists claim that those estimates are absurd and that no war crimes were committed. For a fine, aptly titled introduction to the controversy, see Bob Todashi Wakabayashi, "The Messiness of Historical Reality," in Bob Tadashi Wakabayashi, ed., *The Nanking Atrocity: Complicating the Picture* (New York: Berghahn Books, 2007), pp. 3–28.

44 *"The ruthless bombing from the air":* Quoted in Hulen, "Roosevelt in Plea."

45 *"The immediate aim is, therefore, twofold":* Quoted in Richard R. Muller, "The Orgins of MAD: A Short History of City-Busting," in Henry D. Sokolski, ed., *Getting MAD: Nuclear Mutual Assured Destruction, Its Origins and Practice* (Carlisle, PA: Strategic Studies Institute, U.S. Army War College, 2004), p. 34.

45 *The first "firestorm":* The historian Jörg Friedrich has written a masterful account of the British effort to destroy Germany with fire. His chapters on the weaponry and the strategies used to kill civilians are especially haunting. For the destruction of Hamburg and the desire to create firestorms, see Jorg Friedrich, *The Fire: The Bombing of Germany, 1940–1945* (New York: Columbia University Press, 2006), pp. 90–100; and another fine, unsettling book—Keith Lowe, *Inferno: The Fiery Destruction of Hamburg* (New York: Scribner, 2007).

45 *killed about forty thousand:* Cited in Lowe, *Inferno*, p. 276.

45 *attack on Dresden, where perhaps twenty thousand civilians died:* Long a source of debate, estimates of the death toll in Dresden have ranged from about thirty-five thousand to about half a million. In 2008 a panel of historians concluded the actual number was between eighteen and twenty-five thousand. Cited in Kate Connolly, "International Panel Rethinks Death Toll from Dresden Raids," *Guardian* (London), October 3, 2008.

45 *"de-housing":* Quoted in Sokolski, *Getting MAD*, p. 34.

45 *daytime "precision" bombing:* The American bombing strategy, inspired by the futility of trench warfare during the First World War, sought to avoid unnecessary casualties and to destroy only military targets—a goal more easily achieved in theory than in reality. For the high-minded motives behind the strategy, see Mark Clodfelter, *Beneficial Bombing: The Progressive Foundations of American Air Power, 1917–1945* (Lincoln: University of Nebraska Press, 2010), pp. 1–66.

45 *the Norden bombsight:* For a fascinating account of this "technological wonder," a top secret invention that cost a fortune and never fulfilled the lofty aims of its inventor, see Stephen L. McFarland, *America's Pursuit of Precision Bombing, 1910–1945* (Tuscaloosa: University of Alabama Press, 1995).

46 *forced as many as two hundred thousand Korean women:* The number of Korean women used as sex slaves by the Japanese will never be precisely known. Like the number of Chinese civilians killed in Nanking, it has long been a source of controversy, with Japanese nationalists claiming the actual figure was low. Two hundred thousand is a widely used estimate. For a fine discussion of the issue, see You-me Park, "Compensation to Fit the Crime: Conceptualizing a Just Paradigm of Reparation for Korean 'Comfort Women,'" *Comparative Studies of South Asia, Africa, and the Middle East,* Vol. 30, No. 2, 2010, pp. 204–13. The estimate is cited on page 206.

46 *killed almost one million Chinese civilians with chemical and biological weapons:* The number of Chinese killed by such weapons will never be known. According to the historian Daqing Yang, during the two weeks between Japan's surrender and the arrival of the first American occupying troops, Japanese officials "systematically destroyed sensitive documents to a degree perhaps unprecedented in history." Nevertheless, it has been conclusively established that the Japanese attacked Chinese civilians with weapons containing mustard gas, anthrax, plague, typhoid, cholera, and bacterial dysentery. See Daqing Yang, "Documentary Evidence and Studies of Japanese War Crimes: An Interim Assessment," in Edward Drea, Greg Bradsher, Robert Hanyok, James Lide, Michael Petersen, and Daqing Yang, *Researching Japanese War Crime Records: Introductory Essays* (Washington D.C.: Nazi War Crimes and Japanese Imperial Government Records Interagency Working Group, U.S. National Archives, 2006), pp. 21–56; and Till Bärnighausen, "Data Generated in Japan's Biowarfare Experiments on Human Victims in China, 1932–1945, and the Ethics of Using Them," in Jin Bao Nie, Nanyan Guo, Mark Selden, and Arthur Kleinman, eds., *Japan's Wartime Medical Atrocities: Comparative Inquiries in Science, History, and Ethics* (New York: Routledge, 2010), pp. 81–106.

46 *killed millions of other civilians:* The number of people killed by the Japanese throughout Asia will never be known. Over the years, the estimates of civilian deaths in China alone have ranged from ten to thirty-five million. Although those estimates were made by the Chinese government, they suggest the possible scale of the slaughter. Cited in Wakabayashi, *The Nanking Atrocity,* pp. 4, 8.

46 *the Army Air Forces tried a new approach :* For the decision to abandon precision bombing and firebomb Tokyo, see Wesley Frank Craven and James Lea Cate, eds., *The Army Air Forces in World War II, Volume 5, The Pacific: Matterhorn to Nagasaki, June 1944 to August 1945* (Washington, D.C.: Office of Air Force History, 1983), pp. 608–18; William W. Ralph, "Improvised Destruction: Arnold, LeMay, and the Firebombing of Japan," *War in History,* vol. 13, no. 4, (2006), pp. 495–522; and Thomas R. Searle, "'It Made a Lot of Sense to Kill Skilled Workers': The Firebombing of Tokyo in March 1945," *Journal of Military History,* vol. 66, no. 1 (January 2002), pp. 103–33.

46 *struck Tokyo with two thousand tons of bombs:* Cited in Craven and Cate, *Army Air Forces in World War II,* p. 615.

46 *killed about one hundred thousand civilians:* That number is most likely too low, but the actual figure will never be known. Cited in Ralph, "Improvised Destruction," p. 495.

46 *left about a million homeless:* Cited in Craven and Cate, *Army Air Forces in World War II,* p. 617.

46 *"war without mercy":* See John W. Dower, *War Without Mercy: Race and Power in the Pacific War* (New York: Pantheon, 1987).

46 *About one quarter of Osaka was destroyed by fire:* For the proportions of devastation in Japan's six major industrial cities, see Craven and Cate, *Army Air Forces in World War II,* p. 643.

46 *the portion of Toyama still standing:* The official Army Air Forces history called the amount of destruction in Toyama "the fantastic figure of 99.5 percent." Ibid., p. 657.

47 *"an appropriately selected uninhabited area":* Quoted in Kort, *Columbia Guide to Hiroshima,* p. 200.

47 *"this new means of indiscriminate destruction":* Ibid.

47 *"to make a profound psychological impression":* "Notes of the Interim Committee Meeting, Thursday, 31 May 1945" (TOP SECRET/declassified), p. 4; the full document is reproduced in Dennis Merrill, ed., *Documentary History of the Truman Presidency, Volume 1; The Decision to Drop the Atomic Bomb on Japan* (Frederick, MD: University Publications of America, 1996), pp. 22–38.

47   *"an era of devastation on an unimaginable scale":* "A Peitition to the President of the United States,"
      July 17, 1945; the full document is reproduced in Merrill, *Documentary History of Truman Presi-*
      dency, p. 219.

47   *"continuous danger of sudden annihilation":* Ibid.

47   *Truman's decision to use the atomic bomb:* A number of historians, most notably Gar Alperovitz,
      have argued that President Truman used the atomic bomb against Japan primarily as a means of
      intimidating the Soviet Union. I do not find the argument convincing. See Gar Alperovitz, *The*
      Decision to Use the Atomic Bomb (New York: Vintage, 1996).

48   *between "500,000 and 1,000,000 American lives":* Quoted in D. M. Giangreco, "'A Score of Bloody
      Okinawas and Iwo Jimas': President Truman and Casualty Estimates for the Invasion of Japan,"
      Pacific Historical Review, vol. 72, no. 1 (February 2003), p. 107.

48   *American casualties would reach half a million:* Ibid., pp. 104–5.

48   *more than one third of the American landing force:* The American casualty rate at Okinawa was 35
      percent. Cited in Richard B. Frank, *Downfall: The End of the Imperial Japanese Empire* (New York:
      Penguin, 1999), p. 145.

48   *might require 1.8 million American troops:* For Operation Olympic, the invasion of Kyushu,
      766,700 troops would be used; for Operation Coronet, the invasion of Honshu 1,026,000. Cited
      in ibid., p. 136.

48   *"an Okinawa from one end of Japan to the other":* Quoted in ibid., p. 143.

48   *"Now . . . you'll believe you're in a war":* Quoted in "Unconditional Surrender, Demobilization, and
      the Atomic Bomb," Michael D. Pearlman, U.S. Army Command and General Staff College. Com-
      bat Studies Institute, 1996, p. 7.

49   *"the maximum demolition of light structures":* Quoted in Stephen Walker, *Shockwave: Countdown to*
      Hiroshima (New York: Harper Perennial, 2006), p. 122.

49   *"We should like to know whether the take-off":* See "Letter from J. R. Oppenheimer to Lt. Col. John
      Landsdale, Jr., September 20, 1944," quoted in Chuck Hansen, *The Swords of Armageddon,* vol. 7
      (Sunnyvale, CA: Chucklea Publications, 2007), p. 30.

49   *the president's Target Committee decided:* See "Memorandum for: General L. R. Groves, Subject:
      Summary of Target Committee Meetings on 10 May and 11 May 1945," May 12, 1945
      (TOP SECRET/declassified), reproduced in Merrill, *Documentary History of Truman Presidency,*
      pp. 5–14.

49   *"No suitable jettisoning ground . . . has been found":* Ibid., p. 9.

50   *try to remove the cordite charges from the bomb midair:* Ibid.

50   *"bomb commander and weaponeer":* See Craven and Cate, *Army Air Forces in World War II,*
      p. 716.

50   *"a less than optimal performance":* Quoted in Martin J. Sherwin, *A World Destroyed: Hiroshima and*
      Its Legacies (Stanford, CA: Stanford University Press, 2003), p. 231.

50   *Parsons and . . . Morris Jeppson, left the cockpit:* See Walker, *Shockwave,* pp. 213–17.

51   *leaving about three hundred thousand people in town:* The estimates range from 245,423 to 370,000.
      See Frank, *Downfall,* p. 285.

51   *the temperature reached perhaps 10,000 degrees Fahrenheit:* Estimates of the heat ranged from 3,000
      to 9,000 degrees Centigrade—5,432 to 16,232 degrees Fahrenheit. Cited in "The Effects of
      Atomic Bombs on Hiroshima and Nagasaki," U.S. Strategic Bombing Survey, June 19, 1946,
      pp. 31–32.

51   *a roiling, bubbling sea of black smoke:* The physicist Harold Agnew, who rode in a plane following
      the *Enola Gay,* described the blast to me. Agnew filmed the mushroom cloud as it rose into the air
      and captured the only moving images of the explosion.

51   *98.62 percent of the uranium in Little Boy was blown apart:* Interview with Bob Peurifoy.

51   *Only 1.38 percent actually fissioned:* Ibid.

51   *eighty thousand people were killed in Hiroshima:* According to a study conducted by the U.S. Strate-
      gic Bombing Survey right after the destruction of Hiroshima and Nagasaki, the "exact number of
      dead and injured will never be known because of the confusion after the explosions." The study
      estimated the dead at Hiroshima to be between 70,000 and 80,000. According to the historian
      Richard Frank, the police department in Hiroshima prefecture estimated the number to be about

78,000. Many thousands more died in the months and years that followed. See "The Effects of Atomic Bombs," p. 15; and Frank, *Downfall*, pp. 285–87.

52 *more than two thirds of the buildings were destroyed:* According to Japanese estimates, 62,000 of the 90,000 buildings in Hiroshima were destroyed, about 69 percent. Another 6.6 percent were badly damaged. Cited in "Effects of Atomic Bombs," p. 9.

52 *0.7 gram of uranium-235 was turned into pure energy:* Albert Einstein's equation for converting the mass of an object into an equivalent amount of energy helps to explain why something so small can produce an explosion so large. The energy that can be released, Einstein found, equals the mass of an object multiplied by the speed of light, squared. Since the speed of light is more than 186,000 miles per second, the equation easily produces enormous sums. The estimate of 0.7 grams is based on the quantity of uranium-235 in Little Boy and an assumption that the bomb's yield was 15 kilotons. The power of even a rudimentary nuclear weapon is difficult to convey. The city of Hiroshima was destroyed by an amount of uranium-235 about the size of a peppercorn or a single BB. I am grateful to Bob Peurifoy for helping me to understand the relationship between a nuclear weapon's potential yield and its efficiency.

52 *A dollar bill weighs more:* According to the Federal Reserve, a dollar bill weighs 1 gram.

52 *"the basic power of the universe":* See "President Truman's Statement on the Bombing of Hiroshima, August 6, 1945," reproduced in Kort, *Columbia Guide to Hiroshima*, p. 230.

52 *"We are now prepared to obliterate more rapidly":* Ibid., p. 231.

52 *"an aroused fighting spirit to exterminate":* Quoted in "Effects of Atomic Bombs," p. 8.

52 *putting it together presented more of a challenge:* A report issued the following year, even though heavily censored, suggests the challenges of using Fat Man safely. One early assembly method proved to be unwise: "the overhead chain hoists were dangerous due to long lengths of chain striking the detonators in the sphere." "Nuclear Weapons Engineering and Delivery," Los Alamos Technical Series, vol. 23, LA-1161, July 1946 (secret/declassified), p. 107.

52 *"rebuilding an airplane in the field":* Quoted in Rhodes, *Making of the Atomic Bomb*, p. 590.

52 *Bernard J. O'Keefe noticed something wrong:* For the last-minute, late-night repair work on Fat Man, see Bernard J. O'Keefe, *Nuclear Hostages* (Boston: Houghton Mifflin, 1983), pp. 98–101.

52 *"I felt a chill and started to sweat":* Ibid., p. 98.

53 *flashing red lights on the flight test box:* For the malfunction en route to Nagasaki, see Charles W. Sweeney with James A. Antonucci, and Marion K. Antonucci. *War's End: An Eyewitness Account of America's Last Atomic Mission* (New York: Avon, 1997), p. 209–10.

53 *About one fifth of the plutonium fissioned:* Peurifoy interview.

53–54 *equal to about 21,000 tons of TNT:* The precise yields of the atomic bombs used at Hiroshima and Nagasaki were the subject of disagreement for many years. The rudimentary nature of the measuring equipment and poor documentation of the missions by the United States Army Air Forces created the uncertainty. Estimates of the Hiroshima bomb's explosive force ranged from 6 kilotons to 23 kilotons. According to the most recent study at Los Alamos, the yield of the Hiroshima bomb was 15 kilotons, with a 20 percent margin of error. The yield of the Nagasaki bomb was 21 kilotons, with a 10 percent margin of error. See John Malik, "The Yields of the Hiroshima and Nagasaki Nuclear Explosions," Los Alamos National Laboratory, LA-8819, September 1985.

54 *About forty thousand people were killed . . . at least twice that number were injured:* In 1946 the United States Strategic Bombing Survey estimated the number of deaths in Nagasaki to be more than thirty-five thousand; the following year it raised the estimate to forty-five thousand. The actual number is likely to be much higher and will never be known. See "Effects of Atomic Bombs," p. 15; and Frank, *Downfall*, pp. 285–87.

54 *more than one third of the homes were destroyed:* Of the 52,000 residential units in Nagasaki, 27.2 percent were completely destroyed and 10.5 percent were half burned or destroyed. Cited in "Effects of Atomic Bombs," p. 13.

54 *"bent and twisted like jelly":* The Nagasaki Prefecture Report on the blast is quoted in ibid.

54 *Most of the casualties in Hiroshima and Nagasaki:* The proportions of various causes of death are speculative. As the U.S. Strategic Bombing Survey noted, "Many of these people undoubtedly died several times over, theoretically, since each was subjected to several injuries, any of which would

have been fatal." Nevertheless, an attempt was made to calculate how many people were killed by the different blast effects. Ibid, p. 15.

54   *Flash burns were caused by extraordinarily hot:* For the impact of thermal radiation on human beings, see Glasstone, *Effects of Nuclear Weapons,* pp. 565–76.

54   *"radiation sickness":* For the grim symptoms and survival rate of this ailment, ibid., pp. 577–626.

55   *For decades some historians have questioned:* As Michael Kort has noted, the historiographic debate has focused on a number of questions, including: Was Japan already planning to surrender before the destruction of Hiroshima? How much did the United States know about the Japanese leadership's plans? Was the demand for an unconditional surrender unreasonable? Were the casualty estimates for an American invasion accurate? Did the Soviet declaration of war on Japan—or the two atomic bombs—prompt Emperor Hirohito to accept defeat? Kort's analysis can be found in *Columbia Guide to Hiroshima,* pp. 75–116. For the argument that the Soviet entry into the war proved decisive, see Tsuyoshi Hasegawa, *Racing the Enemy: Stalin, Truman, and the Surrender of Japan* (Cambridge, MA: Belknap Press, 2005). For the argument that the atomic bombs ended the war, see Sadao Asada, "The Shock of the Atomic Bomb and Japan's Decision to Surrender: A Reconsideration," *Pacific Historical Review,* vol. 67, no. 4, (November 1998), pp. 477–512. For the American military's concern that more atomic bombs might have to be used in Japan, see Barton J. Bernstein, "Eclipsed by Hiroshima and Nagasaki: Early Thinking About Tactical Nuclear Weapons," *International Security,* vol. 15, no. 4 (Spring 1991), pp. 149–73. For a thorough and complex look at these issues, see Frank, *Downfall,* pp. 197–364.

55   *"even though we have to eat grass":* The quote comes from "Instruction to the Troops," a radio broadcast by General Anami. The full text can be found in Kort, *Columbia Guide to Hiroshima,* pp. 300–301.

55   *"The enemy has for the first time used cruel bombs":* Quoted in John W. Dower, *Embracing Defeat: Japan in the Wake of World War II* (New York: W. W. Norton, 2000), p. 36.

Potential Hazards

57   *"fire in the hole":* "Report, Major Missile Accident, Titan II Complex 374-7," Statement of Eric Ayala, Airman First class, Tab U-4, p. 2.

59   *"Can my people come back into the control center?":* Quoted in ibid., Statement of Allan D. Childers, First Lieutenant, Tab U-13, p. 2.

59   *"There's got to be a malfunction":* Ibid.

59   *"Well, get over here":* Ibid.

60   *"Holy shit," thought Holder:* Holder interview.

60   *Sid King was having dinner at a friend's house:* Interview with Sid King.

62   *an oxidizer trailer parked on the hardstand had started to leak:* My account of the oxidizer leak is based on interviews with Jeff Kennedy, who was a PTS technician in Little Rock at the time; Gus Anglin, the sheriff who responded to the leak; and Bill Carter, the attorney who represented a local farmer sickened by the fumes. See also Art Harris, "Titan II: A Plague on This Man's House," *Washington Post,* September 22, 1980.

62   *Gus Anglin, the sheriff of Van Buren County, was standing with a state trooper:* Anglin interview.

63   *"I'm the sheriff of the county":* Ibid.

63   *"No, no, we've got everything under control":* Quoted in ibid.

64   *"Sir, get your ass out of here":* Quoted in King interview.

64   *"Boy, he wasn't in too good a mood":* Quoted in ibid.

65   *"green smoke":* Quoted in "Report, Major Missile Accident, Titan II Complex 374-7," Childers statement, Tab U-13, p. 3.

67   *"If the missile blows," Holder said:* Holder interview.

68   *designed to withstand a nuclear detonation with an overpressure of 300 psi:* Cited in Stumpf, *Titan II,* p. 101.

68   *survive an overpressure of 1,130 psi:* Cited in ibid., p. 118.

69   *"Put him in the middle of you guys":* "Report, Major Missile Accident, Titan II Complex 374-7," Childers statement, Tab U-13, p. 4.

70   *"You've got to be kidding me," Holder thought:* Holder interview.

70   *"Get out of here, get out of here":* "Report, Major Missile Accident, Titan II Complex 374-7," Statement of Thomas A. Brocksmith, Technical Sergeant, Tab U-9, p. 1.

PART TWO: MACHINERY OF CONTROL

The Best, the Biggest, and the Most

73   *Hamilton Holt's dream of world peace:* See Warren F. Kuehl, *Hamilton Holt: Journalist, Internationalist, Educator* (Gainesville: University of Florida Press, 1960).

73   *"PAUSE, PASSER-BY, AND HANG YOUR HEAD":* Holt's inscription continues: "This engine of destruction, torture, and death symbolizes the prostitution of the inventor, the avarice of the manufacturer, the blood-guilt of the statesman, the savagery of the soldier, the perverted patriotism of the citizen, the debasement of the human race . . ." The peace monument was vandalized and destroyed in 1943.

74   *About fifty million people had been killed:* The actual number will never be known. I have chosen to use a conservative estimate. See Martin Gilbert, *The Second World War: A Complete History* (New York: Holt Paperbacks, 2004), p. 1.

74   *"destructive beyond the wildest nightmares":* See "General Arnold Stresses Preparedness Need in Statement," *Washington Post,* August 19, 1945.

74   *"Seldom if ever has a war ended":* Quoted in Paul Boyer, *By the Bomb's Early Light: American Thought and Culture at the Dawn of the Atomic Age* (Chapel Hill: University of North Carolina Press, 1994), p. 7. The full text of Murrow's broadcast can be found in Edward Bliss, Jr., ed., *In Search of Light, 1938–1961: The Broadcasts of Edward R. Murrow* (New York: Alfred A. Knopf, 1967), pp. 102–3. "No one is trying to assess the relative influence of the atomic bomb and the Russian declaration of war in bringing about the Japanese defeat," Murrow added, less than a week after Hiroshima's destruction. "People are content to leave that argument to the historians."

74   *The appeal called for the United Nations' General Assembly:* See George C. Holt, "The Conference on World Government," *Journal of Higher Education,* vol. 17, no. 5 (May 1946), pp. 227–35.

74   *"We believe these to be the minimum requirements":* Quoted in ibid., p. 234.

75   *"a world government with power to control":* Quoted in Boyer, *Bomb's Early Light,* p. 37.

75   lowered *"the cost of destruction":* H. H. Arnold, "Air Force in the Atomic Age," in Dexter Masters and Katharine Way, eds., *One World or None: A Report to the Public on the Full Meaning of the Atomic Bomb* (New York: New Press, 2007), p. 71.

75   *"too cheap and easy":* Ibid., p. 70.

75   *"A far better protection":* Ibid., p. 84.

75   atomic bomb's *"very existence should make war unthinkable":* "Memorandum by the Commanding General, Manhattan Engineer District, Leslie R. Groves: Our Army of the Future—As Influenced by Atomic Weapons" (CONFIDENTIAL/declassified), in United States Department of State, *Foreign Relations of the United States, 1946, Volume 1, General; the United Nations* (Washington, D.C.: U.S. Government Printing Office, 1972), p. 1199.

75   *"If there are to be atomic bombs in the world":* Ibid., p. 1203

76   *"a secret armament race of a rather desperate character":* Henry L. Stimson, "Memorandum for the President, Subject: Proposed Action for the Control of Atomic Bombs," September 11, 1945 (TOP SECRET/declassified), reproduced in Merrill, *Documentary History of Truman Presidency,* p. 222.

76   *"The only way you can make a man trustworthy":* Ibid., p. 224.

76   *"We tried that once with Hitler":* Quoted in Walter Millis and E. S. Duffield, eds., *The Forrestal Diaries* (New York: Viking, 1951), p. 96.

76   *"There is nothing—I repeat nothing":* "The Charge in the Soviet Union (Kennan) to the Secretary of State," Moscow, September 30, 1945, in United States State Department, *Foreign Relations of the*

United States: Diplomatic Papers, 1945, Volume 5, Europe (Washington, D.C.: U.S. Government Printing Office, 1967), p. 885.

76   *"highly dangerous":* Ibid.

77   *executed tens of thousands of their citizens:* Within a year of invading Poland during the fall of 1939, the Soviets imprisoned and executed more than twenty thousand Polish officers, policemen, and civilians. And then the Soviet Union denied that fact for more than fifty years. See Anna M. Cienciala, Natalia S. Lebedeva, Wojciech Materski, eds., *Katyn: A Crime Without Punishment* (New Haven, CT: Yale University Press, 2008).

77   *the deaths of perhaps three hundred thousand Japanese:* See Frank, *Downfall,* pp. 325–26.

77   *killed almost as many Russians as the Nazis had:* The actual number killed by Hitler and Stalin remains a subject of debate. Both men were responsible for many millions of deaths. Dmitri Volkogonov, a scholar who gained access to Soviet archives, claimed that Stalin killed about twelve million Russians—not including those who died during the Second World War. According to the historian Timothy Snyder, the Nazis deliberately killed about twelve million civilians, while the Soviets killed about nine million during Stalin's years in power. The historian Anne Applebaum has argued that Snyder's estimates for Stalin seem too low, noting "Soviet citizens were just as likely to die during the war years because of decisions made by Stalin, or because of the interaction between Stalin and Hitler, as they were from the commands of Hitler alone." See Dmitri Volkogonov, *Stalin: Triumph and Tragedy* (New York: Grove Weidenfeld, 1988), p. 524; Anne Applebaum, "The Worst of the Madness," *New York Review of Books,* November 11, 2010; and Timothy Snyder, "Hitler vs. Stalin: Who Killed More?," *New York Review of Books,* March 10, 2011.

78   *"a militaristic oligarchy":* Quoted in Peter Douglas Feaver, *Guarding the Guardians: Civilian Control of Nuclear Weapons in the United States* (Ithaca, NY: Cornell University Press, 1992), p. 100.

78   *The president was given the sole authority:* The historian Garry Wills has argued that the decision to give this unchecked power to the executive branch had a lasting and profound effect on American democracy. See Garry Wills, *Bomb Power: The Modern Presidency and the National Security State* (New York: Penguin Press, 2010). For the constitutional and legal basis for such power, see Frank Klotz, Jr., "The President and the Control of Nuclear Weapons," in David C. Kozak and Kenneth N. Ciboski, eds., *The American Presidency: A Policy Perspective from Readings and Documents* (Chicago: Nelson-Hall, 1987), pp. 47–58.

79   *"We are here to make a choice":* For the full text of Bernard Baruch's remarks, see "Baruch Reviews Portent of A-Bomb," *Washington Post,* June 15, 1946.

79   *"all atomic-energy activities potentially dangerous":* Ibid.

79   *willing to hand over its "winning weapons":* Ibid.

80   *The number of soldiers in the U.S. Army:* In August 1945 the Army had more than 8 million soldiers and by July 1, 1947, it had only 989,664—a remarkably swift dismantling of a victorious military force. See John C. Sparrow, *History of Personnel Demobilization in the United States Army* (Washington, D.C.: Department of the Army, 1952), pp. 139, 263.

80   *from almost 80,000 to fewer than 25,000:* See Bernard C. Nalty, ed., *Winged Shield, Winged Sword: A History of the United States Air Force, Volume 1, 1907–1950* (Washington, D.C.: Air Force History and Museums Program, 1997), p. 378.

80   *only one fifth of those planes:* Ibid.

80   *the defense budget was cut by almost 90 percent:* The United States spent about $83 billion on defense in 1945—and about $9 billion in 1948. Cited in "National Defense Budget Estimates for FYH 2013," Office of the Under Secretary of Defense (Comptroller), March 2012, p. 246.

80   *"No major strategic threat or requirement":* Quoted in Walton S. Moody, *Building a Strategic Air Force* (Washington, D.C.: Air Force History and Museums Program, 1995), p. 78.

80   *the Soviets were "fanatically" committed to destroying:* Kennan's quotes come from his famous "long telegram," whose full text can be found at "The Charge in the Soviet Union (Kennan) to the Secretary of State," February 22, 1946 (SECRET/declassified), in United States State Department, *Foreign Relations of the United States: 1946, Volume 6, Eastern Europe; The Soviet Union* (Washington, D.C.: U.S. Government Printing Office, 1969), pp. 696–709.

80   *an "iron curtain":* For the speech in which Churchill first used that phrase, see "Text of Churchill's Address at Westminister College," *Washington Post,* March 6, 1946.

80–81 *"terror and oppression, a controlled press and radio":* For Truman's speech, see "Text of President's Speech on New Foreign Policy," *New York Times*, March 13, 1947.

81 *the Pentagon did not have a war plan:* The first major study of potential targets in the Soviet Union was conducted in the summer of 1947. For America's lack of war plans, see L. Wainstein, C. D. Creamans, J. K. Moriarity, and J. Ponturo, "The Evolution of U.S. Strategic Command and Control and Warning, 1945–1972," Institute for Defense Analyses, Study S-467, June 1975 (TOP SECRET/RESTRICTED DATA/declassified), pp. 11–14; Ernest R. May, John D. Steinbruner, and Thomas W. Wolfe, "History of the Strategic Arms Competition, 1945–1972," Pt. 1, Office of the Secretary of Defense, Historical Office, March 1981 (TOP SECRET/RESTRICTED DATA/declassified), pp. 21–22; and James F. Schnabel, *The Joint Chiefs of Staff and National Policy; Volume 1, 1945–1947* (Washington, D.C.: Office of Joint History, Office of the Chairman of Joint Chiefs of Staff, 1996), pp. 70–75.

81 *The U.S. Army had only one division . . . along with ten police regiments:* Cited in Steven T. Ross, *American War Plans, 1945–1950: Strategies for Defeating the Soviet Union* (Portland, OR: Frank Cass, 1996), p. 40.

81 *for a total of perhaps 100,000 troops:* In May 1945 the United States had about 2 million troops in Europe; two years later it had 105,000. Cited in "History Timeline," United States Army Europe, U.S. Army, 2011.

81 *The British army had one division:* Cited in Ross, *War Plans*, p. 40.

81 *the Soviet army had about one hundred divisions:* See Schnabel, *Joint Chiefs of Staff, Volume 1*, p. 71.

81 *about 1.2 million troops:* Cited in Ross, *War Plans*, p. 53.

81 *more than 150 additional divisions:* Cited in ibid., p. 33. Some intelligence reports claimed that the Soviet Union had 175 divisions in Europe, with 40 of them ready to attack West Germany. The Pentagon estimates of Soviet troop numbers varied widely—and, according to the historian Matthew A. Evangelista, deliberately overstated the strength of the Red Army. A more innocent motive might have been a desire to prepare for the worst. In any event, by early 1947, the U.S. Army was greatly outnumbered in Europe. See May et al., "History of Strategic Arms Competition," Pt. 1 pp. 37, 139–41; and Matthew A. Evangelista, "Stalin's Postwar Army Reappraised," *International Security*, vol. 7, no. 3 (1982), pp. 110–38.

81 *the Bikini atoll in the Marshall Islands:* For a patriotic account of the test, which somehow inspired the name for a woman's two-piece bathing suit, see W. A. Shurcliff, *Bombs at Bikini: The Official Report of Operation Crossroads* (New York: Wm. H. Wise, 1947).

81 *"Ships at sea and bodies of troops":* "The Evaluation of the Atomic Bomb as a Military Weapon," Enclosure "A," The Final Report of the Joint Chiefs of Staff Evaluation Board for Operation Crossroads, June 30, 1947 (TOP SECRET/declassified), p. 12.

81–82 *"The bomb is pre-eminently a weapon":* Ibid., p. 32.

82 *"man's primordial fears":* Ibid., p. 36.

82 *"break the will of nations":* Ibid.

82 *"cities of especial sentimental significance":* Ibid., p. 37.

82 *if "we were ruthlessly realistic":* Quoted in Marc Trachtenberg, *History & Strategy* (Princeton, NJ: Princeton University Press, 1991), p. 100.

82 *"I don't advocate preventive war":* Quoted in "The Five Nests," *Time*, September 11, 1950, p. 24.

82 *"I think I could explain to Him":* Quoted in ibid.

82 *Support for a first strike extended far beyond the upper ranks of the U.S. military:* Marc Trachtenberg offers a fine summary of American thinking about "preventive war" in *History & Strategy*, pp. 103–7. For other views of the subject, see Russell D. Buhite and W. Christopher Hamel, "War for Peace: The Question of an American Preventive War Against the Soviet Union, 1945–1955," *Diplomatic History*, vol. 14, no. 3, (1990), pp. 367–84; and Gian P. Gentile, "Planning for Preventive War," *Joint Force Quarterly*, Spring 2000, pp. 68–74.

82 *Russell . . . urged the western democracies to attack:* Bertrand Russell and his admirers later denied that he'd ever called for such an attack. But his rejection of pacifism, when dealing with the Soviets, had already been made clear. See "Russell Urges West to Fight Russia Now," *New York Times*, November 21, 1948; Bertrand Russell, "The Atomic Bomb and the Prevention of War," *Bulletin of the Atomic Scientists* (October 1, 1946), pp. 19–21; and Ray Perkins, "Bertrand

Russell and Preventive War," *Russell: The Journal of Bertrand Russell Studies*, vol. 14, no. 2 (1994), pp. 135–53.

82   *"anything is better than submission":* Quoted in *New York Times,* "Russell Urges West to Fight."

82   *Winston Churchill agreed:* See Trachtenberg, *History & Strategy,* p. 105.

82   *Even Hamilton Holt, lover of peace:* See Kuehl, *Hamilton Holt,* pp. 250–51.

83   *"should be wiped off the face of the earth":* Quoted in ibid., p. 250.

83   *the Joint Chiefs of Staff approved HALFMOON:* For an abridged version of HALFMOON, see "Brief of Short Range Emergency War Plan (HALFMOON), " JCS 1844/13, July 21, 1948 (TOP SECRET/ declassified), in Thomas H. Etzold and John Lewis Gaddis, *Containment: Documents on American Policy and Strategy, 1945–1950* (New York: Columbia University Press, 1978), pp. 315–24. For additional details, see May et al., "History of Strategic Arms Competition," Pt. 1, pp. 38–39; Ross, *War Plans,* pp. 79–97; and Kenneth W. Condit, *The Joint Chiefs of Staff and National Policy, Volume 2, 1947–1949* (Washington, D.C.: Office of Joint History, Office of the Chairman of Joint Chiefs of Staff, 1996), pp. 156–58.

83   *an "atomic blitz":* See "Conceptual Developments: The Atomic Blitz," in Wainstein et al., "Evolution of U.S. Command and Control," pp. 11–16.

83   *Leningrad was to be hit by 7 atomic bombs, Moscow by 8:* Cited in Condit, *Joint Chiefs of Staff, Volume 2,* p. 158.

83   *"the nation-killing concept":* Quoted in Wainstein et al., "Evolution of U.S. Command and Control," p. 15.

83   *"a nation would die just as surely":* Quoted in Robert F. Futrell, *Ideas, Concepts, Doctrine, Volume 1, Basic Thinking in the United States Air Force, 1907–1960* (Maxwell Air Force Base, AL: Air University Press, 1989), p. 240.

83   *a "devastating, annihilating attack":* Quoted in Jeffrey G. Barlow, *Revolt of the Admirals: The Fight for Naval Aviation, 1945–1950* (Washington, D.C.: Government Reprints Press, 2001), p. 109.

83   *"It will be the cheapest thing we ever did":* Quoted in Moody, *Building a Strategic Air Force,* p. 109.

84   *"The negative psycho-social results":* The State Department official was Charles E. Bohlen, quoted in Futrell, *Ideas,* vol. 1, p. 238.

85   *the Harmon Committee concluded:* An abridged version of the Harmon Report—"Evaluation of Effect on Soviet War Effort Resulting from the Strategic Air Offensive" (TOP SECRET/ declassified)—can be found in Etzold and Gaddis, *Containment,* pp. 360–64.

85   *reduce Soviet industrial production by 30 to 40 percent:* Ibid., p. 361.

85   *kill perhaps 2.7 million civilians:* Ibid., p. 362.

85   *injure an additional 4 million:* Ibid.

85   *"For the majority of Soviet people":* Ibid.

85   *"the only means of rapidly inflicting shock":* Ibid., pp. 363–64

85   *The Soviets detonated their first atomic device:* For the making of the Soviet bomb, see ibid. David Holloway, *Stalin and the Bomb: The Soviet Union and Atomic Energy, 1939–1956* (New Haven, CT: Yale University Press, 1994).

85   *The yield was about 20 kilotons:* Cited in ibid., p. 218.

86   *Each of its roughly 105,000 parts:* For the extraordinary story of how the B-29 was reverse-engineered, see Van Hardesty, "Made in the U.S.S.R.," *Air & Space,* March 2001; and Walter J. Boyne, "Carbon Copy," *Air Force Magazine,* June 2009.

86   *Soviet Union wouldn't develop an atomic bomb until the late 1960s:* In 1947, General Groves predicted it would take the Soviets another twenty years. See Gregg Herken, "'A Most Deadly Illusion': The Atomic Secret and American Nuclear Weapons Policy, 1945–1950," *Pacific Historical Review,* vol. 49, no. 1 (February 1980), pp. 58, 71.

86   *without a single military radar to search for enemy planes:* See Wainstein et al., "Evolution of U.S. Command and Control," p. 90.

86   *twenty-three radars to guard the northeastern United States:* Cited in ibid., p. 94.

86   *a bitter, public dispute about America's nuclear strategy:* For an excellent overview of the military thinking that led not only to the "revolt of the admirals" but also to Pentagon support for a hydrogen bomb, see David Alan Rosenberg, "American Atomic Strategy and the Hydrogen Bomb Decision," *Journal of American History,* vol. 66, no. 1 (June 1979), pp. 62–87. For the cultural

underpinnings of the revolt, see Vincent Davis, *The Admirals Lobby* (Chapel Hill: University of North Carolina Press, 1967). And for the dispute itself, see Barlow, *Revolt of the Admirals*, p. 109.

87   *"precision" tactical bombing:* See John G. Norris, "Radford Statement Sparks Move for Curb Over Money Powers of Johnson," *Washington Post*, October 8, 1949.

87   *"I don't believe in mass killings of noncombatants":* Quoted in Ibid.

87   *"random mass slaughter":* See "Text of Admiral Ofstie's Statement Assailing Strategic Bombing," *New York Times*, October 12, 1949.

87   *"ruthless and barbaric":* Ibid.

87   *"We must insure that our military techniques":* Ibid.

87   *"open rebellion":* Quoted in William S. White, "Bradley Accuses Admirals of 'Open Rebellion' on Unity; Asks 'All-American Team,'" *New York Times*, October 20, 1949.

87   *"Fancy Dans":* Quoted in ibid.

87   *"aspiring martyrs":* Quoted in Hanson W. Baldwin, "Bradley Bombs Navy," *New York Times*, October 20, 1949.

87   *"As far as I am concerned":* Quoted in *New York Times*, "Bradley Accuses Admirals."

88   *"The idea of turning over custody":* Quoted in David E. Lilienthal, *The Journals of David E. Lilienthal, Volume 2, The Atomic Energy Years, 1945–1950*, (New York: Harper & Row, 1964), p. 351.

88   *"to have some dashing lieutenant colonel decide":* Quoted in Millis and Duffield, *Forrestal Diaries*, p. 458.

88   *"Destruction is just around the corner":* Quoted in Futrell, *Ideas, Volume 1*, p. 216.

88   *Demobilization had left SAC a hollow force:* For a book that makes that point convincingly, see Harry R. Borowski, *A Hollow Threat: Strategic Air Power and Containment Before Korea* (Westport, CT: Greenwood Press, 1982).

88   *almost half of SAC's B-29s failed to get off the ground:* See Thomas M. Coffey, *Iron Eagle: The Turbulent Life of General Curtis LeMay* (New York: Crown, 1986), p. 271.

88   *SAC had just twenty-six flight crews:* Cited in "The View from Above: High-Level Decisions and the Soviet-American Strategic Arms Competition, 1945–1950," Samuel R. Williamson, Jr., with the collaboration of Steven L. Reardon, Office of the Secretary of Defense, October 1975 (TOP SECRET/declassified), p. 118.

88–89   *Perhaps half of these crews would be shot down:* Cited in Wainstein et al., "Evolution of U.S. Command and Control," p. 14.

89   *An estimated thirty-five to forty-five days of preparation:* See ibid., p. 18.

89   *Lindbergh found that morale was low:* See Moody, *Building a Strategic Air Force*, pp. 226–27.

90   *"cut off from normal life":* The quote comes from LeMay's memoir. Curtis E. LeMay with MacKinlay Kantor, *Mission with LeMay: My Story* (Garden City, NY: Doubleday, 1965), p. 32.

91   *a particular form of courage:* American bomber crews had one of the most stressful and dangerous assignments of the Second World War. Remaining in formation meant flying directly through antiaircraft fire; breaking formation was grounds for court-martial. For the pressures of the job and the need for teamwork, see Mike Worden, *Rise of the Fighter Generals: The Problem of Air Force Leadership, 1945–1982* (Maxwell Air Force Base, AL: Air University Press, 1998), pp. 8–11.

91   *more than half would be killed in action:* The typical tour of duty for an American bomber crew was twenty-five missions. A study of 2,051 crew members who flew bombing missions over Europe found that 1,295 were killed or declared missing in action. The study is cited in Bernard C. Nalty, John F. Shiner, and George M. Watson, *With Courage: The U.S. Army Air Forces in World War II* (Washington, D.C.: Air Force History and Museums Program, 1994), p. 179.

91   *"Japan would burn if we could get fire on it":* The prediction was made by General David A. Burchinal, who flew in one of the early firebomb attacks on Japan. Quoted in Richard H. Kohn and Joseph P. Harahan, eds., *Strategic Air Warfare: An Interview with Generals Curtis E. LeMay, Leon W. Johnson, David A. Burchinal, and Jack J. Catton* (Washington, D.C.: Office of Air Force History, 1988), p. 61.

92   *"I'll tell you what war is about":* Quoted in Warren Kozak, *LeMay: The Life and Wars of General Curtis LeMay* (Washington, D.C.: Regnery, 2009), p. xi.

92   *"We scorched and boiled and baked to death more people":* Although more Japanese were probably

killed in Hiroshima and Nagasaki than in Tokyo, LeMay's remark succinctly conveys his view of nuclear weapons. See LeMay, *Mission with LeMay*, p. 387.

92   *"about the darkest night in American military aviation history"*: Ibid., p. 433.

93   *"I can't afford to differentiate"*: Quoted in Kohn and Harahan, *Strategic Air Warfare*, p. 98.

93   *"Every man a coupling or a tube"*: LeMay, *Mission with LeMay*, p. 496.

93   "we are at war now": Ibid., p. 436.

93   *San Francisco was bombed more than six hundred times:* Cited in ibid.

94   *"a* single instrument . . . *directed, controlled"*: The quote, from an article by air power theorists Colonel Jerry D. Page and Colonel Royal H. Roussel, can be found in Michael H. Armacost, *The Politics of Weapons Innovation: The Thor-Jupiter Controversy* (New York: Columbia University Press, 1969), p. 101.

94   *Louis Slotin was tickling the dragon:* For Slotin's accident and its aftermath, see Stewart Alsop and Ralph E. Lapp, "The Strange Death of Louis Slotin," in Charles Neider, ed., *Man Against Nature* (New York: Harper & Brothers, 1954), pp. 8–18; Clifford T. Honicker, "America's Radiation Victims: The Hidden Files," *New York Times,* November 19, 1989; Richard E. Malenfant, "Lessons Learned from Early Criticality Accidents," Los Alamos National Laboratory, submitted for Nuclear Criticality Technology Safety Project Workshop, Gaithersburg, MD, May 14–15, 1996; and Eileen Welsome, *The Plutonium Files: America's Secret Medical Experiments in the Cold War* (New York: Dial Press, 1999), pp. 184–88.

95   *"Slotin was that safety device"*: "Report on May 21 Accident at Pajarito Laboratory," May 28, 1946, in Los Alamos, "Lessons Learned from Early Criticality Accidents."

95   *David Lilienthal visited Los Alamos for the first time:* For the disarray at Los Alamos and the absence of atomic bombs, see Richard G. Hewlett and Francis Duncan, *Atomic Shield: A History of the United States Atomic Energy Commission, Volume 2, 1947—1952* (University Park: Pennsylvania State University Press, 1969), pp. 30, 47–48; May et al., "History of Strategic Arms Competition," Pt. 1, p. 2; Gregg Herken, *The Winning Weapon: The Atomic Bomb in the Cold War 1945–1950* (New York: Vintage, 1982), pp. 196–99; Necah Stewart Furman, *Sandia National Laboratories: The Postwar Decade* (Albuquerque: University of New Mexico Press, 1990), pp. 233–36; and James L. Abrahamson and Paul H. Carew, *Vanguard of American Atomic Deterrence: The Sandia Pioneers, 1946–1949* (Westport, CT: Praeger, 2002), p. 120.

96   *"one of the saddest days of my life"*: Quoted in Herken, *Winning Weapon*, p. 196.

96   *"The substantial stockpile of atom bombs"*: Quoted in Furman, *Sandia National Laboratories*, p. 235.

96   *at most, one:* "Actually, we had one [bomb] that was probably operable when I first went off to Los Alamos: one that had a good chance of being operable," Lilienthal later told the historian Gregg Herken. Although Los Alamos had perhaps a dozen nuclear cores in storage, a shortage of parts made it impossible to put together that many bombs. Colonel Gilbert M. Dorland, who headed the bomb-assembly battalion at Sandia, had an even bleaker view of the situation than Lilienthal. "President Truman and the State Department were plain bluffing," Dorland later wrote. "We couldn't have put a bomb together and used it." For Lilienthal, see Herken, *Winning Weapon*, p. 197. For Dorland, see Abrahamson and Carew, *Vanguard of Atomic Deterrence*, p. 120.

96   *"probably operable"*: Quoted in Herken, *Winning Weapon*, p. 197.

96   *"We not only didn't have a pile"*: Quoted in ibid, p. 235.

96   *"haywire contraption"*: Quoted in Hansen, *Swords of Armageddon, Voulme 1*, p. 133.

96   *Nobody had bothered to save all the technical drawings:* According to the official history of the Atomic Energy Commission, when the original Manhattan Project scientists left Los Alamos, they "left behind them no production lines or printed manuals, but only a few assistants, some experienced technicians, some laboratory equipment, and a fragmented technology recorded in thousands of detailed reports." See Hewlett and Duncan, *Atomic Shield,* p. 134. For the lack of guidance on how to build another Little Boy, see Abrahamson and Carew, *Vanguard of Atomic Deterrence*, pp. 41–42.

97   *He'd wrapped the metal around a Coke bottle:* See Abrahamson and Carew, *Vanguard of Atomic Deterence*, p. 42.

97   *the final assembly of Mark 3 bombs:* Ibid., pp. 60–61.

97   *"a very serious potential hazard to a large area":* Quoted in Hansen, *Swords of Armageddon, Volume 1*, p. 137.

97   *secretly constructed at two Royal Air Force bases:* During the summer of 1946, the head of the Royal Air Force and the head of the United States Army Air Forces had decided that British bases should have atomic bomb assembly equipment, "just in case." See Abrahamson and Carew, *Vanguard of Atomic Deterrence*, pp. 115–17; Ken Young, "No Blank Cheque: Anglo-American (Mis)under-standings and the Use of the English Airbases," *Journal of Military History*, vol. 71, no. 4 (October 2007), 1136–40; and Ken Young, "US 'Atomic Capability' and the British Forward Bases in the Early Cold War," *Journal of Contemporary History*, vol. 42, no. 1 (January 2007), pp. 119–22.

98   *"if one blew, the others would survive":* Quoted in Abrahamson and Carew, *Vanguard of Atomic Deterrence*, p. 119.

98   *parts and cores to assemble fifty-six atomic bombs:* See Wainstein et al.,"Evolution of U.S. Command and Control," p. 34.

98   *deploy only one bomb assembly team overseas:* The AFSWP had two fully trained teams by the end of 1948—but lacked the support personnel to send both into the field at the same time. See ibid., p. 17; and Abrahamson and Carew, *Vanguard of Atomic Deterrence*, pp. 68–69, 150.

98   *Robert Peurifoy was a senior at Texas A&M:* Peurifoy interview.

99   *killed more than two million civilians:* That is a conservative estimate; the Korean War was espe-cially brutal for noncombatants. According to Dong-Choon Kim, who served as Standing Com-missioner of the Truth and Reconciliation Commission of South Korea, "the percentage of civilian deaths was higher than in any other war of the 20th century." For the estimate and the quote, see Dong-Choon Kim, "The War Against the 'Enemy Within': The Hidden Massacres in the Early Stages of the Korean War," in Gi-Wook Shin, Soon-Won Park, and Daqing Yang, eds., *Rethinking Historical Injustice and Reconciliation in Northeast Asia: The Korean Experience* (New York: Rout-ledge, 2007), p. 75.

99   *"prevent premature detonation":* "Final Evaluation Report, MK IV MOD O FM Bomb," "The Mk IV Evaluation Committee, Sandia Laboratory, Report No. SL-82, September 13, 1949 (SECRET/ RESTRICTED DATA/declassified), p. 60.

100   *"integrated contractor complex":* See Furman, *Sandia National Laboratories*, pp. 310–12.

In Violation

101   *Jeff Kennedy had just gotten home:* Interview with Jeffrey Kennedy.

103   *Kennedy thought, "Wow":* Ibid.

105   *"Commander, if you want to tell me how to do my job":* Quoted in ibid.

106   *Sandaker was a twenty-one-year-old PTS technician:* Interview with James Sandaker.

106   *"Well, I got to go":* Ibid.

106   *"All right," Sandaker said:* Ibid.

107   *"baby oil trailer":* See "Report, Major Missile Accident, Titan II Complex 374-7," Statement of Archie G. James, Staff Sergeant, Tab U-42, p. 1.

108   *"Tell it not to land":* Holder interview.

109   *"Jeff, I fucked up like you wouldn't believe":* Quoted in Kennedy interview.

109   *"Oh, David," Kennedy said:* Ibid.

110   *Sam Hutto's family had farmed the same land:* Interview with Sam Hutto.

110   *"We went into, through, and out of the Depression":* Quoted in ibid.

112   *the Air Force provided few additional details:* Interview with Robert Lyford, Governor Bill Clinton's liaison to various state agencies, including the Department of Emergency Services and the Depart-ment of Public Safety. See also "Missile Fuel Leaks; 100 Forced to Leave Area Near Arkansas," *Ar-kansas Gazette*, September 19, 1980; Tyler Tucker, "Officials Had No Early Knowledge of Missile Explosion, Tatom Says," Arkansas *Democrat*, September 25, 1980; and Carol Matlock, "Air Force Listens to Complaints, Says Notification Was Adequate," *Arkansas Gazette*, September 25, 1980.

113   *about fifty thousand gallons of radioactive water leaked:* Cited in "Arkansas Office of Emergency Services, Major Accomplishments During 1979–1980," Attachment 1, Highlights of Response to Emergencies in 1980.

113 *Bill Clinton was an unlikely person:* For a good sense of America's youngest governor in 1980, see David Maraniss, *First in His Class: A Biography of Bill Clinton* (New York: Simon & Schuster, 1996), pp. 352–86; Bill Clinton, *My Life* (New York: Alfred A. Knopf, 2004), pp. 254–89; and Phyllis Finton Johnston, *Bill Clinton's Public Policy for Arkansas: 1979–1980,* (Little Rock, AR: August House, 1982).

113 *"tall, handsome, a populist-liberal":* Quoted in Wayne King, "Rapidly Growing Arkansas Turns to Liberal Politicians," *New York Times,* May 14, 1978.

113 *"He was a punk kid with long hair":* Quoted in Roger Morris, *Partners in Power: The Clintons and Their America* (New York: Henry Holt, 1999), p. 218.

114 *"the Three Beards":* See Maraniss, *First in His Class,* pp. 364–65.

115 *"Captain Mazzaro, we have to get that propane tank":* Kennedy interview.

116 *"Stay here":* Quoted in Powell interview.

116 *"Hell no":* Ibid.

116 *"I'll give you three minutes":* Ibid.

117 *"There's not enough room for two people":* Quoted in ibid.

117 *"Oh, God":* Quoted in Kennedy interview.

117 *"Sir, this is what the tank readings are":* Kennedy interview and "Report, Major Missile Accident, Titan II Complex 374-7," Kennedy statement, Tab U-46, p. 4.

117 *"Where in hell did you get those?":* "Report, Major Missile Accident, Titan II Complex 374-7," Statement of James L. Morris, Colonel, Tab U-60, p. 1.

Megadeath

119 *Fred Charles Iklé began his research:* Interview with Fred Charles Iklé. For his early work on the subject, see Fred C. Iklé, "The Effect of War Destruction upon the Ecology of Cities," *Social Forces,* vol. 29, no. 4 (May 1951), pp. 383–91: and Fred C. Iklé, "The Social Versus the Physical Effects from Nuclear Bombing," *Scientific Monthly,* vol. 78, no. 3 (March 1954), pp. 182–87.

119 *killed about 3.3 percent of Hamburg's population:* Cited in Fred Charles Iklé, *The Social Impact of Bomb Destruction* (Norman: University of Oklahoma Press, 1958), p. 16.

119 *destroyed about half of its homes:* Cited in ibid.

119 *"A city re-adjusts to destruction":* Ibid., p. 8.

119 *British planners had assumed that for every metric ton:* For the lethal efficiencies of Second World War bombing, see ibid., pp. 17–18.

120 *Iklé devised a simple formula:* For the calculations on the relationship between bomb destruction and population loss, see ibid., pp. 53-56.

120 *"the fully compensating increase in housing density":* Ibid., p. 55.

120 *when about 70 percent of a city's homes were destroyed:* Ibid., p. 72.

120 *Project RAND became one of America's first think tanks:* For an unsurpassed account of RAND and its influence on postwar strategic policy, see Fred Kaplan, *The Wizards of Armageddon: The Untold Story of the Small Group of Men Who Have Devised the Plans and Shaped the Policies on How to Use the Bomb* (Stanford, CA: Stanford University Press, 1983). For a more recent look at the history, see Alex Abella, *Soldiers of Reason: The RAND Corporation and the Rise of the American Empire* (New York: Harcourt, 2008.)

121 *"It is not a pleasant task":* Iklé, *Social Impact of Bomb Destruction,* p. viii.

121 *The casualties were disproportionately women:* Cited in ibid., p. 205.

121 *Even in Hiroshima, the desire to fight back survived:* Ibid., p. 180.

122 *"the sheer terror of the enormous destruction":* Ibid., p. 120.

123 *"It is my conviction that a peaceful settlement":* Quoted in Hansen, *Swords of Armageddon,* vol. 2, pp. 85–86.

123 *"the policy of exterminating civilian populations":* Quoted in May et al., "History of Strategic Arms Competition," Pt 1, p. 65.

123 *"a weapon of genocide":* Quoted in Hewlett and Duncan, *Atomic Shield,* p. 384.

123 *"a danger to humanity . . . an evil thing":* For the full text of the statement by Fermi and Rabi, see "Minority Report on the H-Bomb," *Bulletin of the Atomic Scientists,* December 1976, p. 58.

123   *a "quantum leap" past the Soviets:* Quoted in McGeorge Bundy, *Danger and Survival: Choices About the Bomb in the First Fifty Years* (New York: Random House, 1988), p. 204.

124   *"proceed with all possible expedition":* Quoted in "View from Above," p. 203.

124   *"total power in the hands of total evil":* Quoted in Hewlett and Duncan, *Atomic Shield,* p. 402.

124   *most likely "psychological":* Quoted in Herken, *Winning Weapon,* p. 316.

124   *"In that case, we have no choice":* Quoted in Robert H. Ferrell, *Harry S. Truman: A Life* (Columbia: University of Missouri Press, 1994), p. 350.

124   *Albert Einstein read a prepared statement:* See "Einstein Fears Hydrogen Bomb Might Annihilate 'Any Life,'" *Washington Post,* February 13, 1950.

124   *the "hysterical character" of the nuclear arms race:* For the full text of Einstein's statement, see "Dr. Einstein's Address on Peace in the Atomic Era," *New York Times,* February 13, 1950.

124   *the "disastrous illusion":* Ibid.

124   *"In the end, there beckons more and more clearly":* Ibid.

124   *"psychological considerations":* "Effect of Civilian Morale on Military Capabilities in a Nuclear War Environment: Enclosure 'E,' The Relationship to Public Morale of Information About the Effects of Nuclear Warfare," WSEG Report No. 42, Weapons Systems Evaluation Group, Joint Chiefs of Staff, October 20, 1959 (CONFIDENTIAL/declassified), p. 53.

124   *"Weapons systems in themselves":* Ibid.

124   *"information program":* Ibid., p. 54.

125   *"What deters is not the capabilities":* Ibid.

125   *"Any U.S. move toward abandoning or suspending work":* Quoted in Hans Bethe, "Sakharov's H-Bomb," *Bulletin of the Atomic Scientists,* October 1990, p. 9.

125   *the transfer of eighty-nine atomic bombs:* See Wainstein et al.,"Evolution of U.S. Command and Control," p. 31: and Feaver, *Guarding the Guardians,* pp. 134–36.

126   *the transfer of fifteen atomic bombs without cores:* Wainstein et al., "Evolution of U.S. Command and Control," p. 31.

126   *personal responsibility for the nine weapons:* Ibid., p. 32.

126   *the United States had about three hundred atomic bombs:* Ibid., p. 34.

126   *more than one third of them were stored:* Eighty-nine were in Great Britain, fifteen on the *Coral Sea,* and nine on the island of Guam.

126   *the AEC had eleven employees:* See "History of the Custody and Deployment of Nuclear Weapons: July 1945 Through September 1977," Office of the Assistant to the Secretary of Defense (Atomic Energy), February 1978 (TOP SECRET/RESTRICTED DATA/declassified), p. 13.

126   *"Our troops guarded [the atomic bombs]":* Quoted in Kohn and Harahan, *Strategic Air Warfare,* p. 92.

127   *"If I were on my own and half the country":* Quoted in ibid., p. 93.

127   *applied for a patent:* Innovations in nuclear weapon design had been secretly patented since the days of the Manhattan Project. For a fascinating account of how a legal procedure originally created to ensure public knowledge became one used to deny it, see Alex Wellerstein, "Patenting the Bomb: Nuclear Weapons, Intellectual Property, and Technological Control," *Isis,* vol. 99, no. 1 (March 2008), pp. 57–87.

127   *"a bomb in a box":* Quoted in Hansen, *Swords of Armageddon, Volume 1,* p. 182.

128   *"In addition to all the problems of fission":* Quoted in Anne Fitzpatrick, "Igniting the Elements: The Los Alamos Thermonuclear Project, 1942–1952," (thesis, Los Alamos National Laboratory, LA-13577-T, July 1999), p. 121.

129   *The machine was called MANIAC:* The effort to create a hydrogen bomb not only depended on the use of electronic computers for high-speed calculations, it also helped to bring those machines into existence. For the inextricable link between thermonuclear weapon design and postwar computer science in the United States, see "Nuclear Weapons Laboratories and the Development of Supercomputing," in Donald MacKenzie, *Knowing Machines: Essays on Technical Change* (Cambridge, MA: MIT Press, 1998), pp. 99–129; "Why Build Computers?: The Military Role in Computer Research," in Paul N. Edwards, *The Closed World: Computers and the Politics of Discourse in Cold War America* (Cambridge, MA: MIT Press, 1996), pp. 43–73; Francis H. Harlow and N. Metropolis, "Computing and Computers: Weapons Simulation Leads to the Computer Era," *Los Ala-*

mos Science, Winter/Spring 1983, pp. 132–41; Herbert L. Anderson, "Metropolis, Monte Carlo, and the MANIAC," *Los Alamos Science,* Fall 1986, pp. 96–107; N. Metropolis, "The Age of Computing: A Personal Memoir," *Daedalus,* A New Era in Computation, vol. 121, no. 1, (1992), pp. 119–30; and Fitzpatrick, "Igniting the Elements," pp. 99–173.

129   *a mushroom cloud that rose about twenty-seven miles:* See "Progress Report to the Joint Committee on Atomic Energy, Part III: Weapons," United States Atomic Energy Commission, June Through November, 1952 (TOP SECRET/RESTRICTED DATA/declassified), p. 5.

129   *The fireball . . . was three and a half miles wide:* Cited in Hansen, *Swords of Armageddon, Volume 3,* p. 67.

129   *more than a mile in diameter and fifteen stories deep:* See Appendix A, Summary of Available Crater Data, in "Operation Castle, Project 3.2: Crater Survey, Headquarters Field Command, Armed Forces Special Weapons Project, June 1955 (SECRET/FORMERLY RESTRICTED DATA/declassified), p. 60.

129   *yield of the device was 10.4 megatons:* Cited in "Operation Ivy 1952," United States Atmospheric Nuclear Weapons Tests, Nuclear Test Personnel Review, Defense Nuclear Agency, DNA 6036F, December 1, 1982, p. 17.

129   *"The war of the future would be one":* For Truman's remarks, see "Text of President's Last State of the Union Message to Congress, Citing New Bomb Tests," *New York Times,* January 8, 1953.

130   *Project Vista, a top secret study:* For a good account of the study, see David C. Elliott, "Project Vista and Nuclear Weapons in Europe," *International Security,* vol. 11, no. 1 (Summer 1986), pp. 163–83.

130   *an allied army with 54 divisions:* Cited in May et al., "History of Strategic Arms Competition," Pt 1, p. 140.

130   *thought to have 175 divisions:* Cited in ibid., p. 139.

130   *a "trip wire," a "plate glass wall":* Ibid., p. 172.

130   *bring the "battle back to the battlefield":* Quoted in Kai Bird and Martin J. Sherwin, *American Prometheus: The Triumph and Tragedy of J. Robert Oppenheimer* (New York: Vintage 2006), p. 445.

130   *"preventing attacks on friendly cities":* Quoted in Elliott, "Project Vista," p. 172.

131   *"Successful offense brings victory":* "Remarks: General Curtis E. LeMay at Commander's Conference," Wright-Patterson Air Force Base, January 1956 (TOP SECRET/Declassified), NSA, p. 17.

131   *the "counterforce" strategy:* For the thinking behind counterforce, see T. F. Walkowicz, "Strategic Concepts for the Nuclear Age," *Annals of the American Academy of Political and Social Science,* vol. 299, Air Power and National Security, May 1955, pp. 118–27, and Alfred Goldberg, "A Brief Survey of the Evolution of Ideas About Counterforce," prepared for U.S. Air Force Project RAND, Memorandum RM-5431-PR, October 1967 (revised March 1981), NSA.

131   *"Offensive air power must now be aimed":* Quoted in Futrell, *Ideas, Volume 1,* p. 441.

131   *"for us to build enough destructive power":* Quoted in Richard G. Hewlett and Jack M. Holl, *Atoms for Peace and War, 1953–1961: Eisenhower and the Atomic Energy Commission* (Berkeley: University of California Press, 1989), p. 3.

132   *"In the event of hostilities":* "A Report to the National Security Council by the Executive Secretary on Basic National Security Policy," NSC 162/2, October 30, 1953 (TOP SECRET/declassified), p. 22.

132   *"maintain a massive capability to strike back":* "Text of President Eisenhower's State of the Union," *Washington Post,* January 8, 1954.

132   *"a great capacity to retaliate, instantly":* "Text of Dulles' Statement on Foreign Policy of Eisenhower Administration," *New York Times,* January 13, 1954.

132   *"massive retaliation":* The name of the new strategy obscured the fact that General LeMay and the Strategic Air Command had no intention of allowing the United States to be hit first. For Eisenhower's views about nuclear weapons and the threat that the Soviet Union seemed to pose, see Samuel F. Wells, Jr., "The Origins of Massive Retaliation," *Political Science Quarterly,* vol. 96, no. 1 (Spring 1981), pp. 31–52; and Richard K. Betts, "A Nuclear Golden Age? The Balance Before Parity," *International Security,* vol. 11, no. 3 (Winter 1986), pp. 3–32.

132   *the number of personnel at SAC increased by almost one third, and the number of aircraft nearly doubled:* In 1952 the Strategic Air Command had 1,638 aircraft and employed 166,021 people; by

1956 it had 3,188 and employed 217,279. Cited in Norman Polmar, ed., *Strategic Air Command: People, Aircraft, and Missiles* (Annapolis, MD: Nautical and Aviation Publishing Company of America, 1979), pp. 28, 44.

133 *more than one fifth of its funding and about one quarter of its troops:* According to the historian A. J. Bacevich, in 1953 Eisenhower cut the Army's fiscal year 1955 budget from $13 billion to $10.2 billion and lowered the number of troops from 1,540,000 to 1,164,000. See Bacevich, "The Paradox of Professionalism: Eisenhower, Ridgway, and the Challenge to Civilian Control, 1953–1955," *Journal of Military History,* vol. 61, no. 2, (April 1997), p. 314.

133 *"national fiscal bankruptcy would be far preferable":* Quoted in ibid., p. 321.

133 *151,000 nuclear weapons:* For the number of weapons that the Army sought and how it hoped to use them, see "History of the Custody and Deployment," p. 50.

134 *"emergency capability" weapons:* For the definition of the phrase, see "History of the Early Thermonuclear Weapons: Mks 14, 15, 16, 17, 24, and 29," Information Research Division, Sandia National Laboratories, RS 3434/10, June 1967 (SECRET RESTRICTED DATA/declassified), p. 17.

134 *Code-named Project Brass Ring:* See ibid., p. 15; and Hansen, *Swords of Armageddon, Volume 2,* pp. 119–20, 262.

134 *Agnew remembered seeing footage of Nazi tasks:* Agnew interview.

134 *"We've got to find out":* Ibid.

135 *The program, known as Project Paperclip:* For details of the program, see John Gimbel, "U.S. Policy and German Scientists: The Early Cold War," *Political Science Quarterly,* vol. 101, no. 3 (1986), pp. 433–451; Linda Hunt, *Secret Agenda: The United States Government, Nazi Scientists, and Project Paperclip, 1945 to 1990* (New York: St. Martin's 1991); and Tom Bower, *The Paperclip Conspiracy: The Hunt for the Nazi Scientists* (Boston: Little, Brown, 1987).

135 *"rescue those able and intelligent Jerries":* LeMay, *Mission with LeMay,* p. 398.

135 *"Oh yes," Knacke replied:* Quoted in Agnew interview.

135 *Bob Peurifoy led the team at Sandia:* Peurifoy interview.

137 *a temperature of about -423 degrees Fahrenheit:* Cited in Hansen, *Swords of Armageddon Volume 3,* p. 56.

137 *he'd climbed two hundred feet to the top:* Bernard O'Keefe and a friend flipped a coin to see who'd have to disarm the nuclear device. O'Keefe lost, got into a Jeep, and headed to the tower. See O'Keefe, *Nuclear Hostages,* pp. 154–6.

137 *"Is this building moving or am I getting dizzy?":* Quoted in ibid., p. 178.

137 *"My God, it is":* Ibid.

137 *"like it was resting on a bowl of jelly":* Ibid., p. 179.

137 *Shrimp's yield was 15 megatons:* Cited in Hewlett and Holl, *Atoms for Peace* p. 174.

137 *almost three times larger than . . . predicted:* Cited in ibid.

137 *about two hundred billion pounds of coral reef and the seafloor:* The crater dug by the blast was roughly two thousand yards wide, with a maximum depth of eighty yards. As Bob Peurifoy and his son, Steve, a fellow engineer, explained to me, the crater was "an inverted, very-high-aspect ratio, right circular cone." The volume of such a cone is one third of the base area multiplied by the height. According to their calculations, the volume of the Bravo crater was about eighty million cubic yards—and a cubic yard of sandy topsoil weighs about twenty-five hundred pounds. That means the amount of material displaced by the explosion weighed about two hundred billion pounds. To get a visual sense of that amount, imagine a pile of sand and coral the size of a football field that extends about seven miles into the sky. I am grateful to the Peurifoys for these figures. For the dimensions of the crater formed by the Bravo test, see "Operation Castle, Crater Survey," p. 24.

137 *cloud that soon stretched for more than sixty miles:* The mushroom cloud reached a maximum height of about 310,000 feet and a width of about 350,000 feet. See Vincent J. Jodoin, "Nuclear Cloud Rise and Growth" (dissertation, Graduate School of Engineering, Air Force Institute of Technology, Air University, June 1994), p. 89.

138 *The dangers of radioactive fallout:* For a good explanation of how residual radiation is created, how long it can last, and what it can do to human beings, see Glasstone, *Effects of Nuclear Weapons,* pp. 414–501, 577–663.

138 *The "early fallout" of a nuclear blast:* See ibid., pp. 416–42.

139 *A dose of about 700 roentgens is almost always fatal:* See ibid., p. 461.

139 *"Delayed fallout" poses a different kind of risk:* See ibid., pp. 473–88.

139 *an amount of fallout that surprised everyone:* See ibid., pp. 460–61; and Hewlett and Holl, *Atoms for Peace,* pp. 171–82, 271–79.

140 *The villagers had seen the brilliant explosion:* See Hewlett and Holl, *Atoms for Peace,* p. 174.

140 *a Japanese fishing boat, the* Lucky Dragon: The story of the unfortunate crew can be found in ibid., pp. 175–77; and Ralph E. Lapp, *The Voyage of the Lucky Dragon* (New York: Harper & Brothers, 1958).

140 *the fallout pattern from the Bravo test was superimposed:* The map can be found in Hewlett and Holl, *Atoms for Peace,* p. 181.

140 *if a similar 15-megaton groundburst hit:* Ibid., p. 182. Within an area of roughly 6,000 square miles—about 135 miles long and 35 miles wide—the fatality rate among people who did not evacuate or find shelter would be close to 100 percent. See Glasstone, *Effects of Nuclear Weapons,* p. 461.

141 *its first atomic bomb, the "Blue Danube":* Instead of numerical signifiers, the British came up with all sorts of evocative names for their nuclear weapons, including: "Blue Peacock," an atomic land mine; "Blue Steel," an air-launched missile with a thermonuclear warhead; "Green Cheese," a proposed antiship missile with an atomic warhead; "Indigo Hammer," a small atomic warhead for use with antiaircraft missiles; "Red Beard," a tactical bomb; "Tony," an atomic warhead used in antiaircraft missiles; and "Winkle," an atomic warhead developed for the Royal Navy. A thorough list of them can be found in Richard Moore, "The Real Meaning of the Words: A Pedantic Glossary of British Nuclear Weapons," UK Nuclear History Working Paper, no. 1, Mountbatten Centre for International Studies (March 2004).

141 *a yield of about 16 kilotons:* Cited in ibid, p. 3.

141 *"With all its horrors, the atomic bomb":* Quoted in "Debate in House of Commons, April 5, 1954" *Hansard,* vol. 526, p. 48.

141 *Strath submitted his report in the spring of 1955:* For details of the report, see Jeff Hughes, "The Strath Report: Britain Confronts the H-Bomb, 1954–1955," *History and Technology,* vol. 19, no. 3 (2003), pp. 257–75; Robin Woolven, "UK Civil Defence and Nuclear Weapons, 1953–1959," UK Nuclear History Working Paper, no. 2, Mountbatten Centre for International Studies, (n.d.); and Peter Hennessy, *The Secret State: Whitehall and the Cold War* (New York: Penguin, 2003), pp. 132–46.

141 *"render the UK useless":* The quote is from an intelligence report submitted to Strath. See Hennessy, *Secret State,* p. 133.

141 *"The heat flash from one hydrogen bomb":* Quoted in Hughes, "The Strath Report," p. 268.

141 *If the Soviets detonated ten hydrogen bombs:* See Hennessy, *Secret State,* p. 121.

141 *Almost one third of the British population would be killed:* See Hughes, "The Strath Report," p. 270.

141 *the most productive land might "be lost for a long time":* Quoted in ibid., p. 269.

141 *"Machinery of Control":* For the workings of the proposed martial law, see Hennessy, *Secret State,* p. 139; and Hughes, "The Strath Report," p. 270.

142 *"drastic emergency powers," and . . . "rough and ready methods":* Quoted in Hughes, "The Strath Report," p. 270.

142 *Churchill ordered the BBC not to broadcast news:* Ibid., pp. 272–73.

142 *"Influence depended on possession of force":* Quoted in Hennessy, *Secret State,* p. 54.

142 *"We must do it":* Quoted in ibid., p. 44.

142 *build an underground shelter "right now":* Quoted in Allen Drury, "U.S. Stress on Speed," *New York Times,* March 12, 1955.

142 *"we had all better dig and pray":* Quoted in ibid.

142 *"YOUR CHANCES OF SURVIVING AN ATOMIC ATTACK":* "Survival Under Atomic Attack," The Official U.S. Government Booklet, Distributed by Office of Civil Defense, State of California, Reprint by California State Printing Division, October 1950, p. 4.

142–43 *"EVEN A LITTLE MATERIAL GIVES PROTECTION":* Ibid., p. 8.

143 *"WE KNOW MORE ABOUT RADIOACTIVITY":* Ibid., p. 8.

143   *"KEEP A FLASHLIGHT HANDY":* Ibid., p. 19.

143   *"AVOID GETTING WET AFTER UNDERWATER BURSTS":* Ibid., p. 23.

143   *"BE CAREFUL NOT TO TRACK RADIOACTIVE MATERIALS":* Ibid., p. 27.

143   *Val Peterson called for concrete pipelines to be laid:* See Anthony Levieros, "Big Bomb Blast Jolted Civil Defense Leaders; But Program Still Lags," *New York Times,* June 10, 1955.

143   *"Duck and cover," one journalist noted:* See Bernard Stengren, "Major Cities Lag in Planning Defense Against Bomb Attack," *New York Times,* June 12, 1955.

143   *Hoping to boost morale:* The historians Guy Oakes and Andrew Grossman have argued that the underlying goal of Operation Alert and other civil defense exercises was "emotion management"— reassuring the public in order to maintain support for nuclear deterrence. The propaganda value of such drills was considered far more important than their potential usefulness during a Soviet attack. See Guy Oakes and Andrew Grossman, "Managing Nuclear Terror: The Genesis of American Civil Defense Strategy," *International Journal of Politics, Culture, and Society,* vol. 5, no. 3 (1992), pp. 361–403; and Guy Oakes, "The Cold War Conception of Nuclear Reality: Mobilizing the American Imagination for Nuclear War in the 1950's," *International Journal of Politics, Culture, and Society,* vol. 6, no. 3 (1993), pp. 339–63. For an overview of official efforts to protect the nation's capital, literally and symbolically, see David F. Krugler, *This Is Only a Test: How Washington D.C. Prepared for Nuclear War* (New York: Palgrave Macmillan, 2006).

143   *sixty-one cities were struck by nuclear weapons:* For the imaginary attack and the estimated carnage, see Anthony Leviero, "H-Bombs Test U.S. Civil Defense," *New York Times,* June 16, 1955; and Edward T. Folliard, "Tests Over U.S. Indicate Centers Might Suffer Heavily in Raid," *Washington Post,* June 16, 1955.

143   *the corner of North 7th Street and Kent Avenue:* See Anthony Leviero, "U.S. H-Bomb Alert Today; Eisenhower, Top Officials Among 15,000 Slated to Leave Capital," *New York Times,* June 15, 1955.

143   *only 8.2 million people would be killed and 6.6 million wounded:* Cited in ibid.

143–44   *the United States would "be able to take it":* Quoted in Anthony Leviero, "Mock Martial Law Invoked in Bombing Test Aftermath," *New York Times,* June 17, 1955.

144   *more than half of those casualties would be in New York City:* The casualty estimates for the city were quite specific—2,991,285 deaths and 1,776,889 wounded. And yet those numbers did not dim the upbeat reporting of the drill. Cited in Peter Kihss, "City Raid Alert Termed a Success," *New York Times,* June 16, 1955.

144   *"we might—ideally—escape":* Quoted in "Anthony Leviero, "Eisenhower Hails Operation Alert as Encouraging," *New York Times,* June 18, 1955.

144   *"great encouragement":* Quoted in ibid.

144   *"staggering":* Quoted in Betts, "A Nuclear Golden Age?," pp. 3–32.

144   *A new word had entered the lexicon . . . megadeath:* According to the *Oxford English Dictionary,* the word appeared in print for the first time on June 21, 1953, in an Alabama newspaper, the *Birmingham News.*

144   *"The United States experienced . . . total economic collapse":* I read an edited version of this quote in Betts, "Nuclear Golden Age?," p. 14, and then sought out the original in Robert H. Ferrell, ed., *The Eisenhower Diaries* (New York: W. W. Norton, 1981), p. 311.

144   *"It would be perfect rot to talk about shipping troops":* At a White House meeting, Eisenhower lost his cool, pounded the table repeatedly, and said, "You see, actually, the only thing we fear is an atomic attack delivered by air on our cities. God damn it? It would be perfect rot to talk about shipping troops abroad when fifteen of our cities were in ruins. You would have disorder and almost complete chaos in the cities and in the roads around them. You would have to restore order and who is going to restore it? Do you think the police and fire departments of those cities could restore order? Nuts! That order is going to have to be restored by disciplined armed forces." According to Eisenhower's press secretary, the room fell silent, and you could hear a pin drop. Quoted in "Diary Entry by the President's Press Secretary (Hagerty)," Washington, D.C., February 1, 1955, United States State Department, *Foreign Relations of the United States, 1955–1957, vol. 19, National Security Policy* (Washington, D.C.: U.S. Government Printing Office, 1990), pp. 39–40.

144   *"You can't have this kind of war":* Quoted in Gregg Herken, *Counsels of War* (New York: Oxford University Press, 1987), p. 116.

Part Three: Accidents Will Happen

Acceptable Risks

147 *Jimmy Stewart enlisted in the Army:* For a fine account of Stewart's military service, see Starr Smith, *Jimmy Stewart: Bomber Pilot* (Minneapolis: Zenith Press, 2005).

147 *He flew dozens of those missions:* Cited in ibid., p. 263.

147 *"He always maintained a calm demeanor":* The officer was Colonel Ramsay Potts, commander of the 453rd Bomb Group. Quoted in ibid., p. 125.

147 *Stewart visited SAC headquarters:* For the origins of the film, see Hedda Hopper, "General LeMay Briefs Stewart for Film," *Los Angeles Times*, December 27, 1952. The film is also mentioned at some length in the chapter "The Heyday of SAC: The High Point of the Popular Culture Crusade," in Steve Call, *Selling Air Power: Military Aviation and Popular Culture After World War II* (College Station, TX: Texas A&M University Press, 2009), pp. 100–131.

148 *"Toughest Cop of the Western World":* See Ernest Havemann, "Toughest Cop of the Western World," *Life*, June 14, 1954.

148 *"It wouldn't dare":* Quoted in ibid.

149 *a study by the RAND analyst Albert Wohlstetter:* See A. J. Wohlstetter, F. S. Hoffman, R. J. Lutz, and H. S. Rowen, "Selection and Use of Strategic Bases," a report prepared for United States Air Force Project Rand, R-266, April 1954 (SECRET/declassified).

149 *"Training in SAC was harder than war":* The officer was General Jack J. Catton, who served with LeMay for sixteen years. Quoted in Kohn and Harahan, *Strategic Air Warfare*, p. 97.

149 *Rhinelander, Wisconsin, became one of SAC's favorite targets:* See Thomas M. Coffey, *Iron Eagle: The Turbulent Life of General Curtis LeMay* (New York: Crown Publishers, 1986), p. 342.

149 *the SAC battle plan called for 180 bombers:* Cited in Wainstein et al., "*Evolution of U.S. Command and Control,*" p. 257.

149 *the bombardier had aimed at the wrong island:* See Hansen, *Swords of Armageddon, Volume IV*, pp. 160–2.

150 *94 SAC bombers tested the air defense system:* For the results of Operation Tailwind, see Wainstein et al., "Evolution of U.S. Command and Control," pp. 103–4.

150 *Ten Bisons flew past the reviewing stand:* The CIA later admitted its error; the ten that flew past were the only ten in existence. See Donald P. Steury, ed., *Intentions and Capabilities: Estimates on Soviet Strategic Forces, 1953–1983* (Washington, D.C.: History Staff, Center for the Study of Intelligence, Central Intelligence Agency, 1996), p. 5.

150 *more than 100 of the planes:* General LeMay publicly testified that the Soviets already had that many—and he may even have believed it. During a top secret speech to his own officers, LeMay said the Soviet Union would soon be building 300 new bombers a year. For the 100 estimate, see "Bison vs. B-52: LeMay Testifies," *New York Times*, May 6, 1956. For his prediction about Soviet bomber production, see "Remarks: LeMay at Commander's Conference," p. 13.

150 *the Soviets would be able to attack the United States with 700 bombers:* Cited in "Soviet Gross Capabilities for Attack on the US and Key Overseas Installations and Forces Through Mid-1959," National Intelligence Estimate Number 11-56, Submitted by the Director of Central Intelligence, 6 March 1956 (TOP SECRET/declassified), p. 3, in *Intentions and Capabilities*, p. 16.

150 *"It is clear that the United States and its allies":* Quoted in "The Nation: Wilson Stands Ground," *New York Times*, July 8, 1956.

150 *an extra $900 million for new B-52s:* In this case a Democratic Congress approved a major increase in defense spending that a Republican president didn't want. See "Wilson Raps Any Air Fund Boost," *Los Angeles Times*, June 22, 1956, and "House-Senate Group Agrees to Hike Air Force Budget by $900 Million," *Wall Street Journal*, June 29, 1956.

151 *By the end of the decade, the Soviet Union had about 150 long-range bombers:* In 1958, the Soviet Union had about 50 Bison bombers and 105 Bears. Cited in May et al., "History of Strategic Arms Competition," p. 186.

151 *the Strategic Air Command had almost 2,000:* In 1959, SAC had 488 B-52 bombers and 1,366 B-47s. See Polmar, *Strategic Air Command*, p. 61.

151   *such a system would "provide a reasonable degree":* Quoted in Wainstein et al., "Evolution of U.S. Command and Control," p. 201.

151   *at least two hours' warning of an attack:* Cited in ibid., p. 203.

151   *a distance of about twelve thousand miles:* Cited in ibid., p. 207.

151   *almost half a million tons of building material:* Roughly 459,900 tons were transported into the Arctic by barges, planes, and tractor-pulled sleds. Cited in James Louis Isemann, "To Detect, to Deter, to Defend: The Distant Early Warning (DEW) Line and Early Cold War Defense Policy, 1953–1957," dissertation, Department of History, Kansas State University, 2009, p. 299.

151   *temperatures as low as -70 degrees Fahrenheit:* Cited in ibid., p. 304.

152   *"The computerization of society":* I first encountered the quote in Edwards, *The Closed World,* on page 65. The original source is a fascinating book: Frank Rose, *Into the Heart of the Mind: An American Quest for Artificial Intelligence* (New York: Harper & Row, 1984).

152   *America's first large-scale electronic digital computer, ENIAC:* The acronym stood for Electronic Numerical Integrator and Computer.

152   *researchers concluded that the Whirlwind computer:* It is hard to overstate the importance of the Whirlwind computer and the SAGE air defense system that evolved from it. The historian Thomas P. Hughes described the creation of SAGE as "one of the major learning experiences in technological history"—as important as the construction of the Erie Canal. The historians Kent C. Redmond and Thomas M. Smith have called SAGE "a technical innovation of such consequence as to make it one of the major human accomplishments of the twentieth century." And yet one of the great ironies of SAGE, according to the historian Paul N. Edwards, is that it probably wouldn't have worked. "It was easily jammed," Edwards noted, "and tests of the system under actual combat conditions were fudged to avoid revealing its many flaws." It created the modern computer industry—and transformed society—but probably wouldn't have detected a Soviet bomber attack. For these quotes, as well as descriptions of how SAGE influenced the future, see Thomas P. Hughes, *Rescuing Prometheus: Four Monumental Projects That Changed the Modern World* (New York: Vintage, 1998), p. 15; Kent C. Redmond and Thomas M. Smith, *From Whirlwind to Mitre: The R&D Story of the SAGE Air Defense Computer* (Cambridge, MA: MIT Press, 2000), p. 429; and Edwards, *Closed World,* p. 110.

153   *the first computer network:* See Edwards, *Closed World,* p. 101.

153   *contained about 25,000 vacuum tubes and covered about half an acre:* Cited in Hughes, *Rescuing Prometheus,* p. 51.

153   *SAGE created the template for the modern computer industry:* See Redmond and Smith, *From Whirlwind to Mitre,* pp. 436–43; and Edwards, *Closed World,* pp. 99–104.

154   *almost five hours after being sent:* During a SAC command exercise in September 1950 the average transmission time for teletype messages was four hours and forty-five minutes. See Wainstein, et al., "Evolution of U.S. Command and Control," p. 78.

154   *a special red telephone at SAC headquarters:* See ibid., p. 162.

154   *an automated command-and-control system:* It was called the SAC 456L System, or SACCS—the Strategic Automated Command and Control System. It was commissioned in 1958 but did not become fully operational until 1963. See ibid., pp. 169–70; and "The Air Force and the Worldwide Military Command and Control System, 1961–1965," Thomas A. Sturm, USAF Historical Division Liaison Office, DASMC-66 013484, SHO-S-66/279, August 1966 (SECRET/declassified), NSA, p. 12.

154   *from an hour and a half to six hours behind the planes:* See Wainstein, et al., "Evolution of U.S. Command and Control," p. 170.

154   *"I don't think I would put that much money":* Quoted in "Supersonic Air Transports," Report of the Special Investigating Subcommittee of the Committee on Science and Astronautics, U.S. House of Representatives, Eighty-sixth Congress, Second Session, 1960, p. 47.

154   *It extended three levels underground and could house about eight hundred people:* See "Welcome to Strategic Air Command Headquarters," Directorate of Information, Headquarters Strategic Air Command, Offutt Air Force Base (n.d.).

155   *Below the East Wing at the White House:* For Roosevelt's bunker and the construction of a new bunker for Truman, see Krugler, *This Is Only a Test,* pp. 68–75.

155 *an underground complex with twenty rooms:* Cited in ibid., p. 73.

155 *the airburst of a 20-kiloton atomic bomb:* Cited in ibid., p. 70.

155 *Known as Site R:* For details about Site R, see ibid., p. 63–6.

155 *enough beds to accommodate two thousand high-ranking officials:* The actual number was 2,200.
     Cited in Wainstein et al., "Evolution of U.S. Command and Control," p. 232.

155 *the Air Force and the other armed services disagreed:* The Air Force viewed Site R as a military com-
     mand post that should be manned by those who would need to give orders during wartime, not
     used as a refuge for Pentagon officials or unnecessary personnel. See ibid., pp. 226–32.

155 *at Mount Weather, a similar facility:* For the details of this bunker and its operations, see *This Is
     Only a Test*, pp. 106–7, 165–6; Ted Gup, "Doomsday Hideaway," *Time*, December 9, 1991; and
     Ted Gup, "The Doomsday Blueprints," *Time*, August 10, 1992.

155 *Eisenhower had secretly given nine prominent citizens:* CONELRAD, a Web site devoted to Cold
     War history and culture, obtained Eisenhower's letters appointing the men to serve in these
     posts during a national emergency. Ten men were eventually asked to serve, after one resigned
     from his position. See "The Eisenhower Ten" at www.conelrad.com.

156 *Patriotic messages from Arthur Godfrey:* Bill Geerhart, a founder of the CONELRAD Web site,
     has been determined for more than twenty years to obtain a copy of Arthur Godfrey's public ad-
     dress announcement about nuclear war. See "Arthur Godfrey, the Ultimate PSA" and "The Arthur
     Godfrey PSA Search: Updated" at www.conelrad.com. The existence of these messages by God-
     frey and Edward R. Murrow was mentioned in *Time* magazine. See "Recognition Value," *Time*,
     March 2, 1953.

156 *Beneath the Greenbrier Hotel:* See Ted Gup, "Last Resort: The Ultimate Congressional Getaway,"
     Washington Post, May 31, 1992; Thomas Mallon, "Mr. Smith Goes Underground," *American Her-
     itage*, September 2000; and John Strausbaugh, "A West Virginia Bunker Now a Tourist Spot," *New
     York Times*, November 12, 2006.

156 *A bunker was later constructed for the Federal Reserve:* Once known as "Mount Pony," the site is now
     used by the Library of Congress to store old sound recordings and films. See "A Cold War Bunker
     Now Shelters Archive," *Los Angeles Times*, August 31, 2007.

156 *inside the Kindsbach Cave:* See A. L. Shaff, "World War II History Buried in Kindsbach," *Kaiser-
     slautern American*, July 1, 2011.

156 *the code names SUBTERFUGE, BURLINGTON, and TURNSTYLE:* For the story of the Central
     Government Emergency War Headquarters, see Nick McCamley, *Cold War Secret Nuclear Bun-
     kers: The Passive Defense of the Western World During the Cold War* (Barnsley, South Yorkshire: Pen
     & Sword Military Classics, 2007), pp. 248–77, and Hennessy, *Secret State*, pp. 186–205.

156 *a pub called the Rose & Crown:* That detail can be found in Maurice Chittenden, "For Sale: Brit-
     ain's Underground City," *Sunday Times* (London), October 30, 2005.

157 *half a dozen large storage sites:* The AEC had added three more national stockpile sites—Site Dog
     in Bossier, Louisiana; Site King in Medina, Texas; and Site Love in Lake Mead, Nevada.

157 *the president . . . would have to sign a directive:* For the transfer procedure, see Wainstein, et al.,
     "Evolution of U.S. Command and Control," pp. 34–5.

157 *SAC would get the cores in about twelve minutes:* Ibid., p. 35.

157 *Eisenhower approved the shipment of nuclear cores:* Before leaving office, Truman had formally
     granted the Department of Defense the authority to have custody of nuclear weapons outside the
     continental United States—and within the United States "to assure operational flexibility and
     military readiness." But Truman did not release any additional weapons to the military. At the end
     of his administration, the AEC had custody of 823 nuclear weapons—and the military controlled
     just the 9 weapons sent to Guam during the Korean War. Eisenhower's decision in June 1953 put
     the new policy into effect, and within a few years the military had sole custody of 1,358 nuclear
     weapons, about one third of the American stockpile. For the text of Eisenhower's order, see "His-
     tory of Custody and Deployment," p. 29. For the number of weapons in military and civilian
     custody during those years, see Wainstein, et al., "Evolution of U.S. Command and Control,"
     p. 34; and for a thorough account of the power shift from the Atomic Energy Commission to the
     Department of Defense, see Feaver, *Guarding the Guardians*, pp. 128–63.

158 *make the stockpile much less vulnerable to attack:* Secretary of Defense Charles E. Wilson and the

Joint Chiefs of Staff both used this argument. See Feaver, *Guarding the Guardians*, p. 162, and "History of Custody and Deployment," p. 37.

158   *he'd pushed hard for dropping them on Chinese troops:* In a 1952 memo to the secretary of the Army, Nichols argued that the United States should "utilize atomic weapons in the present war in Korea the first time a reasonable opportunity to do so permits." The use of nuclear weapons against military targets in North Korea and air bases in northeast China, Nichols thought, might "precipitate a major war at a time when we have the greatest potential for winning it with minimum damage to the U.S.A." See Kenneth D. Nichols, *The Road to Trinity: A Personal Account of How America's Nuclear Policies Were Made* (New York: William Morrow, 1987), pp. 291–92.

158   *"No active capsule will be inserted":* Quoted in "History of Custody and Deployment," p. 39.

158   *"Designated Atomic Energy Commission Military Representatives":* The acronym for these new keepers of the nuclear cores was DAECMRs. See Feaver, *Guarding the Guardians*, p. 167, and "History of Custody and Deployment," p. 111.

158   *The Strategic Air Command stored them at air bases:* For the list of the bases and the types of nuclear weapons they stored, see "History of the Strategic Air Command, 1 January 1958—30 June 1958, Historical Study No. 73, Volume I 1958 (TOP SECRET/RSTRICTED DATA/declassified), pp. 88–90.

159   *"to provide rapid availability for use":* Quoted in "History of Custody and Deployment," p. 37.

160   *On at least three different occasions:* In one incident, a technician slipped during the test of a Mark 6 bomb and accidentally pulled out its arming wires, triggering the detonators. See "Accidents and Incidents Involving Nuclear Weapons: Accidents and Incidents During the Period 1 July 1957 Through 31 March 1967," Technical Letter 20-3, Defense Atomic Support Agency, October 15, 1967 (SECRET/RESTRICTED DATA/declassified), p. 1, Accident #1 and #3; p. 2, Accident #5.

160   *a "wooden bomb":* For the effort to develop nuclear weapons with a long shelf life, see Furman, *Sandia: Postwar Decade*, pp. 660–66, and Leland Johnson, *Sandia National Laboratories: A History of Exceptional Service in the National Interest* (Albuquerque, NM: Sandia National Laboratories, 1997), pp. 57–8.

160   *"Thermal batteries" had been invented:* For the history, uses, and basic science of thermal batteries, see Ronald A. Guidotti, "Thermal Batteries: A Technology Review and Future Directions," Sandia National Laboratory, presented at the 27th International SAMPE Technical Conference, October 9–12, 1995, and Ronald A. Guidotti and P. Masset, "Thermally Activated ('Thermal') Battery Technology, Part I: An Overview," *Journal of Power Sources*, vol. 161 (2006), pp. 1443–49.

160   *a shelf life of at least twenty-five years:* Cited in Guidotti, "Thermal Batteries: A Technological Review," p. 3.

161   *the Genie, a rocket designed for air defense:* For details about the first air-to-air nuclear rocket, see Hansen, *Swords of Armageddon, Volume VI*, pp. 2–50, and Christopher J. Bright, *Continental Defense in the Eisenhower Era: Nuclear Antiaircraft Arms and the Cold War* (New York: Palgrave Macmillan, 2010), pp. 65–94.

162   *a top secret panel on the threat of surprise attack:* Killian's group was called the Technological Capabilities Panel of the Science Advisory Committee, and "Meeting the Threat of Surprise Attack" was the title of its report.

162   *a "lethal envelope" with a radius of about a mile:* See Hansen, *Swords of Armageddon, Volume VI*, pp. 45–46.

162   *"probability of kill" . . . was likely to be 92 percent:* Cited in ibid., p. 46.

163   *"The Department of Defense has a most urgent need":* Quoted in ibid., p. 21.

163   *Project 56 was the code name:* In an oral history interview, Harry Jordan, a Los Alamos scientist, later described one of the rationales for the tests: "People worried that in shipping these weapons that they could go off accidentally . . . one accidental detonator could go, and would go nuclear in Chicago railroad yards or something." See "Harry Jordan, Los Alamos National Laboratory," National Radiobiology Archives Project, September 22, 1981, p. 1.

163   *"one-point safe":* I am grateful to Bob Peurifoy and Harold Agnew for explaining the determinants of one-point safety to me.

164   *The fourth design failed the test:* Harry Jordan called it "a small nuclear incident." Although the yield was less than one kiloton, it revealed that the weapon design wasn't one-point safe. See "Harry Jordan," p. 2.

164 *"The problem of decontaminating the site":* "Plutonium Hazards Created by Accidental or Experimental Low-Order Detonation of Nuclear Weapons," W. H. Langham, P. S. Harris, and T. L. Shipman, Los Alamos Scientific Laboratory, LA-1981, December 1955 (SECRET/RESTRICTED DATA/declassified), p. 34.

164 *"probably not safe against one-point detonation":* Quoted in Hansen, *Swords of Armageddon, Volume VI,* p. 32.

165 *They argued that if such authority was "predelegated":* "The effective use of atomic warheads in air defense," the Killian report had argued, "requires a doctrine of instant use as soon as a hostile attack has been confirmed." This quote and a thorough examination of the new policy can be found in Peter J. Roman, "Ike's Hair-Trigger: U.S. Nuclear Predelegation, 1953–60," *Security Studies,* vol. 7, no. 4, pp. 121–64.

165 *it was "critical" for the Air Force:* Quoted in ibid., p. 133.

165 *any Soviet aircraft that appeared "hostile":* Quoted in ibid., p. 138.

165 *"strict command control [sic] of forces":* Quoted in ibid.

165 *the French government wasn't told about the weapons:* In January 1952, President Truman authorized the deployment of atomic bombs to Morocco, without their nuclear cores—and without French authorization. See Wainstein, et al., "Evolution of U.S. Command and Control," p. 32.

165 *"a positive effect on national morale":* "Letter, Herbert B. Loper, assistant to the secretary of defense (Atomic Energy), to Lewis L. Strauss, chairman, Atomic Energy Commission," December 18, 1956 (SECRET/declassified), NSA, p. 1.

165 *"The possibility of any nuclear explosion":* The full text of Wilson's press release, issued on February 20, 1957, can be found in Hansen, *Swords of Armageddon, Volume VI,* pp. 37–38. This quote appears on page 37.

166 *"a hundredth of a dose received":* Ibid., p. 38.

166 *"It glowed for an instant":* "National Affairs: The A-Rocket," *Time,* July 29, 1957.

166 *Quarles left the meetings worried:* See "The Origins and Evolution of S²C at Sandia National Laboratories 1949–1996," William L. Stevens, consultant to Surety Assessment Center, Sandia National Laboratories, SAND99-1308, September 2001 (OFFICAL USE ONLY), p. 30.

166 *He rarely took vacations:* These details come from "Quarles Held a Unique Niche," *Washington Post and Times Herald,* May 9, 1959; "Donald A. Quarles, Secretary of the Air Force," Department of the Air Force, Office of Information Services, May 1956, NSA; and George M. Watson, *The Office of the Secretary of the Air Force, 1947–1965* (Washington, D.C.: Center for Air Force History, 1993), pp. 149–63.

166 *Within weeks of the briefings for Quarles:* See Stevens, "Origins and Evolutions of S²C at Sandia," p. 30.

166 *Quarles asked the Atomic Energy Commission to conduct:* See "A Survey of Nuclear Weapon Safety Problems and the Possibilities for Increasing Safety in Bomb and Warhead Design," prepared by Sandia Corporation with the advice and assistance of the Los Alamos Scientific Laboratory and the University of California Ernest O. Lawrence Radiation Laboratory, RS 3466/26889, February 1959 (SECRET/RESTRICTED DATA/declassified), p. 10.

167 *a list of eighty-seven accidents:* Cited in ibid., p. 15.

167 *Sandia found an additional seven:* Cited in ibid.

167 *More than one third . . . "war reserve" atomic or hydrogen bombs:* See ibid., p. 16.

167 *The rest involved training weapons:* See ibid.

167 *a B-36 bomber took off from Eielson Air Force Base:* For a description of the accident see Michael H. Maggelet and James C. Oskins, *Broken Arrow: The Declassified History of U.S. Nuclear Weapons Accidents* (Raleigh, NC: Lulu, 2007), pp. 33–44, and Norman S. Leach, *Broken Arrow: America's First Lost Nuclear Weapon* (Calgary, Ontario, Canada: Red Deer Press, 2008), pp. 75–111.

168 *On at least four different occasions, the bridgewire detonators:* See "Accidents and Incidents Involving Nuclear Weapons," p. 1, Accident #1.

168 *At least half a dozen times, the carts used to carry Mark 6 bombs:* See ibid., p. 8, Incident #1.

168 *Dropping a nuclear weapon was never a good idea:* According to a study released by the Armed Forces Special Weapons Project in 1958, "Extreme shocks can cause failure of one or more of the

presently used safety devices and warhead components, which could contribute to a full-scale nuclear detonation, particularly if the X-unit is already charged." See "A Study on Evaluation of Warhead Safing Devices," Headquarters Field Command, Armed Forces Special Weapons Project, FC/03580460, March 31, 1958, (SECRET/RESTRICTED DATA/declassified), p. 18.

168 *when the Genie was armed, it didn't need a firing signal:* See "Vulnerability Program Summary: Joint DOD-AEC Weapon Vulnerability Program," Armed Forces Special Weapons Project, FC/010 May 1958 (SECRET/RESTRICTED DATA/declassified), p. 44.

169 *a B-29 bomber prepared to take off from Fairfield-Suisun:* For the story of the plane crash and its aftermath, see Jim Houk, "The Travis Crash Exhibit," *Travis Air Museum News,* vol. XVII, no. 3 (1999), pp. 1, 5–11; John L. Frisbee, "The Greater Mark of Valor," *Air Force Magazine,* February 1986; and the accident report reproduced in Maggelet and Oskins, *Broken Arrow,* pp. 65–77.

170 *"a long training mission":* Quoted in "Bomb-Laden B-29 Hits Trailer Camp; 17 Killed, 60 Hurt," *New York Times,* August 7, 1950.

170 *an American B-47 bomber took off from Lakenheath:* I first learned about this accident from a document obtained by the National Security Archive: "B-47 Wreckage at Lakenheath Air Base," Cable, T-5262, July 22, 1956 (SECRET/declassified). The accident report is reproduced in Maggelet and Oskins, *Broken Arrow,* pp. 85–87.

170 *"The B-47 tore apart the igloo":* "B-47 Wreckage at Lakenheath Air Base."

170 *"Some day there will be an accidental explosion":* Morgenstern made the assertion in 1959. Quoted in Joel Larus, *Nuclear Weapons Safety and the Common Defense* (Columbus, OH: Ohio State University, 1967), p. 17–18.

171 *"Maintaining a nuclear capability":* "A Survey of Nuclear Weapon Safety Problems," p. 14.

171 *"Acceptable Military Risks from Accidental Detonation":* Although I did not obtain the Army study, its conclusions are explored in "Acceptable Premature Probabilities for Nuclear Weapons," Headquarters Field Command, Armed Forces Special Weapons Project, FC/10570136, October 1, 1957 (SECRET/RESTRICTRED DATA/declassified).

171 *the acceptable probability of a hydrogen bomb . . . should be 1 in 100,000:* See ibid., p. 4.

171 *The acceptable risk of an atomic bomb . . . set at 1 in 125:* See ibid. p. 4

171 *the "psychological impact of a nuclear detonation":* Ibid.

171 *"there will likely be a tendency to blame":* Ibid.

171 *Human error had been excluded as a possible cause:* Ibid., p. 6.

171 *"The unpredictable behavior of human beings":* Ibid.

171–72 *the odds of a hydrogen bomb exploding . . . should be one in ten million:* Ibid., p. 13.

172 *odds of a hydrogen bomb detonating by accident, every decade, would be one in five:* For a nuclear weapon with a yield greater than 10 kilotons, removed from stockpile storage, the study proposed an accidental detonation rate of 1 in 50,000 over the course of ten years. Putting 10,000 of those weapons into "handling, maintenance, assembly and test operations," therefore, lowered the odds of an accidental detonation to 1 in 5 every decade. See Ibid., p. 14.

172 *the odds of an atomic bomb detonating by accident . . . would be about 100 percent:* For a nuclear weapon with a yield lower than 10 kilotons, removed from stockpile storage, the study proposed an accidental detonation rate of 1 in 10,000 per weapon over the course of ten years. If the United States possessed 10,000 of such weapons, at least one of them would most likely detonate by accident within that period. See ibid., p. 14.

172 *During a fire, the high explosives of a weapon might burn:* See "Factors Affecting the Vulnerability of Atomic Weapons to Fire, Full Scale Test Report No. 2," Armour Research Foundation of Illinois Institute of Technology, for Air Force Special Weapons Center, February 1958 (SECRET/RESTRICTED DATA/declassified), and "Vulnerability Program Summary," pp. 10–20, 58–60.

172 *The time factor for the Genie was three minutes:* Cited in "Vulnerability Program Summary," p. 59.

172–73 *Carl Carlson, a young physicist at Sandia, came to believe:* A short biographical sketch of Carlson—who advocated passionately on behalf of nuclear weapon safety, resigned from Sandia in frustration at one point, and later took his own life—can be found in Stevens, "Origins and Evolution of S²C at Sandia," p. 236.

173 *"the real key":* "A Survey of Nuclear Weapon Safety Problems," p. 28.

173   *the T-249 control box made it easy to arm a weapon:* See ibid., pp. 21–27.
173   *"a weapon which requires only the receipt of intelligence":* Ibid., p. 51.
173   *"always/never":* Peter Douglas Feaver succinctly explains and defines the "always/never problem" of controlling nuclear weapons in his book, *Guarding the Guardians,* pp. 12–20, 28–32.
174   *"a higher degree of nuclear safing":* Quoted in "A Survey of Nuclear Weapon Safety Problems," p. 13.
174   *"Such safing," Quarles instructed:* Quoted in ibid.

The Optimum Mix

175   *"A super long-distance intercontinental":* "Text of Soviet Statement," *New York Times,* August 27, 1957.
175   *a radio signal of "beep-beep":* Some experts speculated, erroneously, that the beeping was part of a Soviet secret code. See Marvin Miles, "Russ Moon's Code Sending Analyzed," *Los Angeles Times,* October 9, 1957.
175   *boasted that Laika lived for a week:* See Max Frankel, "Satellite Return Seen as Soviet Goal," *New York Times,* November 16, 1957.
175   *she actually died within a few hours of liftoff:* Like the Soviet Union's other space dogs, Laika was a stray picked up on the streets of Moscow. She died from excess heat in the capsule. See Carol Kino, "Art: Boldly, Where No Dog Had Gone Before," *New York Times,* November 4, 2007.
176   *"weakened the free world" and "starved the national defense":* Quoted in "Rocket Race: How to Catch Up," *New York Times,* October 20, 1957.
176   *"a devastating blow to U.S. prestige":* Quoted in "Why Did U.S. Lose the Race? Critics Speak Up," *Life,* October 21, 1957.
176   *"plunge heavily" into the missile controversy:* For a fine account of how *Sputnik* affected political and bureaucratic rivalries not only in the United States but also in the Soviet Union, see Matthew Brzenzinski, *Red Moon Rising: Sputnik and the Hidden Rivalries That Ignited the Space Age* (New York: Henry Holt, 2007). The quote by George Reedy can be found on page 213.
176   *"blast the Republicans out of the water":* Quoted in ibid., p. 182.
176   *putting "fiscal security ahead of national security":* Quoted in Christopher A. Preble, "Who Ever Believed in the 'Missile Gap'?: John F. Kennedy and the Politics of National Security," *Presidential Studies Quarterly,* vol. 33, no. 4 (December 2003), p. 806.
176   *"The United States does not have an intercontinental missile":* These quotes can be found in a report prepared by the CIA for the newly elected president, John F. Kennedy: "Compendium of Soviet Remarks on Missiles," February 28, 1961 (SECRET/declassified), NSA.
177   *More than twenty thousand Hungarian citizens were killed:* Cited in Mark Kramer, "The Soviet Union and the 1956 Crises in Hungary and Poland: Reassessments and New Findings," *Journal of Contemporary History,* vol. 33, no. 2 (April 1998), p. 210.
177   *hundreds more were later executed:* Cited in ibid., p. 211.
177   *He was particularly irritated by a secret report:* The report was "Deterrence & Survival in the Nuclear Age," Security Resources Panel of the Science Advisory Committee, November 7, 1957 (TOP SECRET/declassified), NSA.
177   *"It misses the whole point to say":* Quoted in Robert J. Donovon, "Killian Missile Czar: Ike Picks M.I.T. Head to Rush Research, Development," *Daily Boston Globe,* November 8, 1957.
177   *"we have slipped dangerously behind the Soviet Union":* Quoted in "Excerpts from the Comments of Senator Johnson, Dr. Teller, and Dr. Bush," *New York Times,* November 26, 1957.
177   *"just about the grimmest warning":* Stewart Alsop, "We Have Been Warned," *Washington Post and Times Herald,* November 25, 1957.
178   *"locate precise blast locations":* Wainstein, et al., "Evolution of U.S. Command and Control," p. 218. For the science behind the Bomb Alarm System, see "Operation Dominic II, Shot Small Boy, Project Officers Report—Project 7.14: Bomb Alarm Detector Test," Cecil C. Harvell, Defense Atomic Support Agency, April 19, 1963 (CONFIDENTIAL/FORMERLY RESTRICTED DATA/declassified).
179   *The logistics of such a "ground alert":* For the origins and workings of SAC's ground alert, see "The SAC Alert Program, 1956–1959," Headquarters, Strategic Air Command, January 1960 (SECRET/

declassified), NSA, pp. 1–79, and "History of the Strategic Air Command, 1 January 1958—30 June 1958," pp. 25–57.

179 *a mean son of a bitch:* In his memoir, Power belittled the military's role in peacekeeping, defending national security, and maintaining deterrence. "Putting aside all the fancy words and academic doubletalk," he wrote, "the basic reason for having a military is to do two jobs—to kill people and to destroy the works of man." See Thomas S. Power, with Albert A. Arnhym, *Design for Survival* (New York: Coward-McCann, 1964), p. 229.

179 *"sort of an autocratic bastard":* Quoted in Coffey, *Iron Eagle,* p. 276.

179 *The basic premise of SAC's airborne alert:* For the origins of this bold strategy, see "The SAC Alert Program, 1956–1959," pp. 80–140, and "History of Strategic Air Command, June 1958—July 1959," Historical Study No. 76, Volume I, Headquarters, Strategic Air Command (SECRET/RE-STRICTED DATA/declassified), pp. 107–36.

180 *The mission would "fail safe":* The idea of relying on fail-safe procedures to send bombers toward the Soviet Union was first proposed by RAND in a 1956 report. See "Protecting U.S. Power to Strike Back in the 1950's and 1960's," A. J. Wohlstetter, F. S. Hoffman, H. S. Rowen, U.S. Air Force Project RAND, R-290, September 1, 1956, (FOR OFFICIAL USE ONLY), pp. 59–62. For SAC's adoption of fail safe, see "History of the Strategic Air Command, 1 January 1958—30 June 1958," pp. 66–74.

180 *"Day and night, I have a certain percentage of my command":* Quoted in "Alert Operations and Strategic Air Command, 1957–1991," Office of the Historian, Headquarters Strategic Air Command, December 7, 1991, p. 7. Power made the remark at a press conference in Paris, and the boast unnerved some of America's NATO allies. See "Lloyd Defends H-Bomb Patrols by U.S.," *Washington Post and Times Herald,* November 28, 1957.

180 *Designers at the weapons labs had been surprised:* Peurifoy interview. See also "A Review of the US Nuclear Weapon Safety Program—1945 to 1986," R. N. Brodie, Sandia National Laboratories, SAND86-2955, February 1987 (SECRET/RESTRICTED DATA/declassified), p. 11.

181 *"nuclear safety is not 'absolute,' it is nonexistent":* "A Survey of Nuclear Weapon Safety Problems," p. 53.

181 *The odds of a nuclear detonation during a crash or a fire:* According to the Air Force, "There was a 15 percent probability of up to 40,000 pounds of nuclear yield in the event of one point detonation of a weapon requiring the insertion of an in-flight capsule." The Air Force also claimed that "with the sealed pit weapon the plutonium hazard was not significant." See "History of the Strategic Air Command, 1 January 1958—30 June 1958," pp. 78–79.

181 *"operationally unsuitable":* Those are the words of the official SAC history. See ibid., p. 82.

181 *"degrade the reaction time to an unacceptable degree":* Quoted in ibid., p. 83.

181 *"crew morale and motivation":* Quoted in ibid.

181 *The typical air base had only seven dummy weapons:* Cited in ibid.

181 *The AEC refused to allow any fully assembled bombs:* At a briefing on the proposed airborne alert in July 1958, Eisenhower was told that during SAC exercises, "Completely assembled or war-ready weapons have never been flown before." See "Briefing for the President on SAC [Strategic Air Command] Operations with Sealed-Pit Weapons," Briefing Paper, July 9, 1958 (TOP SECRET/declassified), NSA, p. 2.

182 *likely to miss its target by about one hundred miles:* On average, the V-2 went about four miles off-course during a two-hundred-mile flight. An American missile with the same "average error," launched from Colorado and aimed at Moscow, would fly about five thousand miles—and miss the Soviet capital by roughly one hundred miles. For the V-2's accuracy and relevance to the Air Force's missile aspirations, see Donald MacKenzie, *Inventing Accuracy: A Historical Sociology of Nuclear Missile Guidance* (Cambridge, MA: MIT Press, 1993), p. 99.

182 *He wanted SAC to develop nuclear-powered bombers:* Not only did General LeMay believe that such aircraft were essential, his successor, General Power, thought that SAC also needed a Deep Space Force—a fleet of twenty spaceships that could carry nuclear weapons and remain in orbit near the moon for years. The spaceships would be propelled by the detonation of small atomic bombs. The secret effort to build them, "Project Orion," was funded by the Pentagon from 1958 until 1965. The program to develop nuclear-powered bombers lasted from 1946 until 1961. Having a

nuclear reactor on an airplane posed a number of design problems: the shielding necessary to protect the crew would be extremely heavy; without the shielding the crew might be exposed to hazardous levels of radiation; and if the plane crashed, the area surrounding the crash site could be badly contaminated. Nevertheless, LeMay thought these challenges could be overcome. For the story of the Aircraft Nuclear Propulsion (ANP), see Herbert F. York, *Race to Oblivion: A Participant's View of the Arms Race,* (New York: Simon & Schuster, 1970), pp. 60–74. For the attempt to harness "Nuclear Pulse Propulsion" for a Deep Space Force, see George Dyson, *Project Orion: The True Story of the Atomic Spaceship* (New York: Henry Holt, 2002), pp. 193–207.

182 *"the ultimate weapon":* See "SAC [Strategic Air Command] Position on Missiles," letter from General Curtis E. LeMay, commander in chief of Strategic Air Command, to General Nathan F. Twining, chief of staff, U.S. Air Force, November 26, 1955 (SECRET/declassified), NSA.

182 *The interservice rivalry over missiles:* For the fierce bureaucratic warfare over these new weapons, see Michael H. Armacost's *Politics of Weapon Innovation* and Samuel P. Huntington, "Interservice Competition and the Political Roles of the Armed Services," *American Political Science Review*, vol. 55, no. 1 (March 1961), pp. 40–52.

183 a Soviet *"peace campaign":* Through organizations such as the World Peace Council and the World Federation of Scientific Workers, the Soviet Union tried to turn public opinion in Europe against the nuclear policies of the United States. See Laurence S. Wittner, *Resisting the Bomb, 1954–1970: A History of the World Nuclear Disarmament Movement* (Stanford: Stanford University Press, 1997), pp. 86–92.

183 *The Eisenhower administration tried to strike a balance:* For a fine account of the conflicting demands that the president faced, see "Eisenhower and Nuclear Sharing," a chapter in Marc Trachtenberg, *A Constructed Peace: The Making of the European Settlement, 1945–1963* (Princeton: Princeton University Press, 1999), pp. 146–200.

184 *The Mark 36 was a second-generation hydrogen bomb:* See Hansen, *Swords of Armageddon, Vol. V,* pp. 395-7.

184 *at a SAC base in Sidi Slimane, Morocco:* My account of the accident is based primarily on "Accidents and Incidents Involving Nuclear Weapons," pp. 4-5, Accident #24; "Summary of Nuclear Weapons Incidents (AF Form 1058) and Related Problems, Calendar Year 1958," *Airmunitions Letter*, Headquarters, Ogden Air Material Area, June 23, 1960 (SECRET/RESTRICTED DATA/declassified), p. 13; and interviews with weapon designers familiar with the event.

184 *long past the time factor of the Mark 36:* The weapon's time factor was only three minutes. See "Vulnerability Program Summary," p. 58.

184 *fearing a nuclear disaster:* An accident report said the evacuation was motivated by "the possibility of a nuclear yield." See "Summary of Nuclear Weapons Incidents, 1958," p. 13.

185 *"a slab of slag material":* Ibid.

185 *The "particularly 'hot' pieces":* Ibid.

185 *plutonium dust on their shoes:* An accident report mentioned "alpha particles" and "dust" without noting their source: plutonium. See "Accidents and Incidents Involving Nuclear Weapons," p. 5.

185 *"explosion of the weapon, radiation":* The quote is a State Department paraphrase of what the Air Force wanted to say. See "Sidi Slimane Air Incident Involving Plane Loaded with Nuclear Weapon," January 31, 1958 (SECRET/declassified), NSA, p. 1.

185 *The State Department thought that was a bad idea:* See ibid.

185 *"The less said about the Moroccan incident":* The quote is a summary of a State Department official's views, as presented in "Sidi Slimane Air Incident," p. 2.

185 a *"practice evacuation":* "Letter, from B.E.L. Timmons, director, Office of European Regional Affairs, U.S. State Department, to George L. West, political adviser, USEUCOM, February 28, 1958 (SECRET/declassified), NSA.

185 *"In reply to inquiries about hazards":* "Joint Statement by Department of Defense and Atomic Energy Commission," Department of Defense Office of Public Information, February 14, 1958, NSA, p. 1.

185 *Less than a month later, Walter Gregg and his son:* My account of the accident in Mars Bluff is based on "Summary of Nuclear Weapons Incidents, 1958," pp. 8–12; "Mars Bluff," *Time*, March 24, 1958; "Unarmed Atom Bomb Hits Carolina Home, Hurting 6," *New York Times*, March 12, 1958;

and Clark Ruinrill, "Aircraft 53-1876A Has Lost a Device: How the U.S. Air Force Came to Drop an A-Bomb on South Carolina," *American Heritage*, September 2000. Rumrill's account is by far the best and most detailed.

186   *about fifty feet wide and thirty-five feet deep:* The size of the crater varies in different sources, and I've chosen to use the dimensions cited in a contemporary accident report. See "Summary of Nuclear Weapons Incidents, 1958," p. 8.

187   *the plane had just lost a "device":* Quoted in Ruinrill, "Aircraft 53-1876A Has Lost a Device."

187   *"Are We Safe from Our Own Atomic Bombs?":* Hanson W. Baldwin, "Are We Safe from Our Own Atomic Bombs?," *New York Times*, March 16, 1958.

187   *"Is Carolina on Your Mind?":* Quoted in "The Big Binge," *Time*, March 24, 1958.

187   *a nuclear detonation had been prevented by "sheer luck":* Quoted in "On the Risk of an Accidental or Unauthorized Nuclear Detonation," Fred Charles Iklé, with Gerald J. Aronson and Albert Madansky, U.S. Air Force Project RAND, Research Memorandum, RM-2251, October 15, 1958 (CONFIDENTIAL/RESTRICTED DATA/declassified), p. 65.

187   *"the first accident of its kind in history":* "'Dead' A-Bomb Hits U.S. Town," Universal Newsreel, Universal-International News, March 13, 1958.

187   *a hydrogen bomb had been mistakenly released over Albuquerque:* I learned the details of this accident from weapon designers. General Christopher S. Adams—former chief of staff at the Strategic Air Command and associate director of the Los Alamos National Laboratory—tells the story in his memoir, *Inside the Cold War: A Cold Warrior's Reflections* (Maxwell Air Force Base, AL: Air University Press, September 1999), pp. 112–13.

188   *"Well, we did not build these bombers":* Power, *Design for Survival*, p. 132.

188   *Macmillan was in a difficult position:* The United States informed the British when nuclear weapons were being flown into the United Kingdom—but did not reveal when "any particular plane is equipped with special weapons." See "U.S. Bombers in Britain," cable, from Walworth Barbour, U.S. State Department Deputy Chief of Mission, London, to Secretary of State John Foster Dulles, January 7, 1958 (TOP SECRET/declassified), NSA.

188   *argued that nuclear weapons were "morally wrong":* Some members of the C.N.D. wanted Great Britain to disarm unilaterally; others sought an end to hydrogen bomb tests and the use of British bases by American planes. The quote comes from a letter that the organization sent to Queen Elizabeth. See "Marchers' Letter to the Queen," *The Times* (London), June 23, 1958.

188   *"I drew myself," Holtom recalled:* Quoted in Clare Coulson, "50 Years of the Peace Symbol," *Guardian* (U.K.), August 21, 2008. Holtom also described the symbol as the combination of two letters from the semaphore alphabet: "N" for nuclear and "D" for disarmament.

188   *"Imagine that one of the airmen may":* Quoted in Iklé, "On the Risk of an Accidental Detonation," p. 61.

188   *the "world has yet to see a foolproof system":* See "Excerpts from Statements in Security Council on Soviet Complaint Against Flights," *New York Times*, April 22, 1958.

189   *67.3 percent of the flight personnel:* The report was circulated in May 1958. See Iklé, "On the Risk of an Accidental Detonation," pp. 65–66; "CIA Says Forged Soviet Papers Attribute Many Plots to the U.S.," *New York Times*, June 18, 1961; and Larus, *Nuclear Weapon Safety and the Common Defense*, pp. 60–61.

189   *an American mechanic stole a B-45 bomber:* The mechanic had just consumed half a dozen pints of beer after being dumped by his sixteen-year-old British girlfriend. See "Eight Killed in Plane Crashes," *The Times* (London), June 14, 1958; "AF Mechanic Killed in Stolen Plane," *Washington Post*, June 15, 1948; Iklé "On the Risk of an Accidental Detonation," p. 66; and Larus, *Nuclear Weapon Safety and the Common Defense*, p. 61.

189   *more than 250,000 copies of George's novel:* Cited in David E. Scherman, "Everybody Blows Up!," *Life*, March 8, 1963.

189   *Writing under the pseudonym "Peter Bryant":* George had written thrillers for years under a number of other names. After the success of *Red Alert*, he wrote another, even darker, novel about the threat of nuclear war and—before completing a third book on the subject—took his own life at the age of forty-one. For George's work and its influence upon the director Stanley Kubrick, see P. D. Smith, *Doomsday Men: The Real Dr. Strangelove and the Dream of the Superweapon* (New York:

St. Martin's, 2007), pp. 402–30. See also "Peter George, 41, British Novelist: Co-Author of 'Strangelove' Screenplay Is Dead," *New York Times*, June 3, 1966.

189   *"A few will suffer":* Peter Bryant, *Red Alert* (New York: Ace Books, 1958), p. 97.

189   *"the ultimate deterrent":* Ibid., p. 80.

190   *doubts about the idea expressed by LeMay:* President Eisenhower thought that an airborne alert might be useful during an emergency but saw no need for the Strategic Air Command to keep bombers in the air at all times. LeMay agreed with the president, concerned that an airborne alert would be too expensive and would shorten the lifespan of its B-52 bombers. Secretary of Defense Neil H. McElroy and General Nathan F. Twining, head of the Joint Chiefs of Staff, also thought that a full-time airborne alert was unnecessary. But General Powell had made it politically important and a symbol of American power. For LeMay's doubts, see "The SAC Alert Program, 1956–1959," pp. 94–99, 118–29, and "History of Strategic Air Command, June 1958—July 1959," pp. 114–15. For Eisenhower's opposition to making the alert permanent, see "Editorial Note," Document 53, in United States State Department, *Foreign Relations of the United States: 1958–1960, National Security Policy, Arms Control and Disarmament, Volume III* (Washington, D.C.: Government Printing Office, 1967), p. 201. For Twining's opposition and the congressional pressure, see "Memorandum of Conference with President Eisenhower, February 9, 1959," Document 49, in ibid., pp. 49–50.

190   *"positive control":* SAC thought the term was more "absolute in intonation than 'Fail Safe'" and would thwart Soviet attempts to turn world opinion against the plan. See "History of the Strategic Air Command, 1 January 1958—30 June 1958," p. 66.

190   *"the probability of any nuclear detonation":* "Briefing for the President on SAC Operations with Sealed-Pit Weapons," p. 8.

190   *McCone thought that the bombers should be permitted:* See "Memorandum of Conference with the President, August 27, 1958" (TOP SECRET/declassified), NSA, p. 1.

190   *Iklé's top secret clearance had gained him access:* Iklé spoke to me at length about how his research was conducted.

191   *"We cannot derive much confidence":* Iklé, "On the Risk of an Accidental Detonation," p. iv.

191   *"eliminated readily once they are discovered":* Ibid., p. 12.

191   *inadvertently jettisoned once every 320 flights:* Cited in ibid., p. 48.

191   *crash at a rate of about once every twenty thousand flying hours:* The rate of major accidents among B-52s was five per one hundred thousand flying hours. Cited in ibid., p. 75.

191   *twelve crashes with nuclear weapons and seven bomb jettisons:* Cited in ibid., p. 76.

191   *"The paramount task":* Ibid., p. 10.

191   *"makes it necessary to entrust unspecialized personnel":* Ibid., p. 16.

191   *"someone who knew the workings":* Ibid., p. 34

192   *"It can hardly be denied that there is a risk":* Ibid., p. 102.

192   *"one of the most baffling problems":* Ibid., p. 21.

192   *About twenty thousand Air Force personnel:* Six thousand flight officers were assigned to nuclear missions at the time, and an additional sixteen thousand people tested, handled, or maintained the weapons. Cited in ibid., p. 32.

192   *"a history of transient psychotic disorders":* Ibid., p. 27.

192   *A few hundred Air Force officers and enlisted men were annually removed from duty:* Eighty-eight officers and about twice as many enlisted men were "separated or retired from service" in 1956 due to psychotic disorders. See ibid., p. 29.

192   *perhaps ten or twenty who worked with nuclear weapons:* In 1956, the proportion of Air Force officers forced to leave the service because of psychotic disorders was 0.61 per 1,000; the rate among enlisted men was twice as high. Those rates, applied to the roughly twenty thousand Air Force personnel who worked with nuclear weapons at the time, suggest that about ten to twenty of that group would suffer a psychotic breakdown every year. See ibid., p. 29.

192   *"a catalogue of derangement":* Ibid., pp. 120–49.

192   *"A 23-year-old pilot, a Lieutenant":* Ibid., pp. 124–25.

192   *"grandiose, inappropriate, and demanding"* . . . *"eight hours on the B-25":* Ibid., p. 125.

193   *"invested with a special mission":* Ibid., pp. 130–31.

193   *"the authorities . . . covertly wish destruction":* Ibid., p. 131.

193 *"the desire to see the tangible result of their own power":* Ibid., p. 141.

193 *"[An] assistant cook improperly obtained a charge":* Ibid., p. 134.

193 *"Private B and I each found a rifle grenade":* Ibid., p. 135.

193 *"A Marine found a 37-millimeter dud":* Ibid., p. 136.

194 *"the kind of curiosity which does not quite believe":* Ibid., p. 137.

194 *"an accidental atomic bomb explosion may well trigger":* Quoted in ibid., p. 90.

194 *"unfortunate political consequences":* Ibid., p. 83.

194 *"a peaceful expansion of the Soviet sphere":* Ibid., p. 84.

194 *"The U.S. defense posture":* Ibid., p. 95.

194 *put combination locks on nuclear weapons:* Ibid., pp. 99–102.

195 *"If such an accident occurred in a remote area":* "The Aftermath of a Single Nuclear Detonation by Accident or Sabotage: Some Problems Affecting U.S. Policy, Military Reactions, and Public Information," Fred Charles Iklé, with J. E. Hill, U.S. Air Force Project RAND, Research Memorandum, May 8, 1959, RM-2364 (SECRET/RESTRICTED DATA/declassified), pp. vii, 32.

195 *An official "board of inquiry" . . . an "important device for temporizing":* Ibid., p. 62.

195 *"During this delaying period the public information":* Ibid., p. 63.

195 *"avoid public self-implication and delay the release":* Ibid., p. 88.

196 *the electrical system of the W-49 warhead:* Bob Peurifoy and William L. Stevens, who both worked on the electrical system, told me the story of how it became the first warhead with an environmental sensing device. Stevens writes about the Army's resistance to the idea in "Origins and Evolution of S²C at Sandia," pp. 32–34.

196 *"This warhead, like all other warheads investigated":* Quoted in "A Summary of the Program to Use Environmental Sensing Devices to Improve Handling Safety Protection for Nuclear Weapons," W. L. Stevens and C. H. Mauney, Sandia Corporation, July 1961 (SECRET/RESTRICTED DATA/declassified), p. 6. Another study made clear how it could be done: "A saboteur, with knowledge of the warhead can, through warhead connectors, operate any arm/safe switch with improvised equipment." See "Evaluation of Warhead Safing Devices," p. 26.

197 *a "handling safety device" or a "goof-proofer":* Stevens interview.

197 *"to hell with it":* Peurifoy interview.

197 *"environmental sensing device":* Ibid.

197 *A young physicist, Robert K. Osborne, began to worry:* My account of how the one-point safety standard developed is based on interviews with Harold Agnew and Bob Peurifoy, as well as the following documents: "Minutes of the 133rd Meeting of the Fission Weapon Committee," Los Alamos National Laboratory, December 30, 1957; "One-Point Safety," letter, from J. F. Ney to R. L. Peurifoy, Jr., Sandia National Laboratories, May 24, 1993; and "Origin of One-Point Safety Definition," letter, from D. M. Olson, to Glen Otey, Sandia National Laboratories, January 6, 1993.

198 *it could incapacitate the crew:* The goal was to avoid exposing the engine crew to an "immediate incapacitation dose" of radiation. See "Origin of One-Point Safety Definition," p. 1.

198 *Los Alamos proposed that the odds . . . should be one in one hundred thousand:* Agnew interview.

198 *odds of one in a million:* Ibid.

198 *"Testing is essential for weapons development":* Quoted in May, et al., "History of Strategic Arms Competition, Part 1," p. 235.

198 *five hundred long-range ballistic missiles by 1961:* See "Soviet Capabilities in Guided Missiles and Space Vehicles," NIE 11-5-58 (TOP SECRET/declassified), p. 1, in *Intentions and Capabilities,* p. 65.

198 *outnumbering the United States by more than seven to one:* Although estimates varied, amid the controversy over the missile gap, the *New York Times* said that the United States would have about seventy long-range missiles by 1961. Cited in Richard Witkin, "U.S. Raising Missile Goals as Critics Foresee a 'Gap,'" *New York Times,* January 12, 1959.

199 *"entirely preoccupied by the horror of nuclear war":* Quoted in Benjamin P. Greene, *Eisenhower, Science Advice, and the Nuclear Test Ban Debate, 1945–1963* (Stanford: Stanford University Press, 2007), p. 209.

199 *also by defense contractors:* By early 1960, the corporate attacks on Eisenhower were blunt and well publicized. An executive at the General Dynamics Corporation, manufacturer of the Atlas missile, accused Eisenhower of taking "a dangerous gamble with the survival of our people." Among other

sins, Eisenhower had not ordered enough Atlas missiles. See Bill Becker, "'Gamble' Charged in Defense Policy," *New York Times*, February 5, 1960.

199   *"military-industrial complex"*: See "Transcript of President Eisenhower's Farewell Message to Nation," *Washington Post and Times Herald*, January 18, 1961.

199   *"hydronuclear experiments"*: My account of these tests is based on my interview with Harold Agnew as well as this report: "Hydronuclear Experiments," Robert N. Thorn, Donald R. Westervelt, Los Alamos National Laboratories, LA-10902-MS, February 1987.

199   *He authorized the detonations*: George B. Kistiakowsky, the president's chief science adviser, was not convinced, at first, that these experiments were necessary. He thought that "no reasonable amount of safety testing could prove a weapon to be absolutely safe" and that the military should just "accept the responsibility for operational use of devices that had a finite, even though exceedingly small, probability of nuclear explosion." Kistiakowsky later agreed that the one-point safety tests should be done. See George B. Kistiakowsky, *A Scientist at the White House: The Private Diary of President Eisenhower's Special Assistant for Science and Technology* (Cambridge, Mass.: Harvard University Press, 1976), pp. 33, 79.

199   *"not a nuclear weapon test"*: Quoted in Thorn and Westerveldt, "Hydronuclear Experiments," p. 5.

199   *"Are we becoming prisoners of our strategic concept?"*: Quoted in "Memorandum of Conversation," April 7, 1958 (TOP SECRET/declassified), NSA, p. 4.

200   *a "bitter choice"*: Quoted in ibid., p. 9.

200   *a strategy of "flexible response"*: My description of Kissinger's strategic views in the late 1950s is based on his book *Nuclear Weapons and Foreign Policy* (New York: Harper and Brothers, 1957), and his journal article that preceded it, "Force and Diplomacy in the Nuclear Age," *Foreign Affairs*, vol. 34, no. 3 (April 1956), pp. 349–66. For an interesting contemporary critique of limited war theory, see P.M.S. Blackett, "Nuclear Weapons and Defence: Comments on Kissinger, Kennan, and King-Hall," *International Affairs* (Royal Institute of International Affairs), vol. 34, no. 4 (October 1958), pp. 421–34.

200   *Rules of engagement could be tacitly established*: For the proposed limits on nuclear war, see Kissinger, *Nuclear Weapons and Foreign Policy*, pp. 227–33.

200   *a strategy of "graduated deterrence"*: Kissinger's phrase for such a doctrine was "the graduated employment of force." See Kissinger, "Force and Diplomacy," p. 359.

200   *"pause for calculation"*: Kissinger, *Nuclear Weapons and Foreign Policy*, p. 226.

200   *"daring and leadership"*: Ibid., p. 400.

201   *a retaliatory, second-strike weapon*: The vulnerability of Strategic Air Command bases to a Soviet missile attack gave the Navy an opportunity to expand its nuclear role. And the Army eagerly sought to do so as well. In 1959, the Army came up with a plan, "Project Iceworm," that would hide six hundred missiles under the Greenland ice cap. The missiles would be deployed on trains, and the trains would be constantly moved along thousands of miles of railroad track hidden in tunnels almost thirty feet beneath the ice. Hiding the missiles would protect them from a Soviet surprise attack and facilitate their use as retaliatory weapons, like the Navy's Polaris submarines. Despite the Army's enthusiasm for deploying these "Iceman" missiles, none were ever built. See Erik D. Weiss, "Cold War Under the Ice: The Army's Bid for a Long-Range Nuclear Role," *Journal of Cold War Studies*, vol. 3, no. 3 (Fall 2001), pp. 31–58.

201   *"finite deterrence"*: For the historical and intellectual framework of the dispute between the Air Force and the Navy over nuclear targeting, see David Alan Rosenberg, "U.S. Nuclear War Planning, 1945–1960," in Desmond Ball and Jeffrey Richelson, *Strategic Nuclear Targeting* (Ithaca: Cornell University Press, 1986), pp. 35–56. Admiral Burke's opinion on the subject is succinctly conveyed in his memo "Views on Adequacy of U.S. Deterrent/Retaliatory Forces as Related to General and Limited War Capabilities," Memorandum for All Flag Officers, March 4, 1959 (CONFIDENTIAL/declassified), NSA.

201   *"Nobody wins a suicide pact"*: "Summary of Major Strategic Considerations for the 1960–70 Era," CNO Personal Letter No. 5, Office of the Chief of Naval Operations, July 30, 1958, NSA, p. 1.

201   *"the public mind"* . . . *"the professional military mind"*: "The Operational Side of Air Offense," remarks by General Curtis E. LeMay to the USAF Scientific Advisory Board, at Patrick Air Force Base, May 21, 1957 (TOP SECRET/declassified), NSA, p. 2.

201 *"the most humane method of waging war":* "The Air Force and Strategic Deterrence 1951–1960," George F. Lemmer, USAF Historical Division Liaison Office, December 1967, (SECRET/RESTRICTED DATA/declassified), NSA, p. 57.

202 *"weapons must be delivered with either very high accuracy":* "Operational Side of Air Offense," p. 4.

202 *a hydrogen bomb with a yield of 60 megatons:* LeMay argued that such a bomb would have enormous value as a deterrent—and, if used, could wipe out several targets at once. He and General Power wanted to equip SAC's B-52s with these Class A weapons. But Eisenhower refused to test or build them. See "History of the Strategic Air Command, 1 January 1958—30 June 1958," pp. 85–88.

202 *Until 1957 the Strategic Air Command refused to share:* See Ball and Richelson, *Strategic Nuclear Targeting,* p. 50.

202 *hundreds of "time over target" conflicts:* See Wainstein, et al., "Evolution of U.S. Command and Control," p. 182.

202 *"atomic coordination machinery":* See ibid., p. 179.

203 *"It was fatuous to think that the U.S.":* Quoted in Richard M. Leighton, *Strategy, Money, and the New Look, 1953–1956* (Washington, D.C.: Historical Office, Office of the Secretary of Defense, 2001), p. 663.

203 *"an all-out strike on the Soviet Union":* The quote is Kistiakowsky's paraphrase of what Eisenhower said. See Kistiakowsky, *A Scientist at the White House,* p. 400.

203 *the "optimum mix":* For the origins of the term, see Desmond Ball, "The Development of the SIOP, 1960–1983," in Ball and Richelson, *Strategic Nuclear Targeting,* p. 61.

203 *"atomic operations must be pre-planned":* See "Target Coordination and Associated Problems," memorandum from General Nathan F. Twining, Chairman, Joint Chiefs of Staff, to Neil H. McElroy, Secretary of Defense, JSC 2056/131, August 17, 1959 (TOP SECRET/declassified), NSA, p. 1147.

203 *"exactly the same techniques":* See "Conversation Between Admiral Arleigh Burke, Chief of Naval Operations, and William B. Franke, Secretary of the Navy," transcript, August 12, 1960 (TOP SECRET/declassified), NSA, p. 17. It is not clear who recorded the conversation—or whether Burke knew the conversation was being taped.

204 *"The systems will be laid":* Ibid., p. 8.

204 *"The grooves will be dug":* Ibid.

204 *"This whole thing has to be":* Quoted in Ball and Richelson, *Strategic Nuclear Targeting,* p. 54.

204 *as rational, impersonal, and automated as possible:* My account of the SIOP's creation is largely based on "Development of the SIOP"; Scott C. Sagan, "SIOP-62: The Nuclear War Plan Briefing to President Kennedy," *International Security,* vol. 12, no. 1 (Summer 1987), pp. 22–51; "SIOP-62 Briefing: The JCS Single Integrated Operational Plan—1962 (SIOP-62), (TOP SECRET/declassified), Ibid., pp. 41–51; "History of the Joint Strategic Target Planning Staff: Background and Preparation of SIOP-62," History and Research Division, Headquarters, Strategic Air Command, 1963 (TOP SECRET/declassified), NSA; "History of the Joint Strategic Target Planning Staff: Preparation of SIOP-63," History and Research Division, Headquarters, Strategic Air Command, January 1964 (TOP SECRET/declassified), NSA; and "Strategic Air Planning and Berlin (Kaysen Study)," memorandum for General Maxwell Taylor, Military Representative to the President, from Carl Kaysen, Special Assistant to McGeorge Bundy, National Security Adviser, September 5, 1961 (TOP SECRET/declassified), NSA.

204 *the Air Force's* Bombing Encyclopedia: For the origins and the nomenclature of this unusual reference book, see Lynn Eden, *Whole World on Fire: Organizations, Knowledge & Nuclear Weapons Devastation* (Ithaca: Cornell University Press, 2004), pp. 107–9.

204 *a compendium of more than eighty thousand potential targets:* Cited in "SIOP-62 Briefing," p. 44.

204 *twelve thousand candidates in the Soviet Union, the Eastern bloc:* Cited in "Preparation of SIOP-63," p. 18.

204 *A "target weighing system":* See "Background and Preparation of SIOP-62," p. 19.

204 *total value of five million points:* Cited in "Strategic Air Planning and Berlin," Annex B, p. 2.

205 *the "clobber factor":* See "Preparation of SIOP-63," p. 34.

205 *the odds of a target being destroyed . . . at least 75 percent:* Cited in "Strategic Air Planning and Berlin," Annex B, p. 2.

205   *a Jupiter missile, a Titan missile, an Atlas missile:* See ibid., p. 4.

205   *The "alert force" . . . the "full force":* Ibid.

205   *"Tactics programmed for the SIOP":* "SIOP-62 Briefing," p. 48.

205   *attack the Soviet Union "front-to-rear":* For a description of the "'front-to-rear' policy," see "Air Force and Strategic Deterrence," p. 56.

205   *a tactic called "bomb as you go":* See "SIOP-62 Briefing," p. 48.

205   *nuclear weapons solely for city busting:* The quote is from Air Marshal Sir George Mills, who made clear in 1955 that the British much preferred destroying "morale targets"—Soviet cities, not air fields. "Our aim in retaliation," Mills wrote, "is to hit him where it really hurts." See Ken Young, "A Most Special Relationship: The Origins of Anglo-American Nuclear Strike Planning," *Journal of Cold War Studies,* vol. 9, no. 2, 2007, pp. 5–31. The quotes are from pages 11 and 24.

205   *three air bases, six air defense targets, and forty-eight cities:* Cited in ibid., p. 27.

206   *"unnecessary and undesirable overkill":* Quoted in Ball and Richelson, *Strategic Nuclear Targeting,* p. 55.

206   *enough "megatons to kill 4 and 5 times over":* Quoted in Ibid.

206   *"just one whack—not ten whacks":* Quoted in ibid., p. 56.

206   *"I believe that the presently developed SIOP":* "Annex: Extract from Memorandum for the President from the Special Assistant to the President for Science and Technology, dated 25 November 1960," in "Note by the Secretaries to the Joint Chiefs of Staff on Strategic Target Planning," January 27, 1961 (TOP SECRET/declassified), NSA, p. 1913.

206   *"a 100 percent pulverization of the Soviet Union":* Quoted in "Discussion at the 387th Meeting of the National Security Council, Thursday, November 20, 1958" (TOP SECRET/declassified), NSA, p. 5.

206   *"There was obviously a limit":* Ibid., p. 5.

206   *3,729 targets . . . more than 1,000 ground zeros:* Cited in "Strategic Air Planning and Berlin," Annex B, p. 2.

206   *3,423 nuclear weapons:* Ibid., p. 4.

206   *About 80 percent were military targets:* Cited in "SIOP-62 Briefing," p. 50.

206   *295 were in the Soviet Union and 78 in China:* See "Strategic Air Planning and Berlin," Annex B, p. 2.

206   *54 percent of the Soviet Union's population and about 16 percent of China's:* See Ibid., Annex A, p. 2; Annex B, p. 12.

206   *roughly 220 million people:* The population of the Soviet Union was about 210 million at the time; the population of China about 682 million.

207   *Eisenhower agreed to let high-ranking commanders decide:* For the best account of how the military gained the authority to initiate the use of nuclear weapons, see Roman, "Ike's Hair-Trigger," pp. 121–164.

207   *"something foolish down the chain of command":* Quoted in ibid., p. 156.

207   *"very fearful of having written papers on this matter":* The quote is a paraphrase by the author of the memo and can be found in "Memorandum of Conference with the President, June 27, 1958," A. J. Goodpaster (TOP SECRET/declassified), NSA, p. 3.

207   *"It is in the U.S. interest to maintain":* The quote is a paraphrase by the author of the memo and can be found in "Memorandum of Conference with the President, December 19, 1958," John S. D. Eisenhower (TOP SECRET/declassified), NSA, p.1.

Breaking In

208   *Colonel John T. Moser and his wife:* Interview with Colonel John T. Moser.

209   *The two had to rendezvous at a precise location:* For the details of this tricky but essential procedure, see Richard K. Smith, *Seventy-Five Years of Inflight Refueling: Highlights, 1923–1998* (Washington, D.C.: Air Force History and Museums Program, 1998), pp. 38–9.

212   *Leavitt made it clear:* Interview with General Lloyd R. Leavitt.

213   *Of the 119 West Pointers who graduated from flight school:* Cited in Lloyd R. Leavitt, *Following the Flag: An Air Force Officer Provides an Eyewitness View of Major Events and Policies During the Cold War* (Maxwell Air Force Base, AL: Air University Press, 2010), p. 57.

213 *"Landing the U-2," Leavitt wrote:* Ibid., p. 175.

213 *Of the thirty-eight U-2 pilots . . . eight died flying the plane:* See ibid., p. 185.

215 *"ordered everyone to evacuate the control center":* Moser interview.

219 *When Ben Scallorn first reported to Little Rock:* Interview with Colonel Ben G. Scallorn.

219 *4.5 million pounds of steel:* About 2,255 tons of steel were used. Cited in Stumpf, *Titan II,* p. 112.

219 *30 million pounds of concrete:* About 7,240 cubic yards of concrete were used—and a cubic yard of concrete weighs about two tons. Cited in ibid.

219 *a management practice known as "concurrency":* The great advantage of concurrency was that it allowed new weapon systems to be developed quickly; the main disadvantage was that those weapons tended to be unreliable and often didn't work. See Stephen Johnson, *The United States Air Force and the Culture of Innovation: 1945–1965* (Washington, D.C.: Air Force History and Museums Program, 2002), pp. 19–22, 89–94.

219 *one of the largest construction projects ever undertaken by the Department of Defense:* For details of how the silos and launch complexes were built, see Joe Alex Morris, "Eighteen Angry Men: The Hard-Driving Colonels Who Work Against Crucial Deadlines to Ready Our Missile Launching Sites," *Saturday Evening Post,* January 13, 1962; John C. Lonnquest and David F. Winkler, *To Defend and Deter: The Legacy of the United States Cold War Missile Program* (Washington, D.C.: Department of Defense, Legacy Resource Management Program, Cold War Project, 1996), pp. 77–88; and Stumpf, *Titan II,* pp. 99–127.

220 *an area extending for thirty-two thousand square miles:* The launch sites of the 91st Strategic Missile Wing at Minot Air Force Base were set amid 8,500 square miles—about 12 percent of the land in North Dakota. And the sites of the 341st Strategic Missile Wing at Malmstrom Air Force Base were spread out across 23,500 square miles of Montana. See "Fact Sheet," 91st Missile Wing—Minot Air Force Base, April 14, 2011; and "Fact Sheet," 341st Missile Wing—Malmstrom Air Force Base, August 2, 2010.

220 *a population of about ten thousand:* Cited in "History of Air Research and Development Command, July–December 1960" Volume III, Historical Division, Air Research & Development Command, United States Air Force (n.d.), (SECRET/RESTRICTED DATA/declassified), p. 19.

220 *"Like any machine . . . they don't always work":* Quoted in "USAF Ballistic Missile Programs, 1962–1964," Bernard C. Nalty, USAF Historical Division Liaison Office, April 1966 (TOP SECRET/ declassified), NSA, p. 47.

220 *the Snark:* For a wonderful account of this ill-fated missile, see Kenneth P. Werrell, *The Evolution of the Cruise Missile* (Maxwell Air Force Base, AL: Air University Press, 1985), pp. 82–96.

220 *missed by an average of twenty miles or more:* More important, only one out of three Snarks were likely to get off the ground. See ibid., pp. 95–96.

220 *a Snark that was supposed to fly no farther than Puerto Rico:* For the story of the runaway missile, see J. P. Anderson, "The Day They Lost the Snark," *Air Force Magazine,* December 2004, pp. 78–80.

221 *The Army's Redstone missile:* Although its range was short, the missile was so reliable that it was used by NASA to launch America's first astronaut into space. See "History of the Redstone Missile System," John W. Bullard, Historical Division, Army Missile Command, AMC 23 M, October 15, 1965.

221 *Launched from NATO bases in West Germany:* Bob Peurifoy told me about the mismatch between the yield of the Redstone's warhead and the distance that it could fly.

221 *It would take at least fifteen minutes to launch any of the missiles:* For the technical and operational details of the Thor, see Stephen Twigge and Len Scott, *Planning Armageddon: Britain, the United States and the Command of Western Nuclear Forces, 1945–1964* (Amsterdam: Harwood Academic Publishers, 2000), pp. 109–12.

221 *as much as two days to complete its mission:* Ibid., p. 111.

221 *useful for a surprise attack:* For an excellent summary of the inherent flaws of Thor and Jupiter missiles, the intermediate-range weapons that the United States shared with its NATO allies, see Philip Nash, *The Other Missiles of October: Eisenhower, Kennedy, and the Jupiters, 1957–1963* (Chapel Hill, NC: University of North Carolina, 1997), pp. 80–85.

222 *the Atlas missile loomed as America's great hope:* For the definitive account of the Atlas program,

cowritten by one of its managers, see Chuck Walker, with Joel Powell, *ATLAS: The Ultimate Weapon by Those Who Built It* (Ontario, Canada: Apogee Books Production, 2005).

222 a *"fire waiting to happen"*: For the dangers of the Atlas and Titan propellants, see Charlie Simpson, "LOX and RP1—Fire Waiting to Happen," *Association of Air Force Missileers Newsletter*, vol. 14, no. 3 (September 3, 2006). Colonel Simpson is the executive director of the Association of Air Force and worked with Titan I missiles.

222 a *temperature of -297 degrees Fahrenheit*: Cited in Walker, *ATLAS*, Appendix D, p. 281.

222 the *odds of an Atlas missile hitting a target . . . no better than fifty-fifty*: The estimate was sheepishly offered by Major General Thomas P. Gerrity, Commander, Ballistic Systems Division, Air Force Systems Command. Another officer optimistically predicted that the reliability of the Atlas would reach 85 percent. Instead, all of the missiles were deactivated and removed from service within a few years. For the reliability estimates, see "Missile Procurement, Air Force," pp. 529–30.

222 *General Thomas Power . . . thought the odds were closer to zero*: See Jacob Neufeld, *The Development of Ballistic Missiles in the United States Air Force, 1945–1960*, (Washington, D.C.: Office of Air Force History, 1990), p. 216.

222 *During a test run of the first Titan silo*: For more details of the accident, see Stumpf, *Titan II*, pp. 23–26.

222 *about 170,000 pounds of liquid oxygen and fuel*: The missile was fully loaded with propellants.

223 *Donald Quarles was one of the leading skeptics*: A few months before his death, Quarles was strongly attacked by the columnist Joseph Alsop for opposing new missile programs and allowing the United States to fall behind the Soviets. See Joseph Alsop, "Mister Missile Gap," *Washington Post*, April 24, 1959.

223 *how to bring the warhead close to its target*: My description of ballistic missile guidance systems is based on a fine magazine article published more than half a century ago, Maya Pines, "The Magic Carpet of Inertial Guidance," *Harper's*, March 1962; a training manual for Titan II launch officers, "Missile Launch/Missile Officer (LGM-25): Missile Systems," Student Study Guide 3OBR1821F/3121F-V1 through 4, Volume I of II, Department of Missile and Space Training, Sheppard Technical Training Center, September 1968; and an extraordinary book about how missiles hit their targets, Donald MacKenzie, *Inventing Accuracy: A Historical Sociology of Nuclear Missile Guidance* (Cambridge, MA: MIT Press, 1993).

223 *burned for only the first five minutes of flight*: During the booster phase, the first-stage engine of the Titan II fired for about 165 seconds; during the sustainer phase, the second-stage engine fired for about 125 seconds; and during the Vernier Stage, the two small solid propellant engines fired for about 10 seconds. See "Missile Launch/Missile Officer (LGM-25)," p. 3.

224 *about 80 percent of the warheads within roughly a mile of their targets*: Cited in MacKenzie, *Inventing Accuracy*, p. 122.

224 *a leading role in the miniaturization of computers*: See ibid., pp. 159–61, 206–7; Edwards, *Closed World*, pp. 63–65.

224 *all of the integrated circuits in the United States*: See MacKenzie, *Inventing Accuracy*, p. 207. In 1965, the Pentagon was buying 72 percent of the integrated circuits, and the proportion being used in military applications did not fall below half until 1967. See Table 6 in Gregory Hooks, "The Rise of the Pentagon and U.S. State Building: The Defense Program as Industrial Policy," *American Journal of Sociology*, vol. 96, no. 2 (September 1990), p. 389.

225 *It had about 12.5 kilobytes of memory*: This is a rough estimate, used for the sake of simplicity. The Titan II missile's onboard guidance computer could store 100,224 binary bits. They were stored on a magnetic drum memory assembly with 58 tracks. Each track held 64 words (or "bytes") that contained 27 bits. For the sake of comparison, I have converted those 27-bit bytes into today's more commonly used 8-bit bytes. By that measure, the Titan II onboard computer had about 12.5 kilobytes of memory. For the specifications of the computer, see "Missile Launch/Missile Officer (LGM-25)," p. 24. I am grateful to Chuck Penson, Bob Peurifoy, Richard Peurifoy, and Steve Peurifoy for helping me with these calculations.

225 *more than five million times that amount*: Many smartphones now have 64 gigabytes of memory. A gigabyte is equivalent to about 1 million kilobytes. The comparison between the 12.5-kilobyte

memory of a Titan II computer and the 64-gigabyte memory of a smartphone is inexact. But it still conveys an important point: even the rudimentary computing device aboard the Titan II could guide a nuclear warhead almost halfway around the world with remarkable accuracy.

225 *the first missile to employ an inertial guidance system:* For the Nazi efforts in this field, see MacKenzie, *Inventing Accuracy,* pp. 44–60.

225 *the Nazi scientists who invented it were recruited:* Dr. Walter Haeussermann, who played a large role in developing the guidance system of the V-2, was brought to the United States under Project Paperclip and reunited with his former employer, Wernher von Braun. Haeussermann later worked on the guidance systems of the Redstone and Jupiter missiles, left the Army to work for NASA, later headed the Astrionics Laboratory at the Marshall Space Center, and helped devise the mechanisms that guided American astronauts safely to the moon. See Dennis Hevesi, "Walter Haeussermann, Rocket Scientist, Dies at 96," *New York Times,* December 17, 2010.

225 *Circular Error Probable . . . of less than a mile:* See MacKenzie, *Inventing Accuracy,* p. 131.

225 *miscalculated by just 0.05 percent:* During the last fifteen minutes of the Titan II warhead's reentry, it traveled at a speed of about 16,000 miles per hour. It would cover a distance of about 4,000 miles in those fifteen minutes. A measurement error of 0.05 percent would add or subtract about 20 miles from the distance traveled. For the speed of reentry, see Penson, *Titan II Handbook,* p. 169. Maya Pines made a similar calculation in "Magic Carpet of Inertial Guidance," but with a somewhat different result.

225 *The accuracy of a Titan II launch:* My description of a Titan II missile's launch, trajectory, and flight is based on information found in Penson, *Titan II Handbook,* pp. 118–39, 169; Stumpf, *Titan II,* pp. 177–78; and "Final Titan II Operational Data Summary," Rev 3, TRW Space Technology Laboratories, September 1964, p. 3-1. Some of the numbers differ slightly in these sources. For example, Chuck Penson says the missile began to rise 58 seconds after the keys were turned; David Stumpf says 59.2 seconds. I have tried to convey the gist of how a Titan II launch would have unfolded. Penson's account is especially vivid and detailed.

226 *about twenty-three thousand feet per second, faster than a speeding bullet:* An object going 16,000 miles per hour is traveling about 4.44 miles per second—roughly 23,467 feet per second. The velocity of bullets fired from a typical handgun ranges from about 800 to 1,200 feet per second at a distance of 50 yards. The speed of rifle bullets is higher, reaching as much as 4,000 feet per second.

226 *surface temperatures of about 15,000 degrees Fahrenheit:* Although temperatures that high might be encountered briefly, the strong shock wave preceding a warhead as it falls will dissipate a great deal of that heat in the atmosphere. Cited in "Ballistic Missile Staff Course Study Guide," 4315th Combat Crew Training Squadron, Strategic Air Command, Vandenberg Air Force Base, July 1, 1980, p. 3–1.

226 *hotter than the melting point of any metal:* Tungsten's melting point is the highest—6,170 degrees Fahrenheit. Cited in Stumpf, *Titan II,* p. 56.

226 *On the way up, a barometric switch closed . . . On the way down, an accelerometer ignited:* I learned these details from a weapon designer who worked on the W-53 warhead.

226 *set for an airburst . . . at an altitude of fourteen thousand feet:* Cited in Penson, *Titan II Handbook,* p. 135.

227 *At first, perhaps 70 to 75 percent . . . were expected to hit their targets:* Cited in "Missile Procurement," p. 532.

227 *that proportion would rise to 90 percent:* Cited in ibid.

227 *"the biggest guns in the western world":* "Nuclear 'Guns' Ready, Aimed at Likely Foes," *Los Angeles Times,* June 22, 1964.

227 *The first launch crews had to train with cardboard mock-ups:* For the challenges that some of the first crews faced, see Grant E. Secrist, "A Perspective on Crew Duty in the Early Days, the 308th SMW," *Association of Air Force Missileers Newsletter,* vol. 13, no. 4, December 2005, pp. 4–6.

229 *Sergeant Donald V. Green was serving as a referee:* Interview with Donald V. Green.

230 *General LeMay liked to run these tests:* They were prominently featured in the movie *Strategic Air Command* and in the *Life* magazine profile of LeMay, "Toughest Cop of the Western World." The author and historian James Carroll described how his father, a high-ranking security officer at the

Pentagon, spent years attempting acts of "faux sabotage" against LeMay, as part of a friendly rivalry. See James Carroll, *House of War: The Pentagon and the Disastrous Rise of American Power* (Boston: Mariner Books, 2006), pp. 214–19.

235 *"Scallorn, just be quiet":* Quoted in Scallorn interview and Moser interview.

235 *"Roger, General":* Quoted in ibid.

235 *"Little Rock, this is Martin-Denver":* Carnahan's recommendation that nothing be done is the only quote in the entire three-volume accident report that comes from a tape recording of discussions on the Missile Potential Hazard Net. The quote is long, it's verbatim—and it absolves Martin Marietta of responsibility for what later went wrong. The recording was made at Martin-Denver. See "Report, Major Missile Accident, Titan II Complex 374-7," Testimony of Charles E. Carnahan, Tab U-11, pp. 1–2.

241 *"It's hot as hell":* Quoted in "Report, Major Missile Accident, Titan II Complex 374-7," Kennedy statement, Tab U–46, p. 10.

Part Four: Out of Control

Decapitation

245 *a B-52 bomber took off from Seymour Johnson Air Force Base:* My account of the accident is based on interviews with Bob Peurifoy and Bill Stevens, as well as on documents that have been released through the Freedom of Information Act. See "Summary of Nuclear Weapon Incidents (AF Form 1058) and Related Problems—January 1961," *Airmunitions Letter*, No. 136-11-56G, Headquarters, Ogden Air Material Area, April 18, 1961 (SECRET/RESTRICTED DATA/declassified), pp. 1–27; and "Official Observer's Report, Air Accident, Goldsboro, North Carolina," Ross B. Speer, AEC/ALO, February 16, 1961 (SECRET/RESTRICTED DATA /declassified). A good explanation of why the accident was so dangerous can be found in a memo written by Parker F. Jones, the supervisor of Sandia's Nuclear Weapon Safety Department: "Goldsboro Revisited, or How I Learned to Mistrust the H-Bomb, or To Set the Record Straight," Parker F. Jones, SFRD Memo, SNL 1651, October 22, 1969 (SECRET/RESTRICTED DATA/declassified). Joel Dobson offers the best description of the accident itself and the fate of the crew in *The Goldsboro Broken Arrow: The Story of the 1961 B-52 Crash, the Men, the Bombs, the Aftermath* (Raleigh, NC: Lulu, 2011). But Dobson's book is less reliable about the inner workings of the weapons.

245 *Mattocks managed to jump through the escape hatch:* Mattocks should have been killed immediately by the tail of the plane. But the plane was breaking apart as he left it, and the tail was already gone. The B-52 exploded right after his parachute deployed, briefly collapsing it. He landed on a farm in the middle of the night, assured its frightened owners that he wasn't a Martian, got a ride to Seymour Johnson Air Force Base—and got arrested by the guards at the front gate. They had not been informed of the accident, and he couldn't produce any military identification. One of the other crew members who safely escaped from the plane, Captain Richard Rardin, found a ride to the base and arrived at the gate not long afterward. When the guards threatened to arrest Rardin, too, Mattocks managed to convince them that the two men were indeed Air Force officers and that a B-52 had just fallen from the sky. See Dobson, *Goldsboro Broken Arrow*, pp. 55–60.

246 *The Air Force assured the public:* See Noel Yancey, "In North Carolina: Nuclear Bomber Crashes; 3 Dead," *Fort Pierce News Tribune* (Florida), January 24, 1961.

246 *The T-249 control box and ready/safe switch . . . had already raised concerns at Sandia:* Interviews with Peurifoy and Stevens. Some of the limitations of the T-249, known as the Aircraft Monitor and Control Box, had been addressed two years earlier in "A Survey of Nuclear Weapon Safety Problems," pp. 19–23.

247 *all of the weapons were armed:* Stevens interview. See also Stevens, "Origins and Evolution of S²C at Sandia," p. 60.

247 *A seven-month investigation by Sandia:* See ibid.

247 *"It would have been bad news—in spades":* "Goldsboro Revisited," p. 1.

247 *"One simple, dynamo-technology, low-voltage switch":* Ibid., p. 2.

247 *the groundburst of that 4-megaton bomb in Goldsboro:* The amount of fallout would not have been as great as that produced by the far more powerful Bravo test. But the Goldsboro bomb could have spread deadly radioactive material across a large area of the northeastern United States.

247 *"pay any price, bear any burden":* "Text of Kennedy's Inaugural Outlining Policies on World Peace and Freedom," *New York Times,* January 21, 1961.

247 *The story scared the hell out of him:* Interview with Robert S. McNamara.

248 *A B-47 carrying a Mark 39 bomb had caught fire:* Peurifoy and Stevens interviews. See also *Airmunitions Letter,* June 23, 1960, p. 37, and Maggelet and Oskins, *Broken Arrow,* pp. 113–18.

248 *A B-47 . . . caught fire on the runway at Chennault Air Force base:* See *Airmunitions Letter,* June 23, 1960, p. 53.

248 *In the skies above Hardinsburg, Kentucky:* See *Airmunitions Letter,* Headquarters, Ogden Air Material Area, No. 136-11-56B, June 29, 1960 (SECTET/RESTRICTED DATA/declassified, pp. 13–46, Maggelet and Oskins, *Broken Arrow,* pp. 129–32.

248 *a "crunching sound":* Quoted Maggelet and Oskins, *Broken Arrow,* p. 132.

248 *At an air defense site in Jackson Township:* For details of the BOMARC accident, see "Report of Special Weapons Incident . . . Bomarc Site, McGuire AFB, New Jersey," 2702nd Explosive Ornance Disposal Squad, United States Air Force, Griffiss Air Force Base, New York, June 13, 1960 (SECRET/RESTRICTED DATA /declassified); *Airmunitions Letter,* No. 136-11-56C, Headquarters, Ogden Air Material Area, September 8, 1960 (SECRET/RESTRICTED DATA/declassified; and George Barrett, "Jersey Atom Missile Fire Stirs Brief Radiation Fear," *New York Times,* June 8, 1960.

249 *An Air Force security officer called the state police:* See "Jersey Atom Missile Fire."

249 *Fallout from the BOMARC's 10-kiloton warhead:* See "Civil Defense Alerted in City," *New York Times,* June 8, 1960.

249 *The accidents in North Carolina and Texas worried Robert McNamara the most:* McNamara interview. See also "Memorandum of Conversation (Uncleared), Subject: State-Defense Meeting on Group I, II, and IV Papers," January 26, 1963 (TOP SECRET/declassified), NSA, p. 12.

249 *"bankruptcy in both strategic policy and in the force structure":* "Robert S. McNamara Oral History Interview—4/4/1964," John F. Kennedy Oral History Collection, John F. Kennedy Presidential Library and Museum, p. 5.

249 *"The Communists will have a dangerous lead":* Quoted in Desmond Ball, *Politics and Force Levels: The Strategic Missile Program of the Kennedy Administration* (Berkeley: University of California Press, 1980), p. 18. Although Ball's work was written before the declassification of many important national security documents from the Kennedy era, the book's central arguments are still convincing. I also learned a great deal about the Kennedy administration's aims from *How Much Is Enough? 1961–1969: Shaping Defense Program* (Santa Monica, CA: RAND Corporation, 1971), by Alain C. Enthoven and K. Wayne Smith. Enthoven was one of McNamara's most brilliant advisers. For Kennedy's attacks on the strategic thinking of the Eisenhower administration, see Christopher A. Preble, " 'Who Ever Believed in the "Missile Gap"?': John F. Kennedy and the Politics of National Security," *Presidential Studies Quarterly,* vol. 33, no. 4 (December 2003), pp. 801–26.

250 *"We have been driving ourselves into a corner":* Quoted in William W. Kaufmann, *The McNamara Strategy* (New York: Harper & Row, 1964), p. 40.

250 *General Maxwell D. Taylor's book,* The Uncertain Trumpet: Taylor argued that the United States needed "a capability to react across the entire spectrum of possible challenge, for coping with anything from general atomic war to infiltrations and aggressions." He was later a major architect of the Vietnam War. See Maxell D. Taylor, *The Uncertain Trumpet* (New York: Harper & Brothers, 1960), p. 6.

250 *"The record of the Romans made clear":* "Summary of President Kennedy's Remarks to the 496th Meeting of the National Security Council," January 18, 1962 (TOP SECRET/declassified), in United States Department of State, *Foreign Relations of the United States, 1961–1963, Volume VIII, National Security Policy* (Washington, D.C.: U.S. Government Printing Office, 1996), p. 240.

250 *The chief of naval operations, Admiral Arleigh Burke, warned:* Western Europe would suffer radio-

logical effects from a massive American attack on the Soviet Union, but South Korea was likely to receive even worse fallout. See "Chief of Naval Operations Cable to Commander-in-Chief Atlantic Fleet, Commander-in-Chief Pacific Fleet, Commander-in-Chief U.S. Naval Forces Europe," November 20, 1960 (TOP SECRET/declassified), NSA, p. 1.

251 *"whiz kids," "defense intellectuals," "the best and the brightest":* David Halberstam's book on this highly self-confident group remains authoritative: *The Best and the Brightest* (New York: Ballantine Books, 1992).

251 *WSEG Report No. 50:* "Evaluation of Strategic Offensive Weapons Systems," Weapon Systems Evaluation Group Report No. 50, Washington, D.C., December 27, 1960 (TOP SECRET/RESTRICTED DATA/declassified), NSA.

251 *the annual operating costs of keeping a B-52 bomber on ground alert:* See ibid., Enclosure "F," p. 19.

251 *America's command-and-control system was so complex:* Long excerpts from Enclosure "C," the section of WSEG R-50 on command and control, can be found in Wainstein, et al., "Evolution of U.S. Strategic Command and Control," pp. 239–47.

251 *By launching a surprise attack on five targets:* Ibid., p. 243.

252 *By hitting nine additional targets:* Ibid., p. 242.

252 *a 90 percent chance of success:* Cited in ibid.

252 *only thirty-five Soviet missiles:* Cited in Ibid.

252 *Four would be aimed at the White House:* Ibid., p. 243.

252 *"Under surprise attack conditions":* Quoted in ibid., p. 239.

252 *"a one-shot command, control, and communication system":* Ibid., p. 284.

253 *the warning time would be zero:* Cited in ibid., p. 241.

253 *During a tour of NORAD headquarters in Colorado Springs:* My account of this false alarm is based on "'Missile Attack' Terror Described," *Oakland Tribune,* December 11, 1960; "When the Moon Dialed No. 5, They Saw World War III Begin," *Express and News* (San Antonio), December 11, 1960; John G. Hubbell, "You Are Under Attack!, The Strange Incident of October 5," *Reader's Digest,* April 1961, pp. 37–39; and Donald MacKenzie, *Mechanizing Proof: Computing, Risk, and Trust* (Cambridge, MA: MIT Press, 2001), pp. 23–4. MacKenzie obtained an oral history interview with General Kuter that largely confirmed the contemporary accounts of the incident.

253 *a 99.9 percent certainty:* Cited in "'You Are Under Attack!'"

253 *"Chief, this is a hot one":* Quoted in MacKenzie, *Mechanizing Proof,* p. 23.

253 *"Where is Khrushchev?":* Quoted in "'You Are Under Attack!'"

254 *He recalled a sense of panic at NORAD:* Percy later wondered what sort of decision might have been made if the radar signals hadn't been recognized to be a false alarm. See Einar Kringlen, "The Myth of Rationality in Situations of Crisis," *Medicine and War, Volume I,* (1985), p. 191.

254 *"There is no mechanism for nor organization charged with":* Quoted in Wainstein, et al., "Evolution of U.S. Strategic Command and Control," p. 243.

255 *"No other target system can at present offer":* Quoted in ibid., p. 246.

255 *"We have been concerned with the vulnerability":* McNamara learned within weeks of taking office that the command-and-control problems in Europe were severe. These quotes are taken from a report submitted to him in the fall of 1961 by General Earle E. Partridge, a retired Air Force officer who'd been asked to head an investigation of command-and-control issues. "Interim Report on Command and Control in Europe," National Command and Control Task Force, October 1961 (TOP SECRET/declassified), NSA, p. 2.

255 *All of NATO's command bunkers . . . could easily be destroyed:* See ibid.

255 *At best, NATO commanders might receive five or ten minutes of warning:* See ibid., p. 4.

255 *the NATO communications system was completely unprotected:* See ibid., pp. 3–4.

255 *the president could not expect to reach any of NATO's high-ranking officers:* See ibid., p. 5.

255 *"It is imperative that each commander knows":* Ibid.

256 *"Not only could we initiate a war, through mistakes":* Ibid., p. 6.

256 *"A subordinate commander faced with a substantial Russian military action":* "Memorandum from the President's Special Assistant for National Security Affairs (Bundy) to President Kennedy," January 30, 1961 (TOP SECRET/declassified), in *Foreign Relations of the United States, 1961–1963, Volume VIII,* National Security Policy, p. 18.

256   *a top secret report, based on a recent tour of NATO bases:* See "Report of Ad Hoc Subcommittee on U.S. Policies Regarding Assignment of Nuclear Weapons to NATO; Includes Letter to President Kennedy and Appendices," Joint Committee on Atomic Energy, Congress of the United States," February 11, 1961 (SECRET/RESTRICTED DATA/declassified), NSA.

257   *"he almost fell out of his chair":* The adviser, Thomas Schelling, is quoted in Webster Stone, "Moscow's Still Holding," *New York Times,* September 18, 1988.

257   *The Joint Committee on Atomic Energy had been concerned:* My description of the committee's tour of NATO sites and the development of Permissive Action Links is based on "Report on U.S. Policies Regarding Assignment of Nuclear Weapons to NATO"; "Letter, From Harold M. Agnew, to Major General A. D. Starbird, Director of Military Applications, U.S. Atomic Energy Commission," January 5, 1961 (SECRET/RESTRICTED DATA/declassified); Clinton P. Anderson, with Milton Viorst, *Outsider in the Senate: Senator Clinton Anderson's Memoirs* (New York: World Publishing Company, 1970), pp. 165–73; "Command and Control Systems for Nuclear Weapons: History and Current Status," System Development Department I, Sandia Laboratories, SLA-73-0415, September 1973 (SECRET/RESTRICTED DATA/declassified); "PAL Control of Theater Nuclear Weapons," M. E. Bleck, P. R. Souder, Command and Control Division, Sandia National Laboratories, SAND82-2436, March 1984 (SECRET/FORMERLY RESTRICTED DATA/declassified); Peter Stein and Peter Feaver, *Assuring Control of Nuclear Weapons: The Evolution of Permissive Action Links* (Cambridge, MA: Center for Science and International Affairs, John F. Kennedy School of Government, Harvard University, and University Press of America, 1987); Stevens, "Origins and Evolution of S^{2}C at Sandia," pp. 50–52; and my interview with Harold Agnew, who went on the European trip and played an important role in the adoption of PALs.

257   *"I have always been of the belief":* The president's news conference of February 3, 1960, in *Public Papers of the Presidents of the United States: Dwight D. Eisenhower, Containing the Public Messages and Statements of the President, January 1, 1960 to January 20, 1961* (Washington, D.C.: Office of the Federal Register, 1961), p. 152.

257   *"an essential element" of the NATO stockpile:* Quoted in Anderson, *Outsider in the Senate,* p. 170.

258   *a private understanding with Norstad:* See Trachtenberg, *Constructed Peace,* p. 170.

258   *"nearly wet my pants":* Agnew interview.

258   *"All [the Italians] have to do is hit him on the head":* Transcript, Executive Session, Joint Committee on Atomic Energy, Meeting No. 87-1-4, February 20, 1960, NSA, p. 73.

259   *"There were three Jupiters setting there":* Ibid, p. 66.

259   *"Non-Americans with non-American vehicles":* Ibid, p. 47.

259   *"The prime loyalty of the guards, of course":* "Report on U.S. Policies Regarding Assignment of Nuclear Weapons to NATO," p. 33.

260   *French officers sought to gain control of a nuclear device:* I first learned about the attempt from Thomas Reed, a former secretary of the Air Force and adviser to President Ronald Reagan. Reed briefly mentions the episode in a book that he wrote with Danny B. Stillman, a former director of the Los Alamos Technical Intelligence Division: *The Nuclear Express: A Political History of the Bomb and Its Proliferation* (Minneapolis: Zenith Press, 2009), pp. 79–80. The story is told in much greater detail by Bruno Tertrais in "A Nuclear Coup? France, the Algerian War and the April 1961 Nuclear Test," Fondation pour la Recherche Stratégique, Draft, October 2, 2011.

260   *"Refrain from detonating your little bomb":* Quoted in Tetrais, "A Nuclear Coup?," p. 11.

260   *"the dumping ground for obsolete warheads":* "Report on U.S. Policies Regarding Assignment of Nuclear Weapons to NATO," p. 45.

260   *Holifield estimated that about half of the Jupiters:* Transcript, Executive Session, Joint Committee on Atomic Energy, Meeting No. 87-1-4, p. 82.

260   *The chairman of the Joint Chiefs of Staff admitted:* See Nash, *Other Missiles of October,* p. 56.

260   *"It would have been better to dump them in the ocean":* Quoted in ibid., p. 3.

260   *The Mark 7 atomic bombs carried by NATO fighters:* Agnew, Stevens, Peurifoy interviews.

261   *amazed to see a group of NATO weapon handlers pull the arming wires out:* Agnew interview. The bombs lacked trajectory-sensing switches and therefore could detonate without having to fall from a plane. Senator Anderson noted that at Vogel Air Base in the Netherlands "a safety wire designed to keep the firing switch open had been accidentally pulled from a nuclear weapon and that device,

if dropped, would have exploded." See Anderson, *Outsider in the Senate*, p. 172. "Letter, From Harold M. Agnew," p. 8; "Report on U.S. Policies Regarding Assignment of Nuclear Weapons to NATO," p. 37.

261 *A rocket-propelled version of the Mark 7 was unloaded, fully armed:* See "Incidents and Accidents," Incident #3, p. 21.

261 *"During initial inspection after receipt":* See ibid., Incident #1, p. 52.

261 *A screwdriver was found inside one of the bombs; an Allen wrench was somehow left inside another:* See ibid., Incident #1, p. 70.

261 *the training and operating manuals for the Mark 7:* See "Letter, from Harold M. Agnew," p. 2.

261 *"In many areas we visited":* "Report on U.S. Policies Regarding Assignment of Nuclear Weapons to NATO," p. 38.

262 *"far from remote":* Ibid., p. 2.

262 *a mishap on January 16, 1961:* See ibid. and "Incidents and Accidents," Incident #3, p. 38. I was able to confirm where the accident occurred.

262 *the current "fictional" custody arrangements:* "Report on U.S. Policies Regarding Assignment of Nuclear Weapons to NATO," p. 39.

262 *A lone American sentry . . . was bound to start "goofing off":* See ibid., p. 32.

263 *Agnew brought an early version of the electromechanical locking system:* Agnew interview.

263 *The coded switch . . . weighed about a pound:* A weapon often contained two of these switches as a redundancy, to ensure that at least one would work. See "Command and Control Systems for Nuclear Weapons," p. 13.

263 *the decoder weighed about forty:* Ibid., p. 14.

264 *anywhere from thirty seconds to two and a half minutes to unlock:* Ibid., p. 13.

264 *"No single device can be expected to increase":* Quoted in "Subject: Atomic Stockpile, Letter, From John H. Pender, Legal Adviser, Department of State, To Abram J. Chayes, Legal Adviser, Department of State," July 16, 1961 (TOP SECRET/declassified), NSA, p. 4.

264 *"adequately safe, within the limits":* Quoted in ibid.

264 *"all is well with the atomic stockpile program":* Ibid.

265 *Wiesner was deeply concerned about the risk:* See Carl Kaysen, "Peace Became His Profession," in Walter A. Rosenblith, ed., *Jerry Wiesner: Scientist, Statesman, Humanist* (Cambridge, MA: MIT Press, 2003), p. 102.

265 *the locks might help "to buy time":* The quote comes from "Memorandum for the President, From Jerome B. Wiesner, May 29, 1962," in "PAL Control of Theater Nuclear Weapons," p. 84.

265 *"individual psychotics":* Ibid.

265 *prevent "unauthorized use by military forces":* Ibid.

265 *Known at first as "Prescribed Action Links":* See Stein and Feaver, *Assuring Control of Nuclear Weapons*, pp. 36–37.

265 *the broad outlines of his defense policies:* "The decisions of March 1961," Desmond Ball has written, "determined to a very large extent the character of the U.S. strategic-force posture for the next decade." The most important decisions had been made during the first two weeks of the month. See Ball, *Politics and Force Levels*, pp. 107–26. The quote is from page 121.

266 *five of them would inflict more damage:* The comparison was made between five 1-megaton weapons and one 10-megaton—with the larger number of small weapons achieving more blast damage. See Enthoven, *How Much Is Enough?*, pp. 179–84.

266 *the Navy had requested a dozen Polaris subs:* See Ball, *Politics and Force Levels*, pp. 45–46.

266 *Kennedy decided to build 41:* See ibid., pp. 46–7, 116–17.

267 *about half of SAC's bomber crews, if not more:* Cited in "Statement of Robert S. McNamara on the RS-70," Senate Armed Services Committee, March 14, 1962 (TOP SECRET/declassified), NSA, p. 12. This document somehow escaped the black pen of a Pentagon censor—it discloses the nuclear yield and accuracy of the major strategic weapon systems at the time. That information can be found on page 18.

267 *"pipe-smoking, tree-full-of-owls type":* I first encountered this quote in Fred Kaplan's superb *Wizards of Armageddon: The Untold Story of the Small Group of Men Who Have Devised the Plans and Shaped the Policies on How to Use the Bomb* (Stanford: Stanford University Press, 1991), p. 255. It comes

from an article by White about the whiz kids running the Pentagon, "Strategy and the Defense Intellectuals, *Saturday Evening Post*, May 4, 1963.

267 *the proportion of SAC bombers on ground alert . . . on airborne alert*: Policies that Eisenhower had strongly resisted became routine early in the Kennedy administration. During the presidential campaign, Kennedy had promised that SAC would have a round-the-clock airborne alert. For the details of SAC's new alert policies, see "History of Headquarters Strategic Air Command, 1961," SAC Historical Study No. 89, Headquarters, Strategic Air Command, Offutt AFB, Nebraska, January 1962 (TOP SECRET/declassified), NSA, pp. 58–65. For Kennedy's campaign promise, see Ball, *Politics and Force Levels*, p. 18.

268 *"one defense policy, not three"*: Quoted in Jack Raymond, "M'Namara Scores Defense Discord," *New York Times*, April 21, 1963. McNamara had made his opposition to interservice rivalry clear from the start.

268 *the Army was now seeking thirty-two thousand nuclear weapons*: Cited in "Memorandum from Secretary Defense McNamara to the Chairman of the Joint Chiefs of Staff (Lemnitzer)," May 23, 1962 (TOP SECRET/declassified), *Foreign Relations of the United States, 1961–1963, Volume VIII, National Security Policy*, p. 297.

268 *as urgently needed . . . as intercontinental ballistic missiles*: See "History of the XW-51 Warhead," SC-M-67-683, AEC Atomic Weapon Data, January 1968 (SECRET/RESTRICTED DATA/declassified), p. 10.

268 *"appear to be unreasonably high"*: The document that the Army submitted as a reply to McNamara's questions has been heavily censored, and yet the justification for seeking so many nuclear weapons seems clear. The Army wanted to defeat the Soviets on the ground in Western Europe, using "quick kill, quick response weapons." And the author of the report was aware that the request might seem unreasonable. The full quote reads: "At the first reading, the number of weapons suggested appear to be unreasonably high." In any event, the Army's arguments failed to be persuasive. See "Requirements for Tactical Nuclear Weapons," Special Studies Group (JCS), Project 23, C 2379, October 1962 (TOP SECRET/RESTRICTED DATA/declassified), p. 55.

268 *"if the enemy does"*: Taylor criticized the "emotional resistance in some quarters" to providing American troops in Europe with tens of thousands of small nuclear weapons. See "Memorandum from the President's Military Representative (Taylor) to President Kennedy, May 25, 1962 (TOP SECRET/declassified), *Foreign Relations of the United States, 1961–1963, Volume VIII, National Security Policy*, pp. 299–300. The quote is on page 300.

269 *Air Force Intelligence had warned*: According to the Air Force, the Soviet Union would have as many as 950 long-range missiles by mid-1964 and 1,200 by mid-1965. Instead, the Soviets never had more than 209 long-range missiles until the late 1960s. Cited in Raymond L. Garthoff, "Estimating Soviet Military Intentions and Capabilities," in Gerald K. Haines and Robert E. Leggett, eds., *Watching the Bear: Essays on CIA's Analysis of the Soviet Union* (Washington, D.C.: Central Intelligence Agency Center for the Study of Intelligence, 2003), p. 141.

269 *only four missiles that could reach the United States*: Cited in ibid.

269 *the Soviet program had secretly endured a major setback*: A leading Soviet rocket designer wrote the most authoritative account of what came to be known as the "Nedelin Catastrophe." See Boris Chertok, *Rockets and People, Volume II: Creating a Rocket Industry* (Washington, D.C.: NASA History Series, 2006), pp. 597–641.

270 *Tass . . . announced that Nedelin had been killed in a plane crash*: See Osgood Caruthers, "Chief of Rockets Killed in Soviet," *New York Times*, October 26, 1960.

270 *"it would be premature to reach a judgment"*: See "Transcript of the Kennedy News Conference on Foreign and Domestic Matters," *New York Times*, February. 9, 1961.

270 *Eisenhower had thought that twenty to forty would be enough*: Cited in "The Ballistic Missile Decisions," Robert L. Perry, The RAND Corporation, October 1967, p. 14.

270 *Jerome Wiesner advised President Kennedy that roughly ten times that number*: Wiesner thought that about two hundred missiles would be enough. See Ball, *Politics and Force Levels*, p. 85.

270 *General Power wanted . . . ten thousand Minuteman missiles*: Cited in Herbert F. York, *Race to Oblivion: A Participant's View of the Arms Race* (New York: Simon Schuster, 1970), p. 152.

271 *it was "a round number"*: The adviser was Herbert F. York. Quoted in Herken, *Counsels of War*, p. 153.

271 *"a matter of transcendent priority"*: "Memorandum for the Chairman, Joint Chiefs of Staff; Subject: Command and Control," Robert S. McNamara, August 21, 1961 (TOP SECRET/declassified), NSA, p. 1.

271 *"The chain of command from the President down"*: "Letter, From Secretary of Defense McNamara to President Kennedy," February 20, 1961 (TOP SECRET/declassified), in *Foreign Relations of the United States, 1961–1963, Volume VIII, National Security Policy*, p. 39.

271 *"classify the attack, as large or small"*: Wainstein, et al., "Evolution of U.S. Strategic Command and Control," p. 292.

272 *"The first duty of the command and control system"*: Paul Baran, "On a Distributed Command and Control System Configuration," U.S.A.F. Project RAND, RM-2632, Research Memorandum, December 31, 1960, p. 19.

272 *Messages would be broken into smaller "blocks"*: See Paul Baran, "On Distributed Communications Networks," The RAND Corporation, P-2626, September 1962.

274 *a "logical, survivable node in the control structure"*: "Memorandum for the President, Subject: National Deep Underground Command Center as a Key FY 1965 Budget Consideration," Robert S. McNamara, November 7, 1963 (TOP SECRET /declassified), NSA, p. 2,4.

274 *"austere" version or one of "moderate size"*: Ibid., p. 3.

274 *"withstand multiple direct hits of 200 to 300 MT"*: Ibid., p. 1.

275 *While heading a committee on the risk of war by accident*: Thomas Schelling described his concern about the lack of secure communications between the White House and the Kremlin, his role in creating the "hot line," and his admiration for the novel *Red Alert* in an e-mail exchange with me.

The Brink

276 *"Mankind must put an end to war"*: "Text of President Kennedy's Address to the United Nations General Assembly," *New York Times*, September 26, 1961.

276 *"Today, every inhabitant of this planet"*: Ibid.

277 *"peace race". . ."general and complete disarmament"*: Ibid.

277 *"Such a plan would not bring a world free from conflict"*: Ibid.

277 *"Together we shall save our planet"*: Ibid.

277 *"If a general atomic war is inevitable"*: Quoted in "Memorandum of Conference with President Kennedy," September 20, 1961 (TOP SECRET/declassified), in *Foreign Relations of the United States, 1961-1963, Volume VIII, National Security Policy*, p. 130.

277 *Kennedy had just received a memo . . . summarizing how an American first strike*: See "Memorandum from the President's Military Representative (Taylor) to President Kennedy," September 19, 1961 (TOP SECRET/declassified), in ibid., pp. 126–29.

277 *"There are risks as well as opportunities"*: ibid., p. 128.

277 *once again, Berlin was at the center of the crisis*: For the events in Berlin during the Kennedy years, see McGeorge Bundy, *Danger and Survival: Choices About the Bomb in the First Fifty Years* (New York: Random House, 1988), pp. 358–90; Vladislav M. Zubok, "Khrushchev and the Berlin Crisis (1958–1962)," *Cold War International History Project—Working Paper Series*, Working Paper No. 6, Washington, D. C., May 1993; Trachtenberg, *Constructed Peace*, pp. 251–351; Aleksandr Fursenko and Timothy Naftali, *Khrushchev's Cold War: The Inside Story of an American Adversary* (New York: W. W. Norton, 2006), pp. 338–408; and Frederick Kempe, *Berlin 1961: Kennedy, Khrushchev, and the Most Dangerous Place on Earth* (New York: G. P. Putnam's Sons, 2011).

278 *"It is up to the United States to decide"*: Quoted in Fursenko and Naftali, *Khrushchev's Cold War*, p. 364.

278 *"Then it will be a cold winter"*: Quoted in ibid.

278 *the Joint Chiefs of Staff seemed to have few options*: The historian Marc Trachtenberg suggests that Eisenhower's nuclear strategy may have been more "flexible" than was later claimed. But the pressure to launch a full–scale nuclear attack on the Soviet Union—once American and Soviet troops were fighting on a battlefield in Europe—would have been enormous. See Trachtenberg, *Conflict & Stragegy*, pp. 209–12.

279 *It would be "explosive"*: Quoted in Trachtenberg, *Constructed Peace*, p. 289.

279 *"This is the time to create strength"*: "Telegram from the Supreme Allied Commander, Europe (Norstad) to Secretary of Defense McNamara," April 25, 1961 (TOP SECRET/declassified), in United States Department of State, *Foreign Relations of the United States, 1961–1963, Volume XVI, Eastern Europe; Cyprus; Greece; Turkey* (Washington, D.C.: Government Printing Office, 1994), p. 699.

279 *"If a crisis is provoked"*: Quoted in Kempe, *Berlin 1961*, p. 129.

279 *"and we have given our word"*: "Text of Kennedy Appeal to Nation for Increases in Spending and Armed Forces," *New York Times,* July 26, 1961.

279 *"Tell Kennedy that if he starts a war"*: Quoted in Zubok, "Khrushchev and the Berlin Crisis," p. 25.

280 *"[T]he current strategic war plan"*: Quoted in Kaplan, *Wizards of Armageddon*, p. 297.

280 *"spasm war"* . . . *a "ridiculous and unworkable notion"*: "Memorandum of Conversation with Mr. Henry Rowen, Deputy Assistant Secretary of Defense for International Security Affairs," May 25, 1961 (TOP SECRET/declassified), *Foreign Relations of the United States, 1961–1963, Volume VIII, National Security Policy*, p. 82.

281 *"We should be prepared to initiate general war"*: "Memorandum for General Maxwell Taylor, Military Representative to the President, Subject: Strategic Air Planning and Berlin," September 5, 1961 (TOP SECRET/declassified), NSA, p. 3.

281 *more than half the people in the Soviet Union—millions more in Eastern Europe and China:* See ibid, "Annex B, SIOP-62 An Appreciation," Table IX, p. 12.

281 *it would "inevitably" tip off the Soviets:* "Strategic Air Planning and Berlin," p. 3.

281 *"no more than fifteen minutes"*: Ibid., "Annex A, An Alternative to SIOP-62," p. 3.

281 *"we should be able to communicate two things"*: Ibid., Annex A, p. 6.

281 *"less than 1,000,000"*: Ibid., Annex A, p. 3.

282 *"The plan is designed for execution"*: General Lemnitzer made these comments during a meeting with President Kennedy on September 13, 1961. Although these remarks were not directed specifically at Kaysen's proposal, Lemnitzer had been sent it the previous week and did not like it. The quote comes from "SIOP-62 Briefing," p. 50.

282 *"If you have to go, you want LeMay"*: Quoted in "Bomber on the Stump," *Time*, October 18, 1968.

282 *"some portion of the Soviet . . . nuclear force"*: Quoted in Sagan, "SIOP-62: The Nuclear War Plan Briefing," p. 22.

282 *about 16 long-range missiles, 150 long-range bombers, and 60 submarine-based missiles:* See Steven J. Zaloga, *The Kremlin's Nuclear Sword: The Rise and Fall of Russia's Strategic Nuclear Forces, 1945–2000* (Washington, D.C.: Smithsonian Institution Press, 2002), pp. 241–47.

282 *"while small percentage wise"*: "Strategic Air Planning and Berlin, Annex A, An Alternative to SIOP-62," p. 10.

282 *"In thermonuclear warfare"*: Ibid.

282 *kill as many as 100 million Americans:* Two months earlier, Kaysen had calculated how many American lives might be saved by a large-scale civil defense program. In the absence of bunkers and shelters, Kaysen found that the use of one hundred Soviet weapons against American cities would kill between 62 to 100 million people. The American population, at the time, was about 180 million. See "Carl Kaysen, Memorandum for Mr. Bundy, Subject: Berlin Crisis and Civil Defense," July 7, 1961, NSA, Appendix, p. 3.

283 *a "rotten tooth which must be pulled out"*: Khrushchev had made the comparison during his Vienna meeting with Kennedy in 1961. Quoted in "Memorandum of Conversation, Subject: Germany and Berlin; Possible Visit by Khrushchev," October 18, U.S. Department of State, *Foreign Relations of the United States, 1961–1963, Volume XV, Berlin Crisis, 1962–1963* (Washington, D.C.: Government Printing Office, 1994), p. 372.

283 *"It's not a very nice solution"*: Quoted in Kempe, *Berlin 1961,* p. 379.

283 *"Berlin developments may confront us"*: Quoted in "Memorandum to General Lemnitzer, From Maxwell D. Taylor," September 19, 1961 (TOP SECRET/declassified), NSA.

284 *General Power expressed concern that Khrushchev was hiding:* See "Memorandum of Conference with President Kennedy," September 20, 1961, p. 130.

284 *Power advocated an attack with the full SIOP:* Ibid.

284 *"The Western Powers have calmly resolved"*: "Text of Kennedy's Address to United Nations."

284 *"whenever we feel it necessary":* Quoted in Alfred Goldberg, Steven L. Rearden, Doris M. Condit, *History of the Office of the Secretary of Defense: The McNamara Ascendancy, 1961–1965* (Washington, D.C.: Government Printing Office, 1984), p. 162.

285 *"with such a strike, we could in some real sense be victorious":* "Minutes of Oct. 10, 1961 Meeting," October 10, 1961 (TOP SECRET/declassified), in U.S. Department of State, *Foreign Relations of the United States, 1961–1963, Volume XIV, Berlin Crisis, 1961–1962* (Washington, D.C.: Government Printing Office, 1993), p. 489.

285 *A. Selective nuclear attacks:* "Letter from President Kennedy to the Supreme Commander, Allied Powers Europe (Norstad)," October 20, 1961 (TOP SECRET/declassified), in ibid., p. 523.

285 *American tanks were sent to Checkpoint Charlie:* For a feel of the military standoff between American and Soviet armored forces, see Sydney Gruson, "Soviet Advance: 33 Vehicles Are Mile from Crossing Point Used by Americans," *New York Times,* October 27, 1961; Sydney Gruson, "U.S. Tanks Face Soviet's at Berlin Crossing Point," *New York Times*, October 28, 1961; and Sydney Gruson, "U.S. and Russians Pull Back Tanks from Berlin Line," *New York Times*, October 29, 1961; and Kempe, *Berlin 1961,* pp. 455–81.

286 *The mushroom cloud rose about forty miles:* For the story of the "King of All Bombs" by two of its designers, see Viktor Adamsky and Yuri Smirnov, "Moscow's Biggest Bomb: The 50-Megaton Test of October 1961," *Cold War International History Project Bulletin,* Fall 1994.

286 *with enough force to be detected in New Zealand:* See "Transit of Pressure Waves Through New Zealand from the Soviet 50 Megaton Bomb Explosion," E. Farkas, New Zealand Meteorological Service, *Nature,* February 24, 1962, pp. 765–66.

286 *"There was hardly a week":* Bundy, *Danger and Survival,* p. 363.

286 *just before dawn, SAC headquarters in Omaha lost contact:* Sensors for the Bomb Alarm System had been installed at Thule but were not yet operational. For details of the Black Forest incident, see "History of Headquarters Strategic Air Command, 1961," pp. 27–29.

287 *"any maniac at a US military base":* Quoted in Jerry T. Baulch, "Faulty Alert Never Reached Top Command," *Washington Post and Times Herald,* April 4, 1962.

287 *"Highly dispersed nuclear weapons":* McNamara's Athens speech is an important document in the history of the Cold War. The speech was also given my favorite level of classification: COSMIC TOP SECRET. The quote is from "Defense Policy: Statement Made on Saturday 5 May by Secretary McNamara at the NATO Ministerial Meeting in Athens," North Atlantic Council, May 5, 1962 (COSMIC TOP SECRET/NATO RESTRICTED/declassified), NSA, p. 9.

287 *"Our best hope lies in conducting":* Ibid., p. 6.

287–88 *McNamara's remarks were partly aimed at the French:* By maintaining a nuclear force independent of NATO control, France gained an influence disproportionate to its size and power. No matter how hard the United States might try to fight a limited war and restrict its attacks to Soviet military forces, a French decision to use nuclear weapons against Soviet cities would inexorably lead to an all-out war. The French strategy was known as "Deterrence of the Strong by the Weak." "They have understood that we now have the finger on the trigger," Charles de Gaulle, the president of France, once said. "We are becoming as redoubtable as a man walking in an ammunitions depot with a lighter. . . . Of course, if he lights up, he'll be the first to blow. But he will also blow all those around." The quote comes from Bruno Tertrais, "Destruction Assurée: The Origins and Development of French Nuclear Strategy, 1945–1981," in *Getting Mad,* pp. 73–74.

288 *"lead to the destruction of our hostages":* "Statement at Athens," p. 7.

288 *"the catastrophe which we most urgently wish to avoid":* Ibid.

288 *"Not targeting cities—how aggressive!":* Quoted in Fursenko and Naftali, *Khrushchev's Cold War,* p. 442.

288 *"To get the population used to the idea":* Ibid.

289 *If Khrushchev's scheme worked:* Dozens of books have been written about the Cuban missile crisis. I found these to be the most interesting and compelling: Aleksandr Fursenko and Timothy Naftali, *"One Hell of a Gamble": Khrushchev, Castro, and Kennedy, 1958–1964* (New York: W. W. Norton, 1997); Graham Allison and Philip Zelikow, *Essence of Decision: Explaining the Cuban Missile Crisis* (New York: Longman, 1999); Ernest R. May and Philip D. Zelikow, *The Kennedy Tapes: Inside the White House During the Cuban Missile Crisis* (New York: W. W. Norton, 2002); Max Frankel, *High*

Noon in the Cold War: Kennedy, Khrushchev, and the Cold War (New York: Ballantine Books, 2005); and Michael Dobbs, *One Minute to Midnight: Kennedy, Khrushchev, and Castro on the Brink of Nuclear War* (New York: Knopf, 2008). Fursenko and Naftali skillfully include material from the Soviet archives. Frankel covered the crisis for the *New York Times* and brings a firsthand feel to the drama. Allison and Zelikow use the crisis as a means of understanding larger questions of leadership and government behavior. *The Kennedy Tapes*, although based on edited transcripts, allows many of the principal actors to speak for themselves. And Dobbs conveys the simple fact that this is an incredible story, with stakes that couldn't possibly be higher.

289 *twenty-four medium-range ballistic missiles, sixteen intermediate-range ballistic missiles:* Cited in Fursenko and Naftali, *"One Hell of a Gamble,"* p. 188.

289 *forty-two bombers . . . and about 50,000 personnel:* Ibid.

289 *triple the number of Soviet land-based missiles that could hit the United States:* The Soviet Union had about twenty long-range missiles in 1962. Cited in Allison and Zelikow, *Essence of Decision*, p. 92.

289 *"We have no bases in Cuba":* "Letter from Chairman Khrushchev to President Kennedy," April 22, 1961, in U.S. Department of State, *Foreign Relations of the United States, 1961–1963, Volume VI, Kennedy-Khrushchev Exchanges* (Washington, D.C.: Government Printing Office, 1996), p. 12.

289 *"Our nuclear weapons are so powerful":* "Text of Soviet Statement Saying That Any U.S. Attack on Cuba Would Mean War," *New York Times*, September 12, 1962.

290 *their strategic purpose seemed to be a decapitation attack:* Regardless of Khrushchev's actual motive for deploying the missiles, they had the capability to destroy American command-and-control centers with little warning. And that made their presence in Cuba all the more unacceptable for the Kennedy administration. See May, et al., "History of the Strategic Arms Competition," Part 2, pp. 663–68.

290 *"It doesn't make any difference if you get blown up":* "Off the Record Meeting on Cuba," October 16, 1962, in U.S. Department of State, *Foreign Relations of the United States, 1961–1963, Volume XI, Cuban Missile Crisis and Aftermath* (Washington, D.C.: Government Printing Office, 1996), p. 61.

291 *"If we attack Cuba . . . in any way":* May and Zelikow, *Kennedy Tapes*, p. 111.

291 *"We've got the Berlin problem staring us in the face":* Ibid., p. 113.

291 *"almost as bad as the appeasement at Munich":* Ibid.

291 *"LeMay: I think that a blockade":* Ibid., p. 117.

291 *"I just agree with you":* Ibid., p. 122.

292 *"eliminate this clandestine, reckless and provocative threat":* "Text of Kennedy's Address on Moves to Meet the Soviet Build-Up in Cuba," *New York Times*, October 23, 1962.

292 *"move the world back from the abyss":* Ibid.

292 *Nearly two hundred B-47 bombers left SAC bases:* Cited in "Strategic Air Command Operations in the Cuban Crisis of 1962," Historical Study, vol. 1, no. 90, History & Research Division, Strategic Air Command, 1963 (TOP SECRET/RESTRICTED DATA/declassified), NSA, p. 49.

292 *Every day about sixty-five of the bombers circled:* Cited in ibid., p. 97.

292 *"I am addressing you for the purpose":* Quoted in ibid., p. vii.

293 *The American custodians of the Jupiters were ordered:* "The Jupiters," according to the historian Philip Nash, "continued to represent one of the gravest command-and-control problems in the Western arsenal." McNamara was so concerned about unauthorized use of the missiles that he ordered they not be fired, even in response to a Soviet attack on Italy or Turkey. See Nash, *Other Missiles of October*, pp. 125–127.

293 *"an act of aggression which pushes mankind":* "Letter from Chairman Khrushchev to President Kennedy," October 24, 1962, in *Foreign Relations of the United States, 1961–1963, Volume VI, Kennedy-Khrushchev Exchanges*, p. 170.

294 *"Your action desperate":* Quoted in Al Seckel, "Russell and the Cuban Missile Crisis," *Russell: The Journal of Bertrand Russell Studies*, vol. 4, no. 2 (Winter 1984–1985), p. 255.

294–95 *"As I left the White House . . . on that beautiful fall evening":* Robert S. McNamara, *Blundering into Disaster: Surviving the First Century of the Nuclear Age* (New York: Pantheon, 1987), p. 11.

295 *almost one hundred tactical nuclear weapons on the island:* See Fursenko and Naftali, *"One Hell of a Gamble,"* p. 188.

296 *"Absolutely not . . . the Soviet Government did raise the issue"*: Quoted in Nash, *Other Missiles of October*, p. 157.

296 *In order to deflect attention from the charge:* Nash does a superb job of describing how the Kennedy administration covered up the truth and spread the fiction that no secret deal had been made with Khrushchev. See Nash, *Other Missiles of October*, pp. 150–71.

296 *"genuine peace" with the Soviets:* "Text of Kennedy Speech to Class at American U.," *Washington Post and Times Herald*, June 11, 1963.

296 *And a hot line was finally created:* For the history and workings of the hot line, see Desmond Ball, "Improving Communications Links Between Moscow and Washington," *Journal of Peace Research*, vol. 8, no. 2 (1991), pp. 135–59; and Haraldur Þór Egilsson, "The Origins, Use and Development of Hot Line Diplomacy," *Netherlands Institute of International Relations*, Issue 85 in Discussion Papers in Diplomacy, No. 85, March 2003.

296 *"We at the embassy could only pray":* Quoted in Egilsson, "Origins, Use and Development of Hot Line," pp. 2–3.

297 *2,088 airborne alert missions . . . almost fifty thousand hours of flying time:* Cited in "Strategic Air Command Operations in the Cuban Crisis," p. 48.

297 *The case was settled out of court:* For details of the legal battle between Peter George and the creators of *Fail-Safe*, see Scherman, "Everbody Blows UP."

297 *"The whole point of the doomsday machine is lost":* The full title of the film is *Dr. Strangelove or: How I Learned to Stop Worrying and Love the Bomb*. The screenplay was written by Stanley Kubrick, Peter George, and Terry Southern. *Strangelove* was directed by Kubrick and released in 1964 by Columbia Pictures.

298 *"The probability of a mechanical failure":* Sidney Hook, *The Fail-Safe Fallacy* (New York: Stein and Day, 1963), p. 14.

298 *"the Communist determination to dominate the world":* The quote appears on the back cover of *The Fail-Safe Fallacy*.

298 *"'fail safe,' not unsafe":* Roswell L. Gilpatric, "'Strangelove'? 'Seven Days'? Not Likely," *New York Times*, May 17, 1964. A similarly reassuring article had appeared the previous year in a Sunday magazine carried by the *Los Angeles Times* and dozens of other large newspapers. See Donald Robinson, "How Safe Is Fail Safe? Are We in Danger of an Accidental War?," *This Week Magazine*, January 27, 1963.

299 *"The very existence of the lock capability":* "Cable, To General Curtis E. LeMay, From General Thomas S. Power" (SECRET/declassified), NSA, February 17, 1964.

299 *John H. Rubel—who supervised strategic weapon research and development:* Rubel went to work at the Pentagon during the Eisenhower administration and remained there for the first few years of the Kennedy administration, eventually serving as assistant secretary of defense for research and engineering. He spoke to me at length about the trouble with the Minuteman launch procedures and his criticisms of the SIOP. For a man of ninety-three, his memory is astonishing. In a recent book—*Doomsday Delayed: USAF Strategic Weapons Doctrine and SIOP-62, 1959–1962, Two Cautionary Tales* (New York: Hamilton Books, 2008)—Rubel describes his first briefing on the SIOP. He calls the experience a "descent into the deep heart of darkness, a twilight underworld governed by disciplined, meticulous, and energetically mindless groupthink aimed at wiping out half of the people living on nearly one third of the earth's surface." That feeling never entirely left him. Rubel also discussed nuclear weapon issues in an oral history for the John F. Kennedy Library. The entire transcript has been classified, and I've requested it under the Freedom of Information Act.

300 *"an accident for which a later apology":* "The Development of the SM-80 Minuteman," Robert F. Piper, DCAS Historical Office, Deputy Commander for Aerospace Systems, Air Force Systems Command, April 1962 (SECRET/RESTRICTED DATA/declassified), NSA, p. 68.

300 *"completely safe":* The quote comes from an Air Force historian's summary of the Air Force position. See ibid., p. 70.

300 *an independent panel was appointed to investigate:* The panel was headed by James C. Fletcher, who later became the head of NASA. For the Fletcher committee's work, see ibid., p. 71, and Rubel, *Doomsday Delayed*, pp. 17–21.

300 *a series of minor power surges:* The Minuteman launch switches relied on notching motors that
     rotated a single notch when the proper electrical pulse was sent. The turning of the launch keys
     transmitted a series of specific pulses—and once they were received, the notching motors rotated
     the notches, completed a circuit, and launched all the missiles. But a series of small power surges
     could mimic those pulses and activate the motors. The motors might silently rotate, one notch at a
     time, over the course of days or even months, without the launch crews knowing. And then, when
     the final notch turned, fifty missiles would suddenly take off. Rubel interview.

300 *"I was scared shitless":* The engineer was Paul Baran, later one of the inventors of packet switching.
     Quoted in Stewart Brand, "Founding Father," *Wired,* March 2001.

300 *the redesign cost about $840 million:* Cited in Ball, *Politics and Force Levels,* p. 194.

300–301 *To err on the side of safety:* See Dobbs, *One Minute to Midnight,* pp. 276–79; and "Strategic Air
         Command Operations in the Cuban Crisis," pp. 72–73.

301 *"Mr. McNamara went on to describe the possibilities":* "State-Defense Meeting on Group I, II, and
     IV Papers," p. 12.

301 *"to fire nuclear weapons":* Ibid.

301 *"whether or not it was Soviet launched":* Ibid.

301 *"every effort to contact the President must be made":* The predelegation policy from the Eisenhower
     era was largely retained. See "Memorandum from the President's Special Assistant for National
     Security Affairs (Bundy) to President Johnson," September 23, 1964 (TOP SECRET/declassified), in
     U.S. State Department, *Foreign Relations of the United States, 1964-1968, Volume X, National
     Security Policy* (Washington, D.C.: Government Printing Office, 2002), p. 158.

302 *a strategy of "Assured Destruction":* "Draft Memorandum from Secretary of Defense McNamara to
     President Johnson," December 6, 1963 (TOP SECRET/declassified), in *Foreign Relations of the United
     States, 1961–1963, Volume VIII, National Security Policy,* p. 549.

302 *"30% of their population, 50% of their industrial capacity, and 150 of their cities":* Ibid.

302 *the equivalent of 400 megatons:* See Enthoven, *How Much Is Enough,* pp. 207–10.

302 *McNamara said, "Thank God":* "Transcript, Interview with Robert McNamara, March 1986, Part
     2 of 5," WGBH Media Library and Archives.

302 *The move would improve "crisis stability":* Ibid.

303 *The new SIOP divided the "optimum mix":* For the details of SIOP-4, adopted by the Johnson ad-
     ministration in 1966 and still in effect when McNamara left office, see William Burr, "The Nixon
     Administration, the 'Horror Strategy,' and the Search for Limited Nuclear Options, 1969–1972,"
     Journal of Cold War Studies, vol. 7, no. 3 (2005), pp. 42–47.

303 *The number of nuclear weapons in the American arsenal:* At the end of the Eisenhower administra-
     tion, the United States had about 19,000 nuclear weapons. By 1967, the size of the arsenal had
     reached its peak: 31,255 weapons. When McNamara left office, the number had fallen slightly to
     29,561. See "Declassification of Certain Characteristics of the United States Nuclear Weapon
     Stockpile," U.S. Department of Energy, December 1993, and "Fact Sheet, Increasing Transpar-
     ency in the U.S. Nuclear Stockpile," U.S. Department of Defense, May 3, 2010.

303 *the number of tactical weapons had more than doubled:* In 1960 the United States deployed about
     3,000 tactical weapons in Western Europe; in 1968, about 7,000. See Robert S. Norris, William
     M. Arkin, and William Burr, "Where They Were," Bulletin of the Atomic Scientists, November/
     December 199, p. 29.

304 *A centralized command-and-control system . . . had proven disastrous:* The top-down management
     style that McNamara brought to the Vietnam War almost guaranteed an American defeat. "The
     men who designed the system and tried to run it were as bright a group of managers as has been
     produced by the defense establishment of any country at any time," the military historian Martin
     van Creveld has noted, "yet their attempts to achieve cost-effectiveness led to one of the least cost-
     effective wars known to history." McNamara's office determined not only the targets that would
     be attacked but also set the rules for when a mission would be canceled for bad weather and speci-
     fied the training level that pilots had to meet. For Van Creveld, "To study command as it operated
     in Vietnam is, indeed, almost enough to make one despair of human reason." See Martin van
     Creveld, *Command in War* (Cambridge, MA: Harvard University Press, 1985), pp. 232–60. The
     quotes can be found on page 260.

304 *"I don't object to its being called McNamara's war"*: "'McNamara's War' Tag OKd by Defense Chief," *Los Angeles Times*, April 25, 1964.

305 *support for equal rights, labor unions, birth control, and abortion:* Although in 1968 LeMay was considered an archconservative, today he'd be called an old-fasioned liberal. See Jerry M. Flint, "LeMay Supports Legal Abortions," *New York Times*, October 24, 1968; "Wallace Keeps Silent on LeMay Racial View," *Los Angeles Times*, October 24, 1968; and Jerry M. Flint, "LeMay Says He Believes in Equal Opportunity," *New York Times*, October 29, 1968.

305 *"War is* never *cost-effective":* LeMay's feelings about limited warfare are worth quoting at length. "Let me now propose some basic doctrines about war," LeMay wrote. "First, war in any propor- tion, no matter how limited, is a very serious and dangerous business. War is *never* 'cost-effective' in terms of dollars and blood. People are killed. To them war is total. You cannot tell the bereaved wives, children, and parents that today's war in Vietnam, for example, is a counterinsurgency exer- cise into which the United States is putting only a limited effort. Death is final, and drafted boys should not be asked to make this ultimate sacrifice unless the Government is behind them 100 percent. If we pull our punches how can we explain it to their loved ones? Our objectives must be clearly enough defined to warrant the casualties we are taking." Curtis E. LeMay, *America Is in Danger* (New York: Funk & Wagnalls, 1968), p. 305.

305 *"but when you get in it":* "Excerpts from Comments by Wallace and LeMay on the War and Segre- gation," *New York Times*, October 4, 1968.

305 *"We seem to have a phobia":* Ibid.

305 *jeered by protesters yelling,* "Sieg heil": Quoted in "LeMay, Supporter of Dissent, Seems Upset by Hecklers," *New York Times*, October 25, 1968.

306 *the antiwar movement was "Communist-inspired":* Quoted in Jerry M. Flint, "LeMay Fearful Com- munists Threaten American Values," *New York Times*, October 31, 1968.

An Abnormal Environment

307 *a B-52 took off from Mather Air Force Base:* For the Yuba City crash, see *Airmunitions Letter*, No. 136-11-56H, Headquarters, Ogden Air Material Area, April 19, 1961 (Secret/Restricted Data/ declassified), pp. 2–18; "Joint Nuclear Accident Coordinating Center Record of Events," (For Of- ficial Use Only/declassified), n.d.; and Maggelet and Oskins, *Broken Arrow*, pp. 173–93.

307 *"continue mission as long as you can":* Quoted in Maggelet and Oskins, *Broken Arrow*, p. 176.

308 *"a weak point in the aircraft's structure":* The report also noted that the B-52 has "a skin-loaded structure that readily disintegrates upon impact." See "Accident Environments," T. D. Brumleve, J. T. Foley, W. F. Gordon, J. C. Miller, A. R. Nord, Sandia Corporation, Livermore Laboratory, SCL-DR-69-86, January 1970 (secret/restricted data/declassified), p. 58.

308 *On Johnston Island in the central Pacific:* For the missile explosions that occurred during the test series known as Operation Dominic, see Hansen, *Swords of Armageddon, Volume IV*, pp. 382– 445; "Operation Dominic I, 1962," U.S. Atmospheric Nuclear Weapons Tests, Nuclear Test Per- sonnel Review, Defense Nuclear Agency, February 1983; Reed and Stillman, *Nuclear Express*, pp. 136–137; and Maggelet and Oskins, *Broken Arrow, Volume II*, pp. 96–98.

309 *Two thirds of the Thor missiles used in the tests:* Four of the six missile tests ended prematurely. Proj- ect 8C in the Fish Bowl series of Dominic had been carefully planned to determine the effects of a nuclear detonation on a reentry vehicle's heat shield and other components. "The experiment was not completed," a report later said with disappointment, "because after approximately 1 minute of flight the missile blew up." One of the two successful tests had unexpected results. During the Starfish Prime shot, a 1.4-megaton warhead was detonated at an altitude of about 250 miles. The electromagnetic pulse was much stronger than anticipated, damaging three satellites, disrupting radio communications across the Pacific, and causing streetlights to go out on the Hawaiian island of Oahu, about eight hundred miles away. See "Operation Dominic: Fish Bowl Series," M. J. Ru- benstein, Project Officers Report—Project 8C, Reentry Vehicle Tests, Air Force Special Weapons Center, July 3, 1963 (secret/restricted data/declassified), p. 6; "United States High-Altitude Test Experiences: A Review Emphasizing the Impact on the Environment," Herman Hoerlin, a LASL monograph, Los Alamos National Laboratory, Ocotber 1976; and "Did High-Altitude EMP

Cause the Hawaiian Streetlight Incident?," Charles Vittitoe, Electromagnetic Applications Division, Sandia National Laboratories, System Design and Assessment Notes, Note 31, June 1989.

309 *three workers at an Atomic Energy Commission base:* For details of the Medina explosion, see "Run! Three Do; Injuries Are Minor," *San Antonio Express,* November 14, 1963; "'Just Running': Panic in Streets for Few Moments," *San Antonio Light,* November 14, 1963; "Tons of TNT Explode in Weapons Plant," *Tipton* [Indiana] *Daily Tribune,* November 14, 1963; Hansen, *Swords of Armageddon, Volume VII,* p. 272; Maggelet and Oskins, *Broken Arrow, Volume II,* pp. 98–100.

310 *a B-52 encountered severe air turbulence:* For details of the Cumberland Broken Arrow, see *Airmunitions Letter,* No. 136-11-56N, Headquarters, Ogden Air Material Area, March 10, 1964 (SECRET/ RESTRICTED DATA/declassified), pp. 2–17; Dan Whetzel, "A Night to Remember," *Mountain Discoveries* (Fall/Winter, 2007); Maggelet and Oskins, *Broken Arrow,* p. 198.

310 *Another accident with a Mark 53 bomb:* For details of the Bunker Hill Broken Arrow, see "B-58 with Nuclear Device Aboard Burns; One Killed," *Anderson* [Indiana] *Herald,* December 9, 1964; "Memorial Services Held at Air Base," *Logansport* [Indiana] *Press,* December 10, 1964; "Saw Flash, Then Fire, Ordered Plane Abandoned, Pilot Recalls," *Kokomo* [Indiana] *Morning Times,* December 11, 1964; "A Review of the US Nuclear Weapon Safety Program—1945 to 1986," R. N. Brodie, Sandia National Laboratories, SAND86-2955, February 1987 (SECRET/RESTRICTED DATA/ declassified), p. 13; "Remedial Action and Final Radiological Status, 1964 B-58 Accident Site, Grissom Air Reserve Base, Bunker Hill, Indiana," Steven E. Rademacher, Air Force Institute for Environment, Safety, and Occupational Health Risk Analysis, December 2000; and Maggelet and Oskins, *Broken Arrow,* pp. 204–10. After an accident that exposed five hydrogen bombs to burning jet fuel, the Air Force told the *Kokomo Morning Times* that there had been "no danger" of a radiation hazard.

311 *a Minuteman missile site at Ellsworth Air Force Base:* See "Accidents and Incidents," Incident #2, p. 182; and "Review of the US Nuclear Weapon Safety Program," p. 14. The most detailed account can be found in Maggelet and Oskins, *Broken Arrow, Volume II,* pp. 101–9.

312 *a group of sailors were pushing an A-4E Skyhawk:* The story of this long-hidden accident has been told in detail by Jim Little, a retired chief warrant officer with a long career managing nuclear weapons for the U.S. Navy. Little watched the plane roll off the deck of the *Ticonderoga.* His account of the accident can be found in Maggelet and Oskins, *Broken Arrow, Volume II,* pp. 113–16, and in his book, *Brotherhood of Doom: Memoirs of a Navy Nuclear Weaponsman* (Bradenton, FL: Booklocker, 2008), pp. 113–14.

312 *"Brakes, brakes":* Quoted in Little, *Brotherhood of Doom,* p. 114.

312 *recently graduated from Ohio State University:* Webster had flown seventeen combat missions in Vietnam and gotten married the previous year. One of his close friends from high school, Roger Ailes, later the president of Fox News, created a scholarship fund in Webster's name. See William K. Alcorn, "Webster Scholarship to Help City Youths," *Youngstown* [Ohio] *Vindicator,* July 3, 2006.

313 *"responsibility for identifying and resolving":* President Kennedy also asked to be kept informed about "the progress being made in equipping all Mark 7 nuclear weapons assigned to ground alert aircraft with velocity sensing safety devices." He returned to the broader issue just nine days before his assassination, issuing a directive that safety rules be adopted for each weapon in the stockpile. Those rules would have to be approved by the secretary of defense—and shared, in writing, with the president of the United States. See "National Security Action Memorandum No. 51, Safety of Nuclear Weapons and Weapons Systems," May 8, 1962 (SECRET/RESTRICTED DATA/declassified), NSA; and "National Security Memorandum No. 272, Safety Rules for Nuclear Weapon Systems," November 13, 1963 (SECRET/RESTRICTED DATA/declassified).

313 *the Titanic Effect:* Donald MacKenzie mentions the "Titanic effect" in the context of software design. "The safer a system is believed to be," he suggests, "the more catastrophic the accidents to which it is subject." And as a corollary to that sort of thinking, MacKenzie argues that systems only become safer when their danger is always kept in mind. See MacKenzie's essay "Computer-Related Accidental Death," in *Knowing Machines,* pp. 185–213. The Titanic effect is discussed from pages 211 to 213.

313 *an engineer listened carefully to the sounds of a PAL:* The Sandia engineer's name was John Kane,

and in this case his lock-picking skills exceeded those of technicians at the National Security Agency. See Stevens, "Origins and Evolution of S²C," p. 71.

313 *The W-47 warhead had a far more serious problem:* I learned about the unreliability of the W-47 warhead during my interviews with Bob Peurifoy and Bill Stevens. Some of the details can be found in Hansen, *Swords of Armageddon, Volume VI*, pp. 433–41. Hansen called the W-47, without its safing tape, "an explosion in search of an accident." Sybil Francis touched on the subject briefly in "Warhead Politics: Livermore and the Competitive System of Nuclear Weapons Design," thesis (Ph.D.), Massachusetts Institute of Technology, Department of Politic Science, 1995, pp. 152–53.

314 *"almost zero confidence that the warhead would work":* Quoted in Francis, "Warhead Politics," p. 153.

314 *perhaps 75 percent or more:* Cited in Hansen, *Swords of Armageddon, Volume VI*, p. 435.

315 *a B-52 on a Chrome Dome mission:* The Palomares accident was the most widely publicized Broken Arrow of the Cold War. In addition to weeks of coverage in newspapers and magazines, the event inspired a fine book by Flora Lewis, a well-known foreign correspondent, *One of Our H-Bombs Is Missing* (New York: McGraw-Hill, 1967). Randall C. Maydew, one of the Sandia engineers who helped to find the weapon, later wrote about the search in *America's Lost H-Bomb! Palomares, Spain, 1966* (Manhattan, KS: Sunflower University Press, 1977). Barbara Moran made good use of documents obtained through the Freedom of Information Act in writing *The Day We Lost the H-Bomb: Cold War, Hot Nukes, and the Worst Nuclear Weapons Disaster in History* (New York: Ballantine Books, 2009). I relied on those works, as well as on a thorough description of the accident's aftermath—"Palomares Summary Report," Field Command, Defense Nuclear Agency, Kirtland Air Force Base, January 15, 1975—and other published sources.

316 *so poor and remote that it didn't appear on most maps:* See "Palomares Summary Report," p. 18

317 *"450 airmen with Geiger counters":* Quoted in ibid., p. 184.

317 *"unarmed nuclear armament" . . . "there is no danger to public health":* Quoted in ibid., p. 185.

317 *"SECRECY SHROUDS URGENT HUNT":* Quoted in ibid., p. 203.

317 *"MADRID POLICE DISPERSE MOB AT U.S. EMBASSY":* Quoted in ibid.

317 *"NEAR CATASTROPHE FROM U.S. BOMB":* Quoted in ibid.

317 *"There is not the slightest risk":* Quoted in "The Nuke Fluke," *Time*, March 11, 1966.

318 *"the politics of the situation":* "Palomares Summary Report," p. 50.

318 *Almost four thousand truckloads of contaminated beans:* Cited in ibid., p. 56.

318 *About thirty thousand cubic feet of contaminated soil:* According to the Defense Nuclear Agency, about 1,088 cubic yards were removed—roughly 29,376 cubic feet. Cited in ibid., p. 65.

318 *"a psychological barrier to plutonium inhalation":* Ibid., footnote, p. 51.

318 *the American ambassador brought his family:* For this and other efforts to control public opinion, see David Stiles, "A Fusion Bomb over Andalucía: U.S. Information Policy and the 1966 Palomares Incident," *Journal of Cold War Studies*, vol. 8, no. 1 (2006), pp. 49–67.

319 *who claimed to have seen a "stout man":* Quoted in "How They Found the Bomb," *Time*, May 13, 1966.

319 *"It isn't like looking for a needle":* Quoted in Lewis, *One of Our H-Bombs Is Missing*, p. 182.

319 *the first time the American people were allowed to see one:* For the proud display, see ibid., p. 234; Stiles, "Fusion Bomb over Andalucía," p. 64.

320 *"The possibility of an accidental nuclear explosion":* Quoted in Hanson W. Baldwin, "Chances of Nuclear Mishap Viewed as Infinitesimal," *New York Times*, March 27, 1966.

320 *"so remote that they can be ruled out completely":* Quoted in ibid.

320 *"But suppose some important aspect of nuclear safety":* "The Nuclear Safety Problem," T. D. Brumleve, Advanced System Research Department 5510, Sandia Corporation, Livermore Laboratory, SCL-DR-67, 1967 (SECRET/RESTRICTED DATA/declassified), p. 5.

320 *"The nation, and indeed the world, will want to know":* Ibid., p. 5.

320 *a B-52 was serving as the Thule monitor:* The Broken Arrow at Thule has received much less attention in the United States than the one at Palomares. But the Thule accident remains of interest in Denmark because the crash not only contaminated Danish soil with plutonium but also raised questions about the behavior of the Danish government. I found two declassified documents to be especially interesting. The first is "Project Crested Ice: The Thule Nuclear Accident," vol. 1, SAC

NOTES

Historical Study #113, History and Research Division, Headquarters, Strategic Air Command, April 23, 1969 (SECRET/RESTRICTED DATA/declassified), NSA. The other is "Project Crested Ice," a special edition of *USAF Nuclear Safety* magazine that appeared in 1970. The latter has many photographs that show the challenge of decontaminating a large area in the Arctic. A number of recent investigations by Danish authors were also useful: "The Marshal's Baton: There Is No Bomb, There Was No Bomb, They Were Not Looking for a Bomb," Svend Aage Christensen, Danish Institute for International Studies, DIIS Report, 2009, No. 18., 2009; and Thorsten Borring Olesen, "Tango for Thule: The Dilemmas and Limits of the 'Neither Confirm Nor Deny' Doctrine in Danish-American Relations, 1957–1968," *Journal of Cold War Studies*, vol. 13, no. 2 (Spring 2011), pp. 116–47. And I learned much from the documents in Maggelet and Oskins, *Broken Arrow, Volume II*, pp. 125–50.

320 *three cloth-covered, foam-rubber cushions:* For details of the accident and the rescue, see "Crested Ice: The Thule Nuclear Accident," pp. 5–8; "The Flight of Hobo 28," in *USAF NUCLEAR SAFETY*, special edition, vol. 65 (part 2), no. 1 (JAN/FEB/MAR 1970), pp. 2–4; Neil Sheehan, "Pilot Says Fire Forced Crew to Quit B-52 in Arctic," *New York Times*, January 28, 1968; and Alfred J. D'Amario, *Hangar Flying* (Bloomington, IN: Author House, 2008), pp. 233–54. D'Amario served as a copilot on the flight, and he vividly describes what it was like to bail out of a burning B-52 over the Arctic.

321 *about 428 degrees Fahrenheit:* Cited in "Crested Ice: The Thule Nuclear Accident," p. 7.

321 *temperature . . . was -23 degrees Fahrenheit:* Cited in G. S. Dresser, "Host Base Support," in *USAF Nuclear Safety*, p. 25.

321 *windchill made it feel like -44:* The wind was blowing at 9 knots (10.3 miles per hour); the temperature was –23 degrees Fahrenheit; and according to a windchill chart compiled by the National Weather Service, that means the windchill was roughly –44 degrees Fahrenheit. See "Host Base Support," p. 25.

321 *SAC headquarters was notified, for the first time, about the fire:* Ibid., p. 25.

322 *uncovered skin could become frostbitten within two:* Ibid.

322 *But he later worked as a postmaster in Maine:* See Keith Edwards, "Sons Recall Father's Story of Survival in Greenland after SAC Bomber Crash," *Kennebec Journal*, March 17, 2010.

323 *The radioactive waste from Thule filled 147 freight cars:* Cited in Leonard J. Otten, "Removal of Debris from Thule," in *USAF Nuclear Safety*, p. 90.

324 *claims that an entire hydrogen bomb had been lost:* Those claims are convincingly refuted by Christensen "The Marshal's Baton. There Is No Bomb, There was No Bomb, They were Not Looking for a Bomb."

324 *The B-52 . . . had been on a "training flight":* Quoted in Thomas O'Toole, "4 H-Bombs Lost as B-52 Crashes," *Washington Post and Times Herald*, January 23, 1968.

324 *A handful of people within the Danish government:* See Olesen, "Tango for Thule," pp. 123–31.

324 *stored in secret underground bunkers at Thule as early as 1955:* In a recent article for the base newsletter—the *Thule Times*, published by the Air Force Space Command—a retired lieutenant colonel, Ted A. Morris, described a trip to Greenland in May 1955. Morris and his crew flew there in a B-36 bomber, landed, and practiced the loading of a "live war reserve Mk 17" hydrogen bomb that had been stored at the base. The practice of flying to Thule without nuclear weapons and picking them up there seems to have been routine. "How about all those underground ammo bunkers?," Adams wrote. "Maybe you thought they were there for the Greenlanders to use instead of igloos." See Ted A. Adams, "Strategic Air Command at the Top of the World," *Thule Times*, November 1, 2001.

324 *antiaircraft missiles with atomic warheads were later placed at Thule:* See Norris, Arkin, and Burr, "Where They Were," p. 32.

325 *Walske, was concerned about the risks of nuclear accidents:* Bill Stevens spoke to me about Walske's interest in weapon safety. At the time, Walske also served as the head of the Military Liaison Committee to the Atomic Energy Commission. See Stevens, "Origins and Evolution of S²C," p. 85.

325 *range from one in a million to one in twenty thousand:* Stevens interview.

325 *"probability of a premature nuclear detonation":* See "Standards for Warhead and Bomb Premature Probability MC Paragraphs," in Appendix G, Ibid., p. 216.

325 *"normal storage and operational environments":* Ibid.

326 *"the adoption of the attached standards":* "Letter, To Brigadier Military Applications, U.S. Atomic Energy Commission, From Carl Walske, Chairman of the Military Liaison Committee to the U.S. Atomic Energy Commission, 14 March 1968," in Appendix G, ibid., p. 215.

326 *the test of an atomic cannon:* The weapon, nicknamed "Atomic Annie," was fired as the Grable shot in the UPSHOT-KNOTHOLE nuclear tests during the spring of 1953.

326 *trucks, tanks, railroad cars:* For the animals and inanimate objects subjected to the detonation of the Grable atomic artillery shell, see "Shots Encore to Climax: The Final Four Tests of the UPSHOT-KNOTHOLE Series, 8 May–4 June 1953," United States Atmospheric Nuclear Weapons Tests, Nuclear Test Personnel Review, Defense Nuclear Agency, DNA 6018F, January 15, 1982, pp. 127–58; and "Military and Civil Defense Nuclear Weapons Effects Projects Conducted at the Nevada Test Site: 1951–1958," Barbara Killian, Technical Report, Defense Threat Reduction Agency, May 2011. Details of the Grable shot are mentioned throughout the latter report.

326 *more than three thousand soldiers, including Bill Stevens:* For the people involved in the test, see "Shots Encore to Climax," pp. 120–27.

327 *The official list of nuclear accidents:* The Pentagon's "official" list of Broken Arrows now mentions thirty-two accidents, from 1950 until 1980. According to the Department of Defense, an "accident involving nuclear weapons" is "an unexpected event" that results in any of the following: "Accidental or unauthorized launching, firing, or use . . . of a nuclear-capable weapon system" that could lead to the outbreak of war; a nuclear detonation; "non-nuclear detonation or burning of a nuclear weapon or radioactive weapon component"; radioactive contamination; "seizure, theft, or loss of a nuclear weapon," including the jettison of a bomb; "public hazard, actual, or implied." But at least one third of the accidents on the Pentagon's list involved nuclear weapons that were not fully assembled and could not produce a nuclear yield. Far more dangerous, yet less dramatic, accidents—like the unloading of Mark 7 bombs fully armed—have been omitted from the list. Countless mundane accidents posed a grave risk to the public, both actual and implied. For the official list, see "Narrative Summaries of Accidents Involving U.S. Nuclear Weapons, 1950–1980," U.S. Department of Defense, (n.d.).

327 *at least 1,200 nuclear weapons had been involved:* Bill Stevens likes to err on the conservative side, relying on the Pentagon's definition of an "accident." One Sandia weapon report used the term more broadly, including events "which may have safety significance." For the number of these events, see Brumleve, "Accident Environments," p. 154.

328 *"During loading of a Mk 25 Mod O WR Warhead":* "Accidents and Incidents," Incident #8, p. 29.

328 *"A C-124 Aircraft carrying eight Mk 28 War reserve Warheads":* Ibid., Incident #17, p. 63.

328 *Twenty-three weapons had been directly exposed to fires:* Cited in "Accident Environments," p. 69.

328 *blinding white flash:* At Sandia the acronym BWF was used as a shorthand for that phrase, and it was something that nobody there cared to see.

328 *he'd watched a bent pin nearly detonate an atomic bomb:* Stan Spray was not the source of this information.

329 *The Navy tested many of its weapons:* Sandia thought that these "Admiral's Tests" were unnecessary; when electromagnetic radiation triggered the rocket motors of a missile aboard an aircraft carrier, the lab took a different view. See Stevens, "Origins and Evolution of S^2C," pp. 58–60.

329 *Lightning had struck a fence at a Mace medium-range missile complex:* See "Accidents and Incidents," Incident #2, p. 122.

329 *Four Jupiter missiles in Italy had also been hit by lightning:* See ibid, Accident #2, pp. 51–52; Incident #39, p. 69; and Incident #41, pp. 86–87.

329 *Stan Spray's group ruthlessly burned, scorched, baked:* My account of the Nuclear Safety Department's work is based on interviews with Stevens, Peurifoy, and other Sandia engineers familiar with its investigations. Spray has contributed to a couple of papers about the safety issues that were explored: "The Unique Signal Concept for Detonation Safety in Nuclear Weapons, UC-706," Stanley D. Spray, J. A. Cooper, System Studies Department, Sandia National Laboratories, SAND91-1269, 1993; and "History of U.S. Nuclear Weapon Safety Assessment: The Early

Years," Stanley D. Spray, Systems Studies Department, Sandia National Laboratories, SAND96-1099C, Version E, May 5, 1996.

331   a *"supersafe bomb"*: See "Project Crescent: A Study of Salient Features for an Airborne Alert (Supersafe) Bomb," Final Report, D. E. McGovern, Exploratory Systems Department I, Sandia Laboratories, SC-WD-70-879, April 1971 (SECRET/RESTRICTED DATA/declassified).

331   *"under any conceivable set of accident conditions"*: "Project Crescent," p. 7.

331   *mistakenly dropped from an altitude of forty thousand feet*: Peurifoy interview.

331   *"less than enthusiastic about requiring more safety"*: See "Memo, Conceptual Study of Super-Safety," Colonel Richard H. Parker, United States Air Force, Assistant Director for Research and Development, Division of Military Application, May 14, 1968, in "Project Crescent," p. 101.

332   *"We are living on borrowed time"*: Peurifoy interview.

333   *Peurifoy and Fowler went to Washington*: See Stevens, "Origins and Evolution of S²C," pp. 115–16.

333   *The "Fowler Letter"*: "To Major General Ernest Graves, Assistant General Manager for Military Application, Division of Military Application, U.S. Atomic Energy Commission, From G. A. Fowler, Vice President, Systems, Sandia Laboratories, Subject: Safety of Aircraft Delivered Nuclear Weapons Now in Stockpile," November 15, 1974 (SECRET/RESTRICTED DATA/declassified).

PART FIVE: DAMASCUS

Balanced and Unbalanced

337   *James L. "Skip" Rutherford III was working*: Interview with Skip Rutherford.

337   *"It's about the Titan missiles"*: Ibid.

338   *The missiles were old, the airmen said*: I spoke to one of the airmen, who preferred to remain anonymous, and he confirmed Rutherford's account.

338   *Pryor was disturbed by the information*: Interview with David H. Pryor.

338   *other members of Congress were concerned*: Dan Glickman spoke to me about his efforts to retire the Titan II. I'm glad that he saved a copy of the Damascus accident report and donated it to Wichita State University, along with his other congressional papers.

338   *At Launch Complex 533-7, about an hour southeast of Wichita*: My description of the accident in Rock, Kansas, is based principally on "Report of Missile Accident Investigation: Major Missile Accident, Titan II Complex 533-7, Assigned to 381st Strategic Missile Wing, McConnell Air Force Base, Kansas," conducted at McConnell Air Force Base, Kansas, September 22–October 10, 1978. Albert A. Kamas, a Wichita attorney who represented a number of people hurt in the accident, not only shared his memory of the event but also sent me documents, newspaper clippings, and videotaped local news accounts of it. Julie Charlip, who covered the story for the *Wichita Eagle*, graciously shared her reporting on it. And Colonel Ben G. Scallorn, who headed the accident investigation, discussed its findings with me.

339   *Malinger had never been inside a Titan II silo before*: See David Goodwin, "Victim of AF Missile Accident Wanted Only to Be a Mechanic," *Wichita Eagle*, January 18, 1979.

339   *"Oh my God, the poppet"*: "Major Missile Accident, Titan II Complex 533-7," affidavit of Charles B. Frost, Second Lieutenant, Tab U-4, page 3.

340   *"What was the poppet"*: Ibid.

340   *"Get out of here, let's get out"*: Quoted in ibid.

340   *"Where are you?"*: Ibid.

340   *"Come back to the control center"*: Ibid.

340   *"I can't see"*: Quoted in ibid., affidavit of Richard I. Bacon, Jr., Second Lieutenant, Tab U-7.

340   *"Hey, I smell Clorox"*: Quoted in ibid., Frost affidavit, Tab U-4, p. 3.

341   *quickly registered one to three parts per million*: Cited in ibid., p. 5.

342   *"My God, help us, help us, we need help"*: Quoted in ibid., p. 4.

342   *"Hey, door eight is locked"*: Ibid.

342   *"Hey, you guys, get out of here"*: Ibid., p. 5.

342   *"Come help me"*: Quoted in ibid.

342–43   *"This is three-seven. . . . The locks are on the safe"*: Ibid.

343   *"Where's the dep, where's the dep?"*: Quoted in ibid.

343   *"We'll get him later"*: Ibid.

343   *"My God, please help me"*: Quoted in ibid., Affidavit of Keith E. Matthews, First Lieutenant, Tab U-3, p. 4.

344   *"Get them under the fire hydrant"*: Ibid., p. 5.

344   *Jackson . . . climbed the ladder all the way to the bottom in his RFHCO:* It was clearly possible to wear a RFHCO and enter the escape hatch. "Airman Jackson changed helmets," the report said, "and went to the bottom of the air intake shaft (escape hatch) but could not find the entry to the control center." Jackson had never been in it before and climbed down until reaching a pool of water at the very bottom. The darkness and the cloud of oxidizer—not the size of the shaft or the escape hatch—prevented him from getting into the control center. The quote is from page 8 of the report. See also the affidavit of John C. Mock, Jr., technical sergeant, Tab U-25, pp. 1–2. Mock was a PTS team chief and supervisor, but he'd never gone down the escape hatch, either.

345   *Someone hadn't put a filter inside the oxidizer line:* See "Major Missile Accident, Titan II Complex 533-7," p. 10.

345   *someone may have deliberately omitted the filter:* According to Jeff Kennedy, oxidizer would flow more quickly without the filter, and the job could be completed in less time. Some PTS crews were willing to break the rules. But if you wanted to cut corners and not get caught, you also had to remove the O-ring. Otherwise it might clog the line and cause a leak—like it did during the Rock, Kansas, accident. Kennedy interview. See also Julie Charlip, "Missile Workers a Special Breed," *Wichita Eagle,* May 31, 1981.

346   *The Air Force recommended . . . that black vinyl electrical tape be used:* After the accident, the Air Force assembled a team of experts from Boeing, NASA, Martin-Marietta, and other aerospace groups to examine the RFHCOs involved in the Rock, Kansas, accident. They found, among other things, that the suits were vulnerable to leakage at the "glove-cuff interface," especially when a forceful spray of liquid was applied there. Sealing the interface with vinyl electrical tape, the group decided, would be a possible, "very short term solution." See "Class A Ground Launch Missile Mishap Progress Report No. 61," Eighth Air Force Accident Investigation Board, McConnell Air Force Base, September 24, 1978; and Julie Charlip, "Missile Suit Flawed, Says AF Report," *Wichita Eagle,* February 20, 1979.

346   *Carl Malinger had a stroke, went into a coma:* See Goodwin, "Victim of AF Missile Accident."

346   *his mother later felt enormous anger at the Air Force:* Ibid.

346   *failed to "comply with [Technical Order] 21M-LGM25C-2-12":* "Major Missile Accident, Titan II Complex 533-7," p. 11.

346   *"To err is human, . . . to forgive is not SAC policy":* Quoted in Moody, *Building a Strategic Air Force,* p. 469.

346   *Its warhead was more than seven times more powerful:* The single W-56 warhead on the Minuteman II had a yield of about 1.2 megatons. The W-62 warheads carried by Minuteman III missiles at the time had a yield of about 170 kilotons. Each Minuteman III had three of them, for a combined yield of slightly more than half a megaton. The 9-megaton warhead atop the Titan II was far more powerful.

346–47   *the fifty-four Titan IIs represented roughly one third of their total explosive force:* Cited in Walter Pincus, "Aging Titan II Was Time Bomb Ready to Go Off," *Washington Post,* September 20, 1980.

347   *one of Rutherford's confidential sources later told him:* Rutherford interview. See also Pincus, "Aging Titan II Was Time Bomb."

347   *a siren "might cause people to leave areas of safety":* "Letter, From Colonel Richard D. Osborn, Chief Systems Liaison Division, Office of Legislative Liaison, To Senator David Pryor," November 7, 1979, David H. Pryor Papers, University of Arkansas, Fayetteville.

347 *Colonel Richard D. Osborn told Pryor:* Ibid. The sirens could prove especially dangerous, Osborn argued, "during periods of darkness."

347 *one half to two thirds of the Air Force's F-15 fighters were grounded:* The Tactical Air Command considered a plane "fully mission capable" if it could be flown with one day of preparation. In 1978 about 35 percent of TAC's F-15 fighters were fully mission capable; the proportion was about 56 percent in 1980. Cited in Marshall L. Michel III, "The Revolt of the Majors: How the Air Force Changed After Vietnam," dissertation submitted to Auburn University, Auburn, Alabama, December 15, 2006, pp. 290–91.

347 *The Strategic Air Command had lost more than half of its personnel:* In 1961, SAC had 280,582 personnel; by 1978, it had 123,042. The 1961 figure is cited in Polmar, *Strategic Air Command,* p. 72. The 1977 figure comes from Alwyn Lloyd, *A Cold War Legacy, 1946–1992: A Tribute to Strategic Air Command* (Missoula, MT: Pictorial Histories Publishing Co., 1999), p. 516.

347 *"bomber generals" who'd risen through the ranks at SAC:* For the cultural battle within the Air Force, see Mike Worden, *Rise of the Fighter Generals: The Problem of Air Force Leadership, 1945–1982* (Maxwell Air Force Base, AL: Air University Press, 1998).

348 *the inflexible, "parent-child relationship":* Tom Clancy and Chuck Horner, *Every Man a Tiger* (New York: G. P. Putnam's Sons, 1999), p. 96.

348 *"I didn't hate them because they were dumb":* Ibid., p. 86.

348 *"never again be a part of something so insane and foolish":* Ibid., p. 96.

348 *illegal drug use soared:* Decades later, it seems hard to believe how widely the drug culture had spread throughout the American military. Between 1976 and 1981, the Department of Defense rarely performed mandatory drug tests. As a result, a great many servicemen were often high while in uniform. And their access to military equipment provided some unusual opportunities. Operating out of Travis, Langley, and Seymour Johnson air bases, active and retired military personnel imported perhaps $100 million worth of pure heroin into the United States during the mid-1970s. When their drug operation was broken up in 1976, a DEA agent called it "one of the largest heroin smuggling operations in the world." See "U.S. Breaks $100 Million Heroin Ring; Charges GI Group Used Air Bases, Crew," *Los Angeles Times,* March 26, 1976.

348 *about 27 percent of all military personnel were using illegal drugs:* Cited in Marvin R. Burt, "Prevalence and Consequences of Drug Abuse Among U.S. Military Personnel: 1980," *American Journal of Drug and Alcohol Abuse,* vol. 8, no. 4 (1981–2), p. 425.

349 *the Marines had the highest rate of drug use:* Almost half of the young enlisted personnel in the Marines had smoked pot in the previous month. See ibid., p. 428.

349 *About 32 percent of Navy personnel used marijuana:* Cited in ibid., p. 425.

349 *the proportion of Army personnel was about 28 percent:* Cited in ibid.

349 *The Air Force had the lowest rate:* Cited in ibid.

349 *Random urine tests of more than two thousand sailors:* The survey was conducted in December 1980. Cited in "Navy Is Toughening Enforcement Efforts Against Drug Abuse," *New York Times,* July 10, 1981.

349 *Meyer told the* Milwaukee Journal: See "Ex-GI Says He Used Hash at German Base," *European Stars and Stripes,* December 18, 1974.

349 *one out of every twelve . . . was smoking hashish every day:* Cited in "Nuclear Base Men 'Used Hash on Duty,'" *Miami News,* December 17, 1974.

349 *"You get to know what you can handle":* Quoted in "Ex-GI Says He Used Hash."

349 *thirty-five members of an Army unit . . . using and selling marijuana and LSD:* See Flora Lewis, "Men Who Handle Nuclear Weapons Also Using Drugs," *Boston Globe,* September 6, 1971.

349 *Nineteen members of an Army detachment were arrested on pot charges:* See "GI's at Nuclear Base Face Pot Charges," *Los Angeles Times,* October 4, 1972.

349–50 *Three enlisted men at a Nike Hercules base in San Rafael:* See "3 Atom Guards Called Unstable; Major Suspended," *New York Times,* August 18, 1969; and "Unstable Atom Guards Probed," *Boston Globe,* August 18, 1969.

350 *"people from the Haight-Ashbury":* Quoted in "Unstable Atom Guards."

350 *More than one fourth of the crew on the USS* Nathan Hale: Cited in "Men Who Handle Nuclear Weapons."

350   *A former crew member of the* Nathan Hale *told a reporter:* See ibid. The crew member of another ballistic missile submarine thought that smoking marijuana while at sea was too risky, because of the strong aroma. The tight quarters of the sub inspired an alternative. "I do uppers most of the time, but as a special treat, like when I'm on watch, I'll do a little mescaline," the crew member said. Quoted in Duncan Campbell, *The Unsinkable Aircraft Carrier: American Military Power in Britain* (London: Michael Joseph, 1984), p. 224.

350   *The Polaris base at Holy Loch, Scotland:* See G. G. Giarchi, *Between McAlpine and Polaris* (London: Routledge & Kegan Paul, 1984), p. 197.

350   *Nine crew members of the USS* Casimir Pulaski: See "Pot Smoking Sailors Go Home," *Ocala* [Florida] *Star Banner,* January 24, 1977.

350   *a local nickname: the USS* Cannabis: See Andrew McCallum, "Cowal Caught Between Polaris Sailors and McAlpine's Fusiliers," *Glasgow Herald,* April 26, 1984.

350   *"a hippie type pad with a picture of Ho Chi Minh":* Quoted in Lewis, "Men Who Handle Nuclear Weapons."

350   *151 of the 225 security police officers were busted:* See Clancy and Horner, *Every Man a Tiger,* p. 135.

350   *Marijuana was discovered in one of the underground control centers of a Minuteman missile squadron:* See Bill Prochnau, "With the Bomb, There Is No Answer," *Washington Post,* May 1, 1982. According to Prochnau, the arrest occurred in the late 1970s.

350   *It was also found in the control center of a Titan II launch complex:* See "Marijuana Discovery Leads to Missile Base Suspensions," *New York Times,* July 14, 1977; and "15 Suspended After Marijuana Is Found in Titan Silo," *Los Angeles Times,* July 15, 1977.

351   *roughly 114,000 people . . . cleared to work with nuclear weapons:* Cited in Herbert L. Abrams, "Sources of Instability in the Handling of Nuclear Weapons," in Frederic Solomon and Robert Q. Marston, eds., *The Medical Implications of Nuclear War* (Washington, D.C.: National Academy Press, 1986), p. 513.

351   *1.5 percent lost that clearance because of drug abuse:* Of the 114,000 people certified that year under the Personnel Reliability Program, 1,728 lost their certification because of drug abuse—roughly 1.5 percent. See ibid., p. 514.

351   *Colonel John Moser had supervised a major drug bust:* Moser interview.

351   *More than 230 airmen were arrested for using and selling:* See "Drug Probe at Whiteman Air Base," *St. Joseph Missouri News Press,* September 9, 1979; and "Enlisted Airmen Suspended," *Hutchinson* [Kansas] *News,* November 21, 1980.

351   *Marijuana had been found in the control center at a Titan II complex:* Moser interview.

351   *"inaccurate and unreliable":* "Memorandum from the President's Assistant for National Security Affairs (Kissinger) to President Nixon," August 18, 1970, in United States State Department, *Foreign Relations of the United States, 1969–1976, Volume XXXIV: National Security Policy, 1969–1972* (Washington, D.C.: Government Printing Office, 2011), p. 555.

351   *a weapon system . . . "which the Pentagon had been wanting to scrap":* Henry A. Kissinger, *White House Years* (New York: Simon & Schuster, 1979), p. 1221.

351   *Kissinger had offered a deal to the Soviet Union:* See Pincus "Aging Titan II Was Time Bomb."

352   *"You Americans will never be able to do this to us again":* Quoted in Trachtenberg, *History & Strategy,* p. 257.

352   *increased the number of its long-range, land-based missiles from about 56 to more than 1,500:* See Zaloga, *Kremlin's Nuclear Sword,* p. 241.

352   *Its arsenal of submarine-based missiles rose from about 72 to almost 500:* See ibid., p. 244.

352   *a network of underground bunkers:* For a description of the bunker system, see *Soviet Military Power: An Assessment of the Threat* (Washington, D.C.: Government Printing Office, 1988), pp. 59–62.

353   *Kissinger was astonished by his first formal briefing on the SIOP:* See Burr, "'Horror Strategy,'" pp. 38–52. For the strategic thinking of Nixon and Kissinger, I relied largely on Burr's fine article and on Terry Terriff's *The Nixon Administration and the Making of U.S. Nuclear Strategy* (Ithaca: Cornell University Press, 1995).

353   *The smallest attack option . . . almost two thousand weapons:* Cited in "U.S. Strategic Objectives and

Force Posture Executive Summary," National Security Council, Defense Program Review Committee, January 3, 1972 (TOP SECRET/declassified), NSA, p. 29.

353 · *the largest with more than three thousand:* Cited in ibid., p. 28.

353 *a "horror strategy":* Quoted in Burr, "'Horror Strategy,'" p. 63.

353 *"how one rationally could make a decision":* Kissinger was wondering how the Soviet Union could launch such an attack on the United States; but his doubts about the sanity of such a move applied equally to the American war plans of the time. "To have the only option that of killing 80 million people," he said at another meeting, "is the height of immorality." For the first quote, see "Review of U.S. Strategic Posture," NSC Review Group Meeting, May 29, 1969 (TOP SECRET/declassified), NSA, p. 12. For the second, see "Memorandum for Mr. Kissinger, Subject, Minutes of the Verification Panel Meeting Held August 9, 1973," August 15, 1973 (TOP SECRET /SENSITIVE/CODE WORD/declassified), NSA, p. 8.

353 *It was called QUICK COUNT:* For information about the computer model, see N. D. Cohen, "The Quick Count System: A User's Manual," RAND Corporation, RM-4006-PR, April 1964. I learned about Quick Count from another report, one that was "designed to be of use to those who have only a rudimentary knowledge of targeting and the effects of nuclear weapons but who need a quick means of computing civil damage to Western Europe." See "Aggregate Nuclear Damage Assessment Techniques Applied to Western Europe," H. Avrech and D. C. McGarvey, RAND Corporation, Memorandum RM-4466-ISA, Prepared for the Office of the Assistant Secretary of Defense/International Security Affairs, June 1965 (FOR OFFICIAL USE ONLY/declassified). Between pages 19 and 23, you will find a guide to potential blast mortalities in the twenty-four largest cities in Western Europe, derived using Quick Count. The table listing the likely "Incremental Mortalities," "Weapon Order," and "Cumulative Mortalities" is a good example of calm, efficient, bureaucratic madness.

354 *the "obstacle course to recovery":* "Recovery from Nuclear Attack, and Research and Action Programs to Enhance Recovery Prospects," Jack C. Greene, Robert W. Stokely, and John K. Christian, International Center for Emergency Preparedness, for Federal Emergency Management Agency, December 1979. The chart outlining the postattack obstacle course appears on page 7.

354 *"No weight of nuclear attack which is at all probable":* Ibid., pp. 22–23.

354 *NATO nuclear policy "insists on our destruction":* See "Minutes of the Verification Panel Meeting," p. 2.

355 *"I must not be—and my successors must not be":* Quoted in Terriff, *Nixon and the Making of U.S. Nuclear Strategy*, p. 76.

355 *General Bruce K. Holloway . . . deliberately hid "certain aspects of the SIOP":* Quoted in Burr, "'Horror Strategy,'" p. 62.

355 *"with a high degree of confidence":* Another top secret report found that, before the Soviet missiles hit, "it is possible that no President could be sure, with the present warning configuration, that an attack was in progress or that a retaliation was justified." The first statement is quoted in Wainstain, et al., "Evolution of U.S. Strategic Command and Control," p. 424; the second, in ibid., p. 408.

355 *The World Wide Military Command and Control System had grown to encompass:* Cited in "The Worldwide Military Command and Control System: A Historical Perspective (1960–1977)," Historical Division, Joint Secretariat, Joint Chiefs of Staff, September 1980 (SECRET/declassified), NSA, p. 121.

355–56 *The National Emergency Airborne Command Post . . . did not have a computer:* See "Countervailing Strategy Demands Revision of Strategic Forces Acquisition Plans," Comptroller General of the United States, MASAD-81-355, August 1981, pp. 24–25.

356 *the entire command-and-control system could be shut down:* See "Strategic Command, Control, and Communications: Alternative Approaches for Modernization," Congress of the United States, Congressional Budget Office, October 1981, pp. 15–16; and May, et al., "History of the Strategic Arms Competition," Part 2, pp. 605–6.

356 *The system had already proven unreliable:* For the growing problems with the WWMCCS, see "Worldwide Military Command and Control System: Historical Perspective," pp. 93–112; and the chapter entitled "Three WWMCCS Failures," in David Pearson, *The World Wide Military Com-*

mand and Control System: Evolution and Effectiveness (Maxwell Air Force Base, AL: Air University Press, 2000), pp. 71–92.

356 *"A more accurate appraisal"*: Quoted in Wainstein, et al., "Evolution of U.S. Strategic Command and Control," p. 432.

356 *"confused and frightened men making decisions"*: May et al., "History of the Strategic Arms Competition, Part 2, p. 607.

358 *Nixon tried to end the Vietnam War by threatening the use of nuclear weapons:* The details of this risky and unsuccessful plan can be found in Scott D. Sagan and J. Suri, "The Madman Nuclear Alert," *International Security*, vol. 27, no. 4 (2003), pp. 150–83.

358 *"I call it the Madman Theory, Bob"*: Quoted in ibid., p. 156.

358 *nuclear weapons were once again utilized as a diplomatic tool:* For the DEFCON 3 alert in 1973, see Scott D. Sagan, "Nuclear Alerts and Crisis Management," *International Security*, vol. 9, no. 4 (Spring 1985), pp. 122–31.

359 *the administration's bold diplomacy:* The DEFCON 3 alert was part of a complex strategy aimed not only at the Soviet Union but also at the leadership of Egypt and Israel. Kissinger was pleased by the outcome, noting in his memoirs that "we had emerged as the pivotal factor in the diplomacy." See Henry A. Kissinger, *Years of Upheaval* (New York: Simon & Schuster, 1982), p. 612.

359 *"What seems 'balanced' and 'safe' in a crisis"*: Quoted in Sagan, "Alerts and Crisis Management," p. 124.

359 *He argued against the adoption of a launch-on-warning policy:* Iklé's opposition to launching missiles quickly was part of a larger critique of American strategic policy. See Fred Charles Iklé, "Can Nuclear Deterrence Last Out the Century?," *Foreign Affairs*, January 1973, pp. 267–85.

359 *"Launching the ICBM force on attack assessment"*: "The U.S. ICBM Force: Current Issues and Future Options," C. H. Builder, D. C. Kephart, and A. Laupa, a report prepared for United States Air Force Project RAND, R-1754-PR, October 1975 (SECRET/FORMERLY RESTRICTED DATA/declassified), NSA, p. 81.

359 *"accident-prone"*: See "Minutes, National Security Council Meeting, Subject, SALT (and Angola), December 22, 1975" (TOP SECRET/SENSITIVE/declassified), NSA, p. 9.

359 *"the Soviets must never be able to calculate"*: Ibid., p. 9.

359 *"It is not to our disadvantage"*: Ibid.

359 *a military aide carrying the "football"*: The contents of the president's football were described in Bill Gulley, with Mary Ellen Reese, *Breaking Cover: The Former Director of the White House Military Office Reveals the Shocking Abuse of Resources and Power That Has Been the Custom in the Last Four Administrations* (New York: Simon & Schuster, 1980). Despite its lurid subtitle, the book probably offers the most accurate description of the football at the time.

360 *"any emergency order coming from the president"*: See Carroll, *House of War,* p. 354–56. The quote is on page 355. For concerns about Nixon's finger on the button, see also Janne E. Nolan's fine book, *Guardians of the Arsenal: The Politics of Nuclear Strategy* (New York: New Republic Book, 1989), pp. 122–23. A number of the Joint Chiefs thought Schlesinger's remark was a warning that Nixon might attempt a coup d'état. See Mark Perry, *Four Stars: The Inside Story of the Forty-Year Battle Between the Joint Chiefs of Staff and America's Civilian Leaders* (Boston: Houghton Mifflin, 1989), pp. 257–59.

The Wrong Tape

361 *General William E. Odom, attended briefings on the SIOP:* For his effort to change America's nuclear plans, see William E. Odom, "The Origins and Design of Presidential Decision-59: A Memoir," in Sokolski, *Getting Mad*, pp. 175–96.

361 *"Limited Nuclear Options" and "Regional Nuclear Options"*: Ibid., pp. 176–77.

361 *"At times I simply could not believe"*: Ibid., pp. 180, 183.

362 *"absurd and irresponsible"*: Ibid., p. 194.

362 *"the height of folly"*: Ibid.

362 *The SIOP now called for the Soviet Union to be hit with about ten thousand nuclear weapons:* See "Retaliatory Issues for the U.S. Strategic Nuclear Forces," Congress of the United States, Congressional Budget Office, June 1978, p. 6.

362 *"Things would just cease in their world":* Sokolski, *Getting Mad,* p. 180.

362 *Carter had met with the Joint Chiefs of Staff and asked:* See Carroll, *House of War,* pp. 362–64, and Thomas Powers, "Choosing a Strategy for World War III, *Atlantic Monthly,* November 1982.

362 *He thought that one or two hundred missiles:* Right after taking office, President Carter asked Secretary of Defense Harold Brown to prepare a study of what would happen if the United States and the Soviet Union both possessed only 200 to 250 strategic missiles. The study addressed but failed to resolve one of the central questions of nuclear deterrence: How many weapons are enough? "Some have argued that the capability to destroy a single major city—such as Moscow or New York—would be sufficient to deter a rational leader," the study said. "Others argue that a capability for assured destruction of 80 percent or more of the economic and industrial targets of adversaries is necessary and critical." See Brian J. Auten, *Carter's Conversion: The Hardening of American Defense Policy* (Columbia, MO: University of Missouri Press, 2008), p. 146; and "Memorandum for the President, Subject, Implications of Major Reductions in Strategic Nuclear Forces, From Harold Brown," January 28, 1977 (SECRET/declassified), NSA, p. 2.

362 *"the elimination of all nuclear weapons from this Earth":* Carter had also called for the abolition of nuclear weapons in December 1974, when announcing his candidacy for president. See Auten, *Carter's Conversion,* p. 95; and "Text of Inauguration Address," *Los Angeles Times,* January 21, 1977.

363 *"Why the Soviet Union Thinks It Could Fight and Win":* Richard Pipes, "Why the Soviet Union Thinks It Could Fight and Win," *Commentary,* July 1977, pp. 212–34.

364 *To achieve a 95 percent certainty of wiping them out:* President Kennedy's former science adviser, Jerome Wiesner, outlined how difficult it would be for the Soviet Union to win a nuclear war against the United States. "Even after a surprise attack," Wiesner observed, *"U.S. strength would actually be slightly greater than the Soviet Union's."* Indeed, if all the land-based missiles in the United States were destroyed, its submarine-based missiles could still hit the Soviet Union with 3,500 equivalent megatons—almost ten times the explosive force that the Kennedy administration had once thought sufficient to annihilate Soviet society. For these calculations, see Jerome Wiesner, "Russian and American Capabilities," *Atlantic Monthly,* July 1982.

364 *somewhere between two and twenty million Americans:* According to a study conducted in 1979 for the Senate Committee on Foreign Relations, a Soviet attack on missile silos and submarine bases in the United States would kill between two and twenty million people within a month. The wide range of potential fatalities was due to the unpredictability of fallout patterns, which would be largely determined by the wind, rain, and other weather conditions at the time of the attack. See "A Counterforce Attack Against the United States," in "The Effects of Nuclear War," Office of Technology Assessment, Congress of the United States, May 1979, pp. 81–90. The mortality estimates can be found on page 84.

364 *a "countervailing strategy":* In July 1980, President Carter endorsed a new and top secret "Nuclear Weapons Employment Policy." Known as Presidential Directive/NSC-59, it called for a shift in targeting—a renewed emphasis on counterforce, limited war, and the destruction of Warsaw Pact forces while they moved on the battlefield. It sought to "countervail," to resist with equal strength, any Soviet attack. It also sought to provide Carter with the ability to launch on warning. See Odom, "The Origins and Design of Presidential Decision-59," and "Presidential Directive/NSC-59," July 25, 1980 (TOP SECRET/SENSITIVE/declassified), NSA.

364 *The MX missile system embodied the strategic thinking:* For the clearest description of the Carter administration plan for the MX, see "MX Missile Basing," Congress of the United States, Office of Technology Assessment, September 1981. And for a sense of the missile debates at the time, see John D. Steinbruner and Thomas M. Garwin, "Strategic Vulnerability: The Balance Between Prudence and Paranoia," *International Security,* vol. 1, no. 1 (Summer 1976), pp. 138–81; William C. Potter, "Coping with MIRV in a MAD World," *Journal of Conflict Resolution,* vol. 22, no. 4

(1978), pp. 599–626; Wayne Biddle, "The Silo Busters: Misguided Missiles, the MX Project," *Harper's,* December 1979; and William H. Kincade, "Will MX Backfire?," *Foreign Policy,* no. 37 (Winter 1979–1980), pp. 43–58.

365   *scattered across roughly fifteen thousand acres:* See "MX Missile Basing," pp. 64-65.

365   *Eight thousand miles of new roads:* Cited in ibid., p. 61.

365   *About a hundred thousand workers would be required:* Cited in ibid., p. 75.

365   *The total cost of the project was estimated to be at least $40 billion:* Ibid., pp. 13–14.

365   *the computers at the NORAD headquarters:* For the November false alarm, see "NORAD's Missile Warning System: What Went Wrong?," Comptroller General of the United States, Report to the Chairman, Committee on Government Operations, House of Representatives, Comptroller General of the United States, MASAD-81-30, May 15, 1981; "Report on Recent False Alerts from the Nation's Missile Attack Warning System," U.S. Senate, Committee on Armed Services, Ninety-sixth Congress, First Session, October 9, 1980; and Scott D. Sagan, *The Limits of Safety: Organizations, Accidents, and Nuclear Weapons* (Princeton: Princeton University Press, 1993), pp. 225–31.

365   *about four times a day:* There were 1,544 "routine" missile display conferences in 1979. Cited in "Report on Recent False Alerts," p. 4.

365   *triggered by forest fires, volcanic eruptions:* Ibid.

365–66 *a Threat Assessment Conference . . . a few times a year:* Ibid., p. 5.

366   *a Missile Attack Conference had never been held:* Ibid.

366   *A technician had put the wrong tape into one of NORAD's computers:* According to a subsequent investigation, "test scenario data was inadvertently fed into the online missile warning computers which generated false alarms." One could also argue that it was right tape—inserted in the wrong place at the wrong time. See "NORAD's Warning System: What Went Wrong?," p. 13. See also A. O. Sulzberger, Jr., "Error Alerts U.S. Forces to a False Missile Attack, *New York Times,* November 11, 1979.

366   *The computers at NORAD had been causing problems:* See "NORAD's Information Processing Improvement Program—Will It Enhance Mission Capability?," Controller General of the United States, Report to the Congress, September 21, 1978.

367   *the Honeywell 6060 computers were already obsolete:* See "NORAD's Warning System: What Went Wrong?," p. 8.

367   *despite protests from the head of NORAD that they lacked sufficient processing power:* See "NORAD's Information Processing Improvement Program," pp. 13–14.

367   *"due to the lack of readily available spare parts":* Ibid., p. 7.

367   *Many of the parts hadn't been manufactured by Honeywell for years:* Ibid.

367   *twenty-three security officers . . . stripped of their security clearances:* See "AF Guards Disciplined in Drug Probe," *Washington Post,* January 17, 1980.

367   *"FALSE ALARM ON ATTACK SENDS FIGHTERS INTO SKY":* See "False Alarm on Attack Sends Fighters into Sky," *New York Times,* November 10, 1979.

367   *Zbigniew Brzezinski . . . was awakened by a phone call:* For the details of Brzezinski's early-morning call, see Robert M. Gates, *From the Shadows: The Ultimate Insider's Story of Five Presidents and How They Won the Cold War* (New York: Simon & Schuster, 2006), pp. 114–15. Gates tells the story well but conflates the cause of the June false alarm with that of the previous one in November. I tried to confirm the story with Brzezinski, who declined to be interviewed for this book. But he did discuss the incident with Admiral Stansfield Turner, the director of the CIA at the time. See Stansfield Turner, *Caging the Nuclear Genie: An American Challenge for Global Security* (New York: Westview Press, 1997), p. 17.

368   *2,200 missiles were heading toward the United States:* See Gates, *From the Shadows,* p. 114; Turner, *Caging the Nuclear Genie,* p. 17; Sagan, *Limits of Safety,* pp. 231–32.

368   *a defective computer chip in a communications device:* See "Report on Recent False Alerts," p. 7.

368   *The faulty computer chip had randomly put the number 2:* Ibid.

368   *at a cost of forty-six cents:* Cited in "Missile Alerts Traced to 46¢ Item," *New York Times,* June 18, 1980.

369   *Bob Peurifoy became concerned:* Peurifoy interview.

370   *"It's our stockpile. We think it's safe.":* Peurifoy interview. Stevens confirmed that response.

370   *"the magnitude of the safety problems":* This quote comes from a document that Peurifoy used during briefings on nuclear weapon safety at Sandia. On a single page, he assembled quotations from the Department of Defense, the Air Force, and others asserting that the American nuclear stockpile was safe. The original sources, from which the quotes have been drawn, are on file at Sandia. I feel confident that these quotes are accurate. On page 116 of "Origins and Evolution of S²C," Stevens writes that the Pentagon's response to the Fowler Letter "can be characterized as mostly delaying actions in the guise of requiring safety studies of each of the weapons involved."

370   *"The safety advantages gained by retrofitting":* Quoted in "Sandia briefing document."

371   *Modification of any current operational aircraft:* Quoted in ibid.

371   *a six-digit code with a million possible combinations:* See "Command and Control Systems for Nuclear Weapons," p. 40.

371   *the Air Force put a coded switch in the cockpit:* Ibid., p. 12.

371   *The combination . . . was the same at every Minuteman site:* Bruce G. Blair first disclosed this fact in 2004, and the easy-to-remember combination was confirmed for me by a Sandia engineer.

371–72   *cost . . . was about $100,000 per weapon:* Peurifoy interview.

372   *cost about $360 million:* Ibid.

372   *"My dissenting opinion will be brief":* The cartoonist was Sidney Harris and the cartoon originally appeared in *Playboy*, March 1972, p. 208.

373   *During the late 1960s, Stevens had begun to worry:* Stevens interview.

373   *Nozzles on the walls:* The system was called the "sticky foam personnel barrier." In addition to sticky foam, other "active barriers" were considered as a means of protecting nuclear weapons, including cold smoke, aqueous foam, and rigid foam. For a comparison of these active barriers and their merits, see "An Activated Barrier for Protection of Special Nuclear Materials in Vital Areas," Ronald E. Timm, James E. Miranda, Donald L. Reigle, and Anthony D. Valente, Argonne National Laboratory, 1984.

374   *Stan Spray found that one of the bomb's internal cables:* Peurifoy and Stevens interviews.

375   *"base escape":* How long a B-52's engines took to start was one of the most important determinants of whether the plane would get into the air before Soviet missiles arrived—or get destroyed on the ground. For some of the other factors, see "Nuclear Hardness and Base Escape," Rayford P. Patrick, Engineering Report No. S-112, Headquarters Strategic Air Command, Directorate of Aircraft Maintenance, March 31, 1981.

375   *"our B-52s are planned for one-way missions":* See "Minutes, National Security Council Meeting, Subject, SALT (and Angola), December 22, 1975" (TOP SECRET/SENSITIVE/declassified), NSA, p. 5.

376   *A study of all the nuclear weapons in the American arsenal:* A portion of the study has been declassified, and I've filed a Freedom of Information Act request to obtain the rest of it: "An Examination of the U.S. Nuclear Weapon Inventory," R. N. Brodie, November 30, 1977 (SECRET/RESTRICTED DATA/declassified).

376   *The Mark 28 bomb was at the top of the list:* Ibid.

376   *a "retrofit for Enhanced Electrical Safety:* Ibid.

376   *it planned to spend at least $10 billion to equip B-52s:* Cited in "Pentagon Says Even Vast Effort by Soviet Can't Stop New Missile," *New York Times*, November 15, 1978.

377   *Jeffrey A. Zink was pulling an alert:* My account of the Grand Forks accident is based on an interview with Jeffrey A. Zink and on "USAF Mishap Report, Parking Spot A-10, Grand Forks Air Force Base," Headquarters, Fifteenth Air Force, September 29, 1980.

378   *"What have I gotten myself into?":* Zink interview.

378   *"I'll throw up later":* Ibid.

379   *"we're going to die":* Ibid.

379   *"Oh my God, it's the real thing":* Ibid.

380   *"I can't do this":* Quoted in ibid.

380   *"Alpha, Charlie, Delta . . .":* Quoted in ibid.

380   *"Terminate, terminate, terminate":* Quoted in ibid.

381 *"Get in"*: Quoted in ibid.

381 *gusts of up to thirty-five miles an hour:* The mishap report cited gusts of up to thirty knots, and a knot is about 1.15 miles per hour. "USAF Mishap Report," p. 1.

381 *Tim Griffis was at home with his family:* Interview with Tim Griffis.

382 *"What do you think?":* Quoted in Griffis interview.

383 *"Yeah, let me try it":* Ibid.

383 *"Gene, you want to go with me?":* Ibid.

383 *"Yeah":* Ibid.

383 *"Chief, that engine is getting pretty hot":* Quoted in "USAF Mishap Report," p. N-6.

383 *"Yeah, go":* Quoted in ibid., p. N-6.

384 *"Here, somebody wants to talk to you":* Quoted in Griffis interview.

384 *"Mr. Griffis, I want to thank you":* Quoted in ibid.

384 *During a closed Senate hearing, Dr. Roger Batzel:* See Reed Karaim, "Nearly a Nuclear Disaster— Wind Shifted Fire on B-52 Away from Bomb, Experts Say," *Seattle Times*, August 13, 1991. A map showed the potential contamination area.

384 *the cause of the fire in engine number five:* In addition to nearly contaminating Grand Forks with plutonium and/or causing a nuclear detonation nearby, the missing nut caused $442,696 worth of damage to the plane. See "B52H S/N 60-0059 Mishap Engine Investigation" and "Certificate of Damage," in "USAF Mishap Report."

385 *Senator David Pryor once again introduced an amendment:* See Congressional Record—Senate, September 16, 1980, pp. 25468–25470.

385 *at least nine accidents or propellant leaks:* Cited in ibid., p. 25469. See also Tom Hamburger and Elizabeth Fair, "9 Accidents Recorded in State Since January 1978," *Arkansas Gazette*, September 28.

385 *At a launch complex near Heber Springs:* See Hamburger and Fair, "9 Accidents Recorded" and Pincus, "Aging Titan II Was Time Bomb."

385 *More than one third of the entire Titan II force:* Cited in "Aging Titan II Was Time Bomb."

385 *"We have a responsibility to protect the civilians":* Congressional Record, p. 25468.

385 *"Accidents have occurred in the past":* Ibid.

385 *The Air Force had recently submitted a lengthy report:* "Assessment Report: Titan II LGM 25 C, Weapon Condition and Safety," Prepared for the Senate Armed Services Committee and House Armed Services Committee, May 1980.

385 *the accident rate at Titan II sites:* Cited in ibid., p. 1.

385 *"provide a high level of safety":* Ibid., p.3.

385 *"considered by many to be better now than when it was new":* Ibid., pp. 2–3.

385 *The safety record of the W-53 warhead was "commendable":* Ibid., Appendix C, p. 38.

386 *"Airframe rupture":* Ibid., p. 9.

386 *They were being sued by Airman Carl Malinger:* The lawsuits filed by Malinger and the widows of Erby Hepstall and Robert J. Thomas were later settled out of court. According to one news account, the defense contractors agreed to pay Malinger and the other plaintiffs about $500,000 each. See "Lawsuits from '78 Titan Accident Settled Out of Court by Air Force," *Lawrence* (Kansas) *Journal-World*, January 8, 1981.

386 *Skip Rutherford and his wife were at home:* Rutherford interview.

386 *"This is serious":* Ibid.

386 *"Well, how serious?":* Quoted in ibid.

386 *"They tell me it's going to explode":* Ibid.

386 *"You're kidding me":* Quoted in ibid.

387 *"Bob, listen to me":* Ibid.

387 *"What?":* Quoted in ibid.

387 *"Tell Frank to get the hell out":* Ibid.

387 *"How do you know?":* Quoted in ibid.

387 *"You have your sources":* Ibid.

Like Hell

388   *Greg Devlin and Rex Hukle took turns:* Greg Devlin interview.

389   *Jeff Kennedy thought the whole plan was idiotic:* Kennedy interview.

392   *For the next eight minutes, the command post did not hear a word:* "Report, Major Missile Accident, Titan II Complex 374-7," Statement of Jimmy D. Wiley, Staff Sergeant, Tab U-100, p. 3.

392   *Moser thought the warhead had detonated:* Moser interview.

393   *"Get out of here, get out of here":* King interview.

394   *"We just left a bunch of dead people back there":* Ibid.

394   *"Hop in here":* Hutto interview.

395   *"Evacuate, evacuate":* "Report, Major Missile Accident, Titan II Complex 374-7," Statement of Thomas A. Brocksmith, Technical Sergeant , Tab U-9, p. 4.

396   *"I need to get the hell out of here":* Holder interview.

397   *"Screw you":* Sandaker interview.

397   *I just want everything to stop falling:* "Report, Major Missile Accident, Titan II Complex 374-7," Statement of Archie G. James, Staff Sergeant , Tab U-42, p. 2.

398   *"Oh shit, you ain't gonna live through this":* Devlin interview.

398   *"Run, run!":* Ibid.

399   *"Oh, my God":* Ibid.

399   *"Please help, I can't move":* "Report, Major Missile Accident, Titan II Complex 374-7," Statement of John G. Devlin, Senior Airman, Tab U-18, p. 4.

399   *"I have to put you down":* Quoted in Devlin interview.

401   *"Get away from there":* Childers interview.

401   *"Let's go, let's get out of here":* Ibid., and "Report, Major Missile Accident, Titan II Complex 374-7," Statement of Gene M. Schneider, Airman First Class, Tab U-87, p. 3.

402   *"Well, at least I've still got the hair on my arms":* Quoted in ibid., Statement of Allan D. Childers, First Lieutenant, Tab U-13, p. 6.

404   *"Man, ain't that pretty":* Ibid., Testimony of Jimmy E. Roberts, Technical Sergeant, p. 2.

405   *"I'm not going to leave":* Quoted in Green interview.

405   *"Help! Help me. Help me! Can anybody read me?":* Don Green obtained a recording of the radio communications at Launch Complex 374-7 after the accident. The recording was made by a civilian and then given anonymously to KATV-TV in Little Rock. Partial transcripts were also published in the newspaper: "Radio Conversations Detail Rescue Effort by Air Force," *Arkansas Gazette*, September 20, 1980. I'm grateful to Green for making a copy of the tape for me. Kennedy's plea for help can be heard on it.

405   *"Yes, we can hear you":* Transcript, Air Force Radio Traffic, September 19, 1980.

405   *"Help me!":* Ibid.

405   *"Where are you?":* Ibid.

405   *"Where are you, Jeff?":* Ibid.

405   *"Colonel Morris, I'm down here":* Ibid.

405   *"Where are you?":* Ibid.

405   *"I'm down here in your truck!":* Ibid.

406   *"I am not going to die on this complex":* Kennedy interview.

407   *"Oh, my God, help me":* Quoted in Kennedy interview.

407   *"Livy, I'm going for help":* Ibid., and "Report, Major Missile Accident, Titan II Complex 374-7," Statement of Jeffrey K. Kennedy, Sergeant, Tab U-46, p. 14.

407   *"Oh, my God, help me":* Kennedy interview.

407   *"Please, somebody help me":* Ibid.

408   *"Help":* Quoted in "Report, Major Missile Accident, Titan II Complex 374-7," Testimony of George H. Short, Captain, Tab U-90, p. 3.

408   *"Captain":* Quoted in ibid.

411   *"Okay, keep on yelling":* Ibid., Roberts statement, Tab U-77, p. 4.

412   *"Look, we're going to make it out of here":* Ibid., Roberts statement, Tab U-77, p. 5.

412   *"Please don't leave me"*: Quoted in ibid., Roberts statement, Tab U-77, p. 5.
412   *"Great"*: Ibid., Roberts statement, Tab U-77, p. 5.
413   *"Please don't tell my mother"*: Sandaker interview.

Confirm or Deny

415   *Matthew Arnold was taught how to deactivate:* Interview with Matthew Arnold.
415   *"Chlorine is your friend"*: Quoted in ibid.
415   *About one third of the students typically flunked out:* My description of the course work at Redstone and Indian Head is based not only on my interview with Arnold but also on interviews with other EOD technicians who studied at both places during roughly the same period. I also learned a few things about bomb disposal from Peurifoy and Stevens.
418   *SAC headquarters wouldn't even tell Frank Wilson:* See "Local Officials Couldn't Get Information from Military," *Arkansas Gazette,* September 20, 1980.
419   *the whereabouts of "the warhead"*: Transcript, Air Force Radio Traffic.
419   *"Hey, I need one of them masks"*: Anglin interview.
419   *"Oh, you don't need a mask"*: Quoted in ibid.
421   *"dry land drowning"*: See "Fact Sheet, Phosgene Carbonyl Chloride, Military Designations: CG," U.S. Army Chemical Materials Agency (n.d.).
424   *"It's laying in a ditch"*: Transcript, Air Force Radio Traffic.
424   *"Okay, I'd recommend that we wait"*: Ibid.
424   *"Fine with me"*: Ibid.
424   *"Goddamn it, Harold, I'm the vice president"*: This anecdote was told to me by Senator David Pryor and later confirmed by Vice President Walter Mondale.
425   *Peurifoy didn't like hearing that bit of information:* My account of the accident response and render safe procedures at Damascus is based on interviews with Bob Peurifoy, William H. Chambers, Matt Arnold, and other EOD technicians.
425   *None of the work at Los Alamos and NEST had made Chambers feel anxious:* Chambers interview.
429   *About a dozen people in Guy, Arkansas:* See Art Harris, "Residents Near Site of Missile Explosion Complain of Illness," *Arkansas Democrat,* September 26, 1980.
429   *"The Air Force wouldn't tell us a damn thing"*: Quoted in "Air Force Says 'No' to Plea for Inspection," *Arkansas Democrat,* September 21, 1980.
429   *Gary Gray . . . said that he learned more from the radio:* See Lamar James, "Civilians 'Got Cold Shoulder' from Military, Deputy Says," *Arkansas Gazette,* September 21, 1980.
429   *security police stopped Tatom on the access road:* See "Air Force says 'No' to Plea for inspection."
430   *doing "the best they could"*: Quoted in Don Johnson, "Clinton to Talk to Air Force Officials," *Arkansas Democrat,* September 21, 1980.
430   *"I assume they're armed"*: Quoted in "Mondale Avoids Admitting Missile Armed with Warhead," *Arkansas Gazette,* September 20, 1980.
430   *"I believe that the Titan missile system is a perfectly safe system"*: "Transcript, News Conference by Secretary of the Air Force Hans Mark, Friday, September 19, 1980, 4:00 P.M., the Pentagon," David H. Pryor Papers, University of Arkansas, Fayetteville.
430   *"Accidents happen"*: Ibid.
430   *"pretty much the worst case"*: Ibid.
430   *"the emergency teams whose job it is"*: Ibid.
430   *"the emergency procedures worked properly"*: Ibid.
431   *the Titan II accident . . . was its first big, breaking story:* CNN was the only national news network with a live camera at the sight. See Reese Schonfeld, *Me Against the World: The Unauthorized Story of the Founding of CNN* (New York: Cliff Street, 2001), pp. 182–86.
431   *"as a means of reducing or preventing widespread public alarm"*: Quoted in Ellen Debenport, "Air Force Could Have Confirmed Warhead's Presence," United Press International, September 26, 1980.
431   *A newspaper cartoon depicted three Air Force officers:* See "The Air Force on Nukes," *Arkansas Gazette,* September 24, 1980.

432   *"If you're on the military's side"*: Art Buchwald, "Arrivederci, Arkansas," *Los Angeles Times*, October 2, 1980.

432   *"a nuclear conflict"*: Quoted in "Russians Say Accidental Nuclear Explosion Could Touch Off War," Associated Press, September 21, 1980.

432   *"If it's not safe and effective"*: Quoted in "Congressman Wants Inquiry of Missile Silos," *Arkansas Democrat*, September 20, 1980.

432   *"Hey, Colonel, is that what you won't confirm or deny?"*: Quoted in "Titan Warhead Taken to Air Base," *Arkansas Gazette*, September 23, 1980.

The End

433   *Reagan soundly defeated Jimmy Carter*: Reagan got about 51 percent of the popular vote and 489 electoral votes; Carter about 41 percent, and 49 electoral votes. For a contemporary view of the political implications, see David S. Broder, "A Sharp Right Turn: Republicans and Democrats Alike See New Era in '80 Returns," *Washington Post*, November 6, 1980.

433   *"Peace through strength"*: Quoted in Lou Cannon, "Reagan Assures VFW He'll Restore Defenses," *Boston Globe*, August 19, 1980.

433   *America's defense budget would almost double*: In 1980, the United States spent about $134 billion on defense; it spent about $253 billion in 1985. And the following year, it spent about $273 billion. Cited in "National Defense Budget Estimates for FY 2013," Table 7-1, p. 247.

434   *Reagan opposed not only détente*: For the origins of Reagan's anti-Communism and his opposition to arms control agreements with the Soviet Union, see Paul Lettow, *Ronald Reagan and His Quest to Abolish Nuclear Weapons* (New York: Random House, 2005), pp. 10–18.

434   *"motivated by fear of the bomb"*: Quoted in ibid., p. 15.

434   *"the most evil enemy"*: Quoted in ibid., p. 17.

434   *Iklé was still haunted*: Iklé interview.

434   *"assured genocide"*: Iklé, "Can Nuclear Deterrence Last Out the Century?," p. 281.

434   *a "form of warfare universally condemned"*: Ibid., p. 281.

435   *"an auto-da-fé"*: Fred C. Iklé, "The Prevention of Nuclear War in a World of Uncertainty," *Policy Sciences*, vol. 7, no. 2 (1976), p. 250.

435   *Two Air Force reports on the Titan II*: "Report of Missile Accident Investigation: Major Missile Accident, 18–19 September 1980, Titan II Complex 374-7, Assigned to 308th Strategic Missile Wing, Little Rock Air Force Base, Arkansas," Conducted at Little Rock Air Force Base, Arkansas, and Barksdale Air Force Base, Louisiana, December 14–19, 1980, Eighth Air Force Missile Investigation Board, December 1980; and "Titan II Weapon System: Review Group Report," December 1980.

435   *destroyed by three separate explosions*: See "Report, Major Missile Accident, Titan II Complex 374-7," pp. 18–20; Tab I-8, pp. 1–4.

435   *"It may not be important whether the immediate cause"*: Ibid., Tab I-8, pp. 2–3.

436   *the vapor detectors . . . were broken 40 percent of the time*: Cited in "Titan II Review Group Report," pp. 16, B–7, C-25.

436   *the portable vapor detectors rarely worked*: Ibid., pp. 17, B-8.

436   *the radio system . . . was unreliable*: Ibid., pp. B-8, B-9, C-29.

436   *missile combat crews should be discouraged from evacuating*: Ibid., pp. B-9, B-10.

436   *the shortage of RFHCO suits often forced maintenance teams*: Ibid., p. C-28.

436   *the suits and helmets were obsolete*: Ibid., pp. 17, C-40.

436   *the air packs were obsolete*: Ibid., p. C-40.

436   *some of the missile's spare parts were either hard to obtain*: Ibid., p. C-35.

436   *security police officers should always be provided with maps*: Ibid., pp. E-73, E-74.

436   *"modern safing features" should be added to the W-53 warhead*: Ibid., p. D-4.

436   *"modern nuclear safety criteria for abnormal environments"*: Ibid.

436   *a warning siren at every launch complex might be useful*: Ibid., p. 33.

436   *"potentially hazardous" . . . but "basically safe"*: Ibid., p. 1.

436   *"supportable now and in the foreseeable future"*: Ibid., p. x.

436 *Jeff Kennedy was angered by both of the reports:* Kennedy interview.

436 *guidance in the medical literature was scarce:* One of the few good studies on the danger of the oxidizer happened to be published during the same week as the explosion at Launch Complex 374-7. It was written by Air Force physicians. See "The McConnell Missile Accident: Clinical Spectrum of Nitrogen Dioxide Exposure," Lieutenant Colonel Charles C. Yockey, MC, USAF; Major Billy M. Eden, MC, USAF; Colonel Richard B. Byrd, MC, USAF, *Journal of the American Medical Association,* vol. 244, no. 11 (September 12, 1980).

436 *nobody from the Air Force would speak to him, for three days after the accident:* Anderson later told Morley Safer, a correspondent for *60 Minutes,* that the Air Force didn't share information about how to treat victims of oxidizer exposure until "three or four days" after the Damascus accident. Anderson was interviewed for "Titan," *60 Minutes,* November 8, 1981.

436 *"Do not operate the switch":* "Report, Major Missile Accident, Titan II Complex 374-7," Statement of Michael A. Hanson, Tab U-30, p. 7.

437 *Kennedy thought the report was wrong:* Kennedy interview.

437 *Powell . . . blamed himself for Livingston's death:* Powell interview.

438 *Jeff Kennedy was served with a formal letter of reprimand:* For the reprimands sent to Kennedy, see Richard C. Gross, "Titan Accident: Air Force Reprimand for Heroics," United Press International, February 12, 1981; and Walter Pincus, "'Hero' of Titan II Missile Explosion Is Reprimanded by Air Force," *Washington Post,* February 12, 1981.

438 *Air Force regulations permitted a violation of the two-man rule:* In fact, a SAC training video about the Titan II encouraged airmen to break the rule in certain situations. According to the narrator of the video: "Under normal operating conditions, a solitary individual is never allowed inside a no-lone zone. However, during an actual emergency, a lone individual may have to take action to save lives or equipment, if at all possible. If you are working near a no-lone zone and see an emergency in that zone, you will be expected to take action *by yourself* to save the critical component or other equipment from damage, if possible. Yes, your action will be in direct violation of the SAC two-man policy, and you will have to report it as such. However, your action—provided it is taken under an emergency condition—is expected and condoned." This "exception" to the rule is explained in "Nuclear Surety Program, Initial Training, Part 1: History—An Overview," Aerospace Audiovisual Service, U.S. Air Force (n.d.). The tape can be found in the archives of the Titan Missile Museum. According to the museum's archivist and historian, Chuck Penson, the video was most likely recorded some time between 1976 and 1979.

438 *David Powell was given an Article 15 citation:* Powell wasn't charged with using a ratchet instead of a torque wrench—because the socket fell off before the ratchet could be "used." See Carol Griffee, "Airman at Silo Is Disciplined," *Arkansas Gazette,* February 13, 1981.

438 *placed in the psychiatric ward there—along with Greg Devlin:* Kennedy and Devlin interviews.

439 *Bill Carter was an Air Force veteran and a former Secret Service agent:* Carter spoke to me at length about his dealings with the Air Force over its management of the Titan II missiles in Arkansas.

439 *"a substance no more dangerous than smog":* Quoted in Bill Carter and Judi Turner, *Get Carter: Backstage in History from JFK's Assassination to the Rolling Stones* (Nashville: Fine's Creek Publishing, 2006), p. 208.

439 *A few months later, at a ceremony in Little Rock:* Kennedy, Devlin, and Sandaker interviews. See also Walter Pincus, "Eight Honored as Heroes in '80 Titan Missile Blast," *Washington Post,* May 23, 1981.

439 *his local congressman in Maine, David Emery, said that if he took the medal:* Kennedy interview. See also John S. Day, "Behind an Effective Lawmaker—a Good Staff," *Bangor Daily News,* March 19, 1982.

440 *a "temporary medical leave by reason of disability":* Quoted in ibid.

440 *Devlin got a check for $6,400:* Devlin interview.

440 *A study commissioned by the Air Force later questioned:* Peurifoy interview.

440 *"expedite the proposed retrofit of the 28":* "Letter, To Lieutenant General Howard W. Leaf, Inspector General, Headquarters, United States Air Force, From Harold P. Smith, Jr., President, the Palmer Smith Corporation, July 17, 1981" (SECRET/RESTRICTED DATA/declassified), p. 2.

441 *Peurifoy quietly arranged for a unique signal generator:* Peurifoy interview.

441 *expected to cost approximately $1.5 trillion:* Cited in "Economy Can't Absorb Defense Increase," *Washington Post,* October 18, 1981.

441 *About $250 billion would be spent on nuclear weapon systems:* Cited in "Modernizing U.S. Strategic Offensive Forces: The Administration's Program and Alternatives," A CBO Study, Congressional Budget Office, Congress of the United States, May 1983, p. 1.

441 *about fourteen thousand strategic warheads and bombs, an increase of about 60 percent:* The Reagan administration planned to raise the number of warheads from 8,800 to 14,000. Cited in ibid., p. xvi.

442 *a "super-sudden first strike":* See McGeorge Bundy, "Common Sense and Missiles in Europe," *Washington Post,* October 20, 1981.

442 *the "highest priority element":* Quoted in Pearson, *WWMCCS: Evolution and Effectiveness,* p. 264.

442 *"This system must be foolproof":* "Text of the President's Defense Policy Statement: 'Our Plan' to 'Strengthen and Modernize the Strategic Triad . . . ,'" *Washington Post,* October 3, 1981.

442 *greater "interoperability":* Statement of Donald C. Latham, Deputy Undersecretary of Defense (Communications, Command, Control and Intelligence), in "Strategic Force Modernization Programs," Hearings Before the Subcommittee on Strategic and Theater Nuclear Forces of the Committee on Armed Services, United States Senate, Ninety-seventh Congress, First Session, 1981, p. 239.

442 *"to recognize that we are under attack":* Quoted in Bruce G. Blair, *Strategic Command and Control: Redefining the Nuclear Threat* (Washington, D.C.: Brookings Institution, 1985), p. 264.

442 *an unprecedented investment in command and control:* Iklé understood, more than most officials at the Pentagon, the fundamental importance of the nuclear command-and-control system. Once again, a new administration was greeted by the news that the United States lacked the ability to control its strategic forces after a surprise attack by the Soviet Union. A study conducted in the spring of 1981 by Dr. James P. Wade, Jr., an undersecretary of defense, found that the command-and-control system could not assure "an effective initial response to a nuclear attack on the United States"; could not fight a protracted nuclear war; and could not guarantee the "survivability, endurability, or connectivity of the national command authority function." The implications of the Wade study were, essentially, the same as those of WSEG R-50 more than twenty years earlier: the only nuclear war that the United States could hope to win would be one in which it launched first. The quotations in my account of the Wade study are not from the actual document. They come from a summary of it in a document recently obtained by the National Security Archive. See "A Historical Study of Strategic Connectivity, 1950–1981," Joint Chiefs of Staff Special Historical Study, Historical Division, Joint Chiefs of Staff, July 1982 (TOP SECRET/declassified), NSA, pp. 64–65.

442 *spending about $18 billion:* Cited in John D. Steinbruner, "Nuclear Decapitation," *Foreign Policy,* no. 45 (Winter 1981–2), p. 25.

442 *an expansion of Project ELF:* For details of the Navy's ambitious schemes, see Pearson, *WWMCCS: Evolution and Effectiveness,* pp. 287–89; and Lowell L. Klessig and Victor L. Strite, *The ELF Odyssey: National Security Versus Environmental Protection* (Boulder, CO: Westview Press, 1980).

442 *buried six thousand miles of antenna, four to six feet deep:* The ELF antenna grid would have occupied 20,000 of Wisconsin's roughly 65,000 square miles. See Klessig and Strite, *ELF Odyssey,* p. 14.

443 *the "continuity of government":* For a brief description of the new programs, spearheaded in part by Colonel Oliver North, see Thomas C. Reed, *At the Abyss: An Insider's History of the Cold War* (New York: Ballantine Books, 2004), pp. 245–46.

443 *Desmond Ball, an Australian academic, made a strong case:* See Desmond Ball, "Can Nuclear War Be Controlled?," Adelphi Paper #169, International Institute for Strategic Studies, 1981.

443 *John D. Steinbruner . . . reached much the same conclusion:* See Steinbruner, "Nuclear Decapitation."

443 *Bruce G. Blair, a former Minuteman officer:* See Blair, *Strategic Command and Control: Redefining the Nuclear Threat.*

443 *Paul Bracken, a management expert:* See Paul Bracken, *The Command and Control of Nuclear Forces* (New Haven, CT: Yale University Press, 1983).

443 *Daniel Ford, a former head of the Union of Concerned Scientists:* See Daniel Ford, *The Button: The Pentagon's Strategic Command and Control System—Does It Work?* (New York: Simon & Schuster, 1985).

443 *"within bazooka range"*: For the quote by a security expert, see Ford, *The Button*, p. 64.

444 *"its low accuracy and its accident-proneness"*: See "Strategic Force Modernization Programs," p. 59.

444 *on alerts for five months after his first contact with the Soviet embassy*: See Richard Halloran, "Officer Reportedly Kept Job Despite Contact with Soviet," *New York Times*, June 4, 1981.

444 *"a major security breach"*: Quoted in George Lardner, Jr., "Officer Says Cooke Lived Up to Immunity Agreement Terms," *Washington Post*, September 9, 1981. In a legal case full of bizarre details, Cooke made a deal with the Air Force, confessed to the espionage, and received immunity from prosecution. At the time, the Air Force was more concerned about the possible existence of a Soviet spy ring than about the need to imprison this one young officer. But when it became clear that there was no Soviet spy ring and that Cooke had acted alone, the Air Force decided to prosecute him anyway. All of the charges against Cooke were subsequently dismissed by the U.S. Court of Military Appeals on the grounds of "prosecutorial misconduct." See George Lardner, Jr., "Military Kills Lt. Cooke Case," *Washington Post*, February 23, 1982, and "A Bargain Explained," *Washington Post*, February 27, 1982.

444 *Funding would not be provided for a new vapor detection system*: See "Item 010: Toxic Vapor Sensors (Fixed and Portable)" in "Titan II Action Item Status Reports," Headquarters, Strategic Air Command, August 1, 1982.

444 *additional video cameras within the complex*: The Air Force decided that the estimated $18 million cost of adding more cameras did "not justify the marginal benefits." See "Item 0134: L/D TV Camera," in ibid.

444 *"modern nuclear safety criteria for abnormal environments"*: The need to put "modern safety features" inside W-53 warheads had to be balanced against the cost: about $21.4 million for the remaining fifty-two Titan II missiles. Many of the missiles would be decommissioned before the work could be completed. And so none of the warheads were modified. They remained atop Titan II missiles for another six years. See "Item 090: Modify W-53," in ibid.

445 *"It's the dirt that does it"*: Quoted in Ronald L. Soble, "Cranston Demands Official Justify View That U.S. Could Survive a Nuclear War," *Los Angeles Times*, January 22, 1982.

445 *membership in the Campaign for Nuclear Disarmament soon increased tenfold*: Cited in Lawrence S. Wittner, *Toward Nuclear Abolition: A History of the World Disarmament Movement, 1971 to the Present* (Stanford: Stanford University Press, 2003), p. 131. Wittner is the foremost historian of the international effort to eliminate nuclear weapons.

445 *A quarter of a million CND supporters*: Cited in Leonard Downie, Jr., "Thousands in London Protest Nuclear Arms," *Washington Post*, October 25, 1981.

445 *In Bonn, a demonstration . . . also attracted a quarter of a million people*: Cited in John Vinocur, "250,000 at Bonn Rally Assail U.S. Arms Policy," *New York Times*, October 11, 1981.

445 *"On the one hand, we returned to business as usual"*: Jonathan Schell, *The Fate of the Earth and The Abolition* (Stanford: Stanford University Press, 2000), p. 149.

445 *Carl Sagan conjured an even worse environmental disaster*: Sagan became concerned about the atmospheric effects of nuclear war in 1982, and it seems almost quaint today—as global warming looms as a pending threat—that a generation ago Americans worried that the world might get dangerously cold. But the threat of a nuclear winter never went away. And recent calculations suggest that the detonation of fifty atomic bombs in urban areas would produce enough black carbon smoke to cause another "Little Ice Age." For the summation of Sagan's work on the issue, see Carl Sagan and Richard Turco, *A Path Where No Man Thought: Nuclear Winter and the End of the Arms Race* (New York: Random House, 1990). For the latest findings on the global environmental impact of a nuclear war, see Alan Robock, "Nuclear Winter Is a Real and Present Danger," *Nature*, vol. 473 (May 19, 2011).

446 *perhaps three quarters of a million people gathered in New York's Central Park*: The estimates of the crowd varied, from more than 550,000 to about 750,000. See Paul L. Montgomery, "Throngs Fill Manhattan to Protest Nuclear Weapons," *New York Times*, June 13, 1982; and John J. Goldman and Doyle McManus, "Largest Ever U.S. Rally Protests Nuclear Arms," *Los Angeles Times*, June 13, 1982.

446 *"the largest political demonstration in American history"*: See Judith Miller, "Democrats Seize Weapons Freeze as Issue for Fall," *New York Times*, June 20, 1982.

446 *orchestrated by "KGB leaders" and "Marxist leaning 60's leftovers"*: Quoted in Wittner, *Toward Nuclear Abolition*, p. 189.

446 *about 70 percent . . . supported a nuclear freeze*: Ibid., p. 177.

446 *more than half worried*: Cited in Frances FitzGerald, *Way Out There in the Blue: Reagan, Star Wars, and the End of the Cold War* (New York: Touchstone, 2001), p. 191.

446 *one of the most dangerous years of the Cold War*: In *The Dead Hand: The Untold Story of the Cold War Arms Race and Its Dangerous Legacy* (New York: Doubleday, 2009), David E. Hoffman does a masterful job of conveying the threat that year, as an aging, paranoid Soviet leader faced a self-confident and seemingly bellicose American president. The events of 1983 are depicted in pages 54 to 100. Robert M. Gates offers an insider's perspective; he was the deputy director for intelligence at the CIA that year. See "1983: The Most Dangerous Year," a chapter in *From the Shadows*, pp. 258–77.

446 *code-named Operation RYAN*: For another perspective on the events of 1983 and the KGB's role in them, see Benjamin B. Fischer, "A Cold War Conundrum: The 1983 Soviet War Scare," Central Intelligence Agency, Center for the Study of Intelligence, 1997.

446 *the Reagan administration's top secret psychological warfare program*: See "Cold War Conundrum"; and Peter Schweizer, *Victory: The Secret Strategy That Hastened the Collapse of the Soviet Union* (New York: Atlantic Monthly Press, 1994). As Fischer notes, *Victory* may not provide a convincing explanation for why the Soviet Union collapsed, but the book seems to give an accurate description of the Reagan administration's covert activities against the Soviets.

447 *"the focus of evil in the modern world"*: Quoted in Francis X. Clines, "Reagan Denounces Ideology of Soviet as 'Focus of Evil,'" *New York Times*, March 9, 1983.

447 *"Engaging in this is not just irresponsible"*: Quoted in Fischer, "Cold War Conundrum."

447 *"an act of barbarism" and a "crime against humanity"*: Quoted in Flora Lewis, "Leashing His Fury, Reagan Surprises and Calms Allies," *New York Times*, September 11, 1983.

447 *alarms went off in an air defense bunker south of Moscow*: See Hoffman, *Dead Hand*, pp. 6–11.

447 *rays of sunlight reflected off clouds*: See David Hoffman, "'I Had a Funny Feeling in My Gut'; Soviet Officer Faced Nuclear Armageddon," *Washington Post*, February 10, 1999.

448 *two million people in Europe joined protests*: Cited in Joseph B. Fleming, "Anti-Missile Movement Vows to Fight On," United Press International, October 23, 1983.

448 *serious problems with the World Wide Military Command and Control System*: See Pearson, *WWMCCS: Evolution and Effectiveness*, pp. 315-17; and "JTF Operations Since 1983," George Stewart, Scott M. Fabbri, and Adam B. Siegel, CRM 94-42, Center for Naval Analyses, July 1994, pp. 23-31.

448 *"a frustrated Army officer used his AT&T credit card"*: "JTF Operations Since 1983," p. 28.

448 *Able Archer 83*: See Gates, *From the Shadows*, pp. 270-73; Hoffman, *Dead Hand*, pp. 94-95; Fischer, "Cold War Conundrum."

448 *"the KGB concluded that American forces"*: The agent was Oleg Gordievsky. He worked not only for the KGB but also for British intelligence. His quote is from Fischer, "Cold War Conundrum."

448 *A number of the Soviet Union's own war plans*: See Hoffman, *Dead Hand*, p. 94.

449 *About 100 million Americans watched* The Day After: Cited in Robert D. McFadden, "Atomic War Film Spurs Nationwide Discussion," *New York Times*, November 22, 1983.

449 *another B-52 had caught on fire on a runway*: See Phyllis Mensing, "5 Die in B-52 Fire at Air Base," Associated Press, January 27, 1983.

450 *the retrofits were halted . . . because the program ran out of money*: Peurifoy interview.

450 *"The worst probable consequence of continuous degradation"*: "'Hot' Topic!, Nuclear AID [Accidents, Incidents, Deficiencies] Topics," *USAF Nuclear Surety Journal*, no. 90-01, p. 5.

450 *"Naturally, this would be a catastrophe"*: Ibid.

450 *"follow procedures and give the weapons a little extra care"*: Ibid.

450 *A software glitch could launch a Pershing II missile*: Peurifoy and Stevens interviews. See also Stevens, "Origins and Evolution of S^2C," pp. 116-18.

451 *Reagan watched red dots spreading across a map*: See Reed, *At the Abyss*, pp. 233-34.

451 *Reagan's belief in the plan was sincere*: Two well-researched books argue persuasively that Reagan hoped to protect the United States from a nuclear attack and rid the world of nuclear weapons. The

books suggest that Reagan's tough Cold War rhetoric hid a warmer, more peace-loving side. And yet both books fail to place Reagan's subsequent arms control efforts in a wider political context. The massive antinuclear demonstrations in the United States and Western Europe are mentioned on only three of the roughly eight hundred pages in these books—and with disparagement. On October 5, 1982, President Reagan said that the nuclear freeze movement was "inspired . . . by people who want the weakening of America." The huge demonstrations that soon followed no doubt influenced his subsequent behavior, as did his wife Nancy, who strongly supported arms control talks. Reagan's transformation into an outspoken nuclear abolitionist, though heartfelt, followed—and did not lead—American public opinion. Although written without access to many declassified documents, Frances FitzGerald's *Way Out There in the Blue* has a broader perspective. See Lettow, *Ronald Reagan and His Quest to Abolish Nuclear Weapons*; Martin Anderson and Annelise Anderson, *Reagan's Secret War: The Untold Story of His Fight to Save the World from Nuclear Disaster* (New York: Crown, 2009); and Rich Jaroslovsky, "Reagan Blasts Nuclear Freeze Movement, Saying Some Seek 'Weakening of America,'" *Wall Street Journal*, October 5, 1982.

451   *"impotent and obsolete":* "President's Speech on Military Spending and a New Defense," *New York Times*, January 27, 1983.

451   The Day After *left even him feeling depressed:* Thomas Reed, one of Reagan's national security advisers, thought the film "understated . . . the horrors of nuclear war." See Reed, *At the Abyss*, pp. 250, 255.

451   *"A nuclear war cannot be won":* "Transcript of Statement by President," *New York Times*, April 18, 1982.

452   *"The President agreed this could be sorted out":* "Memorandum of Conversation, Hofdi House, Reykjavik, 3:25–6:00, October 12, 1986, United States Department of State (SECRET/SENSITIVE/ declassified), p. 9, in George P. Shultz and Sidney D. Drell, *Implications of the Reykjavik Summit on Its Twentieth Anniversary* (Stanford: Hoover Institution Press, 2007), p. 210.

452   The euphoria . . . *didn't last long:* See Ibid., pp. 211-15.

453   *almost half of the weapons in the American stockpile:* Peurifoy interview.

454   Peurifoy *wrote to the assistant secretary for defense programs:* A more detailed account of the bureaucratic inertia can be found in Stevens, "Origins and Evolution of S²C," pp. 162-66.

454   *"The potential for a nuclear weapon accident":* Quoted in ibid., p. 164.

455   The *Post* ran a series of his articles: See R. Jeffrey Smith, "Defective Nuclear Shells Raise Safety Concerns; U.S. Secretly Repairing Weapons in Europe," *Washington Post*, May 23, 1990; "Pentagon Urged to Ground Nuclear Missile for Safety," *Washington Post*, May 24, 1990; "Pentagon to Await Missile Safety Study; Weapons Will Remain on 'Alert' Bombers," *Washington Post*, May 25, 1990.

455   *"weapon meets all our current safety standards":* Quoted in "Pentagon to Await Missile Safety Study."

455   *"no safety hazards to the public":* Quoted in R. Jeffrey Smith, "A-Missiles Ordered Off Planes; Weapons Grounded Pending Completion of Safety Review," *Washington Post*, June 9, 1990.

456   The Drell Panel on Nuclear Weapons Safety: "Report of the Panel on Nuclear Weapons Safety of the Committee on Armed Services, House of Representatives, 101st Congress, Second Session," Sidney D. Drell, Chairman, John S. Foster, Jr., and Charles H. Townes, December 1990. For Drell's testimony and a discussion of the panel's findings, see "The Report of the Nuclear Weapons Safety Panel," Hearing Before the Committee on Armed Services, House of Representatives, 101st Congress, Second Session, December 18, 1990.

456   *"a realization that unintended nuclear detonations":* The panel singled out the SRAM as the cause of "greatest concern," warning a fire could cause "the potential for dispersal of plutonium, or even of the generation of a nuclear detonation." "Report of the Panel on Nuclear Weapons Safety," p. 25.

456   *"affirm enhanced safety as the top priority":* Ibid., p. 33.

456   A separate study on nuclear weapon safety: "Report to the Congress: Assessment of the Safety of U.S. Nuclear Weapons and Related Nuclear Test Requirements," R. E. Kidder, Lawrence Livermore National Laboratory, July 26, 1991.

456   *Three weapons received an A:* Ibid., p. 4.

456   *General Colin Powell and Secretary of Defense Dick Cheney:* For the decision to change the SIOP

and reduce the number of targets in the Soviet Union, see Colin Powell with Joseph E. Persico, *My American Journey* (New York: Ballantine Books, 1996), pp. 540–41; and Reed, *At the Abyss,* pp. 278-84, 287-92.

457 *Hundreds of nuclear warheads would hit Moscow:* Cited in Reed, *At the Abyss,* p. 283.

457 *"With the possible exception of the Soviet nuclear war plan":* "Speech to the Canadian Network Against Nuclear Weapons," George Lee Butler, Montreal, March 11, 1999.

457 *Butler eliminated about 75 percent of the targets:* Cited in R. Jeffrey Smith, "Retired Nuclear Warrior Sounds Alarms on Weapons," *Washington Post,* December 4, 1996.

457 *National Strategic Response Plans:* See "Memorandum for the Chairman, Joint Chiefs of Staff, From General George L. Butler, Commander in Chief, United States Strategic Command, Subject: Renaming the Single Integrated Operational Plan (SIOP)," September 2, 1992, (CONFIDENTIAL/declassified). This document was obtained through the Freedom of Information Act by Hans M. Kristensen, director of the Nuclear Information Project at the Federation of American Scientists.

457 *"State Committee for the State of Emergency":* For the attempted coup, see William E. Odom, *The Collapse of the Soviet Military* (New Haven: Yale University Press, 1998), pp. 305–46; Hoffman, *Dead Hand,* pp. 369–76; and Mikhail Tsypkin, "Adventures of the 'Nuclear Briefcase': A Russian Document Analysis," *Strategic Insights,* Center for Contemporary Conflict, Naval Postgraduate School, vol. 3, issue 9 (2004).

458 *President George H. W. Bush announced a month later:* See "Remarks by President Bush on Reducing U.S. and Soviet Nuclear Weapons," *New York Times,* September 28, 1991.

459 *"The long bitter years of the Cold War are over":* Quoted in Steve Kline, "SAC, America's Nuclear Strike Force, Is Retired," Associated Press, June 2, 1992.

EPILOGUE

460 *hidden by a repair tag:* Charles Perrow's succinct, unsettling account of the mishap at Three Mile Island can be found in his book, *Normal Accidents: Living with High-Risk Technologies* (Princeton: Princeton University Press, 1999), pp. 15-31.

460 *his shirt caught on the handle of a circuit breaker:* Ibid., pp. 43–44.

460 *A lightbulb slipped out of the hand:* Ibid.

460 *"trivial events in nontrivial systems":* Ibid., pp. 43–46.

460 *"Our ability to organize":* Ibid., p. 10.

461 *"tightly coupled":* Ibid., pp. 89–100.

461 *"No one dreamed that when X failed":* Ibid., p. 4.

461 *"those closest to the system, the operators":* Ibid., p. 10.

461 *"Time and time again, warnings are ignored":* Ibid.

462 *"the highest state of readiness for nuclear war":* Sagan, *The Limits of Safety,* p. 62.

462 *an Atlas long-range missile was test-launched:* Ibid., pp. 78–80.

462 *"so loose, it jars your imagination":* Quoted in ibid., p. 110.

462 *"In retrospect," Melgard said:* Quoted in ibid.

462 *one of the most dangerous incidents:* Ibid., pp. 135–38.

463 *"numerous dangerous incidents . . . occurred":* Ibid., p. 251.

463 *"a stabilizing force":* Ibid.

463 *"Nuclear weapons may well have made* deliberate *war":* Ibid., p. 264.

463 *less by "good design than good fortune":* Ibid., p. 266.

464 *"Fixes, including safety devices":* Perrow, *Normal Accidents,* p. 11.

464 *"Do Artifacts Have Politics?":* The essay can be found in Langdon Winner, *The Whale and the Reactor: A Search for Limits in an Age of High Technology* (Chicago: University of Chicago Press, 1989), pp. 19–39.

464 *"As long as it exists at all":* Ibid., p. 34.

465 *"born secret":* The Atomic Energy Act of 1946 required that "all data concerning the manufacture or utilization of atomic weapons" must be classified, and it created a new legal category for such information: Restricted Data. An amendment to the act in 1954 added another category of secret

knowledge—Formerly Restricted Data—that pertains mainly to the military uses, capabilities, and deployments of nuclear weapons. Despite the apparent meaning of that name, Formerly Restricted Data is still classified information that can't be released to the public without permission from the Department of Energy and the Department of Defense. For insight into the Orwellian world of nuclear secrecy, see Howard Morland, "Born Secret," *Cardozo Law Review*, vol. 26, no. 4 (March 2005), pp. 1401–8; "Restricted Data Declassification Decisions, 1946 to the Present," RDD-8, U.S. Department of Energy, Office of Health, Safety and Security, Office of Classification, January 1, 2002 (OFFICIAL USE ONLY/declassified); and "Transforming the Security Classification System," Report to the President from the Public Interest Declassification Board, November 2012.

465   *"Accidents and Incidents Involving Nuclear Weapons"*: The document, cited previously, is "Accidents and Incidents Involving Nuclear Weapons: Accidents and Incidents During the Period 1 July 1957 Through 31 March 1967," Technical Letter 20-3, Defense Atomic Support Agency, October 15, 1967 (SECRET/RESTRICTED DATA/declassified).

465   *a Genie antiaircraft missile released from a fighter:* Ibid., Incident #33, p. 14.

465   *a Boar missile crushed by the elevator:* Ibid., Incident #3, p. 53.

465   *a Mark 49 warhead blown off a Jupiter missile:* Ibid., Incident #11, p. 34.

465   *smoke pouring from a W-31 warhead atop a Nike missile:* Ibid., Incident #51, p. 89.

465   *the retrorockets of a Thor missile suddenly firing:* The launch pad was evacuated, and when technicians returned to the site they found that the "latch safety pins" were still holding the reentry vehicle atop the missile. "The cause of the incident," the report concluded, "was failure to follow prescribed safety rules for the Thor missile." See ibid., Incident #42, p. 87.

465   *a Mark 28 bomb emitting strange sounds:* Ibid., Incident #9, p. 72.

465–66   *the John Walker spy ring . . . provided about a million documents:* See Pete Earley, *Family of Spies: Inside the John Walker Spy Ring* (New York: Bantam, 1988), p. 358.

466   *so secret that the president . . . wasn't allowed to know it:* Known as the "Venona decryptions," they helped to discover the names or code names of about two hundred Americans spying for the Soviet Union. The chairman of the Joint Chiefs of Staff, General Omar Bradley, made the decision not to tell President Truman. The motive was less sinister than bureaucratic. "Here we have government secrecy in its essence," Senator Daniel Patrick Moynihan later wrote. "Departments and agencies hoard information, and the government becomes a kind of market." Those who know the secrets have great influence over that market. For the decision to keep Truman in the dark, see Daniel Patrick Moynihan, *Secrecy: The American Experience* (New Haven, Yale University Press, 1998), pp. 59–73. The quote appears on page 73.

466   *But the Soviet Union learned the secret:* See ibid., p. 16; and James Earl Haynes and Harvey Klehr, *Venona: Decoding Soviet Espionage in America* (New Haven: Yale University Press, 2000), pp. 47–56.

466   *"Secrecy is a form of government regulation":* See *Secrecy: Report of the Commission on Protecting and Reducing Government Secrecy* (Washington, D.C.: Government Printing Office, 1997). Quoted in Moynihan, *Secrecy*, p. 12.

466   *Cold War documents that were declassified in the 1990s:* See Scott Shane, "U.S. Reclassifies Many Documents in Secret Review," *New York Times*, February 21, 2006.

467   *Chelyabinsk-65, the site of a nuclear weapon facility:* For the tragic legacy of Soviet weapon production, see Vladislav Larin, "Mayak's Walking Wounded," *Bulletin of the Atomic Scientists* (September/October 1999), pp. 20–27, and John M. Whitely, "The Compelling Realities of Mayak," in Russell J. Dalton, Paula Garb, Nicholas P. Lovrich, John C. Pierce, and John M. Whiteley, eds., *Critical Masses: Citizens, Nuclear Weapons Production, and Environmental Destruction in the United States and Russia* (Cambridge, MA: MIT Press, 1999), pp. 59–96.

467   *"arguably the most polluted spot on the planet":* Quoted in Whitely, Dalton et al., *Critical Masses*, p. 67.

467   *well suited to the demands of nuclear command and control:* Bruce G. Blair has written the best guide to the Soviet system. His work on the subject can be found in *The Logic of Accidental Nuclear War* (Washington, D.C.: Brookings Institution, 1993), pp. 59–167, and *Global Zero Alert for Nuclear Forces* (Washington, D.C.: Brookings Institution, 1995). Blair also wrote the introduction for one

of the few works in the field written by a Russian expert: Valery E. Yarynich, *C³: Nuclear Command, Control Cooperation* (Washington, D.C.: Center for Defense Information, 2003). Two other sources, although dated, contain much fascinating information. See Stephen M. Meyer, "Soviet Nuclear Operations," in Ashton Carter, John D. Steinbruner, and Charles A. Zraket, eds., *Managing Nuclear Operations* (Washington, D.C.: Brookings Institution, 1987); and Stephen J. Cimbala, *Soviet C³* (Washington, D.C.: AFCEA International Press, 1987).

467   *"more stringent than those of any other nuclear power":* Blair, *The Logic of Accidental Nuclear War*, p. 107.

467   *the "Perimeter" system:* See Blair, *Global Zero Alert*, pp. 51, 56; Yarynich, *C³*, pp. 137–45, 157–59, 245–48; and Hoffman, *Dead Hand*, pp. 152–54, 421–23.

468   *Sidney Drell regards Bob Peurifoy as one of the leading:* Interview with Sidney Drell.

469   *the nuclear weapon community . . . became outspoken in defense of his cause:* For a good analysis of the sudden interest in nuclear weapon safety, see Frank von Hippel, "Test Ban Debate, Round Three: Warhead Safety," *Bulletin of the Atomic Scientists,* April 1991.

469   *During a Senate debate on the treaty in August 1992:* The senators were discussing an amendment to an energy and water development bill. See "Amendment No. 2833, Energy and Water Development Appropriations Act," Senate, August 3, 1992, Congressional Record, 102nd Congress (1991–1992), pp. S11171–S11222.

469   *"Why is testing of nuclear weapons so important?":* Ibid., p. S11172. The senator was J. Bennett Johnston, Jr., a Democrat from Louisiana.

469   *"we already know that science and technology cries out":* Ibid., p. S11184. The senator was Pete Domineci, a Republican from New Mexico.

469   *"A vote to halt nuclear testing today":* Ibid., pp. S11186–S11187. The senator was William Cohen, a Republican from Maine.

469   *the treaty's opponents argued that nuclear tests:* See Eric Schmitt, "Experts Say Test Ban Could Impair Nuclear-Arms Safety," *New York Times,* October 8, 1999. The National Academy of Sciences recently issued a report contradicting that argument. See *The Comprehensive Nuclear Test Ban Treaty—Technical Issues for the United States,* Committee on Reviewing and Updating Technical Issues Related to the Comprehensive Nuclear Test Ban Treaty, National Research Council of the National Academies (Washington, D.C.: National Academies Press, 2012).

470   *the first "green" nuclear weapon:* A 2007 report claimed that the Reliable Replacement Warhead (RRW) would be "much more than 'just green.'" The new weapon would reduce "potential harm to the environment and . . . improve worker safety." Despite those lofty aims, President Obama eliminated funding for the RRW in 2009. See "Nuclear Warheads: The Reliable Replacement Warhead Program and the Life Extension Program," Jonathan Medalia, CRS Report for Congress, Congressional Research Service, December 3, 2007, p. 20.

470   *"a money grab":* Peurifoy interview.

470   *a study by JASON scientists:* See "Pit Lifetime," JSR-06-335, MITRE Corporation, January 11, 2007.

470   *"nonsense":* Agnew interview.

470   *The Drell panel expressed concern about these warheads:* "The safety issue," it said, "is whether an accident during handling of an operational missile . . . might detonate the propellant which in turn could cause the [high explosives] in the warhead to detonate leading to dispersal of plutonium, or even the initiation of a nuclear yield beyond the four-pound criterion." See "Report of the Panel on Nuclear Weapons Safety," pp. 26–30. The quote can be found on page 29. For a more detailed look at the problem, see John R. Harvey and Stefan Michalowski, "Nuclear Weapons Safety: The Case of Trident," *Science and Global Security, Volume 4* (1994), pp. 261–337.

471   *decrease the missile's range by perhaps 4 percent:* Peurifoy interview.

471–72   *General Wilbur L. Creech had the same sort of lasting influence:* See James C. Slife, *Creech Blue: General Bill Creech and the Reformation of the Tactical Air Forces, 1978–1984* (Maxwell Air Force Base, AL: Air University Press and the College of Aerospace Doctrine, Research and Education, 2004).

472   *1,737 Air Force planes were shot down:* See John T. Correll, "The Air Force in the Vietnam War," Air Force Association, December 2004, p. 26.

472   *the Air Force has lost fewer than 30 planes:* This is my own estimate. The Air Force declined to provide me with a list of combat losses since 2003. "USAF Manned Aircraft Losses 1990–2002," compiled by the Air Force Historical Research Agency, mentions seventeen fixed-wing aircraft shot down during that period—three in missions over the former Yugoslavia and fourteen in Operation Desert Storm. An additional three planes were shot down between 2003 and the fall of 2008, according to "Cost in Airframes," by Michael C. Sirak, *Air Force Magazine,* October 27, 2008. After looking through the United States Air Force Class A Aerospace Mishap Reports for the years 2009 through 2012, I could not find another case of a manned, fixed-wing aircraft brought down by enemy fire. Perhaps a number of the crashes listed were, in fact, combat related. Nevertheless, the Air Force's achievement is remarkable, given that its pilots had flown more than half a million sorties over Iraq and Afghanistan by the spring of 2008. That statistic comes from a chart in Tamar A. Mehuron and Heather Lewis, "The Mega Force," *Air Force Magazine,* June 2008.

472   *units were now given seventy-two hours of warning:* The meaning of the words "no-notice" had clearly evolved over the years. According to a 2008 report on how the Air Force was managing its nuclear arsenal, "so-called 'no-notice' inspections do not begin until 72 hours after the unit is notified." See "Report of the Secretary of Defense Task Force on DoD Nuclear Weapons Management, Phase I: The Air Force's Nuclear Mission," September 2008, p. 37.

472   *a captain or a colonel became the highest-ranking officer:* Ibid., p. 27. According to a study of how the Air Force mistakenly shipped secret nuclear warhead fuzes to Taiwan instead of helicopter batteries, these officers were sometimes not only low ranked but unqualified for their jobs. "There are some leaders with little, dated, or no nuclear experience," the study found, "who hold leadership positions in the Air Force nuclear enterprise." That study is quoted in "The Unauthorized Movement of Nuclear Weapons and Mistaken Shipment of Classified Missile Components: An Assessment," Michelle Spencer, Aadina Ludin, and Heather Nelson. The Counterproliferation Papers, Future Warfare Series No. 56, USAF Counterproliferation Center, January 2012, p. 86.

472   *half of the Air Force units responsible for nuclear weapons failed:* Cited in Joby Warrick and Walter Pincus, "Missteps in the Bunker," *Washington Post,* September 23, 2007.

472   *the nose-cone fuze assemblies of four Minuteman III missiles:* See Spencer et al., "Unauthorized Movement and Mistaken Shipment," pp. 13–14.

472   *On August 29, 2007, six cruise missiles armed with nuclear warheads were mistakenly loaded:* The warheads were loaded on August 29 and discovered the following day. For the official account of what happened, see "Report on the Unauthorized Movement of Nuclear Weapons," the Defense Science Board Permanent Task Force on Nuclear Weapons Surety, Department of Defense, Washington, D.C., February 2008. For a broad look at the management failures that led to the warheads' being left unattended, see Spencer et al., "Unauthorized Movement and Mistaken Shipment." Joby Warrick and Walter Pincus wrote a fine piece about the incident: "Missteps in the Bunker," *Washington Post,* September 23, 2007. And Rachel Maddow includes some disturbing details about it in her book *Drift: The Unmooring of American Military Power* (New York: Crown Publishers, 2012), pp. 231–38.

473   *"significant confusion about delegation of responsibility":* "Report on the Unauthorized Movement," p. 5. The confusion was widespread. Neither the aircraft crew chief nor the pilot of the B-52 had been trained to handle nuclear weapons. And investigators found that the six nuclear weapons were "driven past a security checkpoint . . . but no one checked them as they passed." The quote comes from Spencer et al., "Unauthorized Movement and Mistaken Shipment," p. 12.

473   *nobody was ever asked to sign a piece of paper:* "In the past, there was a requirement for a formal change of custody, physically verified by serial numbers, recorded, and signed on a formal document when weapons moved from breakout crew to convoy crew to crew chief to air crew," the Defense Science Board noted. But at some point those procedures were discontinued—and the movement of nuclear weapons out of the igloo no longer had to be recorded. "Report on the Unauthorized Movement," p. 5.

473   *A maintenance team arrived at a Minuteman III silo:* For the details of this incident, see "United States Air Force Missile Accident Investigation Board Report," Minuteman III Launch Facility

A06, 319th Missile Squadron, 90th Operations Group, 90th Missile Wing, F. E. Warren Air Force Base, Wyoming, May 23, 2008, Robert M. Walker, President, Accident Investigation Board, September 18, 2008.

474 *The fire was most likely caused:* Ibid., p. 4.

474 *it may have occurred five days before the maintenance team noticed:* Ibid.

474 *"unique identifiers" for its nuclear weapons:* The Department of Defense is attempting, with varying degrees of success, to keep track of its vast inventory of weapons, parts, and equipment with "Item Unique Identification" (IUID) technology—the sort of bar codes that supermarkets and electronics stores have used for years. "In the area of Nuclear Weapon Related Material (NWRM)," the head of the Air Force Nuclear Weapons Center testified in 2010, "we continue to gain and refine Positive Inventory Control." The general promised to "lock down all NWRM through unique identifiers and supply chain discipline" but warned "there will be occasional discoveries of newly uncovered assets for years to come." Presumably the weapons themselves are now being scanned, tracked, and stored in the right place. See "Defense Logistics: Improvements Needed to Enhance DOD's Management Approach and Implementation of Item Unique Identification Technology," United States General Accountability Office, Report to the Subcommittee on Readiness, Committee on Armed Services, House of Representatives, May 2012; and "Status of the Air Force Nuclear Security Roadmap," Brigadier General Everett H. Thomas, Commander, Air Force Nuclear Weapons Center, Presentation to the Strategic Forces Subcommittee, Armed Services Committee, House of Representatives, 111th Congress, January 21, 2010, pp. 5, 6.

474 *Each of its twenty B-2 bombers costs $2 billion:* Cited in Tim Weiner, "The $2 Billion Bomber Can't Go Out in the Rain," *New York Times*, August 23, 1997.

474 *And its B-52 bombers haven't been manufactured since:* The last B-52 was made in 1962, and it's still flying. See John Andrew Prime, "B-52 Bomber Marks Major Milestones in 2012," *Air Force Times*, April 9, 2012.

474 *The B-52s are scheduled to remain in service:* See David Majumdar, "Upgrades to Keep B-52s Flying Through 2040," *Air Force Times*, October 4, 2011.

474 *Its mainframe computers had become hopelessly out of date:* The WWMCCS had never worked well. A 1979 study found that its automated data processing program was "not responsive" to local or national needs, "not reliable," and "cannot transfer data . . . efficiently." Other than that, it was a terrific system. The advent of digital communications spelled the end of the WWMCCS. See "The World Wide Military Command and Control System—Major Changes Needed in Its Automated Data Processing Management and Direction," Comptroller General of the United States, Report to the Congress, December 14, 1979, p. ii.

474 *the Global Command and Control System:* See "Global Command and Control System Adopted," news release, United States Department of Defense, No. 552-96, September 26, 1996.

475 *Known by the acronym DIRECT:* See "General Dynamics Awarded $1M DIRECT Emergency Action Message Support Contract," PR Newswire, May 23, 2001; and "DIRECT Messaging System Overview," General Dynamics C4 Systems (n.d.).

475 *a computer failure at F. E. Warren Air Force Base:* For details of the incident, see David S. Cloud, "Pentagon Cites Hardware Glitch in ICBM Outage," *Los Angeles Times*, October 27, 2010, and Michelle Tan, "Equipment Failure Cited in Warren Incident," *Air Force Times*, May 5, 2011.

475 *a report by the Defense Science Board warned:* See "Resilient Military Systems and the Advanced Cyber Threat," Task Force Report, Defense Science Board, Department of Defense, January 2013, pp. 7, 42, 85.

475 *no "significant vulnerability":* See "Hearing to Receive Testimony on U.S. Strategic Command and U.S. Cyber Command in Review of the Defense Authorization Request for Fiscal Year 2014 and the Future Years Defense Program," Committee on Armed Services, United States Senate, 113th Congress, March 12, 2013, p. 10.

475 *an "end-to-end comprehensive review":* See ibid.

475 *"Senator, I don't know":* See ibid., p. 22.

475 *Operation Neptune Spear:* See Mark Bowden, *The Finish: The Killing of Osama Bin Laden* (New York: Atlantic Monthly Press, 2012), pp. 216–64.

476 *The 9/11 Commission Report offers a sobering account:* See National Commission on Terrorist Attacks Upon the United States. *The 9/11 Commission Report: Final Report of the National Commission on Terrorist Attacks Upon the United States* (New York: W. W. Norton, 2004), pp. 1–46.

476 *an attack . . . that lasted about seventy-eight minutes:* The World Trade Center was hit by the first plane at 8:46:40 in the morning; the second plane struck the building at 9:03:11; the Pentagon was hit at 9:37:46; and United Airlines Flight 93 crashed in a field near Shanksville, Pennsylvannia, at 10:03:11. Those seventy-seven minutes and thirty-one seconds were an eternity—compared to the amount of time in which America's command-and-control system was supposed to respond decisively during a Soviet missile attack. For the chronology of that September morning, see *9/11 Commission Report,* pp. 32–33.

476 *His calls to the Pentagon and the White House underground bunker were constantly dropped:* Ibid., p. 40.

476 *they were ordered into the air by a Secret Service agent:* "The President and the Vice President indicated to us," the report notes, "they had not been aware that fighters had been scrambled out of Andrews, at the request of the Secret Service and outside the military chain of command." Ibid., p. 44.

476 *the United States has approximately 4,650 nuclear weapons:* These numbers come from Hans Kristensen, director of the Nuclear Information Project at the Federation of American Scientists. Kristensen has for many years been a reliable source and an indefatigable researcher on nuclear matters. See Hans M. Kristensen, "Trimming Nuclear Excess: Options for Further Reductions of U.S. and Russian Nuclear Forces," Federation of American Scientists, Special Report No. 5, December 2012, p. 15.

476 *About 300 are assigned to long-range bombers:* Cited in Hans M. Kristensen and Robert S. Norris, "U.S. Nuclear Forces, 2013," *Bulletin of the Atomic Scientists* (March/April 2013), p. 77.

476 *500 are deployed atop Minuteman III missiles:* Cited in ibid.

476 *1,150 are carried by Trident submarines:* Cited in ibid.

476 *An additional 200 or so hydrogen bombs:* Cited in ibid.

476 *About 2,500 nuclear weapons are held in reserve:* Cited in ibid.

476 *now known as the Operations Plan (OPLAN) 8010:* For the most detailed investigation of the current OPLAN, see Hans M. Kristensen, "Obama and the Nuclear War Plan," Federation of the American Scientists Issue Brief, February 2010.

476 *"Strategic Deterrence and Global Strike":* Quoted in ibid, p. 7.

477 *Russia, China, North Korea, Syria, and Iran:* Ibid., p. 3.

477 *"Adaptive planning":* Ibid., p. 5.

477 *The United States now plans to spend as much as $180 billion:* See Walter Pincus, "Nuclear Complex Upgrades Related to START Treaty to Cost $180 Billion," *Washington Post,* May 14, 2010.

477 *Russia has about 1,740 deployed strategic weapons and perhaps 2,000 tactical weapons:* Cited in Kristensen, "Trimming Nuclear Excess," p. 10.

477 *France is adding new aircraft and submarines:* For an overview of the world's nuclear powers, the size of their arsenals, and their modernization schemes, see Ian Kearns, "Beyond the United Kingdom: Trends in the Other Nuclear Armed States," Discussion Paper 1 of the BASIC Trident Commission, November 2011. The French weapons program is discussed on page 20.

477 *The United Kingdom . . . approximately 160 warheads:* An additional sixty-five warheads are kept in storage, for a total of 225. Cited in Richard Norton-Taylor, "Britain's Nuclear Arsenal is 225 Warheads, Reveals William Hague," *Guardian* (UK), May 26, 2010.

477 *China is thought to have about 240 nuclear weapons:* Cited in Hans M. Kristensen and Robert S. Norris, "Chinese Nuclear Forces, 2011," *Bulletin of the Atomic Scientists,* November 1, 2011, p. 81. At the moment, there is general agreement that China is increasing the size of its arsenal. But assertions that China has three thousand warheads hidden underground seem unlikely. For China's traditional policy of minimum deterrence, see M. Taylor Fravel and Evan S. Medeiros, "China's Search for Assured Retaliation: The Evolution of Chinese Nuclear Strategy and Force Structure," *International Security,* vol. 35, no. 2 (Fall 2010), pp. 7–44. For a much different interpretation of its nuclear policies, see Bret Stephens, "How Many Nukes Does China Have?," *Wall Street Journal,* October 24, 2011.

477 an "underground Great Wall": See Stephens, "How Many Nukes," and William Wan, "Georgetown Students Shed Light on China's Tunnel System for Nuclear Weapons," *Washington Post*, November 29, 2011.

477 North Korea may already have half a dozen nuclear weapons: See Mary Beth Nikitin, "North Korea's Nuclear Weapons: Technical Issues," CRS Report for Congress, Congressional Research Service, April 3, 2013, p. 4.

477 The yield of North Korea's first weapon test: Cited in ibid., p. 15.

478 "It could go off if a rifle bullet hit it": Quoted in Sagan, *Limits of Safety*, p. 266. The quote originally appeared in Gary Milhollin, "Building Saddam Hussein's Bomb," *New York Times*, March 8, 1992.

478 The ballistic-missile submarines in the Russian fleet: For the deterioration of Russian strategic forces and the potentially destabilizing effects, see David E. Mosher, Lowell H. Schwartz, David R. Howell, and Lynn E. Davis, *Beyond the Nuclear Shadow: A Phased Approach for Improving Nuclear Safety and U.S.–Russian Relations* (Santa Monica, CA: RAND, 2003).

478 the launch of a small research rocket by Norway: For the story of this false alarm, which occurred years after the end of the Cold War, see David Hoffman, "Cold War Doctrines Refuse to Die," *Washington Post*, March 15, 1998.

478 The greatest risk of nuclear war now lies in South Asia: That is my personal view, and unfortunately, a great deal has been written that supports it. *Inside Nuclear South Asia* (Stanford: Stanford University Press, 2009), edited by Scott D. Sagan, contains two particularly good essays: "Revisionist Ambitions, Conventional Capabilities, and Nuclear Instability: Why Nuclear South Asia Is Not Like Cold War Europe," by S. Paul Kapur, and "The Evolution of Pakistani and Indian Doctrine," by Sagan. Another fine book is Feroz Hassan Khan's *Eating Grass: The Making of the Pakistani Bomb* (Stanford: Stanford Security Series, 2012). Paul Bracken's *The Second Nuclear Age: Strategy, Danger, and the New Power Politics* (New York: Times Books, 2012) has a provocative chapter on the risk of nuclear war in South Asia. Bracken has been studying the importance of command and control for more than thirty years. The work of a British academic, Shaun Gregory, seems especially relevant at the moment. Before investigating Pakistan's efforts to maintain its nuclear weapons securely, Gregory wrote a book about nuclear weapons accidents and one about the command and control of NATO forces. I learned much during my conversation with Gregory and from his writing, especially "The Security of Nuclear Weapons in Pakistan," Pakistan Security Research Unit, Brief Number 22, November 18, 2007; "The Terrorist Threat to Pakistan's Nuclear Weapons," *CTC Sentinel*, Combating Terrorism Center at West Point, July 2009, pp. 1–4; and "Terrorist Tactics in Pakistan Threaten Nuclear Weapons Safety," *CTC Sentinel*, Combating Terrorism Center at West Point, June 2011, pp. 4–7.

479 Pakistan has doubled the size of its arsenal since 2006: Cited in Bracken, *The Second Nuclear Age*, p. 162.

479 It now has about 100 nuclear weapons: Estimates range from 90 to 110. Cited in Paul K. Kerr and Mary Beth Nikitin, "Pakistan's Nuclear Weapons: Proliferation and Security Issues," CRS Report for Congress, Congressional Research Service, March 19, 2013, p. 5.

480 a bold attack on the headquarters of the Pakistan army: See Gregory, "Terrorist Tactics in Pakistan," pp. 5–6.

480 Another attack penetrated a naval aviation base: Ibid., pp. 6–7.

480 the roughly seventy thousand nuclear weapons built by the United States: Cited in Stephen I. Schwartz, ed., *Atomic Audit: The Costs and Consequences of U.S. Nuclear Weapons Since 1940* (Washington, D.C.: Brookings Insitution, 1998), p. 102.

480 a success rate of 99.99857 percent: Or to put it another way, if a single nuclear weapon had been stolen or detonated, it would have represented a little more than one thousandth of 1 percent of the entire stockpile.

481 the rate of industrial accidents: Due to variations in record keeping among different countries, any comparison between their accident rates will be imprecise. Nevertheless, the figures that have been compiled do give a sense of relative technological mastery. As the authors of this study found, the "difference in accident rates between developed and developing countries is remarkable." The workplaces in the developed world are much safer; perhaps 350,000 people die on the job every

year, mainly in developing nations. See Päivi Hämäläinen, Jukka Takala, and Kaija Leena Saarela, "Global Estimates of Occupational Accidents," *Safety Science*, no. 44 (2006), pp. 137–56.

481   *That rate is about two times higher in India:* According to the study, the rate of industrial accidents in the United States is 3,959 per 100,000 workers, and the rate in India is 8,763 per 100,000. Ibid., pp. 145, 147.

481   *three times higher in Iran:* The rate in Iran is 12,845 per 100,000. Ibid., p. 153.

481   *four times higher in Pakistan:* The rate in Pakistan is 15,809 per 100,000. Ibid., p. 148.

482   *"A World Free of Nuclear Weapons":* George P. Shultz, William J. Perry, Henry A. Kissinger, and Sam Nunn, "A World Free of Nuclear Weapons," *Wall Street Journal*, January 4, 2007.

482   *"The world is now on the precipice":* Ibid.

482   *the two nations that control about 90 percent of those weapons:* Cited in Madeleine Albright and Igor Ivanov, "A New Agenda for U.S.-Russia Cooperation," *New York Times,* December 30, 2012.

482   *The campaign to eliminate nuclear weapons:* For a fine account of today's antinuclear movement, see Philip Taubman, *The Partnership: Five Cold Warriors and Their Quest to Ban the Bomb* (New York: HarperCollins, 2012). For a detailed look at how such disarmament might occur, see "Modernizing U.S. Nuclear Strategy, Force Structure and Posture," Global Zero U.S. Nuclear Policy Commission, May 2012. And for the opposing point of view, see Rebeccah Heindrichs and Baker Spring, "Deterrence and Nuclear Targeting in the 21st Century," Backgrounder on Arms Control and Nonproliferation, The Heritage Foundation, November 30, 2012.

482   *"Some argue that the spread of these weapons":* "Remarks by President Barack Obama, Hradcany Square, Prague, Czech Republic," The White House, Office of the Press Secretary, April 5, 2009.

482   *"Such fatalism is a deadly adversary":* Ibid.

482   *"a world without nuclear weapons":* Ibid.

483   *an average age of seventy-nine:* Nunn was sixty-eight; Perry, eighty; Kissinger, eighty-three; and Shultz, eighty-six.

483   *Bush's counterforce strategy:* For an analysis of how the Bush administration planned to use nuclear weapons, see Charles L. Glaser and Steve Fetter, "Counterforce Revisited: Assessing the Nuclear Posture Review's New Missions," *International Security*, vol. 30, no. 2 (Fall 2005), pp. 84–126.

483   *"nuclear disarmament fantasy":* Harold Brown and John Deutch, "The Nuclear Disarmament Fantasy," *Wall Street Journal*, November 19, 2007.

483   *"Hope is not a policy":* Ibid.

484   *In 2010 a group of high-ranking Air Force officials:* James Wood Forsyth, Jr.; Colonel B. Chance Saltzman, USAF; and Gary Schaub, Jr., "Remembrance of Things Past: The Enduring Value of Nuclear Weapons," *Strategic Studies Quarterly*, vol. 4, no. 1 (Spring 2010), p. 82.

484   *almost 200 fewer weapons:* A report by the two groups suggested that in the future the United States will need only five hundred nuclear weapons for deterrence. See Hans M. Kristensen, Robert S. Norris, and Ivan Oelrich, "From Counterforce to Minimal Deterrence: A New Nuclear Policy on the Path Toward Eliminating Nuclear Weapons," Federation of American Scientists and the Natural Resources Defense Council, Occasional Paper No. 7, April 2009, p. 44.

484   *the problems with a strategy of minimum deterrence:* The morality of killing civilians as an act of vengeance—after their leaders launched a nuclear attack—has always been an awkward subject for deterrence theorists. In a recent book, the author Ron Rosenbaum questioned the ethics of a retaliatory nuclear strike and urged missile crews to disobey any order to launch: "Nothing justifies following orders for genocide." For a provocative analysis of the issue, see John D. Steinbruner and Tyler Wigg-Stevenson, "Reconsidering the Morality of Deterrence," CISSM Working Paper, Center for International and Security Studies at Maryland, University of Maryland, March 2012; and Ron Rosenbaum, *How the End Begins: The Road to a Nuclear World War III* (New York: Simon & Schuster, 2011). The quote can be found on page 260.

BIBLIOGRAPHY

Reports

"Acceptable Premature Probabilities for Nuclear Weapons," Headquarters Field Command, Armed Forces Special Weapons Project, FC/10570136, October 1, 1957 (SECRET/RESTRICTRED DATA/declassified).

"Accidental War: Some Dangers in the 1960s," Mershon Center for Education in National Security, Housmans (n.d.).

"Accident Environments," T. D. Brumleve, Chairman, Task Group on Accident Environments, Sandia Laboratories, SCL-DR-69-86, January 1970 (SECRET/RESTRICTED DATA/declassified).

"Accidents and Incidents Involving Nuclear Weapons: Accidents and Incidents During the Period 1 July 1957 Through 31 March 1967," Technical Letter 20-3, Defense Atomic Support Agency, October 15, 1967 (SECRET/RESTRICTED DATA/declassified).

"An Activated Barrier for Protection of Special Nuclear Materials in Vital Areas," Ronald E. Timm, James E. Miranda, Donald L. Reigle, and Anthony D. Valente, Argonne National Laboraory, 1984.

"The Aftermath of a Single Nuclear Detonation by Accident or Sabotage: Some Problems Affecting U.S. Policy, Military Reactions, and Public Information," Fred Charles Iklé with J. E. Hill, Research Memorandum, Project RAND, U.S. Air Force, Santa Monica, California, May 8, 1959, RM-2364 (SECRET/RESTRICTED DATA/declassified).

"Aggregate Nuclear Damage Assessment Techniques Applied to Western Europe," H. Avrech and D. C. McGarvey, RAND Corporation, Memorandum RM-4466-ISA, Prepared for the Office of the Assistant Secretary of Defense/International Security Affairs, June 1965 (FOR OFFICIAL USE ONLY/declassified).

"AGM-69A SRAM Explosive Components Surveillance Program Summary Report and FY74 Service Life Estimate," Charles E. Stanbery, et al., Aeronautical Systems Division, Wright-Patterson Air Force Base, AD-A014 428, January 1975.

"Air Force Blue Ribbon Review of Nuclear Weapons Policies and Procedures," Polly A. Peyer, Headquarters, United States Air Force, February 8, 2008.

"The Air Force Role in Five Crises, 1958–1965: Lebanon, Taiwan, Congo, Cuba, Dominican Republic," Bernard C. Nalty, USAF Historical Division Liaison Office, June 1968 (TOP SECRET/declassified), NSA.

"The Air Force and Strategic Deterrence 1951–1960," George F. Lemmer, USAF Historical Division Liaison Office, December 1967 (SECRET/FORMERLY RESTRICTED DATA/declassified), NSA.

"The Air Force and the Worldwide Military Command and Control System, 1961–1965 (U)," Thomas A. Sturm, USAF Historical Division Liaison Office, August 1966 (SECRET/declassified), NSA.

"Airpower and the Cult of the Offensive," John R. Carter, CADRE Paper, College of Aerospace Doctrine, Research, and Education, Air University Press, Maxwell Air Force Base, Alabama, October 1998.

"Alcohol & Drug Use in the Marine Corps in 1983," Peter H. Stoloff and Renee K. Barnow, Center for Naval Analyses, CNR 90, Vol. 1, July 1984.

"Analytical Support for the Joint Chiefs of Staff: The WSEG Experience, 1948–1976," John Ponturo, Institute for Defense Analyses, International and Social Studies Division, IDA Study S-507, July 1979.

"Assessing the Capabilities of Strategic Nuclear Forces: The Limits of Current Methods," Bruce W. Bennett, RAND Corporation, N-1441-NA, June 1980.

"Assessment Report: Titan II LGM 25 C, Weapon Condition and Safety," Prepared for the Senate Armed Services Committee and House Armed Services Committee, May 1980.

"Attack Warning: Better Management Required to Resolve NORAD Integration Deficiencies," Report to the Chairman, Subcommittee on Defense, Committee on Appropriations, House of Representatives, United States General Accounting Office, July 1989.

"The Ballistic Missile Decisions," Robert L. Perry, RAND Corporation, October 1967.

"Ballistic Missile Staff Course Study Guide," 4315th Combat Crew Training Squadron, Strategic Air Command, Vandenberg Air Force Base, July 1, 1980.

"Beyond the United Kingdom: Trends in the Other Nuclear Armed States," Ian Kearns, Discussion Paper 1, BASIC Trident Commission, November 2011.

"A Brief Survey of the Evolution of Ideas About Counterforce," Alfred Goldberg, Prepared for U.S. Air Force Project RAND, Memorandum RM-5431-PR, October 1967 (revised March 1981), NSA.

"Command, Control, and Communications Problems" Ronald A. Finkler, et al., WSEG Report 159, Volume I: Summary, Institute for Defense Analyses, Science and Technology Division, February 1971 (TOP SECRET/declassified).

"Command and Control for North American Air Defense, 1959–1963," Thomas A. Sturm, USAF Historical Division Liaison Office, SHO-S-65/18, January 1965 (SECRET/declassified).

"Command and Control of Soviet Nuclear Weapons: Dangers and Opportunities Arising from the August Revolution," Hearing Before the Subcommittee on European Affairs of the Committee on Foreign Relations, United States Senate, 102nd Congress, First Session, September 24, 1991.

"Command and Control Systems for Nuclear Weapons: History and Current Status," Systems Development Department I, Sandia Laboratories, SLA-73-0415, September 1973 (SECRET/RESTRICTED DATA/ declassified).

"Countervailing Strategy Demands Revision of Strategic Force Acquisition Plans," Comptroller General of the United States, MASAD-81-355, August 5, 1981.

"Custody," Assistant to the Secretary of Defense (Atomic Energy), Office of the Secretary of Defense, November 10, 1960 (TOP SECRET/RESTRICTED DATA/declassified), NSA.

"Defense Logistics: Improvements Needed to Enhance DOD's Management Approach and Implementation of Item Unique Identification Technology," United States Government Accountability Office, Report to the Subcommittee on Readiness, Committee on Armed Services, House of Representatives, May 2012.

"Department of Defense Authorization for Appropriations for Fiscal Year 1986," Hearings Before the Committee on Armed Services United States Senate, Ninety-ninth Congress, 1st Session, 1985.

"Deterrence & Survival in the Nuclear Age," Security Resources Panel of the Science Advisory Committee, Washington, D.C., November 7, 1957 (TOP SECRET/declassified), NSA.

"The Development of the SM-68 Titan," Warren E. Greene, Historical Office, Deputy Commander for Aerospace Systems, Air Force Systems Command, August 1962 (SECRET/FORMERLY RESTRICTED DATA/declassified), NSA.

"The Development of the SM-80 Minuteman," Robert F. Piper, DCAS Historical Office, Deputy Commander for Aerospace Systems, Air Force Systems Command, April 1962 (SECRET/RESTRICTED DATA/declassified), NSA.

"The Development of Strategic Air Command, 1946–1976," J. C. Hopkins, Office of the Historian, Strategic Air Command, March 21, 1976.

"Did High-Altitude EMP Cause the Hawaiian Streetlight Incident?," Charles Vittitoe, Electromagnetic Applications Division, Sandia National Laboratories, System Design and Assessment Notes, Note 31, June 1989.

"Effect of Civilian Morale on Military Capabilities in a Nuclear War Environment: Enclosure 'E,' The Relationship to Public Morale of Information About the Effects of Nuclear Warfare," WSEG Report No. 42, Weapons Systems Evaluation Group, Joint Chiefs of Staff, October 20, 1959 (CONFIDENTIAL/declassified).

"The Effects of Atomic Bombs on Hiroshima and Nagasaki," United States Strategic Bombing Survey, June 30, 1946 (SECRET/declassified).

"The Effects of Nuclear War," Office of Technology Assessment, Congress of the United States, May 1979.

"Electric Initiators: A Review of the State of the Art," Gunther Cohn, Franklin Institute, Prepared for the Picatinny Arsenal, AD266014, November 1961 (CONFIDENTIAL/declassified).

"Enclosure 'I' Changes in the Free World," Weapons Systems Evaluation Group Report No. 50, November 18, 1960 (TOP SECRET/RESTRICTED DATA/declassified).

"The Evaluation of the Atomic Bomb as a Military Weapons," Enclosure "A," the Final Report of the Joint Chiefs of Staff Evaluation Board for Operation Crossroads, June 30, 1947 (TOP SECRET/declassified).

"Evaluation of Programmed Strategic Offensive Weapons Systems," Weapons Systems Evaluation Group Report No. 50, Washington, D.C., December 27, 1960 (TOP SECRET/RESTRICTED DATA/declassified), NSA.

"The Evolution of U.S. Strategic Command and Control and Warning 1945–1972," L. Wainstein, Project Leader, C. D. Cremeans, J. K. Moriarity, and J. Ponturo, Study S-467, International and Social Studies Division, Institute for Defense Analyses, June 1975 (TOP SECRET/RESTRICTED DATA/declassified).

"Exploiting and Securing the Open Border in Berlin: The Western Secret Services, the Stasi, and the Second Berlin Crisis, 1958–1961," Paul Maddrell, Woodrow Wilson International Center for Scholars, Cold War International History Project, Working Paper No. 58, February 2009.

"Factors Affecting the Vulnerability of Atomic Weapons to Fire," Full-Scale Test Report No. 2, Armour Research Foundation of Illinois Institute of Technology, Armed Forces Special Weapons Project Report No. 1066, February 1958 (SECRET/RESTRICTED DATA/declassified).

"The Feasibility of Population Targeting," R. H. Craver, M. K. Drake, J. T. McGahan, E. Swick, and J. F. Schneider, Science Applications, Inc., Prepared for the Defense Nuclear Agency, June 30, 1979 (SECRET/RESTRICTED DATA/declassified).

"Final Evaluation Report, MK IV MOD O FM BOMB," Mk IV Evaluation Committee, Sandia Laboratory, Report No. SL-82, September 13, 1949 (SECRET/RESTRICTED DATA/declassified).

"Final Titan II Operational Data Summary," Rev 3, TRW Space Technology Laboratories, September 1964.

"From Counterforce to Minimal Deterrence: A New Nuclear Policy on the Path Toward Eliminating Nuclear Weapons," Hans M. Kristensen, Robert S. Norris, Ivan Oelrich, Federation of American Scientists & The Natural Resources Defense Council, Occasional Paper No. 7, April 2009.

"Hearing to Receive Testimony on U.S. Strategic Command and U.S. Cyber Command in Review of the Defense Authorization Request for Fiscal Year 2014 and the Future Years Defense Program," Committee on Armed Services, United States Senate, 113th Congress, March 12, 2013.

"Historical Analysis of Command and Control Actions in the 1962 Cuban Missile Crisis," Enclosure A, C&C Internal Memorandum No. 40, August 14, 1964 (TOP SECRET/declassified), NSA.

"A Historical Study of Strategic Connectivity, 1950–1981," Joint Chiefs of Staff Special Historical Study, Historical Division, Joint Chiefs of Staff, July 1982 (TOP SECRET/declassified), NSA.

"History of Air Defense Weapons, 1946–1962," Richard F. McMullen, Historical Division Office of Information, Headquarters, Air Defense Command, ADC Historical Study No. 14, 1962.

"A History of the Air Force Atomic Energy Program: 1943–1953," USAF Historical Division, 1959 (TOP SECRET/RESTRICTED DATA/declassified), NSA.

"History of Air Research and Development Command, July–December 1960," Volume III, Historical Division, Air Research & Development Command, United States Air Force (n.d.) (SECRET/RESTRICTED DATA/declassified).

"History of the Custody and Deployment of Nuclear Weapons: July 1945 Through September 1977," Office of the Assistant to the Secretary of Defense (Atomic Energy), February 1978 (TOP SECRET/RESTRICTED DATA/FORMERLY RESTRICTED DATA/declassified).

"History of the Early Thermonuclear Weapons: Mks 14, 15, 16, 17, 24, and 29," Information Research Division, Sandia National Laboratories, RS 3434/10 (SECRET/RESTRICTED DATA/declassified), June 1967.

"History of Headquarters Strategic Air Command, 1961," SAC Historical Study No. 89, History & Research Division, Strategic Air Command, January 1962 (TOP SECRET/declassified), NSA.

"History of the Joint Strategic Target Planning Staff: Background and Preparation of SIOP-62," History & Research Division, Strategic Air Command, 1963 (TOP SECTRET/declassified), NSA.

"History of the Joint Strategic Target Planning Staff: Preparation of SIOP-63," History & Research Division, Strategic Air Command, January 1964 (TOP SECRET/declassified), NSA.

"History of the Joint Strategic Target Planning Staff SIOP-4 J/K, July 1971–June 1972," Dr. Walton S. Moody, History & Research Division, Strategic Air Command (n.d.) (TOP SECRET/RESTRICTED DATA/unclassified).

"History of the Little Rock Area Office, Corps of Engineers Ballistic Missile Construction Office, 5 October 1960–31 July 1963," Arthur R. Simpson, Army Engineers Ballistic Missile Construction Office, 1963.

"The History of Nuclear Weapon Safety Devices," David W. Plummer and William H. Greenwood, Sandia National Laboratories, Paper Submitted at Joint Propulsion Conference, American Institute of Aeronautics and Astronautics, July 1998.

"History of the Redstone Missile System," John W. Bullard, Historical Division, Army Missile Command, AMC 23 M, October 15, 1965.

"History of the Strategic Air Command, 1 January 1958–30 June 1958," Historical Study No. 73, Volume 1, Headquarters, Strategic Air Command (n.d.) (TOP SECRET/RESTRICTED DATA/declassified).

"History of Strategic Air Command, June 1958–July 1959," Historical Study No. 76, Volume I, Headquarters, Strategic Air Command (n.d.) (TOP SECRET/RESTRICTED DATA/declassified).

"History of the Strategic Air Command: Historical Study #73A SAC Targeting Concepts" Historical Division, Office of Information, Headquarters, Strategic Air Command, 1959 (TOP SECRET/declassified), NSA.

"History of the Strategic Arms Competition, 1945–1972," Ernest R. May, John D. Steinbruner, and Thomas W. Wolfe, Office of the Secretary of Defense, Historical Office, March 1981 (TOP SECRET/RESTRICTED DATA/declassified).

"History of U.S. Nuclear Weapon Safety Assessment: The Early Years," Stanley D. Spray, Systems Studies Department, Sandia National Laboratories, SAND96-1099C, Version E, May 5, 1996.

"History of the XW-51 Warhead," AEC Atomic Weapon Data, SC-M-67-683, January 1968 (SECRET/RESTRICTED DATA/declassified).

"Hydronuclear Experiments," Robert N. Thorn, Donald R. Westervelt, Los Alamos National Laboratories, LA-10902-MS, February 1987.

"Information Bulletin: Intrusion Detection System, AN/TPS-39(V), Radar Surveillance Equipment," Atlas-Titan, Radar Surveillance Security System, Sylvania Electronic Systems, West Mountain View, California, December 1964.

"Interim Report on Command and Control in Europe," National Command and Control Task Force, United States Department of Defense, October 1961 (TOP SECRET/declassified), NSA.

"Job Attitudes: How SAC Personnel Compare with the Rest of the Air Force," Stephen D. Bull III, Air Command and Staff College, Air University, Maxwell Air Force Base, Alabama, 1986.

"JTF Operations Since 1983," George Stewart, S. M. Fabbri, and A. B. Siegel, Center for Naval Analyses, CRM-94-42, July 1994.

"Jupiter: Development Aspects—Deployment," John C. Brassell, Historical Office, Mobile Air Material Area, Brookley Air Force Base, September 1962 (SECRET/declassified), NSA.

"Lessons Learned from Early Criticality Accidents," Richard E. Malenfant, Los Alamos National Laboratory, Submitted for Nuclear Criticality Technology Safety Project Workshop, Gaithersburg, Maryland, May 14–15, 1996.

"Living in the Question? The Berlin Nuclear Crisis Critical Oral History," Benina Berger Gould, Institute of Slavic, East European, and Eurasian Studies, UC Berkeley, Working Paper, March 2003.

"The Magnitude of Initial Postattack Recovery Activities," Richard L. Goen, Stanford Research Institute, Prepared for the Office of Civil Defense, Office of the Secretary of the Army, December 1971.

"The Manhattan Project: Making the Atomic Bomb," F. G. Gosling, National Security History Series, United States Department of Energy, January 2010.

"Manual for Handling Missile Propellants," Facilities Engineering Department, Pan American World Airways, Guided Missiles Range Division, Patrick AFB, Florida, 1958.

"The Marshal's Baton: There Is No Bomb, There Was No Bomb, They Were Not Looking for a Bomb," Svend Aage Christensen, Danish Institute for International Studies, DIIS Report, No. 18, 2009.

"Military Applications of Nuclear Technology," Part 1, Hearing Before the Subcommittee on Military Applications, Joint Committee on Atomic Energy, Ninety-third Congress, April 16, 1973.

"Military and Civil Defense Nuclear Weapons Effects Projects Conducted at the Nevada Test Site: 1951–1958," Barbara Killian, Defense Threat Reduction Agency, DTRA-IR-10-57, May 2011.

"Minimum Nuclear Deterrence Research: Final Report," Gregory Giles, C. Cleary, M. Ledgerwood, Advanced Systems and Concepts Office, Defense Threat Reduction Agency, May 15, 2003.

"Minutes of the Eleventh Explosives Safety Seminar," Vol. 2, Armed Services Explosives Safety Board, Sheraton-Peabody Hotel, Memphis, Tennessee, September 9–10, 1969.

"Missile Launch/Missile Officer (LGM-25): Missile Systems," Student Study Guide 3OBR1821F/3121F-V1 Through 4, Volume I of II, Department of Missile and Space Training, Sheppard Technical Training Center, September 1968.

"Missile Liquid Propellant Systems Maintenance Specialist," Volume 3, Propellant Transfer System, CDC 4551, Extension Course Institute, Air Training Command, February 1983.

"Missile Procurement, Air Force," Hearings Before the Subcommittee on Defense, House Committee on Appropriations, Eighty-seventh Congress, May 16, 1961 (SECRET/declassified), NSA.

"Missile Silo Fire at Little Rock AFB, Arkansas," and "Fire Protection Problems for Special Atmospheres—Including Oxygen," Minutes of Annual Meeting, Federal Fire Council, Washington, D.C., April 5, 1967.

"Modernizing U.S. Nuclear Strategy, Force Structure and Posture," Global Zero U.S. Nuclear Policy Commission Report, May 2012.

"Modernizing U.S. Strategic Offensive Forces: The Administration's Program and Alternatives," a CBO Study, Congressional Budget Office, Congress of the United States, May 1983.

"MX Missile Basing," Office of Technology, United States Government Printing Office, September 1981.

"MX Missile Basing Mode," Hearings Before a Subcommittee of the Committee on Appropriations, United States Senate, Ninety-sixth Congress, Second Session, Special Hearing, Department of Defense, 1980.

"National Defense Budget Estimates for FY 2013," Office of the Under Secretary of Defense (Comptroller), March 2012.

"NATO in the 1960's," National Security Council, November 8, 1960 (TOP SECRET/declassified), NSA.

"Nonstrategic Nuclear Weapons," Amy F. Woolf, CRS Report for Congress, Congressional Research Service, February 14, 2012.

"NORAD's Information Processing Improvement Program: Will It Enhance Mission Capability?" Elmer B. Staats, Comptroller General of the United States, Report to Congress, General Accounting Office, LCD-78-117, September 21, 1978.

"NORAD's Missile Warning System: What Went Wrong?" Comptroller General of the United States, Report to Congress, General Accounting Office, MASAD-81-30, May 15, 1981.

"North Korea's Nuclear Weapons: Technical Issues," Mary Beth Nikitin, CRS Report for Congress, Congressional Research Service, April 3, 2013.

"Nuclear Hardness and Base Escape," Rayford P. Patrick, USAF, Engineering Report No. 5-112, Directorate of Aircraft Maintenance, Headquarters, Strategic Air Command, March 31, 1981.

"The Nuclear Safety Problem," T. D. Brumleve, Advanced System Research Department 5510, Sandia Corporation, Livermore Laboratory, SCL-DR-67, 1967 (SECRET/RESTRICTED DATA/declassified).

"Nuclear Warheads: The Reliable Replacement Warhead Program and the Life Extension Program," Jonathan Medalia, CRS Report for Congress, Congressional Research Service, December 3, 2007.

"Nuclear Weapon Safety," Sandia Corporation with the Cooperation of the Los Alamos Scientific Laboratory and the Ernest O. Lawrence Radiation Laboratory, SC-4630(WD), October 1961 (SECRET/RESTRICTED DATA/declassified).

"Nuclear Weapon Specialist, Volume 4: Bomb Maintenance," Extension Course Institute, Air Training Command, CDC 46350, July 1980 (FOR OFFICIAL USE ONLY).

"Nuclear Weapon Specialist, Volume 5: Rockets, Missiles, and Reentry Systems," Extension Course Institute, Air Training Command, CDC 46350, November 1980 (FOR OFFICIAL USE ONLY).

"Nuclear Weapons Engineering and Delivery," Los Alamos Technical Series, Volume 23, LA-1161 July 1946 (SECRET/declassified).

"Nuclear Weapons Testing at the Nevada Test Site: The First Decade," John C. Hopkins and Barbara Killian, Defense Threat Reduction Agency, May 2011.

"On a Distributed Command and Control System Configuration," Paul Baran, U.S. Air Force, Project RAND, Research Memorandum, RM-2632, December 31, 1960.

"On Distributed Communications Networks," Paul Baran, RAND Corporation, P-2626, September 1962.

"On the Risk of an Accidental or Unauthorized Nuclear Detonation," Fred Charles Iklé with Gerald J. Aronson and Albert Madansky, Research Memorandum, U.S. Air Force Project RAND, RM-2251, October 15, 1958 (CONFIDENTIAL/RESTRICTED DATA/declassified).

"On Weapons Plutonium in the Arctic Environment (Thule, Greenland)," Mats Eriksson, Risø National Laboratory, Roskilde, Denmark, Risø-R-1321(EN), April 2002.

"Operation Castle, Project 3.2: Crater Survey, Headquarters, Field Command, Armed Forces Special Weapons Project, June 1955 (SECRET/FORMERLY RESTRICTED DATA/declassified).

"Operation Dominic: Fish Bowl Series," M. J. Rubenstein, Project Officers Report—Project 8C, Reentry Vehicle Tests, Air Force Special Weapons Center, July 3, 1963 (SECRET/RESTRICTED DATA/declassified).

"Operation Dominic I, 1962," United States Atmospheric Nuclear Weapons Tests, Nuclear Test Personnel Review, Defense Nuclear Agency, February 1983.

"Operation Dominic II, Shot Small Boy, Project Officers Report—Project 7.14: Bomb Alarm Detector Test," Cecil C. Harvell, Defense Atomic Support Agency, April 19, 1963 (CONFIDENTIAL/FORMERLY RESTRICTED DATA/declassified).

"Operation Ivy 1952," United States Atmospheric Nuclear Weapons Tests, Nuclear Test Personnel Review, Defense Nuclear Agency, DNA 6036F, December 1, 1982.

"Operation Upshot-Knothole, 1953," United States Atmospheric Nuclear Weapons Tests, Nuclear Test Personnel Review, Defense Nuclear Agency, DNA 6014F, January 11, 1982.

"The Origins and Evolution of S²C at Sandia National Laboratories, 1949–1996," William L. Stevens, Consultant to Surety Assessment Center, Sandia National Laboratories, SAND99-1308, September 2001 (OFFICIAL USE ONLY).

"Our Nation's Nuclear Warning System: Will It Work if We Need It?" Hearing Before a Subcommittee of the Committee on Government Operations, House of Representatives, Ninety-ninth Congress, First Session, September 26, 1985.

"Pakistan's Nuclear Weapons: Proliferation and Security Issues," Paul K. Kerr and Mary Beth Nikitin, CRS Report for Congress, Congressional Research Service, March 19, 2013.

"PAL Control of Theater Nuclear Weapons," Mark E. Bleck and Paul R. Souder, Command and Control Division, Sandia National Laboratories, SAND82-2436, March 1984 (SECRET/FORMERLY RESTRICTED DATA/declassified).

"Palomares Summary Report," Field Command, Defense Nuclear Agency, Kirtland Air Force Base, New Mexico, January 15, 1975.

"Peace Is Our Profession; Alert Operations and the Strategic Air Command, 1957–1991," Office of the Historian, Headquarters, Strategic Air Command, December 7, 1991.

"Pit Lifetime," MITRE Corporation, JSR-06-335, January 11, 2007.

"Plutonium Hazards Created by Accidental or Experimental Low-Order Detonation of Nuclear Weapons," W. H. Langham, P. S. Harris, and T. L. Shipman, Los Alamos Scientific Laboratory, LA-1981, December 1955 (SECRET/RESTRICTED DATA/declassified).

"The Postattack Population of the United States," Ira S. Lowry, Prepared for the Technical Analysis Branch, United States Atomic Energy Commission, RAND Corporation, RM-5115-TAB, December 1966.

"A Preliminary Report on the B-52 Accident in Greenland on January 21, 1968," Jørgen Koch, Symposium on Radiological Protection of the Public in Nuclear Mass Disasters, Interlaken, Switzerland, May 1968.

"A Primer on U.S. Strategic Nuclear Policy," David M. Kunsman and Douglas B. Lawson, Sandia National Laboratories, SAND2001-0053, January 2001.

"Progress Report to the Joint Committee on Atomic Energy, Part III: Weapons," United States Atomic Energy Commission, June Through November 1952 (TOP SECRET/RESTRICTED DATA/declassified).

"Project Crescent: A Study of Salient Features for an Airborne Alert (Supersafe) Bomb," Final Report, D. E. McGovern, Exploratory Systems Department I, Sandia Laboratories, SC-WD-70-879, April 1971 (SECRET/RESTRICTED DATA/declassified).

"Project Crested Ice: The Thule Nuclear Accident," Vol. 1, SAC Historical Study No. 113, History & Research Division, Headquarters, Strategic Air Command, April 23, 1969 (declassified), NSA.

"Project Crested Ice: USAF B-52 Accident at Thule, Greenland, 21 January 1968," Defense Nuclear Agency, 1968 (SECRET/RESTRICTED DATA/declassified).

"Protecting U.S. Power to Strike Back in the 1950's and 1960's," A. J. Wohlstetter, F. S. Hoffman and H. S. Rowen, U.S. Air Force Project RAND, R-290, September 1, 1956 (FOR OFFICIAL USE ONLY).

"The Quick Count System: A User's Manual," N. D. Cohen, RAND Corporation, RM-4006-PR, April 1964.

"Reconsidering the Morality of Deterrence," John D. Steinbruner and Tyler Wigg-Stevenson, CISSM Working Paper, Center for International and Security Studies at Maryland, University of Maryland, March 2012.

"Record of Decision: BOMARC Missile Accident Site, McGuire Air Force Base, New Jersey," Gary Vest, McGuire Air Force Base, New Jersey, November 20, 1992.

"Recovery from Nuclear Attack and Research and Action Programs to Enhance Recovery Prospects," Jack C. Greene, Robert W. Stokely, and John K. Christian, International Center for Emergency Preparedness, Prepared for the Federal Emergency Management Agency, Washington, D.C., December 1979.

"Reevaluating Nuclear Safety and Security in a Post 9/11 Era," Lisa Brown and Paul Booker, Sandia Report, Sandia National Laboratories, July 2005.

"Remedial Action and Final Radiological Status, 1964 B-58 Accident Site, Grissom Air Reserve Base, Bunker Hill, Indiana," Steven E. Rademacher, Air Force Institute for Environment, Safety, and Occupational Health Risk Analysis, IERA-SD-BR-SR-2000-0017, December 2000.

"Report of Ad Hoc Subcommittee on U.S. Policies Regarding Assignment of Nuclear Weapons to NATO; Includes Letter to President Kennedy and Appendices," Joint Committee on Atomic Energy, Congress of the United States," February 11, 1961 (TOP SECRET/RESTRICTED DATA/declassified), NSA.

"Report to the Congress: Assessment of the Safety of U.S. Nuclear Weapons and Related Nuclear Test Requirements," R. E. Kidder, Lawrence Livermore National Laboratory, July 26, 1991.

"Report of Missile Accident Investigation: Major Missile Accident, 18–19 September 1980, Titan II Complex 374-7, Assigned to 308th Strategic Missile Wing, Little Rock Air Force Base, Arkansas," Conducted at Little Rock Air Force Base, Arkansas, and Barksdale Air Force Base, Louisiana, December 14–19, 1980.

"Report of Missile Accident Investigation: Major Missile Accident, Titan II Complex 533-7, Assigned to

381st Strategic Missile Wing, McConnell Air Force Base, Kansas," Conducted at McConnell Air Force Base, Kansas, September 22–October 10, 1978.

"A Report to the National Security Council by the Executive Secretary on Basic National Security Policy," NSC 162/2, October 30, 1953 (TOP SECRET/declassified).

"The Report of the Nuclear Weapons Safety Panel," Hearing Before the Committee on Armed Services, House of Representatives, 101st Congress, Second Session, December 18, 1990.

"Report of the Panel on Nuclear Weapons Safety of the Committee on Armed Services, House of Representatives, 101st Congress, Second Session," Sidney D. Drell, Chairman; John S. Foster, Jr.; and Charles H. Townes, December 1990.

"Report on Recent False Alerts from the Nation's Missile Warning System," United States Senate, Committee on Armed Services, Ninety-sixth Congress, First Session, October 9, 1980.

"Report of the Secretary of Defense Task Force on DoD Nuclear Weapons Management, Phase I: The Air Force's Nuclear Mission," James A. Blackwell, Jr., Executive Director, September 2008.

——, "Phase II: Review of the DoD Nuclear Mission," James A. Blackwell, Jr., Executive Director, December 2008.

"Report on the Unauthorized Movement of Nuclear Weapons," Defense Science Board Permanent Task Force on Nuclear Weapons Surety, Department of Defense, Washington, D.C., February 2008.

"Report of USAF Aerospace Safety Missile Accident Investigation Board, Missile Accident LGM-25C-62-006, Site 373-4," Little Rock Air Force Base, Arkansas, August 9, 1965.

"Requirements for Tactical Nuclear Weapons," Special Studies Group, Joint Chiefs of Staff, Project 23, October 1962 (TOP SECRET/RESTRICTED DATA/declassified).

"Rescue Mission Report, Special Operations Review Group, Joint Chiefs of Staff, July 16, 1979.

"Resilient Military Systems and the Advanced Cyber Threat," Task Force Report, Defense Science Board, Department of Defense, January 2013.

"Restricted Data Declassification Decisions, 1946 to the Present," U.S. Department of Energy, Office of Health, Safety, and Security, Office of Classification, RDD-8, January 1, 2002 (OFFICIAL USE ONLY/declassified).

"Retaliatory Issues for the U.S. Nuclear Strategic Forces," Congressional Budget Office, Congress of United States, June 1978.

"A Review of Criticality Accidents," William R. Stratton, Los Alamos Scientific Laboratory, LA-3611, January 1967.

"A Review of Criticality Accidents," Thomas P. McLaughlin, Sean P. Monahan, Norman L. Pruvost, Vladimir V. Frolov, Boris G. Ryazanov, and Victor I. Sviridov, Los Alamos National Laboratory, LA-13638, May 2000.

"A Review of the US Nuclear Weapon Safety Program—1945 to 1986," R. N. Brodie, Sandia National Laboratories, SAND86-2955, February 1987 (SECRET/RESTRICTED DATA/declassified).

"The SAC Alert Program, 1956–1959," Headquarters, Strategic Air Command, January 1960 (SECRET/declassified), NSA.

"Security of U.S. Nuclear Weapons Overseas: Where Does It Stand?," Comptroller General of the United States, Report to the Chairman, Subcommittee on Energy, Nuclear Proliferation, and Federal Services, Committee on Governmental Affairs, United States Senate, General Accounting Office, C-EMD-81-2, November 3, 1980.

"The Security of Nuclear Weapons in Pakistan," Shaun Gregory, Pakistan Security Research Unit, Brief Number 22, November 18, 2007.

"Selection and Use of Strategic Bases," A. J. Wohlstetter, F. S. Hoffman, R. J. Lutz, and H. S. Rowen, U.S. Air Force Project RAND, R-266, April 1954 (SECRET/declassified).

"Shots Encore to Climax: The Final Four Tests of the UPSHOT-KNOTHOLE Series, 8 May–4 June 1953," United States Atmospheric Nuclear Weapons Tests, Nuclear Test Personnel Review, Defense Nuclear Agency, 1982.

"60th Anniversary of Trinity: First Manmade Nuclear Explosion, July 16, 1945," Public Symposium, National Academy of Sciences, July 14, 2005.

"Source Book on Plutonium and Its Decontamination," F. C. Cobb and R. L. Van Hemert, Field Command, Kirtland AFB, Defense Nuclear Agency, DNA 3272T, September 24, 1973.

"Soviet Intentions 1965–1985, Volume I: An Analytical Comparison of U.S.–Soviet Assessments During the Cold War," J. G. Hines, E. M. Mishulovich, and J. F. Shull, BDM Federal Inc., September 22, 1995 (declassified), NSA.

"Soviet Intentions 1965–1985, Volume II: Soviet Post-Cold War Testimonial Evidence," J. G. Hines, E. M. Mishulovich, and J. F. Shull, BDM Federal, Inc., September 22, 1995 (declassified), NSA.

"A Soviet Paramilitary Attack on U.S. Nuclear Forces—A Concept," L. G. Gref, A. L. Latter, E. A. Martinelli, and H. P. Smith, Prepared for the Defense Advanced Research Projects Agency, R & D Associates, November 1974 (SECRET/declassified).

"Status of the Air Force Nuclear Security Roadmap," Brigadier General Everett H. Thomas, Commander, Air Force Nuclear Weapons Center, Presentation to the Strategic Forces Subcommittee, House Armed Services Committee, House of Representatives, 111th Congress, January 21, 2010.

"Status of the MX Missile System," Hearing Before the Committee on Armed Services, House of Representatives, Ninety-sixth Congress, Second Session, May 1, 1980.

"Strategic Air Command and the Alert Program: A Brief History," Dr. Henry M. Narducci, Office of the Historian, Headquarters, Strategic Air Command, Offutt AFB, Nebraska, April 1, 1988.

"Strategic Air Command Operations in the Cuban Crisis of 1962," Historical Study, No. 90, Vol. 1, History & Research Division, Strategic Air Command, 1963 (TOP SECRET/RESTRICTED DATA/declassified), NSA.

"Strategic Air Command Participation in the Missile Program, 1 January 1958–30 June 1958," Historical Study No. 72, Historical Division, Office of Information, Headquarters, Strategic Air Command, 1958 (SECRET/declassified).

"Strategic Command, Control, and Communications: Alternative Approaches for Modernization," a CBO Study, Congressional Budget Office, Congress of the United States, October 1981.

"Strategic Warning System False Alerts," Hearings Before the Committee on Armed Services, House of Representatives, Ninety-sixth Congress, Second Session, June 24, 1980.

"Striking First, Preemptive and Preventive Attack in U.S. National Security Policy," Karl P. Mueller, Jasen J. Castillo, Forrest E. Morgan, Negeen Pegahi, and Brian Rosen, RAND, Project Air Force, Santa Monica, California, 2006.

"A Study on Evaluation of Warhead Safing Devices," Headquarters, Field Command, Armed Forces Special Weapons Project, FC/03580460, March 31, 1958 (SECRET/RESTRICTED DATA/declassified).

"Subject: Report of Special Weapons Incident [W 40] Bomarc Site, McGuire AFB, New Jersey," Detachment 6, 2702D Explosive Ordnance Disposal Squadron, USAF, to 2702 EOD Sq, Wright-Patterson AFB, June 13, 1960 (SECRET/RESTRICTED DATA/declassified).

"A Summary of NASA and USAF Hypergolic Propellant Related Spills and Fires," B. M. Nufer, National Aeronautics and Space Administration, NASA/TP-2009-214769, June 2009.

"A Summary of the Program to Use Environmental Sensing Devices to Improve Handling Safety Protection for Nuclear Weapons," William L. Stevens and C. Herman Mauney, Sandia Corporation, July 1961 (SECRET/RESTRICTED DATA/declassified).

"A Survey of Nuclear Weapon Safety Problems and the Possibilities for Increasing Safety in Bomb and Warhead Design," Prepared by Sandia Corporation with the Advice and Assistance of the Los Alamos Scientific Laboratory and the University of California Ernest O. Lawrence Radiation Laboratory, RS 3466/26889, February 1959 (SECRET/RESTRICTED DATA/declassified).

"Survey of Weapon Development and Technology" Sandia National Laboratories, Corporate Training and Development, WR708, February 1998 (SECRET/RESTRICTED DATA/declassified).

"Tech Area II: A History," Rebecca Ullrich, Sandia National Laboratories, SAND98-1617, July 1998.

"Thermal Batteries: A Technology Review and Future Directions," Ronald A. Guidotti, Sandia National Laboratory, Presented at 27th International SAMPE Technical Conference, October 9–12, 1995.

"Thule-2003—Investigation of Radioactive Contamination," Sven P. Nielsen and Per Roos, Risø National Laboratory, Roskilde, Denmark, Risø-R-1549(EN), May 2006.

"Titan II Action Item Status Reports," Headquarters, Strategic Air Command, August 1, 1982.

"Titan II Class A Mishap Report: Serial Number 62-0006, 18 September 1980, Damascus, Arkansas," Eighth Air Force Mishap Investigation Board, October 30, 1980.

"Titan II Launch Facility Accident Briefing, Little Rock Air Force Base, Arkansas," Charles F. Strang, Minutes of the Ninth Explosives Safety Seminar, Naval Training Center, San Diego, California, August 15–17, 1967.

"Titan II Storable Propellant Handbook," Prepared for Air Force Ballistic Systems Division, Bell Aerosystems Company, March 1963.

"Titan II Weapon System: Review Group Report," December 1980.

"Transforming the Security Classification System," Report to the President from the Public Interest Declassification Board, November 2012.

"Trimming Nuclear Excess: Options for Further Reductions of U.S. and Russian Nuclear Forces," Hans M. Kristensen, Special Report No. 5, Federation of American Scientists, December 2012.

"The Unauthorized Movement of Nuclear Weapons and Mistaken Shipment of Classified Missile Components: An Assessment," Michelle Spencer, A. Ludin, H. Nelson, The Counterproliferation Papers, Future Warfare Series No. 56, USAF Counterproliferation Center, January 2012.

"The Unique Signal Concept for Detonation Safety in Nuclear Weapons," Stanley D. Spray, and J. A. Cooper, System Studies Department, Sandia National Laboraties, SAND91-1269, June 1993.

"United States Air Force Missile Accident Investigation Board Report, Minuteman III Launch Facility A06, 319 Missile Sq., 90 Op. Group, 90 Missile Wing, F. E. Warren AFB, Wyoming, May 23, 2008," Robert M. Walker, President, Accident Investigation Board, September 18, 2008.

"United States Defense Policies in 1961," House Document No. 502, Library of Congress, Legislative Reference Service, U.S. Government Printing Office, June 7, 1962.

"United States High-Altitude Test Experiences: A Review Emphasizing the Impact on the Environment," Herman Hoerlin, LASL Monograph, Los Alamos National Laboratory, October 1976.

"United States Nuclear Tests: July 1945 Through September 1992," Nevada Operations Office, United States Department of Energy, December 2000.

"USAF Ballistic Missiles, 1958–1959," Max Rosenberg, USAF Historical Division Liaison Office, July 1960 (SECRET/RESTRICTED DATA/declassified), NSA.

———. "1962–1964," Bernard C. Nalty, USAF Historical Division Liaison Office, April 1966 (TOP SECRET/RESTRICTED DATA/declassified), NSA.

———. "1964–1966," March 1967 (TOP SECRET/RESTRICTED DATA/declassified), NSA.

———. "1969–1970," Jacob Neufeld, Office of Air Force History, June 1971 (TOP SECRET/RESTRICTED DATA/declassified), NSA.

"USAF Mishap Report, Parking Spot A-10, Grand Forks Air Force Base," Headquarters Fifteenth Air Force, September 29, 1980.

"The U.S. ICBM Force: Current Issues and Future Options," C. H. Builder, D. C. Kephart, A. Laupa, a Report Prepared for U.S. Air Force Project RAND, R-1754-PR, October 1975 (SECRET/FORMERLY RESTRICTED DATA/declassified), NSA.

"U.S. Strategic Nuclear Weapons and Deterrence," C. Johnston Conover, RAND Corporation, Santa Monica, California, August 1977.

"U.S. Tactical Nuclear Weapons in Europe After NATO's Lisbon Summit: Why Their Withdrawal Is Desirable and Feasible," Tom Sauer and Bob Van Der Zwaan, Discussion Paper No. 2011-015, Belfer Center for Science and International Affairs, Harvard Kennedy School, 2011.

"The View from Above: High-Level Decisions and the Soviet-American Strategic Arms Competition, 1945–1950," Samuel R. Williamson, Jr., with the collaboration of Steven L. Rearden, Office of the Secretary of Defense, October 1975 (TOP SECRET/declassified).

"Vulnerability Program Summary: Joint DOD-AEC Weapon Vulnerability Program," Armed Forces Special Weapons Project, FC/010, May 1958 (SECRET/RESTRICTED DATA/declassified).

"Weapon System Familiarization, LGM-25 (Titan II)," Course O7R1821F/3121F, Technical Training, Sheppard Air Force Base, Texas, January 1965.

"WSEG Report No. 50, Evaluation of Strategic Offensive Weapons System, Weapons System Evaluation Group, ODDR&E, December 27, 1960 (TOP SECRET/declassified), NSA.

"The Worldwide Military Command and Control System: A Historical Perspective (1960–1977)," Historical Division, Joint Secretariat, Joint Chiefs of Staff, September 1980 (SECRET/declassified).

"The World Wide Military Command and Control System—Major Changes Needed in Its Automated Data Processing Management and Direction," Comptroller General of the United States, Report to the Congress, General Accounting Office, December 14, 1979.

"Worldwide Survey of Alcohol and Nonmedical Drug Use Among Military Personnel: 1982," R. M.

Bray, L. L. Guess, R. E. Mason, R. L. Hubbard, D. G. Smith, M. E. Marsden, and J. V. Rachel, Research Triangle Institute, July 1983.

"The Yields of the Hiroshima and Nagasaki Nuclear Explosions," John Malik, Los Alamos National Laboratory, LA-8819, September 1985.

Journal Articles

Adamsky, Viktor, and Yuri Smirnov. "Moscow's Biggest Bomb: The 50-Megaton Test of October 1961," *Cold War International History Project Bulletin*, Issue 4, Fall 1994.

Allard, Dean C. "Interservice Differences in the United States, 1945–1950—A Naval Perspective," *Airpower Journal*, Winter 1989.

Alperovitz, Gar, and K. Bird. "A Theory of Cold War Dynamics: U.S. Policy, Germany, and the Bomb," *History Teacher*, Vol. 29, No. 3, May 1996, 281–300.

Anderson, Herbert L. "Metropolis, Monte Carlo, and the MANIAC," *Los Alamos Science*, Fall 1986.

Asada, Sadao. "The Shock of the Atomic Bomb and Japan's Decision to Surrender—A Reconsideration," *Pacific Historical Review*, Vol. 67, No. 4, November 1998, 477–512.

Bacevich, A.J. "The Paradox of Professionalism: Eisenhower, Ridgway, and the Challenge to Civilian Control, 1953–1955," *Journal of Military History*, Vol. 61, No. 2, April 1997, 303–33.

Ball, Desmond. "Can Nuclear War Be Controlled?" Adelphi Paper #169, International Institute for Strategic Studies, 1981.

———. "U.S. Strategic Forces: How Would They Be Used?," *International Security*, Vol. 7, No. 3, 1982, 31–60.

———. "Nuclear War at Sea," *International Security*, Vol. 10, No. 3, 1985, 3–31.

———. "Controlling Theatre Nuclear War," *British Journal of Political Science*, Vol. 19, No. 3, July 1989, 303–27.

———. "Improving Communications Links Between Moscow and Washington," *Journal of Peace Research*, Vol. 28, No. 2, 1991, 135–59.

Belletto, Steven. "The Game Theory Narrative and the Myth of the National Security State," *American Quarterly*, Vol. 61, No. 2, June 2009, 333–57.

Bernstein, Barton J. "The Quest for Security: American Foreign Policy and International Control of Atomic Energy, 1942–1946," *Journal of American History*, Vol. 60, No. 4, March 1974, 1003–44.

———. "Eclipsed by Hiroshima and Nagasaki: Early Thinking About Tactical Nuclear Weapons," *International Security*, Vol. 15, No. 4, 1991, 149–73.

———. "The Alarming Japanese Buildup on Southern Kyushu, Growing U.S. Fears, and Counterfactual Analysis: Would the Planned November 1945 Invasion of Southern Kyushu Have Occurred?" *Pacific Historical Review*, Vol. 68, No. 4, 1999, 561–609.

———. "Reconsidering the 'Atomic General': Leslie R. Groves," *Journal of Military History*, Vol. 67, No. 3, July 2003, 883–920.

Betts, Richard K. "A Nuclear Golden Age? The Balance Before Parity," *International Security*, Vol. 11, No. 3, 1986, 3–32.

Biddle, Tami Davis. "Dresden 1945: Reality, History, and Memory," *Journal of Military History*, April 2008, 413–49.

Blackett, P.M.S. "Nuclear Weapons and Defence: Comments on Kissinger, Kennan, and King-Hall," *International Affairs* (Royal Institute of International Affairs), Vol. 34, No. 4, October 1958, 421–34.

Brands, H.W. "The Age of Vulnerability: Eisenhower and the National Insecurity State," *American Historical Review*, Vol. 94, No. 4, October 1989, 963–89.

Bray, R.M., M. E. Marsden, and M. R. Peterson. "Standardized Comparisons of the Use of Alcohol, Drugs, and Cigarettes Among Military Personnel and Civilians," *American Journal of Public Health*, Vol. 81, No. 7, July 1991, 865–69.

Bray, R.M., and L. L. Hourani. "Substance Use Trends Among Active Duty Military Personnel: Findings from the United States Department of Defense Health Related Behavior Surveys, 1980–2005," *Addiction*, Vol. 102, No. 7, 2007, 1092–1101.

Bresler, Robert J., and R. C. Gray. "The Bargaining Chip and SALT," *Political Science Quarterly*, Vol. 92, No. 1, 1977, 65–88.

Briggs, Herbert W. "World Government and the Control of Atomic Energy," *Annals of the American Academy of Political and Social Science*, Vol. 249, January 1947, 42–53.

Brodie, Bernard. "The McNamara Phenomenon," *World Politics*, Vol. 17, No. 4, 1965, 672–86.

Buhite, Russell D., and W. Christopher Hamel. "War for Peace: The Question of an American Preventive War Against the Soviet Union, 1945–1955," *Diplomatic History*, Vol. 14, No. 3, 1990, 367–84.

Burr, William. "The Nixon Administration, the 'Horror Strategy,' and the Search for Limited Nuclear Options, 1969–1972," *Journal of Cold War Studies*, Vol. 7, No. 3, 2005, 34–78.

———, and J. T. Richelson. "Whether to 'Strangle the Baby in the Cradle': The United States and the Chinese Nuclear Program, 1960-1964," *International Security*, Vol. 25, No. 3, 2000, 54–99.

Burt, Marvin R. "Prevalence and Consequences of Drug Abuse Among U.S. Military Personnel: 1980," *American Journal of Drug and Alcohol Abuse*, Vol. 8, No. 4, 1981–82, 419–39.

Carter, Donald Alan. "Eisenhower Versus the Generals," *The Journal of Military History*, Issue 71, October 2007, 1169–99.

Colman, Jonathan. "The 1950 'Ambassador's Agreement' on USAF Bases in the UK and British Fears of US Atomic Unilateralism," *Journal of Strategic Studies*, Vol. 30, No. 2, April 2007, 285–307.

Dyer, Davis. "Necessity as the Mother of Convention: Developing the ICBM, 1954–1958," *Business and Economic History*, Vol. 22, No. 1, 1993, 194–209.

Earle, Edward Mead. "H. G. Wells, British Patriot in Search of a World State," *World Politics*, Vol. 2, No. 2, January 1950, 181–208.

Egilsson, Haraldur Þór. "The Origins, Use and Development of Hot Line Diplomacy," Netherlands Institute of International Relations, Issue 85 in Discussion Papers in Diplomacy.

Elliot, David C. "Project Vista and Nuclear Weapons in Europe," *International Security*, Vol. 11, No. 1, Summer 1986, 163–83.

Enthoven, Alain C. "Defense and Disarmament: Economic Analysis in the Department of Defense," *American Economic Review*, Vol. 53, No. 2, 1963, 413–23.

———. "U.S. Forces in Europe: How Many? Doing What?," *Foreign Affairs*, Vol. 53, No. 3, 1975, 513–32.

Evangelista, Matthew. "Stalin's Postwar Army Reappraised," *International Security*, Vol. 7, No. 3, 1982, 110–38.

———. "The 'Soviet Threat': Intentions, Capabilities, and Context," *Diplomatic History*, Vol. 22, No. 3, 1998, 439–49.

Forsyth, James Wood, Jr., B. C. Saltzman, and G. Schaub, Jr. "Remembrance of Things Past: The Enduring Value of Nuclear Weapons," *Strategic Studies Quarterly*, Vol. 4, No. 1, Spring 2010, 74–89.

Frankel, Sherman. "Aborting Unauthorized Launches of Nuclear-Armed Ballistic Missiles Through Postlaunch Destruction," *Science & Global Security*, Vol. 2, No. 1, 1990, 1–20.

Fravel, M. Taylor, and Evan S. Medeiros. "China's Search for Assured Retaliation: The Evolution of Chinese Nuclear Strategy and Force Structure," *International Security*, Vol. 35, No. 2, Fall 2010, 48–87.

Garwin, Richard L. "New Weapons/Old Doctrines: Strategic Warfare in the 1980s," *Proceedings of the American Philosophical Society*, Vol. 124, No. 4, 1980, 261–65.

Gavin, Francis J. "The Myth of Flexible Response: United States Strategy in Europe During the 1960s," *International History Review*, Vol. 23, No. 4, December 2001, 847–75.

Gentile, Gian P. "Advocacy or Assessment? The United States Strategic Bombing Survey of Germany and Japan," *Pacific Historical Review*, Vol. 66, No. 1, February 1997, 53–79.

———. "Planning for Preventive War, 1945–1950," *Joint Force Quarterly*, Spring 2000, 68–74.

Giangreco, D.M. "Casualty Projections for the U.S. Invasions of Japan, 1945–1946: Planning and Policy Implications," *Journal of Military History*, Vol. 61, No. 3, 1997, 521–81.

———. "'A Score of Bloody Okinawas and Iwo Jimas': President Truman and Casualty Estimates for the Invasion of Japan," *Pacific Historical Review*, Vol. 72, No. 1, February 2003, 93–132.

Gibson, J. William. "Redeeming Vietnam: Techno-Thriller Novels of the 1980s," *Cultural Critique*, No. 19, Autumn 1991, 179–202.

Gimbel, John. "U.S. Policy and German Scientists: The Early Cold War," *Political Science Quarterly*, Vol. 101, No. 3, 1986, 433–51.

Glaser, C.L., and S. Fetter. "Counterforce Revisited: Assessing the Nuclear Posture Review's New Missions," *International Security*, Vol. 30, No. 2, 2005, 84–126.

Goncharov, G.A. "American and Soviet H-Bomb Development Programmes: Historical Background," *Physics-Uspekhi*, Vol. 39, No. 10, 1996, 1033–44.

Graybar, Lloyd J. "The 1946 Atomic Bomb Tests: Atomic Diplomacy or Bureaucratic Infighting?," *Journal of American History*, Vol. 72, No. 4, March 1986, 888–907.

Gregory, Shaun. "The Security of Nuclear Weapons in Pakistan," Pakistan Security Research Unit, Brief No. 22, November 18, 2007.

Guidotti, Ronald A., and P. Masset. "Thermally Activated ('Thermal') Battery Technology, Part I: An Overview," *Journal of Power Sources*, Vol. 161, No. 2, 2006, 1443–49.

Hämäläinen, P., J. Takala, and K. L. Saarela. "Global Estimates of Occupational Accidents," *Safety Science*, No. 44, 2006, 137–56.

Harlow, Francis H., and N. Metropolis. "Computing and Computers: Weapons Simulation Leads to the Computer Era," *Los Alamos Science*, Winter/Spring 1983, 132–41.

Harvey, John R., and Stefan Michalowski. "Nuclear Weapons Safety: The Case of Trident," *Science and Global Security*, Vol. 4, 1994, 261–337.

Harvey, Mose L. "Lend-Lease to Russia: A Story That Needs to Be Told Like It Was," *Russian Review*, Vol. 29, No. 1, January 1970, 81–86.

Herken, Gregg. "'A Most Deadly Illusion': The Atomic Secret and American Nuclear Weapons Policy, 1945–1950," *Pacific Historical Review*, Vol. 49, No. 1, February 1980, pp. 51–76.

Herring, George C., Jr. "Lend-Lease to Russia and the Origins of the Cold War, 1944–1945," *Journal of American History*, Vol. 56, No. 1, June 1969, 93–114.

Hewitt, Kenneth. "Place Annihilation: Area Bombing and the Fate of Urban Places," *Annals of the Association of American Geographers*, Vol. 73, No. 2, June 1983, 257–84.

Holt, George C. "The Conference on World Government," *Journal of Higher Education*, Vol. 17, No. 5, May 1946, 227–35.

Holt, Hamilton. "The League to Enforce Peace," *Proceedings of the Academy of Political Science in the City of New York*, Vol. 7, No. 2, July 1917, 65–69.

———. "The League of Nations Effective," *Annals of the American Academy of Political and Social Science*, Vol. 96, July 1921, 1–10.

Hooks, Gregory. "The Rise of the Pentagon and U.S. State Building: The Defense Program as Industrial Policy," *American Journal of Sociology*, Vol. 96, No. 2, September 1990, 358–404.

Hughes, Jeff. "The Strath Report: Britain Confronts the H-Bomb, 1954–1955," *History and Technology*, Vol. 19, No. 3, 2003, 257–75.

Huntington, Samuel P. "Interservice Competition and the Political Roles of the Armed Services," *American Political Science Review*, Vol. 55, No. 1, March 1961, 40–52.

Iklé, Fred C. "The Effect of War Destruction upon the Ecology of Cities," *Social Forces*, Vol. 29, No. 4, May 1951, 383–91.

———. "The Social Versus the Physical Effects from Nuclear Bombing," *Scientific Monthly*, Vol. 78, No. 3, March 1954, 182–87.

———. "When the Fighting Has to Stop: The Arguments About Escalation," *World Politics*, Vol. 19, No. 4, July 1967, 692–707.

———. "Can Nuclear Deterrence Last Out the Century?," *Foreign Affairs*, Vol. 51, No. 2, January 1973, 267–85.

———. "The Prevention of Nuclear War in a World of Uncertainty," *Policy Sciences*, Vol. 7, No. 2, 1976, 245–50.

Johnson, Robert H. "Periods of Peril: The Window of Vulnerability and Other Myths," *Foreign Affairs*, Vol. 61, No. 4, 950–70.

Jones, Matthew. "Targeting China: U.S. Nuclear Planning and 'Massive Retaliation' in East Asia, 1953–1955," *Journal of Cold War Studies*, Vol. 10, No. 4, 2008, 37–65.

Kanwal, Gurmeet. "Are Pakistan's Nuclear Warheads Safe?," Pakistan Security Research Unit, Brief No. 27, January 24, 2008.

Kincade, William H. "Repeating History: The Civil Defense Debate Renewed," *International Security*, Vol. 2, No. 3, 1978, 99–120.

Kissinger, Henry A. "Force and Diplomacy in the Nuclear Age," *Foreign Affairs*, Vol. 34, No. 3, April 1956, 349–66.

Komer, Robert W. "What 'Decade of Neglect'?," *International Security*, Vol. 10, No. 2, 1985, 70–83.

Kramer, Mark. "The Soviet Union and the 1956 Crises in Hungary and Poland: Reassessments and New Findings," *Journal of Contemporary History*, Vol. 33, No. 2, April 1998, 163–214.

Kringlen, Einar. "The Myth of Rationality in Situations of Crisis," *Medicine and War*, Vol. I, 1985, 187–94.

McNamara, Robert S. "The Military Role of Nuclear Weapons: Perceptions and Misperceptions," *Foreign Affairs*, Vol. 62, No. 1, 1983, 59–80.

Metropolis, N. "The Age of Computing: A Personal Memoir," *Daedalus*, Vol. 121, No. 1, 1992, 119–30.

Mian, Zia, M. V. Ramana, and R. Rajaraman. "Plutonium Dispersal and Health Hazards from Nuclear Weapon Accidents," *Current Science*, Vol. 80, No. 10, 2001, 1275–84.

Moore, Richard. "The Real Meaning of the Words: A Pedantic Glossary of British Nuclear Weapons," UK Nuclear History Working Paper, Number 1, Mountbatten Centre for International Studies, March 2004.

Morland, Howard. "Born Secret," *Cardozo Law Review*, Vol. 26, No. 4, March 2005, 1401–8.

Neufeld, Michael J. "The End of the Army Space Program: Interservice Rivalry and the Transfer of the von Braun Group to NASA, 1958–1959," *Journal of Military History*, Vol. 69, No. 3, July 2005, 737–58.

Newman, Robert P. "Ending the War with Japan: Paul Nitze's 'Early Surrender' Counterfactual," *Pacific Historical Review*, Vol. 64, No. 2, May 1995, 167–94.

———. "Hiroshima and the Trashing of Henry Stimson," *New England Quarterly*, Vol. 71, No. 1, March 1998, 5–32.

Oakes, Guy. "The Cold War Conception of Nuclear Reality: Mobilizing the American Imagination for Nuclear War in the 1950's," *International Journal of Politics, Culture, and Society*, Vol. 6, No. 3, 1993, 339–63.

———, and A. Grossman. "Managing Nuclear Terror: The Genesis of American Civil Defense Strategy," *International Journal of Politics, Culture, and Society*, Vol. 5, No. 3, 1992, 361–403.

Olesen, Thorsten Borring. "Tango for Thule: The Dilemmas and Limits of the 'Neither Confirm Nor Deny' Doctrine in Danish-American Relations, 1957–1968," *Journal of Cold War Studies*, Vol. 13, No. 2, Spring 2011, 116–47.

Park, You-Me. "Compensation to Fit the Crime: Conceptualizing a Just Paradigm of Reparation for Korean 'Comfort Women,'" *Comparative Studies of South Asia, Africa, and the Middle East*, Vol. 30, No. 2, 2010, 204–13.

Perkins, Ray. "Bertrand Russell and Preventive War," *Russell: The Journal of Bertrand Russell Studies*, Vol. 14, Iss. 2, 1994, 135–53.

Pines, Maya. "The Magic Carpet of Inertial Guidance," *Harper's Magazine*, Vol. 224, No. 1342, March 1962, 72–81.

Potter, William C. "Coping with MIRV in a MAD World," *Journal of Conflict Resolution*, Vol. 22, No. 4, 1978, 599–626.

Prados, John. "The Navy's Biggest Betrayal," *Naval History Magazine*, Vol. 24, No. 3, 2010.

Preble, Christopher A. "'Who Ever Believed in the "Missile Gap"?': John F. Kennedy and the Politics of National Security," *Presidential Studies Quarterly*, Vol. 33, No. 4, December 2003, 801–26.

Quester, George H. "Through the Nuclear Strategic Looking Glass, or Reflections off the Window of Vulnerability," *Journal of Conflict Resolution*, Vol. 31, No. 4, 1987, 725–37.

Ralph, William W. "Improvised Destruction: Arnold, LeMay, and the Firebombing of Japan," *War in History*, Vol. 13, No. 4, 2006, 495–522.

Robock, Alan. "Nuclear Winter Is a Real and Present Danger," *Nature*, Vol. 473, May 19, 2011, 275–76.

Roman, Peter J. "Ike's Hair-Trigger: U.S. Nuclear Predelegation, 1953–60," *Security Studies*, Vol. 7, No. 4, 121–64.

Rosenberg, David Alan. "American Atomic Strategy and the Hydrogen Bomb Decision," *Journal of American History*, Vol. 66, No. 1, June 1979, 62–87.

——. "The Origins of Overkill: Nuclear Weapons and American Strategy 1945–1960," *International Security*, Vol. 7, No. 4, 1983, 3–71.

——, and W. B. Moore. "'A Smoking Radiating Ruin at the End of Two Hours': Documents on American Plans for Nuclear War with the Soviet Union, 1954–55," *International Security*, Vol. 6, No. 3, 1981, 3–38.

Sagan, Scott D. "SIOP-62: The Nuclear War Plan Briefing to President Kennedy," *International Security*, Vol. 12, No. 1, Summer 1987, 22–51.

——. "Nuclear Alerts and Crisis Management," *International Security*, Vol. 9, No. 4, Spring 1985, 122–31.

——, and J. Suri. "The Madman Nuclear Alert," *International Security*, Vol. 27, No. 4, 2003, 150–83.

Scott, Len, and S. Smith. "Lessons of October: Historians, Political Scientists, Policy Makers and the Cuban Missile Crisis," *International Affairs*, Vol. 70, No. 4, October 1994, 659–84.

Searle, Thomas R. "'It Made a Lot of Sense to Kill Skilled Workers': The Firebombing of Tokyo in March 1945," *Journal of Military History*, Vol. 66, No. 1, January 2002, 103–33.

Seckel, Al. "Russell and the Cuban Missile Crisis," *Russell: Journal of the Bertrand Russell Studies*, Vol. 4, No. 2, 253–61.

Skidmore, David. "Carter and the Failure of Foreign Policy Reform," *Political Science Quarterly*, Vol. 108, No. 4, 1993, 699–729.

Steinbruner, John D. "Nuclear Decapitation," *Foreign Policy* No. 45 (Winter 1981–1982), 16–28.

——, and T. M. Garwin. "Strategic Vulnerability: The Balance Between Prudence and Paranoia," *International Security*, Vol. 1, No. 1, 1976, 138–81.

Stiles, David. "A Fusion Bomb over Andalucía: U.S. Information Policy and the 1966 Palomares Incident," *Journal of Cold War Studies*, Vol. 8, No. 1, 2006, 49–67.

Sutton, George P. "History of Liquid Propellant Rocket Engines in the United States," *Journal of Propulsion and Power*, Vol. 19, No. 6, 2003, 978–1007.

Tertrais, Bruno. "A Nuclear Coup? France, the Algerian War and the April 1961 Nuclear Test," Fondation pour la Recherche Stratégique, Draft, October 2, 2011.

Thompson, Kenneth W. "The Coming of the Third World War: A Review Essay," *Political Science Quarterly*," Vol. 94, No. 4, 1979, 669–77.

Trachtenberg, Marc. "The Influence of Nuclear Weapons in the Cuban Missile Crisis," *International Security*, Vol. 10, No. 1, 1985, 137–63.

——. "The 'Accidental War' Question," Department of History, University of Pennsylvania, February 14, 2000.

Tsypkin, Mikhail. "Adventures of the 'Nuclear Briefcase': A Russian Document Analysis," *Strategic Insights*, Vol. 3, Iss. 9, 2004.

Twigge, Stephen, and L. Scott. "Learning to Love the Bomb: The Command and Control of British Nuclear Forces, 1953–1964," *Journal of Strategic Studies*, Vol. 22, No. 1, 1999, 29–53.

Varesh, Ron. "Electronic Detonators: EBW and EFI," *Propellants, Explosives, Pyrotechnics*, 21, 1996, 150–54.

Walkowicz, T.F. "Strategic Concepts for the Nuclear Age," *Annals of the American Academy of Political and Social Science*, Vol. 299, Air Power and National Security, May 1955, 118–27.

Walsh, John. "McNamara and the Pentagon: Limits of the 'Management View,'" *Science (New Series)*, Vol. 172, No. 3987, June 4, 1971, 1008–11.

Weathersby, Kathryn. "'Should We Fear This?' Stalin and the Danger of War with America," Woodrow Wilson International Center for Scholars–Cold War International History Project, Working Paper No. 39, July 2002.

Weiss, Erik D. "Cold War Under the Ice: The Army's Bid for a Long-Range Nuclear Role, 1959–1963," *Journal of Cold War Studies*, Vol. 3, No. 3, 2001, 31–58.

Wellerstein, Alex. "Patenting the Bomb: Nuclear Weapons, Intellectual Property, and Technological Control," *Isis*, Vol. 99, No. 1, March 2008, 57–87.

Wells, Samuel F., Jr. "The Origins of Massive Retaliation," *Political Science Quarterly*, Vol. 96, No. 1, 1981, 31–52.

Woolven, Robin. "UK Civil Defence and Nuclear Weapons, 1953–1959," UK Nuclear History Working Paper No. 2, Mountbatten Centre for International Studies (n.d.).

Yockey, Charles C., B. M. Eden, and R. B. Byrd. "The McConnell Missile Accident: Clinical Spectrum of Nitrogen Dioxide Exposure," *Journal of the American Medical Association*, Vol. 244, No. 11, September 12, 1980, 1221–23.

Young, Ken. "A Most Special Relationship: The Origins of Anglo-American Nuclear Strike Planning," *Journal of Cold War Studies*, Vol. 9, No. 2, 2007, 5–31.

———. "No Blank Cheque: Anglo-American (Mis)understandings and the Use of the English Airbases," *Journal of Military History*, Vol. 71, No. 4, 2007, 1133–67.

———. "US Atomic Capability and the British Forward Bases in the Early Cold War," *Journal of Contemporary History*, Vol. 42, No. 1, 2007, 117–36.

Zubok, Vladislav M. "Khrushchev and the Berlin Crisis (1958–1962)," *Cold War International History Project—Working Paper Series*, Working Paper No. 6, Washington, D.C., May 1993.

Dissertations

Fitzpatrick, Anne. "Igniting the Elements: The Los Alamos Thermonuclear Project, 1942–1952," Los Alamos National Laboratory, LA-13577-T, July 1999.

Francis, Sybil. "Warhead Politics: Livermore and the Competitive System of Nuclear Weapons Design," Massachusetts Institute of Technology, Department of Politic Science, 1995.

Isemann, James Louis. "To Detect, to Deter, to Defend: The Distant Early Warning (DEW) Line and Early Cold War Defense Policy, 1953–1957," Department of History, Kansas State University, 2009.

Jodoin, Vincent J. "Nuclear Cloud Rise and Growth," Graduate School of Engineering, Air Force Institute of Technology, Air University, June 1994.

Michel, Marshall L., III. "The Revolt of the Majors: How the Air Force Changed After Vietnam," Auburn University, Alabama, December 15, 2006.

Pomeroy, Steven Anthony. "Echos That Never Were: American Mobile Intercontinental Ballistic Missiles, 1956–1983," Auburn University, Auburn, Alabama, August 7, 2006.

Document Collections

Cantelon, Philip L., Richard G. Hewlett, and Robert C. Williams. *The American Atom: A Documentary History of Nuclear Policies from the Discovery of Fission to the Present*. Philadelphia: University of Pennsylvania Press, 1991.

Coster-Mullen, John. *Atom Bombs: The Top Secret Inside Story of Little Boy and Fat Man*. Waukesha, WI: John Coster-Mullen, 2009.

Etzold, Thomas E., and John Lewis Gaddis. *Containment: Documents on American Policy and Strategy, 1945–1950*. New York: Columbia University Press, 1978.

Ferrell, Robert H., ed. *Harry S. Truman and the Bomb: A Documentary History*. Worland, WY: High Plains Publishing Company, 1996.

Hansen, Chuck. *The Swords of Armageddon (Digital Collection)*. Sunnyvale, CA: Chuklea Publications, 2007.

Kort, Michael. *The Columbia Guide to Hiroshima and the Bomb*. New York: Columbia University Press, 2012.

Maggelet, Michael H., and James C. Oskins. *Broken Arrow: The Declassified History of U.S. Nuclear Weapons Accidents*. Raleigh, NC: Lulu, 2007.

———. *Broken Arrow, Volume II: A Disclosure of Significant U.S., Soviet, and British Nuclear Weapon Incidents and Accidents, 1945–2008*. Raleigh, NC: Lulu, 2010.

May, Ernest R., and Philip D. Zelikow. *The Kennedy Tapes: Inside the White House During the Cuban Missile Crisis*. New York: W. W. Norton, 2002.

Merrill, Dennis, ed. *Documentary History of the Truman Presidency, Volume 1: The Decision to Drop the Atomic Bomb on Japan*. Bethesda, MD: University Publications of America, 1995.

Public Papers of the Presidents of the United States: Dwight D. Eisenhower, Containing the Public Messages and Statements of the President, January 1, 1960 to January 20, 1961. Washington, D.C.: Office of the Federal Register, 1961.

Steury, Donald P., ed. *Intentions and Capabilities: Estimates on Soviet Strategic Forces, 1953–1983.* Washington, D.C.: History Staff, Center for the Study of Intelligence, Central Intelligence Agency, 1996.

United States State Department. *Foreign Relations of the United States: Diplomatic Papers, 1945, Volume V, Europe.* Washington, D.C.: Government Printing Office, 1967.

———. *Foreign Relations of the United States, 1946, Volume I, General, the United Nations.* Washington, D.C.: Government Printing Office, 1972.

———. *Foreign Relations of the United States: 1946, Volume VI, Eastern Europe; The Soviet Union.* Washington, D.C.: Government Printing Office, 1969.

———. *Foreign Relations of the United States, 1955–1957, Volume XIX, National Security Policy.* Washington, D.C.: Government Printing Office, 1990.

———. *Foreign Relations of the United States, 1958–1960, Volume III, National Security Policy, Arms Control and Disarmament.* Washington, D.C.: Government Printing Office, 1996.

———. *Foreign Relations of the United States, 1961–1963, Volume VI, Kennedy-Khrushchev Exchanges.* Washington, D.C.: Government Printing Office, 1996.

———. *Foreign Relations of the United States, 1961–1963, Volume VIII, National Security Policy.* Washington, D.C.: Government Printing Office, 1996.

———. *Foreign Relations of the United States, 1961–1963, Volume XI, Cuban Missile Crisis and Aftermath.* Washington, D.C.: Government Printing Office, 1996.

———. *Foreign Relations of the United States, 1961–1963, Berlin Crisis, Volume XIV, 1961–1962.* Washington, D.C.: Government Printing Office, 1993.

———. *Foreign Relations of the United States, 1961–1963, Berlin Crisis, Volume XV, 1962–1963.* Washington, D.C.: Government Printing Office, 1994.

———. *Foreign Relations of the United States, 1961–1963, Volume XVI, Eastern Europe; Cyprus; Greece; Turkey.* Washington, D.C.: Government Printing Office, 1994.

———. *Foreign Relations of the United States, 1969–1976, Volume XXXIV, National Security Policy, 1969–1972.* Washington, D.C.: Government Printing Office, 2011.

Letters, Diaries, Memoirs, and Oral Histories

Adams, Chris. *Inside the Cold War: A Cold Warrior's Reflections.* Maxwell Air Force Base, Alabama: Air University Press, September 1999.

Alvarez, Luis W., *Alvarez: Adventures of a Physicist.* New York: Basic Books, 1987.

Anderson, Clinton P., with Milton Viorst. *Outsider in the Senate: Senator Clinton Anderson's Memoirs.* New York: World Publishing Company, 1970.

Badash, Lawrence, Joseph O. Hirschfelder, and Herbert P. Broida, eds. *Reminiscences of Los Alamos, 1943–1945.* Boston: D. Reidel Publishing Co., 1980.

Boyle, Peter G., ed. *The Churchill-Eisenhower Correspondence, 1953–1955.* Chapel Hill: University of North Carolina Press, 1990.

Brian, Denis. *The Voice of Genius: Conversations with Nobel Scientists and Other Luminaries.* New York: Basic Books, 2001.

Brown, Harold. *Thinking About National Security: Defense and Foreign Policy in a Dangerous World.* Boulder, CO: Westview Press, 1983.

Brzezinski, Zbigniew. *Power and Principle: Memoirs of the National Security Advisor, 1977–1981.* New York: Farrar, Straus, & Giroux, 1983.

Bundy, McGeorge. *Danger and Survival: Choices About the Bomb in the First Fifty Years.* New York: Random House, 1988.

Carter, Bill, and Judi Turner. *Get Carter: Backstage in History from JFK's Assassination to the Rolling Stones.* Nashville, TN: Fine's Creek Publishing, 2006.

Carter, Jimmy. *White House Diary.* New York: Farrar, Straus, & Giroux, 2010.

Chertok, Boris. *Rockets and People, Volume II: Creating a Rocket Industry.* Washington, D.C.: NASA History Series, 2006.

Clancy, Tom, and Chuck Horner. *Every Man a Tiger.* New York: G. P. Putnam's Sons, 1999.

Clinton, Bill. *My Life*. New York: Knopf, 2004.

Courchene, Douglas E. *Pioneers with Intent: Memoirs of an Air Force Fire Fighter*. Tyndall Air Force Base, FL: Air Force Civil Engineer Support Agency, July 2003.

D'Amario, Alfred J. *Hangar Flying*. Bloomington, IN: AuthorHouse, 2008.

Enthoven, Alain C., and K. Wayne Smith. *How Much Is Enough? Shaping the Defense Program, 1961–1969*. Santa Monica, CA: RAND Corporation, 1971.

Ferrell, Robert H., ed. *The Eisenhower Diaries*. New York: W. W. Norton, 1981.

Gates, Robert M. *From the Shadows: The Ultimate Insider's Story of Five Presidents and How They Won the Cold War*. New York: Simon & Schuster, 2006.

Groves, Leslie R. *Now It Can Be Told: The Story of the Manhattan Project*. New York: Da Capo Press, 1982.

Gulley, Bill, with Mary Ellen Reese. *Breaking Cover*. New York: Simon & Schuster, 1980.

Jordan, Hamilton. *Crisis: The Last Year of the Carter Presidency*. New York: G. P. Putnam's Sons, 1982.

Kelly, Cynthia C., ed. *The Manhattan Project: The Birth of the Atomic Bomb in the Words of Its Creators, Eyewitnesses, and Historians*. New York: Black Dog and Leventhal Publishers, Inc., 2007.

Kissinger, Henry A.. *White House Years*. New York: Simon & Schuster, 1979.

———. *Years of Upheaval*. New York: Simon & Schuster, 1982.

———. *Years of Renewal*. New York: Touchstone, 1999.

Kistiakowsky, George B. *A Scientist at the White House: The Private Diary of President Eisenhower's Special Assistant for Science and Technology*. Cambridge, MA: Harvard University Press, 1976.

Kohn, Richard H., and Joseph P. Harahan, eds. *Strategic Air Warfare: An Interview with Generals Curtis E. LeMay, Leon W. Johnson, David A. Burchinal, and Jack J. Catton*. Washington, D.C.: Office of Air Force History, 1988.

Leavitt, Lloyd R. *Following the Flag: An Air Force Officer Provides an Eyewitness View of Major Events and Policies During the Cold War*. Maxwell Air Force Base, AL: Air University Press, 2010.

LeMay, Curtis E., with Dale O. Smith. *America Is in Danger*. New York: Funk and Wagnalls, 1968.

———, with MacKinlay Kantor. *Mission with LeMay: My Story*. Garden City, NY: Doubleday, 1965.

Lilienthal, David E. *The Journals of David E. Lilienthal, Volume II: The Atomic Energy Years, 1945–1950*. New York: Harper & Row, 1964.

Little, James S. *Brotherhood of Doom: Memoirs of a Navy Nuclear Weaponsman*. Bradenton, FL: Booklocker, 2008.

McNamara, Robert, with Brian VanDeMark. *In Retrospect: The Tragedy and Lessons of Vietnam*. New York: Vintage Books, 1996.

Meyer, Cord. *Facing Reality: From World Federalism to the CIA:* New York: Harper & Row, 1980.

Millis, Walter, and E. S. Duffield, eds. *The Forrestal Diaries*. New York: Viking, 1951.

Nichols, Kenneth D. *The Road to Trinity: A Personal Account of How America's Nuclear Policies Were Made*. New York: William Morrow, 1987.

Nutter, Ralph H. *With the Possum and the Eagle: The Memoir of a Navigator's War over Germany and Japan*. Denton, TX: University of North Texas Press, 2002.

O'Keefe, Bernard J. *Nuclear Hostages*. Boston: Houghton Mifflin, 1983.

Powell, Colin, with Joseph E. Persico. *My American Journey*. New York: Random House, 1995.

Power, Thomas S., with Albert A. Arnhym. *Design for Survival*. New York: Coward-McCann, 1964.

Pryor, David, with Don Harrell. *A Pryor Commitment: The Autobiography of David Pryor*. Little Rock, AR: Butler Center Books, 2008.

Reed, Thomas C. *At the Abyss: An Insider's History of the Cold War*. New York: Ballantine Books, 2004.

Rubel, John H. *Doomsday Delayed: USAF Strategic Weapons Doctrine and SIOP-62, 1959–1962, Two Cautionary Tales*. New York: Hamilton Books, 2008.

———. *Reflections on Fame and Some Famous Men*. Santa Fe, NM: Sunstone Press, 2009.

Schonfeld, Reese. *Me and Ted Against the World: The Unauthorized Story of the Founding of CNN*. New York: HarperCollins, 2001.

Sheff, David, and G. Barry Golson, eds. *All We Are Saying: The Last Major Interview with John Lennon and Yoko Ono*. New York: St. Martin's Griffin, 2000.

Sweeney, Charles W., with James A. Antonucci and Marion K. Antonucci. *War's End: An Eyewitness Account of America's Last Atomic Mission*. New York: Avon Books, 1997.

Vance, Cyrus. *Hard Choices: Critical Years in America's Foreign Policy*. New York: Simon & Schuster, 1983.

Womack, John. *Titan Tales: Diary of a Titan II Missile Crew Commander*. Franklin, NC: Soliloquy Press, 1997.

York, Herbert F. *Race to Oblivion: A Participant's View of the Arms Race*. New York: Simon & Schuster, 1970.

———. *Making Weapons, Talking Peace: A Physicist's Odyssey from Hiroshima to Geneva*. New York: Basic Books, 1987.

Books

Abella, Alex. *Soldiers of Reason: The RAND Corporation and the Rise of the American Empire*. New York: Harcourt, 2008.

Abrahamson, James L., and Paul H. Carew. *Vanguard of American Atomic Deterrence: The Sandia Pioneers, 1946–1949*. Westport, CT: Praeger, 2002.

Ackland, Len. *Making a Real Killing: Rocky Flats and the Nuclear West*. Albuquerque, NM: University of New Mexico Press, 1999.

Air Force Missileers: Victors in the Cold War. Paducah, KY: Association of the Air Force Missileers, Turner Publishing Company, 1998.

Allison, Graham. *Nuclear Terrorism: The Ultimate Preventable Catastrophe*. New York: Times Books, 2004.

———, and Philip Zelikow. *Essence of Decision: Explaining the Cuban Missile Crisis*. New York: Longman, 1999.

Alperovitz, Gar. *The Decision to Use the Atomic Bomb*. New York: Vintage Books, 1996.

Ammerman, Robert T., Peggy J. Ott, and Ralph E. Tarter, eds. *Prevention and Societal Impact of Drug and Alcohol Abuse*. Mahwah, NJ: Lawrence Erlbaum Associates, Inc., 1999.

Anderson, Martin, and Annelise Anderson. *Reagan's Secret War: The Untold Story of His Fight to Save the World from Nuclear Disaster*. New York: Crown Publishers, 2009.

Andrew, Christopher, and Vasili Mitrokhin. *The Sword and the Shield: The Mitrokhin Archive and the Secret History of the KGB*. New York: Basic Books, 1999.

———. *The World Was Going Our Way: The KGB and the Battle for the Third World*. New York: Basic Books, 2005.

Arbatov, Alexei, and Vladimir Dvorkin. *Beyond Nuclear Deterrence: Transforming the U.S.–Russian Equation*. Washington, D.C.: Carnegie Endowment for International Peace, 2006.

Armacost, Michael H. *The Politics of Weapons Innovation: The Thor-Jupiter Controversy*. New York: Columbia University Press, 1969.

Auten, Brian J. *Carter's Conversion: The Hardening of American Defense Policy*. Columbia, MO: University of Missouri Press, 2008.

Ayson, Robert. *Thomas Schelling and the Nuclear Age: Strategy as Social Science*. New York: Frank Cass, 2004.

Ball, Adrian. *Ballistic and Guided Missiles*. London: Frederick Muller, 1960.

Ball, Desmond. *Politics and Force Levels: The Strategic Missile Program of the Kennedy Administration*. Berkeley: University of California Press, 1980.

———, and Jeffrey Richelson. *Strategic Nuclear Targeting*. Ithaca, NY: Cornell University Press, 1986.

Barlow, Jeffrey G. *Revolt of the Admirals: The Fight for Naval Aviation 1945–1950*. Washington, D.C.: Government Reprints Press, 2001.

Berhow, Mark A. *U.S. Strategic and Defensive Missile Systems, 1950–2004*. Oxford, UK: Osprey Publishing, 2005.

Bernstein, Jeremy. *Plutonium: A History of the World's Most Dangerous Element*. Washington, D.C.: Joseph Henry Press, 2007.

Bird, Kai, and Martin J. Sherwin. *American Prometheus: The Triumph and Tragedy of J. Robert Oppenheimer*. New York: Vintage Books, 2006.

Blair, Bruce G. *Strategic Command and Control: Redefining the Nuclear Threat*. Washington, D.C.: Brookings Institution, 1985.

———. *The Logic of Accidental Nuclear War*. Washington, D.C.: Brookings Institution, 1993.

———. *Global Zero Alert for Nuclear Forces*. Washington, D.C.: Brookings Institution, 1995.

Blechman, Barry, ed. *Technology and the Limitation of International Conflict*. Washington, D.C.: Foreign Policy Institute, School of Advanced International Studies, Johns Hopkins University, 1989.

Bliss, Edward, Jr., ed. *In Search of Light: The Broadcasts of Edward R. Murrow 1938–1961*. New York: Knopf, 1967.

Borowski, Harry R. *A Hollow Threat: Strategic Air Power and Containment Before Korea*. Westport, CT: Greenwood Press, 1982.

Bowden, Mark. *The Finish: The Killing of Osama bin Laden*. New York: Atlantic Monthly Press, 2012.

Bower, Tom. *The Paperclip Conspiracy: The Hunt for the Nazi Scientists*. Boston: Little, Brown, 1987.

Boyer, Paul. *By the Bomb's Early Light: American Thought and Culture at the Dawn of the Atomic Age*. Chapel Hill, NC: University of North Carolina Press, 1994.

Bracken, Paul. *The Command and Control of Nuclear Forces*. New Haven, CT: Yale University Press, 1983.

———. *The Second Nuclear Age: Strategy, Danger, and the New Power Politics*. New York: Times Books, 2012.

Brennan, Frederick Hazlitt. *One of Our H Bombs Is Missing*. New York: Fawcett Publications, 1955.

Bright, Christopher J. *Continental Defense in the Eisenhower Era: Nuclear Antiaircraft Arms and the Cold War*. New York: Palgrave Macmillan, 2010.

Bryant, Peter. *Red Alert*. New York: Ace Books, 1958.

Brzenzinski, Matthew. *Red Moon Rising: Sputnik and the Hidden Rivalries That Ignited the Space Age*. New York: Henry Holt, 2007.

Bunn, George, and Christopher F. Chyba, eds. *U.S. Nuclear Weapons Policy: Confronting Today's Threats*. Washington, D.C.: Brookings Institution, 2006.

Burdick, Eugene, and Harvey Wheeler. *Fail-Safe*. New York: McGraw-Hill, 1962.

Burnham, John C. *Accident Prone: A History of Technology, Psychology, and Misfits of the Machine Age*. Chicago: University of Chicago Press, 2009.

Burrows, William E. *By Any Means Necessary: America's Secret Air War in the Cold War*. New York: Farrar, Straus, & Giroux, 2001.

Call, Steve. *Selling Air Power: Military Aviation and Popular Culture After World War II*. College Station, TX: Texas A&M University Press, 2009.

The Campaigns of the Pacific War: United States, Strategic Bombing Survey (Pacific). Washington, D.C.: Government Printing Office, 1946.

Campbell, Duncan. *The Unsinkable Aircraft Carrier: The Implications of American Military Power in Britain*. London: Michael Joseph, 1984.

Carothers, James. *Caging the Dragon: The Containment of Underground Nuclear Explosions*. Alexandria, VA: Defense Nuclear Agency, 1995.

Carroll, James. *House of War: The Pentagon and the Disastrous Rise of American Power*. Boston: Mariner Books, 2006.

Carter, Ashton, John D. Steinbruner, and Charles A. Zraket, eds. *Managing Nuclear Operations*. Washington, D.C: Brookings Institution, 1987.

Cienciala, Anna M., Natalia S. Lebedeva, and Wojciech Materski, eds. *Katyn: A Crime Without Punishment*. New Haven, CT: Yale University Press, 2008.

Cimbala, Stephen J., ed. *Soviet C3*. Washington, D.C.: AFCEA International Press, 1987.

Cirincione, Joseph. *Bomb Scare: The History & Future of Nuclear Weapons*. New York: Columbia University Press, 2007.

Clearwater, John. *Canadian Nuclear Weapons: The Untold Story of Canada's Cold War Arsenal*. Toronto: Dundurn Press, 1998.

Clodfelter, Mark. *Beneficial Bombing: The Progressive Foundations of American Air Power 1917–1945*. Lincoln, NE: University of Nebraska Press, 2010.

Coffey, Thomas M. *Iron Eagle: The Turbulent Life of General Curtis LeMay*. New York: Crown Publishers, 1986.

Cohen, Stephen F. *Soviet Fates and Lost Alternatives: From Stalinism to the New Cold War*. New York: Columbia University Press, 2009.

The Comprehensive Nuclear Test Ban Treaty: Technical Issues for the United States. Washington, D.C.: National Academies Press, 2012.

Condit, Kenneth W. *The Joint Chiefs of Staff and National Policy: Volume II, 1947-1949*. Washington, D.C.: Office of Joint History, Office of the Chairman of Joint Chiefs of Staff, 1996.

Corera, Gordon. *Shopping for Bombs: Nuclear Proliferation, Global Insecurity, and the Rise and Fall of the A. Q. Khan Network*. New York: Oxford University Press, 2006.

Courtois, Stéphane, et al. *The Black Book of Communism: Crimes, Terror, Repression*. Cambridge, MA: Harvard University Press, 1999.

Craven, Wesley Frank, and James Lea Cate, eds. *The Army Air Forces in World War II: Volume Five, The Pacific: Matterhorn to Nagasaki, June 1944 to August 1945*. Washington, D.C.: Office of Air Force History, 1983.

Dalton, Russell J., et al., eds. *Critical Masses: Citizens, Nuclear Weapons Production, and Environmental Destruction in the United States and Russia*. Cambridge, MA: MIT Press, 1999.

Davis, Vincent. *The Admirals Lobby*. Chapel Hill, NC: University of North Carolina Press, 1967.

Defense's Nuclear Agency: 1947–1997. Washington, D.C.: Defense Threat Reduction Agency, U.S. Department of Defense, 2002.

Delgado, James P. *Nuclear Dawn: From the Manhattan Project to the Bikini Atoll*. Oxford, UK: Osprey Publishing, 2009.

Del Tredici, Robert. *At Work in the Fields of the Bomb*. New York: Harper & Row, 1987.

DeVorkin, David H. *Science with a Vengeance: How the Military Created the US Space Sciences After World War II*. New York: Springer, 1992.

Dobbs, Michael. *One Minute to Midnight: Kennedy, Khrushchev, and Castro on the Brink of Nuclear War*. New York: Alfred A. Knopf, 2008.

Dobson, Joel. *The Goldsboro Broken Arrow: The Story of the 1961 B-52 Crash, the Men, the Bombs, the Aftermath*. Raleigh, NC: Lulu, 2011.

Dower, John W. *War Without Mercy: Race and Power in the Pacific War*. New York: Pantheon, 1987.

———. *Embracing Defeat: Japan in the Wake of World War II*. New York: W. W. Norton, 2000.

Drea, Edward, Greg Bradsher, Robert Hanyock, James Lide, Michael Petersen, and Daqing Yang. *Researching Japanese War Crime Records: Introductory Essays*. Washington, D.C.: Nazi War Crimes and Japanese Imperial Government Records Interagency Working Group, U.S. National Archives, 2006.

Drell, Sidney D. *In the Shadow of the Bomb: Physics and Arms Control*. New York: American Institute of Physics, 1993.

———. *Nuclear Weapons, Scientists, and the Post-Cold War Challenge: Selected Papers on Arms Control*. Hackensack, NJ: World Scientific Publishing Company, 2007.

———, and James E. Goodby. *The Gravest Danger: Nuclear Weapons*. Stanford, CA: Hoover Institution Press, 2003.

Duignan, Peter, and Alvin Rabushka. *The United States in the 1980s*. Stanford, CA: Hoover Institution Press, 1980.

Dumas, Lloyd J. *Lethal Arrogance: Human Fallibility and Dangerous Technologies*. New York: St. Martin's Press, 1999.

Dyson, George. *Project Orion: The True Story of the Atomic Spaceship*. New York: Henry Holt, 2002.

Eden, Lynn. *Whole World on Fire: Organizations, Knowledge & Nuclear Weapons Devastation*. Ithaca, NY: Cornell University Press, 2004.

Edwards, Paul N. *The Closed World: Computers and the Politics of Discourse in Cold War America*. Cambridge, MA: MIT Press, 1996.

Farquhar, John Thomas. *A Need to Know: The Role of Air Force Reconnaissance in War Planning, 1945–1953*. Montgomery, AL: Air University Press, February 2004.

Feaver, Peter Douglas. *Guarding the Guardians: Civilian Control of Nuclear Weapons in the United States*. Ithaca, NY: Cornell University Press, 1992.

Ferguson, Charles D., and William C. Potter. *The Four Faces of Nuclear Terrorism*. New York: Routledge, 2005.

Ferrell, Robert H. *Harry S. Truman: A Life*. Columbia, MO: University of Missouri Press, 1994.

FitzGerald, Frances. *Way Out There in the Blue: Reagan, Star Wars and the End of the Cold War.* New York: Touchstone, 2001.

Ford, Daniel. *The Button: The Pentagon's Strategic Command and Control System—Does It Work?* New York: Simon & Schuster, 1985.

Frank, Richard B. *Downfall: The End of the Imperial Japanese Empire.* New York: Penguin Books, 1999.

Frankel, Max. *High Noon in the Cold War: Kennedy, Khrushchev, and the Cuban Missile Crisis.* New York: Ballantine Books, 2004.

Freedman, Lawrence. *The Evolution of Nuclear Strategy.* New York: Palgrave Macmillan, 2003.

Friedrich, Jörg. *The Fire: The Bombing of Germany, 1940–1945.* New York: Columbia University Press, 2006.

Furman, Necah Stewart. *Sandia National Laboratories: The Postwar Decade.* Albuquerque, NM: University of New Mexico Press, 1990.

Fursenko, Aleksandr, and Timothy Naftali. *"One Hell of a Gamble": Khrushchev, Castro, and Kennedy, 1958–1964.* New York: W. W. Norton, 1997.

———. *Khrushchev's Cold War: The Inside Story of an American Adversary.* New York: W. W. Norton, 2006.

Futrell, Robert F. *Ideas, Concepts, Doctrine, Volume I: Basic Thinking in the United States Air Force 1907–1960.* Maxwell Air Force Base, AL: Air University Press, 1989.

———. *Ideas, Concepts, Doctrine, Volume II: Basic Thinking in the United States Air Force 1961–1984.* Maxwell Air Force Base, AL: Air University Press, 1989.

Gaddis, John Lewis. *The Cold War: A New History.* New York: Penguin Press, 2007.

———. *George F. Kennan: An American Life.* New York: Penguin Press, 2011.

Ganguly, Šumit, and S. Paul Kapur. *India, Pakistan, and the Bomb: Debating Nuclear Stability in South Asia.* New York: Columbia University Press, 2010.

Garwin, Richard L., and George Charpak. *Megawatts and Megatons: The Future of Nuclear Power and Nuclear Weapons.* Chicago: University of Chicago Press, 2002.

George, Peter. *Commander-1.* New York: Delacorte Press, 1965.

Ghamara-Tabrizi, Sharon. *The Worlds of Herman Kahn: The Intuitive Science of Thermonuclear War.* Cambridge, MA: Harvard University Press, 2005.

Giarchi, G.G. *Between McAlpine and Polaris.* London: Routledge & Kegan Paul, 1984.

Gibson, Chris. *Vulcan's Hammer: V-Force Projects and Weapons Since 1945.* Manchester, England: Hikoki Publications, 2011.

Gibson, James N. *Nuclear Weapons of the United States: An Illustrated History.* Atglen, PA: Schiffer Publishing, 1996.

Gilbert, Martin. *The Second World War: A Complete History.* New York: Holt Paperbacks, 2004.

Glasstone, Samuel, ed. *The Effects of Nuclear Weapons.* Washington, D.C.: U.S. Government Printing Office, 1964.

Goldberg, Alfred, Steven L. Rearden, and Doris M. Condit. *History of the Office of the Secretary of Defense: The McNamara Ascendancy, 1961–1965.* Washington, D.C.: Government Printing Office, 1984.

Gottfried, Kurt, and Blair, Bruce G., eds. *Crisis Stability and Nuclear War.* New York: Oxford University Press, 1988.

Grayling, A.C. *Among the Dead Cities: The History and Moral Legacy of the WWII Bombing of Civilians in Germany and Japan.* New York: Walker Publishing, 2006.

Greene, Benjamin P. *Eisenhower, Science Advice, and the Nuclear Test Ban Debate, 1945–1963.* Stanford, CA: Stanford University Press, 2007.

Gregory, Shaun R. *The Hidden Cost of Deterrence: Nuclear Weapon Accidents.* Washington, D.C.: Brassey's, 1990.

———. *Nuclear Command and Control in NATO: Nuclear Weapons Operations and the Strategy of Flexible Response.* New York: Palgrave Macmillan, 1996.

Ground Zero Project. *Nuclear War: What's in It for You?* New York: Pocket Books, 1982.

Gusterson, Hugh. *Nuclear Rites: A Weapons Laboratory at the End of the Cold War.* Berkeley, CA: University of California Press, 1998.

———. *People of the Bomb: Portraits of America's Nuclear Complex.* Minneapolis, MN: University of Minnesota Press, 2004.

Hacker, Barton C., and James M. Grimwood. *On the Shoulders of Titans: A History Project of Gemini.* Washington, D.C.: National Aeronautics and Space Administration, Scientific and Technical Information Office, 1977.

Hackett, John. *The Third World War: August 1985.* New York: Macmillan, 1978.

Haines, Gerald K., and Robert E. Leggett, eds. *Watching the Bear: Essays on CIA's Analysis of the Soviet Union.* Washington, D.C.: Central Intelligence Agency Center for the Study of Intelligence, 2003.

Halberstam, David. *The Best and the Brightest.* New York: Ballantine Books, 1992.

Hall, R. Cargill, ed. *Case Studies in Strategic Bombardment.* Washington, D.C.: Air Force Historical Studies Office, 1998.

Hasegawa, Tsuyoshi. *Racing the Enemy: Stalin, Truman, and the Surrender of Japan.* Cambridge, MA: Belknap Press, 2005.

Hastings, Max. *Retribution: The Battle for Japan, 1944–45.* New York: Vintage Books, 2009.

Haynes, James Earl, and Harvey Klehr. *Venona: Decoding Soviet Espionage in America.* New Haven, CT: Yale University Press, 2000.

Hendrickson, Paul. *The Living and the Dead: Robert McNamara and Five Lives of a Lost War.* New York: Vintage Books, 1997.

Hennessy, Peter. *The Secret State: Whitehall and the Cold War.* New York: Penguin Books, 2003.

Heppenheimer, T.A. *Countdown: A History of Space Flight.* New York: John Wiley & Sons, 1997.

Herken, Gregg. *The Winning Weapon: The Atomic Bomb in the Cold War 1945–1950.* New York: Vintage Books, 1982.

———. *Counsels of War.* New York: Oxford University Press, 1987.

Hersey, John. *Hiroshima.* New York: Alfred A. Knopf, 2003.

Hershberg, James G. *James B. Conant: Harvard to Hiroshima and the Making of the Nuclear Age.* Stanford, CA: Stanford University Press, 1993.

Hewlett, Richard G., and Oscar E. Anderson, Jr. *The New World, 1939/1946: A History of the United States Atomic Energy Commission, Volume I.* University Park, PA: Pennsylvania State University Press, 1962.

Hewlett, Richard G., and Francis Duncan. *Atomic Shield, 1947/1952: A History of the United States Atomic Energy Commission, Volume II.* University Park, PA: Pennsylvania State University Press, 1969.

Hewlett, Richard G., and Jack M. Holl. *Atoms for Peace and War, 1953/1961: Eisenhower and the Atomic Energy Commission, A History of the United States Atomic Energy Commission, Volume III.* Berkeley, CA: University of California Press, 1989.

History of the Eighties: Lessons for the Future. Washington, D.C.: Federal Deposit Insurance Corporation Division of Research and Statistics, 1997.

Hoddeson, Lillian, Paul W. Henriksen, Roger A. Meade, and Catherine Westfall. *Critical Assembly: A Technical History of Los Alamos During the Oppenheimer Years 1943–1945.* New York: Cambridge University Press, 1993.

Hoffman, David E. *The Dead Hand: The Untold Story of the Cold War Arms Race and Its Dangerous Legacy.* New York: Doubleday, 2009.

Holloway, David. *Stalin and the Bomb: The Soviet Union and Atomic Energy, 1939–1956.* New Haven, CT: Yale University Press, 1994.

Hook, Sidney. *The Fail-Safe Fallacy.* New York: Stein and Day, 1963.

Hubler, Richard G. *SAC: The Strategic Air Command.* New York: Duell, Sloan and Pearce, 1958.

Hughes, Thomas P. *Rescuing Prometheus: Four Monumental Projects That Changed the Modern World.* New York: Vintage Books, 1998.

———. *American Genesis: A Century of Invention and Technological Enthusiasm, 1870–1970.* Chicago: University of Chicago Press, 2004.

Hunt, Linda. *Secret Agenda: The United States Government, Nazi Scientists, and Project Paperclip 1945 to 1990.* New York: St. Martin's Press, 1991.

Iklé, Fred Charles. *The Social Impact of Bomb Destruction.* Norman, OK: University of Oklahoma Press, 1958.

———. *Every War Must End.* New York: Columbia University Press, 2005.

———. *Annihilation from Within: The Ultimate Threat to Nations.* New York: Columbia University Press, 2006.

Johnson, Leland. *Sandia National Laboratories: A History of Exceptional Service in the National Interest.* Albuquerque, NM: Sandia National Laboratories, 1997.

Johnson, Stephen. *The United States Air Force and the Culture of Innovation: 1945–1965.* Washington, D.C.: Air Force History and Museums Program, 2002.

Johnston, Phyllis Finton. *Bill Clinton's Public Policy for Arkansas: 1979–1980.* Little Rock, AR: August House, 1982.

Kahn, Herman. *On Thermonuclear War.* Princeton: Princeton University Press, 1960.

Kaplan, Fred. *The Wizards of Armageddon: The Untold Story of the Small Group of Men Who Have Devised the Plans and Shaped the Policies on How to Use the Bomb.* Stanford, CA: Stanford University Press, 1991.

Kaplan, Michael, and Ellen Kaplan. *Chances Are . . . : Adventures in Probability.* New York: Penguin Books, 2006.

Kaufman, Burton I., and Scott Kaufman. *The Presidency of James Earl Carter, Jr.* Lawrence, KS: University Press of Kansas, 2006.

Kaufman, Scott. *Plans Unraveled: The Foreign Policy of the Carter Administration.* DeKalb, IL: Northern Illinois University Press, 2008.

Kaufmann, William W. *The McNamara Strategy.* New York: Harper & Row, 1964.

Kearny, Cresson H. *Nuclear War Survival Skills: What You and Your Family Can Do—Before . . . and After.* Coos Bay, OR: NWS Research Bureau, 1982.

Keeney, L. Douglas. *The Doomsday Scenario: The Official Doomsday Scenario Written by the United States Government During the Cold War.* St. Paul, MN: MBI Publishing, 2002.

———. *15 Minutes: General Curtis LeMay and the Countdown to Nuclear Annihilation.* New York: St. Martin's Press, 2011.

Kempe, Frederick. *Berlin 1961: Kennedy, Khrushchev, and the Most Dangerous Place on Earth.* New York: G. P. Putnam's Sons, 2011.

Khan, Feroz Hassan. *Eating Grass: The Making of the Pakistani Bomb.* Stanford, CA: Stanford University Press, 2012.

Kissinger, Henry A. *Nuclear Weapons and Foreign Policy.* New York: Harper and Brothers, 1957.

Klessig, Lowell L., and Victor L. Strite. *The ELF Odyssey: National Security Versus Environmental Protection.* Boulder, CO: Westview Press, 1980.

Kotz, Nick. *Wild Blue Yonder: Money, Politics, and the B-1 Bomber.* Princeton: Princeton University Press, 1988.

Kozak, David C., and Kenneth N. Ciboski, eds. *The American Presidency: A Policy Perspective from Readings and Documents.* Chicago: Nelson Hall, 1987.

Kozak, Warren. *LeMay: The Life and Wars of General Curtis LeMay.* Washington, D.C.: Regnery Publishing, 2009.

Krugler, David F. *This Is Only a Test: How Washington, D.C., Prepared for Nuclear War.* New York: Palgrave Macmillan, 2006.

Kuehl, Warren F. *Hamilton Holt: Journalist, Internationalist, Educator.* Gainesville, FL: University of Florida Press, 1960.

Kunsman, David M., and Douglas B. Lawson. *A Primer on U.S. Strategic Nuclear Policy.* Albuquerque, NM: Sandia National Laboratories, 2001.

Langewiesche, William. *The Atomic Bazaar: The Rise of the Nuclear Poor.* New York: Farrar, Straus, & Giroux, 2007.

Lapp, Ralph E. *The Voyage of the Lucky Dragon.* New York: Harper & Brothers, 1958.

Larus, Joel. *Nuclear Weapons Safety and the Common Defense.* Columbus, OH: Ohio State University Press, 1967.

Leach, Norman S. *Broken Arrow: America's First Lost Nuclear Weapon.* Calgary, Ontario: Red Deer Press, 2008.

Leighton, Richard M. *History of the Office of the Secretary of Defense, Volume III: Strategy, Money, and the New Look, 1953–1956.* Washington, D.C.: Historical Office, Office of the Secretary of Defense, 2001.

Lettow, Paul. *Ronald Reagan and His Quest to Abolish Nuclear Weapons.* New York: Random House, 2005.

Lewis, Flora. *One of Our H-Bombs Is Missing . . .* New York: McGraw-Hill, 1967.

Light, Michael. *100 Suns.* New York: Alfred A. Knopf, 2003.

Lloyd, Alwyn. *A Cold War Legacy: A Tribute to Strategic Air Command 1946–1992.* Missoula, MT: Pictorial Histories Publishing, 1999.

Loeber, Charles R. *Building the Bombs: A History of the Nuclear Weapons Complex.* Albuquerque, NM: Sandia National Laboratories, 2002.

Lonnquest, John C., and David F. Winkler. *To Defend and Deter: The Legacy of the United States Cold War Missile Program.* Washington, D.C.: Department of Defense, Legacy Resource Management Program, Cold War Project, 1996.

Lowe, Keith. *Inferno: The Fiery Destruction of Hamburg, 1943.* New York: Scribner, 2007.

MacKenzie, Donald. *Inventing Accuracy: A Historical Sociology of Nuclear Missile Guidance.* Cambridge, MA: MIT Press, 1993.

———. *Knowing Machines: Essays on Technical Change.* Cambridge, MA: MIT Press, 1998.

———. *Mechanizing Proof: Computing, Risk, and Trust.* Cambridge, MA: MIT Press, 2001.

———, and Judy Wajcman, eds. *The Social Shaping of Technology: Second Edition.* Philadelphia: Open University Press, 1999.

Maddow, Rachel. *Drift: The Unmooring of American Military Power.* New York: Crown Publishers, 2012.

Makhijani, Arjun, Howard Hu, and Katherine Yih. *Nuclear Wastelands: A Global Guide to Nuclear Weapons Production and Its Health and Environmental Effects.* Cambridge, MA: MIT Press, 2000.

Maraniss, David. *First in His Class: A Biography of Bill Clinton.* New York: Simon & Schuster, 1996.

Masters, Dexter, and Katharine Way. *One World or None: A Report to the Public on the Full Meaning of the Atomic Bomb.* New York: New Press, 2007.

Mastny, Vojtech. *The Cold War and Soviet Insecurity: The Stalin Years.* New York: Oxford University Press, 1996.

Maydew, Randall C. *America's Lost H-Bomb! Palomares, Spain, 1966.* Manhattan, KS: Sunflower University Press, 1997.

McCamley, Nick. *Cold War Secret Nuclear Bunkers: The Passive Defence of the Western World During the Cold War.* Barnsley, South Yorkshire: Pen & Sword Military Classics, 2007.

McCullough, David. *Truman.* New York: Simon & Schuster, 1992.

McFarland, Stephen L. *America's Pursuit of Precision Bombing: 1910–1945.* Tuscaloosa, AL: University of Alabama Press, 2008.

McNamara, Robert. *Blundering into Disaster: Surviving the First Century of the Nuclear Age.* New York: Pantheon, 1987.

McPhee, John. *The Curve of Binding Energy.* New York: Farrar, Straus, & Giroux, 1974.

Meilinger, Phillip S., ed. *The Paths of Heaven: The Evolution of Airpower Theory.* Maxwell Air Force Base, AL: Air University Press, 1997.

Midgley, John J., Jr. *Deadly Illusions: Army Policy for the Nuclear Battlefield.* Boulder, CO: Westview Press, 1986.

Miller, Richard L. *Under the Cloud: The Decades of Nuclear Testing.* The Woodlands, TX: Two-Sixty Press, 1991.

Miller, Roger G., ed. *Seeing Off the Bear: Anglo-American Air Power Cooperation During the Cold War.* Washington, D.C.: Air Force History and Museums Program, 1995.

Mojtabai, A.G. *Blessèd Assurance: At Home with the Bomb in Amarillo, Texas.* Boston: Houghton Mifflin, 1986.

Moody, Walton S. *Building a Strategic Air Force.* Washington, D.C: Air Force History and Museums Program, 1995.

Moore, Richard. *Nuclear Illusion, Nuclear Reality: Britain, the United States, and Nuclear Weapons, 1958–64.* New York: Palgrave Macmillan, 2010.

Moran, Barbara. *The Day We Lost the H-Bomb: Cold War, Hot Nukes, and the Worst Nuclear Weapons Disaster in History.* New York: Ballantine Books, 2009.

Morgan, Mark L., and Mark A. Berhow. *Rings of Supersonic Steel: Air Defenses of the United States Army, 1950–1979.* Bodega Bay, CA: Hole in the Head Press, 2002.

Morris, Roger. *Partners in Power: The Clintons and Their America.* New York: Henry Holt, 1996.

Mosher, David E., Lowell H. Schwartz, David R. Howell, and Lynn E. Davis. *Beyond the Nuclear Shadow: A Phased Approach for Improving Nuclear Safety and U.S.–Russian Relations*. Santa Monica, CA: RAND, 2003.

Moynihan, Daniel Patrick. *Secrecy: The American Experience*. New Haven, CT: Yale University Press, 1998.

Mumford, Lewis. *The Myth of the Machine: The Pentagon of Power*. New York: Harcourt Brace Jovanovich, 1970.

Nalty, Bernard C., ed. *Winged Shield, Winged Sword: A History of the United States Air Force, Volume I, 1907–1950*. Washington, D.C.: Air Force History and Museums Program, 1997.

———, ed. *Winged Shield, Winged Sword: A History of the United States Air Force, Volume II, 1950–1997*. Washington, D.C.: Air Force History and Museums Program, 1997.

Nalty, Bernard C., John F. Shiner, and George M. Watson. *With Courage: The U.S. Army Air Forces in World War II*. Washington, D.C.: Air Force History and Museums Program, 1994.

Nash, Philip. *The Other Missiles of October: Eisenhower, Kennedy, and the Jupiters, 1957–1963*. Chapel Hill, NC: University of North Carolina Press, 1997.

National Commission on Terrorist Attacks Upon the United States. *The 9/11 Commission Report: Final Report of the National Commission on Terrorist Attacks Upon the United States*. New York: W. W. Norton, 2004.

Neider, Charles, ed. *Man Against Nature*. New York: Harper & Brothers, 1954.

Neufeld, Jacob. *The Development of Ballistic Missiles in the United States Air Force, 1945–1960*. Washington, D.C.: Office of Air Force History, 1990.

Neufeld, Michael J. *Von Braun: Dreamer of Space, Engineer of War*. New York: Vintage Books, 2008.

Nie, Jing-Bao, Nanyan Guo, Mark Selden, and Arthur Kleinman, eds. *Japan's Wartime Medical Atrocities: Comparative Inquiries in Science, History, and Ethics*. New York: Routledge, 2010.

Nolan, Janne E. *Guardians of the Arsenal: The Politics of Nuclear Strategy*. New York: New Republic Books, 1989.

Nuclear War: What's in It for You?/Ground Zero. New York: Pocket Books, 1982.

Oberg, James E. *Uncovering Soviet Disasters: Exploring the Limits of Glasnost*. New York: Random House, 1988.

Odom, William E. *The Collapse of the Soviet Military*. New Haven, CT: Yale University Press, 1998.

Pearlman, Michael D. *Unconditional Surrender, Demobilization, and the Atomic Bomb*. Fort Leavenworth, KS: U.S. Army Command and General Staff College, Combat Studies Institute, 1996.

Pearson, David. *The World Wide Military Command and Control System: Evolution and Effectiveness*. Maxwell Air Force Base, AL: Air University Press, 2000.

Penson, Chuck. *The Titan II Handbook: A Civilian's Guide to the Most Powerful ICBM America Ever Built*. Tucson, AZ: Chuck Penson, 2008.

Perrow, Charles. *Normal Accidents: Living with High-Risk Technologies*. Princeton: Princeton University Press, 1999.

———. *The Next Catastrophe: Reducing Our Vulnerabilities to Natural, Industrial, and Terrorist Disasters*. Princeton: Princeton University Press, 2007.

Perry, Mark. *Four Stars: The Inside Story of the Forty-Year Battle Between the Joint Chiefs of Staff and America's Civilian Leaders*. Boston: Houghton Mifflin, 1989.

Piszkiewicz, Dennis. *Wernher Von Braun: The Man Who Sold the Moon*. Westport, CT: Praeger, 1998.

Podvig, Pavel, ed. *Russian Strategic Nuclear Forces*. Cambridge, MA: MIT Press, 2004.

Polmar, Norman, ed. *Strategic Air Command: People, Aircraft, and Missiles*. Annapolis, MD: Nautical and Aviation Publishing Company of America, 1979.

Polmar, Norman, and Robert S. Norris. *The U.S. Nuclear Arsenal: A History of Weapons and Delivery Systems Since 1945*. Annapolis, MD: Naval Institute Press, 2009.

Poole, Willard S. *History of the Joint Chiefs of Staff: The Joint Chiefs of Staff and National Policy, Volume VIII, 1961–1964*. Washington, D.C.: Office of Joint History, Office of the Chairman of Joint Chiefs of Staff, 2011.

Priest, Dana, and William M. Arkin. *Top Secret America: The Rise of the New American Security State*. New York: Little, Brown, 2011.

Pry, Peter Vincent. *War Scare: Russia and America on the Nuclear Brink.* Westport, CT: Praeger, 1999.

Redmond, Kent C., and Thomas M. Smith. *From Whirlwind to Mitre: The R&D Story of the SAGE Air Defense Computer.* Cambridge: MIT Press, 2000.

Reed, Thomas C., and Danny B. Stillman. *The Nuclear Express: A Political History of the Bomb and Its Proliferation.* Minneapolis, MN: Zenith Press, 2009.

Rhodes, Richard. *The Making of the Atomic Bomb.* New York: Simon & Schuster, 1986.

———. *Dark Sun: The Making of the Hydrogen Bomb.* New York: Simon & Schuster, 1995.

———. *Arsenals of Folly: The Making of the Nuclear Arms Race.* New York: Alfred A. Knopf, 2007.

Richelson, Jeffrey T. *Defusing Armageddon: Inside NEST, America's Secret Nuclear Bomb Squad.* New York: W. W. Norton, 2009.

Rosenbaum, Ron. *How the End Begins: The Road to a Nuclear World War III.* New York: Simon & Schuster, 2011.

Rosenblith, Walter A., ed. *Jerry Wiesner: Scientist, Statesman, Humanist.* Cambridge, MA: MIT Press, 2003.

Ross, Steven T. *American War Plans, 1945–1950: Strategies for Defeating the Soviet Union.* Portland, OR: Frank Cass, 1996.

Sagan, Carl, and Richard Turco. *A Path Where No Man Thought: Nuclear Winter and the End of the Arms Race.* New York: Random House, 1990.

Sagan, Scott D. *Moving Targets: Nuclear Strategy and National Security.* Princeton: Princeton University Press, 1989.

———. *The Limits of Safety: Organizations, Accidents, and Nuclear Weapons.* Princeton: Princeton University Press, 1993.

———, ed. *Inside Nuclear South Asia.* Stanford, CA: Stanford University Press, 2009

Sagan, Scott D., and Kenneth N. Waltz. *The Spread of Nuclear Weapons: A Debate Renewed.* New York: W. W. Norton, 2003.

Sanger, David E. *The Inheritance: The World Obama Confronts and the Challenges to American Power.* New York: Harmony Books, 2009.

Savranskaya, Svetlana, Thomas Blanton, and Vladislav Zubok, eds. *Masterpieces of History: The Peaceful End of the Cold War in Europe, 1989.* New York: Central European University Press, 2010.

Schaffel, Kenneth. *The Emerging Shield: The Air Force and the Evolution of Continental Air Defense, 1945–1960.* Washington, D.C.: Office of Air Force History, United States Air Force, 1991.

Schell, Jonathan. *The Fate of the Earth and The Abolition.* Stanford, CA: Stanford University Press, 2000.

———. *The Seventh Decade: The New Shape of Nuclear Danger.* New York: Metropolitan Books, 2007.

Schelling, Thomas C. *Arms and Influence.* New Haven, CT: Yale University Press, 2008.

Schnabel, James F. *The Joint Chiefs of Staff and National Policy: Volume I, 1945–1947.* Washington, D.C.: Office of Joint History, Office of the Chairman of Joint Chiefs of Staff, 1996.

Schwartz, Stephen I., ed. *Atomic Audit: The Costs and Consequences of U.S. Nuclear Weapons Since 1940.* Washington, D.C.: Brookings Institution, 1998.

Schweizer, Peter. *Victory: The Reagan Administration's Secret Strategy That Hastened the Collapse of the Soviet Union.* New York: Atlantic Monthly Press, 1994.

Shambroom, Paul. *Face to Face with the Bomb: Nuclear Reality After the Cold War.* Baltimore, MD: Johns Hopkins University Press, 2003.

Sheehan, Neil. *A Fiery Peace in a Cold War: Bernard Schriever and the Ultimate Weapon.* New York: Random House, 2009.

Sherwin, Martin J. *A World Destroyed: Hiroshima and Its Legacies.* Stanford, CA: Stanford University Press, 2003.

Shin, Gi-Wook, Soon-Won Park, and Daqing Yang, eds. *Rethinking Historical Injustice and Reconciliation in Northeast Asia: The Korean Experience.* New York: Routledge, 2007.

Shultz, George P., and Sidney D. Drell. eds., *Implications of the Reykjavik Summit on Its Twentieth Anniversary.* Stanford: Hoover Institution Press, 2007.

———. *The Nuclear Enterprise: High-Consequence Accidents: How to Enhance Safety and Minimize Risks in Nuclear Weapons and Reactors.* Stanford, CA: Hoover Institution Press, 2012.

———, and James E. Goodby, eds. *Reykjavik Revisited: Steps Toward a World Free of Nuclear Weapons.* Stanford, CA: Hoover Institution Press, 2008.

———, Steven P. Andreasen, and James E. Goodby, eds. *Deterrence: Its Past and Future.* Stanford, CA: Hoover Institution Press, 2011.

Shurcliff, W.A. *Bombs at Bikini: The Official Report of Operation Crossroads.* New York: Wm. H. Wise, 1947.

Slife, James C. *Creech Blue: General Bill Creech and the Reformation of the Tactical Air Forces, 1978–1984.* Maxwell Air Force Base, AL: Air University Press and the College of Aerospace Doctrine, Research and Education, 2004.

Smith, Mark E., III. *American Defense Policy.* Baltimore, MD: Johns Hopkins University Press, 1968.

Smith, P.D. *Doomsday Men: The Real Dr. Strangelove and the Dream of the Superweapon.* New York: St. Martin's Press, 2007.

Smith, Richard K. *Seventy-five Years of Inflight Refueling: Highlights, 1923–1998.* Washington, D.C.: Air Force History and Museums Program, 1998.

Smith, Starr. *Jimmy Stewart: Bomber Pilot.* Minneapolis, MN: Zenith Press, 2005.

Smyth, Henry DeWolf. *Atomic Energy for Military Purposes: The Official Report on the Development of the Atomic Bomb Under the Auspices of the United States Government 1940–1945.* Princeton: Princeton University Press, 1945.

Sokolski, Henry D., ed. *Getting MAD: Nuclear Mutual Assured Destruction, Its Origins and Practice.* Carlisle, PA: Strategic Studies Institute, U.S. Army War College, 2004.

Solomon, Frederic, and Robert Q. Marston, eds. *The Medical Implications of Nuclear War.* Washington, D.C.: National Academy Press, 1986.

Soviet Military Power: An Assessment of the Threat. Washington, D.C.: U.S. Department of Defense, Government Printing Office, 1988.

Sparrow, John C. *History of Personnel Demobilization in the United States Army.* Washington, D.C.: Department of the Army, 1952.

Stein, Peter, and Peter Feaver. *Assuring Control of Nuclear Weapons: The Evolution of Permissive Action Links.* Cambridge, MA: Center for Science and International Affairs, John F. Kennedy School of Government, Harvard University, and University Press of America, 1987.

Steury, Donald P., ed. *Intentions and Capabilities: Estimates on Soviet Strategic Forces, 1953–1983.* Washington, D.C.: History Staff, Center for the Study of Intelligence, Central Intelligence Agency, 1996.

Stumpf, David K. *Titan II: History of a Cold War Missile Program.* Fayetteville, AR: University of Arkansas Press, 2000.

Sutton, George P., and Oscar Biblarz. *Rocket Propulsion Elements: Seventh Edition.* New York: John Wiley & Sons, 2001.

Tannenwald, Nina. *The Nuclear Taboo: The United States and the Non-Use of Nuclear Weapons Since 1945.* New York: Cambridge University Press, 2007.

Taubman, Philip. *The Partnership: Five Cold Warriors and Their Quest to Ban the Bomb.* New York: HarperCollins, 2012.

Taylor, Maxwell D. *The Uncertain Trumpet.* New York: Harper & Brothers, 1960.

Technical Manual, USAF Model LGM-25C, Missile System Operation. Tucson, AZ: Arizona Aerospace Foundation, 2005.

Terriff, Terry. *The Nixon Administration and the Making of U.S. Nuclear Strategy.* Ithaca, NY: Cornell University Press, 1995.

Thomas, Evan. *Ike's Bluff: President Eisenhower's Secret Battle to Save the World.* New York: Little, Brown, 2012.

Thompson, Nicholas. *The Hawk and the Dove: Paul Nitze, George Kennan, and the History of the Cold War.* New York: Henry Holt, 2009.

Tillman, Barrett. *LeMay.* New York: Palgrave Macmillan, 2009.

Trachtenberg, Marc. *History & Strategy.* Princeton: Princeton University Press, 1991.

———. *A Constructed Peace: The Making of the European Settlement, 1945–1963.* Princeton: Princeton University Press, 1999.

Tuchman, Barbara W. *The Guns of August.* New York: Ballantine Books, 1994.

Tucker, Todd. *Atomic America: How a Deadly Explosion and a Feared Admiral Changed the Course of Nuclear History*. New York: Free Press, 2009

Turner, Stansfield. *Caging the Nuclear Genie: An American Challenge for Global Security*. New York: Westview Press, 1997.

Twigge, Stephen, and Len Scott. *Planning Armageddon: Britain, the United States and the Command of Western Nuclear Forces, 1945–1964*. Amsterdam, Netherlands: Harwood Academic Publishers, 2000.

United States Strategic Bombing Surveys: European War, Pacific War, The Montgomery, AL: Air University Press, October 1987.

Van Creveld, Martin. *Command in War*. Cambridge, MA: Harvard University Press, 1985.

———. *The Age of Airpower*. New York: Public Affairs, 2011.

Vanderbilt, Tom. *Survival City: Adventures Among the Ruins of Atomic America*. Princeton: Princeton Architectural Press, 2002.

Volkogonov, Dmitri. *Stalin: Triumph and Tragedy*. New York: Grove Weidenfeld, 1988.

Wakabayashi, Bob Tadashi. *The Nanking Atrocity: Complicating the Picture*. New York: Berghahn Books, 2007.

Walker, Chuck, with Joel Powell. *ATLAS: The Ultimate Weapon by Those Who Built It*. Ontario, Canada: Apogee Books Production, 2005.

Walker, Stephen. *Shockwave: Countdown to Hiroshima*. New York: Harper Perennial, 2005.

Watson, George M. *The Office of the Secretary of the Air Force, 1947–1965*. Washington, D.C.: Center for Air Force History, 1993.

Weart, Spencer. *Nuclear Fear: A History of Images*. Cambridge, MA: Harvard University Press, 1988.

Wells, H.G. *The World Set Free: A Story of Mankind*. New York: E. P. Dutton, 1914.

Welsome, Eileen. *The Plutonium Files: America's Secret Medical Experiments in the Cold War*. New York: Dial Press, 1999.

Werrell, Kenneth P. *The Evolution of the Cruise Missile*. Maxwell Air Force Base, AL: Air University Press, 1985.

Williams, Christian. *Lead, Follow, or Get Out of the Way: The Story of Ted Turner*. New York: Times Books, 1981.

Wills, Garry. *Bomb Power: The Modern Presidency and the National Security State*. New York: Penguin Press, 2010.

Wilson, Ward. *Five Myths About Nuclear Weapons*. Boston: Houghton Mifflin Harcourt, 2013.

Winner, Langdon. *The Whale and the Reactor: A Search for Limits in an Age of High Technology*. Chicago: University of Chicago Press, 1989.

Wittner, Lawrence S. *Resisting the Bomb: A History of the World Nuclear Disarmament Movement 1954–1970*. Stanford, CA: Stanford University Press, 1997.

———. *Toward Nuclear Abolition: A History of the World Disarmament Movement, 1971 to the Present*. Stanford, CA: Stanford University Press, 2003.

Worden, Mike. *Rise of the Fighter Generals: The Problem of Air Force Leadership, 1945–1982*. Maxwell Air Force Base, AL: Air University Press, 1998.

Wynn, Humphrey. *The RAF Strategic Nuclear Deterrent Forces: Their Origins, Roles and Deployment. 1946–1969*. London: Stationery Office Publications Centre, 1994.

Yarnynich, Valery E. *C³: Nuclear Command, Control Cooperation*. Washington, D.C.: Center for Defense Information, 2003.

Yenne, Bill. *S.A.C.: A Primer of Modern Strategic Airpower*. Novato, CA: Presidio Press, 1985.

Younger, Stephen M. *The Bomb: A New History*. New York: HarperCollins, 2009.

Zaloga, Steven J. *The Kremlin's Nuclear Sword: The Rise and Fall of Russia's Strategic Nuclear Forces, 1945–2000*. Washington, D.C.: Smithsonian Institution Press, 2002.

Zelizer, Julian E. *Taxing America: Wilbur D. Mills, Congress, and the State, 1945–1975*. New York: Cambridge University Press, 2000.

INDEX